Practicing Texas Politics

SECOND EDITION

HOUGHTON MIFFLIN COMPANY • BOSTON

Atlanta · Dallas · Geneva, Illinois

Hopewell, New Jersey · Palo Alto

London

Preface

The second edition of *Practicing Texas Politics* maintains the same basic structural format as that of the first edition. The total content remains divided about equally between textual material written by the authors and selected readings tied closely to related subjects in the text. Those readers familiar with the earlier 1971 edition will recognize the dual arrangement of the study of Texas politics.

Although the style of selecting, organizing, and arranging the subject matter is essentially the same in the two editions, the content itself has been thoroughly revised and updated. All textual material has been reworked in the light of new developments on both the national and state levels of government. Almost all the readings are new with this edition; that is, only three of the readings from the first edition have been retained in the second. Following is a summary of the major new subjects considered in this edition of *Practicing Texas Politics.*

Chapter 1 contains new and broader information on the people of Texas, both the majority Anglos and the minority blacks, Mexican-Americans, and Indians. The chapter further provides a new perspective on poverty in Texas—about who are its chief victims and why. Finally, there is an account of recent developments in state constitution-making in Texas, and information on the current movement to provide the state with a new constitution by 1975.

Chapter 2 provides analyses of new election laws and their effect on the voting behavior of Texas voters. Among these laws is the Twenty-sixth Amendment to the United States Constitution which established the minimum legal voting age at eighteen. Included also are new rules providing for a permanent voter-registration system for Texas and for a shorter period of time required to establish residence in the state for purposes of voting. Lastly, on Texas political party subjects such as financing party primaries, "ticket-splitting," the rise of *La Raza Unida* Party, and the continuing expansion of the Texas Republican Party, the reader will find the latest information together with a review and analysis of the 1972 election in Texas.

Chapter 3 on the Legislature provides current biographical data on members of the 63rd Legislature and such data are used to characterize the membership of House and Senate and to compare and contrast the memberships of the 62nd and 63rd Legislatures. In addition there are descriptions and analyses of the newly established committee structure and other housekeeping reforms together with the output of the 63rd Legislature's regular session in 1973.

Since the first edition of *Practicing Texas Politics,* the executive branch, considered in Chapter 4, experienced fewer changes than did the legislative branch. However, there were important changes in personnel, both elective and appointive. The effect on the executive branch of the Sharpstown bank scandal is further considered in the second edition and a more detailed view of the politics of administration is provided.

Recent changes in the Texas court system are described in Chapter 5, which also contains proposals for more extensive court reform. This chapter provides new material on the Texas Department of Corrections and the Texas Youth Council. A related reading presents a case study of the trial in Abilene of former House Speaker Gus Mutcher. The purpose of this study is to illustrate the various steps in a criminal trial under Texas law.

Recent court rulings governing public school financing and national legislation providing for a program of revenue sharing are together affecting fundamentally the policies and practices of state and local governments in Texas. These new developments are considered in Chapters 6 and 7. In the latter chapter, projected state revenues for fiscal years 1974 and 1975, together with the 63rd Legislature's appropriations for the biennium, are analyzed.

Finally, an entirely new feature has been added to the second edition, a section designed to encourage students to become involved in the political process—in the practice of Texas politics. This feature is found in the Epilogue, in which the student is advised of various available forms of political participation. The authors hope that the student, after reading this short summary on political involvement, will become more aware of his responsibility as a citizen-participant in democratic government.

As in the first edition, the authors are unable to identify all those who helped in the production of this new edition of *Practicing Texas Politics.* Two fellow political scientists, Jefferson M. Bishop of Texas A&I University and M. Theron Waddell, Jr. of Galveston College read the entire manuscript of the second edition and offered valuable criticism. To them the authors are grateful. Furthermore, the authors want to express their continuing appreciation to Gordon G. Henderson, Wayne Odom, Clyde Wingfield, Beryl Pettus, J. William Davis, and E. Ray Griffin, each of whom read and improved all or part of the manuscript when it was being prepared for the first edition. Finally, to other friends and colleagues, to editors at Houghton Mifflin Company, to departmental secretaries, and to long-suffering wives we owe a continuing debt of gratitude. With these acknowledgements this second edition is dedicated to the students who will read it and who, it is hoped, will be the chief beneficiaries.

Eugene W. Jones
Joe E. Ericson
Lyle C. Brown
Robert S. Trotter, Jr.

Practicing Texas Politics

SECOND EDITION

EUGENE W. JONES

JOE E. ERICSON

LYLE C. BROWN

ROBERT S. TROTTER, JR.

Printed in the U.S.A.
Library of Congress Catalog Card Number: 73-9414
ISBN: 0-395-17164-4

Contents

HERC FICKLEN FROM THE DALLAS NEWS

1

The Context of Texas Politics

Visitors to Texas are as impressed with the size of the Lone Star State as Texans are fond of boasting of her bigness. And certainly her sheer expanse is impressive. Second among the states in size (only Alaska is larger), the flat-to-rolling plains of Texas begin in the west and south, "where the United States begins." Bordering Mexico and the Gulf on the south and extending north to Oklahoma and east to Arkansas and Louisiana, according to Professors Richardson, Wallace, and Anderson: "One can travel 800 miles in a straight line within its borders; Texarkana, on the Arkansas border, is closer to Chicago than it is to El Paso on the Rio Grande."[1] Texas is endowed with an abundance of farm and ranch land and rich in minerals, especially oil, and its people tend to think of their state in terms of four separate and distinct regions: North, South, East, and West Texas. This attitude is better understood when one is aware of the regions' great variety in geography, economy, and ethnic characteristics, as well as in political philosophy and behavior.

Like the other states of the Union, Texas is a product of her past. A victorious struggle for independence and ultimate status as a republic, paralleling the experience of the nation, and a flamboyant and colorful frontier history have each helped to make Texas unique among the fifty states. The influence of this heritage still manifests itself in many ways. *San Jacinto Day,* April 21, and *Texas Independence Day,* March 2, have more meaning for most Texans than does July 4. And, as in all the southern states, the Civil War settled upon Texas the dominance of a single political party, the Democratic, that lasted a hundred years in both state and national politics.

THE ENVIRONMENT OF TEXAS POLITICS

The influences that shape politics are many and varied. They include geography, the extent to which people are concentrated in urban and metropolitan centers, economic characteristics, the degree of freedom of expression, the amount of liberty accorded to political party activity, the spread of educational opportunities, the cultural heritage, and lastly, racial, ethnic, and religious patterns. All these influences have colored Texas politics, but space does not permit elaboration of each. Instead, those thought to have special weight will be examined, and the first among these should be Texas's 11,196,730 people, of whom 10,876,209 are native born, according to the 1970 census.

THE PEOPLE OF TEXAS

In 1541 the *Caddo Indians,* living on the Red River, met Spanish explorers with the greeting *Tayshas,* meaning friendship. The Spaniards responded at length by applying this salutation of friendship to all East Texas Indians and later to their land area. Finally the term was applied to the state of Texas. The story of the Texas Indians cannot be retold here, but their mention serves to remind us that the original people of Texas were Indians who crossed the Bering Strait from Asia. Archaeological excavations in North Texas have revealed Indian burials dating back 37,000 years. These former Asians occupied Texas without challenge from Europeans until the coming of the Spaniards in the 16th century. The American Indian's long struggle with the white man on the North American continent is foretold in the long history of Indian warfare, now familiar to almost every school child. In Texas, as in the nation, the Indian population was never large compared to present-day population densities. The United States Census Bureau reports 17,957 Indians in Texas, based on the 1970 census. (See Reading 1-1 in this chapter.) Some of these Indians now live on reservations. Others have left the reservations, obtained an education, and entered into the economy of the state as businessmen or members of the professions. In every major Texas city are descendants of these original Texans, who were proud people capable of developing a great civilization in the Southwest long before the coming of the white man.

Today, however, the Indian population of Texas is a negligible percentage of the state's total population of eleven million. Racially the state is approximately 70 per cent Anglo, a term loosely used to embrace almost all who are not Indian, Negro, or Mexican-American. Next to the Anglos in number are the Mexican-Americans, followed closely by the blacks. Lastly (and numbered by Texans as Anglos) is a scattering of Germans, East Europeans, Scandinavians, and Asians.

By 1970 Texas had become the fourth most populous state in the Union, surpassed only by California, New York, and Pennsylvania. During the 1960s Texas increased in population 16.9 per cent, as compared to 14.2 per cent for the nation. Its gain in population of 1,617,053 in the decade was the third largest in the nation, exceeded only by gains in California and Florida. This gain enabled the Lone Star State to move from the sixth-ranked to the fourth-ranked in population, surpassing Ohio and Illinois during the decade.

The United States Bureau of the Census refers to two races in Texas, the white and the "Negro and other races (over nine-tenths of which is Negro)."

The census does not separate *Anglos* from *Mexican-Americans.* The bureau indicates that the white race (both Anglos and Mexican-Americans) made up 86.6 per cent of the total population of Texas in 1970 and the "Negro and other races" comprised 13.4 per cent. Subsequent counts made in Texas and based mainly on the results of the Texas Household Survey, commissioned by the Texas Office of Economic Opportunity in 1971, indicate that Negroes alone (discounting the "other races") account for about 12.6 per cent of the total population of Texas. Mexican-Americans in 1960 comprised 14.8 per cent of the Texas population, while the Household Survey shows the 1971 Mexican-American percentage to be 16.8 per cent of the state's population.[2] This leaves 70.6 per cent of the Texas population, not including the blacks and Mexican-Americans. The members of this large majority are commonly referred to by Texans as Anglos.

Blacks first came into Texas as slaves. By 1860 Texas had 182,566 slaves; a hundred years later there were 1,187,125 blacks in the state. By 1971 the black population had reached 1,419,677, approximately 12.6 per cent of the total population. *Black Texans* still live principally in the area where they first settled with their masters, i.e., North, Central, and East Texas, though there are at least a few blacks in all but two of the state's 254 counties.[3] The bulk of the black population lives east of a line drawn from Nueces County (Corpus Christi) north to Travis County (Austin), Tarrant County (Fort Worth), and the Oklahoma border. (See Figure 1-1.) But within this region of the state they have largely abandoned the farms for the great *metropolitan areas* of the state, as Table 1-1 below indicates. (See Reading 1-2 on the concentration of blacks in Houston.)

TABLE 1-1
Black population by metropolitan and nonmetropolitan residence: Texas, 1970

	Metropolitan		
Total	*Inside Central City*	*Outside Central City*	*Nonmetropolitan*
1,067,148	899,249	167,899	352,529

Source: U.S. Bureau of the Census, *1970 Census of Population and Housing. United States Summary,* Final Report PHC(2)-1, Correction Note, Table 5 (Washington, D.C.: U.S. Government Printing Office, 1971), p. 28.

A metropolitan area is composed of a large city and its surrounding *suburban* communities. Though socially and economically integrated, a metropolitan area is composed of separate units of government. The word "metropolitan" comes from the two Greek words "mētēr" (mother) and "polis" (city). The Bureau of the Census identified 247 metropolitan units in the United States in 1971. Texas has 24. (See Figure 1-2.)

The search for employment and a higher standard of living has been the mov-

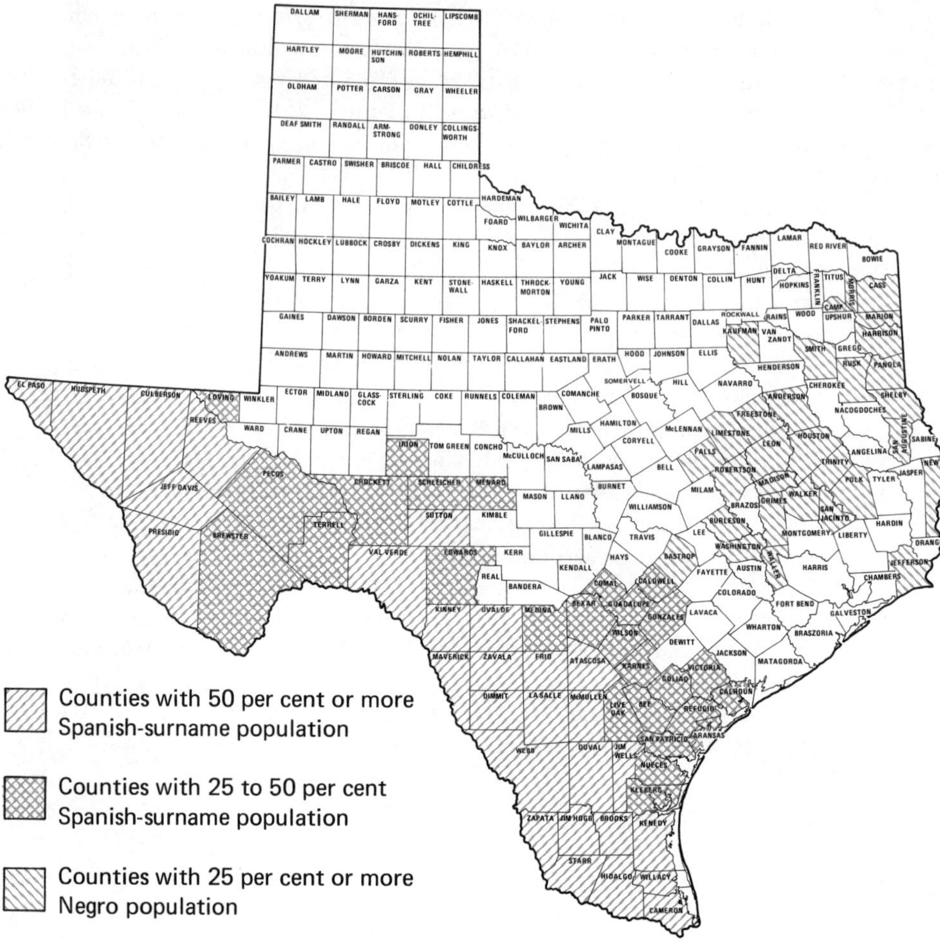

Figure 1-1

Counties with various densities of Spanish-surname and black populations. Source: Summary Selected Demographic Characteristics from Census Data—Fourth Count *(Austin, Tex.: Office of the Governor, Office of Information Services, OIS GR-3, August, 1972), pp. 29-288.*

ing force of this black migration. Heavily concentrated in and near the cities of Houston, Dallas, Fort Worth, San Antonio, and Beaumont-Port Arthur, blacks are employed as nonfarm laborers, craftsmen, and workers in private households and service industries. As we shall see presently, the median income of the black Texan, along with that of the Mexican-American, is about one-half that of his white or Anglo counterpart.

Mexican-Americans, comprising 16.8 per cent of the total population of Texas, are concentrated on the opposite side of the state from the blacks. A line drawn from Calhoun County on the Gulf to Loving County on the New Mexico

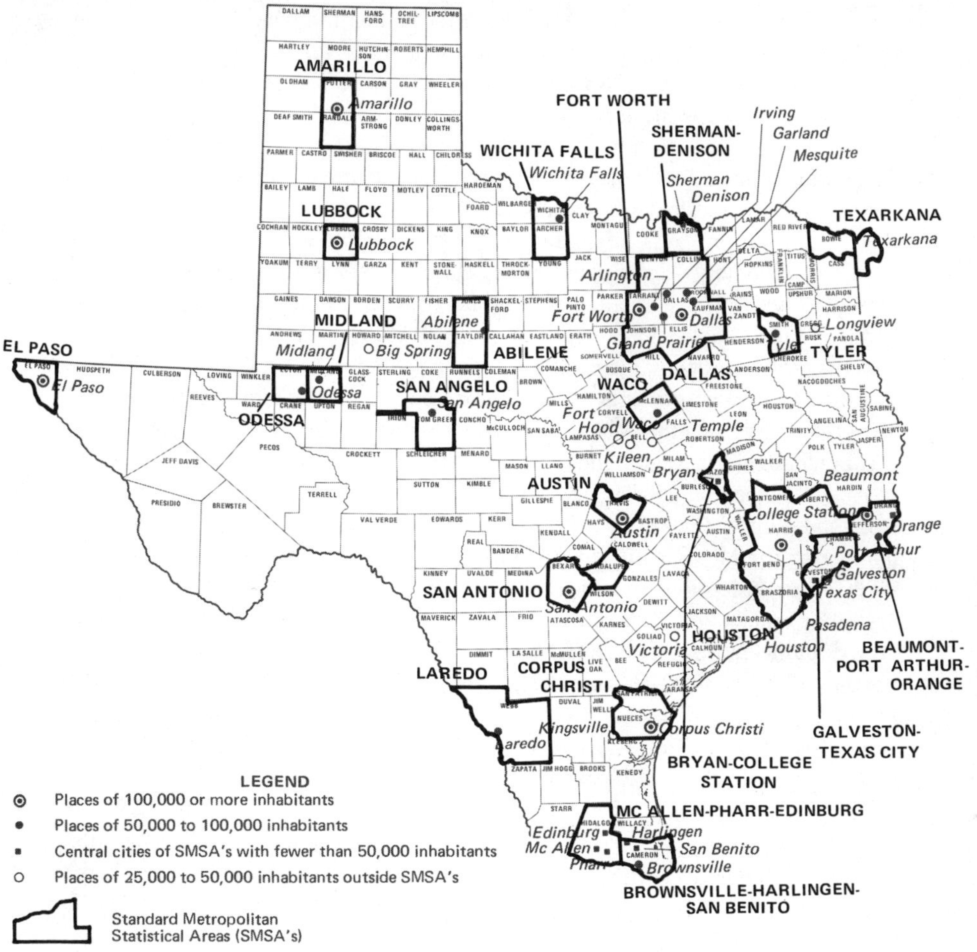

Figure 1-2

Counties, Standard Metropolitan Statistical Areas, and selected places. Source: U.S. Bureau of the Census, General Demographic Trends for Metropolitan Areas, 1960 to 1970. Texas. *Final Report PHC(2)-45 (Washington, D.C.: Government Printing Office, September 1971).*

border would divide the bulk of Mexican-Americans in the southwest from the rest of the population in the east and northeast. (See Figure 1-1.) However, Mexican-Americans are found in all of the state's 254 counties, albeit many of the northern and eastern counties have almost no Spanish-surname people. Twenty-eight counties in which over 50 per cent of the total population have Spanish surnames are located on or close to the Mexican border, while 138 counties in which 10 per cent or less of the total population have Spanish surnames are located in the northern and eastern sections of the state.

Spaniards first saw Texas in 1528. They were the followers of *Panfilo Narvaez,* whose expedition party was shipwrecked on the coast of what is now Texas in that year. Following this brief glimpse of the region, *Francisco de Coronado,* with a band of twenty men, pushed into what is now northwest Texas in 1540. Settlements in connection with Christian missions followed as the Spanish culture was implanted in Texas and the Southwest. Today only a few (approximately 15 per cent) of the state's Mexican-Americans were born in Mexico. Twice that percentage have one or two parents who were born in Mexico. Like the blacks, their income, education, housing, and other social benefits are much below those of the Anglo population.

The Spaniards ruled for nearly three centuries before the Anglos pushed into Texas, but within fifteen years following their first settlement the region was predominantly Anglo, and it has remained so to the present. Only a handful of Anglos resided in Texas in 1821, when Mexico opened its doors to immigrants from the United States. By 1836 there were 30,000. With the Anglos far outnumbering the Mexicans in the region, a majority status which they never lost, it is not surprising that the Anglo culture, rather than the Spanish, became the prevailing culture in Texas. (See Reading 1-3 in this chapter.) After 1821, land-hungry pioneers from the United States, chiefly from the southern states, could obtain title from the Mexican government to almost 5,000 acres of Texas land for the mere promise to pay the nominal surveyor fees. So the wagons rolled into Texas from the East until slowed in 1832 by political developments in Mexico that led apace to the Texas Revolution, independence, and statehood.

For nearly a century shifting populations have marked a way of life in the United States. First was the westward movement; second came the migration from the farm to the city, or urbanization. Lastly, and still in process, is the movement from the central cities to the outer fringes or *suburbs* and to the spreading metropolitan areas. The suburbs are those less densely populated and primarily residential areas circling the central city. (Metropolitan areas, as explained above, include both a large city and nearby suburban units.) Texas has experienced all three of these movements of people. Her westward movement was part of the larger national westward migration. Immigrants entering from the East pushed quickly to the Rio Grande. For a century Texas remained primarily rural. Then came *urbanization,* not suddenly, but once begun, at an accelerated pace. In 1900 Texas was 82.9 per cent rural; by 1970 it was urban by nearly the same percentage and had become the only state in the Union with two cities among the nation's top ten in population. Houston became sixth and Dallas eighth. Like California, Texas and most of its largest cities gained population while other states and several leading cities (St. Louis, Detroit, Cleveland, Baltimore, Philadelphia) declined. Thus Texas was considerably more urban in 1970 than in 1960. It is now experiencing another population redistribution, this time marked by a steady shift from the central city to the outlying suburban regions and to the smaller, outlying towns. This is the process of metropolitanization. Table 1-2 indicates the 1970 concentrations in metropolitan areas.

The increase in population in the 1960s occurred chiefly within the state's

TABLE 1-2
Texas population by race and metropolitan residence: 1970

				Metropolitan		
Total	*White*	*Black*	*Other Races*	*Total*	*Inside Central City*	*Outside Central City*
11,196,730	9,696,569	1,419,677	80,484	8,234,458	5,396,770	2,837,688

Source: U.S. Bureau of the Census, *General Demographic Trends for Metropolitan Areas, 1960 to 1970. Texas.* Final Report PHC(2)-45 (Washington, D.C.: U.S. Government Printing Office, September, 1971), p. 4.

24 standard metropolitan statistical areas (SMSAs), which experienced a growth rate of 23.7 per cent during the decade, a rate significantly higher than that for the state as a whole. By 1970 nearly 74 per cent of the state's people lived in the 24 SMSAs, as compared to 70 per cent in 1960. (See Figure 1-2.) This means that the population outside these areas has steadily decreased as a percentage of the total population, whereas 98 per cent of the entire population increase occurred in the SMSAs. As a further indication of this trend, about 85 per cent of the total metropolitan increase occurred in SMSAs of over half a million population, i.e., the Dallas, Fort Worth, Houston, and San Antonio SMSAs. These four* SMSAs now have over 46 per cent of the population of Texas, whereas in 1960 they had only 40 per cent and in 1950, only 34 per cent. (See Reading 1-4 in this chapter.) The political significance of this concentration of 80 per cent of the state's people into 39 counties is that these few counties potentially control 80 per cent of the vote in Texas. More significantly, it means that the output of state government decisions is answerable largely to the people in 39 of the state's 254 counties. The remaining 215 counties, constituting the bulk of the area but only 20 per cent of the people, will be largely impotent in influencing government policy decisions through the ballot.

Counties located along or near the north-south metropolitan axis (San Antonio SMSA to Sherman-Denison SMSA) and the southeastern metropolitan complex (primarily Corpus Christi, Houston, Galveston, and Beaumont-Port Arthur-Orange SMSAs) are those that gained most of the population. Counties outside these areas, and particularly those in West and South Texas, experienced losses in outmigration or in total population from 1960 to 1970. The greatest single expanse of territory that lost population in the 1960s consisted of the Panhandle, the South Plains, and the Rolling Plains. However, all of West Texas, with few exceptions, decreased in population during the decade; this was in sharp contrast to East Texas, which generally gained. In fact, a line could be drawn north and south, cutting the state down the middle, and generally it would largely divide the counties that increased in population in the 1960s on the east from those that lost on the west side of the line. (See Figure 1-3.) East of the line are the two major metropolitan complexes where the Texas popula-

*In 1973 the Dallas and Fort Worth SMSAs were combined, leaving Texas with twenty-three SMSAs.

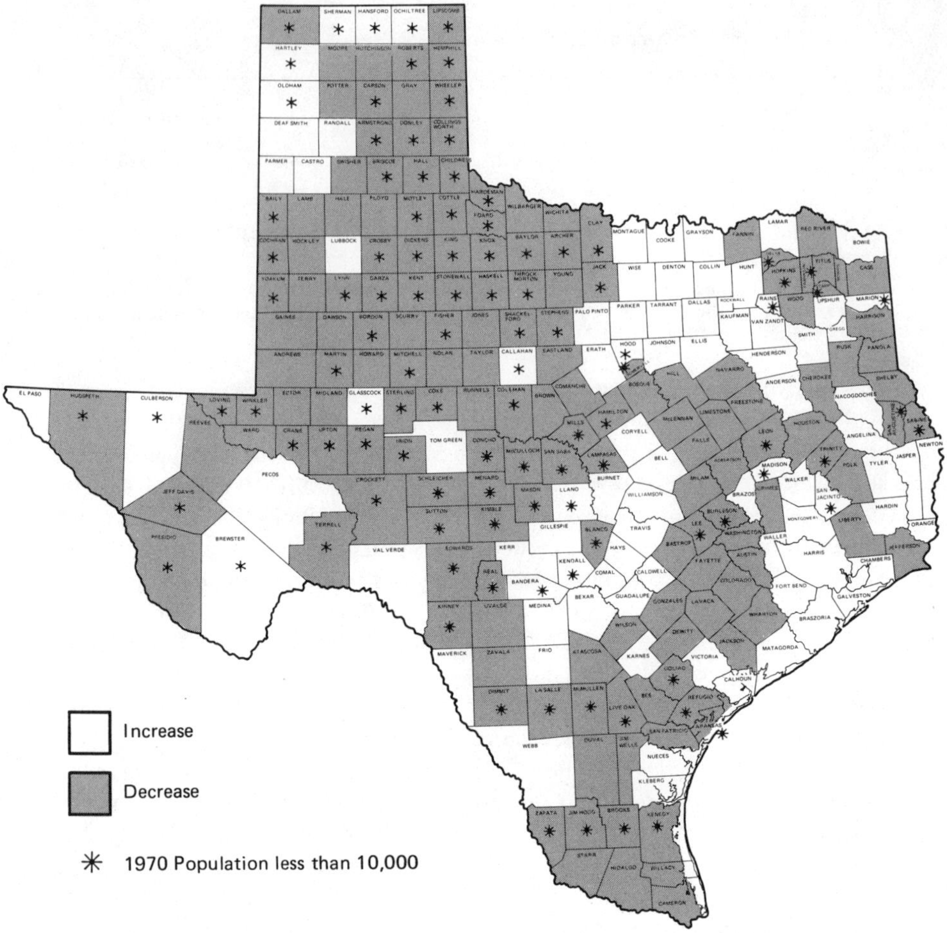

Figure 1-3
1960 to 1970 population increases and decreases in Texas counties.
Source: U.S. Census, Preliminary Reports.

tion is concentrating; on the west side are the nonmetropolitan counties that are losing population or are gaining meagerly. In all likelihood the trend will continue during the seventies. Coastal counties gained noticeably because of attractive residential, recreational, and industrial advantages, and are expected to continue growing. Several areas, especially the Hill Country west of Austin and San Antonio, drew many from other regions of the state because of construction of reservoirs, resorts, and recreational facilities. Deficiencies in water no doubt affected other areas adversely, particularly in West Texas. Conversely, the counties that gained residents lie in those regions of the state with the most rainfall and a dependable water supply.

ECONOMIC AND SOCIAL INFLUENCES

The influence of economic forces upon government and politics has been recognized at least since the time of Aristotle. It is difficult to find fault with "the father of political science," one of the earliest scholars to express his conviction that politics and economics are so interrelated.

Writers of the late eighteenth and early twentieth centuries tied the two together into one science called "political economy." Still later Professor Harold Lasswell of Yale saw politics as the science of "Who Gets What, When and How." And the late Professor V. O. Key, Jr., suggested strongly that Texas politics and economics are not too far apart when he wrote: "The Lone Star State is concerned about money and how to make it, about oil and sulphur and gas, about cattle and dust storms and irrigation, about cotton, banking, and Mexicans."[4]

The earliest influence of economics on Texas politics was the economics of land. This led to a politics of cattle; later came the politics of cotton, and still later that of oil. Today it is all of these, but more: manufacturing, trade, banking, insurance, transportation, service industries, tourism, and a host of lesser economic interests and occupations. Mineral and land resources are measures of a state's economic wealth. In view of this natural wealth, the people of Texas should enjoy one of the highest standards of living among the fifty states. Yet data released in 1972 by the Texas Office of Economic Opportunity reveal that thousands of Texans suffer from low wages, a condition which results in high levels of poverty within the state. Ironically, while this impressive study on poverty in Texas revealed that there are about 2.5 million *poor Texans,* or about 22 per cent of the total population, the *Texas Business Review* reported highly favorable trends in the major sectors of the state's economy.

The United States Bureau of the Census estimated the number of poor people in the United States in 1970 at 25.5 million, or 13 per cent of the population. This was considerably below the figure of 22 per cent for Texas in 1971. In 1971 the maximum gross income for a family of four to be considered poor was $3,800, which amounted to only $2.60 per person per day. On this basis more than one out of five Texans were poor in 1971, or about 2½ million people out of a total of 11 million. Among this army of poor people, 90 per cent of the adults are either currently working or are retired. They are poor because of inadequate income from wages. Although poor people may be found in all of the 254 counties of the state, poverty is particularly acute among certain ethnic groups and in specific geographic regions of the state. Table 1-3 indicates that the very young, the old, and blacks in seven geographic regions of Texas are the most severely deprived. Figure 1-4 outlines the seven regions. Of these, the Lower Rio Grande and East Texas have the largest incidence of poverty (Table 1-3). These two regions also have the largest Negro (East Texas) and Mexican-American (Lower Rio Grande) percentages in comparison to Anglos. East Texas has a high percentage of both blacks and elderly. The Lower Rio Grande has the highest percentage of children under fifteen.

There is a shockingly wide gulf between the economic status of Texas

TABLE 1-3
Selected demographic characteristics and percentage distribution of poor by ethnic group for Survey Regions of Texas and the incidence of poverty in each category

Survey Regions	Incidence of Poverty	Percent Negro Population 1970	Percent Population Aged 65 and Over 1970	Percent Population Aged 0-14 1970	Proportion of Poor Population			Incidence of Poverty		
					Blacks	Mexican-Americans	Anglos	Blacks	Mexican-Americans	Anglos
East	29.0	23.0	13.8	26.8	36.1	2.1	61.9	56.5	*	22.3
Gulf Coast	18.6	19.9	6.7	30.6	41.2	24.6	34.2	36.7	51.9	9.0
Lower Rio Grande	42.2	3.2	8.1	33.7	4.4	79.4	16.2	*	59.3	16.9
North Central	18.0	13.6	8.2	29.4	35.6	11.9	52.5	41.7	29.7	12.2
Central	21.1	13.2	11.3	25.3	32.5	16.4	51.2	50.9	28.3	14.4
Northwest	14.8	5.3	11.0	28.0	17.6	19.1	63.3	*	31.6	10.6
Southwest	23.7	5.1	8.1	31.6	5.2	70.5	24.2	48.0	40.6	10.2
Texas Total	22.0	12.7	8.8	29.8	25.3	34.5	40.2	44.0	45.3	12.6

Source: Texas Office of Economic Opportunity, *Poverty in Texas* (Austin, Tex.: Texas Department of Community Affairs, 1972), p. IV-11; Table A-1; pp. A-1 and A-12.

*Sample size less than 50

Figure 1-4

Survey Regions of Texas. Source: Texas Office of Economic Opportunity, Poverty in Texas *(Austin: Texas Department of Community Affairs, 1972), p. II-3.*

Anglos and that of the two largest minority groups, the blacks and Mexican-Americans. As indicated in Table 1-4, the incidence of poverty among blacks is 44 per cent and among Mexican-Americans, 45.3 per cent, while among Anglos it is only 12.6 per cent. Although the two minority groups constitute slightly less than a third of the total population of Texas (29.4 per cent), they account for nearly 60 per cent of the poor population. More than a fourth of the poor (25.2 per cent) are blacks, though they represent only 12.6 per cent of the total population. (See Reading 1-5 in this chapter concerning the extent of poverty among the blacks in Houston's Fourth Ward.) Over a third (34.5 per cent) of the poor in Texas are Mexican-Americans, though they comprise only 16.8 per cent of the population. Anglos, on the other hand, constitute only 40.3 per cent of the poor, but they account for 70.6 per cent of the Texas population.

TABLE 1-4
Percentage distribution of the total and poor populations and incidence of poverty by ethnic group, 1971

Ethnic Group	Distribution of Total Population	Incidence of Poverty	Distribution of Poor Population
Blacks	12.6	44.0	25.2
Anglos	70.6	12.6	40.3
Mexican-Americans	16.8	45.3	34.5
All Groups	100.0	22.0	100.0

Source: Texas Office of Economic Opportunity, *Poverty in Texas* (Austin, Tex.: Texas Department of Community Affairs, 1972), p. IV-2.

Viewing the spread of poverty according to age in Texas, it is noteworthy that percentages are highest among black and Mexican-American children and among elderly Anglos. This means that the largest numbers of poor people are in the young and old age-groups. In fact, the severest poverty problems in Texas are among children fourteen years of age and younger, and among persons sixty-five years of age and older. Children comprise the largest group (33.7 per cent) within the poor population, while the elderly have the highest incidence of poverty (40.1 per cent). However, the elderly comprise only 18.6 per cent of the poor because they represent only about 9 per cent of the total Texas population. The large number of poor children probably results from the limited incomes of large families, chiefly among Mexican-Americans. Minority group children are about five times more likely to be poor than Anglo children. The poor are heavily concentrated in three ethnic age-groups: black children (11.2 per cent), Mexican-American children (14.7 per cent), and Anglo elderly (13.6 per cent). These three groups represent nearly 40 per cent of all poor people in Texas. According to regional distribution (Table 1-3), poverty for blacks and Anglos is highest in East Texas; and for Mexican-Americans, it is highest in the Lower Rio Grande, where nearly 80 per cent of the poor are Mexican-Americans.

EDUCATIONAL ENVIRONMENT

One prerequisite popularly associated with individual economic achievement is education. Many professional educators are reluctant to look upon education merely as a ladder to economic success. Nevertheless, education is commonly thought to be a strong contributing factor, if not a necessary tool, to advancement in the economic world. The lack of education is likewise cited as a cause of poverty. Whatever the value placed on education, citizens in all the states want the highest-quality education for their children. Consequently, education in the twentieth century has become the most expensive service the state has to offer its citizens. Along with the obligation to expand education budgets, the states have been forced by federal court order to strive for equality of educational opportunity for all their citizens regardless of race or color. To achieve racial balance, the states have been forced to bus schoolchildren from one neighborhood school to another. More recently the whole question of state taxation to finance education has come under attack by the federal courts as discriminatory in its benefits. (The financing of Texas education is discussed in Chapter 7.)

Texas, like all the other states, is now spending a larger percentage of its annual revenue on education at all levels than at any previous time in its history. And like the other states, it is making significant progress. Its educational record in the last decennium, as shown by Table 1-5, is marked by significant increases in the percentages of people who completed various levels of education. Note that for both 1960 and 1970, Texas and the nation are quite similar in the percentages of persons who had not completed high school, but in 1970 Texas exceeded the national average of those who attended or completed college. These are indeed encouraging statistics for Texas.

TABLE 1-5
Percentage distribution of population 25 years old and over by educational group for Texas and the United States, 1960 and 1970

	United States		Texas	
Educational Group	**1960**	**1970**	**1960**	**1970**
Eighth Grade or Less	40.8	27.8	39.7	22.3
Part High School	19.6	17.1	19.2	20.2
High School	21.7	34.0	24.6	28.4
Part College	9.7	10.2	8.8	15.2
College Graduate	8.0	11.1	7.7	13.9
All Groups	99.8	100.0	100.0	100.0

Source: U.S. Bureau of the Census, *Current Population Reports,* Series P-20, No. 207; *U.S. Census of Population: 1960,* Final Report PC(1)-ID; *U.S. Census of Population: 1960,* Final Report PC(1)-45D; Texas Household Survey conducted in May, 1971, for the Texas Office of Economic Opportunity. See Texas Office of Economic Opportunity, *Poverty in Texas* (Austin, Tex.: Texas Department of Community Affairs, 1972), p. III-2.

However, there is another face to Texas education. Table 1-6 indicates the sad plight of the two minority groups in the state when their educational attainment is compared with that of the Anglo population. Although both blacks and Mexican-Americans narrowed the educational gap somewhat in the years 1950-1971, the Anglos continued to exceed the two minority groups. Though all three groups bettered their educational record in the 21 years from 1950 to

TABLE 1-6
Percentage distribution of persons 25 years of age and over in Texas by years of school completed and ethnic group, 1950, 1960, and 1971

Ethnic Group	None	Elementary (1-8)	High School (9-12)	College (1-4+)	Total
Anglo					
1950	1.2	38.1	43.2	17.5	100.0
1960	1.1	31.2	46.5	21.2	100.0
1971	.4	14.5	51.0	33.9	100.0
Nonwhite					
1950	5.9	66.3	22.2	5.6	100.0
1960	5.4	54.8	31.4	8.4	100.0
1971	2.3	29.3	51.2	17.2	100.0
Spanish Surname					
1950	27.8	60.2	9.9	2.0	100.0
1960	22.9	56.8	16.1	4.2	100.0
1971	11.0	47.4	31.8	9.8	100.0

Source: Texas Office of Economic Opportunity, *Poverty in Texas* (Austin, Tex.: Texas Department of Community Affairs, 1972), p. III-5.

1971, a much smaller percentage of the two minority groups participated in the improvement than did the Anglos. And in spite of the fact that the proportion of Mexican-Americans and nonwhites who had no schooling was 60 per cent less in 1971 than in 1950, 58.4 per cent of the Mexican-Americans and 31.5 per cent of the nonwhites had only an elementary school education in 1971, compared to only 15 per cent of the Anglos.

In relating educational attainment to income, it is found that at all educational levels the Anglos are much less likely to be poor, especially at the higher educational levels. Poverty among blacks with a high school education was over four and a half times greater than for Anglos at the same educational level; of those with education beyond high school, Mexican-Americans were five and a half times as likely to be poor as Anglos. About half of both blacks and Mexican-Americans with an eighth-grade education or less were poor.

Studies on the national level have revealed a striking difference in the scholastic attainment levels of Negro and Mexican-American students compared to Anglo students, with the two minority groups scoring much below the Anglos. (See Reading 1-6 in this chapter.) This difference in turn may be partially responsible for the difference in the extent of poverty within educational groups, but it is not likely to be the whole answer. Without a doubt influences other than education play a part in maintaining this condition.

FEDERALISM AND THE TEXAS CONSTITUTION

The federal structure of government, which Governor Terry Sanford of North Carolina referred to as "a system of states within a state," has survived 185 years of stresses and strains including a civil war that almost dismembered the Union. Texas has been a part of the federal union for 129 years and has been governed under the same state constitution for the past 98 years.

THE STATES IN THE FEDERAL SYSTEM

This division between states and central government was accomplished simply by spelling out in the United States Constitution the powers belonging to the central government and permitting the states to exercise all other powers not prohibited to them by the Constitution. The Tenth Amendment to the Constitution reads: "The *powers* not delegated to the United States by the Constitution, nor prohibited by it to the States, are *reserved* to the States respectively, or to the people." Those *powers delegated* to the United States Congress are contained in Article I, Section 8.

This division of powers which created the federal union became operative under the Constitution in 1789 and has remained unchanged to the present time. One may wonder how such a division of governmental powers between the central government on the one hand and the several states on the other could survive unchanged for nearly two centuries amidst the far-reaching social, economic, and political changes that these two centuries have wrought. The truth is that in practice the seemingly rigid arrangement is quite flexible, as the Founding Fathers apparently intended. In their wisdom and foresight they built into the Constitution a governmental framework wherein the three branches of government—legislative, executive, and judicial—could interpret the powers given to Congress in Article I, Section 8. Through this power of interpretation, new meaning may be given to old laws as succeeding needs arise. Thus the Constitution, in effect for nearly two hundred years, serves as the supreme law of the land in this age of the spaceship just as it did in the days of the sailing ship. Although not sovereign and independent like the United States, the individual states may, as Hamilton put it, be sovereign within their own sphere of operation, that is, within the powers reserved to them in the Tenth Amendment. Unlike the relationship between states and counties, the states are not mere subdivisions of the United States created for mere administrative purposes. According to Governor Sanford: "They are, fundamentally, political units within a federal system, wherein both the parts and the whole rest on constitutional bases."[5]

Even though they are political entities with guaranteed powers, the states are hedged in with limitations, both direct and indirect, by the same Constitution that grants them reserved powers. For example, they may not enter into treaties, alliances, or confederations; they may not, without the consent of Congress, participate in interstate or foreign compacts, nor levy imports on one another's products; they must accept the Constitution, acts of Congress, and treaties of the United States as the supreme law of the land; and the Civil War taught them that they are not permitted to secede from the Union. In addition, they may not deny anyone the right to vote because of race, sex, or failure to pay a poll tax; neither they nor the United States may deny or abridge the right of citizens of the United States who are eighteen years of age or older to vote on account of age; they may not deny anyone the equal protection of the laws or the privileges and immunities of citizens of the United States; and finally, they may not deprive anyone of life, liberty, or property without due process of law.

On the other hand, the Constitution provides the states with an imposing list of guarantees. They may not be divided or consolidated against their wishes, and the United States must *protect them against invasion and domestic violence.* The central government also *guarantees to each state a republican form of government.* In addition, the United States Constitution permits the states their own militias, assures them that federal criminal trials will be held within their own borders, guarantees that each state shall have equality of representation in the United States Senate and at least one member in the House of Representatives. Finally the Constitution gives to the states sole power of approving proposed amendments to the national Constitution.

Under this arrangement of divided governmental powers the states have maintained strong positions vis-à-vis the central government in Washington. Just as functions at the national level have expanded, so have they expanded at state levels. Today the states are performing more functions and undertaking more responsibilities than ever before in history. There seems to be no immediate danger that they will be overwhelmed by an all-powerful and paternalistic government in Washington, although this is a profound fear among many citizens. In the mid-1970s there is little evidence that *Harold Laski's* 1939 assessment of American federalism was prophetic:

> The epoch of federalism is over. . . . It is insufficiently positive in character; it does not provide for sufficient rapidity of action; it inhibits the emergence of necessary standards of uniformity; it relies upon compacts and compromises which take insufficient account of the urgent category of time; it leaves the backward areas a restraint, at once parasitic and poisonous, on those which seek to move forward; not least, its psychological results, especially in an age of crisis, are depressing to a democracy that needs the drama of positive achievement to retain its faith.[6]

This is not to say that in the past fifty years the states have not lost functions to the national government; in many cases they have ceased to assume the responsibilities for them. It would be erroneous to presuppose that state functions transferred to Washington are in all cases beneficial to the people of the state. Many of the more conservative-minded have long objected to what they consider a headlong flight of governmental functions to Washington, a greatly accelerated trend since the 1930s. Recent assumptions by the national government of functions previously relegated to the states are most familiar in the fields of education, health, and welfare. One reason for Washington's assumption of state functions since the 1930s has been the lack of state funds to finance the ever-increasing burden of social welfare responsibilities. An inadequate state tax base has led to the surrender to the national government of many responsibilities long accepted as the exclusive prerogative of the states. This trend may have already changed following the enactment by Congress of revenue-sharing legislation, which had started a stream of federal money flowing to the states before the end of 1972. (This subject is considered in more detail in Chapter 7.)

CONSTITUTION-MAKING IN TEXAS

Yet the states cannot entirely blame inability to compete with the national government in raising and spending money for the loss of state functions. Neither can they blame the national government for obsolete and largely unworkable state constitutions. Their own failure to revise their ancient and cumbersome documents has taken its toll upon the general health of the states. One of the most glaring faults of state constitutions is that of excessive length caused by the gradual accumulation of statutory matter. On this subject David Fellman has commented:

> It makes temporary matters permanent. It deprives state legislatures and local governments of desirable flexibility and diminishes their sense of responsibility. It encourages the search for methods of evading constitutional provisions and thus tends to debase our sense of constitutional morality. . . . It hinders action in time of special stress of emergency. It stands in the way of healthy progress. It blurs distinction between constitutional and statute law, to the detriment of both. It creates badly written instruments full of obsolete, repetitious, misleading provisions. Above all, it confuses the public. . . .[7]

The problem of excessive length is a product of the written constitution. The United States was born simultaneously with the advent of the written constitution. Consequently, our entire experience with government has rested quite firmly upon a written basic law. Not only has it been for us a way of government; it has affected materially our whole way of life. Not only are national, state, city, and county governments based on written constitutions (or charters) —so also are student governing bodies on college campuses; private corporations; civic, fraternal, and social clubs and societies; and various other types of organizations, large and small, public and private. Perhaps because of this long experience with written constitutions we have come to accept them as a *sine qua non* of government and have developed great faith in them as a source of governmental strength and stability. Indeed it is difficult for an American, so long accustomed to living under a written constitution, to conceive of government without one.

In the United States the state constitution is the fundamental law of the state. It establishes the government, defines its powers, and imposes restraints. The state constitution is the supreme law of the state, subject only to the United States Constitution, laws, and treaties. But it is more than this. A constitution is a product of history, an expression of political philosophy, a reflection of the moral and social principles of those who adopted it. A constitution should be drafted for the people so the people can read the document. It should be written in simple, concise language. Broad principles need no amendments; legalistic detail does. The specifics of policy and administration should be left to the respective branches of government established by the constitution. The Texas constitution embodies few of these important criteria.

The present constitution of Texas will be one hundred years old in 1976, if it survives that long. It is the sixth constitution to be drafted for Texas. The first, in *1836,* was the *constitution of the Republic of Texas* and was modeled after the United States Constitution. Unlike the present document, it was brief; it contained a minimum of restrictions on government operation. The first state constitution was adopted in 1845 and resembled those of the other southern states in its numerous limitations on legislative powers. A number of executive offices were appointive, but amendments in 1850 converted these to elective offices. Then came the Civil War and the secession of Texas from the Union, a move which resulted in three more constitutions, in 1861, 1866, and 1869. In 1861 the state chose a new constitution adapted to the exigencies of the Confederacy. But within four years it was obsolete and legally invalid within the federal Union. A fourth basic law was therefore adopted in 1866 to restore the state to the Union, but the Reconstruction laws passed by Congress the following year made it illegal. A fifth constitution being necessary, one was drafted by a clamorous and tumultuous constitutional convention in 1868-1869. Supported by the "radical" Republican Congress, it was ultimately ratified by the voters in 1869.

When Reconstruction ended, federal troops were removed, the carpetbaggers withdrew, and Texas was again free to draft and adopt a constitution not dictated by forces from without. And Texas made the most of the situation. Much, therefore, of what went into the 1876 law was motivated by reaction to the excesses of the Reconstruction government under the administration of *Governor E. J. Davis.* So the delegates elected to the 1875 constitutional convention wielded the pen freely, if not acrimoniously, in an attempt to guard themselves and the people of Texas against encroachments and indignities such as had been imposed upon them by the previous administration. They therefore struck out at corrupt administrators, legislators, judges, land speculators, railroad promoters, and those whom they considered voter manipulators. An example of the excessive zeal of the delegates was originally found in Section 4 of Article VI, which provided that "no law shall ever be enacted requiring a registration of voters of this state." They reduced the powers of the governor to a minimum, made executive offices elective, tied the hands of legislators, and made sure that all judges would be popularly elected. Terms of office were reduced to two years, and public services were trimmed to the bone. As a further award to taxpayers, the delegates lowered the salaries of public officials, reduced expenditures for public education, limited the public debt, and restricted the power of the Legislature to tax and spend.

This original constitution, plus 213 amendments, is the document which the voters of Texas indicated in 1972 they wished to have replaced by a new one in

1974. Fortunately or unfortunately, the delegates in 1875 provided a free-wheeling, *flexible amending clause.* The Legislature may propose amendments by a two-thirds majority vote of the membership of each house; such proposals become amendments to the constitution when approved at the polls by a simple majority vote. (Article XVII, the amending provision of the constitution, is contained in Reading 1-7 of this chapter.) As a result of this built-in flexibility, 334 proposed amendments were submitted to the voters by 1972, 213 of these having been approved and adopted. From this lesson in constitution-making-and-amending, Texas voters could have learned that government officials who are restricted from doing wrong are also prevented on occasion from doing good. The moral is, therefore, that an overly restrictive constitution, easy to amend, will soon assume the dimension of a statutory code of laws and thereby cease being a basic fundamental law.

But the voters have partially opened the door to make way for a totally new constitution, which if adopted will be Texas's seventh in 138 years. In November, 1972, Texas voters approved an amendment calling for a constitutional convention composed of the members of the Legislature to assemble in January, 1974, with authority to write a new constitution and submit it to the voters for approval. The convention is instructed by the amendment to consider recommendations submitted by a *constitutional revision commission* appointed by the Legislature in January, 1973. (The text of this amendment is contained in Reading 1-8.)

Excessive length per se is not a valid reason for framing a new constitution. The real case for revision lies within the content of the document, whether long or short, and the impact upon the government it creates. The Texas constitution alone must be blamed for many of the serious faults in the state governmental system it created. Unhealthy restrictions are imposed upon both state and local governments, preventing their maximum effectiveness. There is no need to fear in 1974 the too authoritarian and wasteful administration of the Reconstruction era of a century ago. The reactionary constitution of 1876 does not meet the governmental needs of Texas today. It fails to allow for an active, involved, efficient government that is able to respond to the demands of a highly complex urban society.

The present constitution long discouraged voting in Texas until the federal courts invalidated its restrictive suffrage requirements. The poll tax and annual voter registration were invalidated by federal courts along with constitutional restrictions on the right of military personnel to vote. Federal action voided Texas constitutional provisions limiting counties to one senator and otherwise forced the state to observe the "one man, one vote" rule governing legislative representativeness. These are not the only actions taken by federal courts to broaden the suffrage in Texas and thereby enhance the cause of democracy at the expense of an overly restrictive state constitution. (More information on this subject is contained in Chapter 2.)

The second major reason for a new constitution in Texas is the detrimental effect the present one has on the three branches of government. There are too many harmful *restraints imposed on the Legislature.* The most serious are those related to indebtedness and expenditures and to the length and number of regular sessions in a biennium. The constitution imposes on Texas a "weak" executive that is seriously handicapped in performing as responsibly as it should in a huge industrialized and urbanized state. It has, in short, imposed on the people of Texas one of the most fragmented and disintegrated administrative structures among the fifty states. The judicial department is in turn sorely lacking in structural integration, its benches filled with popularly elected judges, its administrative arm lacking in the soundest business principles.

Nor has local government escaped the deleterious effects of constitutional "safeguards." All 254 of Texas's counties, ranging in population from 164 to nearly 2 million, have the same basic structure of government. The constitution makes no significant distinction between heavily populated, urbanized Harris County and rural Loving County with only 164 inhabitants. No doubt the need for a revised structure of local government in Texas, because of the continuing urban crisis, should receive top priority.

Whether or not Texas citizens obtain a new constitution in 1974, the kind the state needs and to which the people are entitled will depend upon many related interests. A constitution is, first and foremost, *a political instrument.* Its content affects political leaders, interest groups, political parties, and private individuals. Legislators are vitally interested in who writes or revises the constitution. The Texas Legislature is dominant over the executive and judicial departments; undoubtedly the legislators want to keep it that way. In the past the Legislature has been hostile to any move to scrap the present document. Inasmuch as the 1972 amendment provided that the Legislature should name the constitutional revision commission and also sit as a constitutional convention, the legislators have not been overly hostile to the current developments moving toward a new constitution. Because of the dominant position of the Legislature in the Texas governmental structure, many observing citizens are pessimistic of the chances of securing a new constitution calling for a strengthened executive and an integrated court system with appointed rather than popularly elected judges. On the other hand one might expect the Legislature, sitting as the convention, to propose annual sessions of the Legislature with more pay for legislators, removal of legislative restrictions on fiscal operations, and an improved local government structure. An *untouchable clause* in the 1972 amendment forbids any tampering with the Texas Bill of Rights contained in the first article of the constitution.

In an interview with Dr. Janice May on December 1, 1970, Attorney General Crawford Martin referred to numerous constitutional issues that are of vital importance to various interest groups in the state. According to Martin any proposed Texas constitution, either during the drafting stage or when submitted to the voters for approval, will be scrutinized in the light of the approach taken toward the following issues: city-county relationships, state aid to local governments, annual legislative sessions, cabinet system administration, abolition of justices of the peace, the Missouri Plan for the selection of judges, reapportionment of counties, labor-management relations, dual office holding, the state's role in law enforcement, and the pay-as-you-go amendment.[8]

During the decade ending in 1971, eight states[9] adopted new or significantly revised constitutions, while as many states[10] suffered defeats of proposed basic laws. Judging from these performances, Texas should have a fifty-fifty chance of a new constitution. Friends and supporters of a new constitution for Texas include the League of Women Voters, Junior Chamber of Commerce, AFL-CIO, American Association of University Women, Texas Bar Association, leaders of both major political parties, the press, city and county officials, leaders among the judiciary, and a surprisingly large number of private citizens.

However, final ratification by the voters is a formidable and often fatal hurdle; without approval at the polls there can be no new constitution or revision of the old one. Voting publics are fickle indeed when the question is the adoption of a new constitution. Opposition to a single provision, sentence, or clause may cause a voter to reject the "whole thing." This impediment may be overcome by submitting the document piecemeal to the electorate. Either method, however, requires a substantial educational campaign to inform the voting public of the content of the document. As the campaign for a new Texas constitution began in earnest with the passage of the enabling amendment in 1972, many who voted for adoption of the amendment doubtlessly felt that Texas citizens had little to lose by failure of the movement for a new constitution; on the other hand, there was the possibility that a successful movement might bring about a more responsive and efficient state government.

In pursuance of the instructions contained in the 1972 enabling amendment, the 63rd Legislature, in January 1973, appointed a six-member committee to select the constitutional revision commission. This committee, composed of Governor Dolph Briscoe, Lieutenant Governor Bill Hobby, Attorney General John Hill, House Speaker Price Daniel, Jr., Chief Justice of the Supreme Court Joe Greenhill, and Presiding Judge of the Texas Court of Criminal Appeals John F. Onion, announced its selection on February 24 of a thirty-seven-member commission. (See Reading 1-9 for a tabular listing of the name, residence, age, occupation, education, and political party affiliation of each member.) The statute provided that members should be paid $50 per diem "while attending to the business of the commission" and for "time in travel." The commission was instructed to hold six of its full commission meetings in six different areas of the state, the purpose being to encourage citizen communication with the commission.

The 37 names, chosen from a list of approximately 900 names considered, were promptly submitted to the Legislature for final approval. Included were the names of 7 women, 3 blacks (Zan Holmes, Andrew Jefferson, and Earl Lewis), and 4 Mexican-Americans. Those remaining were Anglo males. Thirty members of the commission classified themselves as Democrats, 4 as Republican, 2 as nonpartisan, and 1 as independent. Immediately upon announcement of the commission membership, blacks, Mexican-Americans, Republicans, and women leveled charges of discrimination at the appointing committee. These groups accused the committee of favoritism and failure to provide a commission broadly representative of the state. They called for more representation from the grass roots and, as Texas newspaper columnist Jon Ford expressed it, less representation for "fat cat lawyers and buddies of top state officials." Not only did groups representing blacks, women, Mexican-Americans, and

Republicans feel they were underrepresented; so also did those representing geographic regions–West Texas, Central Texas–and youth. Eight members of the commission were under forty; one was under thirty. The median age was fifty.

Legislators had until March 9 to block these appointments. Prevention of approval could be achieved by a petition signed by a majority of both houses. Such a movement was launched but failed for lack of signatures, and all 37 nominees were approved. Shortly after release of the names of the commission, Tom Vandergriff, mayor of Arlington, resigned his position on the commission and was replaced by James William "Bill" Bass, Canton attorney and former member of the Texas House and the "Dirty Thirty." About two weeks later Harry A. Shufford, former Texas assistant attorney general, resigned and was replaced by Mrs. Ann S. Chappell, research specialist from Fort Worth. The commission held its first meeting on March 10, at which time Chairman Robert W. Calvert, former chief justice of the Texas Supreme Court, appointed seven ad hoc committees:

Budget Preston Shirley, chairman; Mrs. Mary Beth Brient; Wales Madden; and Jim Weatherby.
Office Space and Equipment Mrs. Faye Holub, chairman; Tony Bonilla; Raymond D. Nasher; and Don Rives.
Calendar Ralph Yarborough, chairman; Judge Barbara Culver; M. F. (Mike) Frost; Zan W. Holmes; and L. G. Moore.
Citizens Advisory Judge Andrew Jefferson, Jr., chairman; Loys D. Barbour; Dr. Clotilde García; Bill Hartman; and Mark McLaughlin.
Constitutional Revision Leon Jawórski, chairman; Roy Barrera; Sibyl Hamilton; Mark Martin; and E. L. Oakes, Jr.
Seminar Dr. Janice C. May, chairman; William C. Donnell; Dr. Peter Flawn; W. James Kronzer, Jr.; and Dr. Earl Lewis.
Staff Dr. George Beto, chairman; Beeman Fisher; John Leroy Jeffers; W. Page Keeton; and Honore Ligarde.

Toward the end of March, 1973, the commission heard experts on constitutional law and political science discuss the problems of governing Texas under the 1876 constitution. A style and drafting committee composed of one member from each of the seven ad hoc committees was named on April 13: Mark Martin, chairman; Dr. Earl Lewis; Preston Shirley; W. James Kronzer, Jr.; Dr. Janice C. May; Mrs. Sibyl C. Hamilton; John Leroy Jeffers. Commission hearings began in April at various cities across the state. At these meetings the commission heard a cross section of opinion from citizens who were urged to attend and tell the commission members what changes they felt should be made in the Texas constitution.

On November 1, 1973, the commission submitted its recommendations to the Legislature. Sitting as a *constitutional convention,* the Legislature will begin on January 8, 1974, to consider whatever is submitted to it by the revision commission. The product of the convention could be a totally new constitution, a substantial revision or a series of minor revisions of the 1876 constitution. The convention is instructed by the 1972 enabling amendment to end its labors by

May 31, 1974, unless by a two-thirds majority vote of the convention it extends its life another 60 days. In November the convention's recommendations will be submitted to the voters of Texas for ratification. If a totally new constitution is submitted, the outcome of the referendum will hinge on the campaign, prior to November, to inform the voters of the content of the new document. If popular ratification is achieved, Texas will begin in 1975 to govern itself under its seventh constitution.

NOTES

1. Rupert Norval Richardson, Ernest Wallace, Adrian N. Anderson, *Texas: The Lone Star State,* 3rd ed. (Englewood Cliffs, N.J.: Prentice-Hall, 1970), p. 2.
2. Texas Office of Economic Opportunity, *Poverty in Texas* (Austin, Tex.: Texas Department of Community Affairs, 1972), p. IV-2. See also *Summary Selected Demographic Characteristics from Census Data–Fourth Count* (Austin, Tex.: Office of the Governor, Office of Information Services, OIS GR-3, August, 1972), p. 3.
3. Kennedy and Roberts counties reported no Negro residents. See *Summary Selected Demographic Characteristics* cited in note 2 above. Forty-four other counties reported a Negro population below 50; 21 of these 44 had 10 or fewer blacks in residence.
4. V. O. Key, Jr., *Southern Politics in State and Nation* (New York: Alfred A. Knopf, 1950), p. 254.
5. Terry Sanford, *Storm Over the States* (New York: McGraw-Hill, 1967), pp. 7-8.
6. Harold Laski, "The Obsolescence of Federalism," *New Republic,* May 3, 1939, p. 367.
7. David Fellman, "What Should a State Constitution Contain?" in W. Brooke Graves, *Major Problems in State Constitutional Revision* (Chicago: Public Administration Service, 1960), p. 146.
8. The Texas Urban Development Commission, *The Texas Constitution: Problems and Prospects for Revision* (Arlington, Tex.: The University of Texas at Arlington, October, 1971), pp. 91-92.
9. Michigan, Connecticut, Hawaii, Pennsylvania, Florida, Virginia, Illinois, and North Carolina.
10. New York, Rhode Island, Maryland, Kentucky, Oregon, New Mexico, Arkansas, and Idaho.

KEY TERMS, NAMES, AND CONCEPTS

San Jacinto Day
Texas Independence Day
Caddo Indians
Tayshas

Anglos
Mexican-Americans
black Texans
metropolitan area
Panfilo Narvaez
Francisco de Coronado
suburbs
urbanization
poor Texans
federal system
delegated powers
reserved powers
protection against invasion and domestic violence
guarantee of republican form of government
Harold Laski
constitution of the Republic of Texas, 1836
Governor E. J. Davis
flexible amending clause
constitutional convention in 1974
constitutional revision commission
constitutional restraints on the Legislature
constitution as a political instrument
"untouchable clause" in 1972 amendment

HERC FICKLEN FROM THE DALLAS NEWS

GAL WITH A CLOUT—

Selected Readings

1-1
INDIAN TEXANS HERE MANY YEARS; PEOPLE, CULTURE STILL AN INFLUENCE

Historians estimate [that] scores of Indian tribes have lived in the land we call Texas, at one time or another in history. Perhaps the diverse geography of Texas explains why. What happened to them? Did landhungry Anglo-Americans kill them all, except remnants sent to reservations? Contrary to false ideas advanced in novels, magazines, newspapers, and lately, movies and television, this is not the whole story. Many Indians did die as the white man wrested their land. Probably the least destructive factor was removal to Indian reservations. More

From *People*, II (July-August, 1972), pp. 2-6. *People* is published bimonthly by the University of Texas, Institute of Texan Cultures at San Antonio. Reprinted by permission.

than either of these, it is believed that the great decline in Indian Texan population resulted from two causes: one, European disease (cholera, smallpox, etc.); the other was the killing effect of arbitrary disruption of the Indians' habitat, or the destruction of his ecological balance. Like all other men, the Indian existed in concert with his surroundings.

Still, other Indian Texans made the transition to the white man's world. As a result, the Bureau of Indian Affairs Field Employment Office in Dallas estimates 12,000 Indians live in Dallas County alone. The U.S. Census Bureau says Texas has 17,957 Indians. One thing is sure. The Indian Texan is part of the state's culture in 1972, and he is very much in existence. His blood blends with others in untold thousands of Texans. He contributed familiar place names, including Comanche, Caddo Lake, Tonkawa Creek, Waco, Quanah, Wichita Falls, Waxahachie, and the state's own name–Texas. He and his fellow Indians elsewhere in the nation contributed such words to the American language as coyote, tobacco, caucus, chipmunk, hickory, hominy, and moose–to name a few. His history is on every public library's shelves, and relics of his past in scores of Texas museums.

Texans of Mexican heritage, who make up 37 per cent of the U.S. Mexican population, are descendants of the great Indian cultures of Mexico, some of which had direct connection with Texas Indians. Texas has 2,059,671 Spanish-speaking citizens; many have an Indian heritage. Evidence shows that Indians who peopled this state in pre-recorded history were surprisingly modern men–erect, intelligent, resourceful and courageous. They solved the problems of survival, apparently without the benefit of lessons from ancient civilizations. They were immigrants into Texas, just as later national and racial groups from the Eastern Hemisphere would be. Where the environment was congenial–as in Central Texas and East Texas in recent centuries and other areas in earlier times–they settled down in one place for long periods of time, built villages, farmed, and devised sophisticated cultures.

1-2 INTERPRETATIONS OF THE BLACK POLITICAL EXPERIENCE

Chandler Davidson

Houston, a city of 1.2 million people in 1970, is situated within the country's thirteenth largest standard metropolitan statistical area (SMSA). The Negro population exceeds 300,000 which was approximately the size of Chicago's "Bronzeville" in the thirties when Cayton and Drake undertook their classic study of the black community in that city.[1] Houston lies within Harris County,

From *Biracial Politics: Conflict and Coalition in the Metropolitan South* (Baton Rouge, La.: Louisiana State University Press, 1972), pp. 17-22. Reprinted by permission.

TABLE 1
City of Houston, total and Negro population, 1900-1970

Year	Total Population	Negro Population	Per Cent Negro
1900	44,633	14,608	32.7
1910	78,800	23,929	30.4
1920	138,276	33,960	24.6
1930	292,352	63,337	21.7
1940	384,514	86,302	21.4
1950	596,163	125,400	21.0
1960	938,219	215,037	22.9
1970	1,232,802	316,992	25.7

Source: U.S. Bureau of the Census.

whose 1.7 million population is the largest in the state and is second in growth rate among the country's most populous counties.

As in the case of the larger community, Houston's Negro population is rapidly increasing (Table 1). In 1970, 26 per cent of the city's population was black, indicating a continued reversal of a trend that saw the city's black ratio steadily decline between 1900 and 1950. It is presently the largest Negro concentration in the South, exceeding that of either New Orleans or Atlanta. It is the eighth largest black population in the country.

An important source of this Negro increase is favorable net migration. Bullock has shown that 87.9 per cent of the Negro increase in the city between 1940 and 1950 was the result of migration.[2] A large number of these migrants come from small towns and rural areas in Texas and Louisiana. However, the portrayal of this migration as a movement of southern rural inhabitants to the city is oversimplified. Slightly more than 34 per cent of the Negro in-migrants to Houston between 1955 and 1960 were from other SMSAs.[3] This is considerably less than the percentage of such urban in-migrants in the northern cities, where the proportion is usually more than 60 per cent, but it is higher than that of several other comparable southern ones. In all probability Houston occupies the role of a "stage" city described by the Taeubers: "The redistribution of Negro population from the rural South to northern cities appears to be an indirect process. Few Negroes move directly from Southern farms to Chicago or New York. Negro farmers, croppers, or farm laborers are more likely to move to a nearby southern city. Later they or their children may move to one of the northern cities."[4] As more than 60 per cent of Houston's Negro out-migrants in the period between 1955 and 1960 moved to another SMSA, one can reasonably assume that Houston performs the "service" of acclimating many rural blacks to city life before they make their next move to a northern or western metropolis.

Houston Negroes, like their counterparts elsewhere, are highly concentrated in predominantly nonwhite residential areas. In 1960 the city was rated 93.7 on the Taeubers' index of residential segregation. A score of 100 indicates complete segregation.[5] Everett Ladd, borrowing from the terminology of Charles S. Johnson, has distinguished three types of southern residential patterns. In the "back yard" type, Negro residences are distributed uniformly throughout the city. At the other extreme is the "ghetto" pattern, with a single intense concentration of Negro residences. A third pattern is that of "urban clusters," involving one to three large concentrations of Negroes, as well as up to twenty smaller clusters scattered across the city.[6]

Houston exhibits the latter pattern. There are three main areas of Negro concentration within the city limits, surrounded by numerous smaller clusters. There is also a fourth major area immediately outside the city's northern limits, which is in many ways integral to the Houston Negro community. A fifth area, much smaller than the other four, completes the five major Negro subcommunities. "These areas are more than sheer aggregates of people," writes Bullock. "They constitute virtual social entities, in which the people have strong loyalties toward the section in which they live and quickly identify with them."[7] There are, in addition to these five main areas, more than twenty smaller ones within the city limits.

As in many other American cities, there has been a large increase in the number of Negroes in the core city. Between 1950 and 1960 the total central city population (Negro and white combined) actually decreased by 34,198, while the Negro population rose by 20,299. The proportion of the core city population which was Negro rose from 23.4 per cent to 30.1 per cent in the same period.

Although the Fifth, Fourth, and Third wards are within the core city and have a relatively high population density in terms of people per square mile, they are for the most part free of typically eastern slums, which are characterized by aging tenements and stark high-rise apartment complexes. Rather, the core city residential areas consist primarily of mixed single-family and multi-family dwellings. These are accurately described by a City Planning Commission report: "The predominating housing characteristics of these areas are undersized single-family dwellings crowded together, either upon small lots or with several dwellings upon one lot. Where larger dwellings exist, they too are frequently crowded together and are often occupied by more than one family. The environment created by this type of residential use is usually substandard."[8]

While a high percentage of Houston's Negroes lives in segregated areas, there is extensive daily contact between the two races in the city. One of the reasons for this is a geographical one. The Negro areas are gradually expanding into a north-south belt, cutting the city in half. Movement of whites from one half to the other often requires that they cross through a Negro area. White traffic is particularly heavy through the Third Ward—which lies directly southeast of the main business district—and the Fourth Ward, which is an enclave in the older central business area.

Another reason for this interracial contact is that the Negro community is not economically self-sufficient. The Fifth, Fourth, and Third wards each has an important main street occupied by many small commercial establishments catering to blacks. But the large department stores, banks, theaters, and parks are outside these areas. Further, there is not an old, established Negro commercial and financial district in the city, such as exists in Atlanta or Durham. There is only one Negro-owned bank, opened in 1963, and one Negro savings and loan association, chartered in 1959. Each had less than four million dollars in total assets in 1966. The total resources of the Houston area's banks (not counting savings and loan associations) were more than five billion dollars.

A third reason for extensive interracial contacts lies in the work patterns of the Negro labor force. Most domestics must go outside the Ghetto to work. The same is true for Negroes engaged in lawn care, manual labor, industrial enterprises, and the small but growing white-collar endeavors. Thus, while the majority of white Houstonians do not often pass through Negro residential areas, they meet blacks every day on the city streets, in stores and restaurants, in their own segregated neighborhoods, and of course as servants and laborers in their homes.

To summarize, Houston's history gives evidence of the city's strong identification with the traditions and values which are peculiar to the former slave-owning states who fought against the Union more than one hundred years ago. This is not to deny that the southern mystique is gradually dissipating under the impact of urbanization and the integrating bonds of nationalism. Nor does it contradict the fact that Houston, lying on the periphery of the South, has developed regional loyalties to the Southwest as well. The thesis that Houston is a southern city does imply however that the barriers of caste are a little stronger, the exercise of white power a little more brutal and unashamed, and the intransigence of officials and voters alike to the demands for Negro equality somewhat more unyielding than is the case in the North and West of this nation today.

NOTES

1. Horace Cayton and St. Clair Drake, *Black Metropolis: A Study of Negro Life in a Northern City* (New York: Harcourt, Brace, 1945).
2. Henry Allen Bullock, *Pathways to the Houston Negro Market* (Ann Arbor, Mich.: J. W. Edwards, 1957), p. 31.
3. Karl E. and Alma F. Taeuber, "The Negro Population in the United States," in John P. Davis (ed.), *The American Negro Reference Book* (Englewood Cliffs, N.J.: Prentice-Hall, 1966), p. 126.
4. *Ibid.*, p. 129.
5. Karl E. Taeuber and Alma F. Taeuber, *Negroes in Cities: Residential Segregation and Neighborhood Change* (Chicago: Aldine Publishing Co., 1965), p. 41. The Taeubers (p. 30) explain the index as follows: "The value of the index may be interpreted as showing the minimum percentage of non-whites who would have to change the block on which they live in order to produce an unsegregated distribution—one in which the percentage of non-whites living on each block is the same throughout the city."

6. Everett Carll Ladd, Jr., *Negro Political Leadership in the South* (Ithaca, N.Y.: Cornell University Press, 1966), pp. 52-53. See also Johnson, *Patterns of Negro Segregation,* p. 10 (New York: Harper, 1943).
7. Henry Allen Bullock, *Profiles of Houston Negro Business Enterprises: A Survey and Directory of Their Activities,* mimeographed (Houston, Tex.: Negro Chamber of Commerce, 1962), p. 16.
8. Houston City Planning Commission, *Population, Land Use, Growth* (Houston, Tex.: 1959), p. 78.

1-3
HISTORICAL CIRCUMSTANCE AIDS ANGLO PREDOMINANCE OF TEXAS

The history of Texas was made by, and is inextricably interwoven with, the peoples and governments of many lands. This multiple heritage, perhaps more than any other reason, gives the state its uniqueness among the 50. Yet one of the amazing facts of this history is that Texas–after three centuries of Spanish rule–should within 15 years become predominantly Anglo-American and so remain. Texas' 1820 population, in addition to its Indians, was estimated at 4,000. Then Mexico opened the door to immigration from the United States the following year. By 1836, of the some 38,000 settlers in Texas, 30,000 were Anglos.

The Anglos prevailed not only in numbers. Theirs became the primary language of Texas; their legal and educational institutions were adopted. And the history of Texas has been recorded almost wholly by Anglo-Americans in Anglo-American terms. Too often, however, Anglo predominance of the Texas scene has been credited to the myth of superiority rather than actual historical circumstance. A host of logical and simultaneous factors formed the catalyst for Texas' swift inundation by folk from east of the Sabine.

Of all the people who came here, only the Anglo-Americans had three generations of successful frontiering immediately behind them. In the process they became "professional pioneers," mobile exploiters of the land, which they learned to sell or abandon at will. This was a concept that neither the Mexican nor European ever understood. Acquiring ground–good or bad–they lived with it and passed it on to their posterity. Meanwhile the Anglos swarmed around and over them, always aiming for cheap lands. Impetus was added to the Anglos' experience in 1820, when on the heels of a devastating panic, the United States adopted a new law concerning public lands. No credit and $1.25 cash per acre replaced the small down payment and extended terms on land purchases of former years. In Texas a family could have title to almost 5,000 acres for the "in due time" promise to pay nominal surveyor and impresario fees. Geography, too, conspired in the preponderance of Anglo-American immigration. The Anglo

From *People,* II (March-April, 1972), pp. 2-6. Reprinted by permission.

–crossing from a green, well-forested and watered section into East Texas' piney woods–was as much at home on one side of the border as the other.

In sharp contrast, the European faced a hazardous, expensive sea voyage to this land of which he knew nothing for certain. The journey was far from easy for the Mexican colonist as well. Though technically he lived just across a river, his trek to the watered areas of Texas was over barren mountains and desert. The Anglo-Americans, moreover, were equipped as none others with firsthand knowledge of successful revolution and the establishment of lasting self-government. A few who came to Texas had fought in the American Revolution; many, like Sam Houston, were sons of men in Washington's army. A number had taken part in the formation of state and territorial governments and in constitutional conventions. With this collective know-how, the Anglos moved quickly into positions of leadership when the Texas Revolution began.

1-4
DALLAS IS THE MOST CROWDED CITY
Walter B. Moore

Dallas is Texas' most crowded county. Data just received from the 1970 U.S. Census show that Dallas County has a population of 1,545.2 per square mile of land area, 859 square miles. That is more than 500 persons per square mile greater than the population density in Harris County. The state's most populous county has 1,011 persons per square mile of land area. Its land area is 1,723 square miles. Other populous counties also have a much smaller population density than Dallas. Bexar County (San Antonio) is listed as having 666.5 persons per square mile, and Tarrant County had 832 persons per square mile of land area when the count was made in April, 1970.

Texas continues to be a land of wide open spaces, with only 42.7 persons per square mile average for its 262,134 square miles of land area. That figure, however, represents a significant rise in density from the 1960 average of 36.4 Texans per square mile. In 1950 there were only 29.3 Texans per square mile and the average was 24.3 in 1940. Growing population is the major reason for the rising population density, of course. But the land area is diminishing also because of man-made lakes. Dallas County is shown with a 1970 land area of 859 square miles, whereas the 1960 figure was 892. For Texas, the Bureau of Census gives a land area of 262,134 square miles, a small decrease from the 1960 figure of 262,840. Dallas residents who get a fenced-in feeling from these figures can find consolation in another aspect of the situation. Population density makes an area attractive to businesses that depend upon consumer buying, and that makes Dallas County tops in Texas. Those wanting more breathing space can find that in Texas, too. Many counties have fewer than two persons per square mile and several (Hudspeth, Kenedy and King) have only one resident for each two square miles.

From the *Dallas Morning News,* October 16, 1971. Reprinted by permission.

As Texans move to urban areas, the predominantly rural counties are declining in population density. Eastland County, for example, now has 19 residents per square mile, compared with 20.5 when the 1960 Census was taken. Delta County shows a drop from 21.2 to 17.9 persons per square mile of land area during the decade. There are many others with the same trends.

Comparing Dallas County's density with that of foreign nations is rather startling. The figure of 1,545.2 for our home county compares with an average of 708 per square mile in Japan, 606 in West Germany, 810 in Holland, 818 in Belgium, 415 in India and an estimated 1,200 per square mile in the congested river valleys of Communist China.

With the world's population expected to double in the next three decades unless birth and death rates change drastically, congestion as well as food shortages will be pressing problems. Most acute of those problems will be outside our boundaries, in the poorer nations that now have two thirds of the world's population and a birthrate twice as great as in the more developed countries. That projected growth rate of the world, doubling each 30 years and increasing eightfold during a century, happens to be just about the rate of population growth in the United States between 1800 and 1900—a fact that caused Americans to brag in the past, but now alarms them, according to a new book, *The London Times History of Our Times.*

Here in Texas our population growth rate declined sharply during the 1960s, as compared with previous decades. In fact, the 16.9 per cent gain from 1960 to 1970 was about one third less than the percentage increase during the 1950s and the smallest for any decade on record, except for the 10.1 per cent increase during the depression of the 1930s. With the reduced birthrate and probably smaller net immigration, Texas' rate of growth during the 1970s may not be far from that low of 10 per cent. But that would mean about 1,120,000 more Texans, with most of them likely to locate in Dallas, Houston, Fort Worth and other metropolitan areas.

Ranking near the top in Texas problems, as it does in the U.S. and many other countries, is the need for redistribution of population. Texas has vast areas that need people, but those rural counties aren't likely to attract them unless ways can be found to create jobs and the other human needs and conveniences that most Americans now seek in cities.

1-5
THE AGONIZING DEATH OF AN IGNORED PEOPLE IN FOURTH WARD: LAND THAT HAS NOT BEEN FORGOTTEN
Thomas Wright

Deep in the guts, the bowels of Fourth Ward, a giant yellow tractor plows methodically across a square block of ground. The rigorous effort is not to sow seeds for

From *Forward Times,* December 9, 1972, p. 12B. Published in Houston, *Forward Times* is one of the leading black newspapers in Texas. Reprinted by permission.

the future, but rather, it is to bury the past. Where once there had been life, there now is only raw earth. Where once there had been a house, there now is only rubble. Where once there had been a score of vibrant families, there now is only a lone bulldozer operator grading under his task of demolition.

The Fourth Ward is Houston's Harlem—only worse. Its disenchanted people are poor. Most are old, wrinkled, and frightened. Most are living an existence of despair, a life of hopelessness. Few know what tomorrow will bring. Fourth Ward is a Black neighborhood waiting for something to happen.

Once its narrow brick streets and small houses stretched deep into the pulse-beat of downtown Houston where places like the Humble and Tenneco Building now settle. But today, Fourth Ward is a dying community. Within the last 50 years, more than half the old ward has been razed and what little remains sits in the shadows of advancing skyscrapers and freeways.

Often forgotten, to 7,000 people, Fourth Ward is still home. According to the 1970 census only 90 of the ward's 3,000 housing units were occupied by owners. That figure is even lower now. The rest of the ward is row-after-row of rundown shotgun shack rental property which is owned largely by absentee land-lords—"slumlords" to most people.

Down the narrow streets can be seen little old men and women, draped in heavy coats to protect their thin bodies from the chilly winter air. Tiny children, most ill-clothed and ill-fed, sit on the steps of the mammoth housing project, Allen Parkway Village. Youngsters, most of whom belong in school, stand in front of pool halls and openly smoke marijuana. Every once in a while, a preg-nant teenage girl, a scarf covering her hair rollers and a mask of a forsaken child-hood covering her face, walks swiftly past the corner. Across the street is a row of condemned houses seemingly quaking, waiting for the man with the big yellow tractor.

Like a cancer, the "progress that is in the public interest" is eating away at Fourth Ward. The people there are ignored souls wandering, wondering. But the land is not forgotten. Within a stone's throw of downtown, the fastest growing city in the nation, sit the wooden frame houses with rotting porches occupied by gaunt-eyed people.

Fourth Ward is a tragedy that should never have been allowed to happen. Its saga is one that is nurtured in the hearts of the people living there, but one that affects the lives of the 400,000 Black people in Harris County, for Fourth Ward is the motherland for all Black Houston. . . .

Many of the rent houses are dilapidated. In many, families with seven and eight children try to live in two rooms. In most, there are no sinks, no hot water, floors and walls are rotting, the roof leaks, and hazardous wiring is exposed in almost every house there. And, for the renters, there are always the rats and roaches, health hazards, although some of the old people there try to take a humorous look at their lifestyle.

"Man, the rats here are as big as lions," John Venice said as he leaned back in his handhewn chair, an antique. "I've got a tomcat that is about eight years old and these rats—they look like squirrels—they pull razors on him."

"The rats in my apartment house are as big as cats," seriously intimated Frankie Lee Gipson, a 50-year-old woman who lives on Baldwin Street. "They walk up these stairs better than I do. They cut up the paper and I tell the rent man about it, but nothing ever happens. But that don't stop him from knocking on my door every Saturday asking for his $12.50."

"And the roaches, well, you come by here after sundown and try to hold a conversation, these cockroaches will talk to you," chided Venice. "You think I'm kidding? I don't mean these little roaches you can get rid of with a can of aerosol spray. Hell, these cockroaches will take that spray can away from you."

Venice leaned back, chuckling to himself for a while. Then, the laughter stopped. His voice turned cold, serious, deadly. "Man, renting is the only way we can make it. We're poor people. We got to have at least a roof over our heads and we laugh at these houses sometimes but that's the only way we can make it. We can't cry all the time. These Italian landlords, they're taking our rent money and running to River Oaks to their mansions and we suffer."

For five winters, Seneda D. Mason has lived on Bailey Street. For five winters, she has lived without heat. Her rent is eight dollars a week. Half Black, half Choctaw Indian, she could not have survived those cold winters had it not been for her socialization. She grew up on a neglected reservation in Tulsa, Oklahoma, so "I was ready for the Fourth Ward." This past summer, due to the housing code, Mrs. Mason's landlord (Joe Guarino, the father of one of Houston's most popular district court judges) decided he would fix up her house.

"Instead of really helping me, they've made it worse," Mrs. Mason said, sitting on her cramped front porch, cramped because of the pots of sweet-smelling flowers she keeps to hold down the stench from the open sewer in front of her house. "This summer, they bought me a 10 gallon water heater and they put a sink in the bathroom. They painted it too and all that's going to cost me two extra dollars a week on the rent. But what happened was they didn't fix the bathroom floor after they put in the hot water heater and the sink. Now, I got a gaping hole in that floor."

The hole was about four feet in diameter, "big enough for a child to get through, let alone big rats, lizards or snakes," and the old woman had tried to cover it with a rug and several bricks. A couple of two-by-four's were under the commode to keep it from falling through the opening and onto the ground below the house. For electricity, Mrs. Mason has the old-fashioned "drop cords" that hang from the ceiling. Her daughter sent her an electric heater so she will not freeze this winter, but "I have nowhere to plug it in."

Despite being part Choctaw Indian, Mrs. Mason realizes she is getting too old to endure the icy Houston winters and this year, she is afraid that pneumonia is going to catch up with her, especially with the broken windows caused during the painting, the cracks under the doors, the hole in the bathroom floor, and no place to plug in the heater.

"Fourth Ward is a classic example of urban blight," says the area's newly-elected Black Congresswoman, Barbara Jordan. Jordan–and every other thinking person–knows why Fourth Ward is allowed to languish, an eyesore to the city, a health hazard to the people living there. The area is within a stone's throw of downtown Houston.

Gordon Jennings, the president of the $22 billion development, Houston

Center, has repeatedly said for Houston to continue its phenomenal growth rate, the central business district must expand. Everyone knows that means a jump across the freeway into Fourth Ward unless something is done to save the community from progressing downtown.

Landlords, realizing the value of the property, are simply holding on to it waiting for land values to escalate even further. Speculators are in the area buying what land they can get for $5 a square foot and some are even paying $8 if the property is on West Dallas. "Most of the landowners are just keeping the rental property to pay taxes on the land," indicates James McConn, the area's city councilman. "Some are fixing up the property where it's liveable, but most are content to get by with the bare necessities for those good people living there."

Some of the landlords have gotten tired of contending with tenants and have allowed their buildings to be condemned, but most still stand erect, not torn down by the unsafe buildings demolition crew the city is supposed to use in case landlords refuse to tear down the buildings themselves.

Consequently, young Fourth Warders use the buildings as "dope dens" or they are used by prostitutes who carefully wend their way through the rubble to beds located in the rear of some of them.

The effect of the unliveable conditions of Fourth Ward on the youngsters there has caused a trend that is practically irreversible. Most try to escape their surroundings through the euphoria of dope. Most are unemployed and that means an alternative way to support habits. Crime runs rampant in the Fourth Ward and on the first of the month, old men and women are afraid to cash pension or Social Security checks because they know they are going to be knocked in the head before making it back home to hide their meager funds.

"Brotherman, we don't have nothing here," lamented one teenager. He looked like an ordinary boy, that is, until his arms were glimpsed. There were the ugly tracks—the scars left after scores of hypodermic needles had punctured veins. The tracks were a roadmap of his life of poverty and the attempt to escape from it. "When we want to swim, we have to go all the way to Third Ward, Fifth Ward, Memorial Pool. They used to have a recreation center, but they closed that down. They used to open up the school for us, but they don't do that no more. All we got are a few pool halls and beer joints, so what do they expect us to be. But, man, we wanna live just like other people. To swim, go dancing every Friday night. We're no different from other people. They're just fencing us out—or in, if you want to call this prison that." In one of the condemned houses, this youngster impregnated a 15-year-old girl.

In the middle of that row of condemned houses sits one small, freshly-painted dwelling. To the old man and woman there, it is home. In the back yard, is a rose garden, a fence, some kittens. There, sitting in the middle of filth was someone's dream, the fruit of the work of a lifetime. The tinsel across the fence spelled "Merry Christmas." In the window were candles. Across the door were four words: "God Bless Our Home". And goosebumps run up and down the spine.

1-6
THE EXCLUDED STUDENT

AN UNASSIMILATED MINORITY

Our system of public education has been a key element in enabling children of various ethnic backgrounds to grow and develop into full participants in American life. During the great waves of immigration in the 19th and early 20th centuries, society turned to the schools as the principal instrument to assimilate the millions of children of diverse nationalities and cultures into the American mainstream. By and large, the schools succeeded in accomplishing this enormous task.

In the Southwest, however, the schools have failed to carry out this traditional role with respect to the Mexican-American, that area's largest culturally distinct minority group. There are numerous reasons why they have failed. Many are rooted in the history of the Southwest, which emphasizes the significant differences between Mexican-Americans and other ethnic groups who comprise the rich variety of the American population. What are these differences?

Mexican-Americans are not like other ethnic groups, who are largely descendents of immigrants who came to this country from across the oceans, cutting their ties with their homelands as they sought a new way of life. The earliest Mexican-Americans did not come to this country at all. Rather, it came to them. They entered American society as a conquered people following the war with Mexico in 1848 and the acquisition of the Southwest by the United States. Furthermore, most who have crossed the international boundary since then have entered a society which differs little from the culture they left behind on the other side of the border.

For geographical and cultural reasons Chicanos have, by and large, maintained close relations with Mexico. In contrast to the European immigrant whose ties with the homeland were broken, most Mexican-Americans who crossed the international boundary after the war with Mexico have continued a life style similar to that which they have always known.

Still another distinction is that many Mexican-Americans exhibit physical characteristics of the indigenous Indian population that set them apart from typical Anglos. In fact, some Anglos have always regarded Mexican-Americans as a separate racial group.

The dominance of Anglo culture is most strongly apparent in the schools. Controlled by Anglos, the curricula reflect Anglo culture, and the language of instruction is English. In many instances those Chicano pupils who use Spanish, the language of their homes, are punished. The Mexican-American child often leaves school confused as to whether he should speak Spanish or whether he

From *The Excluded Student: Educational Practices Affecting Mexican-Americans in the Southwest,* Mexican-American Education Study, Report III of the U.S. Commission on Civil Rights (Washington, D.C.: U.S. Government Printing Office, May, 1972).

should accept his teacher's admonishment to forget his heritage and identity.

But this culture exclusion is difficult for the schools to enforce. The Mexican culture and the Spanish language were native to the country for hundreds of years before the Anglo's arrival. They are not easy to uproot. To this day the conflict of cultures in the schools of the Southwest is a continuing one that has not been satisfactorily resolved and is damaging to the Mexican-American people.

The deep resentment felt by many Mexican-American children who have been exposed to the process of cultural exclusion is expressed in the words of a graduate of the San Antonio school system:

"Schools try to brainwash Chicanos. They try to make us forget our history, to be ashamed of being Mexicans, of speaking Spanish. They succeed in making us feel empty and angry inside."

EXCLUSION OF THE SPANISH LANGUAGE

The lack of appreciation for knowledge of a foreign language as well as concern over a deficiency in English have resulted in several devices by school officials to insure the dominance of the English language in the schools of the Southwest.

Some of the more significant justifications for the prohibition include:

1. English is the standard language in the United States and all citizens must learn it.
2. The pupil's best interests are served if he speaks English well; English enhances his opportunity for education and employment while Spanish is a handicap.
3. Proper English enables Mexican-Americans to compete with Anglos.
4. Teachers and Anglo pupils do not speak Spanish; it is impolite to speak a language not understood by all.

Significant data concerning the "No Spanish" rule were gathered by the Commission in its Mexican-American Education Survey. Each district was asked about its official policy regarding the prohibition of Spanish. Each sampled school in these districts also was asked if it discouraged the speaking of Spanish in the classroom and/or on the schoolgrounds.

Few districts reported an official prohibition of Spanish either on the schoolgrounds or in the classroom. Only 15 of the 532 districts which responded to the survey said that they still had a written policy discouraging or prohibiting the use of Spanish in the classroom. Twelve of these districts were in Texas, one each in Arizona, California, and New Mexico. Ten Texas districts also forbid students to speak Spanish on the schoolgrounds as does the one New Mexico district. All but three of the surveyed districts which had a "No Spanish" rule as a policy also had an enrollment that was 50 per cent or more Mexican-American. There was no apparent relationship between the size of the district and the existence of the policy. The following statement of board policy exemplifies the "No Spanish" rule:

Each teacher, principal, and superintendent employed in the free-schools of this state shall use the (English) language exclusively in the classroom and on the campus in conducting the work of the school. The recitations and exercises of the school shall be conducted in the English language except where other provisions are made in compliance with school law.

This statement, following the Texas Penal Code, was enclosed with the Superintendents' Questionnaire and mailed to the Commission from a school district in Texas. It is an example of the near-total exclusion of Spanish by insistence on the exclusive use of English in school work. Texas continues to go so far as to make it a crime to speak Spanish in ordinary school activities. As recently as October 1970 a Mexican-American teacher in Crystal City, Texas was indicted for conducting a high school history class in Spanish, although this case was subsequently dismissed. Another district in Texas which recently "relaxed" its rule against the use of Spanish enclosed this statement:

Effective on September 1, 1968, students were allowed to speak correct Spanish on school grounds and classrooms if allowed by individual teachers. Teachers may use Spanish in classroom to "bridge-a-gap" and make understanding clear.

It should be noted that the school district only allows the use of "correct" Spanish; this often means only the Spanish that is taught in the Spanish class. Many educators in the Southwest regard the Spanish spoken by Mexican-Americans as deficient. Such comments as "the language spoken at home is 'pocho', 'Tex-Mex', or 'wetback Spanish'" were often found in the principals' response to the questionnaire.

The principals' questionnaires also indicated that a relatively large number of schools, regardless of official school district policy, discouraged the use of Spanish in the classroom and on the schoolgrounds. Based on the survey findings, it is estimated that of a projected total of 5,800 schools in the survey area the policies of approximately one-third discourage the use of Spanish in the classroom. About one-half of these schools–15 per cent of the projected total–discourage the use of Spanish not only in the classroom but on the schoolgrounds as well. . . .

A comparison among States presents sharp differences in the frequency of the use of the "No Spanish" rule. In both elementary and secondary schools, in the classrooms and on the schoolgrounds, Texas leads in frequency of application of the "No Spanish" rule. Two-thirds of all surveyed Texas schools discouraged the use of Spanish in the classroom and slightly more than one-third discouraged its use on the schoolgrounds. In the classroom it was applied with at least twice the frequency of most other States. . . .

None of the school principals or staff who responded to the survey admitted to using corporal punishment as a means of dealing with children who spoke Spanish in school. However, at least 3 per cent of the schools did admit to actual discipline of the pupils involved. In one case pupils who violated the "No Spanish" rule were required to write "I must speak English in School."

At the San Antonio hearing one principal testified that in his school–a highly segregated Mexican-American school in El Paso, Texas–students who were found to be speaking Spanish during school hours were sent to Spanish detention class for an hour after school. . . .

Other forms of punishment are revealed in the following excerpts from themes of one class of seventh grade Mexican-American students in Texas. They were written in October of 1964 as part of an assignment to describe their elementary school experiences and their teachers' attitudes toward speaking Spanish in school.

If we spoke Spanish we had to pay 5c to the teacher or we had to stay after school. . . .

In the first through the fourth grade, if the teacher caught us talking Spanish we would have to stand on the "black square" for an hour or so. . . .

When I was in elementary they had a rule not to speak Spanish but we all did. If you got caught speaking Spanish you were to write three pages saying, "I must not speak Spanish in school". . . .

In the sixth grade, they kept a record in which if we spoke Spanish they would take it down and charge us a penny for every Spanish word. If we spoke more than one thousand words our parents would have to come to school and talk with the principal. . . .

If you'd been caught speaking Spanish you would be sent to the principal's office or given extra assignments to do as homework or probably made to stand by the wall during recess and after school. . . .

Although the survey did not uncover instances in which school officials admitted to administering physical punishment for speaking Spanish, allegations concerning its use were heard by the Commission at its December 1968 hearing in San Antonio. . . .

Two San Antonio high school students told of being suspended, hit, and slapped in the face for speaking Spanish. Another young Mexican-American, a junior high school dropout, revealed that one of the reasons he left school in the seventh grade was because he had been repeatedly beaten for speaking Spanish. . . .

The reasoning that motivates administrators and teachers to prohibit or discourage the use of Spanish is not always strictly related to the educational needs of the child. At one San Antonio Independent School District junior high school, which had a 65 per cent Mexican-American enrollment, the Anglo principal testified that he would not be in favor of bilingual instruction past the third grade because:

I think they (Mexican-Americans) want to learn English. And I think that they want to be full Americans. And since English is the language of America, I believe that they want to learn English.

During the course of an interview with a staff attorney prior to the hearing, the same principal stated that he would "fight teaching Spanish past the third grade because it destroys loyalty to America."

Some evidence of a change in traditional attitudes toward the speaking of

Spanish, however, was provided at the San Antonio hearing by Dr. Harold Hitt, Superintendent of the San Antonio Independent School District. He testified that his district had changed its policy toward the use of the Spanish language just 3 weeks prior to the hearing. . . .

Faced by the fact that 47 per cent of all Mexican-American first graders do not speak English as well as the average Anglo first grader, many educators in the Southwest have responded by excluding or forbidding the use of the child's native language in the educational process. In essence, they compel the child to learn a new language and at the same time to learn course material in the new language. This is something any adult might find unusually challenging.

1-7
AMENDING THE CONSTITUTION OF TEXAS: ARTICLE XVII AS AMENDED IN 1972

Section 1. The Legislature, at any regular session, or at any special session when the matter is included within the purposes for which the session is convened, may propose amendments revising the Constitution, to be voted upon by the qualified electors for statewide offices and propositions, as defined in the Constitution and statutes of this State. The date of the elections shall be specified by the Legislature. The proposal for submission must be approved by a vote of two-thirds of all the members elected to each House, entered by yeas and nays on the journals.

A brief explanatory statement of the nature of a proposed amendment, together with the date of the election and the wording of the proposition as it is to appear on the ballot, shall be published twice in each newspaper in the State which meets requirements set by the Legislature for the publication of official notices of officers and departments of the state government. The explanatory statement shall be prepared by the Secretary of State and shall be approved by the Attorney General. The Secretary of State shall send a full and complete copy of the proposed amendment or amendments to each county clerk who shall post the same in a public place in the courthouse at least 30 days prior to the election on said amendment. The first notice shall be published not more than 60 days nor less than 50 days before the date of the election, and the second notice shall be published on the same day in the succeeding week. The Legislature shall fix the standards for the rate of charge for the publication, which may not be higher than the newspaper's published national rate for advertising per column inch.

The election shall be held in accordance with procedures prescribed by the Legislature, and the returning officer in each county shall make returns to the Secretary of State of the number of legal votes cast at the election for and against each amendment. If it appears from the returns that a majority of the votes cast have been cast in favor of an amendment, it shall become a part of this Constitution, and proclamation thereof shall be made by the Governor.

1-8
ARTICLE XVII, SECTION 2, THE TEXAS CONSTITUTION: CONSTITUTIONAL REVISION COMMISSION AND A CONSTITUTIONAL CONVENTION

(*a*) When the legislature convenes in regular session in January, 1973, it shall provide by concurrent resolution for the establishment of a constitutional revision commission. The legislature shall appropriate money to provide an adequate staff, office space, equipment, and supplies for the commission.

(*b*) The commission shall study the need for constitutional change and shall report its recommendations to the members of the legislature not later than November 1, 1973.

(*c*) The members of the 63rd Legislature shall be convened as a constitutional convention at noon on the second Tuesday in January, 1974. The lieutenant governor shall preside until a chairman of the convention is elected. The convention shall elect other officers it deems necessary, adopt temporary and permanent rules, and publish a journal of its proceedings. A person elected to fill a vacancy in the 63rd Legislature before dissolution of the convention becomes a member of the convention on taking office as a member of the legislature.

(*d*) Members of the convention shall receive compensation, mileage, per diem as determined by a five member committee, to be composed of the Governor, Lieutenant Governor, Speaker of the House, Chief Justice of the Supreme Court, and Chief Justice of the Court of Criminal Appeals. This shall not be held in conflict with Article XVI, Section 33 of the Texas Constitution. The convention may provide for the expenses of its members and for the employment of a staff for the convention, and for these purposes may by resolution appropriate money from the general revenue fund of the state treasury. Warrants shall be drawn pursuant to vouchers signed by the chairman or by a person authorized by him in writing to sign them.

(*e*) The convention, by resolution adopted on the vote of at least two-thirds of its members, may submit for a vote of the qualified electors of this state a new constitution which may contain alternative articles or sections, or may submit revisions of the existing constitution which may contain alternative articles or sections. Each resolution shall specify the date of the election, the form of the ballots, and the method of publicizing the proposals to be voted on. To be adopted, each proposal must receive the favorable vote of the majority of those voting on the proposal. The conduct of the election, the canvassing of the votes, and the reporting of the returns shall be as provided for elections under Section 1 of this article.

(*f*) The convention may be dissolved by resolution adopted on the vote of at least two-thirds of its members; but it is automatically dissolved at 11:59 p.m. on May 31, 1974, unless its duration is extended for a period not to exceed 60 days by resolution adopted on the vote of at least two-thirds of its members.

(*g*) The Bill of Rights of the present Texas Constitution shall be retained in full.

1-9
BIOGRAPHICAL DATA FOR MEMBERS OF THE TEXAS CONSTITUTIONAL REVISION COMMISSION
Eugene W. Jones and Lyle C. Brown

History may well classify the thirty-seven members of the Constitutional Revision Commission, along with the 181 members of the 63rd Legislature (see Reading 3-2) as the "fathers" and, perhaps, the "mothers" of Texas' seventh constitution. Certainly the eight women and twenty-nine men who were appointed to the revision commission accepted a solemn responsibility. For years to come, political scientists, lawyers, and others interested in constitution-making across the nation will study their work. Many articles, and perhaps not a few monographs and books, will chronicle their successes and failures. So that instructors and students may know more about the commission members and their qualifications for drafting a new constitution, the authors have compiled the biographical data that are presented in the following table. Data were obtained from questionnaires prepared by the authors and from articles in newspapers and periodicals. Most helpful among newspaper articles was one by Jan Batts headlined "Constitutional Revisionists Ready to Start Burning Deadwood: Impressive Displays of Credentials Posted by Most Commissioners," in the *Fort Worth Star-Telegram,* March 11, 1973.

Name	Residence	Age*	Occupational and Civic Background	Studies at Institutions of Higher Education	Political Party Affiliation
Barbour, Loys D.	Iowa Park	63	Farmer; legislative representative, Texas Farm Bureau for 10 years; helped to organize Texas Farm Bureau and to rewrite its constitution in 1953	none	Democrat
Barrera, Roy R.	San Antonio	46	Attorney; Secretary of State, 1968-1969, by appointment of Governor Connally; former assistant district attorney, Bexar County	Texas Tech/New Mexico A&M/St. Mary's	Democrat
Bass, James William (Bill)	Canton	36	Attorney; farmer; former state representative and member of "Dirty 30"; close friend of Speaker Price Daniel, Jr.	Texas A&M/SMU	Democrat
[1] Beto, Dr. George	Huntsville	57	Professor, Sam Houston State University; former director, Texas Department of Corrections; former president, Concordia College (Austin) and Concordia Theological Seminary (Springfield, Ill.)	Valparaiso (Indiana)/UT, Austin	Democrat
Bonilla, Tony	Corpus Christi	37	Attorney; state director, LULAC; former state representative; South Texas Chairman of "Viva Kennedy" Clubs, 1960; co-founder of PASO; Southwest coordinator for Nixon-Agnew campaign, 1972	Del Mar/Baylor/Houston	Independent
Brient, Mrs. Mary Beth	El Paso	40	Director, Texas League of Women Voters; member of Texas Urban Development Commission, 1970-1971; regional chairman of Citizens for Texas	Baylor/UT, Austin	Democrat

**Calvert, Robert W.	Austin	68	Attorney; retired Chief Justice, Texas Supreme Court; state representative for six years and Speaker, 1937-1939; former county attorney, Hill County	UT, Austin	Democrat
Chappell, Mrs. Ann S.	Fort Worth	29	Campaign director, 1972, for Citizens of Texas, pressure group for new constitution; research associate, Institute of Urban Studies; staff member, Texas Urban Development Commission; research associate for U.S. Department of Housing and Urban Development in Ft. Worth	UT, Austin	Democrat
Culver, Mrs. Barbara G.	Midland	47	County Judge, Midland County; former president, Permian Basin Regional Planning Commission	Whitworth Jr./ Texas Tech/SMU	Republican
Donnell, William G.	Marathon	53	President, Texas and Southwestern Cattle Raisers Association; rancher; board member, American Independent School Districts for 10 years	Texas A&M	Democrat
Fisher, Beeman	Fort Worth	74	Retired board chairman, Texas Electric Service Co.; immediate past president, Texas Water Conservation Association; president of West Texas Chamber of Commerce for 6 years; chairman, Texas Research League, 1971	none	Democrat
Flawn, Dr. Peter T.	San Antonio	47	President, University of Texas at San Antonio; former professor of geological sciences and public affairs and former vice president at University of Texas, Austin	Oberlin/Yale	Democrat
Frost, M. F. (Mike)	McAllen	40	Manager and owner, McAllen Fruit and Vegetable Co.; farmer; vice president, Texas Farm Bureau, 1966-1972	Tulsa/Rice	Democrat

García, Dr. Clotilde	Corpus Christi	56	Physician; board member, Nueces County Community Action and Del Mar College; former member, U.S. Senate Special Committee on Aging	Pan American/ UT, Austin/UT Medical School, Galveston	Democrat
Hamilton, Mrs. Sibyl C.	Dallas	52	Public relations director, Dallas Community College District; Dallas councilwoman, 1965-1969; member of Army Nurse Corps during World War II; former member of national Air Quality Advisory Board; former Dallas County representative to North Texas COG	Shannon West Texas School of Nursing	Republican
Hartman, J. William (Bill)	Beaumont	31	Editor and publisher, *Beaumont Enterprise* and *Beaumont Journal;* member, Texas Advisory Commission on Intergovernmental relations; member, Citizens for Texas; director, Citizens National Bank and Trust of Baytown	Baylor	Democrat
Holmes, Zan W., Jr.	Dallas	38	District Superintendent, Dallas Metropolitan District, United Methodist Church; former assistant director of Dallas War on Poverty; pastor of Hamilton Park Methodist Church; state representative, 1969-1973	Huston-Tillotson/SMU	Democrat
[2] Holub, Mrs. Faye	Austin	52	Business services instructor for Southwestern Bell	none	Democrat
[3] Jaworski, Leon	Houston	67	Attorney; past president of American Bar Association, State Bar of Texas, American College of Trial Lawyers, Houston Bar Association, Houston Chamber of Commerce, and Rotary Club of Houston; Trustee of M. D. Anderson Foundation and Baylor College of Medicine; director, Texas Bill of Rights	Baylor/George Washington	Democrat

Jaworski, Leon (cont.)			Foundation; special counsel to Attorney General of Texas, 1963-1965, 1972-1973; chairman, Governor's Committee on Public School Education, 1966-1969; member, President's Commission on Law Enforcement and Administration of Justice, 1965-1967; member, President's Commission on the Causes and Prevention of Violence, 1968-1969; prosecutor, Nuremberg war crimes trials		
Jeffers, John Leroy	Houston	63	Attorney; president-elect, State Bar of Texas; served for 6 years on Board of Regents, University of Texas, and was president, 1957-1959; assistant criminal district attorney, Bexar County, 1935-1939; former chairman, Texas Bill of Rights Foundation; former faculty member, St. Mary's University and South Texas School of Law	UT, Austin	Democrat
[4] Jefferson, Andrew L., Jr.	Houston	38	Judge, court of domestic relations; former vice chairman, American Bar Association Committee on Organized Crime; member, National Urban League and National Association for the Advancement of Colored People	Texas Southern/ UT, Austin	Democrat
Keeton, Dr. W. Page	Austin	63	Dean, University of Texas School of Law; former president, American Bar Foundation and Association of American Law Schools; member, President's Advisory Committee on Labor-Management Policy, 1966-1969	UT, Austin/ Harvard	Democrat

Kronzer, W. James, Jr.	Houston	53	Attorney; member, advisory commission to the Supreme Court of Texas; member, State Bar grievance committee, Congressional District 22; registered lobbyist for Houston Bar Association and Texas Trial Lawyers Association; member, House Interim Committee on Governmental Immunity	UT, Austin	Democrat
Lewis, Dr. Earl M.	San Antonio	53	Director, Urban Studies Program, and professor of political science, Trinity University; former professor at Howard University and Prairie View A&M; vice president, Texas Urban Development Commission; delegate to the White House Conference on Aging	Tougaloo/ Loyola, Chicago/ Chicago	Democrat
Ligarde, Honore	Laredo	52	Banker; attorney; board chairman, Bank of Commerce of Laredo; vice president, Laredo council of LULAC; state representative, 1962-1972; member, State Democratic Executive Committee, 1960-1964	UT, Austin	Democrat
McLaughlin, Mark	San Angelo	42	Attorney; rancher; director, Texas State Bank and Continental Fidelity Life Insurance Co.; Assistant Attorney General of Texas, 1957-1958; mayor, City of Snyder, 1964; vice chairman, University of Texas at Austin Development Board	Rice/UT, Austin	Democrat
Madden, Wales H., Jr.	Amarillo	45	Attorney; chairman, executive committee of Mesa Petroleum Co.; director, First National Bank of Amarillo; member, Board of Regents, Amarillo College, 1958-1959; member, Board of Regents, University of Texas, Austin, 1959-1965; member, Coordinating Board, Texas College and University System, 1969-1973	Amarillo/ UT, Austin	Democrat

Martin, Mark	Dallas	58	Attorney; commissioner, City of University Park; board chairman, State Bar of Texas; past president, Dallas Bar and Texas Association of Defense Counsel; board member, University of Texas Law School Foundation; counsel for Dallas Independent School District in desegregation suits, 1956-1973	UT, Austin	nonpartisan
[5] May, Dr. Janice C.	Austin	49	Assistant professor of government, University of Texas at Austin; housewife; member, Constitutional Revision Commission, 1967-1968; research associate, Office of the Governor, 1966; former president, American Association of University Women; board member, League of Women Voters, 1964-1970; member and secretary, Travis County Grand Jury, 1962	Minnesota	nonpartisan
***Milburn, Mrs. Malcolm (Beryl)	Austin	52	Housewife; vice chairman of Texas Republican Party, 1969-1972; member, State Republican Executive Committee, 1956-1965; member of Rules Committee, 1972 Republican National Convention	UT, Austin	Republican
Moore, L. G.	Deer Park	37	Representative, International Union of Operating Engineers, AFL-CIO	Oklahoma/Harvard Trade Union Program	Democrat
Nasher, Raymond D.	Dallas	51	Real estate developer; former member of U.S. Commission for UNESCO; executive director, White House Conference on International Cooperation, 1965; member, President's Commission on International Cooperation, 1966-1967; member, President's Committee on Urban Housing, 1967-1968	Duke/Boston	Democrat
Oakes, Elijah L., Jr.	Houston	55	Representative, Ironworkers Local Union #84	none	Democrat

Rives, Don L.	Marshall	38	Attorney; U.S. magistrate, 1965 to present; assistant criminal district attorney, Harrison County, 1959-1961; board member, Harrison County Hospital Association, Marshall Independent School District, and Oak Haven Nursing Home	North Texas/ UT, Austin	Democrat
[6] Shirley, Preston	Galveston	60	Attorney; former associate professor of law, University of Texas School of Law; member and former chairman, Development Board, University of Texas at Austin; director, First Hutchings-Sealy National Bank; past president, Texas Association of Defense Counsel; former member, Charter Review Committee and City Planning Committee, Galveston	TCU/UT, Austin	Republican
Weatherby, Jim Walter	Mountain Home	62	Attorney; rancher; retired president of Charles Schreiner Bank; 15 years' service as county attorney, county judge, district attorney, and district judge	Schreiner/Baylor	Democrat
[7] Yarborough, Ralph W.	Austin	69	Attorney; U.S. Senator, 1957-1970; Assistant Attorney General of Texas, 1931-1934; lecturer, University of Texas School of Law, 1935; state district judge, 1936-1940	U.S. Military Academy/Sam Houston/UT, Austin	Democrat

*Age at time of appointment to Commission
**Chairman
***Vice Chairman
[1] Chairman, committee on staff
[2] Chairman, committee on office space and equipment
[3] Chairman, committee on constitutional revision
[4] Chairman, citizens' advisory committee
[5] Chairman, seminar committee
[6] Chairman, budget committee
[7] Chairman, calendar committee

Rug Beaters — We Got

HERC FICKLEN FROM THE DALLAS NEWS

2

The Politics of Parties and Elections

Government in a democracy looks to active participation by the people in the making of public policies that affect their lives. People participate in the political process through organized political parties, which select candidates for public office and generally set the tone of competition among parties, candidates, and issues. Each voter responds to this three-way challenge as he makes his decisions at the polls. The extent of popular participation in the political process is influenced by these stimuli, but it is affected also by the rules governing such participation. In Texas these rules have undergone great change in recent years. Basically the Texas political structure is not unlike that in the other states, but it bears the marks of the state's historical experiences and total environment. Nevertheless, the growing uniformity of rules governing political participation and the changing social environment are lessening these distinctions and otherwise changing the face of the political process in Texas.

THE ELECTORAL PROCESS

Exercising the right to vote is the most popular expression of political democracy. It is known to more people in a democracy than any other right. Not only do people seem to be more conscious of this important civil right than any other, but it is the most undisputed and accepted of all the personal liberties in a democracy. Exercise of the ballot brings the individual and his government close together for a moment and makes him aware that he is a part of that government. It is through the ballot that the concept of government by the people is given meaning for the masses. At the polls the sovereign voter decides who shall govern.

Participatory democracy via the ballot has not always been as widespread in Texas as it is today. Universal suffrage is a condition only recently realized in the United States. In the exercise of the ballot this nation has not always been as democratic as it is today. In 1780 about 120,000 out of 2 million people of voting age were eligible to vote. This was only 6 per cent of the adult population. The Constitution of the United States, put into effect in 1789, left to the states the power to decide who should be eligible to vote in both state and national elections. When Washington was elected President, only a handful of people in the thirteen states could vote. Voting was limited largely to white male adults, but only those owning property were given the ballot in most states. And even some of these were disqualified because of failure to meet the requirement of church membership.

All of these impediments have been swept away by periodic waves of democracy that have marked the history of the ballot in the United States. The first to go was that of church membership. Most property qualifications were removed in the wave of Jacksonian democracy of the 1820s and 1830s, about the time that Texas entered the Union. By the time of the Civil War all church membership and nearly all property qualifications had been removed. But even these victories for democracy failed to reach women and Negro slaves. Blacks won the first legal victory following the Civil War with the *Fourteenth and Fifteenth Amendments.* The Fifteenth prohibits any state from denying the right to vote to anyone on account of race or color. The Fourteenth forbids any state to deny to anyone the equal protection of the laws. Thus both amendments prohibit government action but not acts by private persons. For the blacks in the South these two amendments proved to be legal victories only, not victories in fact. Following Reconstruction the southern states erected one barricade after another, legal and extralegal; and for the next hundred years the southern Negro was barred from the polls as the Fourteenth and Fifteenth Amendments were reduced to dead letters. In Texas and the other southern states the Ku Klux Klan, the *literacy test,* the *grandfather clause,* the *white primary,* and the *poll tax* largely succeeded in holding the ballot in reserve for whites only.

The work of the Ku Klux Klan is familiar enough as an extralegal force to keep the southern Negro from the polls. The literacy test was a more sophisticated instrument; but when fairly administered, it disqualified many uneducated whites. The grandfather clause in literacy test laws denied the right to vote to an illiterate whose grandfather did not have the right to vote prior to January 1, 1867. Thus white illiterates often qualified for voting, whereas southern blacks could not. This discriminatory legislation was finally declared unconstitutional by the United States Supreme Court in 1915 as a violation of the Fifteenth Amendment.

The so-called white primary, largely a product of Texas ingenuity, was an involved process based upon denying the Negro access to the direct primary rather than to the general election. If, in a one-party state such as Texas, the winner in the Democratic Party primary was always the victor in the general election, the party primary became in effect the real election. Based upon this assumption, in 1923, the Texas Legislature passed a law declaring the Negro ineligible to participate in a Democratic Party primary. This and other white primary legislation were nullified by the United States Supreme Court in *Nixon* v. *Herndon* (1927) and *Nixon* v. *Condon* (1932). Ultimately, however, in *Grovey* v. *Townsend* (1935), the Court upheld a resolution adopted by the Texas state Democratic convention providing that only whites could participate in Democratic Party primary activity, including that of nominating candidates for public office. Since, in the opinion of the Court, no state action was involved in such a resolution by the Democratic Party of Texas, there could be no violation of the Fourteenth or Fifteenth Amendment. This form of racial discrimination at the polls, sanctioned by the Supreme Court in the *Grovey* case, lasted for nine years before the same tribunal declared the practice to be a violation of the Fourteenth Amendment in *Smith* v. *Allwright* (1944). In this case the Court took the position that conduct of party primaries by political parties cannot be separated from state action. Thus, since a state cannot bar blacks from voting in any party primary on account of color, neither can a party carry out such discrimination.

In 1902 an amendment to the Texas constitution provided for payment of a poll tax as a prerequisite for voting. The tax in Texas was nominal, \$1.75, or \$1.50 if the county did not choose to impose a \$.25 tax that was authorized. The plan was not designed as a revenue measure but as a means of discouraging most blacks, Mexican-Americans, and other poor people from registering to vote. In this it succeeded remarkably. Persons with little income frequently failed to pay the poll tax during the designated four-month period from October 1 to January 31. With the ratification of the Twenty-fourth Amendment to the federal Constitution in January, 1964, the poll tax as a prerequisite for voting in national elections was abolished. At that time, however, only five states, including Texas, used the poll tax as a prerequisite. The amendment, of course, still left the states free to require the payment of the tax for voting in state and local elections. Hence Texas continued to require that voters possess a poll tax receipt if they voted in these elections. The federal Voting Rights Act of 1965 directed the Attorney General of the United States to challenge enforcement of poll tax laws in state elections, however; and as a result of action initiated in this way, the United States Supreme Court, in *Harper* v. *Virginia State Board of Education* (1966), invalidated all state poll tax laws. The Court concluded that a state violates the equal protection clause of the Fourteenth Amendment "whenever it makes the affluence of the voter or payment of any fee an electoral standard." The Court also asserted: "Voter qualifications have no relation to wealth nor to paying or not paying this or any other tax. . . . Wealth, like race, creed, or color, is not germane to one's ability to participate intelligently in the electoral process. . . ."

Following this decision the Texas electorate approved a state constitutional amendment which repealed the already defunct Texas poll tax amendment of 1902, and required legislative enactment of an annual voter registration law. In

1967 the Legislature enacted a voter registration law for the state. The effect that discontinuance of the poll tax had upon voter response at the polls is shown by Table 2-1. The numbers who qualified to vote by paying the poll tax during the last two years of the poll tax law compare most unfavorably with the numbers who registered to vote during the first three years without the poll tax law.

TABLE 2-1
Comparison of poll tax receipts with voter registration in Texas

Poll Tax Receipts		**Voter Registration**		
1964-65	*1965-66*	*1967-68*	*1968-69*	*1969-70*
2,411,679	1,577,572	2,982,862	4,073,576	3,400,649

Source: *Texas Almanac,* 1972-1973 (Dallas, Tex.: A. H. Belo Corporation, 1971), pp. 527-528.

Congress added its weight to the effort to further the democratization of the ballot with the passage of a series of election laws in the years 1957, 1960, 1964, 1965, and 1970. These four laws succeeded remarkably in extending the right to vote to more of the previously disenfranchised by providing safeguards against further denial of the ballot. The laws (1) empowered the Attorney General of the United States to obtain court injunctions to prevent illegal denial of the right to vote, (2) provided for the appointment of federal referees to register potential voters in areas where a pattern of denial is found, (3) made unequal administration of voting rights a crime, (4) prohibited the denial of the right to vote because of minor errors in registration, (5) required that all literacy tests be given in writing, (6) suspended literacy tests in states and counties where less than 50 per cent of voting-age residents were registered by November 1 of the election year, (7) provided for the appointment of federal examiners to register persons in these areas, (8) abolished residency requirements of more than thirty days to vote in national elections, (9) suspended literacy tests in all states for five years (from 1970), (10) required all states to provide absentee ballots, and (11) lowered the voting age to eighteen in national primaries and elections.

This imposing body of legislation completed the removal of almost every remaining impediment to exercising the right to vote. In practice these new safeguards were particularly applicable to minority groups. In 1920 women were enfranchised nationally when the states ratified the *Nineteenth Amendment* to the United States Constitution; it forbids denial of the right to vote on account of sex. Effective in 1971, the *Twenty-sixth Amendment* extended the voting privilege in national and state elections to those eighteen years of age and older. The amendment reads: "The right of citizens of the United States, who are 18 years of age or older, to vote shall not be denied or abridged by the United States or any state on account of age."

As a result of this impressive body of constitutional amendments, statutory legislation, and judicial action, the nation has achieved virtual universal suffrage. Today only a few conditions are imposed as prerequisites for voting. Besides the eighteen-year-old *age qualification,* all states require the voter to be a citizen of the United States and of the state in which he resides. Although *state citizenship* does not of itself guarantee the right to vote, it is one of the qualifying conditions that permits the suffrage. The Fourteenth Amendment to the federal Constitution defines both national and state citizenship. It provides that persons born or naturalized in the United States and subject to its jurisdiction are citizens of the United States and of the state in which they reside.

Another qualification for voting required in all states is *residence.* Until 1972 most states required residence of one year in the state, three to six months in the county, and residence in the precinct at the time of voting. One year was the state requirement in Texas; but on March 21, 1972, in *Dunn* v. *Blumstein,* the United States Supreme Court invalidated Tennessee's one-year residence law as a violation of the equal protection clause of the Fourteenth Amendment. Opening the way to the ballot box to 5 million Americans, the Court implied that any required residency period of more than thirty days might be unconstitutional.* The Court pointed out that a lengthy waiting period is unnecessary to guard against fraud and poses an unconstitutional barrier to travel. There is no reason, continued the high tribunal, to suppose that a new resident has less knowledge of election issues than old residents. "Obviously," said Justice Thurgood Marshall, "many longtime residents do not have any." He went on to assert that thirty days "appears to be an ample period of time for the state to complete whatever administrative tasks are necessary to prevent fraud."

Probably about 100,000 of the otherwise qualified voters of Texas were kept from the polls in 1970 by the one-year residency law. This would seem to be a high price to pay for whatever such a law was designed to achieve. An editorial in the *Dallas Morning News* nevertheless took the Court to task for what the paper termed an "invasion of residential requirements" (see Reading 2-1). The *Blumstein* decision, in effect, invalidated one-year residence laws in some thirty states, including Texas. With the primaries only a month away at the time of the Court's ruling, the secretary of state of Texas, as director of elections, replaced the one-year residence requirement with a thirty-day qualification period. This was intended to conform to the period of time suggested by the Court in the Tennessee case.

Another important qualification for voting in Texas is *registration.* The avowed purpose of registration is to help determine in advance whether those desiring to vote have all the qualifications for voting prescribed by law. Following the Civil War, the states generally adopted registration plans whereby voters were required to register periodically, in most instances either annually or every two years. Disadvantages in such frequency of registration were soon recognized, and many states switched to permanent registration. Under the latter system, a

*Since *Dunn* v. *Blumstein* the Court has relaxed somewhat its implied thirty-day maximum by allowing Georgia to impose a fifty-day residency requirement.

voter registers once and remains registered as long as he continues to reside and vote regularly in the county or precinct. This plan is in effect now in at least two-thirds of the states.

Texas had no registration system from 1902 to 1966. Poll tax receipts sufficed as registration certificates. Following the invalidation of the poll tax requirement on the state level by the Supreme Court, the Texas Legislature enacted an annual voter registration law in 1967 requiring that all voters register each year between October 1 and January 31, the same dates encompassing the period for paying the poll tax under the earlier law. This made Texas the only state in the Union requiring annual voter registration and the only state requiring voters to register at least nine months before the general election. It was also one of only three states that closed registration as much as three months before the primary. Finally, Texas had one of the shortest registration periods in the nation; 80 per cent of the states had longer ones. The similarity between the 1902 poll tax amendment and the 1967 registration law was unmistakable: Registration was annual, and the time period for registration was the same.

On January 7, 1971, in *Beare* v. *Smith,* a three-judge federal district court declared the Texas annual voter registration law unconstitutional on the grounds of denial of equal protection of the law guaranteed by the Fourteenth Amendment. The judges directed the Texas Legislature to extend the registration deadline beyond the date of January 31; as a consequence of the early closing date under the 1967 plan, they charged that over 1 million qualified voters were disfranchised each year. This action opened the way for the Legislature to enact a new registration law. On February 5, 1971, Governor Smith signed the first bill passed by the 62nd Legislature; it extended the closing date of the voter registration period from January 31 to February 28, effective in 1971. Nearly six months later the Legislature produced a new registration law enabling Texas to join with most of the other states in the Union having a permanent registration system. Now registration is permanent unless the voter moves his residence from a precinct or fails to vote at least once in a three-year period following registration. He may register at any time but must do so at least thirty days prior to any primary or general election in which he intends to participate. This is indeed a major electoral reform for Texas. Conservatives generally objected to this democratization of the ballot because it tends to increase voting by minority groups and working-class families. In summary, to vote in Texas an individual must have certain qualifications. He must be:

1. A native-born or naturalized citizen of the United States who has reached his eighteenth birthday on or before election day.
2. A resident of the state for at least thirty days immediately preceding the day of the election.
3. A resident of the county for at least thirty days immediately preceding the day of the election.
4. A resident of the election precinct on the day of the election.
5. Registered as a voter for the current year.

Normally those who meet these qualifications are eligible to vote. However, the *Texas Election Code,* following the rule prescribed by the Texas constitution, disqualifies the following persons: lunatics, idiots, paupers supported by the county, and persons convicted of felonies ("except those restored to full citizenship and right of suffrage or pardoned"). It should be noted that disqualification for conviction of a felony is being challenged in the courts in other states and that the disqualification of paupers supported by the county does not include welfare recipients. In fact, any voter disqualification based on pauperism is now a dead letter.

From this overview of suffrage two trends plainly emerge. First, there has been a steady expansion of the suffrage to virtually all persons of both sexes who are eighteen years of age or older. Another trend has been the move toward uniformity of voting policies among the several states. These trends were marked by periodic changes in the law: amendments to the United States Constitution, laws passed by Congress, and opinions rendered by the federal courts. Generally, but not wholly, this democratization of the ballot was forced upon the states by the federal government. From another point of view, the expansion of the ballot was merely a part of the total movement toward more social democracy. One of the reasons why the states lagged behind in expanding suffrage, and why they had to be prodded by federal government action, is that all voting is administered by the states; there is no national election machinery. All elections (national, state, and local) are conducted in and by the states. Another reason is that it is within the states that racial and other forms of discrimination occur. Those who controlled the state lawmaking processes were loath to allow their power base to be undermined by a widening of the suffrage so as to include minority opposition groups. In Texas and the other southern states, those who were disenfranchised by the poll tax, restrictive registration procedures, residence requirements, literacy tests, and other restrictions were mostly from the racial minority groups and the poor. Only federal law could break through this entrenched control of the ballot.

Now that most barriers to use of the ballot have been removed, the way is clear to the voting booth for rich and poor alike, for minority group members as well as for those of the majority, for blacks and browns as well as whites. What has been the response of this newly enfranchised electorate? What has been the response of Texans in the eighteen- to twenty-year age bracket enfranchised by the Twenty-sixth Amendment? What of the blacks, the Mexican-Americans, and the nonpropertied poor, who can no longer be kept from the polls by legal means?

Nationally the 1972 turnout was below normal—about 55 per cent of the voting-age population as compared to slightly over 60 per cent, which has been the national average for the past two decades in presidential election years. This disappointing performance came after addition to the eligible list of the eighteen- to twenty-year-old group and after other liberalizing developments. Voter turnout in Texas has never been equal to the national average, though it has improved in recent years. Table 2-2 shows percentages of the adult population in Texas

TABLE 2-2
Percentages of the adult population who voted in presidential elections (minimum age requirement was 21 years from 1952 to 1968; in 1972 it was 18)

	1952	1956	1960	1964	1968	1972
Texas	42.8	38.1	41.8	45.4	49.8	42.1
United States	62.0	60.1	63.2	62.1	60.7	54.5

Source: *Congressional Quarterly Weekly Report,* November 11, 1972, pp. 2947 and 2650; U.S. Bureau of the Census, *Current Population Reports,* Series P-20, No. 172 (Washington, D.C.: U.S. Government Printing Office, May 3, 1968), p. 2; *Current Population Reports,* Series P-25, No. 479 (March, 1972), p. 9; *Statistical Abstract of the United States 1970* (Washington, D.C.: U.S. Government Printing Office, 1970), p. 370.

who voted in presidential elections between 1952 and 1972. During the same two decades the average turnout for eleven general elections for governor is 31 per cent. The causes of this low turnout are several.

Weak party competition in a one-party state was partially responsible in the past, but this impeding influence is weakening in Texas and was all but exhausted in the 1972 general election. Major reasons for the low percentage in the presidential race nationally and in Texas were the addition of voters in the eighteen- to twenty-year range, a large number of whom were disinterested in the campaign. Another reason was the widely held belief that Nixon would win. National polls indicated that only about 60 per cent of the eligible voters had registered.[1] There is no reason to assume that any larger percentage than this registered in Texas. The large percentage of blacks and Mexican-Americans in the Texas population has added to the state's list of nonvoters. In the 1972 election the Mexican-American vote was higher than in previous years because of the influence of the Raza Unida Party and its gubernatorial candidate, Ramsey Muniz. The black vote, however, continued to be low in comparison to that of Anglos. In the fifty-five black precincts in Dallas County, a record number of blacks registered; but only 50.8 per cent of those who registered later went to the polls and voted. This contrasts to a countywide turnout of 69.2 per cent of registered voters.[2]

In attempting to assess the voter turnout in the November, 1972, election in Texas, it should be remembered that important steps to remove voting restrictions were taken only a short time beforehand. Probably the full impact of these reform measures on voter turnout will not be apparent for some years. More election experiences are needed to gauge their full impact.

PARTY NOMINATIONS

Before an election to public office can take place in a representative democracy, candidates must be nominated. This means that some kind of machinery is needed for the selection of candidates. In the United States, as in most other countries, these means are provided by political parties. Four methods for nominating candidates have been used in this country; self-nomination, the *caucus,* the delegate convention, and the direct primary.

In an earlier day, when life was relatively simple and the population was small, a person interested in running for public office needed only to announce his intention to become a candidate. Use of this device was short-lived. As population increased and as issues became numerous and complex, a more precise and highly organized process became necessary for the selection of candidates. Politicians saw the advantage of combining their strength behind a single candidate with wide enough appeal to be a winner. To accomplish this, the informal conference or caucus arose as a practical means for deciding on one candidate and for galvanizing support behind him. The caucus antedated the party in America, but it was adopted by the parties when they came into being. One of the earliest descriptions of the caucus is contained in John Adams's diary. Describing a political meeting in "Tom Dawes' garret" in 1763, Adams may have given us the first account in American political history of the informal caucus:

> There they smoke tobacco till you cannot see from one end of the garret to the other. There they drink flip [spiced hot cider]. . . . and there they choose a moderator, who puts questions to the vote regularly; and selectmen, assessors, collectors, wardens, firewards, and representatives are regularly chosen before they are chosen by the town.

Even after the appearance of organized political parties, the caucus continued until public opinion forced its demise in the popular sweep of Jacksonian democracy in the 1820s and 1830s. Discarded in accordance with the Jacksonian slogan, "Down with King Caucus," the nation's first organized nominating device was soon replaced by the *delegate convention.* Here, by electing delegates to a nominating convention, the rank-and-file members of a political party were given some voice in the selection of their candidates. With the caucus they had little or none. The period of the delegate convention extended from the 1830s to the end of the nineteenth century. Nominations were made on all levels of government—national, state, and local—by delegates chosen by members of the party. But as time passed, the convention, like the caucus, fell into disfavor. It declined in popular esteem chiefly because it became dominated by party bosses and their political machines; members demanded a more democratic means for the naming of party candidates.

The *direct primary* filled the need of rank-and-file party members. Coming into general usage between 1890 and 1910 (except for selection of candidates for President and Vice-President of the United States, who continued to be chosen by delegates to party conventions), this unique product of American politics permits the party membership to select their candidates directly by going to the polls on primary election day and choosing for each office the person they wish to represent their party against the candidates of opposing parties in the general election. Usually in two-party states the person receiving the most votes (a plurality) for a particular office becomes the party nominee, but in Texas an absolute majority is required for nomination. In the event that a first primary does not produce an absolute majority, a *"run-off" primary* is held later for the top two contenders. Party primaries in Texas are held on the first Saturday in May, six months before the general election in November. Run-off primaries are on the first Saturday in June. This early primary date is criticized because of the long interim period. Most state primaries occur much later. In 1972 ten states held their primaries in August, fourteen in September, and one in October. If the interim between the primary and general election is a period of continuous campaigning, then six months is indeed excessive.

It should be emphasized that no one is elected to government office in a direct primary, even though voters go to the polls and cast ballots. Primaries are held for the purpose of nominating candidates and are therefore party functions. We need to be reminded, however, that party candidates for President and Vice-President of the United States are still selected by national party conventions and that certain party officers such as state, county, and precinct committee members are chosen in most states by party conventions on state and local levels. Although they are party functions, primaries are subject to regulation by Congress and by state legislatures.

Primaries, however, continue to be administered in all states by the political parties that sponsor them and not by the states themselves. Beginning in 1974, a Texas party must nominate candidates by direct primary if its candidate for governor received more than 20 per cent of the votes cast for the office in the preceding general election. A party whose gubernatorial candidate received between 2 and 20 per cent of the vote (La Raza Unida Party in the 1972 election) has the option of employing either primary elections or conventions for the selection of its candidates in 1974; thereafter such a party will be required to use conventions. In order to get one's name on a primary ballot for nomination to a statewide office, the necessary papers must be filed with one's party's state executive committee. The committee certifies the ballot to the local party officers in the counties where the election is administered. One who wishes to have one's name placed on the primary ballot for a local office files with the county executive committee of one's party. This committee prints the ballots, provides the polling places, determines the order of names on the ballot for each office, and canvasses the election returns. The county executive committee also appoints a presiding judge of elections in each precinct in the county, and the judge in turn appoints the clerks who are needed to man the polling place.

Items of cost in operating party primaries include payment of wages to clerks and judges, printing the ballots, and other miscellaneous expenses. Prior to 1972, expenses for the conduct of primaries were paid by assessments made upon the candidates. The county executive committee of the party estimated the cost of the primary in a particular county and apportioned the amount among the candidates. These filing fees had to be paid by the candidates before their names could be printed on the ballots. Fees for candidates for district, county, and precinct offices ranged from $50 to $1,000 or more, depending on the population of the county. Fees for statewide offices and for United States Senator were $1,000; for candidates for the state Legislature they ranged from a nominal amount in small counties to $1,000 in large counties. Texas was the only state with party primaries financed entirely by filing fee payments.

On December 21, 1970, in *Carter* v. *Dies,* a three-judge federal district court in Dallas enjoined enforcement of provisions in the Texas Election Code pertaining to financing of party primaries from fees paid by candidates for nomination. Such fees, ruled the court, violate rights under the United States Constitution when they are used as a revenue-collecting device and as an absolute requirement for candidates to get their names on the party primary ballot. In June, 1971, the 62nd Legislature enacted a "contingent, temporary law" which modified the filing fee requirement for the 1972 primaries. It called for a maximum filing fee of 4 per cent of the full-term salary of the office sought, in some cases a higher amount than that required under the previous law. A person who wished to file for a position on the ballot, but who could not pay the fee, could qualify by filing a petition signed by qualified voters equal in number to at least 10 per cent of the vote cast for the party's candidate for governor in the last general election. The law became effective January 1, 1972.

On January 20, 1972, the same Dallas court, in *Johnston* v. *Luna,* took only a half hour to invalidate the twenty-day-old primary finance law, leaving the political parties of Texas without means for financing the approaching May 6 primaries. Expenses for the approaching primaries would be in the neighborhood of $2 million. At this point neither of the major parties had any immediate plans for raising this much money. Meantime, prior to the February 7 deadline for filing, candidates paid their fees or made "contributions" to their parties equal to the amount of the fees assessed under the law invalidated by the *Carter* v. *Dies* decision. There was still a chance that the United States Supreme Court would overrule the three-judge court panel prior to the May 6 primaries. But on February 24, 1972, in *Bullock* v. *Carter,* the Supreme Court upheld the *Carter* v. *Dies* ruling.

There followed both soul-searching and revenue-searching in Texas. Secretary of State Bob Bullock sought to pay for the primaries from state funds, but Attorney General Crawford Martin ruled that such use of state funds without an express appropriation by the Legislature would violate the Texas constitution. Finally, only hours before the May 6 primaries, Governor Smith called a special session of the Legislature, which promptly appropriated the necessary funds. This appropriation, however, did not provide a permanent solution. It remained for the 63rd Legislature, meeting in regular session in 1973, to enact a permanent law on the financing of primaries.* Expenses for primaries could be reduced somewhat by requiring unitary primaries, wherein all political parties would conduct their primaries at one polling place in each precinct rather than at separate places for each party as now practiced.

*On the last day of the 63rd session, the Legislature enacted a law (SB 11) to finance primaries by way of fees paid candidates in varying amounts and from state funds. See Epilogue for more detail on this subject.

Primaries serve two different purposes in one- and two-party states. In one-party states the primary of the majority party is the determining election, since the nominations occur when various factions and leaders of that party agree on the names of candidates to appear on the primary ballot. This is the pattern still prevalent in state elections in the South, where the Democratic Party holds the dominant position over the weaker Republican Party. Everywhere in the South, however, the Republican Party is making heavy inroads among voters. Texas was a strong one-party state from about 1876 to 1952, but during the last two decades the Republican Party has made steady gains. Nevertheless, in the mid-1970s the Texas Democratic Party is still the majority party in the state, and the primaries still tend to be the determining elections on the state and local levels. In two-party states the primary is much less significant because the final choice occurs at the general election rather than at the primary.

Primaries are of three types: open, closed, and "blanket." The *closed primary* is used in thirty-seven states where the voter is required to identify his party affiliation, either when he registers or when he votes in the party primary, or both. Those who refuse to declare their party affiliation are in turn refused the ballot at the primary. Some voters are resentful of this practice because they feel that it violates the principle of freedom of the ballot. Others contend that since the primary is strictly a party affair through which party members select their candidates for the general election, the party has a moral right to restrict its primaries to its members (see Reading 2-2 for a defense of the closed primary).

Thirteen states,[3] including Texas, use the open primary, wherein voters are not required to declare their party affiliation. Under this plan every registered voter may vote in the primary of his choice; but he cannot vote in more than one primary, except in the state of Washington. Here, under the *blanket primary* system, all eligible voters of all parties are given the same ballot, on which are printed the names of all candidates, the parties with which they are affiliated, and the offices they seek. Voters are free to range across party lines, marking their ballot for the candidates of their choice whatever their party affiliation, though they are allowed to vote only once for each office.

Texas is included here as one of the thirteen states with the *open primary* because the voter is not required to declare the party of his choice at the time of registration. On the party primary ballot, however, the voter will find printed the following party pledge: "I am a Democrat [or the name of the party conducting the primary] and pledge myself to support the nominee of this primary." The pledge is supposed to be binding (see Figure 2-1 for a reproduction of a 1972 primary ballot).

In Texas the bonds of party loyalty are quite loose. Whether the open primary is a cause or an effect of this attitude is moot indeed. At any rate, the practice in Texas of "*ticket splitting*" or "crossing over" and "party piracy" is apparently more common than that of "*party purity*" (see Reading 2-3 on the subject of party purity). In the 1972 primaries, a total of 2,065,748 votes were cast for persons seeking nomination for United States Senator in the Democratic primary; but only 107,648 votes were recorded in the Republican primary.

Nº 1602

OFFICIAL BALLOT

REPUBLICAN PRIMARY ELECTION
MAY 6, 1972
LUBBOCK COUNTY, TEXAS

Vote for the candidate of your choice in each race by placing an "X" in the square beside the candidate's name.

Nº 1602

REPUBLICAN PRIMARY ELECTION
MAY 6, 1972
Lubbock County, Texas

(Note: Voter's Signature to be affixed on reverse side.)

I AM A REPUBLICAN AND PLEDGE MYSELF TO SUPPORT THE NOMINEES OF THIS PRIMARY.

For UNITED STATES SENATOR:

☐ JOHN G. TOWER of Wichita County

For GOVERNOR:

☐ B. THOMAS McELROY of Dallas County
☐ ALBERT BEL FAY of Harris County
☐ JOSEPH ALTON JENKINS of Dallas County
☐ DAVID REAGAN of Grayson County
☐ HENRY C. (HANK) GROVER of Harris County
☐ JOHN A. HALL of Parker County

For TREASURER:

☐ MAURICE ANGLY, JR. of Travis County

For RAILROAD COMMISSIONER:

☐ JIM SEGREST of Bexar County

For COUNTY CHAIRMAN:

☐ JERRY L. "MAC" McDONALD

For PRECINCT CHAIRMAN,
Precinct No. 5:

☐ BILL GOLDSTEIN

Place an "X" in the square beside the statement indicating the way you wish to vote.

THIS REFERENDUM IS AN EXPRESSION OF PUBLIC OPINION ONLY AND HAS NO BINDING EFFECT AS LAW.

☐ **FOR**
☐ **AGAINST**

Are you in favor of a constitutional amendment which would prohibit forced busing of school children or forced consolidation of school districts solely to achieve racial balance?

☐ **FOR**
☐ **AGAINST**

Daylight Saving Time

Figure 2-1
Typical official primary ballot of the state of Texas. Lubbock County, Texas.

Yet the Republican candidate, John Tower, defeated his Democratic opponent, Barefoot Sanders, in the general election with 1,822,877 votes to Sanders's 1,511,985. We cannot assume that most of Tower's supporters refrained from voting in the Republican primary but later turned out in force for the general election. The more realistic assumption would be that thousands of those who voted in the Democratic primary in May later voted Republican in the November general election. This assumption is supported by the following case: The Democratic Party primary in one large precinct (slightly over 2,000 registered voters) in San Angelo required fourteen clerks and vote counters, each working about twelve hours, to operate the polls and tally the votes for 1,268 voters. The Republican polling place in the same precinct required only the party chairman to man the polls. Yet in the general election the same precinct went Republican overwhelmingly in both state and national elections.

In the first primary on May 6, 1972, 54 counties failed to conduct a Republican primary. In the second or run-off primary of the Republican Party in June between Albert Bel Fay and Henry Grover for the party nomination for governor, 57 counties had no primary contest, and 48 others failed to file any returns with the secretary of state. Only 57,008 Republican votes were cast throughout the state in this run-off. Of these, 49,107 came from only 17 counties; of the other 237 counties that conducted primaries, only 7,901 votes were recorded—an average of 33 votes per county. In the Democratic Party run-off for governor between Dolph Briscoe and Frances Farenthold, a total of 1,979,762 votes in 254 counties was recorded with the secretary of state—an average of 7,794 votes per county.

These voting statistics lead one to wonder why the Republican voter turnout is so weak at the primary level and so strong in the general elections—strong enough in 1972 to re-elect Senator Tower and to come close to placing Grover in the governor's mansion. The only answer would seem to be that thousands of voters who are really Republicans prefer to vote in Democratic primaries rather than in their own. One major reason for this is that on the Republican primary ballot in state and local primary elections there are no names of Republican candidates for many offices. In response to this situation Republicans vote in Democratic primaries where the candidates are. Conservative Democrats encourage this practice because they doubt their strength to control Democratic nominations without help from conservative Republicans. Consequently, conservative Democrats oppose any attempt to close their primary to Republicans by enacting a party registration law. One may speculate also on what effect a closed primary would have on this "crossover." Many believe that a "pure primary" law for Texas would strengthen the Republican Party and stimulate more Republican county organizations to conduct primaries in their counties (see Reading 2-4 on how a "party switcher" looks to the future of a strong two-party state for Texas). This assumption would seem to have more weight now that candidates seeking party nominations no longer have to bear the cost of the primaries through payment of fees. More Republicans should now be encouraged to seek nominations, at least for local offices, because of less financial risk at the primary.

GENERAL ELECTIONS

November is traditionally the month for general elections in the United States. Since elections for members of the United States Senate and House of Representatives occur in even-numbered years, Texas, along with twenty-five other states, holds its state and local elections at the same time. Municipal and special district elections in Texas are scheduled for different dates than the biennial general elections. One school of thought in about half of the states is that state and local elections should be held in conjunction with national elections because the result is a larger voter turnout. In the other half of the states the prevailing view holds that state and local election contests tend to be overshadowed by national elections when the two are held simultaneously; thus these states hold separate elections to fill state and local offices.

In addition to the names of nominees of the respective parties, space on the general election ballot is provided also for "independent" and "write-in" candidates. For a new party to place its candidates on the ballot for statewide offices, or for an independent candidate to be similarly listed, a petition bearing signatures of 1 per cent of the total number who voted for governor in the last general election must be submitted to the secretary of state of Texas. This list of signatories, however, may include only names of voters who have not participated in a primary during that year. For example, this was the procedure whereby the Raza Unida Party placed its candidates' names on the 1972 general election ballot. In addition, independent candidates must file for office by February 3, which is prior to the party primaries. Bound by these legalisms, a party candidate defeated for nomination, or a party member disgruntled by the outcome of his own party primary, cannot get his name on the general election ballot merely by becoming an independent.

In the general election Texas uses the *"party-column" ballot* in contrast to the "office-column" type used in many states. Note that the ballot shown in Figure 2-2 lists the candidates in a vertical column according to party, with offices identified in a parallel column to the left. The *Texas Election Code* provides that the party which obtained the highest number of votes in the last gubernatorial election will be listed on the extreme left (strategically the best position since uninformed voters are apt to vote for candidates in the first column), with the next highest parties following. Parties with national candidates only are listed next, followed by a column for independent candidates. Finally, the column farthest to the right is reserved for write-in candidates. If the voter wishes to vote a straight party ticket, he may do so by placing an "x" in the square at the top of the party column. This is the avowed purpose of the party-column type ballot—to encourage the voter to vote a straight party ticket. If he wishes to split his vote, he may pick and choose among party nominees by marking the appropriate squares.

Between biennial general elections, special elections are sometimes called to fill a vacancy in a Congressional or state legislative office and to vote on proposed constitutional amendments, bond issues, and other questions. Special elections to fill vacancies are nonpartisan, so there is no preceding primary election. To obtain a place on the ballot, a person need only conform to

Nº 6532

GENERAL ELECTION

Tom Green County, Texas
November 7, 1972

OFFICIAL BALLOT

Nº 6532
GENERAL ELECTION
Tom Green County, Texas
November 7, 1972
NOTE: Voter's Signature to Be Affixed on the Reverse Side.

INSTRUCTION NOTE:

Vote for the candidate of your choice in each race by placing an X in the square beside the candidate's name.

You may vote a straight ticket (that is, vote for all the candidates of a certain party, and for no candidates outside that party's column) by placing an X in the square beside the name of the party of your choice at the head of the party column. (If you use this straight-ticket method of marking, do not mark squares beside the names of individual candidates.)

Candidates for:	☐ DEMOCRATIC PARTY	☐ REPUBLICAN PARTY	☐ SOCIALIST WORKERS PARTY	☐ RAZA UNIDA PARTY	WRITE-IN
President and Vice-President	☐ GEORGE McGOVERN and R. SARGENT SHRIVER	☐ RICHARD M. NIXON and SPIRO T. AGNEW	☐ LINDA JENNESS and ANDREW PULLEY		
United States Senator	☐ BAREFOOT SANDERS	☐ JOHN G. TOWER	☐ TOM LEONARD	☐ FLORES AMAYA	
U. S. Representative, 21st Congressional District	☐ O. C. FISHER	☐ DOUG HARLAN			
Governor	☐ DOLPH BRISCOE	☐ HENRY C. (HANK) GROVER	☐ DEBORAH LEONARD	☐ RAMSEY MUNIZ	
Lieutenant Governor	☐ BILL HOBBY		☐ MEYER ALEWITZ	☐ ALMA CANALES	
Attorney General	☐ JOHN HILL		☐ THOMAS KINCAID		
Comptroller of Public Accounts	☐ ROBERT S. CALVERT		☐ ANNE SPRINGER		
State Treasurer	☐ JESSE JAMES	☐ MAURICE ANGLY, JR.		☐ RUBEN SOLIS, JR.	
Commissioner of General Land Office	☐ BOB ARMSTRONG		☐ HOWARD PETRICK		
Commissioner of Agriculture	☐ JOHN C. WHITE				
Railroad Commissioner	☐ BYRON TUNNELL	☐ JIM SEGREST		☐ FRED R. GARZA	
Chief Justice, Supreme Court	☐ JOE GREENHILL				
Associate Justice, Supreme Court, Place 1	☐ PRICE DANIEL				
Associate Justice, Supreme Court, Place 2	☐ SAM JOHNSON				
Judge, Court of Criminal Appeals	☐ WENDELL A. ODOM				
State Senator, 25th District	☐ W. E. (PETE) SNELSON				
State Representative, 60th District	☐ TOM MASSEY				
Member, State Board of Education, 21st District	☐ FRANK M. POOL				
Chief Justice, Court of Civil Appeals, 3rd District	☐ JOHN C. PHILLIPS				
District Judge, 51st Judicial District	☐ EARL W. SMITH				
District Judge, 119th Judicial District	☐ GLENN R. LEWIS				
District Attorney, 51st Judicial District	☐ FRANK C. DICKEY, JR.				
District Attorney, 119th Judicial District	☐ ROYAL HART				
County Attorney	☐ GEORGE E. McCREA				
Sheriff	☐ J. ODELL WAGNER				
Tax Assessor-Collector	☐ L. A. (ABE) WALKER				
County Commissioner, Precinct 1	☐ ARLEY GUESS				
Justice of the Peace, Precinct 1, Place 1	☐ RUTH NICHOLSON				
Constable, Precinct 1	☐ L. A. (STEVE) STEVENS				

SAMPLE

Instruction Note: Place an X in the square beside the statement indicating the way you wish to vote.

PROPOSED CONSTITUTIONAL AMENDMENTS

No. 1	☐ FOR ☐ AGAINST	The constitutional amendment to provide annual salaries of $8,400 for members of the Senate and House of Representatives.
No. 2	☐ FOR ☐ AGAINST	The constitutional amendment abolishing the Lamar County Hospital District.
No. 3	☐ FOR ☐ AGAINST	The constitutional amendment to require the commissioners court in all counties of the state to compensate all justices of the peace on a salary basis.
No. 4	☐ FOR ☐ AGAINST	The constitutional amendment providing for a constitutional revision commission which precedes the convening of the members of the 63rd Legislature as a constitutional convention in January, 1974, for the purpose of submitting to the voters a new constitution or revisions of the existing state constitution.
No. 5	☐ FOR ☐ AGAINST	The constitutional amendment allowing certain tax exemptions to disabled veterans, their surviving spouses and surviving minor children, and the surviving spouses and surviving minor children of members of the armed forces who lose their life while on active duty.
No. 6	☐ FOR ☐ AGAINST	The constitutional amendment providing that the various political subdivisions of the State may exempt not less than Three Thousand Dollars ($3,000) of the value of residence homesteads of all persons sixty-five (65) years of age or older from ad valorem taxes under certain conditions.
No. 7	☐ FOR ☐ AGAINST	The constitutional amendment to provide that equality under the law shall not be denied or abridged because of sex, race, color, creed, or national origin.
No. 8	☐ FOR ☐ AGAINST	The constitutional amendment to provide a four-year term of office for the Governor, Lieutenant Governor, Attorney General, Comptroller of Public Accounts, Treasurer, Commissioner of the General Land Office, Secretary of State, and certain statutory State officers.
No. 9	☐ FOR ☐ AGAINST	The constitutional amendment to provide that directors of soil and water conservation districts are not disqualified from holding or being compensated for more than one office.
No. 10	☐ FOR ☐ AGAINST	The constitutional amendment revising provisions on the time and method of proposing amendments to the state constitution and the time and method of publishing notice of proposed amendments.
No. 11	☐ FOR ☐ AGAINST	The constitutional amendment to provide a salary of $22,500 for the Lieutenant Governor and the Speaker of the House of Representatives.
No. 12	☐ FOR ☐ AGAINST	The constitutional amendment permitting State employees, who are not State officers, to serve as members of the governing bodies of school districts, cities, towns, or other local governmental districts, without forfeiting their State salary, and specifying exceptions to the constitutional prohibiton against payment of State funds for compensation to any person who holds more than one civil office of emolument.
No. 13	☐ FOR ☐ AGAINST	The constitutional amendment to set a six percent (6%) weighted average annual interest rate for bonds issued pursuant to constitutional authority presently having a specified interest ceiling.
No. 14	☐ FOR ☐ AGAINST	The constitutional amendment to allow a county to reduce its county permanent school fund and distribute the money to independent and common school districts on a per scholastic basis.

Figure 2-2

Typical official general-election ballot of the state of Texas. Tom Green County, Texas regulations governing filing. In special legislative and congressional races, *run-off elections* are required by law when no candidate in a contest for a recently vacated office obtains a majority of votes in the non-partisan special election.

THE PARTY PROCESS

Party government was a half century old in America when Texas entered the Union. Perhaps some form of political party organization is inevitable wherever governments operate. To most people, a democracy would be inconceivable without political parties. The main purpose of a political party is to gain control of the government in order to be able to determine government policy. It is this purpose that sets parties apart from interest groups, such as labor unions, trade associations, and professional organizations. Interest groups seek to influence public policy without undertaking to control government as a whole. One of the chief cornerstones of democratic societies is the freedom of political party operation. This characteristic above all others sets democracies apart from more authoritarian systems of government. The United States has had a national two-party system since 1800. Minor parties generally have been unable to survive long enough to get a permanent foothold, though it must be conceded that the Republican Party is the one case of a third party that became a major party. But in the face of this exception it is the custom to trace the founding of the two major parties, Democratic and Republican, to Jefferson and Hamilton in 1800.

PARTY ORGANIZATION

Both major parties are quite similar in organization and structure, if not in philosophy. Each has a permanent and a temporary organizational structure. The permanent organization consists of thousands of virtually autonomous party committees on the local, state, and national levels. These committees are little more than nominally tied together to form a "national" party. On the highest level each party has a national committee; on the state level each has fifty state committees. On the county level, if both parties were organized in every county in the nation, each party would have 3,050 county committees. Finally, on the lowest rung of the party hierarchy, each of the two major parties has thousands of precinct committees, though there are some precincts in which only one party is organized. These committees form the *permanent party organizations* of the Democratic and Republican parties throughout the country.

The *temporary party organization* comes into being for a few hours or a few days and then is dismantled until called together the following year, biennium, or quadrennium. The temporary organization is composed of primaries and conventions. The direct primary is organized for one day (two days if there is a run-off primary) to enable the party to nominate its candidates. Conventions, on the other hand, are generally used on the local and state levels to conduct party business, e.g., to elect party leaders and determine party policy. On the national level the convention is used both to determine party business and to select party candidates for President and Vice-President of the United States. This attempt to distinguish between the party primary and the convention is admittedly confusing to some readers because of the many overlapping functions. Suffice it to say that the primary has one major function, that of selecting party candidates for public offices to run in the general election. The convention, on the other hand, has three major functions: (1) on the national level to select party candidates for President and Vice-President every four years; (2) on the state and local levels to conduct party business and select party officers; and (3) in a very few states to select party candidates for a limited number of public offices.

At the bottom of the temporary party structure is the *precinct convention,* which meets biennially in Texas on primary election day. A voting precinct is a small geographic area created by the county commissioners court. It normally contains a few hundred registered voters. The Texas Election Code requires that a precinct contain from 100 to 2,000 voters, except where voting machines are used there may be up to 3,000 voters. On the first Saturday in May, the day of the first primary, both the Democratic and Republican parties hold precinct meetings in almost all of the 5,243 voting precincts in the state's 254 counties. Although all party members who reside in the precinct and who voted in the party primary are eligible to participate, attendance is usually meager. Called to order by the precinct chairman, or by any other person present if the chairman is absent, the convention names a permanent chairman and a secretary. The main business is to elect delegates to the next highest party body, the county convention, which meets one week later. Each precinct may elect one delegate to the county convention for every twenty-five votes or major fraction thereof cast in the precinct for the party's gubernatorial nominee in the last general election.

Depending on how sharp the issues are between the liberal and conservative factions of the party (and this condition applies more to the Democratic Party than to the Republican Party in Texas), the delegates elected to the county convention will more or less represent the views of the majority faction within the precinct convention. Within the Democratic Party this factional division is traceable far back into Texas history and has been sharper at some times than at others. Generally, when factional issues are heated, bitter internecine party battles erupt following the rulings of the credentials committee that favor one delegation over another from a county sending two opposing delegations to the state convention as a result of a split county convention. Thus when such factional division occurs on the precinct level, it is usually based on a statewide or national issue and will therefore carry upward into the county and state conventions.

Each *county convention* elects a convention chairman and a secretary; it also names delegates to the next higher body, the state convention. The state executive committee of each party sets the ratio for the selection of delegates to the state conventions, but the Texas Election Code requires that there shall be one delegate for not less than 300 votes and no more than 600 votes cast for the party's candidate for governor in each county in the last general election. The state convention meets in September of even-numbered years prior to the general election in November. This convention always performs three major duties: It certifies to the secretary of state the party nominees for the approaching general election; it drafts and adopts a party platform; and it selects the members of the party's state executive committee. In presidential election years Texas political parties hold two conventions–the regular September convention just referred to and an earlier one in June commonly known as the *presidential convention.* Delegates selected at the county conventions attend both state conventions each quadrennium. The presidential convention's major duties are also three in number: It selects delegates to the national presidential nominating convention (as many as Texas is allowed according to national party rules); it selects a committeeman and a committeewoman from Texas to serve on the party's national committee; and it selects a slate of potential presidential electors to serve in the Electoral College in the event that the party wins the popular presidential vote in the state (see Reading 2-5).

It is through these thousands of precinct, county, and state conventions that control of the party machinery is exercised. Efforts to gain and hold this control begin in the precinct conventions and rise through the county conventions to the state level. Prior to 1968 the Democratic Party in Texas at all convention levels followed the unit rule in voting; that is, a majority of votes in the delegation controlled the entire delegation vote. This meant that all delegations at state and county conventions voted as a body according to the majority vote of the delegation. Following the 1968 national Democratic convention in Chicago, where the use of the unit rule was abolished on the national level, the Texas Democratic Party also abolished the unit rule. Now, when balloting occurs on issues and in elections, each delegate's vote is counted and applied to the total votes of the convention. The Republican Party in Texas has never made use of the unit rule.

Responding to demands for further reform that would lead to more democratization of the decision-making processes within the political party bodies, the Texas Legislature in 1971 passed a law requiring that major political parties file with the secretary of state of Texas a "set of specific, detailed and written party rules for the conduct of its conventions." The state executive committee of both parties then named special ad hoc committees to draft the rules, and eventually two sets of party rules were drawn up and adopted prior to the May 6, 1972, primaries.

The aura of reform is somewhat less pronounced in the *Republican Party rules* than in those of the Democratic Party. Rule 3 of those adopted by the GOP reads as follows:

> Participation in any Republican convention or meeting including, but not limited to, any primary caucus, any meeting or convention held for the purposes of selecting delegates to a county, district, state, or national convention shall in no way be abridged for reasons of sex, age, race, religion, color, or national origin.

The *Democratic Party rules,* on the other hand, require that steps be taken "to encourage young people, women, and minority groups to seek selection as delegates to party conventions and as members of party committees . . . in reasonable relationship to their presence in their state." At the precinct level, where delegates to the county conventions are chosen, selections by the Democrats are made on the basis of preferences for the various presidential candidates or on the basis of uncommitted status. At the county conventions the precinct delegates again caucus and select by majority vote the number of delegates and alternates to the state convention that each precinct is allotted. At the state convention level the procedures of the two parties become more alike. At least 75 per cent of the Democratic delegates to the national convention are selected by majority vote in each of the thirty-one state senatorial districts. The Republicans elect two delegates from each of twenty-four Congressional districts. The remaining portion of delegates to the two national conventions is selected by each of the two parties on an at-large basis from the total body of delegates present at each of the state conventions. This process of selecting convention delegates, though not as democratic as that provided by the party primary, is a step long overdue in Texas.

The permanent party organization consists of a series of committees and officers at the various levels: precinct, county, and state. The *precinct chairman* is the basic party official. He is elected in each precinct on the primary election ballot. As the Republican Party grows stronger in Texas, the precinct chairmen of both parties will become more prominent figures in party affairs. If the Republican Party is weak in a precinct, the Democratic precinct chairman's job will be more routine, and he may not be active in rounding up support for his party. The reverse is true also. But if both parties are more evenly matched in strength at the polls, both precinct chairmen's positions become more vital at this grassroots level of party activity. In such situations the two chairmen must work hard to get out the vote at election time. Such efforts include encouraging voter registration, instilling interest in party issues, and striving to maintain party unity. The precinct chairman arranges for the precinct convention and serves on the *county executive committee.*

The latter comprises all precinct chairmen in the county and the county chairman, who is elected by his party in the primary on a countywide basis. The county executive committee conducts the primary elections, arranges for the county convention, raises money for the party, campaigns for party candidates in general elections, and maintains party unity and enthusiasm. Of course, a large measure of these responsibilities falls to the county chairman.

The highest permanent party organization of the state is the *state executive committee,* composed of one man and one woman from each of the thirty-one state senatorial districts plus a chairman and vice-chairman, one of whom shall be a man and the other a woman. This committee of sixty-four members is put together at the September state convention, where delegates from each senatorial district choose and place before the convention the names of the two members from their district, and the chairman and vice-chairman are chosen at large. These choices are then ratified by the convention. The state executive committee must canvass the returns and certify the nomination of party candidates chosen at the primaries. It arranges for and conducts the state convention (two conventions in presidential election years), raises money for party candidates, seeks to maintain party unity and strength, and cooperates (sometimes!) with the national committee of the party.

Over and above all party committees and officers in the state looms the figure of the governor as leader of his party. Certain advantages that bolster his party leadership accrue to him from his office; and since he is not limited by the state constitution in the number of terms he may serve, a governor never finds himself in the disadvantageous position of being a lame duck until he announces his decision not to run again or unless he is defeated in the primary. If not a lame-duck governor, he is in a position to influence strongly the party convention and platform and to lead the state delegation to the national convention. In these and other ways the governor of Texas can exercise strong leadership over his party and hence help overcome some of the weaknesses built into the office by the Texas constitution.

MONEY IN TEXAS ELECTIONS

In 1846 Abraham Lincoln, campaigning in Illinois for a seat in Congress, reported spending seventy-five cents—for a barrel of cider. In 1972 John Tower, campaigning in Texas for re-election to the United States Senate, spent $3 million, which is probably a record expenditure for Texas (see Reading 2-6). Perhaps the only moral to this story is that 1846 is not 1972. But long before Lincoln's time the popular concept of American democracy was that all members of the society should have an equal opportunity to strive for and occupy positions of power. This idea is inherent in the recent "one man, one vote" rule of the United States Supreme Court. Money, however, is an effective key for gaining access to public office; and the unequal distribution of wealth in our society creates a situation that makes it extremely difficult for those without money to win public office. The United States Bureau of the Census estimated that in 1972 the number of people in Texas aged eighteen and over was 7,681,000.[4] If a candidate for nomination or election to a statewide office, wishing to economize for lack of funds, were to limit his campaign expenditures to the cost of sending one six-cent postcard announcing his candidacy to every eligible voter in Texas, he would spend half a million dollars for postage alone. From this illustration it is easy to conclude that anyone seeking national or state office must have access to sizeable amounts of money if he expects to communicate with a sufficient number of prospective voters.

The following four observations are important for anyone who is trying to understand the interplay of money and politics in American elections. First, the amounts spent seem exorbitant and dangerously high to the average citizen. Reference was made above to the $3 million spent by Senator John Tower in his bid for re-election. Common Cause, a national organization devoted to reform in government, reported that Governor Preston Smith raised $1.5 million during his re-election campaign in 1970, "mostly on the strength of 8,000 phone calls he made to Texas businessmen—sometimes as many as 500 in a single day."[5] Though on first observation these sums may seem outrageously high, when we realize that the annual cost of operating government in Texas runs into billions of dollars, campaign expenditures on this scale seem more modest if they are viewed as the cost of recruiting elected officials.

Second, money and politics are not a recent American mixture. For example, John Quincy Adams related that while President he was asked "to contribute $5,000 or $10,000 to carry the election of a governor and legislature of Kentucky . . . by the circulation of newspapers, pamphlets, and handbills." Such practices were commonplace, according to the President.[6]

Third, most campaign money comes from big givers. This, too, is an old custom in American politics. In 1850 August Belmont of the Rothschild banking combine contributed $10,000 to James Buchanan's candidacy and thereby became chairman of the newly organized Democratic National Committee. Ten years later, in the Lincoln campaign for President, David Davis, one of his campaign advisers, remarked: "Men work better with money in hand. . . . I believe in God's Providence in this election but at the same time we should keep our powder dry."[7] Today gifts of $1,000 to $5,000 are frequent enough to be commonplace. In the first primary campaign of 1972, Dolph Briscoe, campaigning for the Democratic nomination for governor, reported ten donations of $5,000 each and twenty gifts ranging from $2,000 to $3,500. Ben Barnes, campaigning for nomination for the same office, reported thirty-eight donations ranging from $2,000 to $4,000, five gifts of $5,000, and three donations ranging from $7,000 to $10,000.

Finally, it should be noted that there are no comprehensive and reliable reports available concerning money in Texas politics. Perhaps 90 per cent of this condition is attributable to the laxity of federal and state laws. However, there are grounds for hope that, beginning in 1974, candidates will be faced with tighter federal and state laws governing campaign giving and spending. Two federal statutes were enacted in 1971 on the subject: the Revenue Act of 1971 and the Federal Election Campaign Act of 1971. These laws affect both national and state campaigns.

Briefly, the *Revenue Act of 1971* provides that political contributors may claim tax credit against their federal income tax for 50 per cent of their contributions, up to $12.50, or deductions for the full amount of contributions up to $50. These two forms of tax incentives were enacted into law following lengthy national debate. The purpose was to encourage more people to help finance political campaigns. The *Federal Election Campaign Act of 1971* became effective in April, 1972. This statute applies to financing of campaigns for federal offices (President, Vice-President, and members of Congress). The law abolishes all limits on political contributions except those for candidates themselves and their immediate families; and it provides a system of disclosure of the amounts of all receipts, expenditures, and debts. Political committees that expect to receive or spend more than $1,000 in any year in support of any federal candidate must register with the government. Periodic reports containing complete listings of all contributors or donors of over $100 are required. Continuing reports must be made on surpluses and debts until extinguished. No person may contribute to political campaigns in the name of another. Contributions by candidates (or immediate families) to their own campaigns are limited to $35,000 for the office of United States Senator and $25,000 for members of the House. These provisions of the law are based on the assumption that the voter, having a complete financial picture of the candidate, may decide for himself whether or not that candidate has been given too much, or has spent too much, or both.

Another significant provision of the Federal Election Campaign Act of 1971 relates to spending for advertising, including television, radio, newspapers, periodicals, billboards, and telephone. Such expenditures for federal candidates are limited to ten cents per voting-age person in the area covered by the election (for candidates for Congress, the area covered may be a state or district; for presidential candidates, the United States). Furthermore, no more than 60 per cent of the total allowed for advertising may be expended for television and radio. Broadcasters and newspaper publishers in turn may not charge candidates more than the rate for commercial advertising.[8]

Like the federal election law of 1971, the Texas Election Code places no ceiling on any campaign contributions or expenditures. However, it does require strict reporting of contributions and expenditures. The Code, amended extensively by the *Campaign Reporting and Disclosure Act of 1973,* requires detailed accounting from both donor and candidate. Every candidate for nomination and election to any state, district, county, or municipal office, and every political committee in such elections must designate a campaign manager before accepting contributions or making campaign expenditures. The law makes it illegal for any candidate, political committee, campaign manager, or other person to expend any unlawful contributions. This provision plugs up a gaping loophole in the pre-1973 Code which did not require financial reporting by political committees, managers, or other individuals who spent money in behalf of a candidate without his knowledge or consent. Only the candidate was generally required to file such financial statements. Under the 1973 law both civil and criminal penalties are imposed on those who make unlawful campaign contributions or expenditures. Permissible campaign expenditures are itemized. They include those for travel, advertising, salaries for staff, office rent, and other necessary campaign activity. Under the new law, contributions by both labor unions and corporations are proscribed. This provision, however, is as difficult to enforce as the similar provision in the Taft-Hartley Law on the national level. An individual may contribute his own money, time, and traveling expenses in behalf of a candidate, but may not spend over $100 of his own money for other lawfully funded activities. Neither candidates nor political committees are allowed to receive a contribution in excess of $500 from an out-of-state committee without a written statement providing the name and address of everyone giving more than $100 to that fund.

Candidates and managers of campaign committees must each file a sworn statement with the secretary of state, county clerk, city secretary, or secretary of any other political subdivision. This statement must reveal the amounts and dates of all contributions and expenditures of over $10 and the names and addresses of donors. Three such statements are to be filed in the process of an election campaign. The first filing is to be between the fortieth and thirty-first day before the election (both primary and general election); the second must be filed between the tenth and seventh day before the election. The third statement must be filed no later than the thirty-first day after the date of the election involved. Failure by either candidate or campaign manager to make such reports makes them civilly liable to the state of Texas for triple the amount of such unreported contribution or expenditure. All such statements filed shall be open to public inspection for two years following the election.

The new law establishes watchdog election commissions on the state and county levels to inspect contribution and expenditure statements filed by candidates and managers, and to notify those who fail to file or who make errors in such statements. The county election commission in each county is composed of the chairmen of the county executive committees of the two major political parties and the senior district judge having jurisdiction in that county. The state election commission is composed of the chairmen of the state executive committees of the two major political parties, the chief justice of the Texas Supreme Court, the presiding judge of the court of criminal appeals, one justice of the court of civil appeals appointed by the chief justice of the Supreme Court, one district judge appointed by the presiding judge of the court of criminal appeals, the chairman of one county executive committee of each of the two major parties, and the secretary of state. The county election commission may inspect statements filed with the county clerk or the clerk of any municipality or political subdivision in the county; the state commission may inspect those filed with the secretary of state. In cases of willful violation, each election commission* may take the case to the appropriate county or district attorney for legal action.

Without a doubt the 1973 amendment to the Election Code put more teeth in the state's election law than it had before, and it should aid materially in the prevention of undesirable excesses in political campaigning in Texas.

PARTY AND FACTIONALISM IN TEXAS

From 1865 to 1952 Texas politics signified the Democratic Party. This one-party structural arrangement meant that all shades of political opinion were found within the Democratic Party. Until recently the party was a somewhat loose confederation of farmers and ranchers, oilmen, manufacturers, businessmen, professionals, blue- and white-collar workers, and housewives; conservatives and liberals alike were lodged in the same party. The Republican Party (associated in the minds of all true sons of the Confederacy with Reconstruction, carpetbag rule, military occupation, and Northern dominance) was

*In October, 1973, Attorney General John Hale held the county and state election commissions to be in violation of the Texas Constitution (Opinion H-117).

intolerable to most Texans. Hence all elements of the Texas population, dominated by a conviction that political as well as economic independence was the inherent right of every American, gravitated toward the Democratic Party. Not until the mid-twentieth century did the Republican Party begin to take on a status of political respectability in Texas.

In the years immediately following Reconstruction the conservative element gained control of the Texas Democratic Party. However, for the next forty years the conservative road was a rocky one; there were repeated challenges presented by forces such as the Grange and Greenback movements, Progressivism, and Populism. From the 1870s to World War I demands were made on the conservatives by small farmers, laborers, and the dispossessed, on the one hand, and by financial and corporate interests on the other. National movements had their counterparts in Texas, and some of them had a liberalizing effect on the Democratic Party. But not until 1890 was the liberal element able to gain the governorship. In that year James Stephen Hogg was elected as the state's first liberal governor. Committed to a policy of antibusiness, Hogg's reforms continued to the turn of the century with the help of his successor, Charles A. Culbertson.

In 1907 came another Hogg-endorsed governor, Thomas M. Campbell, who resumed battle for reform. Under Campbell's leadership the Legislature strengthened the antitrust laws, provided for municipal regulation of public utilities, enacted a lobby control law, reformed the tax structure, and enacted a maximum-hours law for railroad workers and a pure-food law. This populist-inspired program was bound to have a permanent impact on the generally conservative atmosphere in the state. In 1915 the redoubtable James E. "Pa" Ferguson was elected as a "businessman's candidate," but he was actually a champion of the dispossessed, especially the poor farmer. "Farmer Jim" managed to serve only one full term and part of another before he was impeached and convicted for financial irregularities and warring on the University of Texas and its Board of Regents. Although he was removed from office, in that short period "Fergusonism" established itself as an issue between rich and poor. Out of office, "Farmer Jim" later succeeded in getting his wife elected in his stead. Under the slogan "Two governors for the price of one," Mrs. Miriam Amanda "Ma" Ferguson ran for governor in 1924, 1926, 1930, 1932, and 1940; she was elected in 1924 and 1932.

Fergusonism antedated the New Deal in Texas. The Fergusons were the liberals of the twenties following the progressive Hogg era. "Pa" and "Ma" took the liberal side on all issues. They opposed prohibition and the Ku Klux Klan, and they favored liberal spending by government to benefit the poor. In that day those southerners who voted wet and opposed the Klan were indeed liberal. Elected essentially by farmers and endowed with great personal appeal to the voter, the Fergusons nevertheless accomplished surprisingly little in the way of lasting liberal reform.

If Fergusonism with all its appeal could not redirect the political current of the decades in which it was so much a part, the Great Depression of the thirties and the ensuing New Deal could. With national, state, and local governments forced to reappraise their responsibilities to their people, the depression of the thirties laid the groundwork for the burning issues of the forties and fifties. Indeed, the influence of New Deal philosophy and legislation could not fail to affect the state for succeeding decades. In Texas its impact on party alignment and political philosophy is still felt in the seventies. In the thirties, Texas began to move toward welfarism. The New Deal strengthened the hand of labor while weakening the favored position of business. Dramatically it made Texans realize that there is another government outside of Austin, a government capable of undertaking limitless activities affecting the lives of individuals.

Inevitably, economic and social developments had to focus on the liberal-conservative alignment within the Democratic Party. These developments hardened that alignment and widened the gulf between liberal and conservative factions. By 1941 the growing factionalism had emerged into open warfare, and in the state conventions from 1944 to 1956 it shook the Democratic Party to its foundation. Thereafter the terms "liberal" and "conservative" had more real meaning to the voter than "Democrat" and "Republican."

In the 1944 state Democratic convention the two factions came to a parting of the ways over the New Deal. One of these, the anti-Roosevelt "*Texas Regulars,*" later qualified for party status and obtained a place on the November presidential ballot in Texas, with Senator Harry Byrd of Virginia as the faction's standard-bearer and presidential candidate. The "Texas Regulars" gradually merged into the South's Dixiecrat or States' Rights Party, but the liberal-conservative alignment within the Texas Democratic Party continued as both sides battled for control of the party machinery.

Liberals suffered two bitter defeats at the hands of the conservatives in the state party conventions of 1952 and 1956, while the state went Republican in the presidential elections of those years. Following the 1956 setback, liberals formed their own organization and called it the "*Democrats of Texas*"; but unlike the "Texas Regulars" they made no attempt to become a new party separate from the regular Democratic Party. Their avowed purpose was to provide a refuge for liberal Democrats, who, they claimed, had been driven from the regular party. The DOT lasted until the 1960 National Democratic Convention, where Lyndon Johnson, considered an arch-conservative by the DOT and the major cause of their grief, destroyed with one stroke the DOT's *raison d'être* by joining the liberal cause as John F. Kennedy's running mate. In that year Texas returned to the Democratic fold with a razor-thin victory by the Kennedy-Johnson ticket, while the conservative Democrats continued in control of the governorship and the state party machinery.

Texas Republicans, on the other hand, taking advantage of the liberal-conservative division in the Democratic Party, continued to widen their own beachhead. In a 1961 special election to fill the United States Senate seat vacated by Lyndon Johnson, Republican John Tower, an unknown political science professor from Midwestern University in Wichita Falls, defeated millionaire conservative "Dollar Bill" Blakely, the conservative Democrats' choice. Throughout the 1960s the Texas vote in the Senate was for the most part canceled out by the opposing votes of conservative Republican John Tower and liberal Democrat Ralph Yarborough, who, like Tower, was first elected to the Senate in a special election. Yarborough won in 1957 to fill a vacancy created when Senator Price Daniel resigned to run for the Texas governorship. Yarborough continued to represent the liberals of Texas in the Senate until ousted in 1970 by Lloyd Bentsen, a conservative Democrat. Through the 1950s and 1960s the governorship continued in the hands of conservative-to-moderate Democratic governors: Allan Shivers, Price Daniel, John Connally, and Preston Smith. Not since the administration of James V. Allred from 1935 to 1939 has Texas had a truly liberal governor.

Thus in the past two decades both liberals and conservatives within the Democratic Party in Texas could point to substantial gains at the polls. Following the two successive Republican victories in Texas in the presidential elections of 1952 and 1956, the state returned to the Democratic fold for the next three presidential campaigns. It gave its approval to such liberals as Kennedy, Johnson (considered liberal by 1964), and Humphrey. The Texas delegation to the United States House of Representatives, though largely conservative compared with states outside the South, has had a sprinkling of liberals during the past two decades. And in a sense the governorship has grown less conservative in practice; without a doubt Governors Daniel, Connally, and Smith took more liberal stances on various issues than their predecessor Allan Shivers had. The state legislature also appears to have grown less conservative since the early 1950s.

The Texas Republican Party waged a discouraging battle for survival until the 1950s. In 1869, during Reconstruction, the GOP won the governorship for the first and only time; it also gained a majority of seats in both houses of the state legislature. But by 1873 the party's honeymoon was largely over in Texas. In that year the Democrats began a statewide rout of the Republican Party, stigmatized in the South by emancipation, military occupation, and carpetbag rule. From then until 1960 the GOP won no seats in the United States Senate and only fourteen full terms for its members in the House of Representatives. Republican membership in the state legislature dwindled to only token representation.

A widening factional division in the Democratic Party, brought on by the New Deal, without doubt aided the cause of Republicanism in Texas and helped indirectly to swing the state to the Republicans in the 1952 and 1956 presidential elections. Only once before, in 1928, had Texas gone Republican in a presidential election. These Republican victories in presidential elections, however, were not matched on state and local levels. There the Democrats remained dominant.

Comparisons of presidential and gubernatorial pluralities in Texas in 1928, 1952, and 1956, while indicating comfortable majority support for Republican presidential candidates, reveal only nominal support for Republican gubernatorial candidates. This situation is described in V. O. Key's midcentury comment on the rise of a new breed in Texas politics: "Indigenous to the South is a strange political schizophrenic, the Presidential Republican. He votes in Democratic primaries to have a voice in state and local matters, but when the Presidential election rolls around, he casts a ballot for the Republican Presidential nominee.

Locally he is a Democrat; nationally he is a Republican."[9] Thus the Republican Party in Texas has undoubtedly capitalized on cleavages within the Democratic Party. Also it has gathered some support as a result of social and economic changes that have followed Texas's transition from an agrarian to an urban and industrialized society—a transition accompanied by the rise of organized labor, the influx of a middle-class white-collar population, and the influx of a number of professionals and technicians from the more Republican areas of the country.

Republican gains of the fifties in Texas were sorely affected in 1964 by the party's disaster nationally; yet only two years later the Texas GOP staged a remarkable comeback, paralleling the Republican rebound across the country. Even in the seemingly unprofitable election year of 1964, Republicans in Texas demonstrated remarkable vitality by winning substantial percentages of votes in the gubernatorial and United States senatorial races. And in the comeback election of 1966, the GOP returned John Tower to the Senate and captured two more seats in the House. In addition, it elected four members to the state legislature, three county judges, eight county commissioners, and six justices of the peace.

Viewed in the same perspective, the 1968 and 1970 elections did not give the Republicans much hope for a permanent beachhead in Texas. Neither of these elections comforted the Texas GOP, and the 1970 showing was an especially bitter blow to the party faithful. With no gains to speak of in 1968, early evaluations of the 1970 returns held out even less hope for the embattled GOP. In the race for the Senate, Bentsen carried 227 of the state's 254 counties, leaving only 27 for his opponent, George Bush, whose campaign drew both President Nixon and Vice-President Agnew to Texas in a desperate attempt to give the GOP two Texas seats in the United States Senate. In the gubernatorial race, Democrat Preston Smith paralleled Bentsen's showing by carrying 234 counties, leaving only 20 for his Republican opponent, Paul Eggers. Control over the United States House delegation remained unchanged, as had been the case in 1968, with three seats retained by the Republicans and the other twenty by the Democrats. Every other statewide race was taken by the Democrats, and the contests for the state legislature were much the same. Thus the Republican Party was left with only one member with statewide identification, Senator Tower.

The 1970 plight of the party was recorded by Jon Ford, whose Sunday column on Texas politics appears on many Texas editorial pages: "The sad sight of fresh young amateurs, who had worked their hearts out, sobbing at the George Bush election night wake in the Shamrock Hilton ballroom, some vowing to leave their home state forever, was the first clue to a widespread feeling of frustration and helplessness among the GOP's." Perhaps more disturbing to the Republicans was the question of what impact the party's poor showing of 1970 in Texas would have on 1972 and its prospects for carrying the state in the presidential race. To bolster his chance of capturing Texas's twenty-six electoral votes in 1972, President Nixon late in 1970 added former Texas Governor John Connally to his cabinet as Secretary of the Treasury; also, he appointed the defeated George Bush to the post of Ambassador to the United Nations.

Judging from the outcome of the 1972 presidential election in Texas, Republicans were undaunted by the discouraging results of the 1970 contests. For the fourth time Texas went Republican—this time by an overwhelming majority. The Nixon-Agnew ticket carried 246 of the 254 counties, with 78 voting Republican for the first time. Only Brooks, Cottle, Duval, Jim Hogg, Maverick, Starr, Webb, and Zapata counties gave a plurality to the McGovern-Shriver ticket. Though the Democratic candidates worked hard to retain the key state of Texas with its 26 electoral votes, they were unable to hold enough of the potential Democratic vote even to come close to a popular plurality of the 3,471,281 votes cast in the presidential race. Despite his agricultural background, McGovern was unable to project a strong appeal to Texas farmers and ranchers. And though Texas voters reacted strongly against the Sharpstown scandal in the May primaries by rejecting most Democratic incumbents, they were unmoved by Democratic reminders of the Watergate scandal associated with the Nixon election campaign. McGovern lost by heavy ratios in the populous counties: Bexar County, 3: 2; Dallas County, over 2: 1; El Paso County, a normally liberal stronghold, 2: 1; Galveston County, 4: 3; Harris County, 2: 1; Tarrant County over 2: 1; Travis County, 4: 3. Statewide McGovern won 33 per cent of the popular vote to Nixon's 65 per cent.

Continuing the 1972 victory march in Texas, United States Senator John Tower had no trouble in winning re-election over his Democratic opponent, *Barefoot Sanders,* 1,822,877 to 1,511,985. Tower, propelled by seemingly endless amounts of money and a strong tail wind from the President's campaign, was able to do well even in a heavily Mexican-American area such as the Lower Rio Grande Valley. Sanders, a self-styled "Lyndon Johnson Democrat," who defeated former United States Senator Ralph Yarborough in a Democratic Party run-off primary, was plagued by lack of money.

In the race for governor, Republican *Henry Grover* came close to an upset victory over Democrat Dolph Briscoe with 1,533,986 votes to Briscoe's 1,633,493. Again money seemed to be a big influence, this time on the side of the Democrats (see Reading 2-7). Briscoe applied doses of television and newspaper exposure both in his two primary contests and in the general election. In the first primary he was forced into a run-off, where he defeated Frances "Sissy" Farenthold. In two other races the Republicans came close to victory when Democratic incumbent Jesse James barely nosed out Republican Maurice Angly, Jr., in the race for state treasurer, and Democratic incumbent Byron Tunnell narrowly held on to his office as railroad commissioner against a strong bid for the position by Republican Jim Segrest. Raza Unida Party candidate Ramsey Muniz and Socialist Workers Party candidate Deborah Leonard received 214,118 and 24,103 votes, respectively, for governor.

In addition to the reelection of Tower to the U.S. Senate, the Republicans pushed their membership in the U.S. House from three to four. In the Texas lower house the GOP increased its number from ten to seventeen, and in the Senate from two to three. On the district level the GOP captured six offices across the state and on the county level forty-six offices in twenty-two counties. Enhancing these significant gains and near victories by the embattled Republican

Party of Texas, there were other contests in which the GOP candidate ran a close race with his Democratic Party opponent. Of equal significance was the number of elections contested by the Republicans. They sought to win 13 of the 31 seats in the Texas Senate, 74 of the 150 seats in the House, and 10 of the 24 positions on the State Board of Education. To quote staff writer Art Wiese of the *Houston Post:*

The Texas Republican Party, which seemed headed for the elephant's graveyard only two years ago, has come roaring back to life with its most resounding election victories in history. While Texas remains essentially a Democratic state, Tuesday's voting results show the GOP is continuing to make slow but steady progress toward becoming a viable second party at the grassroots level.[10]

One may conclude, therefore, that Texas, along with the entire South, will never be as solidly Democratic as it once was. Republicans have made too many inroads since 1952 for the total cause of Republicanism to be lost. Despite the GOP losses of 1970, the sharp gains in 1972 brought Texas closer to becoming a two-party state than ever before. Given more time, probably the Republicans' beachhead will be widened.

Finally, we need to examine the vote of the blacks and Mexican-Americans in the 1972 election to assess their impact in the various contests. The combined populations of the two minority groups approximate 30 per cent of the total population of Texas. This represents enough to count significantly and to affect the outcome of local races in areas where ethnic minority strength can be concentrated. One political weakness within each group is lack of unity. Another is that Mexican-Americans and blacks in Texas are seemingly unable to combine their political strengths to achieve common goals (see Reading 2-8). And rarely have Mexican-Americans been able to concentrate all their strength in one direction or behind one candidate except in a few local elections where they were a strong majority of the population.

There is little in the way of effective political organization among Texas blacks, though it must be observed that they increased their number in the Legislature from three to eight in 1972 and sent one of their own, Barbara Jordan, to the United States House of Representatives. Mexican-Americans made some headway toward unity in their experience with the Raza Unida Party (see Readings 2-9 and 2-10). In the 1972 gubernatorial election Raza Unida candidate Ramsey Muniz more than fulfilled his promise to attract 200,000 votes; but he failed to draw in a significant amount of black support or to concentrate the strength of his own ethnic group. Consequently, the *Texas Observer* commented:

La Raza failed to pull off its base-broadening efforts. With a little more persistence and openness, *La Raza* should be able to bring in the big city blacks, who are as ripe as the young chicanos for a pride-and-power political effort. But this go-round, *La Raza* was unable to convince, for example, some of the key young black leadership in Houston that it really offered anything to blacks.[11]

In closing, it is interesting to note from Reading 2-12 that in the 1972 election, Texas's small Indian population may have learned a lesson in political unity that both blacks and Chicanos have so far failed to learn. (See Reading 2-11 for an interview with a Texas Choctaw Indian on the subject of Indian voting strength in Texas.)

NOTES

1. *Congressional Quarterly Weekly Report,* November 11, 1972, p. 2947. The Gallup Poll corroborated the *Congressional Quarterly Weekly Report* in assessing the causes of the low turnout.
2. *Dallas Morning News,* November 13, 1972.
3. Alaska, Georgia, Idaho, Indiana, Michigan, Minnesota, North Dakota, Tennessee, Texas, Utah, Vermont, Washington, and Wisconsin.
4. U.S. Bureau of the Census, *Current Population Reports,* Series P-25, No. 479 (March, 1972), p. 6.
5. *The Shame of the Cities,* a 15-page pamphlet distributed by Common Cause in 1972. Common Cause is a Washington, D.C.-based and nationally organized people's lobby devoted to achieving reform in national and state government. It was founded by John Gardner, former Secretary of Health, Education and Welfare.
6. Quoted in Joseph B. Shannon, *Money and Politics* (New York: Random House, 1959), p. 16.
7. *Ibid.,* p. 23.
8. For a short, up-to-date, critical analysis of federal financing, see Herbert E. Alexander, *Political Financing* (Minneapolis, Minn.: The Burgess Publishing Company, 1972).
9. V. O. Key, Jr., *Southern Politics in State and Nation* (New York: Alfred A. Knopf, 1950), p. 278.
10. Art Wiese, "Texas Republicans Show Amazing Vitality," *Houston Post,* November 9, 1972.
11. "Election Results and Comments Thereon," *Texas Observer,* December 1, 1972, pp. 4-6. Apparently many of Muniz's 214,118 votes were cast by liberal Anglo voters who refused to support either Briscoe or Grover. La Raza's candidate for the U.S. Senate, Flores Amaya, received only 63,543 votes.

KEY TERMS, NAMES, AND CONCEPTS

Fourteenth Amendment
Fifteenth Amendment
literacy test
grandfather clause
white primary
poll tax
Harper v. *Virginia State Board of Education*
Nineteenth Amendment
Twenty-sixth Amendment

voter age qualification
state citizenship
Dunn v. *Blumstein*
residence requirement to vote
voter registration
Beare v. *Smith* (1971)
Texas Election Code
party caucus
direct primary
"run-off" primary
Raza Unida Party
Ramsey Muniz
Carter v. *Dies*
Johnston v. *Luna*
Bullock v. *Carter*
closed primary
blanket primary
"ticket splitting"
"party purity"
"party-column" ballot
run-off elections
permanent party organization
temporary party organization
precinct convention
county convention
presidential convention
Republican Party rules
Democratic Party rules
precinct chairman
county executive committee
state executive committee
Revenue Act of 1971
Federal Election Campaign Act of 1971
Texas Campaign Reporting and Disclosure Act of 1973
"Texas Regulars"
"Democrats of Texas"
Barefoot Sanders
Henry Grover

C. P. HOUSTON FROM THE HOUSTON CHRONICLE

"After all the rhetoric I'm left with but one question: Is America ready for self-government?"

Selected Readings

2-1
THE VOTE FRAUD DECREE

In its invasion of residential requirements for voting, the Supreme Court has completed the take-over of what was once exclusive state control of voting. The constitutional implications are bad enough; the prospect of vote fraud is probably worse. The justices left everybody guessing when they outlawed Tennessee's 1-year residency requirement as too long but failed to say specifically what is not too much. Thirty days, it was suggested, are enough. Some thirty states, Texas included, require a year's residence, and they are all presumably in the same boat with Tennessee, though hasty reports from most of the states affected suggest that none of them will rush to legislate shorter waiting periods. Some indicate they will await voter suits. But this is mere delay.

Editorial in the *Dallas Morning News,* March 23, 1972. Reprinted by permission.

The residency laws may linger, but die they must because the court has said that voting is a right under the 14th Amendment and not a privilege conferred by states on their citizens. The final slam was not surprising. Beginning with its ratification of the Voting Rights Act of 1965, the court has tossed most of the states' voting-control prerogatives down the throat of the 14th Amendment. "National citizenship" has been the excuse. The latest decision practically abolishes the "state citizen" as a constitutional entity—and on very weak grounds. The court said the State of Tennessee showed no "compelling interest" in setting a year's residency requirement. Compelling interest is a relatively new way of dressing up court take-overs in mock constitutional language.

Three years ago, the court gave this warning: "If a challenged state statute grants the right to vote to some bona fide residents . . . and denies the franchise to others, the court must determine whether the exclusions are necessary to promote a compelling state interest."

Tennessee, like all the other states affected, no doubt thought it had one: purity of the ballot. Brief residency requirements lend themselves to fraud—to the "floating vote," run in and out to control an election. Any address will do for the day, or few days, needed to influence the outcome. States also reason that if an informed electorate is worth having, newcomers should reside in the state long enough to have a grasp of the issues before getting the vote. Nine tenths of all voting is local and state. These issues affect the voter as a state citizen, not [as] an American-at-large. The aim is not bona fide American citizens, as the court ruled, but bona fide state citizens.

But these arguments, compelling as they are, were dismissed almost casually by the court. Waiting periods were treated as "disenfranchisement"—a denial of equal protection of the laws. Seldom has doctrine triumphed over constitutionalism and common sense at such a cost. Even the test itself was of the court's own manufacture. It was a sad day for federalism and an informed electorate, but a great day for Constitution-killing justices and the political corruption that will follow their decree.

2-2
A RECOMMENDED CHANGE OF THE TEXAS ELECTION CODE

The *Texas Election Code* should be amended to provide that each citizen when registering to vote shall designate the political party of which he or she is a member (or no party affiliation). A person becomes a qualified member of the party so designated at the time of registration. Only members of an organized political party, who have designated their party affiliation at the time of their voter registration, may vote in the primary election of that party, subject to procedures to

From *Let's Keep the Republicans Out of the Democratic Primaries* (El Paso, Texas: El Paso County Democratic Executive Committee [1972]). This pamphlet was distributed in Texas during the 1972 primary campaign. Reprinted by permission.

change party affiliation. The Election Code now permits any registered citizen to vote in the primary election of either party.

A large majority of the states have some form of a "party purity" code. The experience in the states with a party purity code is that party members will vote in their own respective primaries, leaving the selection of candidates to the loyal and faithful members of the same party. The change of law will reduce the number of Republicans voting in Democratic primaries.

Since the post-Reconstruction period and until the 1950's, Texans overwhelmingly have been Democrats. Only a small percentage of the electorate related to the Republican Party and to what it then represented. The interests of voting Texans in those days were generally similar and concerned the business of Texas which was mostly a farming, ranching, mineral- and raw material-producing state. In recent decades Texas has progressed dramatically and is now a sophisticated, modern, industrial state. Every segment of the nation's society and economy is reflected and represented in Texas. The political interests of Texans are no longer as similar as they were in the past, but are diverse. The political parties themselves, their positions and goals, have changed considerably and they little resemble the parties by the same names existing some decades ago.

The Republican Party is now, and it is inevitable that it will continue to be, a part of the permanent political structure of Texas. In years gone by when Texans were generally Democratic, political disagreement was carried on and resolved within the Party, but political interests now are widely dissimilar, and basic political differences hereafter will be carried on between the political parties. With the elimination of the poll tax and for other reasons, there exists a much larger voter participation, involving many citizens who before 1950 never formed a significant percentage of the Texas electorate, including Black and Chicano minorities, farm hands and urban labor, and recently, minors. But our Election Code has not kept pace with the changing social and economic conditions of our State. Under the Texas system of open primary elections, any registered citizen may vote in a primary regardless of whether the voter supports the party in whose primary he votes or will support the candidate of such party in the general election. It is clear from the results of the statewide elections of 1968 and 1970 [and 1972—data supplied by authors] that many who supported Republican candidates in the general election were involved in Democratic primaries:

	Primaries		**General Elections**	
	Democratic	*Republican*	*Democratic*	*Republican*
		1968		
Governor	1,749,652	104,765	1,662,019	1,254,333
		1970		
Governor	1,011,300	109,021	1,232,506	1,073,831
U.S. Senator	1,540,763	110,465	1,226,568	1,071,234
		1972		
Governor	2,192,903	114,007	1,633,535	1,533,478
U.S. Senator	2,065,748	107,648	1,511,669	1,822,585

NEED FOR CHANGE

Political parties are not social clubs, but should be meaningful organizations formed to represent and support the views and best interests of their members. If primary elections are unqualifiedly open to all voters, the purpose of the party system is thwarted; it probably would be cheaper, more efficient and have the same result to eliminate primaries and let the candidates submit themselves to a general election. The present system leaves a part of the voters without spokesmen. When Republicans go to the primaries to vote with Democrats, the winning Democratic candidates will often and for obvious reasons be closer to the positions of the Republican Party. This results in a disenfranchisement of a growing and dissatisfied percentage of Texans. Unless the system is corrected there is an increasing probability of third-party movements in Texas, and the possibility of rejection by the Democratic minority of its party's candidates by casting protest votes for the Republican candidates in the general election. The present system of open primaries is unhealthy and it can only cause increasing bitterness, frustration and discord among the good Democrats. This is an age of expanded access to information, an age of awareness. Voters ask political parties for meaningful statements of position and definitions of issues, which can only be achieved by relatively homogenous membership. Party membership unqualified (except to vote in a primary), as the law now stands, results in a poorly organized party and a diffusion of issues, directions, efforts, and appeal.

There is no legitimate reason for voters who do not think like Democrats, and who do not support Democrats, to participate in Democratic primaries. The present Election Code permits a large percentage of Republican and other parties' supporters, contributors and sympathizers to vote in the Democratic primaries. Frequently Republicans voting in a Democratic primary actually choose the Democratic candidate who will face the Republican candidate in November. This is dishonesty, and the worst form of political hypocrisy. The proposed change will establish some permanence in party membership and cause party candidates to be selected by party members and supporters, not by outsiders and competitors.

The proposed change will purify primary elections. Republicans should not object, as it will increase participation in the Republican primaries. Democrats should not be afraid that the change will reduce their chance of victory. The two-party system is established in Texas, but regardless of procedural changes to adapt our electoral process to this reality, Texans will elect Democratic candidates because the principles of our party will be favored.

The present system is weighted in favor of some Texas voters and weighted against a sizeable number of others. Every believer in democracy wants all citizens to share equally in the right to select officials. The true believer in democracy does not want one citizen's vote handicapped while another's vote is favored. Republicans voting in Democratic primaries are assured that their real favorites are being elected in the Republican primaries and they, therefore, influence the results of both primaries. The odds are handicapped and fixed against the loyal Democrat. To be elected these days the traditional Democrat must win the equivalent of a general election in May, and then again in November. The expense to the Democratic candidate is about twice the expense of his Republican opponent, which means that the Republican can afford to spend twice as much as the Democrat for the November race, assuming they have about the same funds. The result is not fair to Democratic candidates and their supporters. In most areas of Texas the vote of many faithful Democrats is cancelled by the unlimited invasion of hostile and biased Republicans into our primaries. *A change is needed, and is needed now.*

THE PRACTICE IN OTHER STATES

The Legal Research Board of the University of Texas School of Law has completed a thorough examination and review of the election codes of each of the fifty states to compare the different systems and procedures used to ensure the purity of primary elections.

Only 12 other states out of the 50 have an open primary similar to that of Texas. Thirty-seven states have laws or party rules which limit in various ways outsider participation in party primaries. Most of the 12 other states with open primaries fall into one of two categories: (1) They are states with at least two active and well-organized political parties, states where the primaries of each party present several attractive choices of candidates, and where the usual activity of each party tends to hold its members in its own primary; (2) they are states which are still in fact one-party [states]. Of the open primary states, only Texas and possibly Tennessee are not one-party states, nor yet are they states where the Republican Party is active and organized enough to hold competitive primaries which keep their members at home.

The Legal Research Board makes the following specific recommendations: (1) Party preferences should be recorded concurrently with initial voter registration; (2) changes in party preference should not be permitted closer than 30 days prior to a primary, and such change should be by affidavit to the appropriate registration official; (3) only voters with registered party preference should be permitted to vote in the party primary. The recommended procedure is the most commonly used among the states and is probably the simplest in practice. The El Paso County Democratic Executive Committee, representing over 45,000 Democratic voters in May, 1970, did in meeting on January 27, 1971, unanimously approve a resolution that the *Texas Election Code* be amended as recommended above by the Legal Research Board.

2-3
PARTY PURITY

There is . . . no party purity in Texas. Voters can switch from primary to primary, year after year. Texas is one of several states that does not require citizens to

From the *New Voter/Houston Post,* March 5, 1972, pp. 9-10. Reprinted by permission.

declare whether they are Democrats, Republicans, independents or followers of any other political group or philosophy when they register to vote. The bonds of party loyalty are loose in Texas, which has an open primary system where any eligible voter can participate. Registered voters in Texas can choose to vote in any party's primary, although in reality primaries normally are held only by the Democratic and Republican parties. Furthermore, any registered voter who participated in the primary of a given party earlier in the day is eligible to attend that party's precinct convention in his voting precinct on primary election night. From there, technically, he can be elected a delegate to the county or district party convention and eventually even become a delegate to the state or national party conventions. A voter can, of course, only participate in the primary of one party in any election year, but there is no legal bar to his switching from primary to primary year after year.

Former U.S. Senator Ralph Yarborough, . . . [a] Texas liberal Democrat, has long favored a "party purity" law that would require Texans to declare their party affiliations when they register to vote and bar them from participating in the affairs of any other parties. The conservative-dominated State Democratic Convention in 1970 defeated a proposal to endorse a "party purity" law, although liberals continue to battle for it. Republicans, who sometimes have been the beneficiaries of the state's lack of a party registration requirement, have remained silent on the issue. Senator Yarborough maintains that thousands of conservative Republicans voted in the 1970 Democratic primary and provided the margin of victory for his conservative Democratic opponent, Lloyd Bentsen. There is some logic in Yarborough's argument because only about 100,000 Texans voted in the Republican primary in 1970. In the general election that year, however, the GOP's senatorial candidate (George Bush) and gubernatorial nominee (Paul Eggers) received more than a million votes apiece. Thousands of conservative Democrats voted for Republican Bush in his losing race to Yarborough in the 1964 general election and most of them were prepared to cross-over again until Bentsen upset Yarborough in the Democratic primary. When that happened, some liberal Democrats, angered by Yarborough's defeat, supported Bush. . . .

Democrats argue that their party has experience on its side since it has held the governorship and controlled the Legislature continuously since 1874. Texas remains essentially a one-party state at the grassroots level and many local and even district races will be, for all practical purposes, decided in the Democratic primary. Persons who don't vote in their primary, therefore, lose their voices in choosing many of their public officials, the Democrats claim. Since Democrats have so thoroughly dominated state politics for the past 100 years they can take credit for what's right about Texas and blame for what's wrong. Understandably, party loyalists feel the good heavily outweighs the bad. The liberal-conservative split within the Democratic ranks provides Texas with the equivalent of a two-party system without even bothering with the GOP, they maintain. It also insures a spirited primary with many hotly-contested races and a chance for persons of all political persuasions to participate. Republicans, by contrast, generally hold small primaries with only a handful of contested races, the Democrats argue, and many of the candidates who win the GOP nomination have virtually no chance of being victorious in the general election.

Republicans counter that they are the only real avenue of political reform in Texas. Only through an increased participation in the GOP primary will the Texas Republican Party be able to build a strong and viable grassroots organization, party members say. A true two-party system in Texas would make government more effective and responsible, they claim, and possibly could prevent political scandals in the future. The Republican Party, although still small, is undeniably growing stronger in Texas. The GOP has managed to elect Tower twice and carried the state for President Eisenhower in 1952 and 1956 and narrowly failed to win it in 1960 and 1968 for President Nixon. Individual votes also carry more clout in the smaller Republican primary than in its Democratic counterpart, GOP partisans point out. Finally, Republicans claim they welcome voters of all philosophies, including liberals and moderates, to their ranks, even though the party is basically conservative at the state level.

Thousands of Texas Democrats are already "presidential Republicans," splitting their general election tickets to vote for GOP candidates in most national and statewide races. These political switch-hitters should take the additional step, Republicans argue, and start participating in the GOP primary too.

2-4
A TEXAS BATTLEGROUND (INTERVIEWS WITH HARRIS COUNTY PARTY ACTIVISTS)
David S. Broder and Haynes Johnson

NANCY PALM, A PARTY SWITCHER

Nancy Palm, a surgeon's wife and self-described "maverick," is one of those conservative Democratic activists who has switched to the Republican Party. She has twice been elected Harris County Republican chairman. A full-time volunteer, with two professional aides, she operates a year-round party operation that is distinguished both by its efficiency and by its independence from the dictates of national and state Republican leaders. Mrs. Palm began this interview by telling of her own, typically Texan political career:

Until 1964 I was generally the type of independent who confuses Texas politics so much, meaning that I voted Democrat in the primary and then Republican in the fall. It's still true of Texas politics that the independent voter who does this, the party-switcher, is the one who controls, who carries the state in all November elections. I had been very active in the Democratic Party, secretary of my precinct, and had been asked a number of times to run for party office. I had also been active in the Republican Party, back to 1952, when I was a precinct organizer for Taft. I know it's a very confused picture, but we have no party registration, so you can move back and forth. It was not until 1964 that I switched permanently to the Republican Party and became a precinct chairman,

From the *Washington Post*, December 26, 1971. Reprinted with permission.

an area chairman, vice chairman of the party, and then won election against a very strong candidate for the party chairmanship.

One reason the Harris County Republicans have been so much more effective than other Republicans in the state of Texas is because during the last four years I have been a full-time county chairman. I have an executive secretary who has been with us about four years, a very competent woman of about 35, and an administrative assistant who is a young fellow who has graduated from Baylor . . . and is going to law school. Our budget for a non-election year is $60,000. During a campaign, we have between 6,000 and 7,000 people we put into the field—all volunteers, of course. In the '68 election, we opened nine area headquarters and canvassed all our precincts with more than 40 per cent Republican votes. We have a vast army of volunteer workers, and that's one reason this county always carries so heavily for the Republicans.

Q. Does it seem to you that the lines between the political parties are getting sharper or dimmer?

A. There's no question that they're getting a very great deal dimmer. This is the reason Mr. (George) Wallace drew such a large vote in Harris County. People feel he represents a more conservative point of view.

Q. Why do you think the differences between the Republicans and Democrats are fading?

A. Because each one is striving for the middle vote. I think the Democrats have enough judgment on a national level to see that it is the independent who decides who is elected President. It disturbs me very much. I think there should be a clearly delineated philosophical difference between the two major parties. And I would prefer to see the Republican Party become the conservative party. Obviously, the Democratic Party has been, in the last 30 years, drifting more and more to the liberal, socialistic philosophy of government. Remember, Harris County's delegation to the national convention went for Ronald Reagan [in 1968]. There has been more disagreement with some of Mr. Nixon's programs here than there has been in other areas. We have a very small group of liberal Republicans. The liberals have found their outlet more in the Democratic Party.

Q. What is your relationship with the state and national Republican organizations?

A. The state party spends an awful lot of money. Whether it is spent wisely is something that you would have to discuss with them. Frankly, we get very little of value out of our state organization. As for the Republican National Committee, except in a presidential election year, that again is rather much of a one-way street. We send them a great deal of statistical material, and we get some value from their publications, but actually not a very great deal.

Q. Are Republicans becoming the "establishment" party in Houston?

A. The power structure in this state is still establishment Democrat. We all know that.

Q. Is the establishment now bipartisan, at least in its political contributions?

A. No, it is not. If the establishment gives to the Republican Party, they give it blind. I mean, they give it in cash, where it can never be traced. There are really very few of the major establishment persons here that are willing to be caught with a Republican Party check in their account.

Q. What did John Connally's coming into the Nixon Cabinet mean in terms of Harris County Republicans, and what do you think it means in terms of the changing party picture?

A. I think those of us that had been on both sides of the fence were very pragmatic about this. It was a move Mr. Nixon felt that he had to make. There was a certain jarring to the party structure, in that overnight a person whom we had considered our opposition all of a sudden was not only a member of the Cabinet but the spokesman for the administration. I would be less than truthful if I did not say this has been somewhat traumatic to the Republican worker. But from a very practical point of view, it was a very smart move on Mr. Nixon's part.

BILLIE CARR, ORGANIZER FOR LIBERALS

Billie Carr, the red-headed chief of precinct organization for the Harris County Democrats, the unofficial organization of liberal Democrats, has been working at grass-roots politics in Houston for 17 years. Her efforts are widely credited with playing a major part in the liberals' victories in intraparty Democratic wars. And, as she makes plain in this interview, as far as she is concerned, the war is far from over:

The Harris County Democrats were organized in 1953, after the official Democratic Party leadership in the state and county went for Eisenhower and even tried to keep Adlai Stevenson's name off the ballot in Texas. Shortly after that time, my husband, who was president of a local labor union, and I went to a legislative workshop in Austin, and we went to call on Allan Shivers, the governor who had led the bolt to Eisenhower. We saw the way the Chicanos who worked for him were being treated, and we argued with him about a bill he was trying to pass to set up a loyalty review board, a "little Joe McCarthy" thing we were fighting. I said to him, "I'm going to go tell the people on you, Governor"—I was really that naive and that young and that dumb—"and they're not going to like what you're doing." And he said, "Little lady, I hold Texas in the palm of my hand," and he put his hand out in front of me. And it infuriated me. I decided nobody ought to be able to say that about a state, no one man ought to have that control. So I came back here, and joined the people who were trying to organize, and I've worked ever since trying to make Allan Shivers out a liar.

I did all the things you're supposed to do. I started calling all the people in my precinct. It had gone 4-to-1 for Eisenhower, but I won (as precinct judge) the first time I ran. The next time I had five precincts, and from there I ended up with all 335 precincts. And in two years, from 1964 to 1966, I personally attended 1,000 meetings in 220 precincts to set up clubs. I met with two people, five people, 10 people, 100 people, whatever showed up. I never let a precinct go until it had enough people to keep going on its own. And in 1966, we elected every liberal we endorsed in this county.

Q. You also served on the state Democratic committee?

A. Yes, briefly. In 1964, when Lyndon Johnson was going to run for President, he suddenly looked around and found he had no organization at all. And he knew we had organization; that's the one thing we did have. And so he decided to have John Connally let some liberals onto the state committee. Connally didn't want me on the committee, but John Crooker, Jr., was in Washington at the time and was talking with Lyndon and said, "You had better go with Billie; she's the precinct organizer." So Lyndon himself told Connally to put me on the committee; so they put me on for two years.

The first meeting we had, they made a motion that we support John Connally's legislative program for the year, and that we send a telegram to every senator and representative, with all our signatures on it, saying please support Connally's program. Marvin Watson was chairman of the committee at the time. So I got up and said, "Mr. Chairman,"—and he didn't recognize me until after I stood up and hollered about four times—"Mr. Chairman, could the governor please tell us what the program is?" I thought that was a very reasonable question. John Singleton, who's now federal judge, but who then was committeeman from Harris County, said, "Billie, why do you have to be so difficult?" And I said, "I just want to know what we're voting on." And the governor got up and said, "Mrs. Carr, I'm going to give my program to the joint session of the senate and house on Wednesday night." So I made a motion that we wait until Thursday to vote for whether we're for the program or not, and I couldn't get a second. There are 62 people on the committee, and I couldn't get a second. And right away, the woman who was sitting next to me moved. And from then on, I was not the most popular person on the committee.

Q. After the liberals established their control of the official Harris County party back in 1958, why did you keep this separate organization going?

A. We kept the separate organization because even if we had a majority on the county committee, it still had the conservative people on that committee, too. It's a matter of meeting with your enemies. There are times when you want to meet among yourselves, to plan on what you're going to do about the enemy, and it's ridiculous to have them sitting there. So we needed this organization, even when we controlled the official party.

Q. Are the fights you really care about the fights within the Democratic Party?

A. Yes, that's right. You have to realize that Texas has been primarily a one-party state. I'm hoping that Texas is coming to the point where it is a two-party state. I'm strongly in favor of that, because it will help us who want to work within the Democratic Party to make it a liberal, progressive party.

Q. What do you think of the move to open a unified Democratic Party headquarters here?

A. From time to time they try that, but they've never had any success, especially when they expect the liberals and conservatives to sort of coalesce. We're not going to let them have any of our records, you know. They're going to be beating us on the head with them in the primaries. We're not going to give them our records, and the conservatives are not going to let us have theirs, either. So you'll have this storefront office that won't mean a damn thing and won't be able to do anything. We're all a little paranoid after all these years, and we're not going to work with them and they're not going to work with us. A couple of people may get together and open an office, but nothing will come out of it.

ED STUMPF, DEMOCRATIC CONSERVATIVE

Ed Stumpf, an executive of a major Houston insurance company, is one of the principal figures in the conservative wing of the Harris County Democratic Party. An unsuccessful candidate for county Democratic chairman in 1958, he has managed the county campaigns for both John Connally and Lieutenant Governor Ben Barnes, Connally's protégé and a candidate for governor in the 1972 primary.

We have something different taking place now. Up until six years ago, if we wanted to fight, we fought among ourselves in the Democratic primary, because the primary was tantamount to election. But certain things have happened. The Republicans are winning elections here. If you look back, you'll see that of the six times Connally ran, he only carried Harris County once, and no Democrat except Ben Barnes has carried Harris County in a contested statewide race since then.

So we've learned we have to get together if we're going to win. With that in mind, we had a meeting the other day of all the elements of the Democratic Party, to discuss opening up an office, a Democratic office in Harris County. This office would not have anything to do with contests within the primary. So everybody can participate. The purpose of the office is to elect a full slate of Democratic candidates in the general election, and we don't care who they are. The fight in the Democratic Party in the past has been between conservatives and labor-liberals. They wanted more of the give-away programs, as we would call them, and we were opposed to that. They wanted heavier taxes on business, and we were opposed to that.

Q. What's the difference between a conservative Democrat and a Republican?

A. The Republicans have always thought the Republican Party was conservative. Now that is an erroneous opinion. Wherever you look, there are the same extremes in the Republican Party as we have in the Democratic Party. They have their Javitses and they have their conservatives. The main differences between a conservative Democrat and a Republican here is that we are convinced that a strong two-party state makes both parties more liberal; whereas, in a one-party state, you can have both conservatism and liberalism within the party, without both parties having to go more liberal in order to pick up the in-between votes.

Q. Why does a two-party state make both parties more liberal?

A. I don't know, but it does. You take Michigan, Illinois, every state that has a strong two-party system. They must all give in to get that independent vote that elects them.

Q. Is that why conservatives like you want to stay in the Democratic Party?

A. That's correct. If you notice, there are very few votes cast in the Republican primary, because that's when the conservative Democrat really wants to make his political philosophy felt. He feels that if he can nominate a conservative in the primary, then he doesn't really have to worry too much about the general.

Q. What is your interest, as a conservative, in having a unified Democratic Party headquarters?

A. It's important to me because I'm convinced the state is going to be run by

Democrats and that the more Democratic representation we have in Washington, the more say we'll have, the better shape we'll be in. If we have all Republican people in Washington and all Democratic people here, we don't have too many doors that we can open. Texas has been so fortunate in the past with Rayburn and Johnson and those people up there who just dominated politics, and all of a sudden we find ourselves without any.

Q. I would guess that there must be many elements in recent Democratic Party programs and platforms that are offensive to you as a conservative.

A. There are. But the package is better than the alternative.

Q. In what way?

A. Well, I just don't think the Republicans have the know-how, the leadership to cope with the problems that come up. When the Republicans get into power, we've seen disregard for those things which we think most important for the Texas economy, such as the depletion allowance. They get in, and the first thing they do is start cutting it down.

Q. What would happen here if Governor Connally formally aligned himself with the Republican Party?

A. It would be extremely shocking. It would have a tremendous effect on Texas. Connally would definitely provide the leadership in the Republican Party that they have not had. But it would surprise me greatly if he did that. It would shock me.

2-5
PRESIDENTIAL CONVENTION POLITICS IN TEXAS–1972
Walter Noelke

The spring of 1972 was an especially critical period for Democrats in Texas and across the nation. Since the preceding decade a showdown had been building up within the national Democratic party between the Old and New Politics. There are several ways to distinguish between Old and New Politics. First, by the degree of continuing participation. Practitioners of the Old Politics tend to be "regulars" or continuing supporters of and participants in a political party, while the New Politicos are "irregulars" in that they are erratic in their involvement, activating only periodically and dependent on the type of campaign and/or issues of a particular election. Second, in terms of purpose, party regulars are party-oriented, while party irregulars are more cued to issues. The Old Politics is built on common concern for the electoral fate of party officeholders; the success of the party is paramount. The New Politics, on the other hand, is based on policy considerations

Dr. Noelke was a delegate to the State Democratic Convention in San Antonio in June, 1972. This article, reflecting his impressions of the convention, was written especially for *Practicing Texas Politics.*

in terms of which the political party is only a means; policy change, not party success, is the major consideration and motivation.

By 1972 several factors were at work in Texas suggesting that a sharp conflict between "regular" and "amateur" politics would surface. First, the national Democratic party had recently adopted a set of new guidelines for the selection of presidential delegates. Known as the McGovern-Fraser rules, the new procedure required that state delegates to the national convention be apportioned according to the presidential preferences of those delegates in attendance at the state convention and be representative of various demographic characteristics within the larger state population including age, sex and race. Second, dramatic political developments had occurred within the state Democratic party. Just a month before the June 13 convention, the party leaders, who were also the incumbents of major state offices, were largely eliminated from office in first and second primaries. Earlier, the Sharpstown State Bank scandal had produced a sharp reaction among Texas Democrats, which defeated the governor, lieutenant-governor, and House speaker in their 1972 bids for re-nomination as candidates for public office. New challengers—until then considered by the electorate to be either political has-beens or unknowns—appeared and seized the reins of the Texas Democratic party.

The third and most unknown element in the new volatile situation was the mood of the Texas political grass-roots. Just a month before the state convention, Texas voters had entered the precinct and county conventions in record numbers and apparently with intense commitment. In many precincts party irregulars outnumbered party regulars, officials, and professionals. Reports from across the state indicated that the rank-and-file was strong and militant.

Significantly, too, the New Politics was neither neutral nor one-sided in its political identification. The newly activated forces contained both conservatives and liberals. From the right came the dedicated supporters of George Wallace, who, only weeks before, had been the victim of an unsuccessful assassination attempt in Maryland. Whereas in 1968 the Wallacites had labored alone to support Wallace's third-party effort, the American Independent Party, in 1972 they were making a successful bid for power within the Democratic party. On the left were the McGovern supporters, buoyed up by their candidate's recent surge across the nation in other state delegate conventions and in presidential primary contests. In Texas, the strength of the McGovern campaign was centered in the urban professional class, racial minority groups, and young voters. With the adoption of the 26th Amendment, young Texans had their first opportunity to participate in a presidential election, and many, especially students, expressed a strong preference for the South Dakotan. Racial minorities, primarily those Mexican-Americans who declined participation in the *Raza Unida* Party, likewise responded favorably to McGovern's appeal. Racial support from the impoverished urban ghettoes and barrios was, in turn, amplified by forces "across town." The growing urban professional class, which had been politicized and activated by Gene McCarthy in 1968, now emerged once again from their gilded ghettoes, the suburbs, to wage holy political battle against the Vietnam War.

Occupying the center were those Democrats who preferred an uncommitted delegation to the national convention. This centrist position was supported by the party professionals, who wanted bargaining leverage at Miami, and by the Humphrey workers, who followed their leader's earlier decision to block a first-ballot nomination for McGovern. Humphrey's forces had hopes of engineering a Miami deadlock or at least of forcing McGovern to modify certain policy positions to which they objected. In sum, the uncommitted strategy represented the Old Politics of professional brokers and the traditional liberalism of the underdog, Hubert Humphrey. Meanwhile, in the June 3 Democratic run-off primary Dolph Briscoe, a Uvalde rancher, won the party's nomination for governor over a liberal reformist candidate, Frances "Sissy" Farenthold. With that victory, the leadership of the approaching state convention was due to pass from Roy Orr, an urban conservative and highhanded parliamentarian, to Briscoe's man, Calvin Guest, a rural conservative who promised a procedurally fair convention.

In line with repeated public promises of a fairly managed state convention, Briscoe announced that the selection of national delegates would be governed by the new party guidelines, which called for proportionate representation based on presidential preferences and demographic characteristics. Also in line with party rule, he stated that more than 75 per cent of the 130 national delegates would be selected by senatorial district caucuses; the balance would be picked by a convention committee on delegates-at-large.

As the June 13 date for the San Antonio convention approached, optimism among the Wallace and McGovern factions ran high; but party regulars, Humphrey supporters, and the undecided all predicted party chaos and disunity. Most committed delegates arrived in the Alamo City early for the convention in order to politic for their presidential favorite, to attend statewide McGovern and Wallace caucuses, and to register maximum strength in their respective senatorial district caucuses to be held Monday afternoon and evening before the convention opened on Tuesday.

The next morning, at the same time that Texas Republicans were assembling for their convention in Galveston, Democratic delegates converged at the convention center on the grounds of the 1968 Hemisfair. Some arrived as early as 8 a.m. After repeated delays, credentials were finally issued to county and district delegates and alternates. At this point, those persons selected as delegates who did not appear for their credentials were replaced by alternates. At least in some county delegations, the absence of uncommitted delegates resulted in a net gain for Wallace and McGovern contingents as their alternates were made voting delegates. And, within many delegations, there were certainly delegate shifts in presidential preferences which distorted earlier county convention preferential totals.

Near mid-day on Tuesday the opening gavel sounded and the convention set about the serious business of "partying." The arena floor was divided into two general seating areas. Delegates occupying the main floor and the lower portions of the bleachers were arranged by senatorial district. The larger urban delegations, such as Houston, Dallas, San Antonio and Fort Worth, were given seats in the center of the floor. Alternates and "guests" occupied the upper reaches of the bleachers. It was this group that kept the voting delegates in a state of tension and anxiety, especially the McGovern supporters. They feared that major convention decisions would be made by voice vote and that this would result in full participation by non-voting alternates and guests, and consequent biased interpretations by the chair. McGovern people also complained that those delegations in which they were strong had not been issued guest passes for family and friends, as had those delegations with uncommitted and Wallace majorities.

Shortly after noon, with all delegations finally seated, the convention began its work under the temporary chairmanship of Roy Orr, Acting Chairman of the State Democratic Executive Committee. He first called for district caucus elections of representatives to the permanent committee on credentials. Delegates from each of the 31 senatorial districts then held their respective caucuses where they were seated on the convention floor and selected one member to serve on the credentials committee. These 31 delegates then left the floor to review earlier decisions made by the temporary credentials committee on contested county delegations.

While this important committee met, the chair recognized the party's nominees for governor, lieutenant-governor, U.S. senator, attorney general, and commissioner of agriculture for the purpose of speaking to the delegates. Gubernatorial nominee Dolph Briscoe made a brief keynote speech, gaining loud applause for his theme of unity based on a healthy diversity of views. His opening statement brought the loudest response: "The day of winner-take-all politics is over." In turn he promised the convention that each faction would receive its fair share of national convention delegates and party committee positions. The other nominees in their turn promised that the Democratic party candidates would defeat all Republican challengers in the November election.

These speeches marked the high point of party unity. Then came the anticipated clash between the Old and New Politics over the seating of convention delegates and election of convention officials. The permanent credentials committee made its report to the convention, confirming the temporary committee's decision to seat all challenged delegations in favor of Wallace supporters. Minority reports filed by liberals were repeatedly voted down by voice vote. Demands for roll call votes were quashed by Mrs. Billie Carr of Houston, a liberal leader, who urged McGovern supporters to hold their political fire. She had in mind a challenge of convention officials, not delegates.

By voice vote the convention confirmed Briscoe's nominee, Calvin Guest, as permanent chairman of the convention. Roy Orr's name was then placed in nomination as Briscoe's choice for the permanent vice-chairman. At this point the liberals revolted. They hastily placed in nomination from the floor the name of Eddie Bernice Johnson, a black Dallasite who had recently won the Democratic nomination for state representative. Then a demand arose from the floor for a roll call rather than voice vote on the vice-chairmanship. After a moment's hesitation, Guest called for a standing vote to determine the method of election and interpreted the result in favor of a roll call. The new party rules providing for such a vote on demand of 20 per cent or more had passed its first test.

Before the vote, supporting speeches for Orr were made by representatives of the conservative and Wallace factions; speeches for Johnson came from liberals and McGovern supporters. Surprisingly, a Wallace woman was escorted to a floor microphone by the liberal leader Mrs. Frances Farenthold and began her speech in support of Johnson by saying: "I may be cutting my political throat." Nonetheless, she continued, she supported Johnson as a woman and felt that "they" were "deserving" of party representation. It was uncertain whether she was referring to females, blacks or liberals. In any case, her speech invited Wallace support in a successful floor revolt. The roll call vote, which took almost two hours, gave Johnson the victory by a vote of 2,125 to 1,795.

This vote, however, was not indicative of the political alignments on the floor. It was the only confirmation throughout the entire convention of the so-called "erosion" thesis. Many amateur delegates felt that the McGovern-Wallace forces would cooperate to erode the strength of the uncommitted delegates who occupied the political center. The assumption was that the conservatives in this middle group could be pressured to go for Wallace while the liberals would eventually commit for McGovern. A second and, as it turned out, more realistic interpretation of the political make-up of the convention was the "shift" thesis. This argument held that the center would not erode under pressure, but rather, would shift—and most likely in the direction of the conservatives. This view was confirmed in the 31 senatorial district caucus elections of national delegates.

The new national party rules, as interpreted and modified by the Texas State Democratic Executive Committee earlier in the year, rejected strict adherence to mathematical formulas based on presidential preferences for selecting either delegates to the national convention or members for the various state convention committees. State party rules read that the convention "shall make every feasible effort to insure that the delegation as a whole reflects in fair proportion the presidential preferences of Democrats throughout the state." The words "feasible effort," "as a whole," and "fair proportion" were loopholes which, in many instances, were used by district caucuses to employ a strategy of alliance between Wallace and uncommitted delegates to defeat McGovern caucus nominees for national delegate slots.

As provided by the new party guidelines, each delegate was allowed to vote for the presidential candidate of his choice immediately upon receiving his credentials and before entering upon the convention floor. The results of this "straw poll" revealed the following percentages of preferences based on 3,864 delegate votes: Wallace, 32.9; McGovern, 27.5; Humphrey, 15.9; uncommitted, 21.9. Translated into the respective numbers of delegates to be chosen by the 31 district caucuses (100 of the 130-member delegation were selected by district caucuses), the poll resulted in the following allocations: Wallace, 33; McGovern, 28; Humphrey, 16; uncommitted, 22. In terms of the total national delegation from Texas, the straw poll indicated the following breakdown among the four preference groups: Wallace, 43; McGovern, 36; Humphrey, 21; uncommitted, 28; total, 128.

On Tuesday afternoon the district caucuses were held on the convention floor. Caucusing was somehow conducted amidst the din and confusion of leadership maneuvers, purposeful delays or speedy balloting, shouts of victory and groans of defeat, heated charges of unfairness, and equally adamant demands for both recounts and revotes. The losers, of whatever persuasion, suffered initial disorganization, ineffective moves to develop rump challenges, and the dulling effect of political defeat. In many cases, a district caucus conducted one key test vote after which the initial winner or coalition swept the balance of delegate and committee positions without effective challenge.

The results of these elections proved that in general the McGovern forces were the principal losers as they were repeatedly outmaneuvered in the various district caucuses. Uncommitted and Wallace caucus factions repeatedly joined to outvote the liberals in the allocation of both delegate and committee slots. Such cooperation, somewhat incongruous on the surface, was expedited by certain political facts of life.

First, Briscoe preferred an uncommitted delegation as did the party regulars and the Orr faction. Second, Humphrey people were hard at work to help stop McGovern on the national scene. Given a choice between Wallace and McGovern, they worked to support the Alabamian, who they supposed had less chance of obtaining the Miami nomination. Third, and most importantly, given the conservative nature of Texas politics, the uncommitted center in the state party will logically move to the right under the pressure of national liberalism during presidential election years.

For whatever reason, the caucus alliances, initiated largely by the Humphrey and uncommitted leaders, worked effectively to exclude the political left. Wallace emerged from the caucus elections with 34 delegates, or two above his district caucus delegate percentage and nine short of his total delegate percentage based on the straw poll. McGovern won only 20 delegates, or minus seven caucus delegates and 16 total delegates. Humphrey, on the other hand, garnered 16 caucus positions, which was the exact number of caucus slots to which he was entitled but minus five total delegate positions. The uncommitted slate won 30 caucus positions, which was eight more caucus delegates than this group was entitled to have, and two more total delegates than it should have had. The results are shown in the following table.

	Percentage of Total Delegates Based on Straw Poll	*Percentage of Caucus Delegates Based on Straw Poll*	*Actual Number of Caucus Delegates*	*Variations from Straw Poll Apportionments*
Wallace	32.9	33	34	+1
McGovern	27.5	28	20	-8
Humphrey	15.9	16	16	0
Uncommitted	21.9	22	30	+8

Clearly, the delegates had not followed the apportionment rule in selecting representatives at the senatorial district caucuses. The committee for selection of delegates-at-large now faced the difficult task of adjusting the preferential imbalances which developed in the district elections. It also had to tackle the problem of demographic discrepancies within the total Miami delegation. And, it had only

30 delegate slots to work with, inasmuch as the districts had chosen 100 of the 130 delegates allotted to Texas by the Democratic National Committee.

As soon as the caucus results were in, Briscoe instructed Will Davis, former party chairman and now one of the major unofficial convention managers, to assure committee adherence to the party's presidential preference and demographic guidelines. The gubernatorial nominee first subtracted three seats from the at-large total for himself and the party's two national committee members. Davis then employed a computer to determine the best method for allocating the remaining 27 delegate positions to achieve a balanced delegation. With this information, the committee finally assembled at 1:15 a.m. on Wednesday, 17 hours after the first delegates arrived for their convention credentials.

While the committee met, delegates on the convention floor idled away the hours sleeping, dozing, staring, eating, drinking, visiting, and, at times, demonstrating. By 2:00 a.m. the convention developed what might be described as the "mass sillies," which had both its light and its unpleasant moments. During the early stage of the long waiting period the delegate mood was somewhat less than tolerant. For the past 18 hours they had listened to angry shouts and had watched the display of hostile banners. Several Wallace people carried banners reading "Legalize Cottonpicking" and "Take cyanide, the best kid trip of all," while some counter-signs read "Five Wallacites for every black man." During one floor demonstration for Wallace, some supporters waved Confederate flags; this activity brought heated protests from liberal delegates. At one point a fist-fight erupted between several Wallacites and a black McGovern delegate from Dallas. Chairman Guest ordered an immediate halt to the affray. His command brought ten to fifteen policemen, who quickly surrounded the Wallace group. The liberals at this point were unable to resist the temptation to repeat a favorite Wallace chant, "Law and Order, Law and Order." After much gavelling from the chair, coupled with threats of forceful removal of unruly delegates, the convention floor lapsed into a brief quiet awaiting the committee reports.

Soon, however, the boredom of the tired delegates was relieved by a spontaneous mass singing. The delegates first sang such old favorites as "The Star-Spangled Banner," "The Eyes of Texas," and "Happy Days Are Here Again." Chairman Guest caught the spirit of the occasion and asked for a song leader from the crowd. One appeared, but after a few more renditions including "Good Night Irene" and "Please Release Me," the convention lost interest in the sing-along and again turned to political bickering. To get around the chairman's gavel and the threat of forceful removal, various contingents took up 'vocal bannering' for their favorite candidate. The Wallacites began to shout "We want Wallace." The McGovern supporters countered with "We want George," throwing the Wallace backers into temporary confusion because of the similarity of both candidates' first names. The whole convention joined in laughter as a small uncommitted delegation took up the chant, "Uncommitted, Uncommitted, Rah, Rah, Rah."

Meanwhile, back in the committee room the delegate-at-large nominating committee had met with an impasse. Davis' computer results indicated that, in terms of the straw poll percentages, the at-large slots would be divided as follows:

Wallace, plus eight delegates, one short of his percentage total; McGovern, plus 14 delegates, two less than his percentage share; and Humphrey, an additional five delegates, which brought him to the precise number entitled by the straw poll. The uncommitted group received three additional at-large slots despite its excess caucus showing. In summary the suggested results were as follows:

	Number of Total Delegation by Straw Poll Percentage	*Actual Number of Caucus Delegates*	*Mathematical At-Large Adjustment*	*Actual At-Large Adjustment*	*Total Convention Delegates*
Wallace	43(32.9%)	34	+ 9	+ 8	42(-1)
McGovern	36(27.5%)	20	+16	+14	34(-2)
Humphrey	21(15.9%)	16	+ 5	+ 5	21(0)
Uncommitted	28(21.9%)	30	- 2	+ 3	33(+5)

Despite the close proximity of the Davis plan to the mathematical ideal, the anti-McGovern forces on the committee at first rejected attempts to balance the delegation along preferential or even demographic lines.[1] However, the chairman, at the direction of Davis, quickly ruled that there was no other option according to the national rules. Delegate slots were then allocated according to preferences, followed by the tedious attempt to balance the delegation in terms of age, race, and sex. According to Davis' analysis, the at-large delegation had to be broken down into 15 women, 17 young people, 6 blacks and 15 Mexican-Americans. Because the uncommitted delegation had been overrepresented in caucus elections, the demographic distribution had to be made among Wallace, McGovern and Humphrey delegates.

At this point, racial balance became the divisive issue because Wallace members categorically refused to accept either a black or a Mexican-American on their 8-member slate, while a Humphrey spokesman rejected the addition of another Mexican-American to his 5-delegate package. Again, at the initiative of Davis, the deadlock was resolved. While Wallace people remained adamant, Humphrey leaders reversed their initial stand. McGovern forces then absorbed the balance of racial members necessary to achieve a balance.[2]

Finally, at 3:00 a.m. the committee reported back to the convention; and, after supporting speeches by both Wallace and McGovern leaders from the floor, the at-large slate was accepted by an overwhelming voice vote. Even though the most underrepresented delegation by presidential preference, the McGovern backers readily accepted the delegation slate. More than likely they hesitated to open the matter to the convention as a whole because of their earlier losses in the caucus elections and their fear that they might once again be the victims of renewed conservative alliances.

Chairman Guest then moved quickly to adjourn the convention. Reluctant to endure long minority reports and threatened roll-call votes, the convention agreed by voice vote to table divisive reports from both the rules and resolutions committees. Mutterings of "railroading" by the chair were heard briefly, but with the critical national delegation fairly balanced by the delegate committee, all the threats of challenges and rump caucuses evaporated. The nation's numerically largest state convention quickly became history as the 6,000 delegates and alternates were released at 3:30 a.m. for welcome sleep, early breakfasts, morning rides home, and favorable press reports.[3]

NOTES

1. The information on the political behavior of the at-large delegate committee is based on the author's personal observations and from an article by R. W. Apple, Jr., "New Rules Not Perfect, But They Work," in the *San Antonio Express-News,* June 18, 1972, p. 8-A.
2. The demographic characteristics of the total delegation–caucus and at-large selections for both delegates and alternates–were representative racially but imbalanced by sex and age. The delegation eventually included 12 blacks and 18 Mexican-Americans. However, the young (18-29 year old group) had 27 per cent of the delegation, shy of the ideal 30 per cent. Women represented 35 per cent, which was 17 per cent short of their 52 per cent total in the larger Texas population.
3. Apple, for example, was very complimentary of Briscoe, Davis, and the convention in general. A *New York Times* political analyst, he said that the convention was one of the three best in the nation in seeking to adhere to the party reform rules.

2-6
THE SELLING OF THE SENATOR, 1972
Art Wiese

Cynics might call it "The Selling of the Senator, 1972." By any standard, however, Republican John G. Tower mounted the most expensive and possibly the most professional, sophisticated campaign in Texas political history to win another six years in the United States Senate last week.

Tower was only pointing out the obvious Tuesday night when he addressed his happy supporters in Wichita Falls after soundly beating Democrat Barefoot Sanders. "This was the best-organized, best-manned and best-financed campaign I've ever seen in Texas," he said. "I've long said that people–not candidates–win

From the *Houston Post,* November 13, 1972, p. 91E. Reprinted by permission. Copyright 1972 The Houston Post.

elections. And you did it." In winning, Tower—along with President Nixon—shattered several old political myths, particularly . . . [that] Republicans cannot win in Texas in high-turnout presidential years. But the senator's re-election was no easy or cheap undertaking.

To begin with, it probably cost more than $2.8 million, which reputedly is the most ever spent in any congressional race anywhere. To raise the cash, Tower used a two-man team: Finance chairman Julian Zimmerman, an Austin businessman who headed the Federal Housing Administration under President Eisenhower, and Brad O'Leary, a St. Louis-bred management consultant who was deputy campaign manager in Republican Jack Danforth's unsuccessful attempt to unseat Senator Stuart Symington, D-Mo., in 1970.

As a pro-business conservative and a two-term incumbent with ranking minority status on the influential Senate Banking, Housing and Urban Affairs Committee, Tower was assured of a sizeable kitty from the outset. Since his re-election was the Texas GOP's main priority, he also received hefty donations (in the $25,000 and up category) from wealthy Republicans and conservative Democrats like John J. Moran of Houston, Edgar Brown of Orange, Sam Wyly of Dallas, Haden Head of Corpus Christi, Rex Cauble of Denton, Bill O'Connor of Victoria and Eddie Chiles of Fort Worth. But the contributions didn't all come from fat cats. Nearly 30,000 persons, most of them just ordinary citizens, chipped in something. The average donation was about $24, only slightly above the national average according to O'Leary. "We realized from the outset that we had to do everything in a very professional manner," says Nola Smith, who managed the Tower campaign. "With the new voter registration laws and the presidential year turnout, we couldn't leave any stone unturned," she said.

For that reason, Tower assembled a huge, experienced staff that included 56 paid employees. Among them were four roaming field men plus full-time campaign coordinators in Houston, Dallas, San Antonio, Fort Worth, El Paso and Wichita Falls. In addition to Mrs. Smith, who ran Tower's Austin office for five years before becoming Texas' first woman chairman of a statewide political campaign, the key staff members included the following: former U.S. Ambassador to Australia Edward Clark, a millionaire Austin Democrat and longtime friend of former President Lyndon B. Johnson and former Senator Ralph Yarborough (Clark was chairman of Texans for Tower, the statewide campaign coordinating committee); Richard Agnich, Tower's administrative assistant and son of Republican national committeeman Fred Agnich of Dallas (the younger Agnich took a leave of absence from Tower's Washington staff to work on campaign strategy, fundraising and scheduling); John Knaggs, an Austin newspaper publisher and political consultant who worked in United Nations Ambassador George Bush's unsuccessful 1970 campaign for the U.S. Senate and has advised many other Republican candidates; Kyle Thompson, former United Press International bureau chief in Austin and one-time press secretary to Governor John B. Connally (he handled press relations and traveled with Tower); Jimmy Banks, former political columnist for the *Dallas Morning News* and ex-press secretary for both Governors Allan Shivers and Price Daniel (Banks—who appeared in some Tower television commercials, handled some press chores and worked with

Democrats who supported the senator—was also a key aide in the 1970 election of U.S. Senator Lloyd Bentsen, D-Tex.); Mrs. Jackie Irby, the Tower campaign research director, who prepared thorough background dossiers on Sanders, Yarborough (whom Sanders defeated in the Democratic primary), and Lieutenant-Governor Ben Barnes (who decided to run for governor instead of challenging Tower); Roger Wallace, who helped establish an intricate, highly-organized campaign in all 254 Texas counties (a first for a Republican candidate) and an extensive telephone canvassing program; Humberto Aguirre, who headed "Tejanos por Tower," the campaign's Mexican-American arm (Aguirre quit Governor Preston Smith's Human Relations Committee in 1970 to campaign for Smith's GOP opponent, Paul Eggers, and then joined Tower).

The Tower effort didn't re-elect its candidate single-handedly, of course. President Nixon's coattails in Texas were long, and Sanders ran a frantic, folksy campaign that was long on charm but short on money. Nevertheless, the organizational work of the Tower troops was, to quote one prominent Democrat, "simply superb." To maximize his dollar-power, the senator pooled some of his resources with the Committee to Re-elect the President. Nixon and Tower shared about 40 telephone centers throughout the state, which canvassed nearly two million Texans in more than a million homes before election day.

Both campaigns also shared the services of Decision Making Information Corporation of Los Angeles, which did extensive polling in Texas on both issues and candidates. (The Tower staff also commissioned issue-oriented opinion samples as early as mid-1971 from the respected Dallas firm of Louis, Bowles and Grace, Incorporated.) The Decision Making Information Corporation polls, reportedly the most thorough and scientific the group had ever taken, showed Tower in late October had a solid base in support with 54 per cent of the electorate—exactly the proportion of the vote received. Based on the polls, the canvasses and other research, Tower predicted he would carry about 175 counties. He won 169.

A major factor in Tower's victory was obviously his advertising image. The campaign relied in that department on Culberson, Heller and Norton, Incorporated, a Houston public relations and advertising firm whose three partners had all worked in Tower's 1966 re-election effort. Robert S. Heller, a leading Tower strategist who also helped elect Bentsen two years ago, said it was obvious immediately that the Republican senator had to start early and campaign hard, particularly in the traditionally Democratic rural areas. "Tower gave us a call a few days before the Bentsen-Bush election and said, 'Win, lose or draw, I want you working for me,'" Heller said.

Tower spent almost all of 1971 and much of early 1972 attending chamber of commerce banquets, barbecues, rodeos and almost any other kind of rural or small-town meeting where a handful of people gathered. The senator is something of a dandy who likes wearing expensive British suits, removable collars and vests. He is forceful but reserved and certainly not ebullient or outgoing in the usual political sense. That rather stiff personality was actually an asset in rural areas, says another of the firm's partners, Jim Culberson. "In a lot of the places he went, people had never seen a United States senator," he remembers. "Even though he shows up in his little English suits, that doesn't hurt him. In small towns, they don't want a guy standing up there in overalls with a twig in his mouth. They want a guy they can respect.... People are more sophisticated than you might think in rural areas. They aren't rubes. Television has made them pretty aware of what's going on."

Sanders' strategists made a major blunder, Heller and Culberson think, in portraying him to the public as a freckle-faced, boyish Andy Hardy figure, an "aw shucks" sort of philosophical politician reminiscent of the late Will Rogers. Heller said the firm just let Tower "be himself and do his own thing" on his television advertisements. He–and the unseen announcers on his commercials–talked about the senator's ties to the Nixon administration: his hawkish, pro-Pentagon view of defense spending; his opposition to busing; and similar hard-line views. The Tower issue polls showed that his rigid conservatism was well-received in Texas, where Heller thinks a subtle shift even farther to the right is occurring in politics.

The advertising campaign began early, in March, 1971, when the first of 10 half-hour documentaries (presented as a public service, free of charge, by many Texas television stations) began running. The programs dealt with rural problems, foreign affairs, busing, bilingual education and other supposedly non-political topics. Once Tower announced for re-election last January, the programs were replaced with five-minute "Report from Washington" commercials, which showed the senator interviewing federal officials like Agriculture Secretary Earl Butz. In rural areas, Tower also began running a 10-minute weekly farm report on radio (a program he now intends to continue). Culberson, Heller and Norton, Incorporated, next bought 600 billboards, again mostly in rural areas.

An early, pivotal decision had been made that Tower must have highly visible Democratic support to make it respectable for rank-and-file Democrats to cross over to vote for him. Through last summer, therefore, radio stations ran dozens of Tower spots in which he was endorsed by Democrats ranging from former Governor Shivers to Del Rio Mayor Alfredo Gutiérrez. On August 25, Tower began doing his own radio and television commercials, often stressing–as did his newspaper advertising–his role as a supporter and friend of President Nixon. The "piece de resistance" of the Tower campaign may have been a full-color rotogravure section inserted in 68 Texas newspapers on September 24. About 3 million copies of the section, depicting Tower's career in the Senate, his views, and his home life, were distributed.

As the campaign reached its climactic final period, Tower's financial superiority dwarfed Sanders, who may have ended up spending only a fifth of what his Republican opponent did. Tower, with his money already raised, bought his TV time unusually early, in late August, to insure access to the best time slots. Sanders had money problems throughout the fall. When he finally got some contributions flowing in October, much of the prime time advertising spots were already reserved. "He ended up running some spots in 1:00 a.m. or on the late movie," said Culberson. "That won't do a candidate any good."

Mrs. Smith–who had to completely reassemble the campaign in a new Austin headquarters after a fire destroyed the original offices last May 9–is perhaps proudest of the Tower staff's direct mail efforts. In all, more than 4 million pieces of campaign literature were channeled to different voter groups like physicians, senior citizens, veterans and so forth.

Dr. Abner McCall, president of Baylor University and a conservative Democrat, mailed 30,000 letters to Texas Baptists in Tower's behalf through the campaign facilities. Clerks sent out more than 1.1 million letters in a single mailing to Democrats and another 300,000 (with accompanying messages from President Nixon) to voters who, telephone canvasses showed, were undecided in the senate race. Notes were also funneled to different groups about specific issues. Anti-busing letters were mailed to voters in areas where busing was especially controversial, for instance, while Mexican-Americans received letters about bilingual education.

The work—and the money—paid off handsomely. Tower carried all of the 27 most populous counties in the state except Galveston County. His electoral strength was remarkably consistent. He received 55.2 per cent of the vote in large counties, 54.1 per cent in medium-sized counties, and 52.4 per cent in rural counties (thus becoming the first statewide GOP candidate to actually win in the rural areas). Tower placed heavy emphasis on the normally Democratic Chicano vote. Preliminary breakdowns give him a healthy 43 per cent of it, compared to only about 32 per cent in his 1966 race. He won many heavily Mexican-American counties like Bexar (San Antonio), Nueces (Corpus Christi), El Paso, Cameron (Brownsville), Hidalgo (Edinburg), and Val Verde (Del Rio). Does all this mean that Tower is, in effect, the best senator money can buy? Mrs. Smith, who admits to being somewhat prejudiced, says not. "Every campaign should raise as much money as it can," she claims. "You're doing your supporters a disservice and taking a chance on losing by not spending everything you receive in contributions."

2-7
THE MEANING OF GROVER'S NEAR MISS
William F. Buckley, Jr.

In search retrospectively of significant political contests last fall, the eye alights on Texas, where the nearest thing to an upset happened. Indeed a headline, on November 8, showed "Grover Leading Briscoe in Gubernatorial Race." Grover? Two days before the election, the *Dallas Times Herald* had reported that "one of the most thorough studies of voting preferences ever conducted" showed Grover with less than 20 per cent of the Dallas County vote. Grover carried Dallas County with 57 per cent of the vote.

The significance of Grover's extraordinary performance running for governor of Texas extends beyond the conventional considerations. Obviously, (a) Grover

From the nationally syndicated column in the *Waco Times-Herald,* December 16, 1972. Reprinted by permission.

was a much stronger candidate than it was assumed he would be; obviously, (b) his opponent, Dolph Briscoe, was a weaker candidate than expected; and obviously, (c) the Republican tide running in Texas was stronger than anyone expected.

Still, there are overtones here of extraordinary interest. The significance of the contest in Texas is that the national Republican organization made very little effort to elect a Republican governor. This was so for a combination of reasons, ranging from delicate to extremely delicate. In ascending order of importance, (a) Candidate Grover is a loner, who does not easily attract the support of other Republican officials, local, state, or national; (b) John Tower, seeking all the support he could find, was not anxious to identify his race with Grover's, fearing that any attempt to do so would be to his disadvantage; (c) the White House people had their narcissistic eyes all but exclusively on Richard Nixon. Their key instrument was of course John Connally, Mr. Texas. Connally was willing to work for the re-election of Richard Nixon, but insisted that for reasons of both credibility and strategy, he needed, as regards other candidates, to be a loyal Democrat, i.e., to support Texan Democrats, however perfunctorily.

Notwithstanding the disadvantages, Hank Grover very nearly took over the Texas statehouse, with all that this means, which is considerable. It is the statehouse that dispenses the patronage, which in Texas is formidable. The Republican disadvantage in the South has always been in state offices. A victory by Hank Grover, which we now know might have been accomplished by the least effort by the White House or by the National Republican Committee, would have consolidated Republican prospects in the South way in advance of what is now happening.

"It was so close," Sam Wood of the *Austin American* wrote, "Democrats and Republicans both recoiled with shock." After the fact, commentators sought to assimilate the race–neck and neck as it turned out, notwithstanding the subsidized assumption that Grover would be overwhelmed. *Time* magazine had described Grover as the "Houston history teacher" who "came out of nowhere," which is true enough, though it hardly accounts for what happened. One might as well have described Humphrey as a "Minneapolis pharmacist who came out of nowhere"–to very nearly win the presidency. Grover had in fact served in the Texas legislature for 12 years, the last six as a state senator. Although he was described as a sectarian richman's candidate, "backed by a cabal of ultraright Houston businessmen" (as *Time* put it), he developed extraordinary support. Five thousand Texans contributed to his campaign.

The *Washington Post,* reaching for straws, came forward with the most extraordinary improvisation of the season by reporting that Grover "spent more than $5 million, using radio and television extensively." In fact Grover spent less than 10 per cent of that sum. And, at that, the few dollars spent during the last few days were personally put up by Grover's campaign director, Philip Nicolaides, the gifted campaign strategist, whose enthusiasm for his client was unconfined. It is as safe to say as anything ever is in this field that a modest fraction of the sum of money the *Washington Post* reported as having been spent by Grover would have been enough to put Grover over the top.

Cui bono? Grover, obviously. And, obviously, the Republican Party of Texas.

But, also, the whole Republican movement in the South, which needs to take roots now, during the period of relative stability with a Republican in the White House. Two years from now the Republicans in Texas will try again for the governorship. Grover's showing suggests he should be given a chance backed by the entire party. His recommendation would synchronize nicely with the Republicanization of George Wallace.

2-8
ETHNIC POLITICS IN WACO: AN ORAL HISTORY INTERVIEW

Rufus B. Spain: The first topic I should like to talk about is your attitude toward white liberals—either in Waco or on a broader scale. Ulysses, will you comment on that?

Ulysses Cosby: I'd like to start off by saying the other day I was some place and someone, a white person, was attempting to be liberal. He was overdoing it, you know. He was very irritating. He was going around trying to do everything for blacks. In other words, they are worse than some of the bigots or whatever you want to call them. Not even giving you an attempt to think for yourself. So many liberals—they say they are liberals—their intent perhaps is good; but in a lot of instances they want to be your mother and father and everything else. And they never really listen to you, is what I'm attempting to say. They always say, "Well, yeah, yeah, that's good, but—" They always come back to their point of view, and your point of view is never really taken into consideration.

Spain: Robert, would you like to add to that?

Robert Gilbert: Yes. I think as far as the white liberals are concerned, their interest in black people is not so much, I feel, out of humanity; it's some kind of thing that they have to satisfy with themselves, and that they've got a bone to pick somewhere, and they use this as one of their means. . . . But what I'm saying is that these people have some really ulterior motives in their efforts. And even if you find a real true liberal, in the sense that here's a guy that will really go all the way with you, he will go so far. He wants you to be gradual. He wants you to accommodate. I haven't been able to find any who you might say are radical in the sense that they are activists themselves. They want to kind of be behind the

This reading is taken from the last of seven interviews tape-recorded between May 18 and November 1, 1972, by Professor Rufus B. Spain of Baylor University. Interviewees are Mr. Cullen Harris, an inhalation therapist at the Veterans Administration Hospital in Waco, who has completed three years of study at Prairie View A&M and McLennan Community College; Mr. Robert Gilbert, a graduate of Baylor University and pastor of Macedonia Baptist Church in Bremond and Good Hope Baptist Church in Chilton; and Mr. Ulysses Cosby, a graduate of Paul Quinn College and a postal clerk in the Waco Post Office. All three interviewees are blacks who have been active in local politics. This interview is part of Baylor University's Program for Oral History. Printed by permission.

scene to put you out to doing things; but as far as them getting out there rolling up their sleeves and getting actively involved in bringing about a change, I don't find that kind of liberal.

I really don't have that much trust in . . . these labels. I'm very careful about it because I have to see a man for what he thinks is just and is fair now. I mean, I've seen some guys who are labelled conservative—like Bob Sheehy [a local lawyer]. I don't have any great love for him; but I have been in meetings where, if he were in charge and things weren't going right for the minority side, he has spoken out for the fair side even though he is conservative. So I think it's what a man does for right at a certain time. I'm going too long on this, but that's the way I feel about it.

Spain: All right. Cullen, do you have any comments on this?

Cullen Harris: Yes. I was speaking of a liberal in the social sense. It does upset me a little bit because if you look at the word in the dictionary—and I've forgotten the exact meaning of the word; it's been some time since I looked at it—but it smacks of condescension, as an individual who's doing you one hell of a favor by treating you as a human being. So, I try to shy away from the word liberal. I try not to think of an individual as a liberal. I try to think of an individual as a person. And sometimes it's difficult to do, due to a person's political leanings and so forth and so on. But I've had some awakenings here, I guess, in the last twelve or fourteen months, from people that I'm sure are conservative in their views as far as politics are concerned, as far as money and finances are concerned, and so forth. But I found that these are the people who in some instances, when you really get down to the nitty-gritty, are the ones who will give you the most support. And maybe it is because they really don't have too much to fear....

Spain: All right. Shall we go on to another topic now? One topic I'd like to get your opinions on is the relations between blacks and Mexican-Americans: two ethnic groups readily recognizable. How do you get along with each other right here in Waco? Robert, would you like to start?

Gilbert: Probably Cullen and Ulysses have had more dealings with the Mexicans than I have, in terms of boards and this type of thing. But the general impression that I get and the little dealings that I've had, it's a stabbing-in-the-back kind of thing where you're looking over your shoulder to see if you're going to get it from them. And they might be looking the same way, you know, from us. I don't know. But I have found that in my little time of working with the EOAC [Economic Opportunities Advancement Corporation] that there definitely is a division and a friction there. . . . There are those who would say that if the Mexican were in power, he would be harder on black people than white people have been. I have seen Mexicans that seemingly have reached the middle class, so to speak, who really do take on a very different attitude in terms of even being identified with their own people. Now, you know, blacks might do the same way. You might find blacks doing the same way. But I find this very strong in Mexicans. I've seen them in board meetings and things where they really cut each other up a great deal more, I think, than we cut each other up. I think we would have more unity if two or three of us were serving on the board together, where it's kind of different with them.

But I can't really put my finger on it; both of us have problems that are similar, particularly economic and so forth. Why is it that we can't form a coalition and get a lot more things done? I think maybe Mexicans might feel that since they've been supposedly classed as white, in a sense, for so long, they feel that they are better than we are anyway. You know, in a sense they do take on a white attitude: "Why do I want to put myself on a level with you, even though I think blacks in their revolution, so to speak, are fifteen years ahead of the Mexicans?" And the Mexican is now, I guess, in the state we were in the mid-1950's or somewhere, trying to make advancements. So I think it's a matter of—I don't even want to use the word "jealousy" or "matter of pride"—but I think each group has its struggle and yet each group wants to be recognized as having made its own accomplishment rather than having the help of the other, one way or the other.

Spain: All right. Cullen, will you comment on this?

Harris: Yes. The Mexican-American is kind of difficult for me to understand as a group of people. When you're working with one Mexican-American, I don't think you have any difficulty. I haven't found this to be so. I think you only run into difficulty when you start dealing with a group. Here in Waco, with the Mexican-Americans that are active in civic affairs, I've found usually you always have three or four with a college education that run the show for the whole shooting match. The masses of the Mexican-American people seem to be unable to do any thinking whatsoever for themselves. Take the [Mexican-American] Alliance for instance. You have about four or five people in the Alliance that completely dominate the Alliance. They do all the thinking. They plan all the strategy—those with a formal education, with a B.S. or maybe a few of them have a master's, I don't know. But their logic defies description. Nobody can understand their logic and the way they go about doing things. Maybe this had to do with their mores and folkways—the close-knit family type of thing where the older people, the grandparents, have a lot to say. They seem to be overprotective of their children. It's almost like you've got a herd leader; and whatever the leader says, nobody ever questions. They go right about it.

I went to Mexico. I've watched the way Mexican-Americans drive cars. Now I might be generalizing this, I don't know; but I noticed that they're terrible drivers. You know, to me, they're terrible drivers; and if you think I'm kidding, go to San Antonio. To me this poses some type of thought process that I'm not familiar enough with. And maybe this is just my attitude. Maybe I'm biased. I don't know. I really don't think I am in this particular case because I've known some. They will switch sides of the horse, you know; when it's to their advantage to be white, they'll be white; when it's to their advantage to be brown, they'll be brown. There's no doubt in my mind about this. They happen to be people of lesser color; maybe not as much as Dr. Spain, but I think in a push, you know, they could pass; and when it's to their advantage to pass, they'll do this. And then, once they find out that they're never fully accepted in the white society, they'll switch back over to the brown side.

In all the dealings that I've had in a group trying to benefit both races, trying to bring about some type of coalition where both parties can progress, I've always met with failure simply because I refuse to feel that Mexican-Americans are the only people that have the answer for me. They cannot tell me what to do. They cannot tell me what to think. Whites cannot tell me what to do. I refuse to let anyone do me this way. And in any instance when we've tried to come to a meeting of minds, so to speak, this is always happening. My good friend, Bob Garibay [a local Mexican-American businessman]—I don't care what you're trying to solve—he'll say, "I'll tell you what you people need to do." Hell, he can't tell me what we people need to do, you know. And this has happened. And we've never been able to come up with any kind of coalition in Waco, as far as I'm concerned, with the Mexican-Americans, even though we've tried many times; and I've been a part of some of this. It's difficult for me to understand. There is friction. I don't know if we'll ever be able to understand one another, in the near future.

Spain: Ulysses?

Cosby: I've met with them I guess as much as any black in Waco. And we sit down and agree in the commission on this Model Cities; and we agree not to support a certain bill because it will not help black or Mexican or even poor white. And we get up and get ready to vote; and when we vote, they vote entirely different from the way we agreed on. But one thing you have to realize (and we have been accused of this in a lot of instances), they put a lot of emphasis on education. The more education that a Mexican has, the more they think that he's supposed to speak for the rest of them—which is not necessarily true. And they're still looking for an identity. I work with a few of them; and the ones I work with, I get along with quite well at work, except one and he has ambitions. But anyway, I like to tell them they're fighting the wrong enemy because we didn't do anything to them. I'm speaking of black people because we can always say this (usually it's a three-way argument or discussion at work when we're going down there): "You aim at attacking the blacks. You say you're going to fill the gap with the black. But we don't have anything. We're trying to gain something. But you had Texas. You owned it. The whites whipped your butts and took it away from you. And now you're turning your swords toward us and we don't even have anything." And this is so true. They aim their swords at the black in the EOAC, which in the beginning they wouldn't even take part in because they didn't want to be a part of it. . . .

At our board meeting the other night, our neighborhood meeting, some of us didn't vote but took part in the discussion. We didn't vote because we're federal employees; but because of Ramsey Muniz's action when he was working for Model Cities in Waco, the blacks out there in my community where I live were going to vote a straight Democratic ticket. And we really don't believe in [Dolph] Briscoe—no way, shape, form or fashion. But they still vote for Briscoe over Ramsey Muniz. One reason, I admit, was to keep from confusing some people who could not vote split ticket. But a lot of us believe that Ramsey would be more harm to us than Briscoe.

Spain: I'm going to ask about that. How many blacks do you think will vote for him? Any significant number?

Cosby: Some of them will and some of them won't.[1] But anyone who has had any dealing with him whatsoever is not going to vote for Ramsey because Ramsey worked in a basically black community and he moved every black he could out and hired Mexican-Americans in there—like the particular time when he was first hired and Model Cities was dealing in East Waco. And every chance he got he moved them. It was so obvious what he was doing, and the people there remember that. . . .

Spain: Do you see any possibility that blacks and Mexican-Americans will get together for political action or social betterment within the near future? What is your experience and thinking about that?

Cosby: In Model Cities they voted against things for Paul Quinn [College] and things of this nature; and there was not a project in the Mexican community; they had not submitted one proposal. They said, "Paul Quinn and the blacks are getting too many projects. Well, you all blacks are just getting too much." So that's the way it is. So finally, after a series of meetings, I said, "Now look, every year we elect a city council." See, it's a strange thing; he [Garibay] got very little Mexican support. The blacks almost put him in. And in his part of town, he got very few; and a large number of those were blacks. And I told him, "I know you're planning to run; I see you off and running right now." And actually I believe you can deal with him; I really believe you can deal with him. And I said, "You guys, you won't cooperate on anything. You blame us for things. Now I guess you're going to blame us for his defeat." And I said, "After the election we can meet with you . . . and just discuss things and lay the cards on the table. If you think the Mexicans will ever get elected to the city council in Waco without the black help, you're crazy. . . ." I told them, "If you ever expect to do anything, you'll have to do it in conjunction with us. You take a little and we take a little, if we can get any control." We outnumber the other people; and, one time on one board, we were able to get some things done when I told them that. And I'm hoping that we can sit down and lay the cards on the table with them. We're not going to try to take everything; we hope the whites are going to stop taking everything. You give a certain amount and we give a certain amount. Kind of spread it around. No sense in the Mexican getting everything or the black or the white.

Gilbert: Ulysses, I'd like to ask you—I noticed in the paper the other day that the Mexicans and the blacks are in control of the Model Cities Board now and that [Vidal] De Leon, I believe, is chairman and you are the vice-chairman.

Cosby: Yes.

Gilbert: Would this change the direction of Model Cities in any way or have any kind of impact on it? . . .

Cosby: I really don't believe so, because you still must get together and vote as a body. And the night I was speaking of, the chairman of the board—I cannot remember his name—was missing; and the Mexican-American was the vice-chairman. Well, he served; and we had a tie vote on whether to spend the $400,000 on the airport. And we discussed this night after night. I guess we must have met twenty times. And I said, "You should come down there." And we agreed; Ramsey [Muniz] was a part of this. We agreed that we would vote *not* to spend that money. . . . See, the city council can change after you vote now. They can overrule, you see; but in the beginning they couldn't.

We got up there, and the chairman at that particular time was—he's in the law department here at Baylor—a young gentleman. He's on the board, anyway; and the Mexican was vice-chairman. The chairman was absent, and it was a tie vote. And the Mexican, who was the chairman and who had been one of the ring-leaders in our meeting, looked at me and said, "Cosby, I know we agreed to do it, but I cannot vote the way we agreed. I'm going to vote in favor of the money going to the airport." Two weeks later they gave him some kind of little bullcorn job. But this is what I had reference to, you see. We had discussed it night after night over there in East Waco at the Model Cities-Urban Design building on Elm Street.

But there is no trust. You cannot imagine—I can't—when you discuss it with other blacks; the blacks trust the white more than they do the Mexican-American. Would you say so?

Gilbert: I would say so.

Spain: So in the immediate future you think there's not much likelihood of close cooperation.

Cosby: I, personally, can't see it. Now in my little meetings, there were a lot of us; and they—the so-called liberal vote, the white vote—the Mexican-American has alienated them. They [whites] are some of their best supporters, but they are not willing to support [Mexican-American members] because they [Mexican-American leaders] urged the Mexicans not to vote for Sissy Farenthold. And since that happened, you go to board meetings there and people who used to, you know, encourage them [the Mexican-Americans] to take part and everything—they have very little to say to them.

NOTE

1. In the gubernatorial election held on November 7, 1972, one week after this interview, the vote in Waco's black precinct 10-C was as follows: Briscoe (Democrat), 1,137; Grover (Republican), 378; Muniz (*La Raza Unida*), 272; and Leonard (Socialist Workers), 0.

2-9
MEXICAN-AMERICAN POLITICS IN TEXAS
John Shockley

Tension, suspicion, and war characterized the early political dealings between Anglos and Mexicans in Texas, and this history of conflict and distrust has

Dr. Shockley has done research in the politics of South Texas and this article was prepared especially for publication in *Practicing Texas Politics.*

continued to play a role in the political relations of the two groups in the state today. In the history of the state no Mexican-American has ever been elected to any top political position. A few Mexicans who sided with the Anglo Texans in the fight over independence played a role in the early politics of the Republic, but with the steady increase in Anglo immigration from the eastern states, Texans of Mexican heritage were shunted aside. In general, they were looked down upon by the Anglos as a defeated minority who were lucky to be allowed to remain in the Lone Star State; and they were subjects of discrimination and segregation.

Only with the coming of the Mexican Revolution of 1910 was there a sharp increase in the proportion of Spanish-speaking people in Texas. During the second decade of this century, many thousands of Mexicans crossed the Rio Grande to seek refuge from the political upheaval and economic hardships which accompanied a period of prolonged civil strife in Mexico. There was some resentment among Anglos over this influx of Mexicans, but the refugees provided a very important pool of cheap labor, especially farm and ranch labor.

Even before the wave of immigration prompted by the Mexican Revolution, Spanish-surnamed people were playing an important political role in some South Texas counties where they constituted a large percentage of the total population. But these counties, concentrated almost exclusively along the border with Mexico, were run by powerful *patrons* or *jefes* owning large amounts of land and controlling the votes of poor, uneducated Mexican-Americans living on their properties. With the arrival of refugees from the Revolution, a small but growing group of middle-class Spanish-speaking citizens emerged and began to organize for the purpose of bettering their lot. Seeking to overcome discrimination and to gain acceptance into Anglo society, they organized the League of United Latin American Citizens (LULAC) in 1929. Disavowing militancy, the middle-class oriented LULAC urged its members to be active in civic affairs; but its membership remained small and had negligible political impact.

World War II brought large numbers of Mexican-Americans into the armed forces. Many of them emerged from this military experience with more pride in being American and with a greater feeling of self-confidence. Consequently, when a funeral home in Three Rivers, Texas, refused to bury the body of a veteran for no other reason than that he was a Mexican-American, the American G. I. Forum was founded under the leadership of Dr. Hector García of Corpus Christi. From its beginning in 1948, the G. I. Forum pursued more aggressive policies than LULAC and appealed to a wider social spectrum of Mexican-Americans. In addition to publicizing acts of discrimination against Spanish-speaking people, the veterans' organization undertook poll tax drives in an effort to qualify more Mexican-Americans for voting.

No significant breakthrough in the election of Mexican-Americans to anything other than minor local offices occurred, however, until San Antonio city councilman Henry B. González was elected to the Texas Senate in 1956. He followed up this election victory with an unprecedented filibuster against segregation legislation designed to prevent Negroes from attending white schools. In 1958 González sought the Democratic party nomination for governor. Although too liberal for most Texans, González garnered over a quarter of a million votes, or about twenty percent of the votes cast in the primary race.

The nomination of John F. Kennedy as presidential candidate of the Democratic party in 1960 served as a further stimulus to Mexican-American political activity in Texas. Kennedy was extremely popular with Spanish-speaking people, both because he was a Catholic and because he expressed concern over the living conditions of most Mexican-Americans. Following Kennedy's election, "Viva Kennedy" clubs in Texas were consolidated into a continuing organization which became known as the Political Association of Spanish-speaking Organizations (PASO). Under the leadership of Bexar County Commissioner Albert Peña and others, PASO attempted to reach the poorest, most impoverished Mexican-Americans and to involve them in political activities. PASO, however, was very quickly weakened by factions within the organization and by their inability to decide upon what strategy to pursue in the endorsement of candidates for office. In the end the organization was unable to maintain the momentum it had developed in the aftermath of the Kennedy election.

The venture for which PASO received widest publicity involved intervention in 1963 in the municipal politics of Crystal City, a town of approximately 10,000 people located 100 miles southwest of San Antonio and famed for its spinach. Although comprising only about 15 percent of the city's population, the Anglo minority had always dominated governmental affairs. In conjunction with the Teamsters Union, which had organized workers at the local Del Monte cannery, PASO supported a group of five Mexican-American candidates for seats on the city council. Following an intensive voter registration drive and a bitter election campaign, the five PASO-backed candidates were elected. None of them had as much as a high school education. Their inexperience and vulnerability, coupled with hostility from the economically dominant Anglo citizens, combined to produce a situation of near chaos in the town's government. Consequently, a newly-formed coalition of Anglos and middle-class Mexican-Americans was able to gain control of the city council in the 1965 municipal election. Nevertheless, Crystal City politics and the political life of other communities in South Texas would never be the same again.

In 1967-1968 a strike was launched in the Lower Rio Grande Valley by low-paid farm workers. The strikers ultimately marched to Austin as a demonstration to publicize the need for a state minimum-wage law. Governor John Connally met the marchers on the highway south of Austin, where he declared that he would neither support their demands for minimum-wage legislation nor meet with them in the capitol. Use of strike-breakers brought into Valley farms from Mexico, arrests of strike leaders by Texas Rangers, and court injunctions eventually broke the farmworkers' strike. But the highly publicized affair further contributed to stimulating political awareness among Mexican-Americans in Texas.

Spurred by the example of black militancy and by the frustrations and failures of earlier attempts at political organization, many young Mexican-Americans in the late 1960s began a search for their own *Chicano* identity. Development of the term Chicano itself signified an increasing desire on the part of many Mexican-Americans to define themselves in their own terms. Their interest in Mexican-American history led to an increased awareness of their prior claim to the Southwest; this, in turn, led to an increased militancy and a greater determination to confront the gringo. But for effective action, there was the need for organization of a broad-based movement that could wield political power. Thus new organizations designed to make Mexican-Americans "masters of their own destiny" were founded with new leadership and new goals.

Most visible of these new groups was the Mexican-American Youth Organization (MAYO), founded in 1967. Led by young and often well-educated Chicanos, MAYO advanced a program designed to fulfill "the destiny of La Raza." Goals for the movement included third party activities that would be completely separate from either the Democratic or Republican parties, Chicano control of public school systems in predominantly Mexican-American communities, and development of Chicano-run businesses and cooperatives that would end economic domination by Anglos.

The first serious attempt to put into practice the goals of MAYO and the Chicano movement occurred in the same town where PASO had earlier tried to develop Mexican-American political power: Crystal City. José Angel Gutiérrez, a native of Crystal City and a founder of MAYO at the time he was studying for his master's degree in political science at St. Mary's University in San Antonio, was instrumental in the organizing activities in the town. Led in part by Gutiérrez, students in Crystal City schools staged a strike in protest of discrimination in school policies. Begun in the fall of 1969, this protest activity carried into the beginning of 1970. It proved to be enormously successful, both for the purpose of obtaining concessions from school administrators and for mobilizing the Mexican-American community for political activities in preparation for school board and city council elections. The resulting takeover of both the school board and city hall was effected under the banner of a new party, La Raza Unida.

Leaders of La Raza Unida hoped to expand its influence to other parts of Texas and the nation. In particular, they sought to gain control of the twenty-odd Texas counties where Mexican-Americans constitute a majority of the population. Elsewhere in the state, their objective was to exercise a balance between rival Anglo groups while raising the political consciousness in their own communities. Progress in this direction proved to be slow, however. Not only did most Anglos oppose the goals and tactics of Chicano activists, but Henry B. González (who in 1961 had become the first Mexican-American ever elected to Congress from the state), opposed the development of a separate Chicano identity and a separate political party. He counseled that the future of Mexican-Americans must lie in the area of integration and cooperation with other forces in the state. Because of all this opposition, gains outside Crystal City came slowly, and defeat was common.

In 1972 La Raza Unida resolved to run candidates not only for local offices in many Texas counties but for statewide offices as well. Heading the Chicano ticket in the November, 1972, general election was Ramsey Muniz, a former Baylor University football player and law school graduate. He polled over 200,000 votes, or about six percent of the total number of votes cast in the governor's race, which saw Dolph Briscoe score a narrow victory over Republican Henry

Grover. Although Muniz's showing could be considered an impressive beginning for a new political party, his vote was less than that of Henry González in his Democratic gubernatorial primary race in 1958. Furthermore, some Mexican-Americans argued that the development of a third party would weaken the support of Mexican-American liberals who sought office through the Democratic party. Supporters of La Raza Unida countered that little had been gained through efforts within the Democratic party, and they insisted that distinctly Chicano-led institutions were needed.

At any rate, two well-known Mexican-American politicians went down to defeat in the Democratic primary in 1972: State Senator Joe Bernal and Bexar County Commissioner Albert Peña. Both San Antonio men sympathized with many of the goals of the Chicano activists. Thus the consequences of organizing a third party did not seem to mean necessarily that Chicano power in the state would grow. But it did mean that greater attention would be focused upon the two million Texans of Mexican heritage, as both Democrats and Republicans were forced to recognize the increasing importance and increasing volatility of the Mexican-American vote.

In summary, it seems that although Mexican-American political power in the state is growing, it is not growing in a unified direction. Tensions and conflict within the community were increasing at the very time that their political involvement was growing. How Mexican-American people and politicians viewed themselves concerning their own identity, their relations with Anglos and with other groups in the state, and their ideas toward changes in the educational, economic, social, and political structures of the state all have become important issues evoking much disagreement. How their power will be utilized, therefore, remains an open question that will be settled only by the interplay of the different segments in the Mexican-American community and in the state of Texas as a whole.

2-10
AZTLAN: CHICANO REVOLT IN THE WINTER GARDEN
José Angel Gutiérrez

As we unpacked our car in the 99 degree temperature of Crystal City, Texas, we vividly recalled the typical suffocating South Texas weather. It was June 20, 1969, and we realized that this sweltering summer before us was to be our orientation course in community development. My wife, Luz, and I had returned to my hometown of Crystal City, Texas (population about 10,000), for the purpose of helping create a model city for Chicano activity. We wanted to begin Aztlan. Aztlan is a Nahautl word in the Aztec language for the Northwestern region of Mexico and, according to Aztec traditions, the place where their tribe

From *La Raza,* I (January, 1971), pp. 36-39. Reprinted by permission.

originated. Presently this geographical area is described as the Southwest in the U.S.

Dimmit, La Salle, and Zavala Counties were to be our community for the next few months and possibly years. This community, known as the Winter Garden area, centers in Dimmit and Zavala Counties. It is north of Laredo, and the area is irrigated from wells and streams to produce vegetables in late winter and early spring. These three counties are dominated by a farming-ranching economy.

Immediately after I had concluded my term as president of MAYO (Mexican-American Youth Incorporated of Texas), Mario Compean, the new president, tapped me for his staff. Mario, Luz, and other staff members, as well as myself, agreed that this area should be the model for Chicano activity. This area was chosen because the economic and political conditions Mexicans are subject to are typical of Texas in general and South Texas in particular. For the past three years, MAYO has engaged in various projects of the state; however, all projects have been mostly experimental and educational in nature.

It should be clarified that MAYO was not intended to be a mass membership organization or a constipated group of reformists. We wanted to be a group of active crusaders for social justice—Chicano style. This demanded that MAYO members be well-versed in one or more problem areas confronting the Mexicano; but more important it meant that the members of MAYO had to experience the frustration of defeat, the joy of victory, and the grind of day-to-day work as well as learning to be real Mexicanos. We wanted to begin Aztlan! Thus, with three years of experimentation, a broad and ambitious program and no money, the Winter Garden area was officially declared a MAYO project, and Aztlan would soon become a reality.

Immediately Luz and I set upon the task of locating other MAYO members in order to begin our model city. The first persons recruited were Linda and Guillermo (Bill) Richey, a VISTA couple from Austin. They joined us in July while they were in La Salle County with their VISTA program. The four of us pushed the program along in the two counties until November. In November we recruited Maria Ynosencio from Crystal City and Severita Lara and Beatriz Mendoza, two high school students. In the neighboring county of Dimmit, David Ojeda and his wife Rosa joined our efforts. A month later, after the national MAYO convention in Mission, Texas, we recruited the needed additional staff: Viviana Santiago, Ruben Barrera, and Alberto Luera. As each addition to the group was made, our efficiency and prospects for success were increased. Our range of expertise grew, and consequently, our offensive strategy was better implemented. In military slang, we were "combat ready." We now had five full-time workers, three counties (with a population of about 30,000) to cover, plus 4,133 square miles, a small grant, and very few friends in the Winter Garden area.

MAYO did have some friends in the area prior to our arrival in Crystal City that summer. Mario Compean, our leader, had repeatedly visited Cotulla and La Salle County. Juan Ptlan, another MAYO member, had retained his Chicano leadership in his hometown of Carrizo Springs in Dimmit County. And also I was still fresh in the memory of many Mexicanos due to the publicity acquired through the media during my tenure as president of MAYO; the term "outside agitator" was not voiced because I was a native of Crystal City in Zavala County. This fact allowed us to do our basic power structure research uninhibited all summer and early fall. In addition, the Chicano community saw us as college-educated Chicanos who had returned to their hometowns in behalf of La Raza. La Raza means "the race"; however, La Raza is a self-descriptive term used among most Spanish-speaking people in this hemisphere.

We were not misguided and mal-informed VISTA volunteers; nor were we white-knight Latin Americans who sought to manage the affairs of the gringo for the gringo. We were young Chicanos who saw and felt things as Chicanos should. We loved and accepted our Mexicanismo and saw brighter things for La Raza. These brighter things were radical ideas indeed to many who heard our comments that long hot summer. To others our ideas were empty dreams long ago abandoned. It seemed to them that a Mexicano was destined to that predicament of always tasting the better fruits of life but never having them. Too many have tasted the strawberries in the field but never with cream and cornflakes. Many of ours have watched over the sirloins and rounds while still on the hoof but never cooked them for an evening meal.

Yet these same ideas seemed very realistic and positive goals. The primary goal was to force the educational system to extend to the Mexican student. Over 70% of the Mexican students in the schools of Crystal City are pushed out or termed "drop-out," if you believe the Mexicano students have some inherent deficiency. These students do not finish the twelfth grade. . . .

The second goal was to bring democracy to those counties, in other words, rule by the majority. The Mexican population far outnumbers the white population. There is not a significant number of black citizens. In most cases the ratio of Chicanos to gringos is about 70% to 30%. . . .

Next to our educational and political goals, our third goal was a direct confrontation with the gringo. We sought to expose, confront, and eliminate the gringo. We felt that it was necessary to polarize the community over issues into Chicano versus gringo. Basically, the difference between the Chicano and gringo, aside from the bad-good guy criteria, is one of attitude. The attitude gringos have of racial superiority, of paternalism, of divine right, of xenophobia, of bigotry, and of animalism is well-known to La Raza. After the gringos were exposed publicly, the next step was to confront their security—status, business, and morality—in order to recognize the enemy in all their involvements of policies, roles, and power manipulations. Once the Chicano community recognized the enemy, then it had the power to eliminate gringo attitudes by not voting for the gringo and not buying from the gringo. Hence, the Chicano community would limit the primitives. Consequently, the Chicano would take power available to the gringo and then attack the colonists' states so evident in South Texas.

The fourth goal of our Aztlan model would be a program of rural economic development, since colonialism still exists in South Texas. Under this economic development the first step would be to replace the existing white managerial functions with Chicano expertise. The transfer of existing businesses from gringo hands to Chicano hands would be the second step. In the last step, La Raza would set upon agri-business, the oil and gas industry, and the modern-day land and cattle barons—the real subversives in America today. . . .

2-11
NATIVE AMERICAN POLITICS

Mrs. Mary Patrick: How are Indians different from other Americans in their response to politics and politicians?
Mr. Richard Lester: The American Indians are folk people. We have folk values that are emotional and spiritual. We do not necessarily vote on dollar-and-cent things. We are not necessarily going to vote for the party that offers us the most programs, the biggest programs. Some politicians never understand that. We vote for what we sense is the man who is nearest to the Indian values. And that may be something intangible. You could create an emotional issue with Indians the night before the election, and they will all go from one party to the other party.
Patrick: Indians comprise a very small percentage of the voters in Texas. In what way can American Indians be most effective in politics in Texas? Should Indians form a separate political party?
Lester: We try to impress upon the minds of our people in Texas that in the present world everyone is bound by bureaucratic regulations. This is a bureaucratic society. If you want to play in the big leagues, then you must play, and learn the rules, and work within the framework. The American Indian needs "more attention and recognition" from politicians in Texas to become an active part of the political process. They have begun to realize that one of the ways to be recognized in the "Great American Mainstream" is by exercising their inherent sovereign right to vote.
Patrick: What has been done to awaken the Indians in Texas to political action?
Lester: The intensive drive to register the Native Americans in the 1972 election in the Dallas-Ft. Worth area was a tremendous success. It was only with the consent of the Dallas Council of Choctaws, 90 days before the election, that we decided to make the registration drive. During that short period we had 4,600 American Indians eligible to vote in Texas. Chairman David Harkins of the Choctaw Council said that by the time of the 1974 election we should have three or four thousand more in the franchise bracket, because the Dallas-Ft. Worth area has ten thousand Indian families.
Patrick: Why have Indians been so unconcerned about politics?
Lester: Lack of enthusiasm of the Indians for voting is no doubt due, in some measure, to lack of interest, and to mixed loyalties, the deepest of which is to the Indian way of life. It is perfectly clear that years of distress and political confusion have not bred the kind of respect for the white man's institutions that encourages the pursuit of social betterment through the medium of the ballot box.
Patrick: In the past American Indians have not been good members of political parties nor good supporters of politicians in their areas. Why has this been true?

Interview of January 15, 1973, between Mrs. Mary Patrick of the Baylor University Program for Oral History and Mr. Richard Lester, Sr., a Choctaw, who in 1958 was the first Indian to come to Dallas under the Bureau of Indian Affairs Relocation Program. Printed by permission.

Lester: A politician coming to the Indians for their support does not come alone: the history of two centuries of betrayal and deception are at the elbow of every candidate. He talks, but the Indian hears other voices. He acts, but the Indians remember previous promises. Whichever way the politician seeks to declare his honesty, no matter how nakedly he attempts to strip himself of the past, he comes with the burden of that past on his neck, like a curse he cannot easily exorcise.
Patrick: Do you think white politicians understand the American Indians?
Lester: For a subject worked and reworked so often in novels, motion pictures, and television, American Indians remain probably the least understood and more misunderstood Americans. Native American Indians defy any single description. They are far too individualistic. They share no common language and few common customs. When the Indians controlled the balance of power, the settlers from Europe were forced to consider their views, and to deal with them by treaties and other instruments.

The pioneers found that Indians in the Southwest had developed a high civilization with safeguards for insuring peace. A northern extension of that civilization, the League of the Iroquois, inspired Benjamin Franklin to copy it in planning the Federation of States. But when the Indians lost their power, they were placed on reservations, lands that were strange to them. It was compulsory outpatient care for the Indian tribes who did not fit into the federal government's official mold.

New Mexico and Arizona were the last states where Indians were legally disenfranchised. The Indians were "given" American citizenship and the "right" to vote by the Act of Congress of 1924. But in New Mexico and Arizona voting rights were denied to reservation Indians until 1948, twenty-four years later. The election victories of the Navajos in recent years were somewhat startling to the political pundits who had not thought they had a chance.
Patrick: Are the Navajo victories you speak of indicative of what we can expect of Indians in the future?
Lester: It was a prophecy of practical politics that was to be quickly fulfilled. Within recent years the powerless and less politically adept tribes have elected more tribesmen to the legislatures than they had in the previous history of the West. Thirty-two Native American Indians are now being seated in ten Western state legislatures and other Indians are taking office as judges, county officials, and others of public trust. It is also noteworthy that several are women. Some of the tribes are beginning to realize that in close elections like we have been having, the Indian can be decisive in a dozen Western states.
Patrick: Is it your opinion then that American Indians can best promote their own welfare by registering and voting together rather than withdrawing from politics as they have done in the past?
Lester: Yes. We have tried to impress upon the Indian's mind living in the 24th Congressional District, in Dallas County, where there are 3,600 registered, that we too could have the "swing vote" if we voted together as Indians. It could be a very "decisive vote" in the state legislature and the state senate race in the Oak Cliff area.

And visions of sugarplums danced in his head —

HERC FICKLEN FROM THE DALLAS NEWS

3

The Legislature

For citizens wishing to maintain the *status quo,* each session of the Texas Legislature brings the disturbing possibility of new taxes, increased spending, more regulation of commerce, new restrictions on industry, and an infinite number of other changes. Yet there are also people who desire the change that new laws can bring, or at least promise; and many individuals and groups agitate constantly and vigorously for specific benefits or protections which only the legislators can authorize. Of course, a popularly elected legislative body is not indispensable. But for a system of truly *representative government,* there can be no substitute for lawmaking bodies composed of members who are voted into office for definite terms by fellow citizens and who exercise power under constitutional limitations. In all of their state constitutions, Texans have entrusted the enactment of bills and the adoption of resolutions to popularly elected legislators. Since the actions of these representatives of the people affect the interests of everyone, it is only natural that legislators should be deeply involved in Texas politics. To gain office, a lawmaker must compete successfully in primary and general election campaigns; and to function effectively, he must establish satisfactory relationships with fellow legislators, executive officials (especially the governor), lobbyists, and others.

SESSIONS

When the 63rd Legislature convened in Austin on January 9, 1973, its members knew that their session would end on or before May 28. This certainty is spelled out in the Texas constitution, which provides for *regular sessions* of not more than 140 days in each odd-numbered year. *Special sessions* lasting not longer than thirty days may be called by the governor at any time, but during special sessions the Legislature may consider only matters placed before it by the governor. Such limits on legislative action are very likely a manifestation of a widely held belief that "the less government, the better" or of the fear that "no man's life, liberty, or property are safe while the Legislature is in session."

There are two reasons why the constitutional limitations prevailing in 1973 might not remain in effect much longer. First, the 63rd Legislature proposed a constitutional amendment providing for a regular session lasting not more than 180 days in each odd-numbered year and another regular session not exceeding sixty days' duration in each even-numbered year. The latter, however, will be restricted to consideration of fiscal matters (i.e., taxes and appropriations) and such emergency matters as the governor submits; also, it can be extended by the governor for an additional thirty days. Other special sessions can be called by the governor at any time. A pay raise for legislators is included in the proposal. If approved by the voters in November, 1973, the amendment becomes effective in January, 1975.

A second reason for possible change in the system of legislative sessions is suggested by the fact that the Legislature will convene in January, 1974, as a constitutional convention. So regardless of action taken on the amendment proposed in 1973, change in legislative sessions may result from the work of the 1974 convention.

SIZE

As in a majority of states, under the Texas constitution of 1876 the lawmaking branch is officially termed the Legislature. Terms used elsewhere include general assembly, legislative assembly, and general court. Nebraska's legislature is *unicameral* or single-house; but Texas and the forty-eight other states have *bicameral,* or two-chamber, lawmaking bodies. The smaller chamber of these bicameral institutions is the senate. In Texas and in forty other states, the larger chamber is called house of representatives; but the remaining states use the terms assembly, house of delegates, or general assembly.

In the forty-nine states with bicameral legislative institutions, the size of the larger chamber ranges from 39 members (Delaware) to 400 (New Hampshire). Texas has 150 members in its House of Representatives. As for state senates, Delaware has the smallest, with 19 members; Minnesota has the largest, with 67. Texas has 31.

DISTRICTING

Since population distribution changes constantly, it is logical to redraw the boundaries of legislative districts periodically in order to ensure equitable representation for the people. For this reason the framers of the Texas constitution stipulated in 1876 that "the Legislature shall, at its first session after the publication of each United States decennial census, apportion the State into Senatorial and Representative districts. . . ." Unfortunately, in the decades that followed the Legislature sometimes failed to comply with this mandate.

Redistricting can be painful to a legislator. It may deprive him of territory where he has strong voter support; it may add to his district an area in which he encounters strong opposition; or it may include the residences of two or more representatives or senators in a new district from which only one of them can be elected. New districts were drawn in 1921, but despite the constitutional requirement, there was no legislative redistricting in Texas following the censuses of 1930 and 1940 (see Table 3-1). Since these two censuses were conducted during a period of rapid urbanization, the inequity of the situation finally led to the adoption in 1948 of a constitutional amendment designed to pressure the Legislature to reapportion after the next census. Under this amendment failure of the Legislature to redistrict during the first regular session following a decennial census brings into operation the *Legislative Redistricting Board.* This board consists of the following five ex officio (i.e., holding other offices) members: lieutenant governor, speaker of the House of Representatives, attorney general, comptroller of public accounts, and commissioner of the general land office. The board must meet within ninety days after the legislative session and carry out the necessary reapportionment within another sixty days. Although adoption of the amendment helped to provide an incentive to the Legislature to redistrict following the 1950 and 1960 censuses (see Table 3-2), other constitutional provisions prevented equality of representation.

From its beginning the constitution of 1876 specified that apportionment of Senate seats was to be based on the number of qualified electors instead of on the total population. This provision resulted in less senatorial representation for some areas of the state, where many people, chiefly for economic reasons, failed to pay the poll tax. Of much greater importance was the stipulation that no county could ever be entitled to more than one senator, regardless of the number of qualified voters. By the beginning of the 1960s, this restriction limited Harris County to a single senator, although it had nearly 13 per cent of the state's population. Inhabitants of Dallas, Bexar, and Tarrant counties also suffered serious underrepresentation in the Senate. The four most populous urban counties, containing the cities of Houston, Dallas, San Antonio, and Fort Worth and having 35 per cent of the population of Texas, were given only 13 per cent of the total number of Senate seats.

A 1936 constitutional amendment sponsored by rural legislators imposed a similar restriction on urban county representation in the House of Representatives. Although calling for reapportionment based on population, the amendment stipulated that no county could have more than seven representatives unless its population exceeded 700,000; thereafter, it was entitled to one additional representative for each 100,000 of population increase. Based on the 1960 census total of 9,579,677, the most equitable ratio of apportionment would have been one representative for every 63,865 Texans (total population divided by 150); however, the 1961 redistricting act fell far short of this ideal. As shown in Table 3-2, the combined population of Bexar, Dallas, Harris, and Tarrant counties amounted to nearly 36 per cent of the state's total inhabitants; but together these four counties were given only 23 per cent of the seats in the Texas House of Representatives. On the other hand, most single-member

TABLE 3-1
Population growth and apportionment: Texas House of Representatives, 1921-1951 (16 selected counties)

1920s, 1930s, 1940s: THREE DECADES OF APPORTIONMENT STAGNATION (NO REAPPORTIONMENT AFTER CENSUSES OF 1930 and 1940)

	Tex. Pop. 1920: 4,663,228 Appor. Ideal: 31,088			County Appor-tion-ment 1921	Tex. Pop. 1930: 5,824,715 Appor. Ideal: 38,831			County Appor-tion-ment 1921	Tex. Pop. 1940: 6,414,824 Appor. Ideal: 42,765			County Appor-tion-ment 1921
COUNTY/Major City	Major City Pop.	County Pop.	County Appor. Quota		Major City Pop.	County Pop.	County Appor. Quota		Major City Pop.	County Pop.	County Appor. Quota	
BEXAR/San Antonio	161,379	202,096	6.5	5	231,542	292,533	7.5	5	253,854	338,176	7.9	5
CAMERON/Brownsville	11,791	36,622	1.2	1	22,021	77,540	2.0	1	22,083	83,202	1.9	1
DALLAS/Dallas	158,976	210,551	6.8	6[a]	260,475	325,691	8.4	6[a]	294,734	398,564	9.3	6[a]
EL PASO/El Paso	77,560	101,877	3.3	3[b]	102,421	131,597	3.4	3[b]	96,810	131,067	3.1	3[b]
GALVESTON/Galveston	44,255	53,150	1.7	2[c]	52,938	64,401	1.7	2[c]	60,862	81,173	1.9	2[c]
HARRIS/Houston	138,276	186,667	6.0	5	292,352	359,328	9.3	5	384,514	528,961	12.4	5
HIDALGO/McAllen	5,331	38,110	1.2	1	9,074	77,004	2.0	1	11,877	106,059	2.5	1
JEFFERSON/Beaumont	40,422	73,120	2.4	3[d]	57,732	133,391	3.4	3[d]	59,061	145,329	3.4	3[d]
LUBBOCK/Lubbock	4,051	11,096	.4	1[e]	20,520	39,104	1.0	1[e]	31,853	51,782	1.2	1[e]
McLENNAN/Waco	38,500	82,921	2.7	3[f]	52,848	98,682	2.5	3[f]	55,982	101,898	2.4	3[f]
NUECES/Corpus Christi	10,522	22,807	.7	1[g]	27,741	51,779	1.3	1[g]	57,301	92,661	2.2	1[g]
POTTER/Amarillo	15,494[h]	16,710	.5	1[i]	43,132[h]	46,080	1.2	1[i]	51,686[h]	54,265	1.3	1[i]
TARRANT/Fort Worth	106,482	152,800	4.9	5[j]	163,477	197,553	5.1	5[j]	177,662	225,521	5.3	5[j]
TAYLOR/Abilene	10,274	24,081	.8	1	23,175	41,023	1.1	1	26,612	44,147	1.0	1
TRAVIS/Austin	34,876	57,616	1.9	2	53,120	77,777	2.0	2	87,930	111,053	2.6	2
WICHITA/Wichita Falls	40,079	72,911	1.2	3[k]	43,690	74,416	1.9	3[k]	45,112	73,604	1.7	3[k]
TOTALS	898,268	1,343,135	42.2	43	1,456,258	2,087,899	53.8	43	1,717,933	2,567,462	60.1	43

Source: *Texas Almanac, 1925*, pp. 30-32; *1931*, pp. 222-223; *1949-1950*, pp. 98-107, 374-375.
[a]Includes one Flotorial District Representative elected with Rockwall and Kaufman Counties (1 FDR with Rockwall and Kaufman). A definition of "flotorial district" is given in footnote 2, p. 156. [b]1 FDR with Hudspeth and Culberson. [c]1 FDR with Chambers. [d]1 FDR with Orange. [e]Gaines, Dawson, Yoakum, Terry, Lynn, Cochran, Hockley and Crosby Counties included in district. [f]1 FDR with Bell and Falls. [g]Jim Wells and Duval Counties included in district. [h]Amarillo census includes city population located in both Potter and Randall Counties. [i]Carson, Armstrong, Randall, Deaf Smith and Oldham Counties included in district. [j]1 FDR with Denton. [k]1 FDR with Wilbarger.

TABLE 3-2

Population growth and apportionment: Texas House of Representatives, 1921-1971 (16 selected counties)

	1950s: DECADE OF DISCRIMINATORY APPORTIONMENT				1960s: DECADE OF FEDERAL COURT INTERVENTION						1970s: DECADE OF URBAN COUNTY DOMINATION?				
	Tex. Pop. 1950: 7,711,194 Appor. Ideal: 51,408				Tex. Pop. 1960: 9,579,677 Appor. Ideal: 63,865						Tex. Pop. 1970: 11,196,730 Appor. Ideal: 74,645				
COUNTY/Major City	*Major City Pop.*	*County Pop.*	*County Appor. Quota*	*County Apportionment 1951*	*Major City Pop.*	*County Pop.*	*County Appor. Quota*	*County Apportionments 1961*	*1965*	*1967*	*Major City Pop.*	*County Pop.*	*County Appor. Quota*	*County Apportionments 1971*	*1973*[a]
BEXAR/San Antonio	408,442	500,460	9.7	7	587,718	687,475	10.8	7	10	10	654,153	830,460	11.1	11+[a]	
CAMERON/Brownsville	36,066	125,170	2.4	3[b]	48,040	151,098	2.4	3[b]	3[c]	3[d]	52,522	140,368	1.9	1+	
DALLAS/Dallas	434,462	614,799	12.0	7	679,684	951,527	14.9	9	14	15	844,401	1,327,321	17.8	18[a]	
EL PASO/El Paso	130,485	194,968	3.8	4	276,687	314,070	4.9	5	5	5	322,261	359,291	4.8	4+	
GALVESTON/Galveston	65,898	113,066	2.2	2	67,175	140,364	2.2	2	2	2	61,809	169,812	2.3	2+	
HARRIS/Houston	596,163	806,701	15.7	8	938,219	1,243,158	19.5	12	19	19	1,232,802	1,741,912	23.3	23+[a]	
HIDALGO/McAllen	20,005	160,446	3.1	3	32,728	180,904	2.8	4[e]	3	3	37,636	181,535	2.4	2++	
JEFFERSON/Beaumont	94,014	195,083	3.8	4	119,175	245,659	3.8	4	4	4	115,919	244,773	3.3	3++	
LUBBOCK/Lubbock	71,747	101,048	2.0	2	128,691	156,271	2.4	3	3[f]	3[g]	149,101	179,295	2.4	2+	
McLENNAN/Waco	84,706	130,194	2.5	3	97,808	150,091	2.4	3	3[h]	3[i]	95,326	147,553	2.0	2	
NUECES/Corpus Christi	108,287	165,471	3.2	4[e]	167,690	221,573	3.5	4	4[j]	4[k]	204,525	237,544	3.2	3+	
POTTER/Amarillo	74,246[l]	73,366	1.4	2[m]	137,969[l]	115,580	1.8	2[m]	2	2	127,010[l]	90,511	1.2	1+	
TARRANT/Fort Worth	278,778	361,253	7.0	7	356,268	538,956	8.4	7	8	8	393,476	716,317	9.6	9+	
TAYLOR/Abilene	45,570	63,370	1.2	1	90,368	101,078	1.6	2	2[n]	2[o]	89,653	97,853	1.3	1+	
TRAVIS/Austin	132,459	160,980	2.6	3	186,545	212,136	3.3	4	4[p]	4[q]	251,808	295,516	4.0	4	
WICHITA/Wichita Falls	68,042	98,493	1.9	2	101,724	123,528	1.9	2	2	2	97,564	121,862	1.6	1+	
TOTALS	2,649,370	3,864,868	74.5	62	4,016,489	5,533,468	86.6	73	88	89	4,729,966	6,881,923	92.2	87*	

Source: *Texas Almanac, 1956-1957,* pp. 417-418; *1964-1965,* pp. 537-538; *1966-1967,* pp. 125-138, 628-629; *1968-1969,* pp. 169-177, 625-626; *1972-1973,* pp. 152-165.

[a]Single-member districts (established by Legislative Redistricting Board for Harris County, 1971; and by federal district court for Bexar and Dallas counties, 1972). [b]Includes one Flotorial District Representative elected with Willacy County (1 FDR with Willacy). [c]1 FDR with Willacy, Kenedy, and Brooks. [d]All representatives elected with Willacy, Kenedy, and Brooks. [e]1 FDR with Kleberg and Kenedy. [f]1 FDR with Crosby. [g]All representatives elected with Hockley and Terry. [h]1 FDR with Coryell. [i]2 representatives elected in northeastern McLennan district; remainder of McLennan with 33,945 inhabitants joined with Coryell to form another district electing the third representative. [j]1 FDR with Kleberg. [k]All representatives elected with Kleberg. [l]Amarillo census includes city population located in both Potter and Randall. [m]1 FDR with Armstrong, Carson, and Randall. [n]1 FDR with Haskell and Jones. [o]Both representatives elected with Jones. [p]1 FDR with Burnet. [q]All representatives elected with Burnet. +Part of county included in 1 other district. ++Parts of county included in 2 other districts. *In addition to the 87 residents who were elected to fill these apportioned seats in the 63rd Legislature, 5 others were elected to represent districts composed of parts of urban counties (Cameron, El Paso, Harris, Hidalgo, and Potter) and 1 or more other neighboring counties: Districts 17, 49, 51, 65, and 71; thus these 16 selected counties could claim a total of 92 residents in the House of Representatives in 1973 and 1974; also, 10 of them shared in the election of representatives who were residents of other counties located in Districts 5, 8, 17, 41, 42, 45, 51, 53, 61, and 76 (see Figure 3-4).

representative districts in rural areas had populations much smaller than 63,865. For example, Wharton County had only 38,152 in 1960, yet it constituted a single-member representative district. Proportionally, inhabitants of Wharton County thus enjoyed nearly three times as much representation in the House of Representatives as the inhabitants of Dallas and Harris counties.

Despite much criticism of districting inequities in Texas and many other states, no relief was available until the United States Supreme Court ruled in *Baker* v. *Carr* (1962) that federal courts might assume jurisdiction over apportionment disputes. Such intervention could be expected whenever failure to redistrict, or discriminatory districting, denied people "equal protection of the laws" as guaranteed by the Fourteenth Amendment to the United States Constitution. Two years later, in *Reynolds* v. *Sims* (1964), the Supreme Court declared that "the seats in both houses of a bicameral state legislature must be apportioned on a population basis." This requirement was based on Chief Justice Earl Warren's assumption that "legislators are elected by voters, not farms or cities or economic interests." Subsequently, in *Kilgarlin* v. *Martin* (1965), a federal district court in Houston declared invalid the Texas constitution's provisions limiting a county to one senator and basing senatorial representation on the number of qualified electors. This court also struck down the provision which specified a limitation on the number of representatives for a single county in the House of Representatives until a population of 800,000 had been attained.

In response to this decision, the Legislature redistricted both the House and Senate in 1965. No longer were the people of Harris, Dallas, Bexar, and Tarrant counties to be represented by a total of only four senators. Under a new districting system based on one senator for every 309,022 inhabitants (total 1960 census population divided by 31), four districts were created within Harris County; and a leftover portion was joined to three adjacent counties to form a fifth district. Tarrant and Bexar counties were given one and two senators, respectively; and parts of these counties were combined with neighboring counties to form two additional senatorial districts. Dallas County was divided into three senatorial districts.

The 1965 redistricting act greatly increased urban county representation in the state's House of Representatives. For example, Harris County's representation increased from twelve to nineteen members. Prior to 1965, Texas law provided for the election of all representatives in *multi-member districts* on an "at-large" basis. Each candidate would file for a numbered place on the ballot (i.e., a two-representative district ballot would list candidates for Place 1 and for Place 2), and voters would indicate separate choices for each contest. The 1965 act continued countywide multi-member districts for all urban counties except Harris, which was divided into three multi-member districts. Two of these districts were apportioned six seats, and the third was given seven. It was probably not by sheer chance that a large portion of the county's Republican voters found themselves isolated in the seven-seat district.

No similar relief was provided for candidates and voters of Dallas County, where all fourteen representatives were to be elected at large. Obviously, the most logical districting arrangement would have involved division of the state into 150 geographically compact, *single-member districts* of approximately the same population.[1] Nevertheless, the revolutionary consequences of such a move were only too apparent to the white, conservative, Democratic majority that controlled the 59th Legislature. In view of the sociopolitical geography of the big-city counties, any system of single-member districts would guarantee subsequent election of an increased number of black, Mexican-American, Republican, and liberal Democratic representatives.

Although attacked in a federal district court on grounds that multi-member districts constituted racial and political *gerrymandering* (a term denoting unfair districting designed to represent disproportionally a faction or party) in violation of the Fourteenth Amendment, these allegations against the 1965 redistricting act were not sustained. The court did, however, declare that the eleven flotorial (usually spelled "floterial" everywhere but in Texas!) districts violated "equal protection of the laws."[2] In sustaining the lower court's ruling in *Kilgarlin* v. *Hill* (1967), the United States Supreme Court also found that population variances among several other districts were unacceptable. In response to this decision, the 60th Legislature redistricted the House of Representatives in 1967. Under terms of this redistricting act, Dallas County's representation was increased by one, flotorial districts were abolished through creation of bicounty or multi-county districts electing two or more members (see Table 3-2), and the ratio of representatives to total population was brought closer to the ideal of one representative for every 63,865 inhabitants.

As a consequence of the 1965 and 1967 redistricting, more and louder big-city voices were heard in the 60th, 61st, and 62nd Legislatures. With a total of eighty-eight, and later eighty-nine, representatives, the sixteen most populous counties in the state acquired majorities in the House of Representatives. These counties also exercised a dominant influence over the selection of a majority of state senators. Furthermore, following the 1960 census, most big cities grew bigger, while the population levels of rural areas remained the same or declined.

Census data for 1970 indicated a population of 11,196,730 Texans; thus the apportionment ratios for state senators and representatives were established at 1:361,185 and 1:74,645, respectively. Redistricting, however, is never a matter of simple arithmetic. During the regular session of the 62nd Legislature in 1971, the Senate was unable to pass a redistricting bill for that chamber; and the House redistricting measure unnecessarily cut so many county boundary lines that it was declared unconstitutional by the Supreme Court of Texas in *Smith* v. *Craddick* (1971). Subsequently the Legislative Redistricting Board undertook the task of House redistricting (see Reading 3-1). The most significant feature of the board's plan was provision for twenty-three single-member districts entirely within Harris County and for one other district encompassing Chambers County and parts of Harris and Galveston counties (see Figure 3-1). Other urban counties were left to elect all of their representatives at large. This produced further litigation; and in January, 1972, a federal district court ruled that at-large election of eleven representatives in Bexar County deprived Mexican-American voters of equal protection of the law and that blacks in Dallas County suffered similar deprivation as a result of the election of eighteen representatives

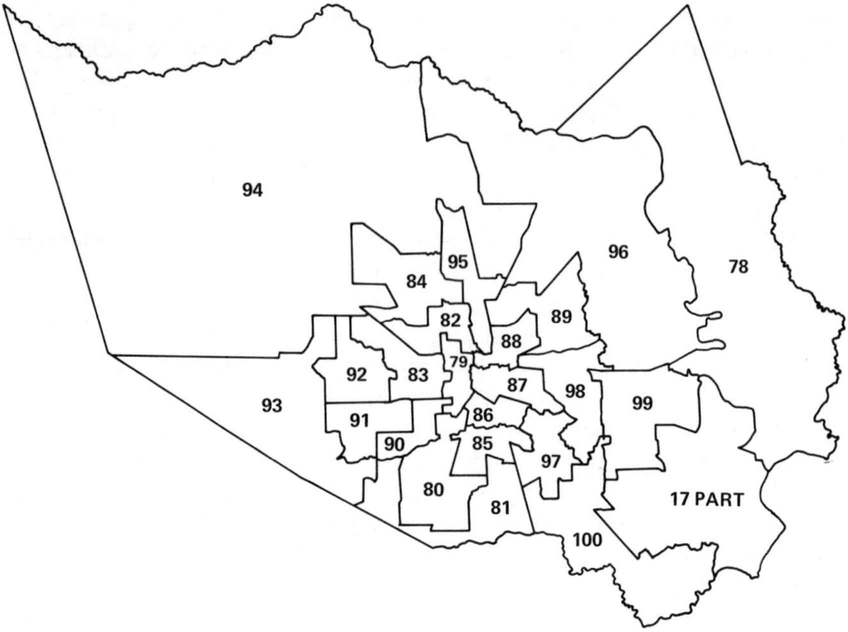

Figure 3-1
Harris County: 23 single-member state representative districts (78-100) plus part of District 17; established by the Legislative Redistricting Board of Texas in October 1971. Source: Texas Legislative Council.

at large. As a result, the court ordered single-member districts for both counties (see Figures 3-2 and 3-3). Furthermore, it was not satisfied with several districts that had populations significantly larger or smaller than the ideal of 74,645 inhabitants per House seat; but the court approved use of the arrangement for the 1972 elections while directing the state to provide for a more acceptable redistricting plan before the end of June, 1973 (see Figure 3-4).

Texas appealed to the United States Supreme Court, but the high court had not decided the case when on May 28, 1973, the 63rd Legislature ended its regular session without carrying out the district court's order. Three weeks later, in *White* v. *Regester,* the Supreme Court upheld the lower federal court's division of Dallas and Bexar counties into single-member districts; but it ruled that the 9.9 per cent difference between the least populated district and the most populated district constituted an acceptable maximum deviation.

The board's redistricting plan for the Senate successfully withstood court challenges (see Figure 3-5). It provides for four senatorial districts entirely within Harris County and incorporates part of this county's territory into Districts 4 and 17, which include neighboring counties. Likewise, Dallas has three senators and Bexar has two, while parts of these counties are included in two additional multi-county senatorial districts. Tarrant County is divided exactly into two senatorial districts. Thus in 1972 voters in four urban counties (Harris,

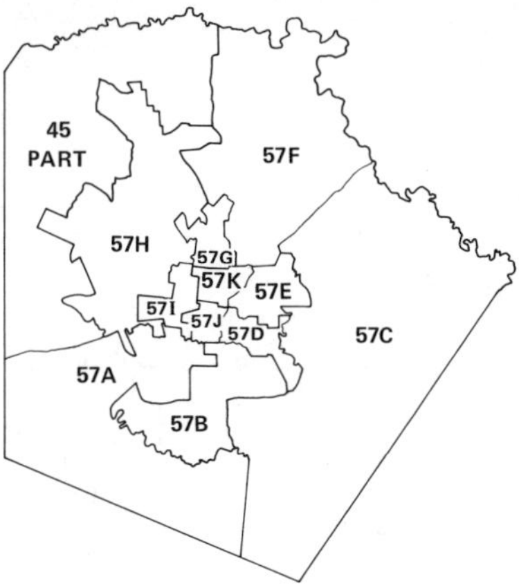

Figure 3-2
Dallas County: 18 single-member state representative districts; established by federal district court order in January 1972. Source: Texas Legislative Council.

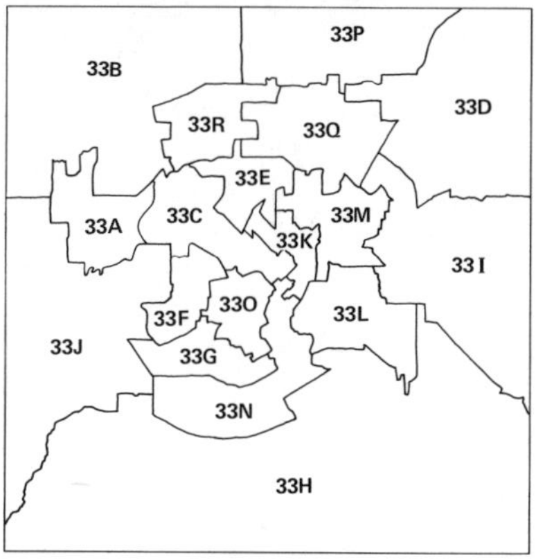

Figure 3-3
Bexar County: 11 single-member state representative districts (57A-57K) plus part of District 45; established by federal district court order in January 1972. Source: Texas Legislative Council.

Dallas, Bexar, and Tarrant) participated in the election of fifteen of Texas' thirty-one state senators.

MEMBERSHIP

As shown in Table 3-3, the Texas constitution establishes five qualifications for membership in the state legislature. Although millions of Texans meet all of these qualifications, biographical data for members of the 63rd Legislature (see Reading 3-2) suggest that opportunities for election to either of the two chambers are more restricted.

TABLE 3-3
Constitutional qualifications for membership in the Texas Legislature

Qualification	House	Senate
Citizenship	U.S. citizen	U.S. citizen
Voter status	qualified Texas elector	qualified Texas elector
Residence in district to be represented	1 year immediately preceding election	1 year immediately preceding election
Texas residence	2 years immediately preceding election	5 years immediately preceding election
Age	21 years	26 years

Source: Constitution of Texas (1876), Article III, Sections 6 and 7.

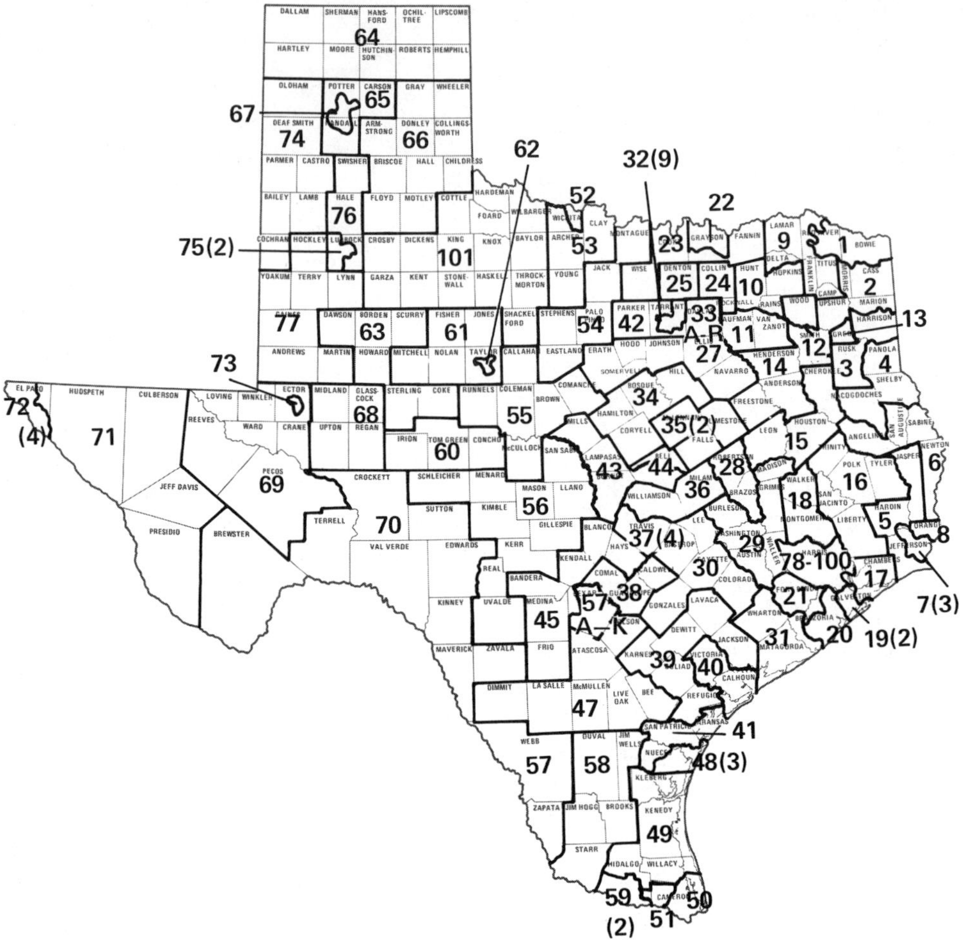

Figure 3-4

Texas state representative districts as enacted in October, 1971, by the Legislative Redistricting Board of Texas and modified in January, 1972, by a federal district court order; effective for 1972 elections. Numbers in parentheses indicate representatives in multi-member districts. Source: Texas Legislative Council.

SEX AND RACE

At the beginning of the 1973 regular session, only six women were serving in the Texas Legislature: Betty Andujar in the Senate and, in the House, Kay Bailey, Eddie Bernice Johnson, Chris Miller, Senfronia Thompson, and Sarah Weddington. Since 51 per cent of the inhabitants of Texas are female, their representation in the Legislature is low. Although the biographical data in Reading 3-2 do not indicate race, it also should be pointed out that there are only eight black

Figure 3-5

Texas state senatorial districts as enacted in October, 1971, by the Legislative Redistricting Board of Texas; effective for 1972 elections. Source: Texas Legislative Council.

representatives in the 63rd Legislature: Anthony Hall, Samuel W. Hudson, Eddie Bernice Johnson, Mickey Leland, Paul Ragsdale, G. J. Sutton, Craig Washington, and Senfronia Thompson (for an account of a sensational personal privilege speech by Mrs. Thompson which rocked the House on April 12, 1973, see Reading 3-3). All of them were elected in three urban counties with single-member districts: Harris, Dallas, and Bexar. Nine Spanish surnames appear on the roster of representatives: Canales, García, Hernández, Montoya, Reyes, Rodríguez, Sánchez, Truan, and Vale; one Mexican-American, H. Tati Santiesteban, serves in the Senate. Both blacks and Mexican-Americans are underrepresented; but black representation increased nearly threefold over the 1971 figure, while the number of Mexican-Americans in the 63rd Legislature is one less than the number for the 62nd Legislature.

PARTY

The beginning of the 63rd Legislative session found the Democratic Party dominating both the House and Senate, but not as heavily as in prior years. Three Republicans, from Tarrant, Dallas, and Harris counties, occupied Senate seats. Seventeen Republican representatives were elected to the 63rd Legislature (Dallas, seven; Harris, seven; Bexar, two; and Midland, one). Although constituting only 9 per cent of the membership of the Senate and 11 per cent of the membership of the House, these twenty Republicans exceeded the number in the 62nd Legislature by nine and constituted a larger minority party representation than had been mustered in any previous Texas legislature in this century.

AGE

As suggested by higher constitutional age qualification, the age level has tended to be higher in the Senate than in the House of Representatives. Table 3-4 shows that at the beginning of the 62nd and 63rd Legislatures there were no senators under thirty years of age, but 11 and 17 per cent, respectively, of the representatives were still in their twenties. The median age was forty-three for senators and thirty-eight for representatives in 1971; in 1973 it was forty-six for senators and thirty-seven for representatives.

PLACE OF BIRTH

Although being born in Texas, or in the United States, is not a formal requirement for election as a member of the state legislature, Table 3-5 shows the 62nd

TABLE 3-4
Age groups of legislators at the beginning of the 62nd and 63rd Legislatures

Age Groups	Percentage of House Members		Percentage of Senate Members	
	1971 (N=150)	*1973 (N=150)*	*1971 (N=31)*	*1973 (N=31)*
21-29	11	17	0	0
30-39	43	42	26	32
40-49	23	22	52	39
50-59	18	13	16	19
60-69	5	5	6	10
70 and above	0	1	0	0

Source: Reading 3-2; and *Practicing Texas Politics*, 1st ed. (1971), p. 121.

TABLE 3-5
State of birth of legislators, 62nd and 63rd Legislatures

State of Birth	Number of Representatives		Number of Senators	
	1971	*1973*	*1971*	*1973*
Arkansas	3	3	2	3
Louisiana	6	3	1	1
Missouri	2	0	0	0
Oklahoma	3	3	0	0
Texas	122	123	26	22
All other states	14	18	1	5
Foreign country	0	0	1	0
Totals	150	150	31	31

Source: Reading 3-2; and *Practicing Texas Politics,* 1st ed. (1971), p. 121.

and 63rd Legislatures to be composed largely of native Texans. Also apparent is the fact that legislators not born in Texas tend to come from bordering states.

OCCUPATION

Traditionally, Texas legislatures have included many attorneys or lawyers, several farmers and ranchers, a few skilled laborers but no unskilled workers, and businessmen of various callings—especially real estate, insurance, and construction activities. The composition of the 63rd Legislature was typical of its predecessors over the past decade or more. At the time of their election, the 181 senators and representatives were directly involved in a variety of professional or business activities. For example, in addition to ninety-two attorneys, there were one or more legislators who could be called upon to broadcast a radio or television program, publish a newspaper, teach a political science class, fill a drug prescription, build and sell a home, issue public relations propaganda, sell insurance, receive a bank deposit, build a swimming pool, embalm a body, drill an oil well, referee a professional football game, audit financial accounts, sell shoes, manage a dairy, nurse a patient, invest money, pilot an airplane, manage a ranch, weld a pipeline, service refinery equipment, or provide the services of a psychologist.

While most legislators have reported only one occupation, others claim two or more occupational interests; and several are executives and serve on the boards of directors of various firms. This large number of occupational backgrounds provides a broad range of expertise in dealing with diverse public problems; on the other hand, the fact that nearly half of the 63rd Legislature's representatives and two-thirds of its senators are attorneys serves to give the legal profession a dominating influence. Although there may be some logic behind the selection of lawyers to make laws, this hardly explains the disproportionate number of attorneys in the Texas Legislature—especially when the

TABLE 3-6
Colleges/universities attended by members of the 63rd Legislature

Institution	Attendance by Representatives	Attendance by Senators
Baylor	12	3
St. Mary's	15	1
Southern Methodist	13	5
Texas A&M	13	2
Texas Christian	8	0
Texas Tech	7	1
University of Texas, Austin	60	16
University of Houston	15	3
All others	102	21
Totals	245	52

Source: Reading 3-2.

drafting of bills and resolutions is chiefly a technical matter handled by the bill-drafting experts staffing the Legislative Council or employed as lobbyists. Lawyers are often more available than other occupational groups as candidates. Even an unsuccessful election campaign provides an attorney with publicity that may attract more clients. In the event of victory, one or more partners may take over much of the legal work of the lawyer-legislator, who devotes part of his time to legislative duties; and the business and government contacts made during the course of legislative service may profit the firm. Clients desiring to delay trial may seek the services of lawyer-legislators because these attorneys are entitled to obtain a continuance or postponement of any case set for trial during a period extending from thirty days before to thirty days after a legislative session. Under a 1973 law, however, a judge may deny this privilege when a lawmaker has been hired to assist other lawyers in handling a case within ten days of the trial or of any proceedings involving it. This new rule does not apply to a new suit or to a suit which a lawyer-legislator is handling alone.

EDUCATION

In government, as in industry, positions of leadership call for college credentials. Thus it is not surprising to find that 146 representatives and 30 senators in the 63rd Legislature have been enrolled in one or more institutions of higher education, and most of them have obtained one or more degrees. Of course, any group containing a large portion of lawyers will certainly include a high percentage of college and university graduates; usually it takes four years of undergraduate education plus three years of law school study to make a lawyer. But lawyer-legislators constitute only slightly more than half of the 176 senators and representatives with college experience. Table 3-6 shows that Texas institutions of

TABLE 3-7
Denominational affiliation of legislators, 62nd and 63rd Legislatures

Denomination	Percentage of House Members		Percentage of Senate Members	
	1971 (N=150)	*1973 (N=150)*	*1971 (N=31)*	*1973 (N=31)*
Baptist	29	30	19	16
Catholic	21	19	13	13
Church of Christ	4	5	3	0
Christian	3	3	3	0
Episcopal	9	7	3	10
Greek Orthodox	1	1	0	0
Jewish	1	0	3	3
Lutheran	3	1	0	0
Methodist	21	20	45	39
Presbyterian	7	10	6	16
Unitarian	1	1	3	3
Unaffiliated	0	2	3	0

Source: Reading 3-2; and *Practicing Texas Politics,* 1st ed. (1971), p. 124.

higher education, especially the Southwest Conference schools, played an important part in educating members of the 63rd Legislature. Significantly, as legislators labor in the Capitol, they are virtually within the shadow of the University of Texas buildings, where many of them have been in attendance for one or more semesters.

DENOMINATIONAL AFFILIATION

Although the Texas constitution contains a detailed requirement for separation of church and state, and although most lawmakers are not particularly famous for piety, religion may play a critical role in the formulation of public policy. Therefore, a legislator's denominational ties and the doctrines of his church must be taken into consideration by political analysts, especially when dealing with legislation involving such issues as birth control, gambling, the sale of alcoholic beverages, state aid to parochial schools, Sabbath observance, and other matters of vital importance to some religious groups but of indifference to others. Table 3-7 shows the denominational affiliations of members of the 62nd and 63rd Legislatures. Two facts stand out clearly: Methodists have constituted disproportionately large groups in the House and Senate, especially in the Senate; and both Catholics and Baptists have been underrepresented, particularly in the Senate. With the exception of four Catholic representatives and one senator, Catholic legislators come from districts on or to the south of a line drawn from Beaumont westward through Houston, San Antonio, Midland, and El Paso. All members of the 63rd Legislature with Spanish surnames were elected in that region. Apparently one of the realities of Texas politics is that Catholic candidates enjoy their greatest success in the large cities and in areas with large numbers of Mexican-Americans. Catholic representatives have doubled in number since the 60th Legislature.

LEGISLATIVE EXPERIENCE

In the legislatures elected between 1935 and 1961, the rate of turnover in the House of Representatives was high. As a result, during every regular session about 40 per cent of the membership was without previous legislative experience, and nearly 30 per cent had served for only one prior term.[3] In the 1960s, the rate of turnover declined significantly; and in the 61st and 62nd Legislatures only 21 and 20 per cent of the representatives were serving a first term (see Table 3-8), although a few others had been elected during interim periods and had not had two full years of legislative experience.

Two developments in 1971 and 1972 helped to produce a high turnover rate for the 63rd Legislature. First, the Sharpstown State Bank scandal discredited Speaker Gus Mutscher and several representatives who supported him (for details concerning this scandal, see Reading 5-3). Secondly, redistricting adversely affected many members of the 62nd Legislature—especially representatives in Harris, Dallas, and Bexar counties, who were confronted with new single-member districts. Conservative, white Democrats who had won multi-member district elections in these urban counties in 1970 were commonly confronted with different political situations in 1972. Some of the new single-member districts could be carried only by candidates supported by black, Mexican-American, Republican, or liberal Democratic majorities. Thus seventy (47 per cent) of the House members who took office in 1973 were without previous legislative experience; furthermore, seven (5 per cent) of the representatives in the 63rd Legislature returned to the House in 1973 after having been out of office for one or more terms.

Table 3-8 shows that only 35 per cent of the senators in each of the 61st, 62nd, and 63rd Legislatures had not formerly served in the House of Representatives for one or more terms; on the other hand, there were only two instances of representatives with former Senate service between 1969 and 1973. Although most representatives are quick to insist that their house is coequal with the Senate, it is apparent that movement from the former to the latter is considered a desirable switch.

Turnover of personnel in the Senate was low in 1969 and 1971, but fifteen senators (48 per cent) in the 63rd Legislature were serving first terms. Ordinarily, only half of the senators face re-election at the same time; but because of redistricting following the 1970 census, all Senate terms ended with the expiration of the 62nd Legislature. At the beginning of the 63rd Legislature, the thirty-one newly elected members drew lots to determine who would be among the sixteen receiving four-year terms and who would have the fifteen two-year terms.

Once elected, senators tend to remain in that chamber longer than representatives usually serve in the House. This situation is explained, in part, by the

TABLE 3-8
Background of legislative experience at the beginning of regular sessions: 61st, 62nd, and 63rd Legislatures

Service in Former Legislatures*	Percentage of House Members			Percentage of Senate Members		
	1969 (N=150)	*1971 (N=150)*	*1973 (N=150)*	*1969 (N=31)*	*1971 (N=31)*	*1973 (N=31)*
No former House service	21	20	47	35	35	35
House service in 1 legislature	35	19	12	19	26	23
House service in 2 legislatures	15	28	15	19	16	16
House service in 3-4 legislatures	19	17	15	23	19	16
House service in 5 or more legislatures	10	15	12	3	3	10
No former Senate service	99	100	99	6	13	48
Senate service in 1 legislature	1	0	0	35	6	10
Senate service in 2 legislatures	0	0	0	3	32	0
Senate service in 3-4 legislatures	0	0	0	35	26	16
Senate service in 5 or more legislatures	0	0	1	19	23	26

Source: Reading 3-2; and *Practicing Texas Politics,* 1st ed. (1971), p. 125.

*Includes periods of interim service of less than the full two years of a legislature; such interim service results from special elections to fill vacancies. Consequently, these figures overstate slightly the amount of former service. Cf. Clifton McCleskey, *The Government and Politics of Texas,* 4th ed. (Boston: Little, Brown, 1972), p. 129.

fact that senators ordinarily enjoy four-year terms, while representatives serve only two-year terms. Yet this distinction does not explain fully why 19, 23, and 26 per cent of the Senate membership in the 61st, 62nd, and 63rd Legislatures, respectively, consisted of those who had served in five or more legislatures, whereas only 10, 15, and 12 per cent of the House membership had compiled such records of service. To some extent, the higher rate of turnover in the House is influenced by the fact that representatives sometimes pass up opportunities for nomination and re-election in order to make a bid for a Senate seat or some other more desirable office. Table 3-9 shows the fate or fortune of members of the 62nd Legislature in 1972. As pointed out above, not only the representatives but also all senators were confronted with expiring terms in that year.

Some legislators simply grow weary of political battle and drop out of politics, seeking a quieter life. Others withdraw because of districting problems, financial difficulties, family opposition to continued political activity, or

TABLE 3-9
Tenure and turnover of members of 62nd Legislature as a result of 1972 elections

Fate or Fortune	Percentage of Members	
	House (N=150)	*Senate (N=31)*
Renominated, reelected, and maintained seat in 63rd Legislature	49	52
Primary defeat in state House contest	17	0
General election defeat in state House contest	1	0
Primary victory by Senate member in state House contest	–	3*
Primary defeat in state Senate contest	12	13
General election defeat in state Senate contest	0	0
General election victory by House member in Senate contest	6	–
Primary defeat in other than state legislative contest	5	16
General election defeat in other than state legislative contest	1	3
General election victory in other than state legislative contest	1	6
Did not seek nomination and election to any public office	9	6

Source: Legislative Reference Library.
*After nomination, this senator withdrew his House candidacy because of prosecution on a theft charge.

employment opportunities that will not permit legislative service. No doubt four-year terms for representatives might help to reduce the attraction which the Senate holds for many representatives—an attraction that lures them away from the House and often leads to electoral defeat. Such terms would also reduce the total cost of campaigning over a period of time, and the reduced financial burdens would encourage some to seek re-election. Another obvious incentive for extended service would be an increase in legislators' salaries and expense allowances.

COMPENSATION

Compensation for legislators takes the form of annual salaries and allowances. *Contingency expense allowances* for senators and representatives are authorized at the beginning of a session by each chamber. For example, in January, 1973, the House resolved that during the 63rd regular session every representative would be allowed to make maximum monthly expenditures of $120 for postage,

$875 for office operations, and $1,400 for staff salaries. The last item was to be expended so as not to exceed the following monthly salary limits: administrative assistant, $750; secretary, $550; administrative aide, $350; and part-time clerk, $250. While not imposing specific limitations on amounts that senators could spend for postage and office operations, the Senate of the 63rd Legislature restricted each member to a total of not more than $5,000 per month for secretarial and other office staff to be employed at salaries ranging from $360 to $1,104 per month during the regular session. At the end of that session the Senate reduced the monthly staff salary allowance during the interim between sessions to $2,800 and the House cut this item to $1,225.

Salaries and per diem allowances for Texas legislators can be changed only by constitutional amendment. In 1960 an amendment was adopted to provide annual salaries of $4,800 for both senators and representatives. The amendment also gave them a *per diem allowance* of $12 a day for the first 120 days of a regular session and for 30 days of each special session. Seven years later another amendment was proposed for the purpose of authorizing salaries of not more than $8,400 per year and extending the $12 per diem to the full 140 days of a regular session. This proposal was rejected by the voters, despite the fact that rising prices had reduced the purchasing power of the 1960 salary and per diem allowance. In 1968 another amendment was proposed which, among other things, would have authorized legislators to fix their own salaries up to the amount paid to district court judges from state funds. This proposal was also rejected at the polls. Then in 1971 an amendment was proposed which called for the establishment of an Ethics Commission with authority to promulgate rules of ethics for state officials and to propose pay increases for legislators. Influenced in part by evidence of legislative corruption involving Speaker Gus Mutscher and others, voters rejected this amendment in a special election held in May, 1971. Before the end of the 62nd regular session, however, another amendment was proposed which would have raised the annual salaries of legislators from $4,800 to $8,400. In November, 1972, this amendment was also voted down. Thus, during the regular session of the 63rd Legislature in 1973, Texas lawmakers were being paid salaries that had been set over a decade earlier, when the cost of living was much lower. In most cases a legislator's secretary received a higher salary than her boss. Under these circumstances, the 63rd Legislature proposed an amendment providing for an annual salary not exceeding $15,000, and a per diem allowance of not more than $18 during regular and special sessions. This same proposal calls for a regular session every year. If approved by the voters in an election held in November, 1973, the amendment becomes effective in January, 1975.

Finally, note must be made of the inadequate travel allowance provided for legislators. Although many constituents expect their legislators to return to the home district from time to time during a session, a travel allowance of ten cents per mile is paid for only one round trip to the capital each session. Furthermore, according to Article III, Section 27 of the Texas constitution, "no member [is] to be entitled to mileage for any extra session that may be called within one day after the adjournment of a regular or called session."

ORGANIZATION

The Texas constitution leaves no doubt as to who will be the presiding officer or *president of the Senate.* This position is assigned to the lieutenant governor. From among its membership the Senate elects a *president pro tempore,* who presides when the lieutenant governor is absent or when that office is vacant. The president of the Senate votes on a bill or resolution only when the membership is evenly divided on the matter.

The presiding officer of the House of Representatives is titled the *speaker.* He is a member of the House and is elected to the office of speaker by his colleagues. Because of the importance of this post, the selection of a speaker involves a great amount of political activity. Lobbyists representing special-interest groups make every effort to ensure the selection of a sympathetic speaker, and aspirants to the position begin to line up support several months or even as much as two or more years before the beginning of a speaker's race. Until 1972 prospective speakers sought to formalize promises of support through use of *pledge cards.* Their objective was to accumulate at least seventy-five signed cards signifying firm commitments. Under this system a representative's prospects for desirable committee assignments and other favors depended greatly on his early signing of a pledge card for the candidate who would later win the speakership. Although Price Daniel, Jr., did not use pledge cards, which had come into bad odor as a result of being associated with domination of the House by his predecessors, he won the speakership in 1973 after eighteen months of campaigning. Daniel reported having spent over $30,000 in this speaker's race.

In performing their duties as presiding officers, both the president of the Senate and the speaker of the House are empowered to recognize members desiring to speak on the floor. They determine the committee to which a bill will be referred and interpret rules of their respective chambers. In addition, and of special importance, is their power to appoint members of all standing and special committees and to designate committee chairmen and vice-chairmen. Until 1973 the speaker appointed all members of standing committees in the House, and there was no seniority system. Consequently, from legislature to legislature the turnover of committee memberships was high. A similar situation with regard to committee appointments prevailed in the Senate.

At the beginning of the 63rd regular session, the House adopted new rules which establish a *limited seniority system* for most *standing committees* (see Reading 3-4). Seniority is based on years of consecutive service as a member of the House. When a new regular session starts, in order of seniority each representative selects a committee on which he desires to serve. If the committee does not already have one-half of its membership filled by seniority selections, the representative then becomes a member. When each representative has chosen a committee on the basis of seniority, the remaining positions (including chairman and vice-chairman) on each committee are filled by appointment of the speaker. Seniority does not apply, however, to membership on the Calendar, Rules, and House Administration committees; all members of these three committees are appointed by the speaker. Moreover, the chairman of the House Administration Committee can be removed by the speaker at any time.

TABLE 3-10
Standing committees and number of members, 63rd Legislature

21 House of Representatives Committees

Agriculture (23)
Appropriations (23)
Business and Industry (23)
Calendars (9)
Criminal Jurisprudence (23)
Education (23)
Elections (21)
Environmental Affairs (21)
Administration (7)
Human Resources (21)
Insurance (21)
Intergovernmental Affairs (23)
Judiciary (23)
Labor (21)
Liquor Regulation (21)
Natural Resources (23)
Reapportionment (21)
Revenue and Taxation (23)
Rules (11)
State Affairs (23)
Transportation (21)

9 Senate Committees

Administration (7)
Economic Development (7)
Intergovernmental Relations (9)
Education (9)
Finance (13)
Jurisprudence (13)
Human Resources (11)
State Affairs (13)
Natural Resources (11)

Another significant change in House rules at the beginning of the 63rd Legislature reduced the forty-five standing committees that had existed in the preceding legislature to twenty-one (see Table 3-10). To ensure that representatives are not forced to divide their efforts among too many committees, membership is limited to not more than three standing committees. Furthermore, because of the special importance of the Revenue and Taxation, Appropriations, and State Affairs committees, no member can serve on more than one of these three. In view of the extra responsibilities of committee chairmen, they are limited to serving concurrently on only one additional committee; and the chairman of the Appropriations Committee is limited to membership on that committee alone.

Under the terms of Senate rules adopted at the beginning of the 63rd Legislature, the number of standing committees was reduced from twenty-seven to nine (see Table 3-10). Chairmen and vice-chairmen are appointed by the lieutenant governor. His power of appointment extends also to the membership of all standing committees, with the exception that "three members of each committee with 10 or less members, and four members of each committee with more than 10 members must be senators who were members of the committee during the previous legislature." A senator serves on not more than three standing committees, and no member of the Senate may serve on more than two of the following committees: Finance, State Affairs, and Jurisprudence. Also, senators are restricted to holding no more than one standing committee chairmanship.

Since standing committees play an important role in the fate or fortune of any bill, the selection of committee personnel goes far toward determining the amount and type of legislative output during a session. Some committees are more important than others; consequently, committee assignments and distribution of chairmanships are important keys to understanding the power structure in each chamber. Members of important committees tend to be "friends" of the presiding officer, while chairmen of the most important committees are "special friends." And in this context, friendship must be defined in terms of loyalty resulting from a desire to achieve common goals.

The Legislative Reorganization Act of 1961 calls for each standing committee to "make a continuing study of matters under its jurisdiction" with a view to formulating and introducing legislative programs. The act also envisions committee work continuing in the interim between sessions. Generally, standing committees have not functioned on a continuing basis, but have terminated their labor at the end of each session. Work which might have been done by these committees has been assigned to special *interim study committees.* For example, the 60th Legislature authorized 55 such interim committees, the 61st Legislature provided for no fewer than 103, and the 62nd went so far as to authorize 162 during its regular session and still others in later special sessions. Subject matter for interim committees has ranged from milk to fire ants and from drug treatment to minimum teaching loads for university faculties. Members of interim study committees have been appointed by presiding officers and sometimes by the governor. In many instances membership has included private citizens as well as senators and representatives. Some interim committees have concluded their work in one or two meetings; others have involved many days of labor by members and by staff personnel. In many instances, however, committees are authorized but appointment of members is never made; also, interim committees may be created but not funded, and thus they are denied financial resources with which to work.

POWERS

All legislative power that is not denied to the state by the United States Constitution or by the Texas constitution is vested in the Texas Legislature. Despite a nationwide trend toward expansion of the influence of the executive branch of government, the Legislature remains the dominant branch of Texas government. The lawmakers have jealously guarded their domain against encroachment by the governor. At the same time, through their control of the public purse, they have made all state agencies and personnel, and to some extent even units of local government, dependent upon them. For this reason, an understanding of the nature and scope of the powers exercised by the Senate and the House of Representatives is of fundamental importance for all who would understand the Texas governmental system. Although there may be some question as to the preciseness of differentiation, we have in the following paragraphs divided the powers of the Texas Legislature into two categories: nonlegislative powers and legislative powers.[4]

NONLEGISLATIVE POWERS

Although the principal powers of the Texas Legislature are exercised through the enacting of civil and criminal statutes, the House and Senate have other important powers which relate only indirectly to the lawmaking function. Both chambers exercise *constituent power* in proposing amendments to the Texas constitution. A proposal is officially made when approved by a two-thirds majority of the membership of each house. As the years have passed and the constitution of 1876 has become more outmoded, this power has been exercised with increasing frequency.

Although largely a formality, at the beginning of each regular session both houses meet in the chamber of the House of Representatives to canvass the general election returns for six executive offices: governor, lieutenant governor, treasurer, commissioner of the General Land Office, attorney general, and comptroller of public accounts. Delivered to the speaker by the secretary of state, the final election returns are opened in the presence of the senators and representatives, and the winners officially declared. In case of a tie vote or of a dispute concerning who should be declared the victor in an electoral contest, a majority vote of the jointly assembled legislators resolves the matter.

Most appointments made by the governor must be submitted to the Senate for approval by two-thirds of the senators present. Thus one chamber of the Legislature is in a position to influence the selection of many important officials. Further legislative control over administrative matters is exercised through passage of laws establishing the various state agencies and defining their responsibilities, through appropriations for support of their operations, and through general supervision of their activities. One form of administrative supervision is the requirement of periodic and special reports to the Legislature. Appointed by the Legislative Audit Committee, the state auditor provides information concerning irregular or inefficient use of funds by administrative agencies. Through the *Legislative Budget Board,* its own budgeting agency, the Legislature is equipped to evaluate administrative operations for the purpose of determining appropriate amounts of financial support. Composed of the speaker, the lieutenant governor, the chairmen of the Senate Committees on Finance and on State Affairs, two other senators, the chairmen of the House Committees on Appropriations and on Revenue and Taxation, and two other representatives, this ten-member board names a director who supervises the work of a staff.

In order to obtain information on problems requiring remedial legislation, the Legislature may subpoena witnesses, administer oaths, and compel the submission of records and documents. Such action may be taken by the two houses as a body or by committees. *Legislative investigations,* which received much publicity in past years, and which led to some reforms, include probes of vice and corruption in Jefferson County, of operations of the Veterans' Land Board, and of shortcomings with regard to regulation of insurance companies.

The House of Representatives has the power to impeach district court judges and judges of appellate courts, although this power is infrequently exercised. The House may also impeach the governor, lieutenant governor, comptroller of public accounts, treasurer, attorney general, and commissioner of the General Land Office. *Impeachment* involves the bringing of charges by a simple majority vote, and it resembles the true bill of indictment returned by a grand jury in felony cases. Following impeachment, judgment is rendered by the Senate; conviction requires a two-thirds vote of senators present. Removal from office and disqualification for holding any other public office under the Texas constitution represents the only punishment that can be imposed by the Senate. But if a crime has been committed by a deposed official, he can be prosecuted like any other person before the state court having jurisdiction over the offense.

LEGISLATIVE POWERS

Using language reminiscent of George Orwell's *Animal Farm,* we may say that whereas all powers exercised by the Texas Legislature are in a sense legislative, some are more legislative than others. Thus the most typical exercise of legislative power is the making of public policy through the passing of bills and adopting of resolutions. Among resolutions there are three types: simple, concurrent, and joint. Each bill and resolution is designated by a number, which indicates the order of introduction during a session; and each type is identified by a distinctive abbreviation, which indicates the chamber of origin.[5]

A *simple resolution,* abbreviated as H.S.R. if originating in the House and S.R. if originating in the Senate, involves action by one house only and is not sent to the governor. Adoption requires a simple majority vote. Matters dealt with by simple resolution include the assignment of desks to members at the beginning of a session, a request for an opinion from the attorney general, or an invitation extended to a nonmember to address the chamber. Prior to the 63rd session, hundreds of resolutions were introduced during every session for the purpose of extending recognition and congratulations to persons who supposedly had performed a worthy deed or had rendered meritorious service in public or private life (see Reading 3-5). As a matter of routine, these resolutions were passed unanimously and without study. To point up the ridiculousness of this procedure, Representative Tom Moore of Waco proposed a resolution calling attention to Albert De Salvo's "noted activities and unconventional techniques involving population control and applied psychology" and commending him "on his outstanding career of public service." The measure passed by a unanimous vote, and only after voting did House members learn that Mr. De Salvo was better known in Massachusetts as the Boston Strangler. As a result of this incident, a House rule now requires that "congratulatory and memorial resolutions shall be limited to those for members and former Members of the Legislature and state and Federal officials and former state and Federal officials." Unanimous consent is required for suspension of this rule. Congratulatory resolutions couched in humorous and satirical language are traditionally passed on the occasion of a representative's birthday (see Reading 3-6). Although some people feel that such resolutions waste time, no doubt this buffoonery may serve the useful purpose of relieving tensions and cooling passions produced by sharp debate and tiresome haggling over more important matters.

A *concurrent resolution* (H.C.R. or S.C.R.) must pass both houses and is sent to the governor, who may sign it, allow it to pass without signature, or exercise his veto power, as in the case of a bill. Typical examples would include resolutions requesting action by the United States Congress or information from a state agency, or adopting joint rules for both houses. An exception is the concurrent resolution to adjourn at the end of a legislative session; this measure is not sent to the governor.

Adoption of a *joint resolution* (H.J.R. or S.J.R.) requires approval by both houses, but the governor's signature is not necessary. A proposed amendment to the Texas constitution exemplifies a joint resolution requiring a two-thirds vote of each house. To date, all proposed amendments to the United States Constitution initiated by Congress, with the exception of the Twenty-first Amendment, have been submitted to state legislatures for ratification. The Texas Legislature has ratified such amendments with joint resolutions adopted by a simple majority of each house.

Before enactment, a proposed law or statute is known as a *bill* (H.B. or S.B.). For purposes of classification, bills may be divided into four categories: local, special, private, and general. A *local bill* affects a single unit of local government (i.e., city, county, precinct) or a group of these units. Usually such bills are passed without opposition if sponsored by all of the legislators from the affected districts. A *special bill* makes an exception to general laws for the benefit of a specific individual, class, or corporation. A *private bill,* for example, authorizes a pension for someone not covered by general pension laws or permits an individual to bring suit against the state. Of greatest importance are *general bills,* which apply to all people or property in all parts of Texas. The subject matter of these bills is suggested by the titles of the numerous standing committees of the Senate and House of Representatives listed in Table 3-10.

PROCEDURE

The Texas constitution calls for regular sessions to be split into three periods for distinct purposes: the first 30 days, for introduction of bills and resolutions, action on emergency appropriations, and confirmation or rejection of recess appointments by the governor; the second 30 days, for consideration of bills and resolutions by committees; and the remainder of the session, which may amount to 80 days if the session runs the full 140 days allowed, for acting on bills and resolutions. Throughout the session action may be taken at any time on emergency matters submitted by the governor. Since the constitution also allows either house to determine by a four-fifths vote its own order of business, it is possible for both the House and the Senate to permit unlimited introduction of bills during the first 60 days. All revenue bills must originate in the House of Representatives; other kinds of legislation may originate in either house. After introduction a bill must pass both houses in the same form in order to become a law. Then it must be signed by the governor, or allowed to pass without his signature, or vetoed by the governor and then passed by a two-thirds vote of each house.

Although the process of turning a bill into a law is not without its complexities, certain basic steps are clearly delineated. In the following paragraphs these steps will be traced from introduction to action by the governor. Location of step numbers in Figure 3-6 should help the reader to visualize the bill's progress. For our purposes, we shall describe the path of a bill that originates in the House of Representatives.[6]

1. Introduction A bill may be introduced by any House member. He can introduce it from the floor after being recognized by the speaker, or he can introduce it by filing four copies with the chief clerk.

2. First reading and referral to committee After receiving the bill, the chief clerk assigns it a number in order of submission and turns it over to the reading clerk for the *first reading.* The reading clerk reads the *caption,* which is a brief summary of the contents, and gives the bill to the speaker. The speaker then assigns the bill to an appropriate committee.

3. Committee consideration and report The committee chairman may refer the bill to a subcommittee for study, after which the entire membership considers the measure in a committee meeting. Many bills are pigeonholed and die in committee. Others are given a hearing at which interested persons receive an opportunity to express their views. If the majority of the committee members decide that the bill should be passed, perhaps with amendments, a favorable report is filed with the calendar clerk. An unfavorable report virtually guarantees the death of a bill. It is the responsibility of the calendar clerk to send all favorably reported bills to the printer, but in the case of a local bill, the reporting committee may recommend that the measure not be printed. With the exception of a general appropriations bill, a printed copy must be placed in the newspaper mailbox of each House member twenty-four hours before the measure is considered on the floor. For a general appropriations bill, delivery must be made to "the newspaper mailbox of each member at least 168 hours during a Regular Session and at least 72 hours during a Special Session before such bill can be considered by the House." (Rule XIX, Sec. 16, House Rules, 63rd Legislature.)

4. Second reading Although bills are supposed to be brought to the floor in order of introduction, various procedures enable legislators to take up bills out of order. At times the entire text of a bill will be read at the *second reading* stage, but reading usually involves reading only the caption. Debate follows, and ordinarily speakers are limited to not more than ten minutes each, unless extra time is granted by a majority vote. The author of a bill, or the committee member reporting on behalf of the committee, is given the privilege of beginning and ending the floor debate with speeches of not over twenty minutes on each occasion. After discussion ends and any amendments are added, a vote is taken on engrossment. If approved by a majority of those voting, the bill is passed to the engrossing and enrolling clerk, who then prepares a copy with all amendments inserted. In the event that the bill contains an *emergency clause* (and

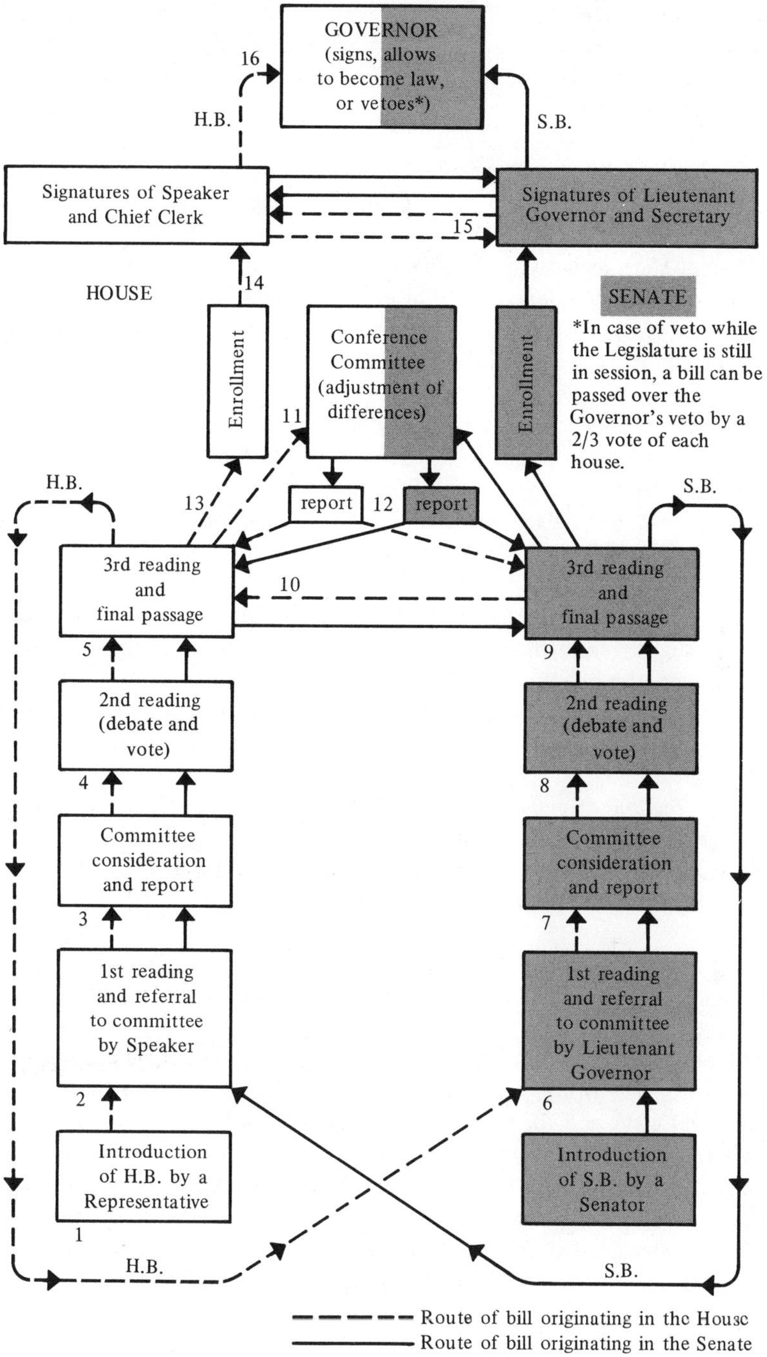

Figure 3-6

Routes followed by bills from legislature to governor (prepared with the assistance of Dr. Beryl E. Pettus, Sam Houston State University).

almost without exception bills are drafted with this clause), a motion may be made to suspend the rules by a four-fifths vote and give the bill an immediate third reading, thus making an exception to the constitutional rule that all bills must be read on three separate days.

5. Third reading Whenever the *third reading* takes place, it is ordinarily by caption only. A simple majority vote is required to pass the bill at this reading. Amendments may still be added at this stage, but such action requires a two-thirds vote. Until recently, amendments added on third reading were attached to the bill as engrossed riders. Now, however, following the addition of an amendment a new printing is made, checked over by the engrossing and enrolling clerk, and stamped "Engrossed–Third Reading."

6. First reading (Senate) After passage on the third reading in the House, the chief clerk transmits the bill to the Senate (where it retains the original House number) and adds a statement certifying passage. In the Senate, the House bill's caption is read by the reading clerk; then the lieutenant governor (or, in his absence, the president pro tempore) assigns the bill to committee.

7. Senate committee consideration and report Senate committee procedure differs only slightly from that in the House. If a majority of committee members favor passage, the bill is given a favorable report. Senate committees usually can be depended on to give House bills favorable treatment, although amendments may be added.

8. Second reading (Senate) As in second readings in the House, the Senate at this stage debates the bill, considers amendments, and puts the measure to a vote. According to Senate procedure, bills are taken up out of order by a two-thirds vote; passage requires a simple majority.

9. Third reading (Senate) If passed on the second reading, a third reading can come immediately, assuming that rules are suspended by the required four-fifths vote.

10. Return to the House After passage by the Senate, a House bill is returned to the chief clerk and then sent to the engrossing and enrolling clerk. The latter has the responsibility for supervising the preparation of a perfect copy of the bill and for its delivery to the speaker. If one or more amendments have been added in the Senate, these changes must be voted on in the House. If the House is not prepared to accept the amended bill, the ordinary procedure is to request a conference. Otherwise, the bill will die unless one of the chambers reverses its position.

11. Conference committee When the two houses agree to send the bill to conference, each presiding officer appoints five members to serve on the *conference committee.* Attempts will be made to adjust differences and produce a compromise version acceptable to both houses. At least three Senate members and three House members must reach agreement before the committee can recommend a course of action to the two houses.

12. Conference committee report The conference committee's recommended settlement of the questions at issue must be fully accepted or rejected by each house. Amendments may not be added; but both houses may agree to return the report to the committee or, at the request of the House, the Senate may accept a proposal for a new conference.

13. Enrollment When a conference report has been accepted by both houses, the bill is sent to the engrossing and enrolling clerk of the House for preparation of a perfect copy. The Rules Committee determines if the enrolled copy is correct and then reports it to the House.

14. Signatures of chief clerk and speaker When the enrolled conference committee report is received in the House, the reading clerk of the House reads the bill by caption only. It is then signed by the chief clerk, who certifies the vote by which it passed, and signed by the speaker.

15. Signatures of secretary and lieutenant governor Next the engrossing and enrolling clerk of the House takes the bill to the Senate where it is read by caption only. Then the bill is signed by the lieutenant governor and by the secretary of the Senate, with certification of the vote by which it passed.

16. Action by the governor While the Legislature remains in session, the governor has three options: sign the bill; allow it to lie on his desk for ten days, exclusive of Sundays, after which time it becomes law without his signature; or veto the measure and return it to the House with a message giving a reason for his action. A two-thirds majority vote in each house can override the chief executive's veto, but such action is unlikely. No *veto* has been overridden in Texas since 1941 during the administration of Governor W. Lee (Pappy) O'Daniel. If the legislative session ends before the ten-day period has expired, there is no possibility of overriding a veto. After the expiration of a session, the governor has twenty days, including Sundays, in which to veto all undesirable legislation and file the rejected measures with the secretary of state. A measure not vetoed by the governor automatically passes at the expiration of the twenty-day period. Ordinarily, acts of the Legislature do not take effect until ninety days after adjournment. Exceptions to this rule include general appropriation acts and emergency measures. The latter must be identified by an emergency statement in the text or preamble and must pass each house by a two-thirds majority of the total membership.

INFLUENCE

In theory, elected representatives should be influenced mostly, if not exclusively, by their constituents. In practice, however, many of the actions of legislators bear little relationship to the needs or interests of the "folks back home." To be sure, Texas senators and representatives are not completely indifferent to the voters; yet many of them fall far short of being truly representative. One problem is that large numbers of citizens are uninterested in most affairs of state and have no opinions about how their representatives should act in dealing with public problems. Others may have opinions but are inarticulate or too busy to attempt to communicate with their legislators. Many citizens remain ignorant of what happens in Austin because of inadequate press coverage of legislative affairs, but this situation has improved in recent years. Consequently, lawmakers are apt to yield to the influence of powerful forces that are ever present in Austin seeking to court or coerce them: the presiding officers, the governor, and the lobbyists.

GOVERNOR

Earlier we saw the roles of legislative leaders, and the governor's veto power has been noted. It is also important to point out that the ever-present threat of executive veto plays an equally important part in legislative behavior. Even though a bill might prove to be popular with many senators and representatives, knowledge that the governor will oppose the measure is often sufficient to discourage its introduction. After all, a governor's veto has not been overridden in thirty years. Likewise, a legislator may support a bill that is backed by the governor even though he may consider it to be injurious to the interests of his constituents, who may never learn of his action, especially if there is no roll call vote. Even if they do, they may be far away and election time still many months ahead. Meanwhile, the governor is close at hand and may offer some tangible rewards for a legislator's cooperation: reciprocal support for one of his own bills, an appointment to some state office for a job-seeking friend, or merely the promise of future favors.

There is nothing illegal about such actions, but they do suggest a contradiction between the representative ideal and the reality of executive influence. Yet the governor also considers himself to be a representative—a representative of all the people of Texas. He has been elected on a platform of promises, and he feels a compulsion to promote his programs. Thus legislators must be influenced to ensure the success of the governor's plans for taxing, spending, building, healing, and educating, among others. And if there is any doubt as to what the governor wants, he will probably outline his policies in messages from time to time. Extensive popular acceptance of the chief executive's ideas will make opposition difficult, even though a legislator's own constituents are adversely affected by them.

COURTS AND ATTORNEY GENERAL

An act that may be politically expedient and even popular with constituents may also be unconstitutional. Thus in their lawmaking all legislators are influenced by what courts have done or may do with regard to a contemplated legislative action. Usually senators and representatives do not wish to spend time and invest political capital in legislative efforts that will be struck down by the judges. Therefore, they may turn to the attorney general for an opinion regarding the constitutionality of a proposed measure. It is also true that an opinion may be sought as a device to justify killing a bill in committee or as a delaying tactic (see Reading 3-7).

LOBBY

As for the influence of the lobby on legislative behavior, opinions are varied. In many minds all *lobbying* carries with it the stench of corruption; others see lobbyists as performing a useful role in supplying information and serving as links with organized groups of constituents. For underpaid legislators, the free food and entertainment provided by well-financed representatives of labor, manufacturing, religion, and other special interest groups merely constitute a well-deserved fringe benefit. They will insist that they can consume a lobbyist's food and drink—and even accept his assistance in financing an election campaign—without selling out the interests of their constituents in particular and the public in general. Yet there is the nagging fact that special interests spend large amounts of money to influence legislative action that would not otherwise be taken as a matter of individual initiative or in response to requests by constituents (see Reading 3-8).

Under the terms of the Lobby Registration Act of 1957, lobbyists were required to register with the chief clerk of the House of Representatives and to make monthly reports of money spent for lobbying activities during legislative sessions. Failure to register or to render truthful reports constituted a felony offense, but no particular enforcement agency was specified. During the sixteen years that this law remained in force, there was little evidence that it had the intended effect of publicizing lobby activities. As time passed, fewer lobbyists bothered to register, and all informed observers agreed that more lobby money was spent than was reported. Finally, in the wake of the Sharpstown Bank scandal, it became apparent that Texas voters expected that the 63rd Legislature would enact a new law on this subject, along with other reform legislation.

REFORM

The bribery conspiracy trial and conviction of Speaker Gus Mutscher, House Administration Committee Chairman Tommy Shannon, and the speaker's aide, Rush McGinty, attracted nationwide attention in the spring of 1972. Before the end of the year no fewer than four other legislators or former legislators had been convicted on charges of failure to account for state funds, nepotism, theft of House-provided stamps by false pretext, and theft of a state warrant. This evidence of corruption prompted demands for reform. Confident that he would be named speaker for the 63rd Legislature, late in 1972 Price Daniel, Jr., and his supporters prepared nine bills to be introduced in January, 1973. Publicized as the speaker's reform package and strategically given the first nine House Bill numbers, these bills total over 100 double-spaced, legal-size pages and cover a multitude of details. Some of the reform provisions encountered strong opposition, especially in the Senate, but seven of the bills were passed by both houses. Nevertheless, weakening amendments were added and a considerable amount of horse-trading was done in conference committee sessions—in some cases as late as May 28. Consequently, the matter of reform was the subject of much legislative debate and public comment during the first five months of 1973. Even the Apache Belles of Tyler Junior College made a contribution to the cause. One day in March a half dozen members of this drill team appeared in the House gallery; and, according to the *Texas Observer,* "They turned their gold laméd posteriors to the brass rail overlooking the House floor and pertly displayed hand-lettered placards which spelled out R*E*F*O*R*M."

The subject of 21 called conference committee meetings and many times amended before it passed on the last day of the session, the ethics bill, H.B. 1, is designed to ensure that a state officer shall not have any interest that "is in substantial conflict with the proper discharge of his duties in the public interest." To this end the measure requires the filing of an annual financial statement with the secretary of state in April by every "elected officer" (member of the legislature, executive or judicial official elected in a statewide election, judge of a court of civil appeals or district court, member of the State Board of Education); "salaried appointed officer" (one who is authorized to receive a salary as opposed to per diem or other compensation); "appointed officer of a major state agency" (member of one of 27 boards and commissions ranging from the Texas Industrial Commission to the School Land Board); and "executive head of a state agency" (an executive director, commissioner, administrator, chief clerk, or other officer serving as the highest executive or administrative official of a state agency—including university chancellor and president of a public senior college or university). These officials are required to report their sources of income (in categories of less than $1,000, $1,000 but less than $5,000, or $5,000 or more), real estate and securities, personal loans in excess of $1,000, gifts received that are valued over $250, and a list of executive positions and directorships held in corporations. The statement must cover also the financial activities of a spouse and dependent children. An "appointed officer" (secretary of state, member of the governing board of a state-supported institution of higher education, or officer of a state agency who is appointed for a term of office) need only report if he acquires or divests himself of a substantial interest in a business regulated by a state agency, or if he owns a substantial interest in an entity that does business with the state. A candidate for an elected office must submit a financial statement within 30 days after the filing deadline. Originally the bill provided for enforcement by a 12-member State Ethics Commission, but the final version leaves enforcement to the district attorneys. All statements required by this *ethics legislation* become matters of public record and can be examined by any interested person.

Concerning registration and reporting of activities designed to influence legislation, H.B. 2 is another reform measure that was passed on the last day of the 63rd Legislature's regular session. This law requires *lobby registration* of a person who spends more than $200 in a calendar quarter (not including the cost of his food, travel, and lodging) for "communicating directly with one or more members of the legislative or executive branch to influence legislation." Also required to register are persons who are paid for lobbying activities or who lobby as part of their regular employment. The full name and address of every person paying a membership fee or making a contribution of more than $500 a year to a lobbyist or his employer must also be reported. Periodic *lobby reports* must include a list of supported or opposed legislation as well as a breakdown of expenditures into the following categories: postage and telegraph; publication and advertising; travel and fees; entertainment; gifts, loans, and political contributions; and other expenditures. Registration and reporting required by this law are made to the secretary of state; enforcement is the responsibility of the attorney general, county attorneys, and district attorneys. Significantly, this lobby control measure provides coverage of lobby activity throughout the year, with monthly reports filed during a legislative session and quarterly reports made thereafter.

Both H.B. 3 and H.B. 6 were enacted for the purpose of preventing unnecessary secrecy in government. The former requires that meetings of the legislature, its committees, and other bodies associated with the legislature, must be open to the public under most circumstances; and the same bill extends this *open meetings rule* to city councils, county commissioners courts, school boards, and governing bodies of other political subdivisions. Similarly, H.B. 6 lays down an *open records rule* that offices within the legislative and executive branches of the state government, along with those of units of local governments (excluding the judiciary at all levels), shall normally be open to the public and that copies of such materials are to be made available at reasonable rates.

House Bills 7, 8, and 9 deal with the office of the speaker. The first of these, which would have prevented a speaker from succeeding himself for a second term, was declared to be unconstitutional by the attorney general. This ruling held that such a change could be effected only through a constitutional amendment. Both H.B. 8 and H.B. 9 were enacted. The former requires that a candidate for the office of speaker must report to the secretary of state all loans and contributions of money, services, and other things of value received on behalf of his campaign. Also to be reported are the names and addresses of lenders and contributors, and of persons to whom payment in excess of $10 is made. Corporations and unions are prohibited from lending or giving money or any other thing of value, either directly or indirectly, to aid or to defeat a candidate for the speakership. H.B. 9 defines the crime of *legislative bribery*. Under the terms of this law it is a felony offense for anyone to attempt to influence a member of the House or a candidate for the House in voting for a speaker by promising particular committee or subcommittee assignments or appointment to a chairmanship or vice-chairmanship of a committee or subcommittee. Also prohibited are attempts to influence the election of a speaker through promises or threats with regard to any legislation or appropriation, employment for any person, or economic benefit to any person.

H.B. 4, the Campaign Reporting and Disclosure Act, provided a significant reform by way of an amendment to the *Texas Election Code.* It tightens up the *Code* and provides better safeguards against fraudulent or otherwise undesirable campaign activities. This measure is considered in more detail in Chapter 2.

Of Daniel's nine reform bills, only H.B. 5 was defeated in the Senate. This measure sought to limit conference committees to the function of reconciling differences between House and Senate versions of a bill. Thus a conference committee would have been prohibited from changing or omitting any text not in disagreement or adding text on any matter not included in either the House or Senate version. Similar restrictions were outlined with regard to items of appropriation and tax items. In spite of a long history of flagrant abuse of power by conference committees during prior legislatures, a majority of the senators insisted that the matter had been adequately covered by House and Senate rules in the 63rd Legislature and need not be made the subject of a statute.[7]

NOTES

1. For a description of a comprehensive model designed along these lines by Professors Luther G. Hagard and Samuel B. Hamlett, see August O. Spain, "State Legislative Redistricting in Texas," in *Legislative Redistricting in Texas,* edited by John M. Claunch, Arnold Foundation Monographs XIII (Dallas, Tex.: Southern Methodist University, 1965), pp. 1-14; detailed maps of districts proposed by Hagard and Hamlett are included in this publication.
2. As indicated in Tables 3-1 and 3-2, the flotorial district was a device for providing representation for a county with insufficient population to warrant a representative and which did not border other counties to which it could be joined for the purpose of making the required total. Such a county was combined with a neighboring county which already elected one or more representatives but which had a population surplus in excess of the apportionment ideal. All the voters in the resulting flotorial district then participated in the election of a single representative. For example, under the 1965 districting act, Kleberg County (population 30,053) was joined to Nueces County (population 221,573 and forming District 45 with 3 representatives) for the purpose of creating a flotorial district (District 46f) representing all of the voters of both counties.
3. See William E. Oden, "Tenure and Turnover in Recent Texas Legislatures," *Southwestern Social Science Quarterly,* XL (March 1965), 371-374.
4. This terminology has been employed by Wilbourn E. Benton, *Texas: Its Government and Politics,* 3rd ed. (Englewood Cliffs, N.J.: Prentice-Hall, 1972), pp. 130-136.
5. Each regular session brings forth an avalanche of bills and resolutions. Concerning the 63rd Legislature, the Texas Legislative Council reported 1,749 bills introduced in the House and 997 introduced in the Senate. Three hundred of the latter and 388 of the former passed both houses and were sent to the governor, who vetoed 30.

6. For more detailed description of the lawmaking process, see Dick Smith, *How Bills Become Laws in Texas,* 2nd ed. (Austin, Tex.: Institute of Public Affairs, University of Texas, 1970).
7. The June 15, 1973, issue of the *Texas Observer* is devoted to end-of-the-session activities of the 63rd Legislature.

KEY TERMS AND CONCEPTS

representative government
regular session
special session
unicameral
bicameral
redistricting
Legislative Redistricting Board
ex officio
Baker v. *Carr*
Reynolds v. *Sims*
Kilgarlin v. *Martin*
multi-member district
single-member district
gerrymandering
Kilgarlin v. *Hill*
Smith v. *Craddick*
White v. *Regester*
contingency expense allowance
per diem allowance
president of the Senate
president pro tempore
speaker
pledge card
limited seniority system
standing committee
interim study committee
constituent power
Legislative Budget Board
legislative investigation
impeachment
simple resolution
concurrent resolution
joint resolution
bill
local bill
special bill
private bill
general bill
first reading
caption
second reading
emergency clause
third reading
conference committee
veto
lobbying
ethics legislation
lobby registration
lobby report
open meeting rule
open records rule
legislative bribery
Campaign Reporting and Disclosure Act of 1973

HERC FICKLEN FROM THE DALLAS NEWS

Selected Readings

3-1
REDISTRICTING THE TEXAS HOUSE OF REPRESENTATIVES, 1971-1973
William C. Adams

Redistricting of a state legislature seems guaranteed to generate political fireworks. These controversies assume special significance because redistricting influences the composition of subsequent legislatures and thus may determine the fate of future issues. From 1971 to 1973 the struggle to redistrict the Texas House of Representatives involved some remarkable battles in the Legislature, in state courts, and finally in the Supreme Court of the United States. Two questions will be considered: Through what process were the new 1972 districts created? What was the political impact of these new districts?

This previously unpublished article is based on a paper the author presented March 22, 1973, at the annual meeting of the Southwestern Political Science Association in Dallas, Texas.

The U.S. Supreme Court's rulings in *Reynolds* v. *Sims,* 337 U.S. 533 (1964), and in later cases have required that population figures generally supersede other factors in the drawing of new districts. Population equality among representative districts was held to be a right under the U.S. Constitution; it cannot be subject to the whims of legislatures. So the 1970 census determined the thrust of necessary districting changes and provided the framework within which redistricting conflicts would be fought.

Since the previous census in 1960, important shifts had occurred in the relative distribution of population throughout Texas. Gains in the proportionate share of the state's population were concentrated in the North Texas area around Dallas and Fort Worth, in the Harris County (Houston) area, and in a Central Texas corridor from San Antonio to Austin to Killeen. From the beginning it was apparent that increases in representation for these booming regions would have to be granted largely at the expense of parts of West and South Texas as well as scattered, medium-sized cities which lost population during the 1960s (e.g., Abilene, Amarillo, Beaumont, Harlingen, Port Arthur, Waco, and Wichita Falls). Changes indicated by 1970 population data were not minor; for example, the four counties containing Houston, Dallas, San Antonio, and Fort Worth together deserved about ten new House seats. Before examining the 62nd Legislature's response to its redistricting responsibility,.two crucial issues should be noted: county lines and multi-member districts.

The U.S. Supreme Court's "one man, one vote" standard requires that districts be substantially equal in population to the ideal district (state's population divided by the number of seats). Texas' 1970 population was 11,196,730. To have 150 equally populated districts, each would have the ideal population of 74,645. So if, for example, the largest district contained 78,377 people (5% above the ideal) and the smallest had 70,913 (5% below the ideal), there would be a "maximum deviation" or "variance" of 10%.

Article III, Section 26, of the Texas Constitution of 1876 specifies that a House district is to consist of one entire county or several entire counties, and does not permit the division of a county in order to join a segment of it with other counties to form a district. But to minimize the population differences among districts and thus comply with Supreme Court rulings, in the 1960's Texas had been forced to start selectively violating this provision in the state constitution. Still, as one Texas Attorney General put it, counties were to be split "only to the extent necessary to carry out the mandate of the Supreme Court." Certain types of county splitting were viewed as greater departures from the spirit of the Texas Constitution than were others. This problem of drawing equal districts which bisect few counties was aggravated by a widespread uncertainty as to the amount of population disparity among districts which the Supreme Court would tolerate. Most people agreed that districts which varied as much as 20% or 30% from the ideal would be unacceptable—but what about 5% or 10%?

A second area of debate centered around multi-member districts. Traditionally, if a county had two or more representatives, they filed for "places" and ran "at large" in a countywide multi-member district. Although urbanization in

Texas resulted in metropolitan counties with as many as fifteen seats, the Legislature had never bothered to carve up such counties into single-member election districts. Instead, the custom of multi-member districts was continued. One variation was that in 1967 three multi-member districts were employed for Harris County; other major multi-member districts remained countywide. Occasionally, multi-member districts involved two or three counties.

Advocates of this system of multi-member districts contended that it (1) promoted strong, united, civic-minded urban delegations and (2) prevented petty, boss-dominated, "ward-style" politics. Large multi-member districts generally worked to favor the election of conservative Democrats. Opponents of multi-member districts, on the other hand, argued that this system (1) minimized competition by necessitating huge campaign expenditures, (2) made some districts so large that representatives could not be genuinely responsive to their constituents, and (3) denied representation to relatively large groups which still might constitute minorities countywide. Clearly, single-member districts would enhance the prospects of Republican, liberal Democrat, Negro, and Mexican-American candidates.

Reverberations of the Sharpstown State Bank scandal, including dramatic challenges to Speaker Gus Mutscher and the House leadership, provided the setting for redistricting in the tense 62nd Legislature. All major committees were packed with allies of the Speaker, and the House Committee on Congressional and Legislative Districts was no exception. The chairman of the redistricting committee was Delwin Jones of Lubbock, a loyal Mutscher supporter.

A small group of Republicans and liberal Democrats championed single-member districts; but, without support on the House floor, their efforts produced little except press releases. So while controversy on many other matters boiled throughout the regular session in 1971, redistricting simmered quietly until the closing hours. Then, late in May, only four days before adjournment, Rep. Jones unveiled House Bill 783. The ensuing furor over redistricting climaxed the turbulent five-month period.

H.B. 783 continued multi-member districts in urban counties, but newspaper headlines were derived from another aspect of the bill. Critics charged that the plan was an act of desperation designed to salvage the political fortunes of Gus Mutscher by "purging" his opponents through blatant gerrymandering. This "mutschermandering" put many members of the reform coalition known as "the Dirty Thirty" into districts with other incumbents; in Central Texas, for example, three enemies of the Speaker were thrown together in the same district. At the time, Jones insisted that such matchings had been unavoidable. Later, however, he was quoted as saying that he had done his "dead-level best to eliminate liberal House members," that the Dirty Thirty was a bunch of "nobodies" who just "wanted something to bellyache about," and that he hoped he had "made it impossible for some of those people to get re-elected."[1]

Through hours of bitter and prolonged debate, the Mutscher forces defeated repeated attempts to thwart their proposal. On final passage, H.B. 783 received 90 "yeas," 51 "nays," and 1 "present not voting." A tradition of mutual non-interference in the other house's apportionment bill protected the measure in the Senate, and Governor Smith signed it.

Republican Representative Tom Craddick's district was Midland County. Under the Mutscher-Jones plan, Midland County was split: half was in a district stretching eastward to Abilene; the remainder was in a district that extended as far south as the Mexican border. Craddick and other Republicans brought suit in a state district court. They argued that in twenty-three instances counties such as Midland had been bisected unnecessarily. District Judge Herman Jones of Austin agreed; and, on appeal, the Texas Supreme Court ruled unanimously that since the county splitting had not improved population equality among the districts, H.B. 783 constituted an unjustifiable violation of the Texas Constitution (*Smith* v. *Craddick,* 471 S.W. 2d 375 [1971]).

The Texas judiciary has usually been self-restraining, that is, reluctant to void acts of the Legislature. Never before had the state courts thrown out an apportionment statute, so no one was quite sure what the next step should be. Eventually, the Texas Supreme Court decided that the Legislative Redistricting Board, which had never been used, was the appropriate agency to design the new House districts (*Mauzy* v. *Legislative Redistricting Board,* 471 S.W. 2d 570 [1971]). Created by a 1948 constitutional amendment, the five-member, *ex officio* Board is charged with redistricting the state in the event the Legislature does not act during the first regular session following each decennial federal census.

In the fall of 1971, the Legislative Redistricting Board produced a new districting arrangement for the Texas House. This plan, drawn under the direction of Lieutenant Governor Ben Barnes, avoided the county-cutting errors of H.B. 783 and provided single-member districts for Harris County. For the first time, multimember districts had been abolished in a metropolitan Texas county. Nonetheless, many people were not satisfied; they wanted 150 single-member districts.

Consequently, several suits were filed, this time in federal court, against the Board's redistricting plan. Four suits were heard together before a three-judge panel in Austin in January, 1972.[2] These judges quickly decided that multimember districts diluted the votes of Dallas Negroes and San Antonio Mexican-Americans in violation of the "equal protection" clause of the Fourteenth Amendment (*Graves* v. *Barnes,* 343 F. Supp. 704 [1972]). For relief, the court ordered immediate implementation of single-member district plans for Dallas and Bexar counties. (For the 1972 elections, the court suspended the requirement that a candidate must reside in his district; county residency was sufficient.) Furthermore, the court decided that the 9.9% maximum deviation among the districts did not satisfy the "one man, one vote" standard. Having ordered single-member districts in Dallas and Bexar counties, the court permitted 1972 elections under the remainder of the Board's plan; however, the federal judges directed the Legislature to redistrict so as to reduce population disparities by the end of June, 1973.

The U.S. Supreme Court had refused the state's request to stay the implementation of the lower court's decision until the Supreme Court itself could hear the case on appeal. Thus, the 1972 elections became the first in Texas' history with representatives elected from single-member districts in metropolitan counties. Dallas and Bexar counties, using the court-drawn districts, and Harris County, with the Redistricting Board's districts, soon experienced some interesting political developments.

Single-member districts in Texas' three largest counties brought changes in both the election contests and in the type of winners. Multi-member districts had produced fairly low levels of competition in Democratic party primaries, and virtually no competition in Republican primaries. Drastically reducing campaign costs and creating winnable Republican seats, single-member districts prompted more people to seek nomination. In fact, over twice as many primary candidates per seat filed in 1972 as had filed in 1968 or 1970. Another aspect of increased competition was that in 1972 not one incumbent in these three counties was unopposed for re-election. Previously, incumbents were often without any opposition in primary and general elections.

An exceptionally high proportion of the incumbent representatives failed to run for re-election in 1972. While the stock fraud scandal is commonly cited as having instilled a reluctance among incumbents to face the public, another plausible factor was the radically different constituencies which had been created by single-member districts. Obvious differences between their former and their prospective constituencies must have discouraged many office-holders from making re-election bids.

In Dallas, for years, the conservative Democratic establishment had successfully fielded and elected a slate of candidates. With the introduction of single-member districts, the opportunity for such slating activity was effectively destroyed. Breaking up large multi-member districts into small constituencies permitted the election of candidates with distinctive partisan, ethnic, and ideological characteristics. Previously, their supporters had constituted submerged minorities in countywide constituencies.

Indeed the new composition of delegations sent to the 63rd Legislature represented the most obvious impact of single-member districts. Predictions of greater "minority" representation were fulfilled. Republican representation from these three metropolitan counties was more than doubled by the 1972 elections. Dallas increased from 1 to 7 its number of GOP House members, Bexar from 0 to 2, and Harris from 6 to 7. Only 2 blacks, 1 each from Dallas and Houston, had served in the 62nd Legislature. For the 63rd, that number jumped to 8, drawing 1 from San Antonio, 3 from Dallas, and 4 from Houston. Although no additional Mexican-American representatives were elected from Dallas (0) or Houston (1), San Antonio increased from 1 to 4. Also, it was apparent that the total number of liberal Democrats representing these counties increased with the implementation of single-member districts. Under the new system, third-party candidacies, such as those of La Raza Unida, will probably have greater chances of success; although none were elected in 1972.

Together, Harris (23), Dallas (18), and Bexar (11) counties fully elect 52 representatives; parts of Harris and Bexar counties are joined to other counties for the purpose of electing two additional representatives. These 54 representatives constitute over one-third of the House membership. Most of the changes which occurred in the composition of the Texas House after the 1972 elections can be attributed to the new delegations that these three counties elected under the new single-member district arrangement. Well over two-thirds of Harris, Dallas, and Bexar representatives in the 63rd Legislature were freshmen—almost twice the proportion of first-term members chosen from the rest of the state. The only blacks in the Texas House were those elected from these three counties. All of the new 1972 Republican representatives resided in one of these three largest counties.

On June 18, 1973, in *White* v. *Regester,* the U.S. Supreme Court ruled on the state's appeal of the federal district court's decision. Part of that decision was overruled and part was sustained. By a 6-3 vote, the high court rejected the lower court's conclusion that the 9.9 per cent maximum deviation between Texas House districts was too great to be tolerated under the Equal Protection Clause of the Fourteenth Amendment. Speaking for the majority, Justice Byron White asserted that state reapportionments "are not subject to the same strict standards applicable to reapportionment of congressional seats. . . ." In explaining this position, White wrote,

> We do not consider relatively minor population deviations among state legislative districts to substantially dilute the weight of individual votes in the larger districts so as to deprive individuals in these districts of fair and effective representation. . . . [W]e cannot glean an equal protection violation from the single fact that two legislative districts in Texas differ from one another by as much as 9.9 per cent, when compared to the ideal district.

Thus, there would be no need for another statewide House redistricting to reduce population differences among districts.

Turning to the issue of multi-member districts, White stated that they are not necessarily unconstitutional; however, the Supreme Court unanimously upheld the district court's action in creating single-member districts for Dallas and Bexar counties, where there was evidence that multi-member districts had been "used invidiously to cancel out or minimize the voting strength of racial groups." With regard to the situation in Dallas, White took note of the lower court's finding that only two black representatives had been elected in that county since the Reconstruction era and that both had been selected as candidates by the Dallas Committee for Responsible Government, "a white-dominated organization that is in effective control of Democratic Party candidate-slating in Dallas County." Continuing with an account of the district court's findings, he observed, "That organization . . . did not need the support of the Negro community to win elections in the county, and it did not therefore exhibit good-faith concern for the political and other needs and aspirations of the Negro community." Taking notice of the fact that as late as 1970 the Dallas Committee for Responsible Government was using racial campaign tactics in defeating candidates who had overwhelming black support, White found no reason for interfering with the district court's judgment regarding Dallas.

As for the situation in San Antonio, the Supreme Court found that the Mexican-Americans of Bexar County constitute "an identifiable class" for application of the Equal Protection Clause of the Fourteenth Amendment. White noted that most Mexican-Americans have resided in San Antonio's West Side barrio with poor housing, low income, and high rates of unemployment. As for the political consequences of discrimination, restrictive voter-registration procedures, and multi-member districting, he presented the findings of the district court:

> The residual impact of this history reflected itself in the fact that Mexican American voting strength remained very poor in the county and that, although they now occupy a plurality in Bexar County, only five Mexican Americans since 1880 have served in the Texas Legislature from that county. Of these, only two were from the barrio area. The district court also concluded that the Bexar County Legislative Delegation was insufficiently responsive to Mexican American interests.

Thus the U.S. Supreme Court endorsed the finding of the lower court that multi-member districts in Bexar County "invidiously excluded Mexican Americans from political life."

As a result of *White* v. *Regester,* the issue of a 9.9 per cent population disparity among Texas House districts was laid to rest; likewise, the question of single-member districts for Bexar and Dallas counties was resolved. On the other hand, the judicial door was opened for litigation attacking the nine remaining multi-member districts: Tarrant County (Fort Worth) with 9 seats; El Paso (El Paso) and Travis (Austin) counties each with 4 seats; Nueces (Corpus Christi) and Jefferson (Beaumont-Port Arthur) each with 3 seats; and McLennan (Waco), Galveston (Galveston), and Lubbock (Lubbock) counties each with 2 seats. A suit was immediately filed against Tarrant county's especially vulnerable multi-member district. Shortly thereafter, suits were filed for the purpose of obtaining single-member districts for the other eight counties having multi-member districts. Whether they can withstand judicial scrutiny or will be divided into single-member districts became an important subject for future court battles. Given their political histories and minority populations, multi-member districts for some or all of these counties may soon be ordered.

One final implication deserves mention. Not only do single-member districts advance Texas toward genuine two-party status by the immediate election of more Republicans to the House; these districts also promote a liberal-conservative realignment of the Texas electorate and the two parties.

Traditionally, conservative Democrats have owed much of their domination of statewide offices to spring primary victories made possible through the ballots of many people who later voted Republican in the fall general election. An enlarged and meaningful Republican primary, drawing conservative votes away from the Democratic primary, certainly would help liberals secure Democratic nominations. By increasing the importance of Republican primaries, single-member districts have just that effect. In 1972, a Republican House nomination became much more valuable; for the first time, there were even some metropolitan districts where winning the GOP primary was tantamount to winning the general election. If more conservatives defect to the Republican primary, the balance should be tipped toward more liberal victories in the Democratic primary; this development, most politicos are convinced, would then further accelerate the movement of Texas conservatives into the Republican Party.

NOTES

1. *Temple Daily Telegram,* July 31, 1971; cf. *Austin American,* August 3, 1971.
2. *Graves* v. *Barnes,* dealing with Texas Senate districting, was the lead case; *Regester* v. *Bullock, Mariott* v. *Smith,* and *Archer* v. *Smith* involved Texas House districting. The opinion for all four suits is cited as *Graves* v. *Barnes* (1972). On appeal to the U.S. Supreme Court, the Texas House districting litigation was styled *White* v. *Regester,* 93 S. Ct. 2332 (1973).

3-2
BIOGRAPHICAL DATA FOR MEMBERS OF THE 63RD LEGISLATURE OF THE STATE OF TEXAS, 1973-74
Lyle C. Brown

With the exception of scattered newspaper articles and election campaign materials, there is an almost complete lack of published information concerning individual members of the Texas Legislature. Although it is generally known that most legislators are male Democrats and that many are lawyers, exact data on these characteristics and others are not available for classroom use. In order to fill this gap, an effort has been made to compile data that will help to reveal significant characteristics of members of the 63rd Legislature. A questionnaire was sent to each legislator; all of them responded. When compilation was completed, copies of data tables were sent to each senator and representative. Response on the part of legislators, both with regard to providing corrections and to making comments on the accuracy and utility of the data, suggests that the final revision constitutes a reliable compilation that can be used with good effect by instructors and students. Hopefully, this data will help readers to visualize each legislator as a human being who has been the subject of specific environmental and cultural influences as a result of his place of residence, occupation, educational experience, denominational affiliation, and legislative tenure. Four students gave invaluable assistance in the compilation of data: Baldemar Alarcón (Texas A & I University) and Judy Johnson, Vicki Stark, and Elizabeth Fonseca (Baylor University). [See table of biographical data, pp. 166-176.]

3-3
HE CALLED HER HIS MISTRESS
Thomas Wright

There was a time in the history of this democracy when Black women were forced to smile coyly and swallow their pride whenever a white man decided he wanted to hurl a racist-sexist joke in their direction. The white man's preoccupation with the Black woman's sexual mystique has long been the undertone in much backwoods

From *Forward Times* (Houston, Texas), April 21, 1973, p. 8B. Reprinted by permission.

PART 1 *Senate*

Dist./Place	Name	Political Party	Residence	Date of Birth	Place of Birth	Occupation	College and/or University Attended	Religious Affiliation	Continued Election to Senate since Election Year	Years Prior Legislative Service	Member of House (H) and/or Senate (S) of Former Legislatures
1	A. M. Aikin, Jr.	D	Paris	10/09/05	Aikin Grove, Tex.	Attorney/ Merchant	Cumberland	Methodist	1936	40	H:43–44; S: 45–62
2	Peyton McKnight, Jr.	D	Tyler	12/10/24	Alba, Tex.	Independent oil operator	East Texas/Texas A&M/UT, Austin	Episcopal	1972	2	H: 51
3	Don Adams	D	Jasper	12/18/38	Jasper, Tex.	Attorney	Baylor	Methodist	1972	4	H: 61–62
4	*D. Roy Harrington	D	Port Arthur	11/12/07	Indian Bayou, La.	Retired refinery technician/ Co-owner of drugstore	none	Methodist	1958	16	H: 55–57; S: 58–62
5	*William T. (Bill) Moore	D	Bryan	04/09/18	Wheelock, Tex.	Attorney	Texas A&M/ UT, Austin	Baptist	1948	26	H: 50; S: 51–62
6	James P. (Jim) Wallace	D	Houston	04/08/28	Sidon, Ark.	Attorney	Arkansas/Houston	Baptist	1970	2	S: 62
7	*Robert A. (Bob) Gammage	D	Houston	03/13/38	Houston, Tex.	Attorney/Law school professor	Del Mar/Corpus Christi/Sam Houston/UT, Austin	Baptist	1972	2	H: 62
8	*O. H. (Ike) Harris	R	Dallas	06/05/32	Denton, Tex.	Attorney	North Texas/SMU	Methodist	1967	7	H: 58; S: 60–62
9	*Ronald (Ron) Clower	D	Garland	10/01/40	Stamps, Ark.	Attorney	SMU/UT, Austin	Episcopal	1972	0	
10	William C. (Bill) Meier	D	Euless	08/01/40	Waco, Tex.	Attorney	Tarleton/UT, Austin	Presbyterian	1972	0	
11	Chet Brooks	D	Pasadena	08/18/35	Prescott, Ariz.	Businessman	San Angelo/San Jacinto/UT, Austin	Methodist	1966	10	H: 58–59; S: 60–62
12	Mrs. Betty Andujar	R	Fort Worth	11/06/12	Harrisburg, Pa.	Housewife	Wilson	Presbyterian	1972	0	
13	*Walter H. Mengden, Jr.	R	Houston	10/25/26	Houston, Tex.	Attorney	UT, Austin	Catholic	1972	2	H: 62
14	Charles F. Herring	D	Austin	06/01/14	McGregor, Tex.	Attorney	UT, Austin	Catholic	1956	16	S: 55–62
15	*Jack Ogg	D	Houston	09/07/33	Kansas City, Mo.	Attorney	Houston/South Texas College of Law	Episcopal	1972	6	H: 60–62
16	*Bill Braeklein	D	Dallas	12/20/20	Los Angeles, Calif.	Attorney	SMU	Presbyterian	1972	6	H: 60–62

17	*A. R. (Babe) Schwartz	D	Galveston	07/17/26	Galveston, Tex.	Attorney	Texas A&M/ UT, Austin	Jewish	1960	17	H: 54–55; S: 56–62
18	*William N. (Bill) Patman	D	Ganado	03/26/27	Texarkana, Tex.	Attorney	UT, Austin	Methodist	1960	12	S: 57–62
19	*Glenn H. Kothmann	D	San Antonio	05/30/28	San Antonio, Tex.	Real estate/ Cattle	Texas A&M	Methodist	1970	12	H: 55, 57–59, 61; S: 62
20	*Michael (Mike) McKinnen	D	Corpus Christi	06/12/39	Los Angeles, Calif.	President, KIII-TV	Redlands/Harvard	Methodist	1972	0	
21	John A. Traeger	D	Seguin	07/06/21	Wichita Falls, Tex.	Retail merchant/ Real estate	Texas Lutheran	Methodist	1972	10	H: 58–62
22	*Tom Creighton	D	Mineral Wells	02/26/27	Mineral Wells, Tex.	Attorney	UT, Austin	Baptist	1960	12	S: 57–62
23	Oscar Mauzy	D	Dallas	11/09/26	Houston, Tex.	Attorney	UT, Austin	Unitarian	1966	6	S: 60–62
24	*Grant Jones	D	Abilene	11/11/22	Abilene, Tex.	Insurance agent	SMU/Pennsylvania	Methodist	1972	8	H: 59–62
25	W. E. (Pete) Snelson	D	Midland	03/28/23	Grandfalls, Tex.	Advertising executive	UT, El Paso/ Northwestern	Presbyterian	1964	8	H: 57; S: 59, 61–62
26	Nelson W. Wolff	D	San Antonio	10/27/40	San Antonio, Tex.	Attorney/Vice president, building supplies company	St. Mary's/UT, Austin/Sam Houston/ Houston/Texas Southmost	Methodist	1972	2	H: 62
27	Raul L. Longoria	D	Edinburg	02/22/21	La Grulla, Tex.	Attorney	UT, Austin	Catholic	1972	10	H: 57, 59–62
28	H. J. (Doc) Blanchard	D	Lubbock	12/21/23	Denison, Tex.	Attorney	Texas Tech/SMU	Methodist	1962	14	H: 55–56; S: 58–62
29	*H. Tati Santiesteban	D	El Paso	11/03/34	El Paso, Tex.	Attorney	New Mexico Military Inst./UT, Austin	Catholic	1972	6	H: 60–62
30	Jack Hightower	D	Vernon	09/06/26	Memphis, Tex.	Attorney	Baylor	Baptist	1964	10	H: 53; S: 59–62
31	*Max Sherman	D	Amarillo	01/19/35	Viola, Ark.	Attorney	Baylor/UT, Austin	Presbyterian	1970	2	S: 62

*Serving first half of 4-year term; other senators drew 2-year terms at the beginning of the regular session.

PART 2 *House of Representatives*

Dist./ Place	Name	Political Party	Residence	Date of Birth	Place of Birth	Occupation	College and/or University Attended	Religious Affiliation	Continued Election to House since Election Year	Years Prior Legislative Service	Member of House (H) and/or Senate (S) of Former Legislature
1	Ed Howard	D	Texarkana	04/13/37	Hot Springs, Ark.	Discount stores executive	Abilene Christian/ SMU	Ch. of Christ	1968	4	H: 61-62
2	Doyce R. Lee	D	Naples	09/02/40	Marietta, Tex.	Attorney	Texarkana/East Texas/UT, Austin	Baptist	1972	0	
3	Ben Z. Grant	D	Marshall	10/25/39	De Ridder, La.	Attorney	Panola/Northwestern La./ UT, Austin	Ch. of Christ	1970	2	H: 62
4	Roy Blake	D	Nacogdoches	03/29/28	Nacogdoches, Tex.	Insurance agency owner/ Owner & mgr. of retail shoe store	Texas A&M/ Stephen F. Austin	Methodist	1972	0	
5	Herman Adams, Jr.	D	Silsbee	07/16/42	Kirbyville, Tex.	Public school administrator	UT, Austin	Methodist	1972	0	
6	Arthur (Buddy) Temple	D	Diboll	02/26/42	Texarkana, Ark.	President, real estate company	UT, Austin	Episcopalian	1972	0	
7-1	Terry Doyle	D	Port Arthur	01/14/39	Port Arthur, Tex.	Attorney	La. Tech/UT, Austin	Catholic	1970	2	H: 62
7-2	Pike Powers	D	Beaumont	05/01/41	Houston, Tex.	Attorney	Lamar Tech/SMU/ UT, Austin	Presbyterian	1972	1	H: 62
7-3	Carl A. Parker	D	Port Arthur	08/06/34	Port Arthur, Tex.	Attorney	UT, Austin	Baptist	1962	10	H: 58-62
8	Wayne Peveto	D	Orange	04/05/39	Orange, Tex.	Attorney	Sam Houston/ Houston	Baptist	1972	0	
9	George L. Preston	D	Paris	12/18/29	Lamar Co., Tex.	Attorney	East Texas/South Texas College of Law	Ch. of Christ	1972	4	H: 56-57
10	James Dee Cole	D	Greenville	11/03/37	Cumby, Tex.	Vice president, telephone company	UT, Austin	Methodist	1960	12	H: 57-62
11	William (Bill) Hollowell	D	Grand Saline	07/22/28	Grand Saline, Tex.	Attorney	Baylor/UT, Austin	Baptist	1972	10	H: 55-59
12	Billy H. Williamson	D	Tyler	11/14/27	Nachitoches, La.	Attorney	Baylor	Baptist	1965	8	H: 59-62

13	John Allen	D	Longview	12/16/26	Cunningham, Tex.	Radio station executive	Paris Jr/UT, Austin	Ch. of Christ	1959	14	H: 56-62
14	Fred Head	D	Troup	02/22/39	Troup, Tex.	Attorney	Tyler Jr/SMU	Methodist	1966	6	H: 60-62
15	Emmett H. Whitehead	D	Rusk	10/09/25	Cisco, Tex.	Newspaper publisher/ Radio station and TV cable co. owner	Sam Houston	Methodist	1972	0	
16	Price Daniel, Jr.	D	Liberty	06/08/41	Austin, Tex.	Attorney	Baylor	Methodist	1968	4	H: 61-62
17	Ed R. Watson	D	Deer Park	07/20/20	Wallisville, Tex.	Refinery worker/President Chem. & Atomic Workers local union	Houston/San Jacinto Jr.	Baptist	1972	0	
18	Jimmie C. Edwards III	D	Conroe	08/06/48	Cleveland, Tex.	USMC, retired	Sam Houston	Baptist	1972	0	
19-1	Ed Harris	D	Galveston	05/19/20	Trinity, Tex.	Attorney	Southwestern/ Wisconsin	Methodist	1962	10	H: 58-62
19-2	Andrew Z. Baker	D	Galveston	10/22/19	Bienville Parish, La.	Attorney	South Texas College of Law	Unitarian	1972	0	
20	Neil Caldwell	D	Alvin	11/13/29	Gulf, Tex.	Attorney	UT, Austin	Baptist	1960	13	H: 56-62
21	Joe A. Hubenak	D	Rosenberg	07/02/37	Frenstat, Tex.	Accountant	Houston	Catholic	1968	4	H: 61-62
22	Ben Munson	D	Denison	07/25/42	Sherman, Tex.	Attorney	Notre Dame/UT, Austin	Catholic	1972	0	
23	Bill Sullivant	D	Gainesville	01/19/40	Gainesville, Tex.	Attorney	UT, Austin	Baptist	1972	0	
24	Bob Hendricks	D	McKinney	10/02/25	Farmersville, Tex.	Attorney	SMU	Methodist	1966	6	H: 60-62
25	Walt Parker	D	Denton	07/23/17	Ft. Worth, Tex.	Building contractor/ Rancher/ National Football League official	North Texas/ TCU	Methodist	1968	4	H: 61-62
(no district 26)											
27	Forrest Green	D	Corsicana	12/11/21	Kirven, Tex.	Rancher	UT, Arlington	Baptist	1972	0	
28	Bill Presnal	D	Bryan	04/26/32	Bryan, Tex.	Dairy farmer	Texas A&M	Methodist	1968	4	H: 61-62
29	Latham Boone III	D	Navasota	12/13/39	Navasota, Tex.	Attorney	Texas A&M/ South Texas College of Law	Episcopal	1972	0	
30	John Wilson	D	LaGrange	07/09/39	San Antonio, Tex.	Part owner retail western store & real estate business/Rancher	UT, Austin/ Southwest Texas	Baptist	1972	0	

31	Donald R. (Tom) Uher	D	Bay City	12/16/37	Bay City, Tex.	Attorney	Texas A&I/ UT, Austin	Presbyterian	1967	6	H: 60-62
32-1	Charles W. Evans	D	Hurst	02/19/39	Jacksonville, Fla.	Attorney	UT, Arlington/ SMU	Baptist	1972	0	
32-2	Bill Hilliard	D	Fort Worth	05/24/16	Martin, Tenn.	Insurance	SMU	Baptist	1970	2	H: 62
32-3	Winthrop Curtis (Bud) Sherman	D	Fort Worth	12/02/14	Melrose, Mass.	Public relations	Washington (St. Louis)	Episcopal	1964	8	H: 59-62
32-4	Gibson D. (Gib) Lewis	D	Fort Worth	08/22/36	Oletha, Tex.	President, Lewis Tape and Label Products	Sam Houston/ TCU	Ch. of Christ	1970	2	H: 62
32-5	Tom Schieffer	D	Fort Worth	10/04/47	Fort Worth, Tex.	Investments management	UT, Austin	Presbyterian	1972	0	
32-6	Joe Spurlock II	D	Fort Worth	01/29/38	Fort Worth, Tex.	Attorney	Texas A&M/ UT, Austin	Lutheran	1970	2	H: 62
32-7	David Finney	D	Fort Worth	09/29/33	Fort Worth, Tex.	Attorney	TCU/Chicago/ UT, Austin	Methodist	1962	10	H: 58-62
32-8	Ms. Chris Miller	D	Fort Worth	06/15/26	Boston, Mass.	Public relations consultant	Wheaton (Ill.)/ Mills/TCU	Unitarian	1972	0	
32-9	Doyle Willis	D	Fort Worth	08/18/08	Kaufman, Tex.	Attorney/ Rancher	UT, Austin/ Georgetown (Washington, D.C.)	Methodist	1972	18	H: 50-52, 61; S: 53-57
33	Charles C. (Kit) Cooke III	D	Cleburne	07/06/47	Cleburne, Tex.	Attorney	Baylor	Baptist	1972	0	
33-A	Robert E. Davis	R	Dallas	08/19/41	Fort Worth, Tex.	Attorney	Vanderbilt	Episcopal	1972	0	
33-B	A. J. (Al) Korioth	R	Dallas	12/06/28	Sherman, Tex.	Home builder	St. Edwards/ Austin College	Catholic	1972	0	
33-C	Samuel W. Hudson III	D	Dallas	11/06/40	Houston, Tex.	Attorney	Texas Southern	Methodist	1972	0	
33-D	Jerry Russell	D	Garland	02/07/37	Gorman, Tex.	Attorney	North Texas/ SMU	Baptist	1972	0	
33-E	Robert B. Maloney	R	Dallas	01/31/33	Dallas, Tex.	Attorney	SMU	Episcopal	1972	0	
33-F	Chris V. Semos	D	Dallas	06/02/36	Dallas, Tex.	Businessman/ Restaurateur	SMU	Gr. Orthodox	1966	6	H: 60-62
33-G	Richard S. Geiger	D	Dallas	02/21/36	Dallas, Tex.	Attorney	Texas A&M/SMU	Episcopal	1972	0	
33-H	Ben Atwell	D	Hutchins	08/04/15	Hutchins, Tex.	Attorney	UT, Austin	Christian	1950	22	H: 52-62
33-I	T. H. McDonald, Sr.	D	Mesquite	11/20/00	Bedias, Tex.	Real estate	Sam Houston/ UT, Austin	Baptist	1972	0	
33-J	James S. (Jim) Vecchio	D	Grand Prairie	10/28/31	Cleveland, Ohio	Attorney	Case-Western Reserve	Catholic	1972	0	
33-K	James A. Mattox	D	Dallas	08/29/43	Dallas, Tex.	Attorney	Baylor/SMU	Baptist	1972	0	
33-L	Joe Hawn	D	Dallas	05/08/15	Sherman, Tex.	Realtor	none	Baptist	1968	4	H: 61-62
33-M	Frank Gaston	R	Dallas	09/19/28	San Francisco, Calif.	Media consultant/Broadcast journalist	Stephen F. Austin/ Houston/SMU	Methodist	1972	0	

33-N	Paul B. Ragsdale	D	Dallas	01/14/45	Jacksonville, Tex.	Sociologist	UT, Austin	Methodist	1972	0	
33-O	Mrs. Eddie Bernice Johnson	D	Dallas	12/03/34	Waco, Tex.	Professional nurse/Personnel counselor	St. Mary's (Ind.)/TCU/North Texas/Texas Woman's	Baptist	1972	0	
33-P	Richard P. Reynolds	R	Richardson	09/23/27	Franklin Co., Ohio	Vice President, Ben Griffin Enterprises/Retail bookstore owner	Ohio State	Methodist	1972	0	
33-Q	E. Ray Hutchison	R	Dallas	09/16/32	Rockwall, Tex.	Attorney	SMU	Methodist	1972	0	
33-R	Fred J. Agnich	R	Dallas	07/19/13	Eveleth, Minn.	Independent investments	Minnesota	Presbyterian	1970	2	H: 62
34	Jerry (Nub) Donaldson	D	Gatesville	02/03/43	Gatesville, Tex.	Attorney	Baylor/UT, Austin	Baptist	1972	0	
35-1	Lane Denton	D	Bellmead	12/18/40	Waco, Tex.	Educator	Baylor/UT, Austin	Baptist	1970	2	H: 62
35-2	Lyndon Olson, Jr.	D	Waco	03/07/47	Waco, Tex.	Law student—clerk/Business interests	Baylor	Presbyterian	1972	0	
36	Daniel J. Kubiak	D	Rockdale	03/19/38	Reagan, Tex.	Publisher/Real estate developer/Author	UT, Austin/Midwestern	Catholic	1968	4	H: 61-62
37-1	Larry Bales	D	Austin	03/09/40	Kyle, Tex.	Attorney	UT, Austin	Baptist	1972	0	
37-2	Sarah R. Weddington	D	Austin	02/05/45	Abilene, Tex.	Attorney	McMurry/UT, Austin	Methodist	1972	0	
37-3	Don W. Cavness	D	Austin	04/22/28	San Antonio, Tex.	Real estate/Insurance	UT, Austin	Baptist	1962	10	H: 58-62
37-4	Wilson Foreman	D	Austin	08/30/26	Eastland, Tex.	Pool builder/Rancher/Excavation & concrete contractor	UT, Austin/Pan American	Baptist	1970	14	H: 55-60, 62
38	Bennie Bock II	D	New Braunfels	05/17/42	Lockhart, Tex.	Attorney	UT, Austin/St. Mary's	Episcopal	1972	0	
39	Tim Von Dohlen	D	Goliad	10/20/43	Cuero, Tex.	Attorney/Pharmacist/Rancher	UT, Austin	Catholic	1970	2	H: 62
40	Joe Wyatt	D	Bloomington	12/12/41	Victoria, Tex.	Auditor	UT, Austin	Catholic	1970	2	H: 62
41	Leroy J. Wieting	D	Portland	02/28/27	Runge, Tex.	Corporation executive	Texas A&I/Corpus Christi	Baptist	1962	10	H: 58-62
42	W. G. (Bill) Coody	D	Weatherford	05/08/34	Wallis, Tex.	College professor	Sam Houston/TCU	Methodist	1972	0	

43	Camm Lary, Jr.	D	Burnet	11/26/41	Blanco, Tex.	Attorney	Texas A&M/ UT, Austin	Ch. of Christ	1972	0	
44	John R. Bigham	D	Belton	07/05/38	Belton, Tex.	Construction contractor	Temple Jr./ Central Texas/ Mary Hardin-Baylor/Baylor	Baptist	1968	4	H: 61-62
45	John H. Poerner	D	Hondo	11/21/32	D'Hanis, Tex.	Banker/Rancher/ Land developer	St. Mary's	Catholic	1969	4	H: 61-62
(no district 46)											
47	Jon P. Newton	D	Beeville	06/04/41	Postville, Iowa	Attorney	UT, Austin	Methodist	1970	2	H: 62
48-1	L. DeWitt Hale	D	Corpus Christi	06/10/17	Caddo Mills, Tex.	Attorney	UT, Austin	Baptist	1964	20	H: 46, 53-57, 59-62
48-2	Carlos F. Truan	D	Corpus Christi	06/09/35	Kingsville, Tex.	Insurance agent	Texas A&I	Catholic	1968	4	H: 61-62
48-3	Joseph J. (Joe) Salem	D	Corpus Christi	12/29/20	Corpus Christi, Tex.	Jeweler/Real estate developer-builder	none	Catholic	1968	4	H: 61-62
49	Gregory Montoya	D	Elsa	01/23/17	Corpus Christi, Tex.	Farmer/Businessman/ University administrator	Texas A&M/ UT, Austin/ Texas A&I/ UCLA/Del Mar	Catholic	1972	2	H: 59
50	Henry Sánchez	D	Brownsville	05/15/31	San Benito, Tex.	Investments	St. Mary's	Catholic	1967	6	H: 60-62
51	Menton J. Murray	D	Harlingen	10/25/07	Dayton, Ohio	Attorney	UT, Austin/Rice	Catholic	1948	24	H: 51-62
52	Dave Allred	D	Wichita Falls	11/27/33	Austin, Tex.	Writer	TCU/Columbia	Christian	1966	6	H: 60-62
53	Charles A. Finnell	D	Holliday	09/16/43	Wichita Falls, Tex.	Attorney/ Oil producer	UT, Austin/ St. Mary's	Methodist	1966	6	H: 60-62
54	Joe Hanna	D	Breckenridge	05/19/20	Lawton, Okla.	Real estate	Tarleton/UT, Austin	Baptist	1970	2	H: 62
55	Lynn Nabers	D	Brownwood	03/31/40	Brownwood, Tex.	Attorney	North Texas/ Howard Payne/ Baylor	Baptist	1968	4	H: 61-62
56	James E. (Jim) Nugent	D	Kerrville	06/24/22	San Angelo, Tex.	Attorney/ Businessman	Texas A&M/UT, Austin	Baptist	1960	12	H: 57-62
57	William N. (Billy) Hall, Jr.	D	Laredo	08/20/40	Laredo, Tex.	Associate newspaper publisher	UT, Austin	Catholic	1972	0	
57-A	Frank Madla	D	San Antonio	01/23/37	San Antonio, Tex.	College instructor	St. Mary's/Our Lady of the Lake	Catholic	1972	0	
57-B	A. L. (Tony) Dramberger	D	San Antonio	05/18/08	Seguin, Tex.	Real estate broker	none	Catholic	1966	6	H: 60-62
57-C	Joseph F. Sage	R	San Antonio	08/24/20	Pottsville, Pa.	Attorney	Trinity/ St. Louis/Drake	Catholic	1972	0	

57-D	Ronald (Ron) Bird	D	San Antonio	12/10/36	St. Louis, Mo.	Food concessionaire	LSU/Washington (St. Louis)/ St. Mary's	Catholic	1972	0	
57-E	G. J. Sutton	D	San Antonio	06/22/09	San Antonio, Tex.	Mortician	Wilberforce	Baptist	1972	0	
57-F	James R. Nowlin	R	San Antonio	11/21/37	San Antonio, Tex.	Attorney	Trinity/UT, Austin	Presbyterian	1972	4	H: 60-61
57-G	Frank Lombardino	D	San Antonio	01/27/27	New York, N.Y.	Credit assoc. owner	San Antonio/ St. Mary's	Catholic	1966	6	H: 60-62
57-H	Wayland A. Simmons	D	San Antonio	08/15/40	San Antonio, Tex.	Attorney	Texas A&M/ St. Mary's	Baptist	1970	2	H: 62
57-I	R. L. (Bob) Vale	D	San Antonio	12/04/31	Roma, Tex.	Attorney	St. Mary's	Catholic	1964	8	H: 59-62
57-J	Joe L. Hernández	D	San Antonio	11/03/33	Galveston, Tex.	Attorney	Tulane/UT, Austin/St. Mary's	Catholic	1972	0	
57-K	Matt García	D	San Antonio	11/07/27	San Antonio, Tex.	Attorney	St. Mary's	Catholic	1972	0	
58	Terry Canales	D	Premont	11/13/45	Kingsville, Tex.	Attorney	St. Mary's	unaffiliated	1972	0	
59-1	Felix McDonald	D	Edinburg	09/13/12	Mexia, Tex.	Attorney	UT, Austin	Methodist	1972	8	H: 58-61
59-2	Lindsey Rodríguez	D	Hidalgo	05/21/32	McAllen, Tex.	Farmer/Real estate salesman	Texas A&I/Pan American	Methodist	1970	5	H: 57-58, 62
60	Tom Massey	D	San Angelo	03/05/31	San Angelo, Tex.	Attorney/ Cattle breeder	Texas A&M/ UT, Austin	Methodist	1972	0	
61	Elmer Martin	D	Colorado City	06/24/15	Colorado City, Tex.	Farmer/Rancher	Sul Ross/Howard County Jr.	Methodist	1972	0	
62	Frank W. Calhoun	D	Abilene	04/15/33	Houston, Tex.	Attorney	Texas Tech/UT, Austin	Methodist	1966	6	H: 60-62
63	Renal B. Rosson	D	Snyder	12/24/19	Stephens Co., Tex.	Attorney/ Rancher	Texas Tech/UT, Austin	Baptist	1958	14	H: 56-62
64	L. Dean Cobb	D	Dumas	05/16/36	Marlin, Tex.	Attorney	UT, Austin/ Baylor	Presbyterian	1968	4	H: 61-62
65	Bryan Poff, Jr.	D	Amarillo	12/24/37	Fort Worth, Tex.	Attorney	TCU/UT, Austin	Baptist	1970	2	H: 62
66	Phil Cates	D	Pampa	01/06/47	Pampa, Tex.	Cabot Corp., oil & gas div., accounting dept.	West Texas	Baptist	1970	2	H: 62
67	Ben Bynum	D	Amarillo	04/16/43	Amarillo, Tex.	Director of operations, printing and publications firm	UT, Austin	Presbyterian	1970	2	H: 62
68	Thomas Russell (Tom) Craddick	R	Midland	09/19/43	Beloit, Wis.	Investments	Texas Tech	Catholic	1968	4	H: 61-62

69	Richard C. Slack	D	Pecos	12/20/14	Pecos, Tex.	Attorney	Texas A&M/ St. Mary's	Presbyterian	1952	20	H: 53-62
70	Hilary B. Doran, Jr.	D	Del Rio	08/16/36	Del Rio, Tex.	Attorney	Southwest Texas/ UT, Austin	Presbyterian	1966	6	H: 60-62
71	James J. (Jim) Kaster	D	El Paso	07/04/33	El Paso, Tex.	Travel agent/ Pilot	UT, El Paso	Episcopal	1970	2	H: 62
72-1	Ralph (Skip) Scoggins	D	El Paso	09/02/31	El Paso, Tex.	Attorney	UT, El Paso/UT, Austin	Episcopal	1972	4	H: 59-60
72-2	Charles F. Tupper, Jr.	D	El Paso	10/01/42	El Paso, Tex.	Attorney	UT, El Paso/UT, Austin	Presbyterian	1970	2	H: 62
72-3	Ronald D. Coleman	D	El Paso	11/29/41	El Paso, Tex.	Attorney	UT, El Paso/UT, Austin	Presbyterian	1972	0	
72-4	Luther Jones	D	El Paso	08/22/46	Corpus Christi, Tex.	Attorney	UT, El Paso/St. Mary's	Methodist	1972	0	
73	John Hoestenbach	D	Odessa	11/29/43	Gulfport, Miss.	Attorney	Texas Tech/UT, Austin	Lutheran	1972	0	
74	Bill Clayton	D	Springlake	09/11/28	Olney, Tex.	Farmer/ Businessman	Texas A&M	Baptist	1962	10	H: 58-62
75-1	Elmer L. Tarbox	D	Lubbock	03/07/16	Bishop, Okla.	Real estate broker/Sporting goods patents	Texas Tech	Methodist	1966	6	H: 60-62
75-2	R. B. (Mac) McAlister	D	Lubbock	08/21/11	Brownwood, Tex.	Chairman of board, radio & TV co.	Texas Tech/ Daniel Baker	Baptist	1968	4	H: 61-62
76	James E. (Pete) Laney	D	Hale Center	03/20/43	Plainview, Tex.	Farmer	Texas Tech	Ch. of Christ	1972	0	
77	E. L. Short	D	Tahoka	10/02/25	Lynn Co., Tex.	Farmer/ Rancher/Cottonseed processing business	Texas A&M	Methodist	1969	4	H: 61-62
78	Joe Allen	D	Baytown	01/27/40	Baytown, Tex.	Banker	Lee/Houston	Presbyterian	1966	6	H: 60-62
79	Ronald (Ron) Waters	D	Houston	11/16/49	Houston, Tex.	Student/Small business owner	Houston	unaffiliated	1972	0	
80	Joseph (Joe) Pentony	D	Houston	05/27/38	Philadelphia, Pa.	Psychologist	UT, Austin	Catholic	1972	0	
81	Woodrow (Woody) Denson	D	Houston	03/24/40	Beaumont, Tex.	Attorney	Houston	unaffiliated	1972	0	
82	John H. Whitmire	D	Houston	08/13/49	Hillsboro, Tex.	Student	Houston	Baptist	1972	0	
83	Larry A. Vick	R	Houston	09/15/41	San Antonio, Tex.	Law clerk	Abilene Christian/ Houston	Ch. of Christ	1972	0	

84	Hawkins Menefee	D	Houston	02/09/45	Washington, D.C.	Urban research	Austin College/ UT, Austin	Presbyterian	1972	0	
85	Anthony Hall	D	Houston	09/16/44	Houston, Tex.	Businessman	Howard	Baptist	1972	0	
86	Craig A. Washington	D	Houston	10/12/41	Longview, Tex.	Attorney	Prairie View A&M/Texas Southern	Baptist	1972	0	
87	Ben T. Reyes	D	Houston	02/16/47	Burton, Tex.	Community relations consultant/ Student	Texas Southern	Catholic	1972	0	
88	George (Mickey) Leland	D	Houston	11/27/44	Lubbock, Tex.	Clinical pharmacist	Texas Southern	Catholic	1972	0	
89	Mrs. Senfronia P. Thompson	D	Houston	01/01/39	Booth, Tex.	Teacher	Texas Southern/ Prairie View A&M	Catholic	1972	0	
90	Kay Bailey	R	Houston	07/22/43	Galveston, Tex.	Attorney/TV reporter	UT, Austin	Episcopal	1972	0	
91	William J. (Bill) Blythe, Jr.	R	Houston	08/15/35	San Antonio, Tex.	Investments/ Brokerage/ Ranching	UT, Austin/London School of Economics	Baptist	1970	2	H: 62
92	A. S. (Sid) Bowers	R	Houston	10/07/47	Victoria, Tex.	Stockbroker	Virginia/South Texas College of Law	Catholic	1970	2	H: 62
93	Milton E. Fox	R	Houston	07/28/26	Tulsa, Okla.	Petroleum consultant	Tulsa/UT, Austin	Presbyterian	1972	0	
94	Donald (Don) Henderson	R	Houston	08/25/49	Houston, Tex.	Vice president, iron company/ Insurance agent	Tulane/Houston	Episcopal	1972	0	
95	Raymond E. (Gene) Green	D	Houston	10/17/47	Houston, Tex.	Journeyman printer	Houston	Christian	1972	0	
96	Lindon Williams	D	Houston	12/27/32	Broaddus, Tex.	Investments	Houston	Baptist	1966	6	H: 60-62
97	Gene Jones	D	Houston	07/21/34	Corrigan, Tex.	Attorney	Houston/South Texas College of Law	Baptist	1972	0	
98	R. C. (Nick) Nichols	D	Houston	07/15/28	Norflett, Ark.	Welder/United Steelworkers staff	none	Baptist	1968	5	H: 60-62
99	James A. (Jim) Clark	D	Pasadena	09/15/23	Lovelady, Tex.	Vice President, International Longshoremen local union	Houston	Baptist	1966	6	H: 60-62
100	Ray Barnhart	R	Pasadena	01/12/28	Elgin, Ill.	Construction	Marietta/Houston	Methodist	1972	0	
101	William S. (Bill) Heatly	D	Paducah	09/03/12	Mart, Tex.	Attorney	Decatur Baptist/ Baylor	Christian	1954	18	H: 54-62

folklore. Some thought that day was over, but Thursday [April 12, 1973], on the floor of the State Legislature, Rep. Senfronia Thompson was compelled to strike what must be considered a blow for not only Black women, but all women.

In a personal privilege speech, Thompson delivered a blistering assault on Rep. C. C. "Kit" Cooke, the 25-year-old attorney from Cleburne. The attractive Black woman from Houston told her colleagues Cooke has insulted her as a Black, as a woman, and as a member of the Texas House of Representatives. Rep. Thompson intimated that while she was attending a luncheon Thursday, she walked in to the tune of Cooke saying, "Here comes my beautiful mistress."

"I told him I was not his mistress," Rep. Thompson told this reporter. "He asked me, 'You mean you would not make love with a white man?' and I told him that was against my culture." To this 33-year-old mother of three children, "making love to a white is against my culture because I am Black, I am married, [and] because this is not what I'm here to do. There are too many serious things I am here in Austin for." This statuesque woman reminded all her colleagues she was virtually alone in Austin, without her husband, and she was required to defend herself.

It is no secret that some of the lawmakers are prone to think that every woman around the state capitol is "available." One woman reporter intimated to this newsman she has overheard several legislators say, "I'm sure glad these secretaries around here can't make personal privilege speeches or we'd be cooking here"—a remark she said came after Thompson's attack on Cooke. "I've had some of these guys pinch me on the behind," the reporter revealed, "but what could I do? I've got to interview these sexual degenerates. What Rep. Thompson did wasn't done for Black women only," this white woman said. "It was a blow for all of us here at the capitol."

When it was made known that Rep. Thompson was going to make the speech attacking Cooke's "sexist-racist" actions, several influential members of the legislature reportedly attempted to talk Thompson out of doing that. When that would not work, she said, they began threatening her, doing something that must be considered tantamount to blackmail. "They told me that if I stood up for what I believed was right that I would never get another piece of legislation through this House," Rep. Thompson hotly indicated. "They were all saying what Cooke did was a joke. But I know one thing, if I had been a white woman, they never would have joked with me like that."

Cooke told reporters, "We were just kidding around. She took it wrong. I really think she got upset about nothing." To Thompson, Cooke and many other members of the House took the incident "too lightly." "But I can appreciate their feelings," she curtly said, "because they've never been Black!"

Several overt attempts were made to stop Thompson's personal privilege speech. One came when Rep. Bob Davis of Dallas raised a point of order declaring her speech was not germaine to her legislative duties. When House speaker Price Daniel allowed Rep. Thompson to continue, she told the House:

Several of you have asked that I refrain from taking public action, but I want to put the House on notice that I will not tolerate racial or sexual insults whether they are delivered by a fool with no forethought or done in a vicious manner calculated to bring my outrage.

This is a personal matter, but it reveals an attitude that each of us needs to pry out. There used to be a horror among white men with racist values that all Black men were after their white women. I can imagine what their reaction would have been had this kind of insult delivered to me been delivered by a Black man to a white woman.

Consider what your reaction would have been had your wives or husbands been subjected to insults because of their sex or their color.[1] I do not hesitate. I do not believe there is any room left in this state for sexism or racism and I would hope you feel the same.

The point is simple. We will never root those maladies out of Texas unless we start with ourselves in this House of Representatives.

Mr. Speaker and members, I deem my position as a member of this House a high honor, but my character rises above everything and no sacrifices can be made where my character is at stake.

We are here to make laws for the general good and the morals of this State.

I, Mr. Speaker, would like to put this House on notice that another incident like this one will leave me with no other alternative except take matters into my own hands.

Rep. Thompson said that last paragraph of her delivery before the House simply means that she will take legal action if necessary to see to it that sexist and racist slurs are forever banned from the lips of members of the Legislature.

This marks the second time in less than a year that Rep. Thompson has been insulted because she is Black and a woman. Last year, at the Rice Hotel in Houston, she—along with another Black person—was ordered out of the Old Capital Club, one of those "exclusive, members-only bastions of segregation" in the South. At that time, Rep. Thompson threatened suit unless the situation at the club was corrected. There was a rash of apologies from the hotel management, indicating someone made a "big mistake."

When the first-term legislator finished her speech, there was no applause, not even from members of the Legislative Black Caucus. Immediately after she sat down, Rep. Neil Caldwell of Alvin went to the podium to make amends for Cooke. "I appreciate the lady's feelings, and I assure you the person who made the remarks is sorrier than I am. It was ill-advised, but not intended. Goodness knows, we all have made such remarks," Caldwell said. After his speech Caldwell received a round of applause.

"I certainly felt there was a need for me to stand up for my reputation," Rep. Thompson said, "so in a sense, personality was a part of my own motivation. Most of the white representatives seem to think that personal reasons were the only motivation for me to make the speech. And it seems like they all missed the point."

Most of the predominantly white male membership of the House seemed to feel, after six hours of buzzing conversation about his sexual slur, the remarks about Rep. Thompson being a "mistress" and her unwillingness to have sexual relationships with white men were spoken in jest by one of the thoughtless and flippant members of the House. Had the insult not been both sexist and racist, Rep. Thompson said she might have been inclined to overlook Cooke's remark since she is committed to passing the bills she now has on the House calendar. "However, any bill I may want passed is not necessarily as important as the need to destroy the kind of racism and sexist attitude that led to the remarks that were made to me."

To Thompson, what most of the members of the House fail to realize is that women, "and particularly Black women," are constantly being subjected to this type of "joke."

If I were white, this kind of joke would never have been made even by the most immature member of the House.

Therefore, I was not defending myself by striking out against one individual, but rather, I felt I had to stand up for all women. I had to attack an attitude that made people think one could degrade a person with insults to her race or sex. I had to point out the remarks were merely symptoms of an attitude that every member of this Legislature needs to work to erase.

The people I represent have long suffered because this attitude is engrained in the white American culture; and everywhere racism surfaces, whether in jest or seriousness, I feel it is my duty to speak out against it. If I let this type of thing pass for personal political expediency, I would not be doing the job people sent me here to do. The people of my district did not vote for me because I was willing to abandon my principles.

You do not change these things by remaining silent nor do you remain true to yourself or your constituents or your conscience.

Since making that speech defending the essence of Black womanhood against the sexist attacks by white men, Rep. Thompson says she has received hundreds of letters from women across the state, all of them telling her she has done the right thing—she has spoken out against this attitude. Perhaps more horrifying, or rather, surprising was that members of that House had the audacity to attempt blackmail to keep this legislator from dragging into the open the stinking filth that has been festering in this society for centuries.

Now, all Texas will be watching those who attempt to block Rep. Thompson's legislation.

NOTE

1. What Texas legislators might do under such circumstances is a matter of conjecture. However, in an editorial concerning the Cooke-Thompson affair, the editor of one of the most widely circulated Black newspapers in Texas called attention to the fact that in March, 1973, by a vote of 21-2, the Tennessee State Senate called for the appointment of a committee for the purpose of investigating remarks made on the Vanderbilt University campus by one of its members, Senator Avon Williams. This Black senator is reported to have declared, "White women accomplish anything they want in the bedroom . . . so all the injustice and inequality that goes on in this country lies at the feet

of white women." Later, Williams defended his remark with this statement: "It was the highest tribute given any person that he might influence another toward equality and justice. White men did indeed take advantage of Black women for years, and that's the reason I happen to be more white than Black." See the editorial, "R-E-S-P-E-C-T . . . That's What Black Women WANT," *Forward Times,* April 21, 1973, p. 12A.

3-4
THE 63RD LEGISLATURE CONVENES
Charles Deaton

As the 63rd Legislature convened in Austin in January, 1973, it had perhaps more potential for reform than any legislature in years. Both the Senate and the House were full of brand-new members, and many of the missing incumbents had been closely identified with some of the politicians and practices that had angered the voters.

Veterans from the 62nd Legislature did not see too many familiar faces. There were 77 brand-new representatives (out of 150), and 15 new senators (out of 31), and much of this turnover could be attributed to either the Sharpstown Scandal or to the new single-member districts in Houston, Dallas, and San Antonio.

The great Sharpstown Scandal, and a number of smaller scandals, created a highly unfavorable climate for incumbents in the primaries in the spring of 1972. The running feud in the 62nd Legislature between Speaker Gus Mutscher's loyal followers and the Dirty Thirty, an assortment of liberal Democrats and conservative Republicans, helped draw attention to the scandals. Mutscher, his successor Rayford Price, and a number of important committee chairmen and vice-chairmen all found themselves victims of the voters' wrath.

Dirty Thirty members who ran for re-election did extremely well, winning 17 of 18 races. The one who lost, Charles Patterson of Taylor, was "paired" by redistricting with another Dirty Thirtian, Dan Kubiak of Rockdale. Dirty Thirtian Fred Head knocked off Speaker Price in a bitter East Texas contest, paving the way for Price Daniel, Jr. (whose name was on the Dirty Thirty letterhead) to become Speaker of the 63rd Legislature.

The single-member districts in the state's three largest cities also produced a large turnover; 39 of the 53 representatives from these cities are freshmen. Perhaps the most significant change occurred in Dallas, where the conservative Democratic establishment's slate had won for decades, edging by the liberals in May and the Republicans in November. Both minorities had clamored for the change to S-M-D's for years, saying the crumbs allowed to them by the system (2 liberals, 1 Republican) were not enough. The change proved them correct, and Dallas' 18-member delegation this time includes 7 Republicans and 5 liberals.

This article is based on the author's observations at first hand of the 63rd Legislature. He is the editor and publisher of *Texas Government Newsletter,* a weekly publication prepared especially for college classroom use.

The Senate moved visibly to the right, as five of its sometime liberals were replaced by conservatives. By latest count, about 20 or 21 of the 31 can be classified as conservative. This change may make the Senate the "last hope" for the blocking of establishment-opposed bills. Republicans increased their number in the Senate from two to three; but the number of women remained the same—one. (A new senator, Mrs. Betty Andujar, is a Republican from Fort Worth.)

With brand-new presiding officers, both houses got to work on reform bills and rules designed to prevent some of the questionable practices from the past.

In the House, the new Speaker was Price Daniel, Jr. Like the new lieutenant-governor, he comes from a politically prominent family, his father having served as a representative, a Speaker, a Governor, a U.S. Senator, and now a Texas Supreme Court justice. Elected from an East Texas-Gulf Coast district, Price, Jr., usually had in the past been on the fringes of the liberal minority in the House. In the tumultuous 62nd session, he was identified with the Dirty Thirty; however, he split away from them on a few key votes, causing some of the more dedicated Dirty Thirty members to have certain reservations about him.

Daniel, a young-looking 31, had not been taken seriously back in 1971 when he announced his speakership race; but a long winding trail of ability and luck ended when he was elected without opposition on January 9, 1973. Running strong on reform proposals, he found many supporters in the freshman members, and he even got an endorsement from the Texas AFL-CIO.

His committee assignments completely shook up the old order in the House. The big three chairmanships, Appropriations, Revenue and Taxation, and State Affairs, went respectively to Neil Caldwell, Terry Doyle, and Dave Finney. Daniel took care of his area as 10 of the 21 chairmanships went to Gulf Coast members. The 62nd session's Dirty Thirty came out in good shape as eight of its returning 18 members got chairman positions. The number of these important positions that went to either a Gulf Coast or a Big City member made it possible that the House might move away from its rural-dominated stands of the past.

The presiding officer in the Senate was newly-elected Lieutenant-Governor William P. Hobby, Jr. A 41-year-old Houston millionaire publisher, Hobby comes from a well-known Texas family, too. His father was elected Lt. Governor back in 1916 and became Governor when Governor Jim Ferguson was impeached in 1917; his mother, Oveta Culp Hobby, served in President Eisenhower's cabinet as the nation's first Secretary of Health, Education, and Welfare. The socially-prominent family also controls the *Houston Post,* and with this background of political, social, and journalistic prominence, it was only natural for Bill Hobby, Jr., to enter into politics.

He displayed his political ability in the Senate by winning an early fight to restore some of the power stripped from the lieutenant-governor by a special session held following Gus Mutscher's Abilene trial. At stake was the power to make committee assignments. In the past, the lieutenant-governor had a completely free hand in this, but the special session installed a seniority system taking most of this power away. Hobby insisted on a middle position where he could name most of the committee members.

Upon his announcement of committee assignments, it became clear that the old Senate hands were retaining their power. The chairman of the powerful Finance Committee, for example, was veteran Senator A. M. Aikin of Paris, and the State Affairs Committee stayed in the hands of Senator W. T. "Bill" Moore of Bryan. Both Aikin and Moore had previously held the positions.

The rules changes that attracted attention in the early days of the session were perhaps more far-reaching in the House. Highlights of their changes are:

1. Number of committees reduced from 45 to 21.
2. Maximum of three committee assignments per member; committee chairman allowed to serve on only one other committee; Chairman of Appropriations Committee not allowed to serve on any other committee; members not allowed to serve concurrently on more than one of the following committees: Appropriations, Revenue and Taxation, State Affairs.
3. Committees given power to subpoena witnesses and records upon 2/3 vote of the committee.
4. Testimony before committees and subcommittees required to be tape-recorded unless suspended by a 2/3 vote of the committee.
5. Proceedings of the House required to be tape recorded.
6. Complete records of all committee proceedings required to be kept.
7. Five-day notice required for committee hearings; two-hour notice required for committee meetings; committee meetings while House in session prohibited without permission from the House.
8. Limited seniority system installed with up to 50% of committee membership (exclusive of chairman and vice-chairman) to be filled by seniority. This does not apply to Calendar, Rules, and Administration Committees.
9. Stricter controls created on the placing of bills on the local and consent calendars.
10. Conference committees limited to adjusting differences in House and Senate bills.
11. Cost analysis (fiscal note) required for bills requiring state expenditures.
12. Chief clerk may furnish certified copies of bills lost in legislative process.

The Senate also made some changes in their rules, including:

1. Number of committees reduced from 27 to 9.
2. Limited seniority system installed with the lieutenant-governor appointing the chairman, vice-chairman, and all but three of the remaining members of nine-member committees, and all but four of the larger committees.
3. Votes on confirmation of gubernatorial appointments to be public (discussion of the nominees will remain closed to the public).

Some of the reform ideas in the House were also introduced in statutory form, thus making it harder for future legislatures to ignore them. Among the measures proposed by Speaker Daniel and introduced by various members were a new ethics law with stronger financial disclosure provisions, a new, far-reaching lobby regulation bill, a new campaign financing law with enforcement power given to the ethics commission, a shield law for reporters, a law limiting future Speaker to one two-year term, and a law revising the legislative continuance statute.

The members of the 63rd Legislature faced many problems as they came to Austin: public school financing, redistricting, ethics and conflict-of-interest laws for public officials—all these and many more were waiting. This legislature also faced the herculean task of rewriting the Texas Constitution, a job that would begin in January of 1974.

3-5
GUS MUTSCHER'S RESOLUTION COMMENDING FRANK W. SHARP FOR HIS RELIGIOUS LEADERSHIP TOWARD ECUMENICAL BROTHERHOOD AND CONGRATULATING HIM AS A JESUIT "FOUNDER"

HSR 32 ADOPTED BY THE HOUSE ON AUGUST 11, 1969

Whereas, In an almost unprecedented action, the Catholic Church, on Wednesday, August 13, 1969, will name a Methodist, Frank W. Sharp of Houston, Texas, a "Founder" of the 429-year-old Jesuit order; and

Whereas, Pope Paul is expected to grant a special audience to this distinguished Texas builder, banker, and real estate man, and in bestowing the Jesuit honor the Catholic Church passes another milestone toward ecumenical brotherhood; and

Whereas, Frank W. Sharp has been a civic and Methodist lay leader in Southeast Texas since he went to Houston from Palestine, Texas, in the early days of the depression; his residential subdivision of Sharpstown is one of the outstanding of its kind in the United States; and

Whereas, The fourth American to receive the carefully-screened Jesuit honor, Mr. Sharp is the only non-Catholic in a series of royal and princely patrons older than America for whom each of the 33,800 members of the Church's largest order is specifically obliged to say or hear a mass every month; and

Whereas, Although various honors of the Catholic Church are bestowed on its friends—Catholics, Protestants, and Jews—often enough so that they sometimes appear to be automatic rewards for generosity, Mr. Sharp's honor is a carefully-chosen tribute to a Protestant without scholarly pretensions who took the responsibility of welcoming the order into a firmly Protestant community; the Reverend John Blewett, a scholar from Fond du Lac, Wisconsin, who is making the arrangements for Mr. Sharp and his party of Protestant Texans, said: "The Church is facing the problem of adapting to the unification of the whole human family. This honor is granted to Mr. Sharp not simply for his generosity, but because he has personally worked with courage and foresight to render possible the establishment of a Jesuit preparatory school in a community where it would not necessarily be automatically welcome"; and

This document was not published in the *House Journal* of August 11, 1969; a Xerox copy of the original resolution was obtained with the assistance of Rep. Lane Denton.

Whereas, Mr. Sharp gave property worth about $3 million, plus some $4 million in special bequests, to help the 12-year-old Strake College Preparatory School, which has a faculty of 16 Jesuits and several laymen who teach 375 pupils in Sharpstown; the school is named for the late George Strake, a Catholic, who helped to start it; and

Whereas, "Founder" has a special meaning laid down by the earliest Jesuit jurists in the years after 1540, when the order was founded by Ignatius Loyola, a Spanish missionary, and some 200 jurists worked until 1558 to write the rules of the order; the resulting constitution is comparable to the American Constitution as an early blueprint for self-government by consensus, and nowhere in the constitution does it say that founders must be Catholics; and

Whereas, In modern as well as historical times the Jesuits have a screening system to sort out nominees for the name of "founder," and in Mr. Sharp's case the initiative came from the Reverend Michael R. Kennelly, S.J., the order's presiding figure in Houston, who secured the approval of his superior, the New Orleans Provincial John Edwards, S.J.; and

Whereas, In becoming a "founder," Mr. Sharp takes his place beside John Andrew Creighton, founder of Creighton University in Omaha, and Michael Cudahy, the Chicago meat-packer who helped start Loyola; another founder of recent times is Mrs. Anna Brady, a church historian and journalist residing in Rome, who gave her Long Island Estate to the Jesuits; and

Whereas, Mr. Sharp has been invited by the Jesuits to have two Protestant churchmen, with whom he often works, accompany him to Rome: Dr. Charles C. Allen, a Methodist author and pastor of Mr. Sharp's own church, and Dr. William Hinton, pastor [sic] of the Houston Baptist College, which has also benefited from Mr. Sharp's generosity; also expected to be in the party are Astronaut James A. Lovell and Senator Edward Kennedy, a former roommate of Mr. Sharp's son-in-law, Claude Hooten; and

Whereas, The House of Representatives of the 61st Legislature desires to recognize Frank W. Sharp, a distinguished Texas Methodist lay leader, and to congratulate him upon the signal honor to be bestowed upon him by the Catholic Church, now, therefore, be it

Resolved, That the House of Representatives of the 61st Legislature, 1st Called Session, by this Resolution highly commend Frank W. Sharp of Houston, Texas, for his religious leadership toward ecumenical brotherhood, and congratulate him as a Jesuit "Founder"; and, be it further

Resolved, That a copy of this Resolution, under the official seal of the House of Representatives, be prepared for Mr. Sharp as an expression of appreciation to him and in all good wishes on the occasion of his award and special audience with Pope Paul.

Mutscher

3-6
CONGRATULATING REPRESENTATIVE FRANCES "SISSY" FARENTHOLD ON HER BIRTHDAY

HSR 80 ADOPTED BY THE HOUSE ON OCTOBER 17, 1972

Whereas, On October 2, 1926, in the Sparkling City by the Sea, better known as Corpus Christi, there was born Frances "Sissy" Tarlton, ~~unbeknownst to the Texas Rangers~~;[1] and

Whereas, Sissy is a descendent of many great Texans, including a lawyer, a teacher, a school superintendent, a legislator, and a Confederate Army Officer; and

Whereas, the untamed spirit of these famous Texans was born into Sissy and earned her the title of "the Melancholy Rebel"; and

Whereas, Sissy married George Farenthold, a flashy Belgian cook, whose unpublished cookbook, inspired by Sissy's frequent, extravagant adventures in the kitchen, would surely outsell "Shadow on the Alamo", ~~the bible of the 62nd Legislature~~;[2] and

~~Whereas, Sissy's name is now a household word in Texas; at least in the households of a former Land Commissioner, a former Speaker of the House, an almost-former Lieutenant Governor, an almost-former Governor, an almost-former Attorney General, and several disappointed financial promoters; and~~[3]

~~Whereas, Sissy's campaign for Governor of Texas is a model of clean, progressive politics; the kind of politics which must come to this state and nation if we are to end the era of "private government"; and~~[4]

Whereas, Sissy's campaign for governor of Texas is a model of clean, progressive politics; the kind of politics which attracted the attention of this state and nation, and

Whereas, Sissy's quality of leadership was again recognized at the 1972 Democratic National Convention when her name was placed in nomination for the Vice-Presidency; an act which is sure to be repeated; and

Whereas, Sissy, rarely missing a roll call in the Texas House of Representatives, appears to have boundless energy and enthusiasm, as is demonstrated in her efforts as National Co-Chairwoman of "Citizens to Elect McGovern/Shriver"; and

Whereas, Sissy, George Farenthold, and their entire family continue to serve the people of Texas with sincerity, strength, and compassion; and

~~Whereas, Sissy deserves many honors for her service such as dedicating, in her name, either the House Hearing Room or a new park at 11th and Congress in Austin; and~~[5]

Whereas, With her many admirable traits, her loyalty and enthusiasm, Frances Tarlton Farenthold deserves the highest recognition by her fellow members, the

Printed in the *House Journal,* October 17, 1972, pp. 456-457, 464-466. The fact that this birthday resolution was passed only after being amended suggests that some representatives did not appreciate the humor of the Dirty Thirty members who sponsored the measure.

occasion of her birthday is an appropriate time to recognize Sissy and her accomplishments; now, therefore, be it

Resolved, That the House of Representatives of the 62nd Legislature, Fourth (going on Fifth) Called Session, congratulate Sissy Farenthold on the celebration of her birthday and commend her for her distinguished contributions in bringing good government to Texas; and, be it further

Resolved, That official copies of this resolution, under the Seal of the House of Representatives, be prepared for Frances Tarlton Farenthold as a memento of her service in the House and as a token of the affection and esteem of her colleagues for her.

NOTES

1. Deleted by amendment offered by Rep. John Traeger.
2. Deleted by amendment offered by Rep. John Traeger.
3. Deleted by amendment offered by Rep. John Traeger.
4. Deleted by amendment offered by Rep. Hilary Doran.
5. Deleted by amendment offered by Rep. John Traeger.

3-7
FUNCTIONS OF THE OPINIONS OF THE TEXAS ATTORNEY GENERAL IN THE STATE LEGISLATIVE PROCESS
Beryl Pettus

By state constitution and statute, the attorney general of Texas is the major legal adviser of state legislative and administrative officials. With respect to the former, an advisory opinion in 1944 asserted that the state cannot pay a legal fee to attorneys for advice concerning the legality of proposed legislation (*Ops. Att. Gen. Tex.*, C-6066, 1944 [Opinions are identified hereafter by number and year only.]). The effect of that unchallenged opinion has been to give the attorney general an exclusive function of advising legislators concerning the legality, including constitutionality, of bills.

Utilizing what Alan Isaak calls the "system-affecting" approach to functional analysis,[1] a clearer determination of the effects of formal, written advisory opinions of the state's attorney general in the Texas legislative system can be made. How authoritative, in practice, is the advice of the state's chief legal officer? What consequences or effects do the opinions have for legislative actors?

OPINIONS ADDRESSED TO THE LEGISLATURE

Legislative actors requested the attorney general's advice 132 times during the decade of the 1960's. Although the opinions pertained to a variety of subjects, of particular concern to the legislature were measures having to do with its own limited affairs: legislative powers, organization, and procedure, 25; taxes and taxation, 10; statutory construction, 9; appropriations, 9; legislators' travel expenses, 6; federal relations, 4; general state government, 4; and special districts and authorities, 8. The remaining opinions were spread rather evenly over a wide list of subjects.

Figuring prominently in requests for opinions by legislators were questions of constitutionality. And bills, rather than statutes or administrative actions, were at issue in 56 of 65 instances in which a question of constitutional conflict was broached by the legislature.

This author's research suggests that legislative committee chairmen and presiding officers perceive the written opinions of the attorney general and the opinion process, which takes a minimum of three weeks, as basic to a strategy by which bills may be killed outright or destroyed by delay. Given the authoritative character of advisory opinions, another possible strategy may be for a sponsor to gather support for a bill under attack by attempting to obtain a favorable opinion and to gain time to round up additional support within the legislature itself.

Various observers have remarked about the reluctance of most standing committees to take responsibility for killing bills in committee. As a result, within limitations of time (including restrictions imposed by the constitutionally limited 140-day regular session), most standing committees report all bills for floor action. An alternative is to ask the attorney general for an opinion about a bill's application, structure, or constitutionality. In fact, however, the chief legal officer returned findings of unconstitutionality in only half of his opinions on this matter in the 1960's.

An interesting phenomenon with respect to requests for opinions by legislative officers is that about 50 per cent of them are withdrawn by the requesting legislative official when the officer is notified that the opinion is ready for release to him and to the press.[2] This behavior of squelching opinions can be explained only in terms of changed strategic considerations surrounding the bills in question—such as the assurance of the necessary floor strength for defeat or passage, the culmination of attempts to compromise or fail to compromise differences, or the decision to shift legislative priorities for the session.[3]

AUTHORITATIVE CHARACTER OF THE OPINIONS

Analysis demonstrates that both the legislative actors and the governor accept as authoritative the opinions of the attorney general which advise that bills are constitutionally defective. Thirty-one bills were so adjudged during the last decade. Of these measures, three were draft bills, only one of which had been drawn up by a legislative committee; and it did not pass the legislature. Of the remaining twenty-eight bills, two had been sent to the executive for signature, only to be the subject of requests by the governor for rulings by the attorney general on their constitutionality. The governor promptly exercised an executive veto upon the advice of unconstitutionality.

Twenty-six bills were before the legislature when either a legislative actor or the governor requested opinions asking about their constitutionality. Only three of these proposals were passed and sent to the governor; the other twenty-three expired with the end of the legislative sessions. Two of the three passed bills were amended before passage to embody exactly the changes suggested by the attorney general to cure unconstitutionality, and they were subsequently signed into law by the governor.[4] The single bill passed "uncorrected" by the legislature in the face of the attorney general's objections to its constitutionality, a rider which purported to give the comptroller of public accounts power to pre-audit claims, was vetoed by Governor John Connally.

Thus, the support score of the legislature on bills declared by the attorney general to contain constitutional defects was 96.3 per cent, while that of the governor was 100 per cent. The support by the legislative-gubernatorial combination was 100 per cent. No bill which was declared unconstitutional by the attorney general during the 1960's became statute. Thirty-four other bills about which questions of constitutionality were raised were adjudged to be constitutionally adequate. Of these proposals, thirteen (38.2 per cent) were enacted into law.

The passage of a large proportion of the bills which were ruled constitutionally adequate, when cast against the fact that only one bill which was adjudged unconstitutional was passed and sent to the governor, supports the proposition that some opinion requests are made in a sincere effort to obtain advice and help. This finding emphasizes the function of advisory opinions as aids in the making and codifying of law or in the setting of guidelines for administrative action, rather than as part of a strategy to garner additional authoritative support for bills or to destroy bills. While, in general, a conservative ideological affinity existed between committee majorities and personnel staffing the Office of the Attorney General, no evidence of existence of any tacit understanding to engage in a strategy to kill bills was found. On the contrary, the writer was most favorably impressed by the independence of mind, fairness, legal acuity, and objectivity of the chairman and vice-chairman of the opinion committee and of other assistant attorneys general who were commonly called upon to consider legal arguments, to arrive at decisions, and to write opinions. Further, the opinion-writing process often involved as many as ten different people in the preparation of a single opinion, making any attempts at collusion extremely difficult to hide and to execute.

One particularly clear example of the use of an advisory opinion by a committee chairman to destroy a bill occurred in 1969, when the chairman of the Senate State Affairs Committee requested advice as to whether a bill, ostensibly having the primary purpose of regulating coin-operated machines, was primarily a regulatory act or a revenue measure. The attorney general ruled that the bill was a tax bill which was constitutionally prohibited from arising in the Senate (M-370, 1969). Such revenue measures must originate in the House.

The total volume of measures killed in any single session by rulings of unconstitutionality, or through losses due to use of the opinion requests as a stalling device, was not large. The input of bills during the 59th through the 61st Legislatures in regular sessions was approximately 6,300 bills, of which 62 per cent, or some 4,000, failed of passage. Only twenty-four measures during the three legislatures were labeled unconstitutional by advisory opinions, and that many or more are estimated to have fallen by the device of requests for opinions which were written but which were withdrawn upon the request of committee chairmen. Thus, only approximately 1.5 per cent of the total bills which failed of passage were lost because of the authoritative intervention of the attorney general in the legislative system.

THE SPECIAL CASE OF BRACKET BILLS

One class of bills, called population bracket bills because they contain limiting population figures within brackets, is particularly susceptible to selective punitive action. The Texas Constitution, while prohibiting thirty classes of local or special legislation, does not contain a blanket prescription against such bracketing. Whether a bill is a permissible bracket measure, or local or special legislation prohibited by the fundamental law, may be only a matter of judgment of effect.[5]

A tidal wave of bracket legislation is passed biennially by the Texas legislature.[6] Only twelve bills and statutes were held by the attorney general to violate the constitutional prohibition against local or special legislation; however, these measures did amount to 14.6 per cent of the total acts declared unconstitutional.

In the case of the statutes declared by the advisory opinions to have the constitutional defect of being local or special legislation, the legislature judiciously ignored the measures. That is, no effort was made in any succeeding legislative session to repeal or amend the statutes so labeled. It was as though the attorney general's opinions had served to exempt from the law those local governmental officials who complained. In the absence of court challenges, the statutes remained efficacious for all the other local governments in Texas which were included within the population brackets. That the opinion request may have been used by local officials as a means of obtaining desired exemptions is seen in the fact that almost all of the bracket measures which were presented to the attorney general for advice were declared to be local or special legislation prohibited by the Constitution.

In the case of bills adjudged by the chief legal officer as local or special legislation, the legislative authorities demonstrated total acceptance of the attorney general's rulings, at least for the session during which the opinions were issued. The legislative leadership's request for advisory opinions on only a small portion of the several score of bracket bills passed during any legislative session can be viewed as almost entirely punitive.

CONCLUSIONS

The opinions of the Texas attorney general are treated as authoritative in Texas; that is, the officials to whom they are addressed generally abide by their conditions and prescriptions. This is especially true of the members of the legislature and the governor, who together gave total acceptance during the 1960's of advice of unconstitutionality rendered by the State's chief legal officer.

A number of functions may be attributed to the advisory opinions in the legislative system. Chiefly, the opinions presented a means by which bills could be removed from the legislative process temporarily or permanently without any member taking direct responsibility for the action. Motives apparently included taking punitive action against selected legislators, decreasing the number of bills for floor consideration, and honestly desiring advice and help in making and codifying the law in Texas.

NOTES

1. Alan Isaak, *Scope and Methods of Political Science* (Homewood, Ill.: The Dorsey Press, 1969), p. 223.
2. Interview with Mr. Kerns Taylor, Chairman, Opinion Committee, Office of the Attorney General, Austin, Texas, August 4, 1970.
3. Besides the requests for formal, written opinions, the Office of the Attorney General is also hit by a barrage of requests for "unofficial advice" about bills. The substance of such advice and the effect, if any, on legislative output cannot be gauged because of the absence of official records. Given the authoritative position of the attorney general in the Texas political system, some strategic importance—in terms of remarks already made—can be attached to this large volume of unofficial advice accorded the legislative actors on bills under their consideration.
4. One of these two bills, a tax measure handled in C-402, 1065, was subsequently declared constitutional by the Supreme Court of Texas in *Smith* v. *Davis,* 426 S. W. 2d 827 (1968). Few cases involving statutes or administrative actions on which opinions have been rendered are ever adjudicated. When they are, the courts, too, usually accept as authoritative the advisory opinions. Indeed, some court opinions contain large portions of the attorney general's reasoning.
5. The Texas courts permit statutes to contain a classification on the basis of population if the category is "reasonable," relevant to a statewide purpose, touches on a subject in which the people at large may be interested, or permits other localities to enter the class if at some future census or in some future circumstance they qualify. See Texas Legislative Council, *Laws Based on Population,* Report No. 57-3 (Austin, Tex.: Texas Legislative Council, December, 1962), p. 4.
6. The Legislative Council reported that the "constitutional restrictions [against local or special laws] are being successfully evaded . . . particularly in the area of county and local governmental affairs, by a resort to population and other classification devices." Further, "it is common practice in the Legislature for such acts to be handled on the local and uncontested bills calendar. This virtually assures their passage without opposition and without much deliberation

on the part of members of the Legislature." Finally, "a high percentage of population laws relate to subjects concerning which the Legislature is prohibited from enacting local or special laws." The tabulation by the Council of population bracket laws then apparently in effect (1962) was some 204 pages in length on legal-size paper, two columns to the page. *Ibid.,* pp. 3 and 5.

3-8
HOW TO WIN FRIENDS, INFLUENCE PEOPLE AND STAY HONEST: A *TEXAS OBSERVER* INTERVIEW WITH TOM BASS

Bass I guess it's the teacher in me, but I found that during the Legislature frequently a relatively new member would come to me and ask some suggestions on being in the Legislature. I began to develop a couple of ideas, and they're so common-sense that unfortunately they're overlooked most of the time. . . .

One thing, learn the rules. Now, surprising as it would seem, there are literally just a handful of members of the House who do know the rules. People, for example, like DeWitt Hale and Jim Nugent, those two are sort of in a class by themselves, and most members sort of enjoy watching them when they are in action against one another. Because those two members do know the rules so well, it generally doesn't make any difference who is speaker; they're going to land on their feet, because any speaker is going to want those two guys working with him rather than working against him.

Observer It seemed that the times that the Dirty Thirty was most effective was on procedural motions.

Bass Well, . . . I didn't pay you to say that, but my role with the Dirty Thirty, more than anything, was the rules adviser, if you please. I never considered myself, obviously, in the category of Nugent or DeWitt Hale, but, I think, right below them a half a dozen or a dozen members know the rules pretty well. And it doesn't take too much to get into that particular category. (This coming [63rd] session I think Hilary Doran will probably be in that category, just a step below DeWitt [Hale] or Nugent, but real sharp on the rules.)

So few members do know the rules that the handful that do their homework and learn them have a distinct advantage over the majority of the members.

Observer Do you need a lawyer's brain?

From *The Texas Observer,* February 2, 1973, pp. 14-16. Tom Bass, now a Harris County commissioner, spent ten years in the Texas House of Representatives and was a member of the Dirty Thirty.

Bass No, I don't think you need a lawyer's brain. You have to think logically. You have to be able to read legalese in a sense, because the rules sometimes get a little complex, but I don't think anybody who is intelligent enough to get elected to the Legislature lacks the intelligence to become an expert on the rules.

But if you attempt to use the rules you'd better have them down pat because, if you don't, the first time you blunder people like Hale and Nugent will pick you up and cut you off. You should plan ahead as much as you can, and in a fight you should have your floor manager so you'll know who is really keeping up with that particular issue and whose lead to follow if it becomes very murky. But you can study and you can study and you can learn the rules, but you're going to have to learn a few by mistake.

Second, and this sounds cynical as hell, but I still think it's good: Never be disappointed in any other member. That is, don't place your complete trust in another member. You may have some good friends. You may work together with them real fine, but there has got to be some issue where that other person has to vote differently from you when you feel that he should be voting your way. So I think you have to recognize that there are political considerations. There's no other member who's going to see everything exactly the way you do, and if you put your total faith and trust in another person and they let you down, this is very disappointing. If you recognize this from the start, you'll not be disappointed when you're betrayed, so to speak.

The third thing is just simply use your intelligence. Too many of these guys up here in the past have reacted either through emotion or pressure. Emotion in that they're afraid the voter will think such and such, or pressure, maybe, from some special-interest group, which is the obvious one we think of. But . . . subtle pressure . . . is sometimes exerted. You know, the best lobbying technique is the good-old-boy approach. He doesn't pressure you, he doesn't ask you for anything, but he gradually gets to be a friend and then an issue comes along, and you think, "Well, I don't feel too strongly on this, but Jim is for it and Jim's a good old boy, so I'll vote for it." But if you use your intelligence and look at the issue when it comes up and vote it the way you really think you should—and this sounds idealistic as hell—but I think in the long run you're really better off.

Observer What criteria did you use for deciding what was right and wrong?

Bass Well, this is a very subjective type of thing. And this is why I never personally criticize another member on any vote he may take, because given the same circumstances under which he is operating, I may vote the same way he does. In my case, it was a combination of things. Usually I try to vote my constituency. But, if it was something I felt real strongly on, I would definitely vote my conscience rather than my constituency. And this is where I think a lot of them are afraid to do this. But I think in the long run the voters tend to respect you more when you occasionally differ with them.

Now, when it came to this [Sharpstown State Bank] stock scandal thing, for example, I had all along told my classes that I could work with the system and not betray my own morality or ethic. So that I did try to work with the system, and when I failed to do that I would just lick my wounds and go home, so to speak. But I kept trying. I kept plugging. But the stock scandal turned out to be something that I, in my own conscience, felt was different. Morally or ethically the House leadership had betrayed the House in their handling of the Sharpstown bill. I could no longer support that administration.

Observer What I'm interested in is how you got on the team in the first place.

Bass Okay. In 10 years in Austin I was never considered part of the establishment. I was always a maverick. But the last two or three sessions I was up here I had learned the rules and I had made myself politically strong at home so that I usually led the ticket when it came for reelection, and I had the confidence of the Harris County delegation to be twice selected chairman of that delegation. So, without ever actually becoming part of the establishment, I found myself in the situation where they would prefer to give me a few positions of influence just so that I would not cause too much trouble.

Prior to the stock scandal, I had in a sense sort of modeled myself after DeWitt Hale. That is, I felt that if I could become strong enough in the rules that I wouldn't have to really worry about being one of the first 30 to line up with the speaker. As long as I lined up with him early enough that I wasn't one of the outcasts, I would get a pretty good assignment. I had moved from the appropriations committee to the rules committee, both of which I consider good assignments.

I liked Gus [Mutscher] personally. And he did like me personally. I don't know that he does any more, but this political acceptability at home, knowledge of the rules, and personal friendship with the man put me in the position that I was in. This, of course, made it difficult for me to break, because I did feel I owed a certain allegiance to the man.

Observer I've been fascinated by the degree to which emotions and personal loyalty take part in the legislative process. For example, at the end of the last session it got terribly bitter. Even without the special emotion and tension that marked the last Mutscher session it seems to me when people spend so much time together they tend to lose their perspective and what happens within that little group becomes so important. . . . Did you ever find a way to just back off from it?

Bass Apparently, more so than the average and it may be my nature. I didn't acquire any close personal friendships with other members of the House. There was a mutual respect, but literally up until the very midst of the Dirty Thirty fight, when you just had to be together, there was no member of the House that I automatically voted with. But politicians are gregarious by nature, and it's awfully easy to fall into a pattern of being too closely aligned with a clique and lose your perspective. A freshman should be aware that this tendency exists and guard against it.

Literally, if a legislator is so inclined, and the word gets around, just about every expense in Austin—breakfast, lunch, supper, clubs, you name it—can be picked up by a lobbyist. But this is where the individual legislator is going to have to make some judgments. I'm convinced we can never pass a law to regulate lobbyists. Now, I'm not saying there shouldn't be some laws on the book, but I'm saying if you get a lobbyist and a legislator alone in a hotel room there's no way that you can keep $500 to $1000 from changing hands if neither one of them is going to tell anyone else. You're not going to be able to eliminate the influence of the lobby, so you have to keep close tabs on the elected officials. And when you catch 'em, boy, make an example out of them. I don't know any flat rule. My own rule of thumb was that anything a lobby group offers all 150 members I have no qualms in accepting, but anything he wants to offer me individually, that's usually where I draw the line.

Observer Is it physically, socially possible to move around in legislative circles without meeting the lobby?

Bass I think the average freshman likes to make at least one meeting of every group that comes along, and maybe this isn't bad the first time around. But after I made the round, I doubt that in a 140-day session I made it to more than half a dozen evening sessions. I doubt that I had more than two or three luncheons. Now it's not necessary to be as anti-social as I was, but it's easy to get too social, to get too close to the lobbyists and other members, and without really realizing it get obligated.

I think the lobby has got to try because this is the first time in over a decade that a speaker, I'm convinced, was elected without substantial help from lobby groups. I think this frightens a lot of them to death, and so they have got to get organized and do what they can with the members. Prior to this time, for the last couple of sessions, man, the lobby just had to deal with the speaker for all practical purposes, and that was it.

Observer I was wondering if something might be done, for example, about some of the attitudes which I found not only hypocritical and generally distasteful, but actually debilitating last time. And this is the famous thing when after an attack on Mutscher someone would get up and rail against the attacker in terms of "This is an insult to the integrity of this honorable body." The vast amount of time that is wasted in self-praise and "the great dignity of this Legislature," which everyone has been thrashing all over all of the time.

Bass What develops up here is what I called Capitolitis. All I mean by this is that you begin to study your own navel too much in this fishbowl atmosphere up here and you sort of lose touch with what's going on elsewhere. There's a tendency to be only interested in what other members of the House and the people immediately think of you. And if you do something that upsets them, then this is wrong, you see.

You sort of lose touch with the real values and you're only concerned with—I won't call them false values—but the limited values of the House membership.

And obviously any group, family or any group, is self-serving. We like to think we're great. So when somebody attacks us we react defensively and the House reacts defensively.

Observer Maybe we ought to make a law that requires legislators to be bussed home on weekends. How many sessions does it take for a House member to become either a useful member of the team or a threat?

Bass Well, if you get a session like last time, you can do it by the end of your first session. Lane Denton is a good example of that. I think Lane Denton, although obviously he could not pass legislation last session, was still a threat from the news media coverage point of view to the Mutscher team. This is unusual though. . . . Normally, you're doing pretty good if by the end of your second session or the beginning of your third you're really able to move along exercising influence. But there can be exceptions; this is because most members don't really concentrate on what's going on.

These members coming into the 63rd session, I think they literally do have a mandate to exercise independence and integrity and judgment. I told a couple of new members earlier, I said, "Now we shed blood all last session, it's time for *you* this session to be able to do something."

Even if we can't get as much progressive legislation as we'd like, if at least we can modestly reform the House structure in the way that it operates, then we're set up for when we can pass progressive legislation.

"It's a bird; it's a plane; no, it's Briscoe!"

HERC FICKLEN FROM THE DALLAS NEWS

4

The Executive

Long considered the pinnacle of success in Texas politics, the governorship of Texas is a paradoxical office. On the one hand, political leadership, widespread publicity, and prestige are the inevitable rewards for serving as chief executive of the state. "Figurehead" and "paper tiger" also describe the Texas governor because of constitutional limitations and administrative structure.

HISTORICAL PERSPECTIVE

The office of the governor of Texas suffers from a distrust of executive power that has some effect upon the governor's office in every state in the Union. This sense of distrust has roots which go all the way back to the colonial period of American history. It was only logical then that the governorships, created by the state constitutions after the Revolutionary War, were weak offices commanding little respect from the electorate. Professor William Young correctly characterized the governorship as an office which "was conceived in mistrust and born in a strait jacket, the creature of revolutionary assemblies."[1]

JACKSONIAN INFLUENCE

The typical state constitution allowed the governor to serve only one term and gave him no veto power over legislation. In all the states except Massachusetts and New York, the governor was named by the legislature. This situation prompted a perceptive observation by Alexis de Tocqueville: "In America the legislature of each state is supreme, nothing can impede its authority, since it represents that majority which claims to be the sole origin of reason."[2]

Even though the legislature began falling into disrepute during the Jacksonian period, the executive could not gain appreciably in power and prestige. Election to the office was gradually taken from the legislature and placed in the hands of the people. However, the Jacksonian influence of electing all the major offices in state government proved to be a bane rather than a boon for the governorship. Escalation in the number of elected officers at the state level was best represented in this example by Professor Leslie Lipson, who noted that New York had 10 agencies in 1800, 81 in 1900, and 170 in 1925. Illinois had 5 elected officials and 3 administrative agencies in 1848. By 1870 it had 25 independent agencies and by 1916, prior to reorganization, 191 agencies had elected heads.[3] Although a *reorganization movement* of state executive departments was begun under the leadership of Illinois Governor Frank Lowden in 1917, the southern states, including Texas, refused to follow this trend. They retained the Jacksonian concept of popularly elected officials, i.e., governor, lieutenant governor, attorney general, treasurer, comptroller, and others.

RECONSTRUCTION EFFECT

The current executive office in Texas is a reflection not only of the Jacksonian influence but also of the overall negative attitude toward the office of governor during the Reconstruction era. Led by Radical Republicans, Texans were forced to live under the authoritarian rule of Governor E. J. Davis, who epitomized the wrath of those men in the national government seeking to punish the South for its part in the Civil War.

Included in Davis's program were such items as denying voting privileges to many leading white citizens, allowing many blacks to vote, and establishing military rule in the place of civil due process.[4] All these actions, which were sanctioned by the Reconstruction Act of 1867, resulted in a hue and cry for a new constitution to replace the one adopted in 1869. Accordingly, the constitutional convention of 1875 drafted a new constitution, which was ratified by the people in 1876 (see Chapter 1 for a discussion of the constitution).

The Texas executive office, provided for in *Article IV of the constitution of 1876,* is a product of the history of that office as it developed in the South. That history is characterized by, first, an inherent distrust of executive power; second, the Jacksonian influence of electing executive officials; and, finally, the reactionary attitude of Texas toward government per se following the carpetbag rule of the Davis regime.

RECRUITMENT AND REWARDS

The road to the governorship is an arduous one, despite the deceptive ease with which some men have attained the office. No description of the Texas governorship would be complete without an examination of how the office is filled.

QUALIFICATIONS

Legal qualifications for the office are minimal. The governor must be at least thirty years of age, a United States citizen, and a resident of Texas for five years immediately preceding his election. These minimal qualifications might lead one to think that anyone could win the office. Extralegal restraints imposed on the office, however, are numerous and limit the number of *gubernatorial aspirants.* History has shown that the typical Texas governor is a white, Anglo-Saxon, Protestant, middle-aged, Democratic lawyer-businessman who has had previous experience in public affairs, usually in state government. To be sure, Governor Dolph Briscoe conforms to this mold (see Reading 4-1).

ELECTION

Superimposed upon constitutional prerequisites are the candidate's political and personal affiliations with influential lobbyists, lawyers, and leading citizens in the larger cities of Dallas, Houston, Fort Worth, San Antonio, and Austin. In short, the "establishment's" role in the recruitment of Texas governors cannot be underestimated, as witnessed by the close ties of the influential Austin law firm of Clark, Denius, Winters, et al., with the candidacies and administrations of three recent governors: Allan Shivers, Price Daniel, and John Connally.

A word of caution is offered here, however, with respect to the "establishment's" role in the election of the Texas governor. As exemplified by the 1972 gubernatorial election, the "establishment's" man can be overexposed to the public, which results in rejection by the voters of lower-keyed candidates. Among the candidates in the 1972 Democratic primary, Lieutenant Governor Ben Barnes unquestionably had the strongest support of the banking-business community, leading newspapers, and influential Texans. Yet the voters spurned him along with Smith, who was seeking a third term. Neither Briscoe nor liberal "Sissy" Farenthold were officially endorsed by the "establishment," but both surfaced as the run-off candidates. The aftermath of the Sharpstown banking scandal certainly contributed to the defeat of both Smith and Barnes, but the electorate served notice on the "establishment" that their support does not guarantee that it will capture the governor's office.

REMOVAL

Only one governor has been removed from office by the impeachment process in Texas. In 1917 Governor James Ferguson was impeached by the House of Representatives and convicted by the Senate on charges of misapplication of public funds (see Reading 4-2). The impeachment process is the only method of removing a Texas governor, as there is no constitutional provision for popular recall. As provided in Article IV of the Texas constitution, the House of Representatives initiates the impeachment proceedings and investigates the charges, while the Senate judges the case.

COMPENSATION

The governor's salary is set by the Legislature. Currently the Texas governor receives an annual salary of $63,000, which is second only to the $85,000 annual salary received by New York governors.[5] The constitution also allows the governor to reside in the governor's mansion, an imposing structure located at 10th and Colorado streets in Austin. Fringe benefits include allowances for staffing and maintaining the mansion and use of a state-owned limousine and an airplane.

With the adoption of a 1972 constitutional amendment increasing the term of office from two to four years, with no limitation on the number of years a Texas governor may serve, the opportunity for a governor to lead the state has increased. Selecting and supervising his personal staff are two key tests of his leadership.

THE GOVERNOR'S STAFF

"The governorship is preeminently a political office,"[6] notes one authority in state government. A brief look at the development of the Texas governor's personal staff would support such an observation, since the "politics" of functioning as the state's chief executive has given rise to a larger, more complex bureaucracy. As late as 1963 the *governor's office* was staffed by 68 full-time and 12 part-time employees.[7] Carrying out a campaign pledge to offer the state new leadership, John Connally reorganized the governor's office. Ten years later the staff of the governor had grown to some 250 employees, who assist the governor in many areas, as the organizational chart for Governor Briscoe's staff shows (see Figure 4-1).

In addition, the increasing demands upon state government to seek federal funds for welfare and other social services caused the Legislature to create the Office of Federal-State Relations, which works under the governor's direction. The Department of Community Affairs is coordinated by the governor, although it is also separately funded.

One of the innovations begun during Governor Preston Smith's administration was the overall planning process that included the *Goals for Texas* program. In order to give gubernatorial leadership in planning and coordinating programs to meet the future needs of the state, Smith expanded the governor's office to include an assistant for program development, with six directors reporting to the executive assistant.

To illustrate the scope of the governor's office, one division (Planning Coordination) includes offices for the following areas: information center, planning and development, regional services, natural resources, human resources, transportation, and special programs.

In the final analysis, the governor's office reflects two significant developments in state government. First, there has been a nationwide trend to personalize the office so that every interested citizen will have the opportunity to have access to one of the governor's assistants, or perhaps even to the chief executive. As Lockard indicates: "The ideal governor is responsive to the public demands and seeks to give the impression that he is concerned with every man's problem and that not only his office but his own broad shoulders are appropriate repositories for the worries and fears of the people."[8] Second, the increasing

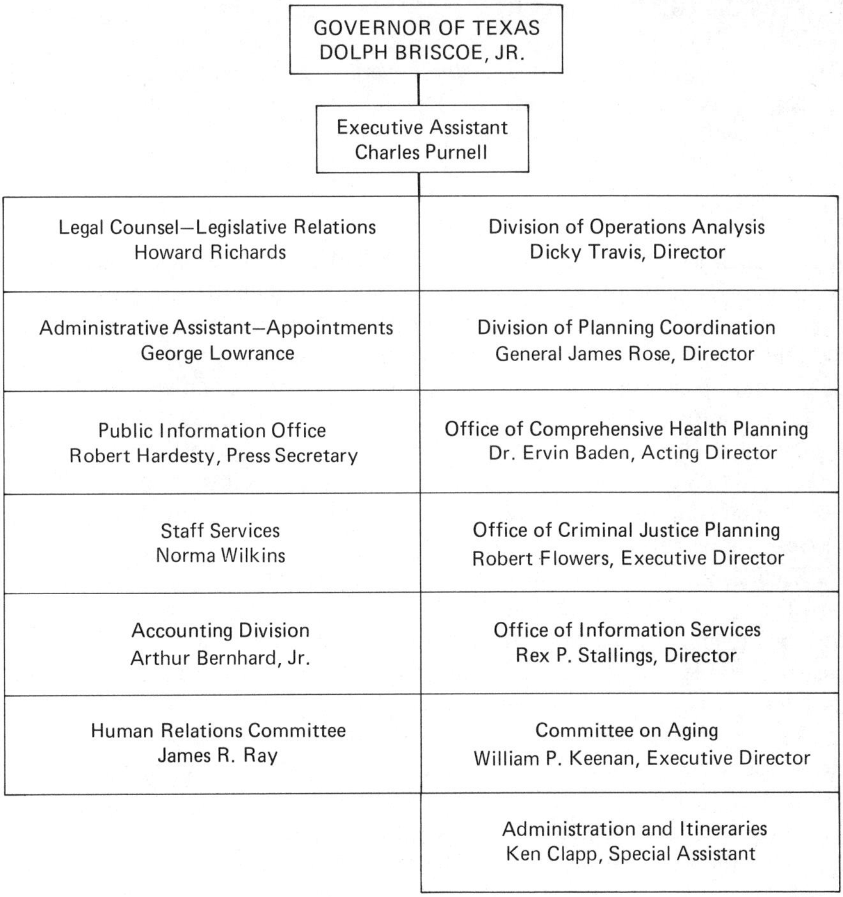

Figure 4-1
The principal staff-members of the Texas governor's office.

importance of intergovernmental relations involving cities, councils of governments, interstate councils, and federal aid has resulted in an enlargement of the governor's office. The passage of revenue-sharing legislation by the Congress will focus more attention on the governor's office as a broker between the federal government and the cities.

One might argue that "protecting the chief" is still the primary function of the governor's staff and that patronage is freely dispensed in staffing the gubernatorial aides. But such an argument is a tenuous one in Texas, where the complexity of handling large sums of money and coordinating programs that affect millions of people require that staffing be based more on a man's expertise than on political "pull."

Staffing of the governor's office is done without Senate confirmation. Thus, responsible only to the governor, his aides assist him in carrying out the formal and informal powers bestowed upon him by the constitution, custom, and practice.

POWERS OF THE GOVERNOR

Few formal powers are granted to the governor by the state constitution and legislation. His political acumen and popularity with the electorate are his principal tools in overcoming the limitations of the office.

APPOINTIVE

A fundamental tenet of executive power, whether in government, business or education, is the power to appoint and remove individuals in the organization. *Appointive power* is the most significant lever which the Texas governor holds over the state's board-commission system, but it has its limitations. First, some of the more powerful boards and commissions are not appointive, but elective. As an example, the Railroad Commission is a three-member elective body which regulates the oil and gas industries in Texas as well as intrastate transportation. The governor's hands are virtually tied in influencing the direction of the Railroad Commission because the three commissioners are elected by the people for six-year overlapping terms.

Second, the problem of the governor's being an *ex-officio member* of many boards and commissions, but still not being able to appoint or remove the elective board members, often results in uncontrolled waste and corruption. A cogent example of this problem is the case of the Veterans' Land Board scandal during the last administration of Governor Allan Shivers.

Hints of a possible scandal in Shivers's administration began in a series of stories published in the *Cuero Record,* a small weekly newspaper in South Texas. Ken R. Towery, managing editor of the *Record,* became suspicious when he discovered that some of Cuero's realtors were entertaining blacks and Mexican-Americans. His journalistic investigation produced these startling facts: Cuero blacks and Mexican-Americans, some of whom were war veterans, were signing land-purchase papers for vague reasons. Both minority groups thought they were to get free land from the state or receive a bonus of some kind. They obtained a bonus, but not from the state. Land promoters paid them for their signatures on applications for state loans with which to buy land.[9]

State Senator Dorsey Hardeman requested the Senate Investigating Committee to study the veterans' land program. By the end of December, 1954, the position of Land Commissioner Bascom Giles, a popularly elected official, had become so untenable that he refused to take his oath of office on January 1, 1955. Giles was later convicted and served a prison sentence for defrauding the public. The principal basis for his conviction was collusion with the land promoters in the form of "kickbacks." Money was allegedly returned to Giles for having allowed this scheme to be carried out.

This scandal contributed to the weakening of the political power of Allan Shivers. The governor was an ex-officio member of the Land Board, which was responsible for such fraudulent activity. Other members of this three-man board were the land commissioner and the attorney general. Shivers personally denied any involvement in the scandal and later commented on the governor's problems in seeing that the laws are faithfully executed:

This is an anomaly in the Texas setup: While in general policy matters and vital administrative functions the Texas governor has responsibility without authority, in the case of the vast detail work of the ex-officio boards he has authority without the time to exercise proper responsibility. This type of board should be replaced by an appointive board.[10]

Third, the governor is hampered by the fact that most of the 200-odd boards and commissions are governed by members who serve for six-year, overlapping terms of office. A new governor is forced to live with carry-overs from previous administrations who may or may not be supportive of him and his programs. With the two-year term of office (until 1975), a governor had to serve for at least two terms before he could appoint enough board-commission members who were his people.

Finally, the constitutional requirement of senatorial confirmation (twenty-one "aye" votes) coupled with the political necessity of "senatorial courtesy" often thwart gubernatorial appointments. "Senatorial courtesy" involves the governor's consulting the senator from the district of the appointee in an attempt to gain support for his confirmation. But political courtesy alone is sometimes not sufficient. Although confirmation usually is obtained, the Texas Senate can block qualified appointees for political or personal reasons. A case in point was the senatorial rejection of Larry Teaver, appointed by Governor Preston Smith to the chairmanship of the three-member State Insurance Board. Long an advocate of the controversial "no-fault" insurance plan for automobile owners, Teaver was denied his appointment because of intense pressure from insurance lobbyists and lawyers who specialize in automobile accident litigation.

Aside from his personal staff and vacancies on a board or commission, the governor appoints the secretary of state, the adjutant general, the commissioner of labor statistics, and the director of the Department of Community Affairs, each requiring senatorial confirmation. Vacancies in the state judiciary and the United States Senate and the Railroad Commission are filled by gubernatorial appointment and remain effective until the next election. Vacancies in the state legislature and the Texas delegation in the United States House of Representatives are filled by the voters in special elections, which are called by the governor.

REMOVAL

In creating the numerous boards and commissions, the legislature gives the governor appointive power but virtually no *removal power.* Lack of removal power causes the Texas governor to be more of a figurehead than a chief administrator of the state's bureaucracy. Persons directly responsible to the governor, such as his staff and statutory officials (for example, the director of the Department of Community Affairs) are subject to his removal power. On the other hand, the administrative business of state government, which is carried out by the boards and commissions, is removed from the governor's direct control. Informal pressure to resign or to accept another appointment may be resorted to by the governor in dealing with a board member, but this is not as effective as direct removal power. Impeachment by the House of Representatives, with conviction by the Senate, is the only constitutional method of removing state officials who serve on boards and commissions; this procedure is rarely employed.

MILITARY

The governor is commander in chief of the state military forces except when the President of the United States places the Texas National Guard, including air and ground forces, under federal orders. Acting under gubernatorial orders, the state adjutant general may mobilize the Texas National Guard to enforce the law, repel invasion, curb insurrection and riot, and maintain order in times of natural disasters such as tornadoes and floods. In rare cases he may declare martial law to restore order. Martial law has been used sparingly and with discretion by Texas governors. Interestingly enough, the last time *martial law* was invoked was in 1943 by Senator A. M. Aikin, who was acting governor during the absence of Governor Coke Stevenson and the lieutenant governor. Faced with a race riot, local officials requested that martial law be declared in Beaumont; it was invoked only temporarily until order could be restored.[11]

The governor also has some control over state law enforcement through his power to appoint, with Senate approval, the three members of the Public Safety Commission, who serve six-year, overlapping terms. The commission-appointed director of public safety oversees a staff of some 3,500 employees in the Department of Public Safety. Included in the department's responsibilities are state police, traffic supervision, driver licensing, motor vehicle inspection, and criminal law enforcement in cooperation with local and federal agencies.

When circumstances demand swift and direct action, it is sometimes necessary for the governor to assume command of the Texas Rangers, a branch of the Department of Public Safety. Such action occurred in 1951, when Governor Allan Shivers ordered the Rangers into Mansfield to restore order during a race riot.

BUDGETARY

There is a duality in Texas government relative to budget drafting and legislative implementation. Since 1951 the governor has been empowered to present a budget to the Legislature at its regular session. The Legislature, however, is more inclined to follow the recommendations of the Legislative Budget Board, which is independent of gubernatorial control.

Here political and personal wrangling can result in an executive-legislative deadlock over which budget to accept. Such an impasse was demonstrated in the 61st Legislature. A majority of the legislators, including Speaker Gus Mutscher and Lieutenant Governor Ben Barnes, wanted a one-year budget or a "pay-as-you-go" approach to state finance. Governor Preston Smith, however, advocated a two-year appropriations bill in compliance with Texas's biennial approach to state government. When the Legislature sent the one-year bill to the governor for his signature, he exercised the postadjournment prerogative in vetoing the measure. The governor was then forced to call a special session of the Legislature for the purpose of drafting a two-year budget which he could support and sign into law.

Thus the dual nature of the budgetary power creates a situation in which neither the governor nor the Legislature has final authority. The net result is all too often fiscal irresponsibility, waste, and lack of public accountability in handling the state's budgetary needs. The governor's *budgetary power* has been further reduced by an attorney general's opinion which forbids his transferring funds from one agency to another. Also, the governor has no impoundment power over appropriated funds.

LEGISLATIVE

Perhaps the most stringent test for a Texas governor's leadership is the biennial struggle for *legislative power* between the governor and the Legislature. His program for the next two years is spelled out in his "State of the State" address delivered at the beginning of each regular session of the Legislature. In addition, he delivers his budget message, special messages during the course of the regular session, and a farewell message at the conclusion of his term of office. How successful the message power is in promoting a harmonious relationship between governor and Legislature depends to a large degree upon external variables such as the timing of special messages vis-à-vis volatile issues, the support of powerful legislative committee chairmen for the governor's program, and the personal persuasiveness of the governor in outlining his program.

The governor possesses a strong *veto power* over legislative acts. For example, he may veto any item in an appropriation bill, while permitting enactment of the rest of the bill. Hence, the *item veto* gives him an effective bargaining position with individual legislators in the delicate game of "pork-barrel" politics (see Reading 4-3). The item veto, coupled with the infrequency with which the Legislature overrides the executive veto, gives the Texas governor a formidable weapon in dealing with recalcitrant legislatures. In contrast, the President of the United States does not possess an item veto.

Unlike the President of the United States, however, the governor of Texas cannot employ the *pocket veto.* The President exercises the prerogative of neither signing nor vetoing a bill within ten weekdays after its passage, thus allowing the measure to become law without his signature. But if he "pockets" a bill that is presented to him within ten weekdays before adjournment, his failure to act automatically kills the measure. The Texas governor has a different course. He may exercise a *post-adjournment veto.* That is, he can veto a bill within twenty days after a legislative session has ended and thus deprive the Legislature of the opportunity to override his veto in that session.

The governor also has the power to call the Legislature into special sessions, each of which, as we saw in Chapter 3, is limited to thirty days. There is no limit to the number of special sessions a governor may call. Although each special session is restricted to those topics which the governor submits for consideration, new business may be introduced, unless some member of either house raises a point of order that is sustained by the presiding officer. Failure of the presiding officer to support the governor's wishes will allow other items of business to come before the special session.

It may thus be argued that the governor's legislative role is a relatively strong one. Personal cajolery and astute balancing of the conflicting interests in the Legislature can place the governor in a strong leadership role vis-à-vis the Legislature.

JUDICIAL

The Texas governor has few formal *judicial powers.* That is, as Chapter 5 will relate, the state's judiciary is outside the governor's direction or influence in that all of the judges are elected, except for municipal court judges. The governor may exert influence on the judiciary by the power to appoint district and appellate court judges when a vacancy results from death or resignation (about 75 per cent of all urban-district judges were initially appointed). An overlapping mixture of personal friendship, state bar association activity, and qualifications as a jurist form the principal criteria for the governor's selection. The governor has no removal power over the state's judges.

What judicial powers the Texas governor does possess are found in relationship to the state's penal system. Working with the Board of Pardons and Paroles, a three-member board consisting of one member appointed by the governor, one by the chief justice of the Supreme Court, and one by the presiding judge of the court of criminal appeals, the governor may invoke executive *clemency.* The act of reducing a sentence assumes different forms.[12] *Parole* grants a release from prison on condition of future good behavior before the prisoner's term has expired and is granted by the board subject to the approval of the governor. *Pardon* is granted by the governor upon recommendation of the board and may occur before or after imprisonment. A full pardon means forgiveness for the offense, and restoration of full civil rights. A *reprieve* temporarily suspends execution of the penalty imposed. That is, the governor, without board recommendation, may grant one thirty-day reprieve in a death-sentence case; requests for such a reprieve usually are granted. The board may recommend additional reprieves. *Commutation of sentence* reduces a sentence or fine and is recommended by the board subject to approval by the governor.

EXTRALEGAL

Any description of the governor's office would be incomplete without including a word about the governor's involvement in political and ceremonial functions. In the eyes of Texans the impressive office in the eastern wing of the Capitol occupies center stage. Its occupant is often asked to serve as a symbol of the people of Texas. He could never hope to fill all of the requests made of him to speak and to participate in dedications, ceremonies, and humanitarian causes. However, within the limits of time and his own sense of priorities, the governor does attempt to make his role as chief public relations officer an effective one. The width and depth of this role cannot be fully measured, but its significance should not be underestimated in determining the political popularity of a governor.

The governor is also the head of his political party, and as such he must exercise astute political judgment in attempting to reconcile the various factions within his party. Since Reconstruction days the governor's office, as we have seen, has been in the control of the Texas Democratic Party. The conservative faction within the party has been dominant, with the exceptions of the administrations of James S. Hogg (1891-1896), James Ferguson (1915-1917), and James V. Allred (1935-1939).

THE PLURAL EXECUTIVE

Democratic control of the other executive offices in Texas' executive department also continues. Politically speaking, such control has contributed to the lack of responsiveness to the hue and cry for administrative reform in Texas government.

LIEUTENANT GOVERNOR

Considered by many political observers to be the most powerful official in Texas government, the lieutenant governor functions more in the legislative arena than in the executive branch. Article IV of the state constitution, nevertheless, places the lieutenant governorship in the executive branch. Upon the death, resignation, or removal by impeachment of the governor, the lieutenant governor ascends to the governorship. Receiving a salary of only $4,800, the holder of the office is in a position to have significant influence in state affairs. He serves a four-year term with no limitation on the number of terms.

The powers of the lieutenant governor are discussed in more detail in Chapter 3; here, however, they need a brief summary. Constitutionally, he is the presiding officer of the Senate (two-year term), with the right to vote in the case of a tie. By statutory provisions, he is a member of the Legislative Budget Board and of both the Legislative Audit Committee and the Legislative Redistricting Board. By the Rules of the Senate, he has tremendous influence in the legislative process because he appoints members to standing and conference committees and determines the order in which legislation is brought before the Senate.

The office of lieutenant governor has grown in importance primarily because of its impact on legislation. Moreover, as a steppingstone to the governorship or some other office, the lieutenant governorship is the prized objective of many political aspirants. Governor Allan Shivers and Railroad Commissioner Ben Ramsey perhaps contributed more to the power and prestige of the office than any other two living former lieutenant governors.[13] Shivers, who served as governor while Ramsey was lieutenant governor, combined strong personal friendship with an uncommon political acumen to wield power in the legislative and executive branches for about seven years (1949-1956).

The 1972 Democratic primary race for the lieutenant governorship was indicative of the high political stakes inherent in the office. The contest involved three state senators (Ralph Hall of Rockwall, Wayne Connally of Floresville, and Joe Christie of El Paso), Houston newspaper publisher William Hobby, and Odessa businessman William Jones.

Interestingly enough, the Republicans offered no candidates. Attacking Hall and Connally as being "in" politicians who supported the Sharpstown banking bills, Hobby successfully forced Connally into a run-off and then emerged as the winner of that contest. Hobby reported expenditures of more than $750,000 in the primary race, while Connally spent $254,570.

ATTORNEY GENERAL

Another constitutional executive is the attorney general, who serves as the state's lawyer by giving advisory opinions and representing the state in civil litigation. Overseeing a staff of some 160 assistants, the attorney general has the opportunity to influence public policy in many areas.

Receiving a salary of $33,000 set by the Legislature and possessing a four-year term of office (no limitation) the attorney general's office is sought by many Texas lawyers. The 1972 Democratic primary for attorney general also produced a new winner in the person of Houston lawyer John Hill, who had run unsuccessfully for governor in 1968. The late Crawford Martin was seeking a fourth two-year term. Hill had no Republican opponent in the general election.

COMMISSIONER OF THE GENERAL LAND OFFICE

Since its creation under the constitution of 1836 and subsequent retention by the present constitution, the Land Office has grown in power and responsibility. Exercising broad powers such as awarding oil, gas, and sulphur exploration leases, serving as chairman of the Veterans Land Board, and sitting as ex-officio member of numerous boards responsible for handling various public lands, the land commissioner is one of the more powerful elected state officials. Commissioner Bob Armstrong of Austin unseated Jerry Sadler in 1970 and was elected for a second two-year term in 1972. His salary is also $33,000 and he serves a four-year term (no limitation).

COMMISSIONER OF AGRICULTURE

One of the largest departments in the executive branch (580 employees), the Department of Agriculture is directed by a statewide elected commissioner (salary $33,000), who serves for a four-year term with no limitation on the number of terms. Since 1940 Commissioner John White has directed this department, which has the responsibility of enforcing agricultural laws and providing service programs for Texas farmers and consumers.

COMPTROLLER OF PUBLIC ACCOUNTS

A popularly elected official with a four-year term and unlimited succession, the comptroller of public accounts (salary $33,000) is the principal tax administrator of the state. Since 1949 the office has been filled by Robert S. Calvert, who was eighty years old when re-elected in 1972 (see Chapter 7 for a more detailed discussion of his duties).

STATE TREASURER

The treasury function is essentially one of receiving state funds and administering depositories for state funds authorized and approved by the State Depository Board, of which the treasurer is a member. Jesse James (salary $33,000), at age sixty-nine, was sworn in for his seventeenth term in 1972. He serves a four-year term with unlimited succession (see Chapter 7 for a more detailed description).

RAILROAD COMMISSION

Created during the administration of Governor James S. Hogg (1891-95), the regulatory responsibilities of the three-member Railroad Commission include a broad range of governmental regulations (see Reading 4-4). Current commissioners are Mack Wallace, Ben Ramsey, and Jim Langdon, each of whom is elected for a six-year, overlapping term on a statewide ballot and receives a salary of $33,000.

STATE BOARD OF EDUCATION

Created by statute in 1949, the State Board of Education consists of twenty-four members, who are elected from Texas' congressional districts for six-year, overlapping terms. The principal duties of the policy-making body include the following: appointment of the commissioner of education (chief administrative officer of the Texas Education Agency) with senatorial confirmation, passage on rules and policies recommended by the commissioner of education, execution of contracts for the purchase of textbooks, direction of the investment of the Permanent School Fund, and appointment of the fifteen-member State Textbook Committee. The board does not attempt to usurp local school district autonomy, but it does set policies to meet state educational needs, which are recommended by the commissioner or required by statutes passed by the Legislature.

THE ADMINISTRATIVE PROCESS

The preceding offices, along with the governor, constitute Texas's *plural executive,* as prescribed in Article IV of the state constitution. They are part of a sprawling bureaucracy which contributes to an already decentralized administrative system.

BOARDS AND COMMISSIONS

For all practical purposes, the administrative structure in Texas is more closely tied to the legislative than to the executive branch. The majority of the 200-odd *boards and commissions* are created by the Legislature and can be reorganized or abolished by statute. In most cases the governor appoints members of these boards and commissions to six-year, overlapping terms. Generally, board members meet occasionally, but the daily work of the agency is conducted by a board-appointed executive director and his staff.

The business of these boards and commissions includes a broad spectrum of governmental matters: election administration, property control, public land, external relations, public safety, regulation of business, health regulation, conservation of natural resources, highways, hospitals, institutions for the handicapped, correctional institutions, education, recreation, public welfare, pensions, retirements, fine arts, Indian affairs, and examining boards for the professions and crafts.[14] A strong case probably could be made for each of the boards and commissions, since most of them perform necessary functions. The overriding question involves not the "why" of the *bureaucracy* but the "where." Under the present structure, the governor has little direct control over the many important functions each of these boards carries out. This has resulted in a disintegrated system with little accountability to the governor, and even less to the general public.

The significance of the boards and commissions is clearly seen in the magnitude of the programs they oversee and the financial requirements needed to implement the programs. An insight into the complexity of Texas's bureaucracy is perhaps best achieved by examining selected departments and public policy areas.

Highways Spanning over 69,000 miles (the largest state highway system in the nation), Texas highways are managed by a three-member commission, appointed by the governor with Senate concurrence. Actual administrative control is given to the state highway engineer, who is appointed by the board. The state is divided into twenty-five district organizations, which operate under the supervision of the state highway engineer's headquarters in Austin.

With the passage of the Federal Highway Act in 1965, Texas was allotted the largest portion of the 42,000 mile Interstate Highway System (3,166 miles). In addition, the State Highway Commission oversees an extensive farm-market road system. In 1972 a new $20.1 million program was approved by the commission for the development of 436 miles of secondary roads in Texas.

Two of the more important issues confronting the future of Texas highways include mass urban transit systems and increased expenditures for highway maintenance and construction (see Chapter 6 for a discussion of the urban transit problem). It is estimated by State Highway Commissioner DeWitt C.

Greer that Texas needs to spend an additional $718 million on highways in 1973 to maintain an adequate standard for its highway system. Furthermore, Greer indicated that inflation has boosted construction prices so that it now takes $1.58 to buy the highway construction which cost $1.00 only ten years ago (1962).[15]

Welfare Perhaps the most controversial public policy area has been welfare, which takes many forms under the general heading of public assistance. Traditionally, control of Texas welfare programs has rested with the commissioner of public welfare, appointed by the three-member State Board of Public Welfare with concurrence by the Senate. The four areas of public assistance programs include Old Age Assistance, Aid to the Blind, Aid to Families with Dependent Children, and Aid to the Permanently and Totally Disabled. Financing these programs has involved use of federal (75 per cent) and state (25 per cent) funds. The board called upon the Legislature to provide the Welfare Department with $373 million for fiscal 1974, which began on September 1, 1973, and $424 million for fiscal 1975.

In the public's view the most controversial program is Aid to Families with Dependent Children (AFDC). Stigmatized by widespread illegitimacy of the children of families on AFDC welfare (27 per cent) and a high ratio of minority-group children (51 per cent Negro, 36 per cent Mexican-American, and 12 per cent Anglo), the total welfare program is victimized by negative public opinion.[16] Negativism was reflected in 1968 when Texas voters turned down a state constitutional amendment which would have raised the ceiling for state appropriations to the welfare program.

Taken in total perspective, however, the AFDC program in 1970 ranked third among the public assistance programs (medical payments, 47.5 per cent; Old Age Assistance, 34 per cent; AFDC, 14 per cent; Aid to the Permanently and Totally Disabled, 3.6 per cent; and Aid to the Blind, 0.9 per cent).[17] Furthermore, percentages of populations on welfare rolls in Texas' largest cities—Houston (2.9 per cent) and Dallas (3.6 per cent)—are relatively small when compared to those in Boston, New York, Baltimore, St. Louis, San Francisco, and Philadelphia. Each of these cities has more than 10 per cent of its population on welfare.[18]

Faced with spiraling welfare costs and lack of administrative coordination from the governor, two significant proposals for reform emerged in the early 1970s. First, both Governor Preston Smith and Lieutenant Governor Ben Barnes recommended that the state get out of the welfare field altogether and turn the program over to the federal government exclusively. Second, the Senate Interim Committee on Welfare Reform proposed a "Department of Human Resources," which would combine the programs of the State Department of Public Welfare and related programs, such as mental health and rehabilitation,[19] and would be directly responsible to the governor.

At the close of the 92nd Congress, the Supplemental Security Income Act was passed, which abolished the existing state-administered welfare programs of Old Age Assistance, Aid to the Blind and Aid to the Permanently and Totally

Disabled, effective January 1, 1974. Joint state-federal financing of the AFDC program will continue.

Education Problems in public education are multitudinous, whether analyzed in terms of financial support (discussed in Chapter 7), racial balance (discussed in Chapter 6), or levels of attainment (discussed in Chapter 1). Texas's administrative structure for public education tends to compound the problems by its multi-level arrangement. At the elementary-secondary level one sees general policies (i.e., teacher certification requirements, textbook lists, etc.) handed down by the twenty-four-member State Board of Education acting in conjunction with the Texas Education Agency and the board-appointed commissioner of education. Locally each district is governed by a popularly elected board, which sets local policy. In addition, some counties retain a county school board and superintendent (see Chapter 6 for a discussion of this office). Educational officials at both state and local levels must also conform to stringent federal guidelines in terms of racial mix in both student bodies and faculties for the purpose of receiving federal aid under such laws as the Elementary and Secondary Education Act of 1965.

Although local autonomy in public education has been a jealously guarded right of Texas communities, more state control, particularly in the area of financial support, coupled with increased federal aid, seem imminent in Texas's future. At the state administrative level, the Texas Urban Development Commission has recommended the establishment of a state Office of Equal Education Opportunity in the Texas Education Agency to administer state-federal compensatory programs and to identify and eliminate ethnic inequity in Texas.[20]

Lack of gubernatorial direction and responsibility for the overall level of the state's public education is vividly revealed in the foregoing administrative structure. That is, the State Board of Education, members of which are relatively unknown to the voting public, are popularly elected. Vested with broad policy decisions affecting some 2.7 million schoolchildren, the board appoints the state commissioner of education, who is responsible to the board rather than to the governor.

Higher education is also the recipient of loose state coordination from the governor's office. The governor does appoint the eighteen-member Coordinating Board of Colleges and Universities, in addition to members who serve on fifteen Boards of Regents for the respective colleges and universities. The Coordinating Board has authority over such matters as creating new departments, adding or deleting degree programs, and setting long-range goals for the state's higher-education needs. Individual institutions, however, are governed directly by their own boards, which appoint the chief administrative personnel for each school. Competition for state appropriations causes most of Texas's colleges and universities to lobby the Legislature and to develop political leverage with key lawmakers, rather than to look for gubernatorial leadership.

Junior or community colleges are governed by independent, countywide boards or are a part of a local school district. The Coordinating Board also has some power over the two-year colleges; for example, proposed new districts must be approved by the board. But Texas has no state-directed administrative authority over the junior colleges, such as is currently operating in California.

STATE REGULATION

The terms "duplication" and "overlapping functions" would apply to governmental regulation in Texas. Perhaps the issues of air and water pollution best serve to exemplify the problem of a multi-agency approach to state regulation. With the growth of Texas's metropolitan areas, air and water pollution have increasingly emerged as a major concern for the inhabitants of Texas' larger cities. When the individual citizen seeks relief from air pollution, he is confronted with a myriad of state agencies which are involved in some way with the problem. According to the office of the Texas attorney general, they include: (1) the Air Control Board, (2) the Water Quality Board, (3) the Water Development Board, (4) the Parks and Wild Life Department, (5) the State Department of Health, (6) the Railroad Commission and (7) the Water Rights Commission.

As one commentator editorialized on this multi-agency problem, ". . . if you go to Austin seeking relief from pollution, you will need a list of government agencies, a city map and probably your lawyer."[21] With the creation of the Environmental Protection Agency at the national level, it appears that more federal involvement in the regulation of air and water pollution is imminent unless integration of Texas agencies involved in the problem results in more concentrated control at the state level.

State regulation also extends to such areas as banking (the State Banking Board, the Finance Commission, and the State Securities Board), insurance (the State Insurance Board), oil and gas (the Railroad Commission), labor health standards (the Occupational Safety Board), and numerous occupations and professions. By noting examples of how board members are selected and how they conduct their business, one gains further insight into Texas' administrative process.

POLITICS OF ADMINISTRATION

Hidden by the bureaucratic maze and isolated from direct reprisal from the chief executive in the form of removal, the boards and commissions can function according to the dictates of related special-interest groups. Little attention is given to this situation until graft or scandal is discovered. Then the sharp glare of adverse publicity catapults a particular board into statewide exposure. The Texas Liquor Control Board irregularities of 1968 resulted in the creation of a new agency to regulate the liquor industry, the Alcoholic Beverages Commission, composed of three members appointed by the governor with Senate approval (see Reading 4-5).

Also, special-interest groups having influence in the Legislature and with the governor can wield power with regard to policy-making and appointments to the boards and commissions. The following recent examples of interest-group activity vis-à-vis boards and commissions are noteworthy.

Airlines In April, 1972, the Texas Aeronautics Commission, composed of six members appointed by the governor, canceled the certificates of four commuter airlines: R.W.K. Airlines, Houston Commuter Airlines, National Flight Center, and King Flight Service. Charged with regulating intrastate air passenger and freight transportation, this six-member commission demonstrated a propensity to safeguard the interests of the big airlines which provide both intrastate and interstate service, e.g., Texas International, Braniff International, and Southwest Airlines.

Vending-machine Industry A second example of special-interest domination of state commissions was revealed in the appointments to the newly created Texas Vending Commission. Under the terms of the 1971 statute creating this commission, it is composed of six members appointed by the governor (three to represent the industry and three to represent the general public) and three ex officio members: the consumer credit commissioner, the attorney general, and the director of the Department of Public Safety. In appointing members representing the coin-operated vending-machine industry, not only did Governor Preston Smith select all his appointees from the big companies (including a chairman who had made a large financial contribution to Smith's re-election campaign in 1970), but he also appointed as representatives of the general public two commissioners with business ties to the industry.

Optometry One of the most important areas of administrative activity involves the licensing and regulation of many professions and vocations. Some thirty-eight boards regulate professions ranging from architecture to vocational nursing. All too often a conflict of interest in the governance of these professions hampers the professional ethics and performance of those involved. Such a case was recently demonstrated in a controversy involving the Texas Optometry Board. A six-member board created to regulate the state's optometrists, the members are appointed by the governor and must be licensed optometrists who have practiced in Texas five years preceding their appointment. For many years there has been a battle between a group of optometrists who oppose chain-type operations, such as Texas State Optical, and those who favor the chains. One member of the board had obtained a license to establish branch offices of his practice in several Texas cities under the 1955 law creating the Board of Examiners in Optometry. Three members of the current board voted to hold a public hearing after the North Texas Optometric Society challenged the legality of the member's license. Final disposition of the case is still pending, but it exemplifies the difficulties in regulating a multi-million-dollar industry when board members have vested interests within the profession.

Insurance Legislative interference with administrative business poses another problem for the boards and commissions. When a powerful legislator, armed with the power to determine appropriations for a board, is involved in a state-regulated business, special favors are often bestowed upon him. As an example, it was recently disclosed that an insurance firm, owned by Representative W. S. Heatly of Paducah, had failed to submit annual financial reports to State Insurance Department auditors as required by law. The State Insurance Department is governed by the State Board of Insurance, composed of three members appointed by the governor with Senate approval. Until March 7, 1972, Heatly was chairman of the House Appropriations Committee, which passes upon all state agency budgets. Apparently fearing budgetary reprisal from Heatly, State Insurance Commissioner Clay Cotten authorized Ira Goodrich, head of the Insurance Department's title section, to grant Heatly's firm a new license. Goodrich acknowledged that out of 547 title agencies in Texas, only Heatly's firm had been permitted to flout the audit requirement.

Created to protect the public interest, the state's boards and commissions obviously do not function as was originally intended. Endless debate can be provoked by any proposal for remedying the defects of these agencies, but most citizens will agree with an opinion expressed in the December 30, 1971, issue of the *San Angelo Standard Times:* "As a matter of good principle, no board or commission charged with regulating any business should be dominated by members of the regulated business. The conflict of interest is bad for business and for the public, and it tends to compromise high government officials."[22]

Underlying, if not undermining, the administrative structure of Texas government is a *spoils system* that staffs thousands of state offices on the basis of friendships in the Legislature or in the governor's office (see Reading 4-6). Lack of a state civil service program with competitive examinations for many state positions may result in the appointment of an incompetent, or political "hack," who serves his time with little regard for professional ethics or the public interest. Currently only eleven state agencies staff on a merit basis, the largest of which are the Departments of Public Safety, Health, Welfare, Mental Health and Mental Retardation, and the Texas Employment Commission. Supervision of employment based upon competitive examinations is carried out by the Merit System Council, composed of three members who serve for six-year terms and are appointed by the Texas Employment Commission.

PROPOSED REFORMS

Concerned groups and professions (such as the League of Women Voters, editorial writers, and political scientists) have consistently gone on record as favoring a drastic overhaul of the executive branch. A major reform was instituted by Texas voters in 1972 with the passage of a constitutional amendment providing a four-year term for the governor, with no limit on succession of terms. Other reforms, however, are needed in order to make the Texas governor an effective chief executive.

CABINET SYSTEM

The administrative jungle of state government is perhaps the focal point in any discussion about needed reforms in the executive branch. Aside from the lieutenant governor, the governor should have appointive power, with Senate concurrence, for the offices of attorney general, comptroller, treasurer, land commissioner, and the three-member Railroad Commission, which would serve as a *state cabinet.* Direct removal by the governor for these offices would allow him to take the reins of state government. As we have seen, special interests, coupled with voter apathy toward the executive offices other than those of governor and lieutenant governor, tie the governor's hands with regard to seeing that the laws are faithfully executed.

CONSOLIDATION

Some 200 boards and commissions create an unwieldy bureaucracy for the governor. Studies of the board-commission system have long advocated a reduction and consolidation to some fifteen to twenty departments. Again, appointment of department heads by the governor with Senate concurrence, along with gubernatorial removal, would strengthen the governor's hand.

EXECUTIVE BUDGET

The newly adopted four-year term for governor gives additional impetus to reforming his budgetary powers. At present the governor shares the budget-making function with the Legislature, which, because of its close ties with the various state agencies, can often ignore the governor's recommendations. Unquestionably, the power of appropriation should reside in the Legislature; but fiscal responsibility demands that the governor and his budgetary staff recommend a unified budget for the state agencies.

Perhaps the most convincing evidence for executive reform in Texas appears in a study by Professor Joseph Schlesinger. Following an in-depth comparison of the formal powers of governors, Professor Schlesinger concludes with the following statistics:

> To arrive at a general rating of the governor's formal powers we have combined the four measures of each governor's strength: his tenure potential, and his appointive, budgetary and veto powers. The maximum possible rating is 19, found only in New York. The lowest rating is 7, found in *Texas,* North Dakota, Mississippi, and South Carolina.[23]

Texas could significantly strengthen the powers of its governor and still leave him weaker than the chief executive in many other states.

APPENDIX

Governors of Texas (1874-1973)

Governors	Term	Distinctions in Office
Richard Coke	1874-76	Present constitution was written
Richard B. Hubbard	1876-79	First governor under the constitution of 1876
Oran M. Roberts	1879-83	First governor to come from the "Tyler Gang"
John Ireland	1883-87	Brought an end to the "fence cutting" war in West Texas
Lawrence S. Ross	1887-91	"Man of the People"–mediocrity in Texas government
James S. Hogg	1891-95	Railroad Commission was created
Charles A. Culberson	1895-99	The "Quiet Era" of Texas politics
Joseph D. Sayers	1899-1903	Left Congress for the governorship
Samuel W. T. Lanham	1903-07	Col. House instrumental as his campaign manager in his election
Thomas M. Campbell	1907-11	First leftist in the governorship
Oscar B. Colquitt	1911-15	Fought prohibition–led to administrative squabbles
James E. Ferguson	1915-17	Only governor to be impeached and convicted
William P. Hobby	1917-21	Began an amicable era in Texas's relations with Mexico
Pat M. Neff	1921-25	First governor to point up high cost of being governor of Texas
Miriam A. Ferguson	1925-27 1933-35	First woman governor of Texas
Dan Moody	1927-31	Laid the foundation for the creation of the Board of Pardons and Paroles
Ross S. Sterling	1931-33	Maintained martial law in East Texas oil fields for six months
James V. Allred	1935-39	Texas's most liberal governor
W. Lee O'Daniel	1939-41	First governor to make extensive use of the radio both in campaigns and while in office
Coke R. Stevenson	1941-47	First governor to break two-term tradition
Beauford H. Jester	1947-49	First governor to begin movement for constitutional revision in Texas
Allan Shivers	1949-57	Longest tenure in office–helped to carry Texas for President Eisenhower and the Republican party in both the 1952 and 1956 presidential campaigns
Price Daniel	1957-63	Used the special sessions more than any governor since Dan Moody

John Connally	1963-69	Tourist promotion and creation of Coordinating Board for Higher Education
Preston Smith	1969-73	*Goals for Texas* program
Dolph Briscoe, Jr.	1973-	

NOTES

1. William Young, "The Development of the Governorship," *State Government,* XXXI (Spring, 1958), 178.
2. Alexis de Tocqueville, *Democracy in America* (New York: Alfred Knopf, 1945), pp. 87-88.
3. Leslie Lipson, *The American Governor, from Figurehead to Leader* (Chicago: University of Chicago Press, 1939), pp. 2-3.
4. Fred Gantt, Jr., *The Chief Executive in Texas, A Study in Gubernatorial Leadership* (Austin, Tex.: University of Texas Press, 1964), p. 29.
5. *The Book of the States, 1970-71* (Lexington, Ky.: The Council of State Governments, 1970), p. 156.
6. Duane Lockard, *The Politics of State and Local Government,* 2nd ed. (New York: The Macmillan Co., 1969), p. 339.
7. Gantt, *op. cit.,* p. 103.
8. Lockard, *op. cit.,* p. 338.
9. "One for the Record," *Time,* March 7, 1955, pp. 84-85.
10. Allan Shivers, University of Houston television interview, quoted in Gantt, *op. cit.,* p. 164.
11. Gantt, *op. cit.,* p. 163.
12. *Guide to Texas State Agencies,* 3rd ed. (Austin, Tex.: Institute of Public Affairs of the University of Texas, 1970), pp. 134-135.
13. J. William Davis, *There Shall Also Be a Lieutenant Governor* (Austin, Tex.: Institute of Public Affairs of the University of Texas, 1967).
14. For a complete listing of the boards-commissions, see the *Texas Almanac and State Industrial Guide, 1972-73* (Dallas: A. H. Belo Corp.), pp. 616-628.
15. The *Texas in Action Report* (Austin, Tex.: Executive Services, Inc., October 2, 1972), p. 33.
16. Senate Interim Committee on Welfare Reform, *Breaking the Poverty Cycle in Texas* (Austin, Tex.: 1970), p. 13.
17. *Ibid.,* p. 35.
18. Texas Urban Development Commission, *Urban Texas: Policies for the Future* (Arlington, Tex.: Institute of Urban Studies, The University of Texas at Arlington, November, 1971), p. 158.
19. Senate Interim Committee on Welfare Reform, *op. cit.,* p. 39.
20. Texas Urban Development Commission, *op. cit.,* p. 184.

21. As quoted in Fred Pass, "One Texas Environmental Agency?" *Dallas Morning News*, December 2, 1972.
22. *San Angelo Standard Times*, December 30, 1971.
23. Joseph A. Schlesinger, "Politics of the Executive," in Herbert Jacobs and Kenneth W. Vines, eds., *Politics in the American States* (Boston: Little, Brown and Co., 1965), p. 209.

KEY TERMS AND CONCEPTS

reorganization movement
Article IV of the constitution of 1876
gubernatorial aspirant
governor's office
Goals for Texas
appointive power
ex-officio member
removal power
martial law
budgetary power
legislative power
veto power
item veto
pocket veto
post-adjournment veto
judicial powers
clemency
parole
pardon
reprieve
commutation of sentence
plural executive
boards and commissions
bureaucracy
spoils system
state cabinet

BOB TAYLOR FROM THE TIMES HERALD

Selected Readings

4-1
TEXAS' NEW GOVERNOR
Weldon Hart

Dolph Briscoe, Jr. has to be the prototypal example of the hometown boy who made good, in Uvalde and in most of the far-flung precincts of Texas.

His position as favorite son was magnified statewide when his general election victory November 7 confirmed what the electorate had been expecting for many months: The next Texas governor is going to be Dolph Briscoe.

The 1972 Democratic primaries produced two memorable developments in the governor's race. The first primary brought a thunderbolt, the elimination of Governor Preston Smith and the favorite Lt. Governor Ben Barnes. Briscoe's presence at the head of the list was not as startling as State Representative Frances (Sissy) Farenthold's strong showing as runner-up.

From the *Texas Star,* November 26, 1972, pp. 6-7. Reprinted by permission.

Not really too surprising, either, was Briscoe's runoff victory in June. But the end result—Briscoe as governor—would have been a long-odds bet in the beginning.

Five of the last seven Texas governors have been, in a broad sense, "South Texans," but none of the others represented an area as thinly populated as the southwestern sector where Briscoe grew up. Counties touching Uvalde average less than 10,000 population, only a fourth of the statewide average. A lot of room is left for ranches, and Dolph Briscoe owns or leases half a dozen of them. The total acreage under his brand is about one million; the largest unit is the fabulous Catarina, 165,000 acres, dotted with fish-filled lakes and stretching out of Dimmit County across a corner of Webb to the Rio Grande.

The Kingpin of Briscoe's cattle operations is Briscoe Ranches, Inc., of which he is president. A practicing environmentalist before the word became popular (he won the outstanding conservation rancher award in 1958), Dolph is noted for taking barren, drouth-burned cactus and mesquite land and turning it into lush green pastures.

Next to the cattle business, Briscoe comes over strong in the banking business. He is chairman of the board at both the First State Bank in Uvalde and the Security State Bank in San Antonio, and a director of the Alamo National Bank of San Antonio. Some claim Briscoe had to line up places to store his money; others say that he, like most cattlemen, just wanted to be sure he could borrow when he needed to.

Seriously, Dolph Briscoe knows what it means to be short of cash. His late father, Dolph Sr., went broke in the cattle business twice and came back twice, finally leaving to his only son what Dolph calls "a very fine ranching business."

While granting "We've been fortunate enough to make it grow," young Briscoe is reluctant to call himself a wealthy man. One reason is his innate modesty—but the main reason is because, by his definition, a man doesn't really "get rich" in an operating business like a cattle ranch. A good year is when enough's left over to start another.

"We have no cinch income from investments or yields from bonds," he explained to a newspaper friend. "Ours is an operating business that requires considerable working capital."

He doesn't add, although he might, that a bad year could make a cattle fortune disappear pretty fast.

You can understand why Briscoe, an essentially conservative man financially, can say—and mean it: "I've never considered myself wealthy."

Be that as it may, Dolph Briscoe is a highly regarded man in his own habitat and beyond. He has been prominent, popular and successful all his life in Uvalde, to an extent that might have been dangerous to his personality if he hadn't been immune to excesses. He was born in Uvalde, April 23, 1923, and graduated from Uvalde High School in 1939 as valedictorian. He was graduated from the University of Texas in 1943; finished up World War II as a GI in the CBI Theater in Southeast Asia.

Aided by his pretty young wife Janey (born Betty Jane Slaughter of Austin) and encouraged by hometown friends, Dolph ran for and won a place in the Legislature. When old acquaintances remember him as a "liberal" in the House, he believes they're remembering only part of the story.

"I served four terms in the House and never had an opponent—didn't have one when I quit. I represented a very conservative area, and, I'm convinced, represented it satisfactorily," Briscoe says.

Briscoe was aligned with some of the young firebrands in the House—people like Maury Maverick, Jr., Jim Sewell, D. B. Hardeman—in what started as a fight with Governor Allan Shivers over farm-to-market roads. The details have long been forgotten, but the general effect remains vivid: By opposing Shivers, widely identified as the conservative leader of the state, Briscoe came to be classed as a "liberal." (He might have been called a member of the "Dirty Thirty," except that name wasn't in use then and, besides, Briscoe had a lot more than 30 colleagues. It turned out, in fact, that the young rebels gave Shivers what amounted to his only legislative defeat in a record stay as governor—an event that Shivers and Briscoe don't talk about these days.)

What Briscoe was defending against dilution was the "Colson-Briscoe Bill," $15 million a year from general revenue for farm-to-market roads. (It was still in effect in 1972, $360 million worth of roads later.)

After three reelections in the House, Briscoe checked out. His voting record for eight years was described most adequately, perhaps, as moderate-conservative. He had a test on bills: "I tried to vote on every issue for what I thought was best for the state."

Briscoe turned more seriously to business and family matters after 1957. He and Betty Jane already had two children, Janey (now 21) and Dolph III (now 18), more generally known around Uvalde as Chip. Cele, 15, finished off the home roll that year. Not surprisingly, the Briscoe offspring are well-knit and fair of face; both parents are very handsome people. They are an Episcopalian family.

Honors continued to come Dolph's way: Named one of the five outstanding young Texans by the Jaycees in 1958; president of the Texas & Southwestern Cattle Raisers Association, 1960-61; winner of the Knapp-Porter Award for distinguished service to agriculture, given by the Texas Agricultural Extension Service in 1966; president of the South Texas Chamber of Commerce, 1967-68; "Mr. South Texas" at the Laredo George Washington's Birthday celebration in 1967; a Silver Beaver with the Boy Scouts of America in 1968 (he is a director in Region Nine); chairman of the National Livestock and Meat Board, Chicago; trustee of the Texas A&M Research Foundation; Chairman of the Board of Trustees, Mohair Council of America, 1966-70, and so on and on.

Not to be overlooked on the list is his position as president of the Southwest Animal Research Foundation, which is the outfit that does an amazing control job on the familiar and obnoxious screwworm. Briscoe was one of the first stock raisers to "buy" the process and has supported it faithfully and aggressively. Except for occasional reinfestation out of Mexico, this natural enemy of cattle, deer and other animals both wild and domestic has been effectively restrained in Texas.

Speaking of wild things, such as bucks and birds, the Briscoe ranches are teeming with game of many sorts. The ranches are hunted conservatively in season by Briscoe and his guests. The giant Catarina is ideally equipped as a "guest ranch," although it is much more than that. Over a hundred people can bed down in the ranch house. On-ranch travel is by converted Land Rovers with an unobstructed view and shooting room on top for hunters. Friends say it fits Dolph's idea of sportsmanship and fair play to shoot from the top of a swaying bus, traveling hard over rough cowtrails, at a running target two or three hundred yards away. To say the least, Briscoe is a thoroughgoing outdoorsman, both proficient and cautious when bullets are flying.

A question is bound to occur about this time to a reader somewhat uninitiated in political whims and ambitions:

Why does a fellow like Dolph Briscoe want to be governor?

Why would a man in the prime of life (49), in good health, fortunate and happy with a charming family, secure in the home country he loves, blessed with ranch holdings that produce good cash crops (good enough, for example, so that Briscoe could spend $350,000 of his own money in his fourth-place finish in the 1968 Democratic primary), honored and popular in civic life, modest and unassuming in public life, with an unblemished reputation in private life—why would Dolph Briscoe trade all that for a political job likely to pay more in blood and tears than in coin of the realm?

The man himself admits it's a good question. One that's hard for a modest man to answer. A man such as Dolph Briscoe is reluctant to say he wants to be governor because he thinks he can do the job better than anyone else. And it isn't a case of over-confidence, or ignorance of what the assignment includes. A lifelong Democrat, he has friends—and enemies—on both sides.

Although Briscoe has held no other state office than that of representative and has been out of politics since 1957, he knows there are more brickbats than bouquets headed his way. He has already received some of the former, even though he actually isn't governor yet: His experiences with McGovernites, Wallaceites, laborites, and the delicately poised groups of extreme liberals and intense conservatives have already taken some hide off at the party conventions. In a manner neither entirely critical nor laudatory, Briscoe has been referred to as an "amateur" in dealing with the tough questions from racial and economic groups not entirely pleased with anyone or anything. And, although not a babe in the political woods exactly, Briscoe probably rates the label of an "amateur" going about a rugged job in a naive sort of way.

It could be, on the other hand, that the uncertain course of politics and government in Texas these last few years has left the electorate so gun-shy it can't tell the difference between naiveté and candidness. Jaundiced commentators, cynical about political motives, might not take Briscoe at face value—which, according to his friends back in the ranch country, is about the only safe way to take him.

It's rather an odd thing to say, but the best answer to that "why-run-for-governor" question could be a direct quotation from one of his own pieces of campaign literature. Usually campaign literature is best hidden away in the "forget" file. With Briscoe it might be different. Here is what he said about seeking the office:

"I'm proud to be a native Texan, and I feel a commitment to serve the people of our great state.

"I pledge . . . that I'll be free to act in the interest of the people, with no ties to political machines or financial interests that will keep me from putting the public's interest first."

Whether Dolph Briscoe will be able to "act in the interest of the people" is another good question and one that only the passing months will answer. All you can really count on—according to the evidence at hand—is that he definitely means to try.

4-2
THE CASE AGAINST "PA" FERGUSON
Felton West

"Why they impeached old Jim Ferguson for less than that."

That remark has been made frequently during the past year, and impeachment has been suggested for state officials accused of taking stock profits which allegedly influenced their official acts. What the comparison shows, however, is that there are a good many Texans who don't remember their Texas history very well. The present-day officials who are involved in stock scandals are in bad repute, and some of them have been indicted. But to set the record straight, Farmer Jim wasn't playing around with any kid stuff, either.

While most adult Texans probably know that Ferguson was once a Texas governor and that he was impeached, there may not be many who recall the full story of his deportment. James Edward Ferguson, a high-school dropout in Bell County, taught himself law and became a successful small-town farmer and banker. A political unknown in 1914, he ran for governor advocating a "business administration" and won the election. He appealed strongly to the tenant farmers and spoke their language. Someone called him the "master of rural English." But some of the city slickers liked him, too. After all, he was a banker as well as a farmer, and the "business administration" part sounded good to the captains of industry. "We are agin high taxes," "Pa" Ferguson roared. "We are agin high rent."

The new governor got along well with the Legislature during most of his first term, winning nearly all of his objectives and making some acknowledged governmental improvements. In 1916, the governor's race was between two Methodist preachers' sons, Ferguson and Charles H. Morris of Winnsboro. Ferguson won again, but by this time he was under attack. His "business administration" was not very businesslike, it was said, and there was extravagance and mishandling of state funds.

The governor feuded with the Legislature, the attorney general and the courts about the legality of using state money to pay the governor's grocery bill and supplement his $4,000 salary. He lost that argument and refunded $2,403.55

From the *Texas Star,* December 26, 1971, pp. 12-14. Reprinted by permission.

of the public funds. It was not the first nor the last of his difficulties, but he might not have been impeached except for an all-out war he waged against the University of Texas. That controversy led to serious investigation that disclosed a shocking accumulation of irregularities.

Charging payroll padding, graft and misuse of public funds at U.T., Ferguson made war of the kind calculated to be popular with his rural supporters. He called for abolishing fraternities and labeled faculty members "day dreamers," "butterfly chasers" and "two-bit thieves." He tried to tell the university administrators and board of regents how to spend their legislative appropriation and was ignored. He demanded the firing of five faculty members, and the regents investigated, and then ignored him again. Governor Ferguson used pressure in trying to get some regents to resign, and he tried to pack the board with regents who would obey his orders. He got action, but not the kind he wanted. The result was senate opposition, court actions and an aroused U.T. student body, which marched to the Capitol in protest. (Ferguson called it a "mob.")

While temperatures rose, Ferguson eventually did get the board of regents packed to his satisfaction. Six professors were fired. He wasn't through. On June 2, 1917, the angry governor shocked an uneasy Texas citizenry by vetoing the entire $1.6 million appropriation for the university and its medical branch. People feared that the schools would have to close. That was Ferguson's fatal mistake. He had managed to live through some others.

Prior to that time, resolutions had been introduced in both the House and Senate calling for an investigation of the governor for misuse of public funds, violations of the banking laws, and other irregularities, but Ferguson talked both houses out of the investigations. A subsequent House resolution, calling for impeachment if charges against the governor were true, resulted in a committee investigation that censured him for the way he paid his grocery bill and for being indebted far in excess of the law's allowance to his own Temple State Bank; but the committee refused to recommend impeachment.

The governor's troubles were not over by any means. On July 21, he was questioned by the Travis County grand jury and six days later was indicted along with several of his appointees. He was accused of seven instances of misapplying public funds, one of embezzlement and one of diversion of a public fund. Ferguson claimed a "frame-up" and said he had never misused a nickel of state money. The grand jury indictments never went to court, and Ferguson announced his third-term candidacy. But House Speaker F. O. Fuller had called the House to convene on August 1 to consider impeaching the governor. Though Ferguson claimed the action was not legal, the attorney general upheld the speaker.

When it became apparent that a quorum of the House would attend, Ferguson tried to take the offensive by calling a special session of the whole Legislature for August 1 to appropriate again for the University of Texas. The same U.T. funds he had vetoed were approved again, but that was only a sideshow. For about three weeks the House investigated 13 charges Fuller made against Ferguson. Then it returned 21 articles of impeachment (analogous to indictments), suspended Ferguson and turned the government temporarily over to Lt. Governor William P. Hobby on August 25.

After a trial that began August 30, the Senate on September 25 found Ferguson guilty of 10 of the charges (by far more than the needed two-thirds majorities in most cases) and voted 25-3 to bar him from ever holding state office again. Nine of the sustained charges were considered violations of law, the tenth "official misconduct" that was bad public policy. Three involved his war on U.T. He was found guilty of trying to set aside laws putting control of the university under the regents by telling regents what to do and purging them for not doing his bidding–in one case trying to influence a regent by remitting $5,000 due the state. Five other sustained charges alleged misapplication of funds. Three were that he placed or had placed state funds in the Temple State Bank, more than one-fourth of which he owned, for his own and other stockholders' benefit. The prosecution claimed $354,000 of the secretary of state's funds were in Ferguson's bank at one time, some of it actually carried there by the governor.

Although he claimed an accounting mistake was responsible, the Senate also found him guilty of having had a $5,600 personal debt paid from some of the state money at his bank. Because he induced the Temple bank to lend him more than $150,000, when state law would have allowed it to lend no more than $37,500 to one individual, the Senate convicted him of not carrying out his duty to respect and enforce the banking laws. Ferguson had laughed off that charge, saying the Legislature should be proud of a governor who could borrow that much. Lastly, the Senate found him guilty of "official misconduct" and contempt of the House for refusing to say where he got some $156,000 in mysterious cash while in office. Rumors were rife that he had received the cash from various special interests. Ferguson claimed he had borrowed it from personal friends, but refused to identify them. Trying to evade the consequences of the judgment, he resigned the day before it took effect and claimed it did not apply to him. He later lost a court appeal on this question.

He spent the rest of his life seeking vindication in one way or another from the voters, many of whom obviously thought he got a raw deal. Defeated by Hobby in the 1918 gubernatorial campaign, he ran unsuccessfully as the American (Know-Nothing) Party presidential candidate in 1920 and for the United States Senate in 1922. In 1924, offering two governors for the price of one, he got his wife, Miriam A. "Ma" Ferguson elected governor–the first woman so elected in Texas. They lost her governor's races in 1926 and 1930, but bounded back to the office in the 1932 voting, only to be turned out again after two years and to lose again in their last hurrah in 1940.

Farmer Jim's supporters continually hoped to clear his name and restore his right to hold office with an amnesty act expunging his impeachment from the record. In "Ma's" first term, she got such an act passed, but under her successor, Governor Dan Moody, it was rescinded. So her husband went to his grave in 1944 still legally locked out of the office he was so good at winning. Amazingly, though, he had remained a power in Texas politics for 30 years, hated by his enemies but well loved by rural folk and many of the city slickers.

Ferguson's was no Mickey Mouse operation, as the record shows. It is too early to compare him with any of the present-day state office holders, however, because their complete story has not yet unfolded.

4-3
THE GOVERNOR'S VETO IN TEXAS: AN ABSOLUTE NEGATIVE?
Fred Gantt, Jr.

THE VETO IN TEXAS

Despite the fact that the governorship in Texas is widely acclaimed as being a constitutionally "weak" office, it nevertheless is regarded generally as having a "strong" veto power. A recent comparative evaluation of formal gubernatorial powers in all states ranked the governor's office in Texas as one of the four weakest among American state executives (along with Mississippi, South Carolina, and North Dakota). The same study, however, placed Texas among the states having a strong veto power.[1] In such a paradoxical situation, the importance of the gubernatorial veto as a check upon the legislative process becomes especially significant within the Texas context.

All five constitutions under which Texas has operated as a state in the union have provided for the executive veto. Consistently, the constitutions have strengthened the position of the governor in this regard. The first Reconstruction Constitution of 1866 granted him the item veto on appropriations; the Constitution of 1876 lengthened the time for consideration of bills sent to him, and also permitted him to exercise a post-adjournment veto, which in actuality gives him the power of life and death over a proposed bill coming to him after the legislature has adjourned. Article IV, Section 14 of the Texas Constitution contains the veto power as currently practiced. Under the terms of its provisions, the governor has ten days, excluding Sundays, to act upon a bill while the legislature is still in session. If he objects, he returns it to the house of origin along with a message stating his objections. After reconsideration, the legislature may override the veto by a vote of two-thirds of the members present in both houses. However, if the legislature has adjourned, the governor has twenty days to consider, and if he vetoes the measure, he files a message with the secretary of state, thus spelling death for the measure. If he does not act within the time specified, the bills become law without signature. In view of these provisions, which probably encompass the Texas executive's strongest constitutional power, a governor's position in the making of public policy is considerably enhanced, because as one writer concluded, "A fairly good correlation can be observed between the states which have strong constitutional provisions on the subject and the frequency and firmness with which the veto has recently been exercised."[2]

From *Public Affairs Comment,* Vol. XV (Austin, Tex.: Institute of Public Affairs, The University of Texas at Austin, March, 1969), pp. 1-4. Reprinted by permission. This is an abridged version of the original article.

VETOES UNDER THE CONSTITUTION OF 1876

After the executive office was established as a "weak" one by the limitations placed upon it by the Constitution of 1876, there seems to be little doubt that the veto has been the single most important means of gubernatorial control over public policy in Texas during the past nine decades. Indeed, it is true that most Texas governors have played a vitally important role in the history of the state through their wise use of the veto. Through this power, they have frequently been the "watchdog" of the public interest. No doubt the judicious use of the prerogative best explains its continued importance today.

As indicated in Table 1, the twenty-four governors who have served under the Constitution of 1876 returned 308 messages to the legislature in which they exercised the negative. Only twenty-five vetoes were overridden by the necessary majority, which gives the governors a most respectable batting average of .919. Also impressive has been the use of the post-adjournment veto, which was first allowed by the Constitution of 1876. Up to January, 1969, approximately two-thirds of the gubernatorial vetoes—628 of 936—have been sent to the secretary of state after adjournment of the legislature; in most cases, such action was the death knell of the measure, with little chance of revival. It is virtually impossible to determine the exact number of cases in which matters killed in this fashion were brought up in later sessions, but it is the opinion of former Governor Coke Stevenson, who also served as presiding officer of both houses of the legislature, that the number is quite negligible. He expressed the opinion that if a governor vetoes a bill after adjournment this usually means its final and irrevocable death.[3] Former Governor Stevenson's belief was corroborated by a study of the subject in Illinois which concluded: "It seems to be the general opinion of experienced legislators that instances are rare indeed in which vetoed bills are reintroduced and passed without first having undergone sufficient amendment to meet, or at least to compromise, the objections to the veto."[4]

TABLE 1
Vetoes by Texas governors under the constitution of 1876

Years	Total Number of Vetoes	Vetoes during Session	Number Over-ridden	Per Cent Over-ridden	Post-Adjournment Vetoes
*1876-1920**	298	117	7	2.35	181
1921-1930	213	34	6	2.82	179
1931-1962	330	143	12	3.63	187
1963-1968	95	14	0	0.00	81
Totals	936	308	25		628

Source: Compiled from journals of the House of Representatives and Senate, Texas Legislature, and veto messages, Office of Secretary of State.

*Includes vetoes by Richard Coke, who served under both the Constitution of 1869 and the Constitution of 1876.

THREAT OF VETO

One of the intangibles to be taken into consideration in assessing the veto power necessarily must be the success of "threats" by executives to exercise the prerogative. Although it is difficult to determine with any degree of accuracy just how much weight is carried by such tactics, the inevitable conclusion must be that the threat of veto is a force immeasurable but felt. In the early part of this century, the then leading specialist on the governorship detected a "new role" for state executives, i.e., the role as legislative leader. Writing in 1912, Professor John A. Fairlie expressed the belief that a governor wielded larger influence over legislation through his power of disapproval than was indicated by the number of bills disapproved.[5] His idea is no less valid today. If it is known that bills will be disapproved, they will not be passed, or they may be changed to meet the governor's objections prior to passage. Legislators may also be encouraged to vote for bills known to be favored by the governor in return for his support (and coincidentally failure to veto) on bills in which they are especially interested.

An examination of journals of the Texas legislature reveals that from time to time governors have threatened the veto with some success. It is apparent also that the threat of veto has been used less within the past quarter of a century than formerly. This, no doubt, has resulted from the increasing attempt to reconcile differences in advance: today, it is quite common for legislators and the executives to confer on proposals even before they are introduced in order to exchange views on the matters. In many cases, differences are resolved and the need to threaten a veto is eliminated. Most governors would prefer not to exercise the negative, or threat thereof, blatantly, but would rather work out differences on an informal basis. Such discussions provide a reduction in the number of vetoes and also a better understanding between author and governor.

AN ABSOLUTE NEGATIVE?

The experience of Texas governors with the veto power through the years has produced some interesting conclusions. Paramount among such observations is the all-powerful nature of the veto. Today, it remains one of the most important –if not the most important–formal grants of power through which the executive makes his impact upon public policy in the state. This influential position of the veto has probably been sustained by the fact that governors have not abused the trust given to them in its exercise, and over the long range, most have been conscientious and judicious when using it. The longer a governor remains in office, the more valuable the veto becomes to him as an instrument of public policy-making. Likewise, the trend toward freer discussion and understanding between executive and legislative branches has caused some decrease in the use of the veto in the years since World War II. The fact that the power is there and available for use in the event no compromise is effected is probably as significant to the governor's influence as in cases where the power is actually used. Taking into consideration that the mathematical probability of a gubernatorial veto being overridden is small indeed, most legislators would prefer to avoid a situation which would force the issue by having their bills vetoed. They know full well that the two-thirds vote in both houses needed to override the governor's judgment is hard to muster. Experience in securing such a vote is not on their side.

Despite the convincing case for the all-powerful nature of the gubernatorial veto in Texas, it probably would still be unsafe to allege that the veto is absolute. At the same time, it certainly is safe to say that it is a "strong" power in a "weak" office. Not only have governors of the past ninety years been upheld in their veto actions more than 97 per cent of the time, but it has now been more than a quarter of a century since the last executive was reversed by the lawmakers. That incident occurred in 1941 when W. Lee O'Daniel was overridden for the twelfth time. The experience of so long a period—twenty-eight years—during which five executives have been sustained consistently in the exercise of the prerogative would seem to augur well for future governors in their use of the veto. If it is not yet an absolute negative, the veto in Texas may be well on the way to becoming so.

NOTES

1. Herbert Jacob and Kenneth N. Vines, eds., *Politics in the American States* (Boston: Little, Brown, 1965), pp. 227-229. See also Thad L. Beyle, "The Governor's Formal Powers: A View From the Governor's Chair," *Public Administration Review,* Vol. XXVIII (November/December 1968), pp. 540-545.
2. Frank W. Prescott, "The Executive Veto in Southern States," *Journal of Politics,* Vol. X (November, 1948), p. 99.
3. Personal interview with former Governor Stevenson, August 4, 1968.
4. Glenn R. Negley, "The Executive Veto in Illinois," *American Political Science Review,* Vol. XXXIII (December, 1939), p. 1053.
5. John A. Fairlie, "The State Governor," *Michigan Law Review,* Vol. X (March, 1912), p. 383.

4-4
RAILROAD COMMISSION—WITH LOSS OF SPARE RESERVES, ROLE OF COMMISSION CHANGES
Stephen Gardner

Oil allowables in Texas, after moving sharply upward for several months, finally reached maximum production in April [1972]. With demand for petroleum

From the *Business Review,* October, 1972, pp. 1-5. Reprinted by permission.

products continuing to rise faster than domestic reserves, production is very apt to remain at this level. And without a drastic change in price conditions or import policies, there is little likelihood that the Texas Railroad Commission will again be called on to limit the output from fields in the state because of insufficient markets.

For nearly a quarter century, the commission held production in Texas at less than capacity. During that time, the nation's demand for crude oil more than doubled, surging from less than 2.2 million barrels a day in 1948 to more than 5.3 million in 1971. But while demand for crude increased, the discovery of new reserves slowed. Where 21,519 wells were completed in Texas in 1956, for example, only 8,114 were completed in 1970. As the gap between demand and reserves closed, production in Texas came closer to its peak—which it may have already passed.

Texas has long been the nation's leading oil-producing state, supplying at least a third of all domestic crude. By regulating the flow of wells in Texas, the Railroad Commission was able to smooth out fluctuations in the nation's oil markets. In the 1950's the state accounted for about three-fourths of the nation's reserve capacity, and shut-in capacity was believed to amount to as much as 38 per cent of production.

This spare capacity gave Texas the flexibility needed to stabilize markets—a capability that sometimes stood the United States and other countries in good stead. In the Suez crisis of 1957, for example, interruption of the flow of oil from the Middle East could have left Europe in dangerously short supply had Texas' spare capacity not been used to help narrow the gap.

In Louisiana, where production has been increasing (from about a tenth of the domestic crude in 1950 to about a fourth in 1970), the Department of Conservation has followed a stabilization strategy similar to that of the Texas Railroad Commission. But since prorationing on the basis of demand was instituted first in Texas and this state has continued to be the major producer, the Railroad Commission has been generally recognized as the agency shouldering the burden of curtailing output. With spare capacity also stretched to the limit in Louisiana, that state's regulatory agency is in no position to take over the stabilization function that the Railroad Commission has performed since the oil glut in the East Texas field in the early 1930's.

The matter of the nation's crude production being regulated by an agency of one of the states has not been without controversy. With most of the country's production concentrated far from its major consumption areas, differences in regional interests were to be expected. But even so, the prorationing of production in Texas on the basis of market demand has long been part of a broad though informal federal policy regarding crude markets, prices, and imports.

Capacity production from Texas fields leaves no spare capacity for smoothing out short-term fluctuations in demand for crude. As a result, a major change in the role of the Texas Railroad Commission has become almost certain. The implications of the change, however, are much greater for the U.S. Government than for the Texas Railroad Commission.

HOW CONTROLS ARE SET . . .

Two basic but closely related considerations have been taken into account in regulating the flow of oil from Texas fields. One has been conservation. The other has been market demand—or was, at least, as long as the state had spare reserves.

The matter of conservation is handled in terms of the maximum production considered efficient for each field. This barrel-per-day rate—called *maximum efficient production*—is the limit at which wells can be produced without damaging the field. Once established, the rate is ordinarily left unchanged until producers show that the field can be produced at a higher rate without eventual damage to the field.

The matter of market demand is decided monthly. On the basis of projected demand for Texas crude, the Railroad Commission prorations production for the coming month as a percentage of maximum efficient production. This proration rate is the *allowable.*

Conservation controls are needed to maintain pressure in a field. If the field is produced too fast, it loses the pressure that drives oil through the formations to the well. Where water provides the pressure, there is the added danger that water might push past the crude and isolate large amounts of oil that could otherwise have been produced.

In new fields, where the pressure is usually good anyway, producers are assigned special *discovery rates* for the first two years or until the eleventh well is drilled. Use of these special rates gives the discoverer time to determine the production characteristics of the field and an opportunity to recover some of his exploration costs. The rapidity of this early flow apparently does no damage to the potential of the field and provides an incentive for further exploration.

When the discovery rate no longer applies, the commission sets the maximum rate of production it will allow for that field, based on characteristics of the field and experience with other Texas fields of similar spacings and depths. Rates arrived at in this manner are called *yardstick allowables.* Producers can ask the commission for a higher rate, and special hearings are held for that purpose. But the producer has to show that an increase in output will not eventually reduce the field's potential, and the final decision is up to the commission.

When production begins to fall off enough to show that the field is about depleted, wells are classed as *strippers,* and to encourage production of all the oil accessible, the commission removes its production controls. All told, Texas strippers produce as much oil as the state's largest field.

To determine market demand, the commission holds monthly meetings at which refiners estimate the amounts of Texas crude they expect to buy over the following month. In addition to these estimates—called *nominations*—the commission considers crude inventories and stocks of petroleum products and reviews demand forecasts prepared by the Bureau of Mines.

Then an allowable must be determined that will provide the production needed to meet demand. As one step in its determination, the commission estimates the production from wells exempt from prorationing. Most of these are, of course, discoveries and strippers, neither of which are subject to market demand prorationing but which, together, account for a considerable amount of production and a large number of wells. Nearly half the wells in the state last year, for example, were strippers, but they produced only about a tenth of the state's crude.

As another step, the commission takes into account the production of wells that are not subject to *effective* prorationing. These wells are in fields that cannot be produced at market demand levels—either because of their depletion or because of conservation problems that develop when they move toward the maximum rates of production originally set for them.

Successive increases in allowables over the past few years have brought increasingly weaker responses in production—primarily because of fields that cannot be held at high rates of output. Some older fields, while still far from ready for the stripper category, simply no longer have the potential to reach the rates of output originally set as their maximums. As a result, full flow from many fields is less than the allowable.

Output of other fields is held back by the conservation problems that full production would create. Output from three of the state's largest fields—the East Texas field, the Kelly-Snyder field in West Texas, and South Texas' Tom O'Connor field—being held back because of difficulties in processing the volume of natural gas that flows as a byproduct of their oil production and because of special reservoir problems that did not become evident until the fields were pushed to their maximum outputs.

Altogether, only 13 per cent of the state's 178,500 wells were subject to effective prorationing in June 1971—when allowables were still little more than 75 per cent of maximum efficient production. But those wells produced nearly four-fifths of the state's crude. In fact, wells in fewer than 100 of the state's more than 8,000 fields provided about two-thirds of its production.

With nominations established for the following month and a fairly close estimate of the production exempt from effective stabilization controls, the commission has been in a position to announce the new allowable as a percentage of maximum efficient production. But with most wells operating too far below maximum efficiency for the allowable to apply and nominations running close to the state's total capacity, the commission has had to allow practically maximum production. Without a reversal in the situation—which seems highly unlikely—the commission can no longer regulate output in terms of market demand. Conservation has again become the commission's primary function—maybe its only function.

. . . AND WHY

Concern for conservation was the reason for prorationing on the basis of market demand in the first place. Resources were wasted if they were underpriced, as oil was in the depression. And in those early days of the Texas fields, conservation was difficult. In the absence of production controls, producers pumped oil as fast as they could, regardless of the future of the field. Producers owning only part of a field could not be kept from draining off their neighbors' reserves. As a result, even though prices were low, the drive was to deliver oil before the price—or the reservoir—fell further.

The concept of a rate of maximum efficient production is an outgrowth of the first efforts in Texas to protect owners' correlative rights to oil by preventing withdrawals so rapid they damage the recovery of oil from the field as a whole. In the heat of cutthroat competition in early Texas fields, oil was withdrawn at damaging rates—often faster than companies could transport, refine, or even store the oil. Earthen dams were often used to hold crude, wasting oil, damaging the land, polluting water, and creating fire hazards.

Prorationing on the basis of market demand, on the other hand, emerged in response to the closely connected problem of price cutting that accompanied overproduction. As demand fell off during the depression and the supply ballooned with discovery of the East Texas field (which suddenly pushed Texas reserves far in excess of the nation's total demand for crude), crude prices fell to 10 cents a barrel. Martial law had to be declared to keep peace among producers competing for markets. With prices falling, market allocation of resources failed.

The first efforts to introduce some stability into the crude market were undertaken at the federal level—in the same spirit in which the Government sought to help other depressed industries. But with the striking down of the National Recovery Administration—which had adopted a petroleum code calling for import restrictions, minimum crude prices, control of new reservoirs, demand limitations, and the allocation of production among states and producers—the burden of control passed to the states.

Congress moved to encourage production control at the state level by passing legislation supporting controls in producing states. The Connally Hot Oil Act prohibited interstate shipment of oil to escape state regulation. And although the Interstate Oil Compact Commission had no authority for limiting production, this federally sponsored agency gave producing states a forum for considering regulatory problems.

Temporary federal controls were imposed during World War II, and by the end of the war, many state officials and industry leaders were convinced that production control filled an economic and conservation need and that controls could be effectively administered. Several states passed conservation regulations for the first time, and some states that had controls strengthened them.

As spare capacity increased in the early postwar years, producers in Texas shared only modestly in the increases in production and heavily in the decreases, opening the Railroad Commission to criticism that its procedures were used to manipulate prices. The commission, however, mindful that its regulations were always conservation-oriented, has answered that prorationing was never used except to prevent the accumulation of unstable inventories and to meet seasonal, and occasionally emergency, demands. It merely accepted prices set in the crude market.

Some of the problems of regulating Texas oil have related to imports. Except for a few years in the 1920's, the United States was a net exporter of oil until 1948. Tariffs were applied to imports in the early 1930's, and import quotas were used for a while. But with the development of low-cost reserves in the Middle East, imports began to rise in the late 1940's, reaching the point where they accounted for nearly a fourth of the 5.5 billion barrels of petroleum products used in the United States last year.

Voluntary restraints were tried to slow the inflow of foreign oil in 1955. Such restraints could not be relied on, however, and as the flow continued, the Railroad Commission absorbed the impact on domestic markets by cutting back on allowables in Texas, adding further to the nation's reserves.

The Suez crisis and accompanying shutoff of oil from the Middle East delayed any Government action on imports until 1959, when quotas were imposed. Two policies were adopted. On the West Coast, where producing areas were operating at capacity, imports were simply allowed to make up the difference between production and consumption. But on the East Coast, which is linked to the rest of the country by an interlacing of pipelines as far west as the Rockies, imports were held to 9 per cent of domestic production in hopes of stimulating the further development of domestic reserves.

But as demand for energy continued to rise relative to reserves, quotas had to be eased. Since 1962, the Government has tried to hold imports at 12.2 per cent of the domestic production of oil and gas liquids. Residual oil for heating and industrial purposes has been imported with very few restrictions, especially since 1966.

A SHIFT IN DECISION-MAKING

With demand leaving little (if any) reserve capacity and the country depending increasingly on imports, the Texas Railroad Commission can no longer effectively regulate production to meet market demand. Responsibility for regulating market conditions and the adequacy of supply has passed essentially from state to federal government. Only through a coordination of imports, offshore lease sales, and taxing and pricing practices can an effective policy any longer be administered.

The Texas commission will, of course, continue its efforts to conserve the state's crude resources. In fact, with allowables at 100 per cent, its efforts at conservation are more difficult than ever, especially in preventing wasteful reservoir conditions. The commission's responsibility for seeing that salt water is reinjected into original formations or allowed to evaporate under control conditions, for example, becomes increasingly difficult at high levels of production. So does its responsibility for restricting the flaring of byproduct gas. When production levels were lower, prorationing took care of most problems of conserving natural gas.

The commission's concern with conservation has not changed with fields running at full capacity. What has changed is national policy.

4-5
OPEN SALOONS: EIGHTEEN MONTHS BEFORE THE BAR
Jack Keever

Grinning and shaking his head, Senator Joe Christie sipped black coffee and mused about liquor. The El Paso senator rarely drinks, but he worked for over four years to allow people in Texas to order cocktails in public places. He was widely praised in some circles; widely censured in others. "I wonder now," he said, "what all the damn struggle was about."

Eighteen months before, Governor Preston Smith had signed Christie's bill legalizing—subject to local option—the public sale of mixed drinks. During the signing ceremony, Smith asserted, "It is a relief to have this issue settled in Texas once and for all. . . ." But was the issue settled, the long and turbulent history of liquor legislation in Texas at an end? Texans have been quaffing in open saloons for more than a year now. What can be concluded from the experience so far? Has honesty supplanted the hypocrisy implicit in "private" clubs as Christie hoped it would? Have mixed drinks brought in more tourists and money as Preston Smith anticipated? Has booze by the shot been a boon or—as a West Texas evangelist prophesied darkly—has it propelled the state "to hell in a hand-basket"? Should Texans lift their glasses in toast or fling them to the floor in horror?

The quaff or curse question is not easily resolved, for muddying the fire-waters are two potent factors:

1. The remnants—legal, political and psychological—of more than 100 years of intense, statewide wet-dry warfare.
2. The continuing warfare. Though the Great Texas Whiskey War may have gone to the wets at the state level, skirmishes continue in the counties, cities and precincts.

Efforts to control liquor in Texas go back as far as 1858, when the legislature prohibited the sale of whiskey to "wild Indians," but serious attempts to ban alcohol only fermented with the arrival of the United Friends of Temperance in the state in 1870. These bar-baiters put the squeeze on lawmakers until they passed a local option law in 1876 which permitted as few as 20 voters in a precinct to call a "wet-dry" election. The Friends were joined in their efforts to wean Texas in the early 1880's by the Women's Christian Temperance Union. Together they compelled a statewide vote on a prohibition amendment. It failed 220,637 to 120,270, but many northern counties voted dry in the process. Since then liquor has been on the ballot or on the voters' tongues in virtually every statewide election. Historians Seth McKay and Odie Faulk said that for nearly 30 years after 1900, "Texans measured all candidates for office, from governor to constable, on the basis of whether they were 'wets' or 'drys'."

That first election defeat only whetted the drys' thirst for victory. They

From the *Texas Parade,* November 1972, pp. 24-33. Reprinted by permission.

persisted and forced referendums in 1908 (the drys won but the legislature paid no heed); in 1911 (the wets won), in 1914 (the wets doused the drys), and in 1916 (the drys again). None of these elections had the profound effect, however, of a 1917 law prohibiting the sale of alcoholic beverages within 10 miles of a military base. At the time, the state was virtually one big armed encampment and thus virtually dry. Then from 1918 to 1920, the Texas Legislature fell into the swing of Hoover's "noble experiment," okaying first the 18th Amendment and then the Volstead Act, bringing in Prohibition. While altering the state constitution to comply with repeal, however, the Texas Legislature inserted a prohibition against "open saloons," thereby forbidding the public sale of mixed drinks, and made "wet-dry" a local option.

Wets countered the open-saloon prohibition with private clubs, which were permitted to serve booze to members in even the most parched counties, and the legendary "brown paper bag." As Christie pointed out repeatedly, the private club was usually little more than a legal facade, where to become a member required only registering at the door or paying a token fee. These clubs flourished. Even now, though 92 counties remain officially "dry," an official of the Alcoholic Beverage Commission says, "There is not a county in the state without a private drinking club." In restaurants and beer bars of wet counties, liquor was often underfoot. Erect brown bags twisted around the silhouettes of bottles peopled the floors of these places, as management of local law usually required they be kept beneath the table and out of sight. Visitors to the state were understandably confused. Russian poet Yevgeny Yevtushenko, who visited Dallas in the 1960's, told of his reactions: "In the Soviet Union," he said, "America is cowboys, jazz, some kind of fabled land offering the possibility of unusual corruptions. Just imagine if I tell them about Dallas. There I had to go out and buy a bottle of vodka and conceal it inside my jacket to bring it inside the restaurant, hide it under a table so no one would see it and then pour it secretly into tomato juice."

Every effort to alter the situation met heated opposition, as Christie found out during his campaign. Time and time again, these strong and fervent soldiers of prohibitionism—aided by powerful organizations—trampled down the wets' attempts to make liquor available by the drink, or by the minibottle, or only at restaurants or under varied other schemes. Even Governor John Connally, considered by many as the most politically powerful first man in state history, failed in several attempts to push liquor legislation through. One of the primary reasons was the Texas Baptist General Convention. During Christie's campaign, the Convention's executive board called on Texas' 1.8 million Baptists to oppose liquor by the drink and asked its 4,400 Baptist churches to contribute $25 each—or a total of $110,000—to defeat the amendment. But the attitudes of Texans and some churchmen were changing. A 1941 sampling of public opinion had shown 69 per cent of the populace favored sale of liquor by the bottle but only 31 per cent were for booze by the drink. By 1970, 67 per cent had come to favor the sale of liquor-by-the-drink on a local option basis. Finally, the public voted to repeal the prohibition against open saloons 979,868 to 914,481, permitting the Legislature to write a liquor-by-the-drink bill, which in turn passed.

When Governor Smith signed the bill into law, he said, "It will bring in more people who will spend money and will have a tremendous impact on the economy of our state." Joe Christie, whose efforts for liquor-by-the-drink may have cost him the lieutenant governor's race, explained his persistence: "I viewed it as a law enforcement issue. We injected a wholesome, honest, well-enforced law into a dishonest system." But were they overly optimistic? For though the Great Whiskey War is apparently ended at the state level, the drinking laws of Texas remain a mishmash.

The wet-or-dry status of an area is still a matter of local option to be voted on according to city or justice of the peace precincts or counties. And while they lost to the wets statewide, the drys still hold strongly-fortified bastions of at least official sobriety, count thousands of powerful and fervent soldiers in their ranks and persist in violent attacks on any wet who encroaches their domain. The war may be over but skirmishes continue at the local level. The law ushering in mixed drinks also grandfathered 46 counties which had previously approved the constitutional amendment. Besides these 46, only 13 counties have joined okayed mixed drinks. A toll-call of counties would go: 92 wholly dry; 31 counties completely wet; 115 permitting the sale of beer, wine and liquor in parts of the county; 14 counties allowing only the sale of beer; and two okaying only beer and wine up to 11 per cent alcohol.

Obviously, "Can a man get a drink here?" remains a good question of geography nearly everywhere in Texas, for a county may be wet or dry, cities may booze or not, and even subsections of cities may approve or disapprove. Strong evidence of the resulting confusion can be had simply by studying the figures of the Alcoholic Beverage Commission and the State Treasury, which disburses revenues from alcohol taxes. The Beverage Commission lists 92 counties as wholly dry but disbursed alcohol tax refunds to 174 counties for a total of 266 counties. Texas has only 254 counties. But remember the ABC official's statement that "there isn't a county in Texas without a private club." Before passage of the mixed-drink law almost 2,000 private clubs were licensed by the state. As of mid-September 1972, this number had dropped to 1,051, with 370 of these being fraternal organizations and exempt from paying a licensing fee.

Obviously, large numbers of "private" clubs switched to open bars, for as the number of clubs was falling, the open-bar tally machine was clacking away. At this writing, establishments licensed to sell mixed drinks total 1,634. The transition can be expensive. A non-exempt private club pays a licensing fee based on its membership which averages about \$2 a member (the minimum being 250 members or \$500). There is no maximum. On the other hand, a public mixed-drink license costs \$2,000 the first year, \$1,500 the second year, \$1,000 the third year and \$500 the fourth and all following years. But the moment the state fee drops to \$500, the county and city can add \$250 each for themselves, making the running fee \$1,000 a year. The state's stamp of approval on the sale of beer and wine for on-premises consumption costs only \$25.

Further complicating the life of aspiring inn-keepers are a few other handicaps. First, unlike other retailers, he is not free to deal with wholesalers or manufacturers. He must buy his line from a retail package store, thus adding yet another markup to the price of a mixed drink. Second, the tightest squeeze on corn is the tax squeeze. Whenever a gallon of 100 proof leaves the distiller's bonded warehouse, the federal government collects $10.50. If the proof is less, the feds pick up a percentage equal to the proof. When that gallon arrives in Texas, the distributor pays another $2.00 state tax. If the bottle is sold retail to a private citizen, he pays four or five percent sales tax. If sold to a bar, the inn-keeper pays a 10 per cent tax on the gross receipts derived from the resale of that liquor. All of these taxes are, of course, reflected in the high price of a drink. By comparison, beer carries a $3 federal tax and a $5 state tax on each barrel, or 31 gallons.

Tax monies were, of course, one of the prime selling points for mixed-drink legislation—as they have been for virtually all liquor legislation—at both state and local levels. The enabling legislation for mixed drinks provided that 15 per cent of the mixed-drink taxes collected in a county be returned to the county and likewise for the city. Proponents had estimated these tax collections statewide as high as $1.5 million a month. While collections have yet to reach that lofty figure, they are drawing near. In August, the state picked up $1,466,309 in drinking money, the highest to that date. Altogether, state taxes on liquor in 1972 totaled $95,046,606.82, of which $15,573,936.16 came from taxes on mixed drinks. Through June 30, 1972, the state had disbursed $2,178,490.87 of these mixed-drink taxes to the counties and $2,038,751.70 to the cities. A quick look at the breakdown of these disbursements reveals which are the most spirited towns in Texas: Houston, $180,476.09; Dallas, $138,298.42; San Antonio, $46,546.81; Fort Worth, $30,274.14; and El Paso, $29,060.70. As might be expected, the counties which include these cities are the wettest in Texas.

While the tax kettle has been heating up, things have been cooling down in the law enforcement division. Fines for liquor law violations have steadily declined over the three past fiscal years from $312,011.32 in 1969-70 to $264,553.27 in 1970-71 to $183,869.45 in 1971-72. As to law enforcement problems, Christie still maintains there is "no correlation" between liquor-by-the-drink and increased traffic accidents. He claims "the best yardstick" of this was the September 1, 1972, decrease in automobile insurance rates, reducing them by 11 per cent on a statewide average. The Department of Public Safety can't agree or disagree with Christie. It just doesn't have the statistics. A spokesman said, "It's difficult to tell if they (drunk drivers) had a jug in the car, tanked up at home or had been to a bar."

Protests that liquor-by-the-drink would result in more alcoholics also have not been proved. Officials at the Texas Commission on Alcoholism say they have not compiled statistics since liquor-by-the-drink passed, but they do not personally feel it "materially affects the rate of alcoholism." Of the 25 counties rating highest in admissions to hospitals for alcoholism, 19 are dry.

Governor Smith's prediction that liquor-by-the-drink would attract more tourists is also difficult to judge. The Highway Department did count a higher than usual 8.9 per cent increase in automobile visitors to Texas in 1971. And the Texas Tourist Council said the number of visitors arriving by bus, rail and plane from out of state also had increased. But as the Council says, neither increase "could be tied to any one thing."

But one group isn't bothering to weigh the pros and cons: The Texas

Restaurant Association. Their cup runneth over for, according to a survey of restaurants which have gained public drink licenses, liquor-by-the-drink has been a real shot in the arm for dining out. Of the 700 eateries surveyed, all reported increases in business—most said 10 to 15 per cent more trade, some told of gains as high as 50 per cent. Walt Erdmann, executive assistant to the president of the Texas Restaurant Association, told *Texas Parade,* "There was no noticeable trailing off as the novelty wore off, and more and more people are associating an evening out with a cocktail before dinner. It has surpassed our expectations in acceptance by the public . . . One of the more significant comments is that it is helping to control rowdyism through individual servings (of drinks) in place of the brown bag. With individual servings, you can gauge what a person is drinking and refuse to serve him if he's drinking too much. But you couldn't take a man's brown bag away."

Regardless of the favorable comments, the drys continue the battle. Texas Alcohol Narcotics Education, Inc., a non-profit organization supported by 19 religious denominations, still insists mixed drinks have brought about an increase in drunkenness, arrests for drunkenness and police costs. The Rev. R. R. Holton of Dallas-based TANE said there were 207 murders in Dallas County in 1971 and 138 were in the only wet area of the county and all the others were within 10-15 blocks of a bar or liquor store. He said the Oak Cliff section of Dallas (population 400,000) "had a drastic drop in police incidents and 30 per cent decrease in crime the first year after it went dry." The Rev. Holton hopes TANE will have a report on the effects of liquor-by-the-drink in Lubbock within six months. "We feel liquor-by-the-drink has made things worse," Holton says, but he admits, "We don't have the facts to back it up."

While he waits for proof, the Rev. Holton and his fellows may be losing the last great battle for public support, for the after-work-happy-hour-drink culture seems to be growing as fast as the drink-before-dinner custom. The Houston *Post* recently poured forth the wheres and hows of moving in the happy hour world. Several bars surveyed in Austin have been unofficially chosen as the spot for after-work quickies by neighboring companies. And, in Dallas, a few have earned the lucrative recognition—among the male populace at least—as good "dating bars."

In short, the drinking patterns that dominate the East are, though still in infancy, growing in Texas. Instead of being merely a place to swill liquor, the public bar is fast becoming a social institution.

4-6
THE STATE OF STATE EMPLOYMENT

Texas is a growing state. Our budgets have increased substantially over the past twenty years. Our tax base has been broadened and increased repeatedly. This

From the *Texas in Action Report* (Austin, Tex.: Executive Services, Inc., August 21, 1972), pp. 39-47. Reprinted by permission.

growth affects the State employees of Texas directly and uniformly. For while experiencing an ever-increasing demand for additional State services, Texas has not kept pace with the private sector in salary scale and wage benefits for its 63,000-plus employees. It is a fact that wages of public employees of the State of Texas have increased at a rate far BELOW the increase in salaries in the economy in general.

Some State employees are currently so inadequately paid that they could be termed the "working poor." As of February, 1972, 23.5 per cent of the classified State employees could not raise a family of three children on their State salary without falling below the poverty income level used by the Office of Economic Opportunity. Further, over three-quarters of the State's classified workers earn lower wages than those defined by the Bureau of Labor Statistics as necessary to maintain a "moderate standard of living." That is what the Texas Public Employee Association has been trying to correct—this inequality in the economic marketplace. The Texas standing compares poorly with other facets of the economy—business, industry, and Federal government.

The State must compete with other employers for workers in various labor markets. Their wages have followed the national pattern of increasing at record rates during the past several years. The State of Texas has not followed suit. Available data on counterpart occupations in private industry and Federal government indicate that salary levels have risen sharply since 1968. Even though State employees perform on an equal level, State salaries have steadily lost ground.

State government continues to be one of the fastest growing segments of the economy. Demand and supply conditions would evidence a trend toward higher rates of growth in earnings of State employees. In Texas, this is not the case. We rank 45th nationwide in the number of State employees per 10,000 population—yet far down the pay scale at 33rd in average monthly earnings of full-time State employees.

One indirect index of productivity is the number of employees per 10,000 in the population. Of the five most populous states, our low ratio of employees per 10,000 population demonstrates that the cost of State government in Texas is nominal compared to that of other states. Productivity measures show that Texas employees tend to carry a heavier work load than comparable workers in other states. Texas adult welfare programs had the highest average caseload per worker and lowest administrative cost ratio of any program in the United States. Holding occupational classifications constant, it is clear that for the vast majority of jobs State employees' salaries fall below those paid by Federal, municipal, and private sectors in Texas.

One of the most significant competitors for workers in the State is the Federal government. In June, 1971, the number of Federal civilian employees in Texas totaled 162,791. Moreover, Federal employment is concentrated in the same labor market where the bulk of State employment is located. Texas State employees' average earnings are a fraction of Federal average earnings. Since 1969, authorized increases in salaries of Federal government employees have amounted to 26.5 per cent, while Texas employees have received authorized increases of only 17 per cent.

State employment over the nation is more stable and has fewer layoffs than many industries; yet, in Texas, approximately one out of four State workers left his job during the last fiscal year. The State loses costly manhours and dollars in recruiting and training replacements for workers who have left. "Inadequate salary" was the reason listed for leaving by 19.3 per cent of the State's 9,893 resignations for the year ending August 31, 1971. Turnover was highest in the lowest occupational categories and inversely related to salary level. Rates ran from a high of 47.3 per cent in salary group 2 to a low of 4.5 per cent in salary group 19 (62.8 per cent of all classified employees worked at step two or lower as of February, 1972). Turnover in 1971 dropped from previous years. The decline reflects, to a large extent, the nationwide economic downturn. People are less likely to leave a job when they face few alternative opportunities.

Successful administration of government depends on the efficiency and dedication of its employees. The State would be able to reward and retain its better workers if funds for individual merit increases were authorized and appropriated. Merit raises improve employee morale and help separate experienced workers from new entrants. Fringe benefits are no longer a "fringe area." Approximately $1 out of every $4 earned by employees in the United States comes in a form other than wages and salaries. Texas lags behind the Federal government and the private sector, especially in providing vacation allowances and health and insurance programs. Texas workers must take their paychecks to the market. The rise in prices of consumer goods and the figure on the paycheck do not tally. Even though the average earnings of Texas classified employees increased 66.6 per cent over the period 1963-1971, consumer prices increased 32.3 per cent during the same period. Almost half the money gains made by State employees have been eroded away by inflation.

Some might contend that Texas salaries are low because the cost of living in Texas is low compared to the national average. However, even when adjustment is made for the cost of living in Texas, State employees are paid at a lower rate than are employees of other states. Furthermore, the relative position of Texas workers has declined over recent years, especially in our metropolitan centers.

State salary adjustments are a necessity if Texas is to compete in the labor market. Employees for the State doing similar work should be paid on a similar scale to those in other sectors: business, private industry and Federal government. The key principals are equity and competition—and the statistics and data prove that Texas is not a viable contender in the marketplace. The State has fewer employees to carry on governmental functions than do other states, yet pays these productive workers at a lower rate than the average for all states. Texas government has the ability to pay for wage increases without resorting to untapped sources. The vetoed raise (appropriated by the 62nd Legislature in Regular Session) for the second half of the biennium—together with funds for merit increases and improved vacation allowances—would amount to a gross increase of less than two per cent in State expenditures. Suitable compensation can help Texas attract and retain more productive workers. If it assists in reducing turnover costs, the total net costs of such a raise may be even lower. The State can save money.[1]

NOTE ON SOURCE

1. Data on Texas State government by Texas State Classification Office; data on private industry computed from Bureau of Labor Statistics, Area Wage Surveys (for various Texas cities), "Office, Professional, and Technical Occupations; Men and Women Combined." Table A-3: data on Federal government from Bureau of Labor Statistics, *National Survey of Professional, Administrative, Technical, and Clerical Pay, June, 1970* (Washington, D.C.: U.S. Government Printing Office, 1971); step 4 was used as a pay line for each grade. Data on Houston municipal government from Bureau of Labor Statistics, *Municipal Government Wage Survey: Houston, Texas, March, 1971* (Dallas, Tex.: Bureau of Statistics, Region VI Office, 1971).

"Superior Court, County of Baxley, Honorable John L. Mills presiding. And now . . . Heeeere's Johnny!"

5

The Judiciary

The accusers explain why the seventy-year-old, barefoot, bearded army veteran should be found guilty of heresy and of corrupting the minds of the young. He speaks in his own defense without the assistance of a lawyer. By a margin of about thirty votes the jury of 500 fellow citizens renders a verdict of guilty. The law does not prescribe a specific punishment, but the prosecution proposes a sentence of death. Then the convicted man counters with an offer to pay a fine equivalent to a few dollars, but immediately raises the sum to a few hundred dollars when his friends volunteer to back him with their own money. However, the jury opts for capital punishment. About a month passes before an executioner brings the condemned man a cup containing a poisonous brew. Determined to be a good citizen to the end, Socrates drinks knowingly but without resistance. Death comes slowly yet apparently without pain. His friends are sad, and a young political scientist named Plato becomes quite disillusioned with the politics of the times.

Obviously, these events did not take place in Texas in 1974 but in Greece in 399 B.C. Was the machinery of justice adequate? Did the accused receive a fair trial? Did the punishment fit the crime? By contemporary Texas standards, these questions must be answered in the negative. But what will be said of today's judicial institutions and procedures by the men and women who study them in the year 4500 A.D.? No doubt they will conclude that our legal system was quaint at best and inhumane or inefficient at worst. But contemporary Texas courts and laws are the products of a culture that has its roots in ancient Athens as well as in the Rome of Cicero, the England of Sir Edward Coke, and the Virginia of Jefferson and Marshall. Thus we may expect our judicial experience to make some contribution to the type of justice that will evolve for others, who someday will be separated from us by as many years as we now are from the days of Socrates. Meanwhile all Texans should understand the laws, judicial institutions, and procedures that have been developed for the protection of life, liberty, and property in this state in the 1970s.

In all, there are over 2,000 courts in Texas. Most of them have a single judge, but some have three, five, or nine judges. A large majority of the state's courts hear both *civil cases* (e.g., suits involving property rights or noncompliance with the terms of a contract) and *criminal cases* (e.g., prosecution for theft). Some courts are limited to civil cases, whereas others handle only criminal cases. Also, there are courts of *original jurisdiction* only; these tribunals are limited to trying cases being heard for the first time. Other courts are restricted to hearing appeals from lower courts and thus have *appellate jurisdiction* only. Still other courts enjoy both original and appellate jurisdiction.

STATE LAW IN TEXAS

Regardless of jurisdiction, Texas courts have the responsibility of interpreting and applying the law. This responsibility is established in the statutes enacted by the Legislature, in the state constitution, and in the body of *common law* based on custom and usage, which dates back to the days of medieval England. Newly enacted bills, concurrent resolutions, and joint resolutions passed in each legislative session are published under the title *General and Special Laws of the State of Texas.* For more ready reference, these laws are also arranged by subject matter and are codified in part in *Vernon's Annotated Statutes of the State of Texas,* published by the Vernon Law Book Company of Kansas City, Missouri.[1] Judges, lawyers, and interested citizens are kept up to date on changes in Texas law through Vernon's Supplementary Service, which provides periodic pamphlets and cumulative annual pocket parts to supplement the bound volumes.

In addition to piecemeal changes resulting from routine legislation, pressure occasionally mounts for extensive revision of rules of procedure or an entire legal code. Thus in 1965, after years of such pressure from judges, lawyers, and the public—particularly as a result of several United States Supreme Court decisions concerning due process of law—the Legislature for the first time in over a century acted to revise the Code of Criminal Procedure. At the same time a committee of the State Bar of Texas, chaired by Dean Page Keeton of the University of Texas School of Law, began work on a revision of the state's 117-year-old Penal Code. After five years of labor, the committee submitted its draft proposal to the Legislature in January, 1971. Opposed by many prosecuting attorneys who complained that this draft reduced penalties for many crimes, it was never brought up for a vote by the 62nd Legislature.

Avoiding the thorny issue of narcotics control, the County and District Attorneys Association and a reconstituted State Bar committee produced a revised draft which was studied, debated, amended, and finally passed as S.B. 34 by the 63rd Legislature at the end of its 1973 regular session. The new Penal Code condenses a century's collection of criminal statutes into a well organized body of law, but probably its most distinctive contribution is the establishment of a system of graded penalties. As shown in Table 5-1, there are three degrees of *felonies* for which penitentiary sentences and/or fines can be imposed, and there are three classes of *misdemeanors* for which fines and/or jail sentences are

TABLE 5-1
Noncapital offenses and penalties for first offenders under the Texas Penal Code

Selected Criminal Acts	Category of Offense	Maximum Fine	Period of Confinement
Aggravated rape, aggravated robbery, aggravated sexual abuse, murder, burglary of a habitation	1st degree felony	no fine	5-99 yrs. or life
Theft of property valued at $10,000 or more, injury to a child, rape, robbery, sexual abuse	2nd degree felony	$10,000	2-20 yrs.
Theft of property valued at $200 or more but less than $10,000, bigamy, burglary of a vehicle, credit card abuse, impersonating a peace officer, incest	3rd degree felony	$5,000	2-10 yrs.
Theft of property valued at $20 or more but less than $200, barratry, burglary of coin-operated machine, compensation for past official favor, cruelty to animals, false alarm or report	Class A misdemeanor	$2,000	1 yr. maximum
Theft of property valued at $5 or more but less than $20, disrupting a meeting or procession, endless chain scheme, evading arrest, harassment	Class B misdemeanor	$1,000	180 days maximum
Theft of property valued under $5, gambling, indecent exposure, issuance of a bad check, prostitution, public intoxication, shooting on a public road	Class C misdemeanor	$200	none

Source: S.B. 34 passed by the 63rd Legislature, Regular Session; signed by the governor on June 14, 1973.

outlined. Repeated felony convictions result in punishment for the next higher degree of felony. Repeated misdemeanor convictions require minimum jail sentences or bring punishment for the next higher class of misdemeanor.

After passing the Penal Code bill, the 63rd Legislature revised the state's drug laws with the Controlled Substances Act. Table 5-2 illustrates the system of graded penalties as applied to unlawful activities involving four groups of hard drugs and other controlled substances. Under previous legislation, possession or sale of marijuana in any quantity constituted a felony punishable by two years to life imprisonment. The new law outlines lesser penalties for marijuana offenses

TABLE 5-2
Drug offenses under Texas law

Selected Drugs	Unlawful Manufacture or Delivery, or Possession with Intent to Manufacture or Deliver*	Unlawful Possession
Codeine, heroin, lysergic acid diethylamide (LSD), metapheta-mine ("speed"), methadone, morphine, opium	1st degree felony	2nd degree felony
Mescaline, hashish, psilocyn	3rd degree felony	3rd degree felony**
Amphetamines (e.g., "bennies," "dexies"), barbiturates (e.g., "blue devils," "yellow jackets"), methaqualone ("love drug"), harvested peyote***	3rd degree felony**	Class A misdemeanor
Medicinal mixtures with limited quantities of drugs (e.g., cough syrups with codeine)	Class A misdemeanor	Class B misdemeanor

Source: H.B. 447 passed by the 63rd Legislature, Regular Session; signed by the governor on June 14, 1973.

*Deliver and delivery are defined to mean transfer from one person to another; it also includes an offer to sell. Proof of an offer to sell requires corroboration by someone other than the person to whom the controlled substance was offered.

**Judge may reduce to Class A misdemeanor after conviction or in initial prosecution.

***Exemption is granted for use in religious ceremonies of the Native American Church; however, this exemption "does not apply to a member with less than 25% Indian blood."

(see Table 5-3). Further, as regards marijuana or any other controlled substances, in a first offense case the trial judge may grant a "conditional release" and the defendant does not have a conviction on his record after a probationary period of not more than two years.

S.B. 34 (the Penal Code bill passed by the 63rd Legislature) did not provide capital punishment for any crime, but murder is classified as a first degree felony carrying possible penalties of 5 to 99 years or life imprisonment. On the last day of the 1973 regular session, however, both houses accepted a conference committee report on H.B. 200 which specifies that a murderer commits *capital murder* if he

1. murders a peace officer or fireman who is acting in the lawful discharge of an official duty and who the person knows is a peace officer or fireman;
2. intentionally commits the murder in the course of committing or attempting to commit kidnapping, burglary, robbery, aggravated rape, or arson;
3. commits the murder for remuneration or the promise of remuneration or employs another to commit the murder for remuneration or the promise of remuneration;

TABLE 5-3
Marijuana offenses under Texas law

Delivery (offer to sell or sale of any quantity, or gift of ¼ ounce or more)	3rd degree felony*
Delivery of less than ¼ ounce as a gift	Class B misdemeanor
Possession of over 4 ounces	3rd degree felony*
Possession of 2 to 4 ounces	Class A misdemeanor
Possession of 2 ounces or less	Class B misdemeanor

Source: H.B. 447 passed by the 63rd Legislature, Regular Session, and signed by the governor on June 14, 1973.
*Judge may reduce to Class A misdemeanor after conviction or in initial prosecution.

4. commits the murder while escaping or attempting to escape from a penal institution; or
5. while incarcerated in a penal institution, murders another who is employed in the operation of the penal institution.

Although H.B. 200 originally provided for a mandatory death penalty, the Senate insisted on an amendment which makes a life sentence possible for any of the five crimes under certain circumstances. Thus the conference committee report which was accepted by both houses specifies that after a jury has found a defendant guilty of a capital offense it must consider the following issues:

1. whether the conduct of the defendant that caused the death of the deceased was committed deliberately and with the reasonable expectation that the death of the deceased or another would result;
2. whether there is a probability that the defendant would commit criminal acts of violence that would constitute a continuing threat to society; and
3. if raised by the evidence, whether the conduct of the defendant in killing the deceased was unreasonable in response to the provocation, if any, by the deceased.

If the jury unanimously answers each of the three questions in the affirmative, the convicted murderer must be given the death sentence, which is carried out at Huntsville in the electric chair ("Sparky") after automatic review by the Court of Criminal Appeals. If ten or more of the twelve jurors agree that the answer to one of the issues is "no," the defendant receives a life sentence and may become eligible for parole within twenty years.

Governor Briscoe signed H.B. 200 on June 14, 1973. At the time of this writing, no one has been sentenced to death under the statute. Some informed observers, however, have expressed doubts regarding its constitutionality in view of the United States Supreme Court's ruling in *Branch* v. *Texas* (1972), which struck down the state's former capital punishment law. In that case the high court objected to a Texas statute which gave a jury unlimited discretion in determining whether the death penalty would be applied upon conviction of

ORGANIZATION AND JURISDICTION OF TEXAS COURTS

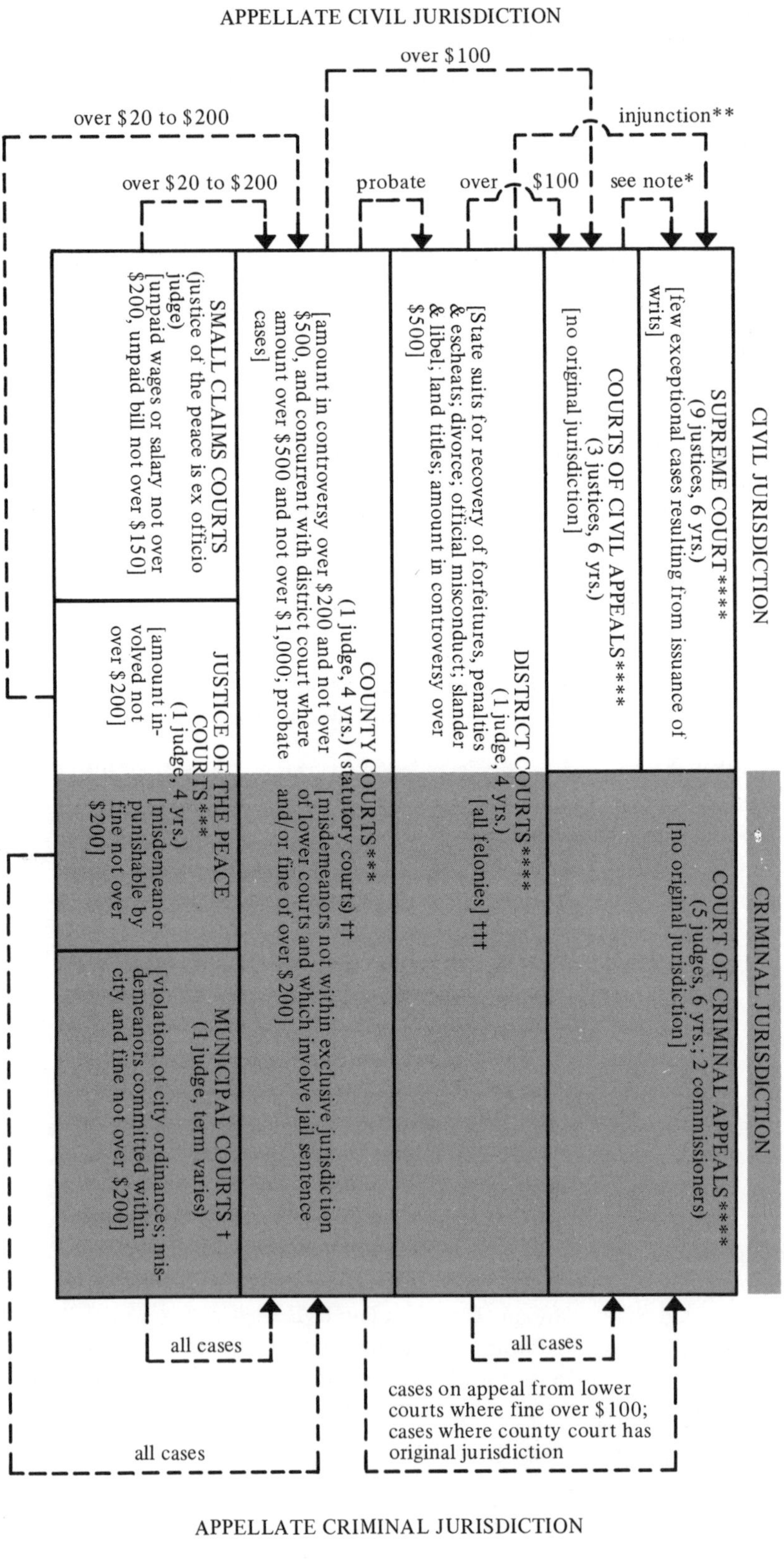

Figure 5-1

Organization and jurisdiction of Texas courts: For each court the number of judges and length of term of office are given within parentheses; original jurisdiction is described within brackets.

- * *The Supreme Court hears appeals from courts of civil appeals under the following circumstances: when members of a court of civil appeals disagree on a material question of law, when a court of civil appeals renders a decision contrary to a decision by the Supreme Court or by another court of civil appeals, when an act of the Legislature has been held unconstitutional, when a case involves state revenues, when the Railroad Commission is a party to a case, when it appears that a court of civil appeals has made an error of substantive law affecting a judgment.*
- ** *When a district court has ruled a statute or administrative order of a state board or commission to be unconstitutional and has issued an interlocutory or permanent injunction preventing enforcement, appeal may be taken directly to the Supreme Court.*
- *** *Vacancy filled by county commissioners court until next general election.*
- **** *Vacancy filled by governor until next general election.*
- \+ *Vacancy filled according to provision of city charter.*
- ++ *Some counties have separate statutory courts (35 county courts at law, 4 county criminal courts at law, 6 county criminal courts, 3 county civil courts at law, 1 county criminal court of appeals, 5 probate courts, and 2 "county courts"). County courts at law with civil jurisdiction exercise it concurrently with district courts in cases where the amount in controversy is over $500 and not over $5,000.*
- +++ *The Legislature has removed jurisdiction of misdemeanor cases from the county courts of 12 counties and has given it to district courts.*

rape by force, a capital offense under the penal code in effect at that time (see Reading 5-1).

COURTS AND JUDGES

Admittedly, the Texas judicial system is complex, but an understanding of the basic organization and jurisdiction of the state's courts is not impossible—especially if approached on a court-by-court basis (see Figure 5-1). Article V of the Texas constitution is titled "Judicial Department." As amended in 1891, the first section of this article declares that state judicial power "shall be vested in one Supreme Court, in Courts of Civil Appeals, in a Court of Criminal Appeals, in District Courts, in County Courts, in Commissioners Courts, in courts of Justices of the Peace and in such other courts as may be provided by law." Each county does have a commissioners court, composed of four elected commissioners and presided over by the county judge; however, this court is an administrative and quasi-legislative body. Although, properly speaking, it is not a court, it is empowered to issue writs and can cite persons for contempt. Not included among the courts listed in Article V are the municipal courts in incorporated cities, towns, and villages, which play an important role in the administration of justice in Texas.

MUNICIPAL COURTS

Previously known as corporation courts, the judicial bodies of the cities, towns, and villages in Texas have, since September, 1969, been officially termed *municipal courts.* Because most of their cases involve violations of motor vehicle traffic regulations, municipal courts are often referred to as "traffic courts." Qualifications, terms of office, and methods of selection and removal of municipal judges vary in accordance with individual city charter provisions. The mayor of a general-law city* functions as municipal judge unless the council provides for the election or appointment of someone else to hold this office. Usually the municipal court judge of a home-rule city is named by the council. Large cities may have one or more full-time judges, but most municipal judicial personnel serve in a part-time capacity and hold court for a short period each day or on certain designated days of the week.

Municipal courts have neither civil nor appellate jurisdiction. Their original and exclusive criminal jurisdiction extends to all violations of city ordinances, which are legislative acts of city councils. Also, in Class C misdemeanors resulting from violations of state laws within city limits, municipal courts share concurrent original jurisdiction with justice of the peace courts in cases where punishment is limited to fines of $200 or less.

Although neither a justice of the peace nor a municipal court judge can impose jail sentences, a convicted person who is able but unwilling to pay a fine can be forced to "lay out" his fine (i.e., go to jail) at the rate of $5 per day. Until the time of the United States Supreme Court's ruling in *Tate* v. *Short* (1971), poor people as well as those who were able to pay were jailed for nonpayment of a fine. Now a low-income person is commonly allowed to pay a fine on the installment plan. If because of language or action a person is held in contempt of court by a municipal judge, that person may be jailed for up to twenty days for each act of contempt or fined $200, or both jailed and fined.

With the exception of Wichita Falls, Texas cities do not have municipal

*Cities and towns of less than 5,000 population may be chartered only under the general law of the state; those larger than 5,000 may, by a majority vote of their residents, adopt their own charter for purposes of home rule. See Chapter 6, page 317.

courts of record with court reporters to record proceedings.[2] Proceedings are usually informal. Only a relatively small number of defendants request trial by jury. Defendants usually plead guilty, as in most cases heard in trial courts at other levels. Only a few retain a lawyer, since the fine resulting from conviction will often amount to less than a lawyer's fee.

JUSTICE OF THE PEACE COURTS

It is the constitutional responsibility of the commissioners courts in each county to create at least four and not more than eight justice of the peace precincts. In some lightly populated counties, however, only one or two justice of the peace precincts have been created. This conflicts with the Texas constitution, but additional justices are simply not needed. Qualified voters of each precinct elect one *justice of the peace* for a term of four years, but whenever a precinct contains a city with a population of 8,000 or more, two justices may be elected. Thus there is the possibility that a single county might have as many as 16 justices of the peace. In 1973 Harris County became the first to have this many. Large urban counties and South Texas counties, though the latter are not necessarily large in population, tend to have greater numbers of justices than other counties. The total number for the state is over 900; only a dozen are Republicans.

Neither previous legal training nor experience is required for the position by law, but a few justices of the peace are law school graduates and may retain a private legal practice while serving in office. In an effort to improve the quality of justice administered by justices of the peace in Texas, the 62nd Legislature enacted H.B. 168. This statute requires that a justice of the peace who is not a licensed attorney must, within one year from the date of his first election, successfully complete a forty-hour course in the performance of the duties of his office. Persons already in office August 29, 1971, were allowed one year in which to take the course. Exempted by a "grandfather clause" were justices of the peace who had served two or more terms at the time of enactment. The statute specifies that the course must be taken in an "accredited state-supported school of higher education."

The official duties of justices of the peace in urban areas often constitute a full-time job. On the other hand, in a rural precinct there may be few cases to be tried. Thus compensation for the post, which is determined by the commissioners court of each county, ranges from practically nothing to $21,600 per year in Harris County.

Justices of the peace are subject to removal for official misconduct, drunkenness, or incompetency through jury trial before a district court. They may also be removed by the Supreme Court on recommendation of the *State Judicial Qualifications Commission,* a body of four judges appointed by the Supreme Court, two lawyers appointed by the State Bar, and three lay members appointed by the governor.

Justice of the peace courts have both criminal and civil jurisdiction. In all cases their jurisdiction is original. In criminal matters justice of the peace courts may try Class C misdemeanors where the maximum penalty is a fine of $200, but any conviction may be appealed to the county court for a new trial. Also, a justice of the peace is empowered to punish a person held in contempt of court with a maximum fine of $200 or a maximum jail sentence of twenty days, or both. In addition to trying Class C misdemeanor cases, justices of the peace are authorized to issue warrants for search and arrest. Furthermore, they conduct preliminary hearings to determine whether persons arrested on criminal charges shall be jailed, released on bond, or simply released pending possible grand jury indictment leading to a district court trial or the filing of an information leading to a county court trial.

Civil jurisdiction of the justice of the peace courts extends to "cases where the amount in controversy is $200 or less, exclusive of interest, of which exclusive original jurisdiction is not given to the District or County Courts." If a judgment is for $20 or less, the justice of the peace court is the state court of last resort. As far as state law is concerned, its decision is final, but there is the possibility of appeal to the United States Supreme Court if a federal constitutional question is involved. This is true also of the decisions of other Texas courts which for certain types of cases are courts of last resort.

Since 1953 a justice of the peace has also functioned as a judge of his precinct's *small claims court.* For a total of $5 in fees ($8 if a jury is requested by either party), anyone desiring to collect unpaid wages or salary not exceeding $200, or to collect a bill amounting to not more than $150, may bring his case before a small claims court. Since these proceedings are not highly structured, the assistance of a lawyer is not required. When the amount in controversy exceeds $20, the losing party may appeal to the county court.

In addition to his judicial duties, a justice of the peace serves as an ex officio notary public; and, as in the case of other Texas judges, he may perform marriages. Also, he functions as *coroner* when the commissioners court has not named a county medical examiner. Thus, although few justices of the peace can claim any type of medical training, most of them are required to determine by inquest the cause of death when someone dies without the presence of witnesses or when death takes place under circumstances indicating the possibility of foul play. If a justice determines that an autopsy should be performed, he may request the county health officer to do it; or, if the commissioners court is prepared to pay up to $300, he may procure the services of some duly licensed and practicing physician with training in pathology.

COUNTY COURTS

The Texas constitution specifies that each county shall have a court of record and that the voters shall elect a county judge for a term of four years. These judges, the constitution stipulates, "shall be well informed in the law of the State." In fact, this provision simply means that they must have the political appeal necessary to be nominated, probably through the Democratic Party primaries, and to be elected. As of May, 1973, only Bee, Kerr, Lipscomb, Midland, and Runnels counties had Republican judges. As with other county and precinct officers, a county judge may be removed from office as a result of a district court jury trial wherein he is found guilty of incompetency, official misconduct, habitual drunkenness, or other legally prohibited acts. He can also be removed by the Supreme Court of Texas on recommendation of the Judicial Qualifications Commission. A vacancy in the office of county judge is filled through appointment by the county commissioners court. Since the state constitution designates the county judge as "a conservator of the peace," he is entitled to carry a pistol.[3] Salaries for county judges vary widely, ranging from $6,000 to $33,000 per year, depending on various laws and in most cases on the discretion of the commissioners court.

Most county courts have both original and appellate civil and criminal jurisdiction, but criminal jurisdiction is denied when the county has a criminal district court, unless the Legislature has expressly conferred such criminal jurisdiction. Acting under the authority of Article V, Section 22 of the state constitution, the Legislature has removed jurisdiction over misdemeanor cases from the county courts of Cass, Hidalgo, Hill, Johnson, La Salle, Marion, Real, Red River, Robertson, Stephens, Titus, and Wharton counties. Original criminal jurisdiction includes Class C misdemeanors which are not within the exclusive jurisdiction of the justice of the peace courts and all Class A and Class B misdemeanors. When a county court sentence specifies confinement of a convicted person, this sentence is served in the county jail.

Appellate criminal jurisdiction extends to cases originating in justice of the peace courts and municipal courts. A county court's appellate jurisdiction is final with regard to cases involving fines of $100 or less; when greater fines are imposed, appeal may be taken to the court of criminal appeals. Civil cases are heard on appeal from justice of the peace courts when the amount in controversy is greater than $20. Jurisdiction is final with regard to those cases in which the amount in controversy does not exceed $100. When a case is appealed to the county court from a justice of the peace court or from a municipal court which is not a court of record, the case must be tried *de novo.* The lack of recorded testimony in the original trial necessitates a complete retrial of the case before the county court.

The Texas constitution gives the county courts exclusive jurisdiction in all civil cases involving $200 to $500, exclusive of interest. However, the county courts do not have jurisdiction in suits for recovery of land. Whether a civil case falling within the $500 to $1,000 range will be tried in a county or a district court depends on the party filing suit, since the courts have *concurrent jurisdiction* in such suits.

County judges must hear criminal cases at least once a month and hold a "term for civil business" at least once every two months. The state constitution also provides that county courts "shall dispose of probate business, either in term time or vacation as may be provided by law." In designating the county courts as probate courts, the constitution specifies that "they shall probate wills, appoint guardians of minors, idiots, lunatics, persons *non compos mentis* and common drunkards, grant letters testamentary and of administration, settle accounts of executors, transact all business appertaining to deceased persons, minors, idiots, lunatics, persons *non compos mentis* and common drunkards, including the settlement, partition and distribution of estates of deceased persons and to apprentice minors, as provided by law." Appeal of probate cases is taken to a district court.

In twenty-six counties with large populations, the burden of probate, civil, and criminal cases has become too heavy for the *constitutional county court* to handle. Thus the Legislature has established a total of fifty-six *statutory* or *special courts* in these counties, Dallas County has ten statutory courts. Variously titled county probate courts, county courts at law, county civil courts at law, county courts for criminal cases, county criminal courts, and county criminal courts of appeals, these statutory courts relieve the constitutional county judge of a portion, and sometimes all, of his judicial duties. As the chief administrator of county business matters, the county judge in a metropolitan area often has little time for purely judicial matters. Usually he will continue to hear probate cases.

Qualifications for statutory court judges vary; in some counties these judges must have had from two to five years of experience as practicing lawyers. In 1971 the 62nd Legislature increased the civil jurisdiction of all "county courts at law, county civil courts, and other statutory courts exercising civil jurisdiction corresponding to the constitutional jurisdiction of the county court in civil cases." These statutory courts now have civil jurisdiction concurrent with that of the state's district courts when the amount in controversy involves between $500 and $5,000, exclusive of interest. Since the jurisdiction of the 254 constitutional county courts is fixed by Article V of the Texas constitution, this statute had no effect on their concurrent civil jurisdiction.

DISTRICT COURTS

The principal trial courts of Texas are the *district courts* created by the Legislature under Article V, Section 7, of the state constitution. Each court has a single

Figure 5-2
*State district courts in Texas (includes new courts established by the 63rd Legislature, 1973)***

220 district courts (identified by arabic numerals only; a -2 following a number, e.g., 9-2 for Montgomery, Polk, San Jacinto and Trinity, counties indicates a 2nd district court)
10 criminal district courts (C)
23 special domestic relations courts (DR)
6 juvenile courts (J)

* *Courts will not become operative until January 1975.*
** *Prepared with the assistance of Judith A. Lloyd and Rafael Rodríguez. Source: Texas Civil Judicial Council,* Forty-fourth Annual Report 1972 *(Austin, 1973), pp. 261-266; and 63rd Legislature, S.B. 52.*

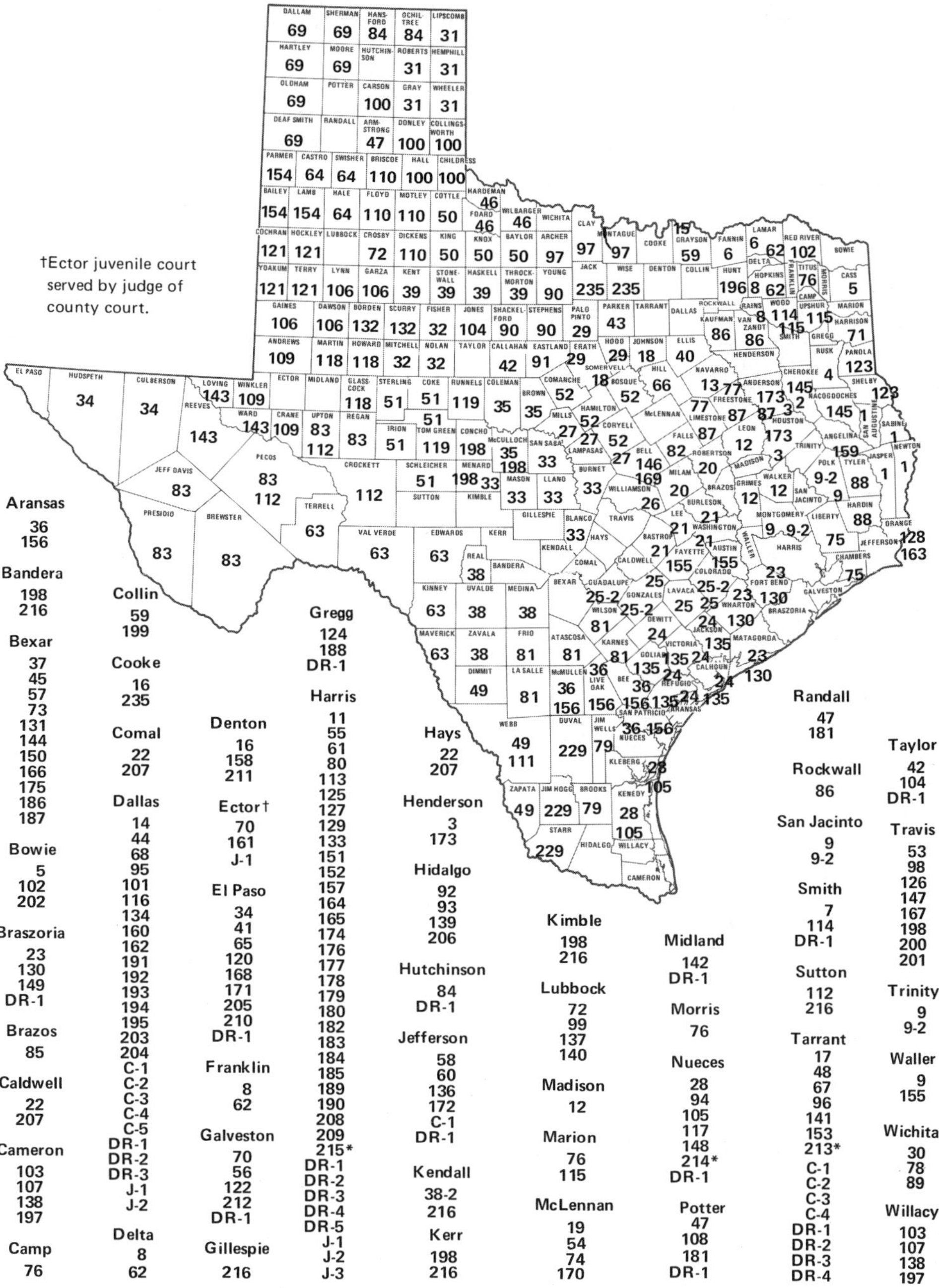

†Ector juvenile court served by judge of county court.

Aransas
36
156

Bandera
198
216

Bexar
37
45
57
73
131
144
150
166
175
186
187

Bowie
5
102
202

Braszoria
23
130
149
DR-1

Brazos
85

Caldwell
22
207

Cameron
103
107
138
197

Camp
76

Collin
59
199

Cooke
16
235

Comal
22
207

Dallas
14
44
68
95
101
116
134
160
162
191
192
193
194
195
203
204
C-1
C-2
C-3
C-4
C-5
DR-1
DR-2
DR-3
J-1
J-2

Delta
8
62

Denton
16
158
211

Ector†
70
161
J-1

El Paso
34
41
65
120
168
171
205
210
DR-1

Franklin
8
62

Galveston
70
56
122
212
DR-1

Gillespie
216

Gregg
124
188
DR-1

Harris
11
55
61
80
113
125
127
129
133
151
152
157
164
165
174
176
177
178
179
180
182
183
184
185
189
190
208
209
215*
DR-1
DR-2
DR-3
DR-4
DR-5
J-1
J-2
J-3

Hays
22
207

Henderson
3
173

Hidalgo
92
93
139
206

Hutchinson
84
DR-1

Jefferson
58
60
136
172
C-1
DR-1

Kendall
38-2
216

Kerr
198
216

Kimble
198
216

Lubbock
72
99
137
140

Madison
12

Marion
76
115

McLennan
19
54
74
170

Midland
142
DR-1

Morris
76

Nueces
28
94
105
117
148
214*
DR-1

Potter
47
108
181
DR-1

Randall
47
181

Rockwall
86

San Jacinto
9
9-2

Smith
7
114
DR-1

Sutton
112
216

Tarrant
17
48
67
96
141
153
213*
C-1
C-2
C-3
C-4
DR-1
DR-2
DR-3
DR-4

Taylor
42
104
DR-1

Travis
53
98
126
147
167
198
200
201

Trinity
9
9-2

Waller
9
155

Wichita
30
78
89

Willacy
103
107
138
197

Figure 5-2
State district courts in Texas

judge whose district is identified by number. When two districts are given the same number, they are distinguished by designating one of them "2nd." In predominantly rural areas a district may include two or more counties; other districts consist of one county; and more densely populated counties contain identical or overlapping jurisdictions of two or more districts (see Figure 5-2). In all of these districts, judges sit separately.

In order to meet constitutional qualifications for election to the four-year term, a candidate for the district court must be a citizen of the United States and must have resided in the district for two years immediately prior to election; moreover, he must be a lawyer licensed to practice in Texas. As a guarantee that he has had practical legal experience, the constitution further stipulates that he "shall have been a practicing lawyer or a judge of a Court of this State, or both combined, for four years next preceding his election." Given current political realities, an informal qualification is Democratic Party affiliation; in 1973 there were only three Republican district judges in Texas, one of whom was judge of a domestic relations court.[4]

In the event of death, resignation, or removal of a district court judge, the vacancy is filled by an appointment by the governor. Removal may be effected through impeachment by the House of Representatives and conviction by the Senate or through action by the Supreme Court on the recommendation of the Judicial Qualifications Commission. District court judges receive a basic annual salary of $25,000 which is paid by the state. Also, they may receive supplemental pay from the county or counties forming their districts; but a district court judge's annual combined salary and supplemental pay must be at least $1,000 less than that received by the judges of the court of civil appeals in whose supreme judicial district his court is located.

The state constitution requires that each district court judge shall "hold regular terms of his court at the County Seat of each County in his district at least twice in each year." Most judges of the 240 district courts are authorized to try both criminal and civil cases, although statutes frequently specify that a court shall give preference to one or the other. Ten special district courts have been set up in some predominantly urban counties for the purpose of handling only criminal cases. Other special district courts consist of 6 juvenile courts and 23 domestic relations courts. All criminal jurisdiction is original; and except within twelve counties where the Legislature has removed jurisdiction over misdemeanor cases from county to district courts, it is limited to felonies. Felonies have accounted for about one-fourth of the cases tried in district courts in recent years (for example, see Figure 5-3). Until 1973 the theft of property valued at $50 or more constituted a felony; however, under the new Penal Code stolen property must be valued at $200 or more to constitute a third degree felony. In view of this reclassification, we can expect district courts to handle fewer theft cases in the future. Obviously, rising prices have an effect on felony statistics in Texas. But there is one type of felony that is not affected by price: theft of livestock (horses, cattle, sheep, goats, and swine) is always a felony regardless of the value of the stolen animal. Appeal following a felony conviction is taken to the court of criminal appeals.

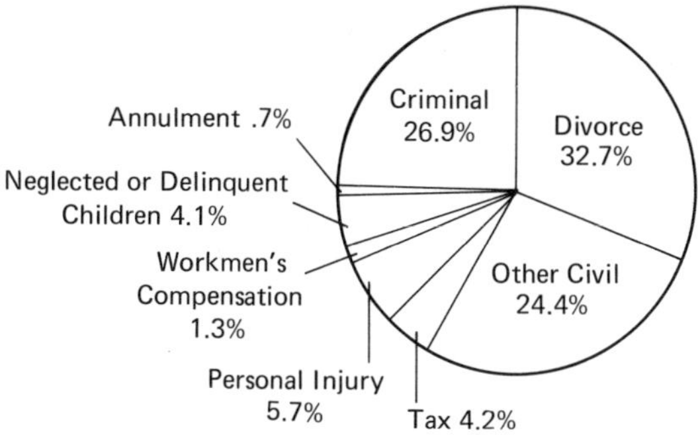

Figure 5-3
District courts: categories of cases filed, 1972. Reproduced from Texas Civil Judicial Council, Forty-fourth Annual Report, 1972 *(Austin, 1973), p. vi.*

Original civil jurisdiction of the district court extends to suits by the state of Texas to recover forfeitures, penalties, and escheats;* divorce cases; cases involving official misconduct; slander and libel suits; suits involving disputed land titles; suits involving seizure or attachment of property valued at $500 or more; contested elections; and all suits "where the matter in controversy shall be valued at or amount to $500, exclusive of interest." If the amount in the controversy exceeds $500 but is not more than $1,000, the case falls within the concurrent jurisdiction of district and county courts. In cases involving more than $1,000, the district court has exclusive original jurisdiction except in the counties where the Legislature has established special or statutory county courts at law with civil jurisdiction corresponding to the constitutional jurisdiction of the county court. These courts have civil jurisdiction concurrent with that of the district courts when the amount in controversy involves between $500 and $5,000, exclusive of interest. Appeal of a civil case from a district court is taken to a court of civil appeals. The district court's own appellate jurisdiction is limited largely to probate cases originating in a county court within the district; however, it also hears appeals from statutory county courts in cases involving mental illness and alcoholic hospitalization proceedings.

Few people will dispute the adage "Justice delayed is justice denied." Yet one of the most common problems facing American courts is that of crowded dockets, which cause long delays before cases can be heard. In an effort to minimize this problem, the district courts of Texas have been grouped into nine *administrative judicial districts* (see Figure 5-4). For each of these nine districts the governor appoints a district judge as presiding judge. The presiding judge is responsible for calling a conference of district judges within his area at least once a year for the purpose of receiving reports on the state of court dockets. Various circumstances may cause a backlog of cases to build up: Significant growth of

*Reversion of property to the state in the absence of legal heirs or claimants.

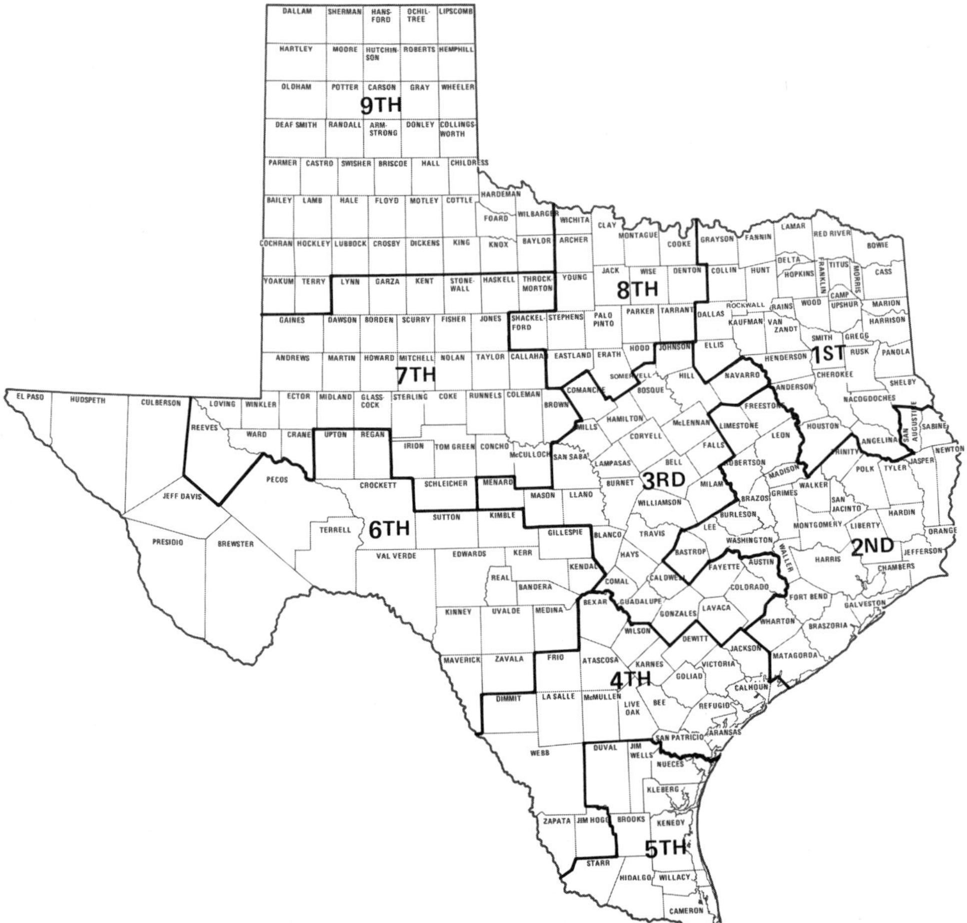

Figure 5-4

*Administrative judicial districts of Texas**

**Prepared with the assistance of Judith A. Lloyd. Source: Texas Civil Judicial Council,* Forty-fourth Annual Report, 1972 *(Austin, 1973), pp. 273-276.*

District	Presiding Judge	District	Presiding Judge
First	*Dallas A. Blankenship (Dallas)*	*Sixth*	*Marvin Blackburn, Jr. (Junction)*
Second	*Max M. Rogers (Huntsville)*	*Seventh*	*C. V. Milburn (Odessa)*
Third	*Herman Jones (Austin)*	*Eighth*	*Louis T. Holland (Montague)*
Fourth	*Peter Michael Curry (San Antonio)*	*Ninth*	*Howard C. Davison (Lubbock)*
Fifth	*José R. Alamía (Edinburg)*		

population and increased commercial activity often give rise to a larger volume of litigation; changing social and economic conditions may be accompanied by a rapidly spiraling crime rate; and illness, old age, or sloth on the part of a judge may cause him to fall far behind, even with a normal load of cases.

In many instances the only solution to the problem of an overloaded docket is legislative action to establish additional courts. On a short-term basis, however, the problem may be attacked by using the services of retired judges, if they are able and willing to serve, or by temporary transfer of judges with relatively light dockets to districts where large numbers of cases are awaiting trial. Arranging such assignments is the responsibility of the presiding judges; but a district judge may not be compelled to accept an assignment. When the caseload for each judge in an administrative judicial district is so great that crowded dockets cannot be cleared through reassignment of judicial personnel within the district, the chief justice of the Supreme Court can assign judges from other administrative judicial districts if they are willing to serve (see Table 5-4).

In spite of these arrangements, during 1972 the district courts of Texas fell farther behind in their efforts to clear crowded dockets (see Table 5-5). Beginning the year with 274,603 cases pending, the courts added 285,509 cases to their dockets (new cases filed, cases reinstated, and other cases added) in the following twelve months, while disposing of 283,133 cases. Thus the judges ended 1971 with 276,979 cases pending, or 2,376 more than had been pending at the beginning of the year. Of course, many civil suits never actually come to trial but are filed in order to preserve procedural rights in case the parties are unable to reach out-of-court settlement. This is especially true of personal injury and workmen's compensation cases.

Official statistics indicate that during 1972 the average number of case dispositions per district court judge was 1,156, including 558 nonjury trials and 21 jury trials. Many criminal cases are dropped for want of prosecution. At the end of the year, however, each judge had an average of 1,131 cases pending.[5]

COURTS OF CIVIL APPEALS

Under Article V, Section 6 of the Texas constitution, the Legislature has created fourteen *supreme judicial districts;* and voters in each district elect a three-justice *court of civil appeals* (see Figure 5-5). The individual elected as chief justice and the two associate justices of each court must have the constitutional qualifications of justices of the Supreme Court: Each must be thirty-five years of age, a resident of Texas, and a citizen of the United States; and he must have ten years of experience as a practicing lawyer, or ten years of combined experience as a practicing lawyer and judge of a court of record. The six-year terms of office are staggered so that one seat on the court becomes vacant every two years. Each associate justice receives a state salary of $35,000 per year and a chief justice receives $35,500. Supplemental pay is received from counties within each supreme judicial district, but the combined salary and supplemental pay must be at least $1,000 less than the yearly salary received by an associate justice of the Supreme Court. Justices may be removed through impeachment by

TABLE 5-4

Assignments of active and retired judges in administrative judicial districts for the purpose of clearing crowded dockets, 1972

District	Assignment of Judges within District (and Days Served)		Assignment of Judges to Other Districts (and Days Served)		Total Assignments within and without District (and Days Served)		Total Assignments (and Days Served)
	Active	*Retired*	*Active*	*Retired*	*Active*	*Retired*	*Active & Retired*
1	89 (264)	86 (326.5)	7 (15)	8 (42)	96 (279)	94 (368.5)	190 (647.5)
2	21 (84)	29 (455)	2 (1)	0 (0)	23 (85)	29 (455)	52 (540)
3	52 (99)	3 (13)	22 (90)	2 (5)	74 (189)	5 (18)	79 (207)
4	7 (17)	10 (52)	5 (17)	3 (19)	12 (34)	13 (71)	25 (105)
5	14 (2)	9 (0)	0 (0)	0 (0)	14 (2)	9 (0)	23 (2)
6	NR (NR)	NR (NR)	NR (NR)	NR (NR)	NR (NR)	NR (NR)	NR (NR)
7	12 (34)	2 (3)	5 (50)	0 (0)	17 (84)	2 (3)	19 (87)
8	39 (53)	48 (172)	13 (89)	12 (83)	52 (142)	60 (255)	112 (397)
9	12 (6)	14 (35)	0 (0)	0 (0)	12 (6)	14 (35)	26 (41)
TOTALS	246 (559)	201 (1,056.5)	54 (262)	25 (149)	300 (821)	226 (1,205.5)	526 (2,026.5)

Source: Texas Civil Judicial Council, *Forty-fourth Annual Report, 1972* (Austin, Tex.: 1973), p. 205.
NR indicates no report.

TABLE 5-5
District court statistics for 1972

Type of Case	Cases Pending 1 January 1972	New Cases Filed	Cases Reinstated	Other Cases Added	Total Cases on Docket	Cases Disposed of	Cases Pending 31 December 1972
Personal injury	27,439	15,915	193	207	43,754	17,680	26,074
Workmen's compensation	4,013	3,758	26	42	7,839	3,933	3,906
Divorce	58,043	91,859	484	109	150,495	92,217	58,278
Annulment	597	1,880	63	0	2,540	1,798	742
Dependent & neglected or delinquent children	6,100	11,462	966	4	18,532	10,949	7,583
Tax	39,995	11,792	89	8	51,884	12,042	39,842
Other civil cases	82,130	68,605	782	1,069	152,586	73,003	79,583
All criminal cases	56,286	75,700	96	400	132,482	71,511	60,971
GRAND TOTALS	274,603	280,971	2,699	1,839	560,112	283,133	276,979

Source: Texas Civil Judicial Council, *Forty-fourth Annual Report, 1972* (Austin, Tex.: 1973), pp. 183-192.

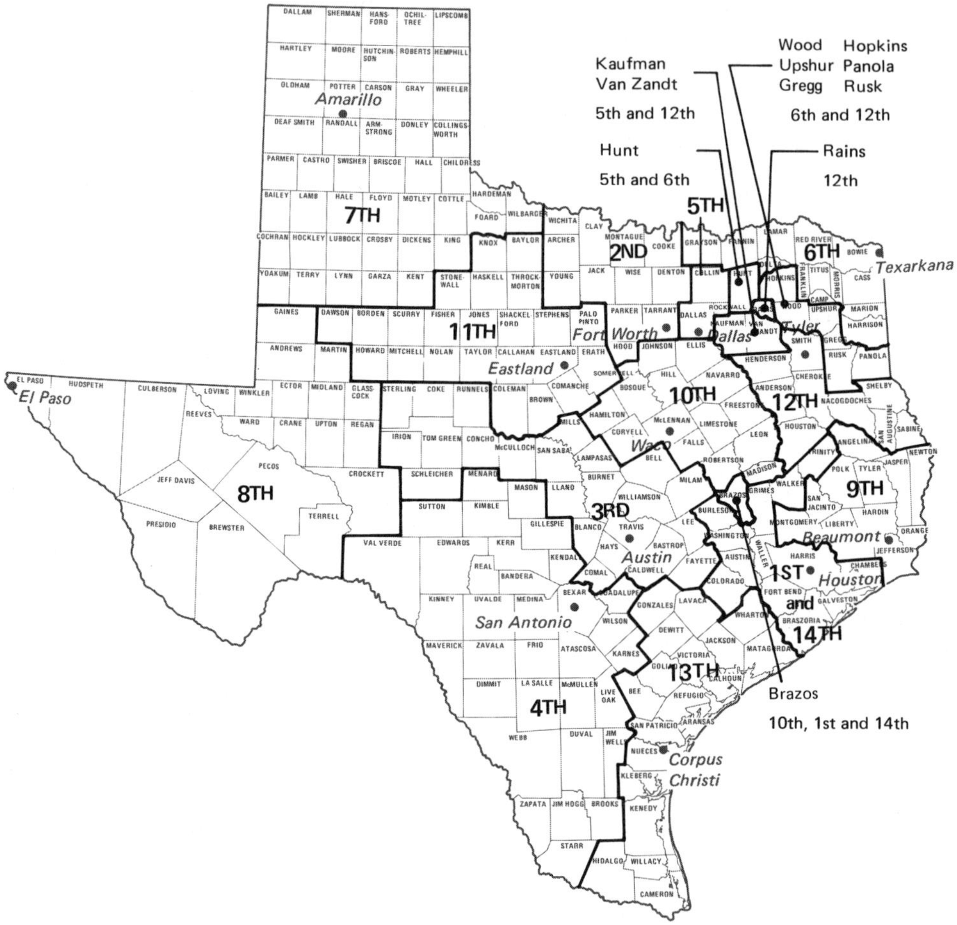

Figure 5-5
Supreme judicial districts for fourteen courts of civil appeals

the House of Representatives and conviction by the Senate, or they may be removed by the Supreme Court as it acts on the recommendation of the Judicial Qualifications Commission. The governor makes appointments to fill vacancies until the next general election.

Jurisdiction of these courts, as this title implies, is limited to hearing appeals of civil cases from county and district courts. Final jurisdiction is exercised in cases involving divorce, slander, boundary disputes, elections held for purposes other than choosing government officials (e.g., bond elections), and appointment of receivers or trustees.

Members of a court of civil appeals sit *en banc,* i.e., together, when a case is heard. Two justices constitute a quorum. Each court begins its term on the first Monday in October and remains in session until the first Monday in July of the following year, with adjournments as deemed appropriate. As directed by the Supreme Court, cases may be transferred from one court of civil appeals to another for the purpose of equalizing dockets. Official statistics for the calendar year 1972 indicate that the courts of civil appeals were able to keep abreast of the tide of incoming cases. On January 1 there was a total of 586 cases pending in the fourteen courts. During the following twelve months, 1,397 new cases were filed, 190 cases were received from and 193 cases were transferred to other courts, 13 rehearings were granted, and 1,392 cases were heard.

Thus by the end of December, 1972, there were 601 cases pending, which represented an increase of 15 cases on the dockets during the course of the calendar year. Of these pending cases 528 had been on the dockets less than six months; 65 had been pending from six to twelve months; and eight had been pending over twelve months. The average time between the date of filing and disposition was less than five months.[6]

COURT OF CRIMINAL APPEALS

Texas's highest criminal court is the *court of criminal appeals.* Elected on a statewide basis for six-year terms, its five judges must have the same qualifications as justices of the courts of civil appeals and of the Supreme Court. One of the judges is elected as presiding judge and holds this position for six years. Terms of office are staggered so that not more than two judges must be elected or reelected every two years. Vacancies are filled through gubernatorial appointment and may occur as the result of death, resignation, impeachment by the House of Representatives and conviction by the Senate, or action by the Supreme Court on recommendation of the Judicial Qualifications Commission. Judges sit *en banc;* three constitute a quorum; and the agreement of three members is required for reaching a decision. The salary for a court of criminal appeals judge is $40,000 per year; the presiding judge receives an additional $500. In 1971 the Legislature authorized appointment by the court of two commissioners to assist the judges. The commissioners hear appeals, but their opinions must receive approval by a majority of the court's judges before such opinions are handed down. Salary and qualifications for commissioners are the same as for judges of the court of criminal appeals.

As the name implies, this court hears criminal cases on appeal from lower courts. It is also empowered to issue writs of habeas corpus and, as provided by law, other writs necessary for the enforcement of its jurisdiction. Since the Supreme Court of Texas has no criminal jurisdiction, judgments of the court of criminal appeals are final. The constitution specifies that the court shall function during a nine-month term beginning on the first Monday in October and extending to the last Saturday in June. Thus it has no power to hear cases during the three-month vacation period. Although the constitution has authorized the Legislature to provide for sessions of the court of criminal appeals "at the state capital and two other places (or the capital city)," the Legislature has determined that all meetings shall be held in Austin.

The court of criminal appeals began the calendar year 1972 with 655 cases pending. During the following twelve months it docketed 1,394 new cases and reinstated 35 others. In this same period it disposed of 1,285 appeals from district and county courts. In addition, the court granted relief in 15 docketed cases of habeas corpus and writs of mandamus; it denied relief in 17 cases of these categories; and it otherwise disposed of another 4 cases. Thus the court of criminal appeals disposed of a total of 1,321 docketed cases during the year; and at the end of December, 1972, there were 763 cases pending.[7]

SUPREME COURT

Like the Supreme Court of the United States, the *Supreme Court of Texas* has nine members: a chief justice, who is elected as such, and eight associate justices. Elected on a statewide basis for six-year terms, at the time of election each must have the following qualifications: He must be a citizen of the United States and of Texas; he must be 35 years of age; and he must have experience as a practicing lawyer, or as lawyer and judge in a court of record combined, for at least ten years. Three terms expire every two years so that the presence of experienced justices on the court will be assured. Removal can be effected only through impeachment in the House of Representatives and conviction by the Senate. A vacancy caused by removal, death, or resignation is filled by the governor's appointee until the next general election. As for other appellate court judicial personnel, their salaries are determined by the Legislature; under the terms of the Judicial Act of 1973, each justice is paid $40,000, with the chief justice receiving an extra $500.

Although most Texans pay little attention to the court or its members, this tribunal receives more publicity than any other, and its work is of special interest to judges of other courts and to the more than 24,000 lawyers in the state.[8] Despite the great expense of statewide campaigning for election, the power and prestige of the office have attracted the candidacies of prominent lawyers, especially those with previous experience as county and district attorneys, and judges of district courts and courts of civil appeals. Receiving an appointment to the court to fill a vacancy created by death or resignation, as in the case of the 1970 appointment of former Governor Price Daniel, gives the incumbent an advantage when he runs for election to a full term, but stiff competition can be expected in this first contest. After winning an election, justices are generally unopposed in their bids for subsequent terms.

The justices of the state's highest court have tended to be considerably older than the minimum age stipulated in the constitution. A study made in mid-1969 showed that the ages of Supreme Court justices ranged from forty-eight to seventy-two, the average being fifty-nine. As to total years of service on the court, the range was from less than a year to nineteen years, with an average of nine years.[9]

Lacking criminal jurisdiction, the Supreme Court of Texas is "supreme" only in the field of civil law. And because it has only the most limited original jurisdiction, practically all of its work involves hearing appeals from lower courts, especially the courts of civil appeals. This appellate jurisdiction is spelled out by both constitutional provision (Article V, Section 3) and legislative statutes. Constitutionally, the Supreme Court hears appeals from courts of civil appeals under the following conditions: (1) when there has been a disagreement among members of an appellate court on a material question of law; (2) when a court of civil appeals renders a decision that conflicts with a decision of the Supreme Court or of another court of civil appeals; and (3) when an act of the Legislature has been held unconstitutional. In addition to these constitutional grants of jurisdiction, the Legislature has authorized appellate jurisdiction over the following: (1) cases involving state revenues; (2) cases to which the Railroad Commission is a party; and (3) cases where it appears that an error of substantive law affecting the judgment has been made by a court of appeals, except for the Legislature's having conferred final jurisdiction on those courts. The Legislature has also authorized direct appeal to the Supreme Court from any district court which declares a statute or an administrative order by a state board or commission to be unconstitutional and which issues an interlocutory or permanent injunction preventing enforcement.

The court's limited original jurisdiction can be traced to the constitutional provision that the court or any of its members is empowered to issue certain writs, including writs of mandamus, for the purpose of restraining or directing "any judge, or Court of Civil Appeals or judges thereof, or any officer of the State Government, except the Governor." To the list of officials subject to Supreme Court writs have been added political party officers. Consequently, as Professor Sinclair has noted, a person wrongfully denied a place on a primary ballot may appeal directly to the Supreme Court in search of immediate relief.[10] The Supreme Court is also empowered to issue writs of habeas corpus for relief of persons who have been jailed on grounds that they have violated a court order in a civil case.

Much of the Supreme Court's work involves handling applications for writ of error. This writ is requested by a party who alleges that a court of civil appeals has erred on a question of law. If as many as three justices favor issuing the writ, the case is docketed as a *regular cause* and, unless waived, is scheduled for argument in open court. Between January 1 and December 30, 1972, a total of 603 applications for writs were considered, and 87 were granted.* During this period the court heard 79 writ of error cases.[11]

In addition to hearing motions and applications and deciding cases, the Supreme Court performs other important functions. It is responsible for making rules of civil procedure, which become law unless specifically rejected by the Legislature. And for the purpose of equalizing the dockets of courts of civil appeals, the Supreme Court is empowered to transfer cases. To cope with this same situation at the district court level, the chief justice of the Supreme Court can request a district court judge to move temporarily into another administrative judicial district in order to assist in clearing a crowded docket.

Finally, the Supreme Court has a role in the training and licensing of lawyers,

*Until docketed as a "regular cause," an application for writ of error, writ of mandamus, or writ of habeas corpus is known as a case "other than a regular cause."

some of whom become judges. The court has the authority to approve Texas schools of law, which enroll about 5,500 students,[12] though accreditation is largely in the hands of the American Bar Association. But the court appoints members of the Board of Law Examiners, which passes on the qualifications of persons seeking to practice law in Texas and certifies the names of successful applicants to the Supreme Court. A license to practice is issued by the court after a formal ceremony; it is at this point that the lawyer obtains membership in the *State Bar of Texas* and is obligated to pay dues for its support.

Although the State Bar of Texas is a professional organization dedicated to promoting the interests of lawyers and encouraging a high level of ethical conduct, it is also an administrative agency of the state, with power to discipline, suspend, and disbar attorneys. Monthly issues of the *Texas Bar Journal* frequently publish reports of such actions. Rules and regulations for the bar are proposed by the Supreme Court or by bar members who file their proposals, supported by a petition bearing the signatures of a minimum of 10 per cent of the bar's membership, with that court. Proposed rules and regulations are adopted by a vote of members of the State Bar.

In addition to its influence over attorneys, the Supreme Court exercises certain controls over judges, as has been noted. At the recommendation of the Judicial Qualifications Commission, it can censure, retire, or remove judges of lower courts—even judges of the coequal court of criminal appeals.[13]

JUDICIAL PROCEDURES

Texans, much like their counterparts in other states, are interested spectators of the judicial process. They crowd courtrooms to witness sensational trials; they avidly watch televised versions of trials, both real or fictional; and they read unbelievable quantities of books about the legal process. Moreover, they actively participate in the judicial process to a far greater degree than in the work of the legislative or executive branches of their state government. At some time in his life virtually every American will have to go to court as a litigant, a witness, or a juror. As a *litigant,* for example, he may find himself a party to a civil case arising from damages growing out of an automobile accident, or from marital relations involving questions of divorce or child custody. Or he may find himself a party in a criminal case where he is accused of violating the theft, traffic, or homicide statutes of the state, or a tax case where the state or local government is attempting to recover taxes he has failed to pay. As a *witness* he may be summoned to testify in any type of case brought before the trial courts of the state. As a *juror* he may be called upon to help decide the fate of his fellow men in both civil and criminal cases. In still another capacity he may be elected a county judge or a justice of the peace. For these reasons he should be especially cognizant of what happens in the Texas courtroom, and he should have some understanding of the judicial procedures employed.

Courts, like all other such institutions, must operate under rules of procedure whereby the rights of all concerned are protected and general order and decorum are maintained. American courts have developed two different sets of rules of procedure, one for civil cases and another for criminal cases. Texas constitutional law requires the Legislature to develop rules of criminal procedure, but it permits the state Supreme Court and the civil courts under its supervision to develop their own rules upon authorization of and approval by the Legislature. A summary of court procedures used in Texas should help to prepare the citizen to evaluate the performance of his judicial system, and it should acquaint him with the stage on which he may well play a role as a participant.

CIVIL PROCEDURE

Even though the Texas constitution adopted in 1876 provides that the Supreme Court may make rules of civil procedure not inconsistent with the laws of the state, the Legislature did not permit the court much opportunity to exercise this power before 1941. The result was that an elaborate body of rules had been built up over the years but had become outmoded and unduly formal in nature. Following an active campaign for procedural reform led by the State Bar of Texas and the Texas Civil Judicial Council,[14] the Legislature in 1939 enacted legislation, effective in 1941, which repealed all statutes dealing with procedures in civil cases. At the same time the Supreme Court was vested with power to make rules of procedure in civil cases, although the Legislature could disallow some or all rules adopted. With the help of the State Bar of Texas and other interested persons, the Supreme Court promulgated the Rules of Civil Procedure, which, together with amendments, constitute the basis for all civil actions in Texas today.

Civil cases deal primarily with property rights and domestic relations. Thus they usually involve disputes between persons (according to American law, corporations are regarded as legal persons). These cases are normally begun in county and district courts with the filing of a *petition* by the injured party, who is known as the *plaintiff.* This petition, a written document, contains the plaintiff's grievance against the defendant and the remedy to which he feels he is entitled. The petition is filed with the clerk of the county or district court where the action is contemplated, whereupon the clerk issues a *citation.*

The citation, directed to the sheriff or to a constable in the defendant's county of residence, is accompanied by an attached copy of the plaintiff's petition and indicates when an answer is due. A true copy of the citation is served upon the defendant, directing him to answer the charges against him. If the defendant elects to contest the suit, he must file a written *answer* to the plaintiff's charges, in which he states his reason for believing the plaintiff is not entitled to the remedy for which he has sued.

When the case goes to trial, either party has the option of demanding a jury determination of the facts. If a jury is not demanded, the trial judge determines both facts and law. If a jury determines the facts after receiving instructions from the judge, then the judge's only duty is to apply the law to those predetermined facts.

A civil jury is composed of six or twelve persons—six in the county court and twelve in the district court—drawn from a much larger panel of qualified jurors summoned to assist the judge in this particular term of court. Formal panels are not always called for county courts, particularly in the smaller Texas counties. When a jury trial is requested in such courts, prospective jurors are sometimes literally brought in off the courthouse grounds and the city streets. *Qualifications for jury service* are determined by the Legislature. It is said that all persons who are citizens of the United States and of the state of Texas, eighteen years of age, sound of mind, morally straight, able to read and write, and who are not convicted felons or under indictment or other legal accusation of theft or of any felony, are eligible for jury duty and have a patriotic if not a legal responsibility to serve when called. In actual fact, those who have served as jurors in the district court for six days or more in the past six months, or six days or more during the previous three months in the county court, or those who have served as jury commissioners within the past twelve months, are prohibited from serving again in those periods. Persons unable to read and write may serve if there is an insufficient supply of qualified jurors.

In 1971 the Legislature reduced to two the number of *mandatory exemptions from jury duty*. Formerly, a long list of occupational exemptions virtually guaranteed that many of the state's best-educated citizens would never be required to perform jury service. Those now exempted are persons over sixty-five years of age and females who have legal custody of a child or children under the age of ten years. Nevertheless, judges still retain the prerogative of excusing others from jury duty under unusual circumstances. A person who is legally exempt from jury duty may avoid reporting as summoned if he files a signed statement with the court clerk at any time before the day on which he is scheduled to appear.

All prospective jurors, known as *veniremen,* are now chosen by the use of a *jury wheel.* In the past, jury commissioners tended to make use of property tax rolls as the sources of names for prospective jurors, since those rolls are readily accessible and contain sufficient names for many jury panels. This practice has been declared unconstitutional; consequently, slips with names taken from voter registration lists are now placed in a hollow wheel that is turned so as to produce random selection. Since many females do not own taxable property, the old system of selecting names of possible jurors had a discriminatory effect. Today it is not uncommon to find a female majority on a jury panel.

On a date and at a time determined by the judge, the trial begins. By then all interested parties should have had an opportunity to file their petitions, answers, or other pleas with the court. All of these written instruments constitute the pleadings in the case and form the basis of the trial. They should show the court the precise issues in dispute. Except under unusual circumstances, the trial will take place in the county of the defendant's residence.

Before the trial gets under way, the jury must be selected. Initially, the judge examines the prospective jurors to determine if all are legally qualified and if those who have asked to be excused have valid reasons for being relieved of jury duty. Attorneys for the parties are then permitted to examine the jury panel to ascertain whether any of the prospective jurors should be disqualified because of partiality, prejudice, or kinship. Such persons are excused by the judge for "cause," without limitation on the number. Attorneys for plaintiff and defendant are each allowed to exclude six persons in a district court and three at the county court level by *peremptory challenges,* i.e., because they want to exclude them for any or no reason. From those remaining the trial jury is chosen.

As the trial opens the plaintiff's petition and the defendant's answer are read or, in some instances, extemporaneously explained to the jury by their respective lawyers. The plaintiff then presents his case. By calling witnesses who give verbal testimony or by producing written documents—deeds, contracts, depositions, and the like—he offers all admissible evidence supporting the contentions of his petition. The defendant has the opportunity to contest the relevance or admissibility of all evidence introduced by the plaintiff and to cross-examine the plaintiff's witnesses. After the plaintiff has presented his case, it is the defendant's turn. He presents his defense by submitting his evidence, which can be challenged by the plaintiff. The judge is the final authority as to what evidence may be introduced by all parties, though exceptions to his rulings may be used as grounds for appeal.

After all parties have finished their presentations, the judge writes a *charge to the jury,* submits it to all parties for their approval, makes changes suggested by them if he chooses, and reads it to the jury. In his charge the judge instructs the jury on rules for deliberation, defines various terms, and submits the "special issues" or questions for fact-finding upon which the court bases its judgment. After the charge is read, the attorneys make their appeals to the jury, whereupon the jury retires to deliberate. At least ten jurors must agree to a decision in a district court and five in a county court. A court decision is known as the *verdict.* On the basis of that verdict the judge prepares his written opinion, known as the *judgment* or *decree of the court.* Either party may then file a motion for a new trial based on the reasons why he believes that he has not had a fair trial. If the judge agrees, he orders a new trial; if not, the case may be appealed. In each appeal a complete written record of the trial is sent to the appellate court.

In the appellate court the case is heard by a panel of judges without the assistance of a jury. The appellate court proceeds on the basis of the record sent up from the lower court, which includes *briefs,* that is, the written arguments prepared by the attorneys for the interested parties, oral arguments from the attorneys, and questions from the bench directed to the attorneys. At the conclusion of the arguments the judges take the case to conference, where they discuss it among themselves and arrive at a decision on the basis of a majority vote. One of those voting in the majority is assigned the task of writing an opinion embodying the decision of the court and stating its major reasons for reaching that decision. Minority opinions in the form of dissents or concurrences may also be filed but do not affect the ultimate decision in the particular case. Under extraordinary circumstances civil appeals may be taken from county or district courts to the Supreme Court of Texas, but the usual route of appeals is from those trial courts to the courts of civil appeals and then in some instances to the Supreme Court.

CRIMINAL PROCEDURES

Although often revised, the Texas Code of Criminal Procedure remained substantially unchanged from its adoption in the early days of statehood until recently. The 1965 revision, with substantial amendment in 1967, was necessary for reasons other than the antiquated provisions of the previous code, adopted in 1856. In large measure, changes were necessary to bring Texas procedures into line with United States Supreme Court rulings regarding confessions, arrest, and searches and seizures. Other changes resulted from pressure by the State Bar of Texas, which had spent thousands of dollars and hundreds of man-hours in a statewide campaign for revision, and from a long-standing policy of systematic statute revision on the part of the Texas Legislature.

A storm of criticism that tended to fall into two distinct categories, administrative and popular, greeted the new code. The first kind of criticism stemmed from lawyers, judges, and certain law-enforcement officers; and it centered on their anticipated difficulties in administering the new code. The second kind came especially from elected prosecuting attorneys, who presumably believed they were expressing the concern of their constituents. They contended that the code was too lenient in punishing criminals and would thus encourage rather than deter crime. Their outspoken criticism is probably traceable to public agitation for "law and order" and to public outcries against those United States Supreme Court decisions on rights of the accused that had made revision necessary in the first place. Many criminal lawyers, however, hailed the code as a better, long-overdue guarantee of individual rights.

In response to the popular agitation, the Legislature in 1967 enacted some important amendments to the 1965 code. For example, the minimum time period a convict must serve before he is eligible for parole was extended to one-third of his sentence or twenty years, whichever is the shorter. Other changes allow law-enforcement officers to arrest without warrant persons committing crimes in their presence and permit those officers to arrest "suspicious" persons. Generally, the amendments eased restrictions on the activities of law-enforcement officers.

The "revised" code made some 200 changes in criminal procedures, of which the following were probably the most significant:

An accused person is assured that he will be provided with *counsel* (that is, with the services of an attorney, more commonly referred to as a lawyer) in any criminal case, felony or misdemeanor, if the crime of which he is accused is punishable by confinement in prison or jail.

"Without unnecessary delay" any person arrested must be taken before a *magistrate* (justice of the peace), who, in turn, must immediately inform him of the charge or charges against him and of his legal rights. These include the rights to consult with counsel, to remain silent, to have an attorney present during any questioning by law-enforcement officers or prosecuting attorneys, to have an attorney appointed for him if he is indigent, and to an examining trial. The magistrate must also inform the accused person that he is not required to make any statement and that if he does so, it may be used against him at a subsequent trial. If a lawyer is appointed by the court, he must be paid a "reasonable fee" by the county in which the prosecution was begun—at least $50 a day, and not less than $250 a day in a *capital felony* (i.e., capital murder) case.

Written or oral confessions obtained from persons under arrest may be used as evidence against them only if the confession is voluntarily given—and then provided the accused was warned of his right of counsel prior to and during questioning, and of his right to remain silent, and was told that any confession he made might be used against him. Incriminating oral statements made in the presence of an officer prior to arrest may be received in evidence, but generally they must be in writing and signed by the accused.

Except in a capital felony case, the defendant may waive jury trial regardless of his plea—guilty, not guilty, or no contest (*nolo contendere*). When the defendant has waived a trial by jury, the Texas judge determines the punishment to be imposed; and in cases where a jury trial is requested, the judge may also determine the penalty unless the defendant requests that the jury be allowed to do so. In both cases, a separate hearing on the penalty is held, at which the person's prior criminal record, general reputation, and other relevant factors may be introduced. Under the new code husbands and wives are now permitted to testify against each other but only at trials involving crimes of violence against children under sixteen, child desertion, incest, or willful refusal to support a minor child.

Simplification of criminal appeals procedures has been achieved by eliminating many of the technicalities of old appeals practices. The defendant's lawyer can now prepare his appeal to the court of criminal appeals with more confidence that it will be technically correct and that it will be heard. In addition, trial courts have been given what is really appellate power over their own cases, in that they can grant motions for a new trial in many more cases without the necessity and expense of an appeal to the court of criminal appeals.

In criminal trials the procedure is much the same as that for civil cases. A criminal trial, however, proceeds on the basis of a formal accusation. Texas criminal procedure recognizes two types of accusations: a written statement prepared by a grand jury and called an *indictment* is used in felony cases, and an *information* based on the complaint of any creditable person is filed in misdemeanor cases. A grand jury is composed of twelve persons. They are selected from a list of fifteen to twenty county residents with qualifications of trial jurors. A jury commission, composed of three to five "intelligent citizens" from different parts of the county, is appointed by the district judge and prepares the list. Then the judge examines those persons listed and selects twelve for grand jury service. At each term of the district court the grand jury meets to inquire into felony cases. Answers to inquiries stem from the juror's own knowledge or from information supplied by the district attorney representing the state or by any other creditable person (see Reading 5-2).

Sessions of the grand jury are secret. Jurors and witnesses are sworn to keep secret all they hear in grand jury sessions. If after investigation the grand jury decides there is sufficient evidence to warrant a trial, it prepares, with the aid of the prosecuting attorney, an indictment—a written statement accusing some person or persons of a particular crime. A vote of only nine grand jurors is required to return an indictment. An indictment is referred to as a *true bill;* failure to indict constitutes a *no bill.*

For misdemeanor prosecutions grand jury indictments are not required. Any creditable person may file a *complaint*—a sworn statement asserting that he has good reason to believe that a certain individual has committed a particular offense. On the basis of this complaint the district or county attorney may prepare, if he so chooses, an information, which is a document that formally charges the accused with the offense.

When a criminal case is called to trial in a district court, the accused defendant pleads guilty, not guilty or no contest to the charges. In a homicide case, a *special venire* or panel composed of hundreds of persons may be called and examined before a jury of twelve is ultimately selected. In all cases since the recent revisions in criminal procedure, prospective jurors may be examined as a group even in a capital felony case, except when the state or a defendant demands the right of individual examination. Whether they are examined collectively or individually, the judge is required to question prospective jurors concerning the principles of reasonable doubt, burden of proof, presumption of innocence, and prior opinion. Those *veniremen* who indicate by their answers that they cannot be fair and impartial are excused from serving on the case. In a capital felony case, both the prosecution and the defense are allowed to challenge prospective jurors either peremptorily (up to fifteen per side) or for good cause (an unlimited number). A *challenge for cause* is evaluated by the judge, who must decide if the cause is sufficient. Only ten peremptory challenges are allowed per side in noncapital felonies and five or less in misdemeanor cases. The first twelve veniremen not excused by the district judge nor challenged peremptorily by the parties to the case make up the trial jury and are known as jurors.

After the jury has been selected, the indictment or information is read by the prosecuting attorney. The jury is thus informed of the basic allegations of the state's case. The state then calls its witnesses and introduces any other evidence supporting the indictment. The defense may challenge the truth or relevance of the evidence presented and is allowed to cross-examine all witnesses and challenge all evidence. Next, the defense presents its case, calling its witnesses and submitting other evidence subject to attack by the prosecution. Witnesses for both the prosecution and the defense may be recalled to the stand for additional questioning and cross-examination.

Before the arguments of state attorneys and defense attorneys are presented to the jury, the judge charges the jury concerning the law applicable to the case. In his charge the judge may in no way indicate his opinion of the defendant's guilt or innocence, nor may he influence the decision of the jury in any substantial way. Both the prosecution and the defense must have an opportunity to examine and raise objections to the charge. Both must also be given an opportunity to address arguments to the jury before it retires to reach a verdict, but the prosecution makes the concluding address.

Before retiring to deliberate on a verdict, jurors may not discuss the case among themselves. The twelve-man jury of the district court and the six-man jury of the county court may determine only questions of fact, but the six-man juries of justice of the peace and municipal courts decide questions of both fact and law. A unanimous decision is required for the jury to reach its verdict. In the event of a *"hung jury,"* when jurors are hopelessly split on their decision, the judge declares a mistrial, discharges the jurors, and orders a new trial with another jury.

When the jury brings its verdict before the court, the judge may choose to disregard the finding and order a *new trial* on the ground that, in his judgment, the jury has failed to arrive at a verdict that achieves substantial justice. In a jury trial the sentence may be fixed by the jury if the convicted person so requests; otherwise, the judge determines the sentence. (Reading 5-3 provides the history of a highly publicized case from indictment to post-trial motions.)

REHABILITATION

Suspended sentences are no longer authorized, but *probation* is commonly granted. In misdemeanor cases juries and judges alike may grant probation; in felony cases the judge may grant probation regardless of jury recommendations. Although free from confinement, a probationer must shun criminal companionship, avoid committing criminal acts, report periodically to a probation officer, and comply with other conditions that may be imposed by the court. Noncompliance can result in revocation of probation and confinement for the full length of the sentence.

A misdemeanor sentence is served in a county jail. These local penal institutions are also used for holding persons awaiting trial if they have not been released on bail. Jail facilities vary in quality, but usually these county institutions are completely lacking in rehabilitation programs involving academic instruction, vocational training, and counseling. The high cost of jail construction has caused many county governments to "make do" with facilities built half a century or more ago. Meanwhile, the crime rate continues to rise and more prisoners are thrown into overcrowded cells. Conditions in urban counties tend to be especially bad.

Convicted male felons serve penitentiary sentences in thirteen units administered by the *Texas Department of Corrections* (see Reading 5-4). All of these units are located in the southeastern part of the state. Goree Unit, at Huntsville, is the fourteenth unit; it houses the state's female prisoners. Also located at Huntsville is the administrative headquarters of the director of the prison system. This official is named by the *Board of Corrections,* and the nine members of this board are appointed by the governor with the consent of the Senate for six-year terms.

Despite the fact that most penitentiary inmates are employed in a variety of jobs, ranging from cultivation of food crops to production of braille textbooks and motor vehicle license plates, each prisoner costs the taxpayer over $4.00 per day. Most convicts are eventually released or paroled after serving sentences with "time off for good behavior" according to a point system that provides an incentive for good conduct. Nearly one-fifth, however, can be expected to return and serve a second sentence; and some of these will eventually be released, only to come back as "lifers" following a third felony conviction. To combat such *recidivism,* prisoners receive instruction and training designed to equip them with the means for self-support upon release. Those who have not completed the third grade are required to attend prison school. Many learn useful skills while working in prison industries (e.g., print shop, laundry, cardboard carton factory, canning plant, garment factory); some obtain high school diplomas; and over 1,200 (including a few, no doubt, who are studying this textbook) are enrolled in accredited college courses, either through extension or correspondence. Upon leaving the penitentiary, each prisoner is given $100 and, if requested, a new suit and shoes.

After having served one-third of his sentence or twenty years, depending on which is the lesser, a prisoner is eligible to apply for *parole.* Application is made to the *Board of Pardons and Paroles,* which has three members appointed for six-year terms; one member each is named by the chief justice of the Supreme Court, the presiding judge of the court of criminal appeals, and the governor. On the recommendation of this board, paroles are granted by the governor. A parolee is in a status similar to that of a probationer. He must report to a parole officer as directed and must refrain from all illegal or immoral conduct; otherwise, the parole will be revoked and the parolee will be returned to the penitentiary to serve out his sentence.

JUVENILE DELINQUENCY

Generally, young people between the ages of ten and seventeen are dealt with in *juvenile courts* when they commit acts that would be classified as felonies or misdemeanors if committed by adults. A young person within this age group is classified as a "delinquent child" not only for violating penal laws but also for knowingly associating with thieves, vicious or immoral persons, or for knowingly visiting a house of ill repute or any place where a gambling device is operated. In each county there is a court of record that is designated as a juvenile court. Usually this is a district court, but some county judges are authorized to act as juvenile court judges. Not all juvenile offenders, however, are dealt with in these juvenile courts. As a result of a recent change in Texas law, provision is made for *discretionary transfer* from juvenile to regular courts of young people fifteen and sixteen years of age whose criminal conduct merits sterner justice.

The *Texas Youth Council,* composed of three members appointed by the governor and approved by the Senate for six-year terms, names an executive director who is responsible for supervising the care and rehabilitation of over 2,500 juveniles. Schools for delinquent boys have been established at Gatesville and Giddings; delinquent girls are committed to schools maintained by the Texas Youth Council at Gainesville, Crockett, and Brownwood. Also under the administration of the council are state homes caring for about 1,000 dependent and neglected children at Corsicana, Waco, and Monahans. Official records reveal common background problems: divorce or separation of parents and illegitimacy. Without doubt, juvenile delinquency is often the result of adult irresponsibility.

REFORM

Important elements of any system of justice are laws, judicial personnel, court structure, legal procedures, and rehabilitation of criminals. As has been pointed out, the 63rd Legislature took positive action with regard to a draft proposal submitted by the State Bar Committee on Revision of the Texas Penal Code. There has been continuing reform of the Rules of Civil Procedure since 1941; and the Texas Code of Criminal Procedure underwent a thorough revision in 1965 and was substantially amended two years later. Rehabilitation of adult criminals and juveniles has received more attention by state authorities in recent years, but county governments lag far behind in this area. Modernizing changes in the areas of judicial personnel and court organization have been insignificant, but there are indications that a restructuring of the Texas court system is imminent.

A constitutional amendment approved in 1948 established a contributory retirement system for district and appellate judges. Although not completely satisfactory, this system at least provides some assurance of security after long and satisfactory service for district and appellate court judges; however, the total absence of such a system for other judges only compounds the problem of securing and retaining quality people in those positions. Likewise, the Legislature has provided reasonable compensation for judges at the district court level and above; salaries of other trial judges, however, are fixed by county commissioners courts. Consequently, the revenue-raising capacity of each county is a major factor in determining the salaries that are paid to county judges and justices of the peace. Nevertheless, a 1972 constitutional amendment, which abolished the last vestige of compensation on a fee basis for justices of the peace, represents some progress.

Constitutional and statutory laws in Texas have long provided several formal methods for removing incompetent or incapacitated judges from office once elected, but few have in fact been removed except by voters failing to re-elect them. A 1965 constitutional amendment produced at least a partial reform by providing that the offices of district and appellate judges should become vacant when the judge reaches the age of seventy-five or from seventy to seventy-five if the Legislature should so order. As an added inducement, the Legislature has offered judges an extra 10 per cent in retirement pay if they leave office at the age of seventy. The same amendment established a Judicial Qualifications Commission to hear complaints and make recommendations to the Supreme Court regarding removal of appellate and district court judges. Another amendment, approved by the voters in 1970, granted this power to the commission with respect to all justices and judges.

County jail conditions constitute one of the most important challenges to reformers in the field of criminal justice. With federal judges threatening to order the release of prisoners kept in overcrowded, substandard jails, it is apparent that counties must provide more jail space and better care of prisoners. New regional jails serving several counties represent another possible solution to the jail problem. Space problems can be overcome by constructing new facilities or reducing jail populations. Since over one-fifth of all arrests are for the offense of drunkenness, and since many of these offenders are confined for varying periods of time, jail populations can be significantly reduced by detoxification programs administered outside the jails. When alcoholism is viewed as a disease rather than as a crime, it is apparent that penal institutions are hardly appropriate places for the handling of drunks. But the enormity of this problem is suggested by the Texas Commission on Alcoholism, which estimates that nearly half a million Texans must be classified as alcoholics.

For many years one of the strongest advocates of streamlining the state's court system has been Robert W. Calvert. In 1972, during his last year of active service as chief justice of the Supreme Court of Texas, he organized and headed the *Chief Justice's Task Force for Court Improvement.* Composed of members of House and Senate committees responsible for judicial matters, prominent lawyers, and distinguished judges, the task force prepared a complete revision of the judiciary article of the Texas constitution and presented this draft to the 63rd Legislature when it convened in January, 1973. Previously, in an effort to publicize the work of the task force and to involve citizens across the state in the court reform movement, during the fall of 1972 seven regional and one statewide court improvement conferences were held. Also, task force members accepted speaking engagements that afforded opportunities to impress upon Texans the importance of communicating their support of the task force's work to members of the 63rd Legislature (see Reading 5-5).

Two constitutional amendments were prepared by the task force. Consisting of about 1,000 words, Amendment No. 1 would replace all of Article V of the 1876 Constitution, which has about 5,000 words. It calls for an integrated judicial pyramid headed by a single Supreme Court with both criminal and civil jurisdiction. Membership is to consist of the "Chief Justice of Texas" and eight other justices, but during a transitional phase the five members and two commissioners of the court of criminal appeals are to be added to the nine members of the present Supreme Court. No new justice is to be named until the membership of that court is reduced below nine by attrition. Courts of civil appeals are to be reorganized as courts of appeals with authority to hear criminal as well as civil cases. District courts are to be established in districts drawn by the Legislature or "by an agency acting under authority of law." Present overlapping districts and special district courts are to be eliminated. As determined by the Legislature, a system of county courts is to be established to perform all judicial functions currently handled by county courts, county courts at law, justice of the peace courts, and municipal courts. All county judges must be lawyers. The Legislature will provide for the election of district attorneys, district clerks, sheriffs, county clerks, and, as it deems necessary, county attorneys. The chief justice of Texas is designated as the administrative head of the state court system and, as authorized by rules of administration, is to transfer cases between courts of appeals and temporarily assign judges or any qualified lawyer to any court. Also, he is to serve as chairman of a fifteen-member Judicial Council that is empowered to propose rules of administration for all courts, such rules becoming effective when approved by the Supreme Court.

Amendment No. 1 calls for the nonpartisan election (no party identification of candidates on the ballot) of all judges and justices for six-year terms, but Amendment No. 2 outlines a different system for naming judicial personnel. It proposes a Missouri Plan arrangement for merit selection of appellate court judges. Under terms of the second amendment, a vacancy on the Supreme Court and the courts of appeals would be filled by the governor with one of three nominees presented by a seven-member Judicial Nominating Commission, one of whom would be the chief justice of Texas. Then, after a period of not less than ten months, the appointed judicial official would run against his record in a general election for the purpose of obtaining a six-year term. This amendment specifies that judges of district courts and county courts are to be elected for six-year terms by nonpartisan elections or, if provided by the Legislature, "by appointment by the Governor from lists of nominees presented to him by district nominating commissions."

Although the draft amendments were not accepted by the 63rd Legislature in its regular session, sufficient public interest and legislative support were created to ensure that the same or similar plans would be considered by that Legislature when it convened as a constitutional convention in 1974. Significant progress has been made in recent years with regard to reform of the state's laws. Now it would appear that the major task at hand is that of restructuring the court system—either through amending the Constitution of 1876 or through adopting a new constitution providing for a judicial system better suited to the needs of Texans living in the last quarter of the 20th century.

NOTES

1. The word "annotated" refers to the extensive notes on cases which have been before the courts. These notes provide valuable information concerning judicial interpretations of the laws. *Vernon's Annotated Statutes* consists of five series of volumes: *Vernon's Annotated Constitution of the State of Texas* (cited as *Vernon's Ann. Tex. Const.*), *Vernon's Annotated Revised Civil Statutes* (cited as *Vernon's Ann. Civ. St.*), *Vernon's Annotated Penal Code* (cited as *Vernon's Ann. P. C.*), *Vernon's Texas Rules of Civil Procedure* (cited as *Vernon's Ann. Rules Civ. Proc.*), and *Vernon's Annotated Code of Criminal Procedure* (cited as *Vernon's Ann. C. C. P.*). Although used primarily by lawyers, these volumes (especially *Vernon's Ann. Tex. Const.*) can be consulted with profit by political science students and other nonlawyers.
2. See *General and Special Laws of the State of Texas Passed by the Regular Session of the Sixty-First Legislature* (1969), Vol. II, pp. 2255-2263, for

S.B. 392 authorizing creation of one or more municipal courts of record in the city of Wichita Falls.

3. See *Hooks* v. *State,* 158 S. W. 808 (1913). This citation refers to a court of criminal appeals decision handed down in 1913 and reported in Volume 158 of the *Southwestern Reporter,* beginning on p. 808. Printed by the West Publishing Co. of Minneapolis, Minn., since 1887, the *Southwestern Reporter* publishes opinions rendered by the Texas courts of civil appeals, the court of criminal appeals, and the Supreme Court. After the first 300 volumes were published, a second series was begun in 1928.
4. In November, 1972, a total of 142 district, criminal district, domestic relations, and juvenile court judgeships were on the ballot. (A Republican was elected at midterm as the domestic relations judge in Gregg County.) In Harrison County a Republican incumbent retained the 71st district judgeship without Democratic opposition, and in Ector County a Republican incumbent defeated a Democratic opponent to retain the 161st district judgeship. Two Republicans in Dallas County, two in Harris County, and one in Gregg County were unsuccessful in attempts to win district judgeships; however, Democratic candidates were without opposition in winning the remaining 135 district judgeships. Likewise, there were no Republican candidates on the ballot for the courts of civil appeals, the court of criminal appeals, and the Supreme Court.
5. Texas Civil Judicial Council, *Forty-fourth Annual Report, 1972* (Austin, Tex., 1973), pp. 191-193.
6. *Ibid.,* p. 39.
7. *Ibid.,* p. 33.
8. For a listing of legal firms and practicing lawyers in each county, see the *Texas Legal Directory,* published annually by Legal Directories Publishing Corp., Los Angeles, Calif.
9. For additional information and statistics on the recruitment of justices, see T. C. Sinclair, "The Supreme Court of Texas," *Houston Law Review,* Vol. VII (September, 1969), pp. 23-41.
10. *Ibid.,* p. 43.
11. Texas Civil Judicial Council, *Forty-fourth Annual Report, 1972,* p. 21.
12. For a report on legal education in the state's eight law schools (Baylor, Texas Southern, St. Mary's, Southern Methodist, South Texas, Texas Tech, Houston, and the University of Texas at Austin), see "The Law School Story," *Texas Bar Journal,* Vol. XXXV (November 22, 1972), pp. 1029-1034.
13. Sinclair, *op. cit.,* pp. 42 and 66.
14. In addition to compiling and reporting statistics relating to the operation of the district and appellate courts of the state, the Texas Civil Judicial Council makes a continuous study of court operations, receives and considers suggestions for improving the administration of civil justice, formulates methods for simplifying civil procedure, and investigates matters touching the administration of civil justice that are referred to it by the Legislature or the Supreme Court. Council membership is composed of nine appointed

members (7 lawyers and 2 nonlawyers, 1 of whom must be a journalist) and nine ex officio members, including the chief justice of the Supreme Court or some other justice of that court appointed by him.

KEY TERMS AND CONCEPTS

civil case
criminal case
original jurisdiction
appellate jurisdiction
common law
General and Special Laws of the State of Texas
Vernon's Annotated Statutes of the State of Texas
felony
misdemeanor
capital murder
municipal court
justice of the peace
State Judicial Qualifications Commission
small claims court
coroner
de novo
concurrent jurisdiction
constitutional county court
statutory or special county court
district court
administrative judicial district
supreme judicial district
court of civil appeals
en banc
court of criminal appeals
Supreme Court of Texas
regular cause
State Bar of Texas
litigant
witness
juror
petition
plaintiff
citation
answer
qualifications for jury service
mandatory exemptions from jury duty
veniremen
jury wheel
peremptory challenge
charge to the jury
verdict
judgment or decree of the court
brief
counsel
magistrate
capital felony
nolo contendere
indictment
information
grand jury
true bill
no bill
complaint
special venire
veniremen
challenge for cause
"hung jury"
new trial
probation
Texas Department of Corrections
Board of Corrections
recidivism
parole
Board of Pardons and Paroles
juvenile courts
discretionary transfer
Texas Youth Council
Chief Justice's Task Force for Court Improvement

JEFFREY J. MONAHAN: BY PERMISSION OF CASE & COMMENT

"The judge said we are not to discuss the case with anyone."

Selected Readings

5-1 CAPITAL PUNISHMENT: THE COURT OF CRIMINAL APPEALS OF TEXAS IS OVERRULED BY THE SUPREME COURT OF THE UNITED STATES

I. ELMER BRANCH V. THE STATE OF TEXAS [Tex. Cr. App., 447 S.W. 2d 932 (1969)]

The offense is rape by force; the punishment, death.

The record reflects that the victim, a widow, lived alone some twelve miles north of Vernon and a distance of about two blocks from the home of her son. Testifying at the trial she positively identified appellant as the Negro man who, about 2 A.M., after gaining entrance into her house through a window by force, ravished her and had sexual intercourse with her, and after demanding and taking money she had in her coin purse and threatening to repeat his act, finally drove away. She immediately ran to her son's home and reported the matter. She described her assailant as being a young Negro man, wearing dark trousers and tennis shoes. Her son relayed the information to the sheriff by telephone and told the sheriff that the suspect was believed to be in an automobile headed toward Vernon.

The sheriff immediately alerted all officers in the area by radio, requesting them to stop any car containing colored subjects coming into Vernon from the north. Within minutes a vehicle driven by appellant pulled into a service station on the north side of Vernon. Police officers of the City of Vernon observed that he was wearing tennis shoes and dark trousers which were unzipped, and detained him until other officers arrived.

The tennis shoes worn by appellant were compared with the footprints found near the house in which the offense was committed and they matched. . . .

Ground of error No. 3 presents the contention that the judgment of conviction with punishment assessed at death violates the Fifth, Eighth, and Fourteenth Amendments to the Constitution of the United States; and poses the question of whether capital punishment inflicted as a punishment for "a crime less than murder" constitutes cruel and unusual punishment within the meaning of the Eighth Amendment, and whether when inflicted in a rape case involving a Negro defendant and a Caucasian complaining witness such a defendant has been deprived of equal protection of law under the provisions of the Fifth, Eighth, and Fourteenth Amendments. . . .

Ground of error No. 3 is overruled. . . .

The judgment is affirmed.

II. ELMER BRANCH V. STATE OF TEXAS, 92 S.Ct. 2726 (1972) [Justice William O. Douglas]

In these three cases [*Furman* v. *Georgia, Jackson* v. *Georgia,* and *Branch* v. *Texas*] the death penalty was imposed, one of them for murder, and two for rape. In each the determination of whether the penalty should be death or a lighter punishment was left by the State to the discretion of the judge or of the jury. In each of the three cases the trial was to a jury. They are here on petitions for certiorari which we granted limited to the questions whether the imposition and execution of the death penalty constitutes "cruel and unusual punishments" within the meaning of the Eighth Amendment as applied to the States by the Fourteenth. I vote to vacate each judgment, believing that the exaction of the death penalty does violate the Eighth and Fourteenth Amendments.

That the requirements of due process ban cruel and unusual punishment is now settled. *Louisiana ex rel Francis* v. *Resweber,* 329 U.S. 459; *Robinson* v. *California,* 370 U.S. 660. It is also settled that the proscription of cruel and unusual punishments forbids the judicial imposition of them as well as their proscription by the legislature. *Weems* v. *United States,* 217 U.S. 349. . . . The words "cruel and unusual" certainly include penalties that are barbaric. But the words, at least when read in light of the English proscription against selective and irregular use of penalties, suggest that it is "cruel and unusual" to apply the death penalty—or any other penalty—selectively to minorities whose numbers are few, who are outcasts of society, and who are unpopular, but whom society is willing to see suffer though it would not countenance general application of the same penalty across the boards. . . .

A study of capital cases in Texas from 1924 to 1968 [Rupert C. Koeninger,

"Capital Punishment in Texas, 1927-1968," *Crime and Delinquency*, Vol. XV (January, 1968), pp. 132-141] reached the following conclusions:

> Application of the death penalty is unequal: most of those executed were poor, young, and ignorant.
>
> Seventy-five of the 460 cases involved codefendants, who, under Texas law, were given separate trials. In several instances, where a white and a Negro were codefendants, the white was sentenced to life imprisonment or a term of years, and the Negro was given the death penalty.
>
> Another ethnic disparity is found in the type of sentence imposed for rape. The Negro convicted of rape is far more likely to get the death penalty than a term sentence, whereas whites and Latins are far more likely to get a term sentence than the death penalty.

Warden Lewis E. Lawes of Sing Sing said [*Life and Death in Sing Sing* (1928), pp. 155-160],

> Not only does capital punishment fail in its justification, but no punishment could be invented with so many inherent defects. It is an unequal punishment in the way it is applied to the rich and to the poor. . . .

Former Attorney General Ramsey Clark has said [*Crime in America* (1971), p. 355], "It is the poor, the sick, the ignorant, the powerless and the hated who are executed." One searches the chronicles in vain for the execution of any member of the affluent strata of this society. The Leopolds and Loebs are given prison terms, not sentenced to death. . . .

Branch, a Black, entered the rural home of a 65-year old widow, a White, while she slept and raped her, holding his arm against her throat. . . . The record is barren of any medical or psychiatric evidence showing injury to her as a result of Branch's attack.

He had previously been convicted of felony theft and found to be a borderline mentally deficient and well below the average IQ of Texan prison inmates. He had the equivalent of five and a half years of grade school education. He had a "dull intelligence" and was in the lower four percentile of his class.

We cannot say from facts disclosed in these records that these defendants were sentenced to death because they were Black. Yet our task is not restricted to an effort to divine what motives impelled these death penalties. Rather we deal with a system of law and of justice that leaves to the uncontrolled discretion of judges or juries the determination whether defendants committing these crimes should die or be imprisoned. Under these laws no standards govern the selection of the penalty. People live or die, dependent on the whim of one man or of 12. . . .

In a Nation committed to Equal Protection of the laws there is no permissible "caste" aspect of law enforcement. Yet we know that the discretion of judges and juries in imposing the death penalty enables the penalty to be selectively applied, feeding prejudices against the accused if he is poor and despised, poor and lacking political clout, or if he is a member of a suspect or unpopular minority and saving those who by social position may be in a more protected position. In ancient Hindu law a Brahmin was exempt from capital punishment. And in those days "Generally, in the law books, punishment increased in severity as social status diminished" [Spellman, *Political Theory in Ancient India* (1964), p. 112.] We have, I fear, taken in practice the same position, partially as a result of making the death penalty discretionary and partially as a result of the ability of the rich to purchase the services of the most respected and most resourceful legal talent in the Nation.

The high service rendered by the "cruel and unusual" punishment clause of the Eighth Amendment is to require legislatures to write penal laws that are evenhanded, nonselective, and nonarbitrary, and to require judges to see to it that general laws are not applied sparsely, selectively, and spottily to unpopular groups.

A law that stated that anyone making more than $50,000 would be exempt from the death penalty would plainly fail, as would a law that in terms said that Blacks, those who never went beyond the fifth grade in school, or those who made less than $3,000 a year, or those who were unpopular or unstable should be the only people executed. A law which in the overall view reaches that result in practice has no more sanctity than a law which in terms provides the same.

Any law which is nondiscriminatory on its face may be applied in such a way as to violate the Equal Protection Clause of the Fourteenth Amendment. *Yick Wo* v. *Hopkins,* 118 U.S. 356. Such conceivably might be the fate of a mandatory death penalty, where equal or lesser sentences were imposed on the elite, a harsher one on the minorities or members of the lower castes. Whether a mandatory death penalty would otherwise be constitutional is a question I do not reach.

I concur in the judgments of the Court [Justice Brennan, Justice Stewart, Justice White, and Justice Marshall filed separate opinions in support of judgments; Chief Justice Burger, Justice Blackmun, Justice Powell, and Justice Rehnquist filed separate dissenting opinions in this 5 to 4 decision].

5-2
THE GRAND JURY IN TEXAS: A CASE STUDY
Robert A. Carp

Article I of the Texas Constitution declares that "no person shall be held to answer for a criminal offense, unless on an indictment of a grand jury, except in cases in which the punishment is by fine or imprisonment, otherwise than in the penitentiary. . . ." By incorporating this clause into the Texas Bill of Rights, the Texas Fathers sought to provide the state's citizens with the same privilege which is guaranteed all United States citizens in the Fifth Amendment to the national

This previously unpublished article is printed by permission of the author.

Constitution, which likewise declares that "no person shall be held to answer for a capital or otherwise infamous crime, unless on a presentment or indictment of a grand jury."

What is a grand jury, and what is it supposed to do? The grand jury is established to bring to trial persons accused of public offenses upon just grounds and to protect the people against unwarranted prosecution, either by the government or by any person motivated by private enmity. The grand jury determines whether there is sufficient preliminary evidence to warrant the trouble and expense of a trial, and an affirmative finding will result in the return of an indictment (or a true bill). The case will then be brought before the petit (trial) jury, which decides the actual guilt or innocence of the accused. While a trial jury is impaneled to try one case only, the grand jury's life is for a full term of the court, which in Texas may extend from three to six months (depending on the county involved) and may include the determination of over a thousand individual cases. In Texas, at least nine of the twelve grand jurors must vote to indict before the accused can be brought to trial.

The process of selecting grand jurors in Texas is as intricate as it is arbitrary. Unlike many of its sister states which non-discriminately select the names of grand jurors from a lottery wheel containing the names of hundreds of potential jurors, Texas grants jury commissions almost unlimited discretion to compile a small list of names from which the grand jury is impaneled. The local district judges select not less than three nor more than five qualified persons from different parts of the county to serve as jury commissioners. After taking a comprehensive oath and receiving a set of instructions from the district judges, the commissioners secure from the district clerk the last tax assessment roll of the county and a list of those who are either exempt or disqualified from service on the grand jury (e.g., persons previously convicted of a felony). With this information in hand, the commissioners are free to select sixteen prospective grand jurors who meet broadly defined statutory standards. The names of those selected are written down in numerical sequence, placed in a sealed envelope, and delivered to the district judge in open court. When the list is opened, the judge conducts an inquiry as to their qualifications, and the first twelve who are qualified are impaneled as the grand jury.

Historically most jurists have argued, and the courts have officially determined, that grand juries, like trial juries, should be representative of the population of the community as a whole. Although there is still considerable uncertainty about how this goal is to be achieved, the U.S. Court of Appeals for the Fifth Circuit has determined that the Constitution requires that members of Texas grand juries represent "a fair cross section . . . [of the] community's human resources. . . ." (366 F.2d at 14). In light of this judicial determination it is fair then to ask the question: how representative are Texas grand juries of the county populations from which they are selected? This is largely an empirical question, and for a partial answer we may compare the results of a recently completed study of grand jurors in Harris County (Houston), Texas, with the 1970 census figures for this same county.

This study, which sampled Harris county grand jurors between 1969 and

1972, provided the following data profile of the county's grand jury members:[1]

Sex

Male	81%
Female	19%

Race

Anglo	82%
Negro	15%
Mexican-American	3%

Age

21-35 years–10%
36-50 years–42%
51-65 years–38%
Over 65 10%
(Median age is 51)

Education

Some high school	3%
High school degree	8%
Some college	34%
College degree	32%
Graduate degree	23%

(Median education is 16 years or a college degree)

Income

Under $5,000	1%
$5,000 to $10,000	3%
$10,000 to $15,000	25%
$15,000 to $20,000	16%
Over $20,000	55%

(Median family income is approximately $25,000)

Employment

Business Executive	37%
Employed worker	14%
Proprietor	8%
Professional	20%
Housewife	8%
Retired	13%

Thus, the typical Harris County grand juror is an Anglo-Saxon male college graduate about fifty-one years of age who is quite likely to earn over $20,000 per year while working either as a business executive or as a professional man. How does this profile compare with what the 1970 census data indicate about the "typical" resident of the county? A brief summary of these data reveals the following about the citizens of Harris County: 49% are male and 51% are female; the median age is 25; 69% are Anglo, 20% are Negro, and 11% are Mexican-American; the median education is 12 years (a high school degree); and the median family income is $10,348.[2] These figures reveal clearly that even by rudimentary standards Harris County grand juries do not meet the judicial criterion of "a fair cross section . . . [of the] community's human resources." Grossly underrepresented are women, young people, Negroes, Mexican-Americans, the poor, and those with less extensive educational backgrounds.

The civil libertarian-liberal is likely to react to the above conclusion with horror: "How are the young, the minorities, the poor and the oppressed to be accorded due process of law when they are not proportionally represented among those who administer the laws?" Such a critic would do well, however, to consider what numerous investigations reveal about the attitudes of high-status persons toward dissident and minority factions in our society. Studies by Stouffer, Lipset, and Hyman and Sheatsley, for example, reveal that higher-status people (i.e., those with at least a college degree and who are in the professions or who are business leaders) are significantly *more* likely to be solicitous towards the rights of ethnic minorities and social dissidents than are those who come from the lower end of the social spectrum.[3] Thus the liberal might well think long and hard before "blowing the whistle" on this portion of our judicial establishment.

The same day the grand jury is impaneled it usually begins to hear cases. How well prepared is the average Texas grand juror to perform his important and responsible task of determining whether there is "probable cause" for a citizen to be formally indicted for a crime and to be put on trial? In Harris County all new grand jurors are provided with a training program of sorts which entails three different aspects: a *voluntary* one-day training seminar conducted primarily by police and sheriff's department officials; two booklets pertaining to grand jury instructions and procedures, one written by the District Attorney and the other prepared by the county Grand Jury Association; and, finally, an in-depth, give-and-take discussion between the grand jury and an experienced member of the District Attorney's staff.

How adequately does this training program prepare the grand jurors for their work? Let us examine each aspect of the program separately. First of all, the series of lectures by law enforcement officials appears to be of limited utility for the novice grand juror. Not only do these lectures come several days *after* the formal work of the grand jury has begun, but most grand jurors tend to agree with an evaluation which is included in a recent grand jury report: "The day-long training session was interesting, but for the most part the lectures were irrelevant to the primary functions of a Grand Jury, and many of us noted rather unsubtle political overtones in the formal presentations."[4] Interviews with a score of former grand jurors and a content analysis of grand jury reports reveal that the primary function of the law enforcement lectures is to explain and to "plug" the work of the respective departments rather than to provide the grand juror with substantive insights into what his grand jury duties entail.

The booklets prepared separately by the District Attorney and the Harris County Grand Jury Association are well-written and provide a good summary of the formal duties and functions of the grand jury. However, since these booklets are not provided until the first day of jury service, the earliest they could be read is after the grand jury has put in one full day of work, which usually means hearing at least fifty cases. More important, however, is the fact that interviews with former grand jurors suggest that very few jurors bother to read and study these booklets. This statement by one former grand juror is typical:

> Yes, I took the books home with me that first night and I glanced through them, but I can't say I really read them. I figured that we'd meet our problems as we came to them, and that's about what happened. If we had a question during our deliberations, one of us would usually say, "Let's see if the booklet says anything about this." That's how we used the books when I was on the jury. I don't think any of us actually read them as such.

The give-and-take discussion between the grand jury and an assistant district attorney is usually scheduled for the first day, and it is the final part of the grand juror's formal on-the-job training. When such a discussion does indeed occur, it appears to be of some utility in acquainting grand jurors with their new duties. However, this comment by a recent member of a grand jury was far from uncommon:

Yes, we were supposed to meet with one of the D.A.'s at the end of the first day, and he was supposed to explain to us what the hell was going on. But can you believe this? They [the assistant district attorneys] presented us with so many cases on our first day, it got to be five o'clock, and we didn't have time for anyone to explain to us what we were supposed to be doing. We heard dozens of cases that first day, and when I got home that night I was just sick. I told my wife, "I sure would hate to be one of those guys who had his case brought before us today."

How long does it take, then, for the average grand juror to understand substantially what the duties, powers, and functions of a grand jury are? The results of the questionnaire survey of former Harris County grand jury members reveal that the typical grand juror does not claim to substantially understand his basic purpose and function until well into the third full working session of the grand jury. Using the typical daily workload of 1971 as a base (58 cases per working session), this means that the grand jury hears a minimum of 116 cases before its members even claim to understand their primary duties and functions. Since the average grand jury in 1971 dealt with 1328 cases, the data suggests that most grand jurors stumble through the first 8 per cent of their cases without fully knowing what is incumbent upon them.

Once into its work, how much time does the average grand jury spend with each case to determine whether the state has sufficient evidence to place a man on trial for a felony offense? While the evidence suggests considerable variation in the amount of time spent deliberating on the various categories of cases, the data reveal that the typical grand jury spends only five minutes per case. (In 1971, twelve Harris County grand juries spent an estimated 1344 hours deliberating on 15,930 cases.) This average time of five minutes includes the assistant district attorney's summary of the case and his recommendation as to how the case should be decided (about 90 seconds per case), the hearing of testimony by whatever witnesses are called, and the actual secret deliberations by the grand jury on each case individually. By anyone's standards, "justice" is indeed swift!

The evidence also suggests that some types of cases receive considerably more grand jury attention than do others. The questionnaire results indicate that the amount of time spent conducting "extensive investigations" for each category of cases is in this order, beginning with the greatest amount of time: crimes of passion (e.g., murder, rape), drug cases, forgery and embezzlement, victimless sex crimes (e.g., sodomy), driving while intoxicated, theft, burglary, and robbery. Thus, while a grand jury might spend several hours investigating one of the numerous drug or rape cases, they might spend less than a minute dealing with the average burglary or robbery case.

In addition, one may conclude that the grand jury becomes more efficient as its term progresses; that is, it is able to deal with a larger number of cases per hour toward the end of its term than at the beginning. Such was the opinion of 84 per cent of former grand jurors who responded to the questionnaire. To illustrate, the 177th Grand Jury, which sat between November, 1971, and February, 1972, spent an average of 7.4 minutes per case during its first six sessions, but only 5.9 minutes per case during the final six working days.

What types of cases cause the greatest amount of internal dissension among Texas grand juries, that is, with which cases is there most likely to be less than a unanimous vote among grand jurors? Before responding to this question, it should perhaps first be noted that there is a rather high degree of unanimity in the voting patterns of most Harris County grand juries. This is confirmed by interviews with former grand jury members and by examining the voting record of the previously mentioned 177th Grand Jury: of the 918 cases heard by that Grand Jury, a less than unanimous vote occurred in a mere 42 cases (5 per cent). On those types of cases where internal disagreement occurred, the questionnaire results reveal that dissension occurred in this order, beginning with the most significant category of cases: drug cases, crimes of passion, victimless sex crimes, forgery and embezzlement, driving while intoxicated, theft, burglary, and robbery. For the 177th Grand Jury, which disagreed only 5 per cent of the time, the rate of disagreement on victimless sex crime cases was as high as 33 per cent, for example. Such findings are not too surprising when one considers that cases in the first three categories are not only likely to be the most serious and complex, but they are also the cases about which society as a whole seems to be most divided as to whether such offenses are really crimes at all or whether they are merely the actions of social dissidents or psychopaths.

One final question about the internal dynamics of Texas grand juries is worthy of exploration: with which type(s) of cases is there likely to be the greatest amount of disparity between the assistant district attorney's recommendation as to the "correct" disposition of the case and the actual determination made by the grand jury? Questionnaire data place such disagreement as to category of cases in this order, beginning with the greatest amount: drug cases, crimes of passion, victimless sex crimes, driving while intoxicated, forgery and embezzlement, theft, burglary, and robbery. For the 177th Grand Jury under study, whose rate of disagreement with the district attorney's staff averaged only 6 per cent, the rate of disagreement with drug cases was 28 per cent; with victimless sex crimes, 27 per cent; and with crimes of passion, 17 per cent. Thus, these types of cases which caused the greatest amount of disharmony between district attorney and grand jury are the same types of cases which resulted in the largest degree of internal discord among individual grand jurors. The reasons for this are in all probability the same: cases involving marijuana, rape, and sodomy involve highly complex issues which not all members of society regard as truly criminal in nature and, therefore, worthy of public indictment.

SUMMARY

There are several impressions about the composition and inner workings of Texas grand juries which the author would like to emphasize. First, the data strongly suggest that the make-up of the grand jury is not truly representative of the community at large since there is a marked bias in favor of higher status elements of society. Lest the civil libertarian despair, however, other social science data tell us that higher status persons are more likely to be solicitous of the rights of the accused than are lower social status citizens. Thus, Texas grand juries probably contribute to civil libertarianism not in spite of their non-representative character—but directly because of it.

Second, it seems fair to conclude that whatever their potential for according full due process to the accused, Texas grand juries fall woefully short of the mark. This is so partly because of a patently inadequate training program for newly-selected grand jurors. Since grand jurors do not learn systematically from an independent source the full measure of their duties, powers, and prerogatives, there exists the strong potential that they will become "rubber stamps" of the district attorney's office. This is not to suggest that all grand juries become mere tools of the district attorney, but the potential for this result is by no means minimal. In addition to the haphazard training program, the never-ending stream of cases with which grand juries are daily bombarded places a second obstacle in the path of a full and fair hearing for all those accused of crimes. Given the generally vague and inaccurate nature of the police reports and of the district attorney's file on the accused—about which a majority of grand jurors frequently complain—five minutes per case is certainly not enough time to spend on the determination of probable cause. As one former grand jury foreman lamented in an interview,

> Oh, once in a while we'd catch the D.A. in a mistake, and we'd send him back to do his homework. But for every error we caught, we felt that ten must have slipped by us. You see, there were just so many cases. The D.A.'s office wanted us to just keep cranking 'em out. "If an error was made here [at the grand jury stage], the trial jury would surely make it right later on," we were told. That's a crazy way to do business, but what could we do. There were so many cases.

Finally, the data reveals that some of the complex social problems which divide society as a whole, such as marijuana and hard-drug laws, the possible pathology of the murderer and the rapist, the permissibility of "abnormal" sexual relations between consenting adults, all manifest themselves in the give-and-take of grand jury deliberations. This is evidenced by the comparatively high level of disagreement on the resolution of cases dealing with these subjects, not only among individual members of the grand jury but also between the grand jury and the district attorney's staff.

This study concludes by reaffirming both the need and desirability of the grand jury in Texas, by acknowledging the great capacity of these judicial bodies to further the cause of civil liberties, and by sadly noting that our state's grand juries are best characterized by their potential than by what they are permitted to deliver.

NOTES

1. A three-part study was conducted by the author. Part I included a case-by-case content analysis of the 918 cases considered by the 177th District Court Grand Jury which met in Houston, Texas, between November, 1971, and February, 1972, and on which he served as a member. The second part was a series of in-depth interviews with former Harris County grand jury members. Part III consisted of a questionnaire mailed to all persons who served on Harris County grand juries between 1969 and 1972. The author acknowledges the considerable help provided him by Mr. Gary Orloff of the University of Houston School of Law in the preparation of the questionnaire.
2. *Census Tracts (Houston, Texas): Standard Metropolitan Statistical Area* (Washington, D.C.: U.S. Department of Commerce, 1972), pp. 1, 34, and 100.
3. Samuel A. Stouffer, *Communism, Conformity, and Civil Liberties* (New York: Doubleday, 1955), p. 139; Seymour M. Lipset, *Political Man* (Garden City, N.Y.: Doubleday, 1960), p. 104; Herbert H. Hyman and Paul B. Sheatsley, "Attitudes Toward Desegregation: 1942-1963," *Scientific American,* Vol. CCXI (July, 1964), pp. 16-23. In the South, however, a very high level of education is necessary before anti-Negro attitudes are basically modified. See Donald R. Matthews and James W. Prothro, *Negroes and the New Southern Politics* (New York: Harcourt Brace Jovanovich, 1966).
4. 177th Criminal District Court Grand Jury, Report of the November 1971 Grand Jury for the 177th Criminal District Court, Houston, Texas, 1972, p. 1.

5-3
TEXAS V. MUTSCHER: PRINCIPALS OF THE SHARPSTOWN BANK SCANDAL FACE TRIAL
Richard P. Stark

On September 9, 1969, at the close of the Second Called Session of the 61st Legislature of the State of Texas, Representative Bill Clayton's H.S.R. 64 honoring Speaker Gus F. Mutscher, Jr., was adopted unanimously. In view of later revelations which were to bring Mutscher before the bar of justice as a convicted felon, the laudatory language employed now sounds like a bad joke:

Whereas, It is the pleasure of the House of Representatives, through this Resolution, to express sincere appreciation to the outstanding leader of the House of Representatives, the Honorable Gus Mutscher; and

Whereas, During this 61st Legislature, 1st and 2nd Called Sessions, the dedication, fairness, and courtesy of Speaker Mutscher enabled him to make the many difficult decisions with integrity and with a sincere outlook for the well-being of the people of Texas; now, therefore, be it

This is a previously unpublished article and is printed by permission of the author.

Resolved, That Members of the House of Representatives express deep appreciation to Speaker Gus Mutscher and commend him for his wisdom as a presiding officer, for his knowledge of the legislative process, and for the easy-going and objective, yet decisive, manner which enabled him to lighten tense situations and assure progress in the House of Representatives.

One year later, the Securities and Exchange Commission (SEC) began an investigation which led to the filing of a civil action in the Dallas court of U.S. District Judge Sarah T. Hughes (*SEC* v. *National Bankers Life Insurance Company et al.*, CA-3-4432-B). In its complaint, the SEC named thirteen corporate defendants and fifteen individual defendants, including Frank W. Sharp of Houston. Misconduct was charged on two counts: one described the sale of unregistered securities in violation of the Securities Act of 1933, and the other noted the use of "manipulative and deceptive devices" to defraud in violation of the Securities Exchange Act of 1934. It was the contention of the SEC that the defendants had manipulated the common stock of National Bankers Life Insurance Company (NBL), had misled the public as well as state and federal agencies, and had sought to conceal financial self-dealing.

Furthermore, the SEC charged that the defendants had attempted to avoid further regulation of certain banks by the Federal Deposit Insurance Corporation (FDIC) by seeking to induce Texas law-makers to enact legislation allowing state bank deposits to be insured by a state insurance corporation. According to the SEC, defendants sought to further this proposed legislation by causing large sums of money to be loaned to certain legislators, legislative employees, and members of the executive branch for the purchase of NBL stock. Although they were not listed among the defendants, high-ranking Texas political figures were said to have been given opportunities to make large profits from speculation in stock purchased with money obtained through unsecured loans from the Sharpstown State Bank of Houston. Frank W. Sharp controlled both the insurance company and the bank; moreover, it was he who desired passage of the state bank deposit insurance legislation.

According to depositions obtained by the SEC and made public at the time the civil action was filed in Dallas, stock purchases were made by Speaker Mutscher, his father, aides S. Rush McGinty and F. C. Schulte, Speaker Pro Tempore Tommy Shannon, Governor Preston Smith, Democratic State Executive Committee Chairman Elmer Baum, and House Appropriations Committee Chairman William S. Heatly. Moreover, these deals were made during the days that two state bank deposit insurance bills were under consideration by the Second Called Session of the 61st Legislature. Although the bills were passed at this special session, both were later vetoed by Governor Smith after substantial profits had been made by him and the other aforementioned parties.

Public hearings in connection with the SEC suit began February 8, 1971, in Dallas before Judge Hughes. Subsequently, twenty-seven of the defendants were placed under temporary injunction; none of the defendants was dismissed; and a trial on the merits of the case was set for August 30.[1] Despite the great amount of publicity given to the SEC case during the spring and summer of 1971,

Mutscher was able to maintain control over the Regular Session of the 62nd Legislature and its First Called Session. The only significant threat to Mutscher took the form of Representative Frances Farenthold's resolution, introduced on March 10, 1971, which proposed creation of a joint Senate-House committee to investigate fully the involvement of public officials in the stock scandal. Opposed by Mutscher's defenders, the Farenthold resolution was easily defeated on March 15 by a vote of 118-30; at the same time, the resolution's supporters were branded "the Dirty Thirty" by a scornful lobbyist. In time, however, this pejorative appellation was to become a respected title; and the proud Speaker was to be forced to step down from his high office.

If, because of political factors, the House was unwilling to take action, Mutscher, Shannon, and McGinty were not immune to prosecution in a state district court. Thus it is that the wheels of justice turn for some powerful politicians as well as for common citizens. Even in sensational cases involving the great and the near-great, justice is meted out via established procedures; and to appreciate fully the drama of any trial, one must understand both the background of the case as well as the procedures of the court. Such is the situation with regard to the case of *Texas* v. *Mutscher,* one of the most publicized trials in Texas history.

On September 16, 1971, Judge Hughes handed down an unequivocal decision in the SEC case. She found evidence of stock manipulation, dealings in unregistered stock, and a "scheme and device to defraud." Although the judge determined that illegal stock transactions had occurred, her judgment included neither prison terms nor fines but did permanently enjoin the defendants from selling unregistered stock and from employing manipulative devices in any future stock transactions. The ruling did not assert that state officials involved in the case (although not named in the SEC suit) were aware of any wrongdoing; but by association, it did pull Mutscher and others more deeply into the mire of scandal.

INDICTMENT

Concluding months of intensive investigation by Travis County District Attorney Bob Smith and a Travis County grand jury, on September 23, 1971, indictments were returned against Mutscher, Shannon, and McGinty. Mutscher was charged with conspiracy to accept a bribe and with accepting a bribe, but Shannon and McGinty were charged only with the first offense. According to the bribery indictment, Mutscher allegedly accepted from Sharp, through the Sharpstown State Bank, a personal loan of $130,000 and aggregate loans of $179,258.76 for employees, associates, and relatives. In return, it was charged, Mutscher had employed his "vote and influence and powers of his offices . . . to procure and assist in procuring the passage of certain legislation." The conspiracy indictments contended that in July, 1969, the three defendants conspired to accept a bribe and subsequently permitted money to be deposited in their names in the Sharpstown bank, having accepted the money from Sharp "under the pretense and semblance of profits" which they made from deals involving National Bankers Life Insurance Company Stock.

In addition to the indictments, the grand jury issued a special report which criticized the Texas Legislature for its handling of the 1969 banking bills. Although no other indictments were returned at that time, the grand jury rebuked unnamed high state officials for questionable practices. Furthermore, the report of the grand jury declared, "Some Texas lawmakers . . . were too busy granting political favors and being influenced in exchange for 'turning a fast buck' to be concerned about good government for the people. There is dire need of reform so that good laws for the protection and well-being of our citizens might be passed."

PRE-TRIAL ACTIVITY

Despite demands by Mutscher's political opponents—in particular, the Dirty Thirty—he refused to resign from his office as Speaker. Mutscher and his two cohorts denied guilt and expressed confidence in their efforts to gain acquittal. On October 7, four members of the Dirty Thirty (Lane Denton, Tom Moore, David Allred, and Walter Mengden) urged Governor Preston Smith to call a special session of the legislature in order to allow House members the opportunity to declare the speakership vacant, to elect a new Speaker, and to act upon reform legislation. The Governor did not heed the suggestion. On that same day, in arraignment proceedings held before 167th District Court Judge Thomas D. Blackwell in Austin, Mutscher and his co-defendants entered pleas of "not guilty" to the charges on which they had been indicted two weeks earlier. December 2, 1971, was set as the date for a hearing on pre-trial motions; a jury trial was scheduled for January 10, 1972.

In mid-November, Judge Hughes amended her previous judgment in the SEC case. Included among her findings of fact was the following: "During the period January 1, 1968 through January 18, 1971 defendant Sharp, directly and through defendant [John] Osorio and others, attempted to obtain passage of legislation, concerning insurance of deposits in state banks by a state chartered insurance company, by causing stock of NBL to be sold to certain State officials in the legislative and executive branches and by causing SSB [Sharpstown State Bank] to finance purchases of NBL stock by those persons."[2] Although Judge Hughes did not name any of those state officials, her finding disclosed that "someone" had entered into a bribery conspiracy with Sharp.

Two weeks after Judge Hughes issued her final judgment in the SEC case, Judge Blackwell opened pre-trial hearings in Austin for Mutscher, Shannon, and McGinty. Both the defense and the state requested a change of venue, but for different reasons. The defense sought a change because of intensive adverse publicity in the Austin area. On the other hand, the state contended that a fair trial was not possible in the capital city because many potential jurors were public employees who were subject to a fear of the loss of their jobs as a result of the Speaker's influence. In response to these pleas for a change of venue, Judge Blackwell moved the Mutscher case from Austin to Abilene on December 2. Thus, the trial was scheduled for the 104th District Court of the State of Texas before Judge J. Neil Daniel.

Much of the pre-trial polemics focused on the manner in which the case would be prosecuted. The question was settled at the February 10 pre-trial hearing in Judge Daniel's court when Travis County District Attorney Bob Smith (chief prosecutor in the case) announced his decision to prosecute the three defendants on charges of conspiring to accept a bribe but not to prosecute Mutscher on the bribery charge (at least at that time). One other decision reached by Daniel during the day ordered jury selection to be on an individual basis, a procedure normally utilized only in capital cases.

DEFENSE COUNSEL

The trial began on February 28, 1972, with counsel for both the defense and the prosecution being allowed eighteen peremptory challenges in the process of jury selection. Defense counsel was headed by Frank Maloney. Assisting Maloney were Richard "Racehorse" Haynes of Houston and Davis Scarborough of Abilene, representing Mutscher; Joe Shannon, Jr., of Fort Worth and Bob Hanna of Abilene, representing Tommy Shannon; and A. L. "Dusty" Rhodes of Abilene, representing McGinty. Defense counsel not only sought to eliminate persons unfavorably influenced by news media accounts of the scandal and those prejudiced against politicians, but also attempted to determine if prospective jurors objected to borrowing money to finance stock market speculation. District Attorney Smith, aided by Travis County Assistant Attorney Harold Jacquet and Abilene District Attorney Ed Paynter, merely reviewed the indictments and the applicable laws at the start of the sessions and then spent little time questioning individuals. On the other hand, the defense resorted to more lengthy interrogation in an effort to discern persons unduly influenced by factors noted above.

Although all of the early subpoenas were issued at the request of the prosecution, those filed by the defense counsel on the first day of the trial drew greatest attention. According to the *Abilene Reporter-News,* "political implications ran rampant" when the defense summoned both Governor Smith and Lieutenant Governor Barnes as potential witnesses, for both had vigorously endeavored to dissociate themselves from the Mutscher case. Furthermore, on the second day of proceedings, the defense subpoenaed still more notables, including Louie Welch, Houston's mayor, and Doug Sanders, a nationally famed professional golfer. It was the opinion of most political observers that the defense planned to demonstrate that Sharp's arranging of the loans and stock purchases included a variety of persons and that the three defendants had received no special consideration from the Houston financier.

THE JURY

On the morning of the fourth day of proceedings, a jury of eight women and four men was selected from a forty-eight-person jury panel. Comprising the jury were six Baptists, five Methodists, and one member of the Christian Church; the average

age of the twelve jurors was slightly under thirty-nine years. A McMurray College student, twenty-eight-year-old Larry E. Yerger of Abilene, was selected as foreman of the jury. Shortly after the jury was selected, Judge Daniel read to them the indictment of the defendants. Then in his brief opening statement, District Attorney Smith told the jurors that the state would prove that the defendants had accepted bribes from Sharp and subsequently had pushed through the Legislature the controversial banking bills. During the remarks, Daniel sustained an objection by Maloney to overrule Smith's attempt to emphasize that testimony of eyewitnesses was not needed to prove a conspiracy case. No statements were made at that point by counsel for the defense, since they preferred to wait until the time of presentation of their side of the case.

WITNESSES FOR THE STATE

Following the opening statements, Gus F. Mutscher, Sr., father of the Speaker, appeared to present documents demonstrating his transactions with Sharp and with NBL. The first witness to testify verbally was F. C. "Sonny" Schulte, the Speaker's aide from Brenham, who stated that he purchased 2,000 shares of NBL stock in July of 1969 on the advice of Mutscher and McGinty but was unaware of any connection between the 1969 banking insurance bills and the stock investments.

That same afternoon Sharp himself took the stand to offer testimony coinciding with depositions given seven months earlier to the SEC. (In 1971 he had been granted immunity from further federal or state prosecution and had been handed a three-year probated sentence after pleading guilty to federal charges of minor bank and stock law violations. During preliminary questioning of prospective jurors in Abilene, defense counsel emphasized that Sharp was a convicted felon; however, District Attorney Smith countered with the declaration that "the evidence will show that he [Sharp] is the defendants' friend, not ours.") Sharp swore that he and Mutscher had discussed a state program to insure bank deposits for over a year prior to passage of the 1969 banking bills. Concerning the highly significant issue of his principal motivation for seeking a state banking insurance program, the Houston financier told the court that he had hoped to escape federal regulation of his banking activities. However, Daniel instructed the jury to disregard the statement when he sustained an objection by Maloney that Sharp's remarks contradicted previously admitted evidence. The evidence was in the form of a letter to Mutscher (dated February 19, 1969) in which Sharp claimed that the bills (yet to be drafted at that time) would provide state insurance supplementary to existing FDIC coverage (rather than in lieu of federal protection).

During testimony the following day, March 3, Sharp recounted his frequent contacts with Mutscher and McGinty during the Regular Session of the 61st Legislature. He recalled having, in effect, approved loans from the Sharpstown State Bank to Mutscher and his associates for the purchase of NBL stock. However, at no time during his testimony did Sharp use the phrase "tacit understanding" to describe his agreement with Mutscher (a phrase which he had used in giving his deposition to the SEC). According to the *Waco Tribune-Herald,* however, Sharp did say (with reference to Mutscher), "He knew I needed help, and I knew he needed help." Defense counsel chose not to cross examine Sharp but did reserve the right to do so later in the trial.

Following Sharp to the stand were John Ragley, assistant manager of the Rice Hotel in Houston, and Mrs. Carol Price, former assistant cashier for the Sharpstown State Bank. With testimony from these two witnesses, the state sought to connect the defendants even more closely to Sharp through records of Houston hotel stays and records of the bank loans. Concluding the day's testimony was Mrs. Sharon Gilleon of Houston, Sharp's former private secretary. Mrs. Gilleon provided the court with a notebook in which she had recorded all incoming and outgoing telephone calls for her former boss, and her testimony (based on that log) indicated several probable conversations between Sharp and Mutscher between July and September, 1969. In a determined effort to minimize the significance of the telephone calls, defense attorney Haynes pointed out that the names of numerous notables appeared in the notebook, including Governor Smith, Lieutenant Governor Ben Barnes, astronaut Alan Shepard, and U.S. Senator Edward M. Kennedy.

When Mrs. Gilleon completed her testimony the next day, Elmer Eugene Palmer, an Austin attorney, testified that he had drafted the two bank deposit insurance bills at the request of John Osorio (an associate of Sharp and President of NBL until July, 1970)[3] and had delivered them to Representative Shannon. Palmer insisted that the bills would have provided deposit insurance supplementary to, but not in lieu of, FDIC coverage; but the *Houston Post* reported that District Attorney Smith did prompt Palmer to agree that neither of the bills specifically guaranteed the continuation of FDIC protection. The *Post* also reported that during the course of questioning Palmer, District Attorney Smith implicated Governor Preston Smith with the declaration, "I think it is going to become quite clear that the Governor is a co-conspirator. . . ."

On March 7, the pace slowed somewhat as testimony produced a protracted argument concerning the purpose and potential effect of HB 72 and HB 73. State Banking Commissioner Robert E. Stewart appeared as yet another prosecution witness, opining that the bills would not have accomplished their intended purpose. Sam O. Kimberlin, Jr., executive vice president of the Texas Bankers Association, succeeded Stewart on the witness stand, testifying that Palmer's bill would have allowed state banks to discontinue FDIC coverage if they so desired. Final witnesses of the day were State Insurance Commissioner Clay Cotten and the former vice president of Ling and Company, Harold W. Lehrmann. According to the *Abilene Reporter-News,* Lehrmann's testimony, which continued through the next morning, identified records of the following purchases of NBL stock: 4,115 shares each for Shannon and McGinty for $45,779.38 (at $11.125 per share); 10,000 shares for Gus F. Mutscher, Jr., for $130,000 (at $13.00 per share); 5,000 shares for Mutscher, Sr., for $65,000 (at $13,00 per share); and 2,000 shares for Schulte for $22,250 (at $11.125 per share).

Representative Charles Patterson, testifying that defendant Shannon had informed him that the controversial banking bills would have created a state deposit insurance corporation to operate in lieu of the FDIC, was the last witness of the March 8 session. Patterson, who voted against the measures, said that no one had exerted pressure on him with regard to his vote. During the afternoon of March 8, defense attorney Joe Shannon requested that subpoenas be served to twenty-eight members and former members of the Texas House of Representatives who had served in the Second Called Session of the 61st Legislature in 1969.

On the afternoon of March 9, Joseph P. Novotny, president of Sharpstown State Bank, testified that the decision to give loans to Mutscher and his cohorts for the purchase of NBL stock had been Sharp's decision only. While cross-examining the witness, Maloney noted that in addition to the loans made to the Mutscher group, a similar loan had been made by Sharp to two other persons at approximately the same time. In re-direct questioning, District Attorney Smith returned to the issue of the unidentified loans, and Novotny indicated that the loans were to Governor Smith and to Elmer Baum, Chairman of the State Democratic Executive Committee of Texas. None of Novotny's testimony dealt with the relationship between the bank loans and the passage of Sharp's desired legislation, but he did affirm that the sale of the stock was made to the Jesuit Fathers, Inc., of Houston.

At the time of the stock deal the Jesuit Fathers of Houston were headed by Father Michael Kennelly, who had also served as an honorary director of the Sharpstown State Bank. His association with Sharp had begun in 1959 when Kennelly moved to Houston to establish Strake Jesuit College Preparatory School. Sharp was a financial adviser to the Jesuits and gained their confidence through a series of generous gifts of stock and land, including the land on which the school was located. In turn, the Catholic clergymen had been used by the Houston banker to further his personal financial welfare. Thus, on several occasions, the Jesuits had obtained loans from the Sharpstown State Bank and then had allowed Sharp to use the money for his business ventures. It was Kennelly who took the initiative to have Sharp (a Methodist) named "founder" of the Jesuit Order in 1969.

Kennelly, who at the time of the Abilene Trial was President of Loyola University in New Orleans, appeared voluntarily as a prosecution witness on Friday, March 11. He testified that on September 11, 1969 while acting on behalf of the Jesuits, he purchased NBL stock from Mutscher and his associates. The priest added that on the following day he purchased similar stock from Baum and Governor Smith. According to Kennelly, the Jesuits bought over 33,000 shares of NBL stock at $20.00 per share (although the average market price at the time was only $14.75 per share) on the advice of Sharp. Succeeding Kennelly on the witness stand was Mrs. Betty Jordan, Novotny's former secretary. Financial figures revealed during Mrs. Jordan's testimony indicated the defendants made the following profits after repaying the loans and interest: Mutscher, $18,365.44; Shannon, $23,582.40; and McGinty, $13,582.40 (a combined profit of $55,530.24).

CHARGE TO THE JURY

When court resumed on Monday morning, March 13, District Attorney Smith announced that the state would rest its case. Later that afternoon, following a brief recess, the defense announced it would rest its case without calling any witnesses and without cross-examining Sharp. The unusual move was explained by defense counsel as having been taken on the ground that the state did not have "one piddling iota of evidence to prove a positive agreement among the defendants." District Attorney Smith described the surprising development as a "calculated risk."

Daniel sequestered the jury for the duration of the trial, and court was recessed until the following day. In his charge to the jury on March 14, the judge noted laws applicable to the case and instructed jurors that the defendants' failure to testify was not to be considered against them. The judge stressed that a conviction for conspiracy should not result unless the jury determined that evidence proved "beyond a reasonable doubt that there was a positive agreement to commit a felony."

CLOSING ARGUMENT

Closing arguments were begun by state's attorneys Jacquet and Paynter, who sought to emphasize the importance of the case and to cast doubt on the legality of the stock transactions in question. Maloney then established the pattern for defense arguments by attacking Sharp, by questioning his credibility as a witness, and by emphasizing the necessity of having to prove the existence of a positive agreement to accept a bribe. Attorney Joe Shannon reiterated the emphasis on the "guidelines of the law," and Hanna argued particularly in defense of defendant Tommy Shannon. Concluding defense arguments, Haynes begged for acquittal and urged the jurors not to be stampeded into returning a conviction. District Attorney Smith terminated the arguments with a methodical recapitulation of the state's evidence and pictured the defendants as having initiated the conspiracy. Moreover, the district attorney sought to emphasize that the defendants were charged with conspiring among themselves and not with Sharp. Throughout the final day, various invocations and appeals to conscience were voiced as the emotional setting made its impact upon the participants in the trial. Bob Smith concluded the oratory by telling the weary jurors, "You are the conscience of this community and you are the conscience of the state. It is up to you to write the standard of acceptable conduct."

VERDICT AND SENTENCES

If Mutscher, Shannon, and McGinty were percipient with regard to omens, they knew what the future held. On March 15, 1972—the Ides of March and the unlucky thirteenth day of trial proceedings—the Abilene jury found each of the defendants guilty of conspiracy to accept a bribe. Defense attorneys withdrew their motion that the jury assess punishment, and the task was left to Judge Daniel. District Attorney Smith recommended a five-year probated sentence for each of the defendants, and defense counsel requested that their clients be considered for probation. Daniel responded by setting the punishment for each defendant at five years in the Texas Department of Corrections and announcing that the sentences would be probated.

POST-TRIAL MOTIONS

On March 24, attorneys Maloney and Shannon filed motions for a new trial on behalf of their clients, contending in part that circumstantial evidence presented by the state was insufficient and that the charge to the jury was improper. In addition to filing the motions for a new trial, the lawyers requested that Daniel not act on the motions until the filing of amended motions within the designated period. Motions for a new trial were denied by Daniel on April 19, 1972. On that same day, Maloney filed notices of appeal for all three defendants in the 104th District Court. Thus, the case was to go before the Court of Criminal Appeals in Austin in an appellate procedure likely to extend into 1973 and even later.

The conscience of the state—an eight-woman, four-man jury—had spoken in Old Abilene Town. These plain people had accepted the state's evidence of a conspiracy among public officials; and without a doubt, the twelve West Texans had acted in accord with the sentiments of the vast majority of their fellow citizens. Nevertheless, while many legislators and citizens turned their attention to the need for governmental reform, the "Abilene Three" stubbornly stood their ground and maintained their innocence.

Subsequent to the Abilene trial, the defendants resigned their House offices; but both Mutscher and Shannon retained their seats and unsuccessfully sought nomination for re-election in 1972. At the same time, former opponents of Mutscher (most notably the group of dissident representatives known as the Dirty Thirty) became more influential within the House; and at the beginning of 1973, it appeared that anti-Mutscher liberals would be increasingly effective in the 63rd Legislature. At the time of this writing, in mid-February, 1973, the most recent development in the Sharpstown Bank scandal has been the filing of a civil suit by the Houston Educational Foundation. Once known as the Jesuit Fathers of Houston, the Houston Educational Foundation has charged that Sharp's manipulations on behalf of prominent political figures in Texas caused the Catholic organization to sustain heavy financial losses, to be the object of unjustifiable claims totalling about four million dollars, and to suffer loss of a "well-established ability to obtain regular and sizable charitable donations." Minimum damages of $11,500,000 have been sought. Included among the defendants in this civil suit are Sharp, Mutscher, Smith, Baum, Osorio, Kennelly, Welch, and sixty-six others.

NOTES

1. *Securities and Exchange Commission* v. *National Bankers Life Insurance Co. et al.*, 324 F.Supp. 189 (1971).

2. *Securities and Exchange Commission* v. *National Bankers Life Insurance Co. et al.*, 334 F.Supp. 444, 449 (1971).
3. On January 23, 1973, Osorio was found guilty on federal charges involving conspiracy and embezzlement of over $600,000 from the NBL pension fund for the purpose of manipulating the price of NBL stock. The case was tried in a U.S. district court in Amarillo. Prior to the trial, which began on January 15, Sam E. Stock and Donald A. Akins (both charged along with Osorio) pleaded guilty to minor charges; both Stock and Akins appeared as prosecution witnesses. Following his conviction, Osorio claimed that the government obtained criminal indictments against him only after he refused to say that he had "bought off" former Lieutenant Governor Ben Barnes in connection with Sharp's two bank bills in 1969.

5-4
A REPORT ON TWO UNITS OF THE TEXAS DEPARTMENT OF CORRECTIONS
Gary Morton

HUNTSVILLE—Twenty miles north of this Texas town stands the Chapel of the Prodigal Son. It is probably more aptly named than most churches in the "free world" because the chapel is incorporated within the confines of the Ferguson Unit of the Texas Department of Corrections. Its aim is to aid in the return to society of 1,501 "prodigal sons" housed in the unit.

The "free world" is what prisoners call the everyday society most people know. Most of the inmates here were convicted of narcotic or drug-related crimes, assistant warden John Mathis said. "Fourteen per cent of our prisoners are here on drug charges," he told members of the Waco Police Department's recruit class recently touring the facilities. "Probably as many as 40 per cent of the others are here for drug-related crimes."

Ferguson is a unit designed for first-time offenders between 17 and 25 years old, although a few older prisoners are kept here whose skills are necessary to the running of the prison. The entire Texas Department of Corrections (TDC) system aims at being as nearly self-supporting as possible, including using skills of various prisoners and teaching skills to others. One often hears arguments from both the left and the right on the inadequate effect of prisons. Those on the left claim the prisons only intensify the criminal element without any rehabilitation; those on the right claim prisons are "country clubs." At Ferguson and at nearby Ellis, where the Waco recruits toured prison facilities, neither are correct. Both units have strong programs aimed at rehabilitation in conjunction with providing for the needs of the TDC system. Both regiment the lives of the prisoners to such a degree they could in no sense be thought of as country clubs.

From the Waco *Times-Herald* (February 12 and 14, 1973). This is an edited version of the original report and is reprinted by permission of the Waco *Times-Herald*.

An average day begins at 6 a.m., when prisoners are aroused. At Ferguson, most of the prisoners work in fields, as the unit is responsible for much of the raw vegetable and fruit supply for the TDC system. "They call it 'work' out in the field," Mathis said. "It's a 'job' when they get some inside duty."

After awakening, prisoners have breakfast and are taken to the fields. During all meals there is no talking. The cafeteria is for eating and for eating alone. The inmates return for lunch and go to the fields again in the afternoon. When they return to the housing quarters in the evening, they strip down in a courtyard and are thoroughly searched before taking a shower. Later they eat dinner. After dinner, prisoners are given "day time" for socializing and recreation. The day room, equipped with dominoes and a television set, is open until 10 p.m. except in certain conditions. "We learned real quick with Monday night football you can't have a completely arbitrary time for cutting off the television," Mathis said with a grin. Lights go off in the prisoners' quarters at 10:30 p.m.

While the stress is on farming at Ferguson, there is an emphasis on education of the prisoners within the entire TDC system through the Windham Independent School District—the only school district in the state without any geographical boundaries. It was set up by the Texas legislature expressly for the TDC system in order to give it an opportunity to raise the educational level of its inmates. Indicative of the source of much crime is the 6.9 educational achievement level—not quite seventh-grade level—at Ferguson. The district offers courses from elementary to high school levels and works at the student's level. In addition, the TDC has a cooperative program with Lee Junior College in Baytown for an associate degree program. Much of the educational stress is on practical vocational education. Among the courses in vocational education offered at Ferguson are upholstery, automotive mechanics and body repairs, and broom and mop making. Many of the TDC's own fleet of vehicles are taken care of at Ferguson at a rate to be expected in the "free world," and the mops and brooms are sent to other prisons and state agencies.

Most of the funds for the schooling of prisoners, as well as for recreational and religious activities, come from the annual Texas Prison Rodeo and from profits of the commissaries of the various units. An example of the self-supporting nature of the TDC system is the cost of feeding prisoners. Mathis said prisoners are fed three meals a day with meat served at each meal. Prisoners can take as much food as they want but are expected to eat all they take. "It costs 54 cents a day per inmate for food," Mathis said. "Only 12 cents a day goes to the outside for spices and things we can't produce ourselves." Even during the winter, the TDC is able to feed prisoners with the system's own food because all excess raw vegetables and fruit are canned at another unit.

One of the most punishing aspects of the system is the visiting regulations. Inmates may receive visitors for only two hours every two weeks except in certain circumstances. Only if a person travels a great distance to see the prisoner will the prison officials consider granting more visiting time, and then Mathis said it is usually held to four hours. There is no physical contact inside the visiting room. Prisoners are stripped and searched before entering and upon leaving the visiting room. If the guest wishes to buy cigarettes or something for the prisoner to eat, it must be from the commissary. Even then, the goods are opened by a guard before given to the prisoner. Anything left over is destroyed.

Guards inside Ferguson and other housing units of the TDC system carry no weapons. But the security is still there, and the prison staff, perhaps as much as ever, is regarded as the boss. It's noticeable walking down the halls of Ferguson. Inmates give the right of way to guards and visitors immediately. They look inquisitively when a tour passes but say nothing. They know the rules of the game. Those rules center around parole regulations, especially concerning "PIP" (Participation in Programs) points, Mathis said. Prisoners must have at least 80 points, based on attitude and work, to be eligible for parole.

Prisoners are sent to a Diagnostic Center at Huntsville before being assigned to any particular unit. After being assigned, the prisoner enters the unit as a "first-class" prisoner. This means he earns 20 extra days' time for each 30 days he serves. As a result, a first-class prisoner can be paroled in three years for a five-year sentence.

An interesting anecdote underlining the importance of PIP points to prisoners involves the Chapel of the Prodigal Son. "We used to give PIP points for religious involvement," Mathis said. "When we stopped giving points for this, church attendance dropped in half. The minister said he was elated because all his trouble-makers were gone."

As one enters the Ellis Unit of the Texas Department of Corrections 13 miles northeast of Huntsville, he knows immediately he doesn't want to end up here. There is a sense of tense security at Ellis which envelops one when he walks into the best-known—and probably worst-feared—unit of the TDC. Perhaps it is the dread and awe of knowing Death Row was here which cause the tenseness. Perhaps it is the high wall in the main hallway blanketed with closed-circuit television sets. Perhaps it is the firing range as one enters the gate to the prison grounds. It's a completely different atmosphere than at the nearby Ferguson Unit. While the regulations are still the same as at Ferguson, the security of the unit seems to hang in the air.

Eight prisoners still remain on the now-defunct Death Row, assistant warden Paul Fields said. The eight are filing writs for new trials instead of accepting the commuted sentences Gov. Preston Smith ordered after the U.S. Supreme Court overruled death penalty laws last summer. Death Row is like any other cellblock at Ellis in appearance. However, even more so than the rest of the unit, a tenseness overwhelms Death Row. Even among prisoners in the TDC, Ellis is referred to as the "jail." The looks of the prisoners are different—a glance at them tells one they are the more hardened criminals.

Still, even at Ellis, the main emphasis appears to be on the rehabilitation of prisoners. There's the educational system like the one at Ferguson to help educate the 1,530 inmates. There are also "jobs" inside the prison proper, and away from the fields which border the Trinity River, which help prisoners learn various trades for work in the outside world. One of the most unusual jobs at Ellis is in the denture factory. It offers prisoners the profession of dental technician, a good-paying job in the free world. The factory produces 500 dentures a month. "It's the top job here," Fields said. "Everyone knows they can get a good-paying job if they work up here."

While Ferguson seems aimed more at the agricultural needs of the TDC system, Ellis is responsible for much of the clothing and many of the shoes for both the TDC and other state agencies. Inside the shoe factory at Ellis, which produced more than 82,000 shoes, 20,000 belts, and 3,000 saddle accessories the last fiscal year, prisoners learn a trade which will enable them to get a job in the free world after they are released. Currently the prison is working on a large shoe order from the Gary Job Corps Center at San Marcos. School buses from independent school districts throughout the state are sent to Ellis for body work and refurbishing, yet another job aimed at helping the prisoner find work outside after his release. The handles for brooms and mops made at Ferguson are manufactured at Ellis.

There is farm work at Ellis, though on a smaller scale than at Ferguson. After breakfast and lunch, the inmates go in squads to the fields. They count off in pairs and take their white caps off as they pass through the gates so guards can make sure they are in the right squad. Fields said the white uniforms now used by the system are an improvement in security over the traditional striped uniforms. "If someone gets loose out in the fields, it's a lot easier to see them if they're dressed in all white instead of stripes," he said. As the inmates walk to the fields, an armed guard on horseback follows close behind and oversees their work. The guard is trained to shoot if a prisoner attempts to escape.

Fields' approach toward handling prisoners is simply to care for them. "The judge sets the punishment," Fields said. "We just care for them and make sure they stay here until their time's up." While once again the guards carry no weapons in the main quarters, the guard still has the upper hand. Fields attributes the discipline inside the prison to the Participation in Programs points. "The point system is our best means of discipline here," he said. "They know they won't get out on parole if they don't have the points." Parole officers won't even consider a possible parole for a prisoner who has less than 80 points out of over 200 possible.

As aptly named as the Chapel of the Prodigal Son at Ferguson is the Chapel of Reconciliation at Ellis, which features a full-length stained-glass window. Some aren't ready to reconciliate, however, according to an escape attempt Fields told about. Two prisoners broke through the window and fled over two barbed wire fences during a service. They were caught within an hour.

Neither Ferguson nor Ellis are the "country clubs" some conservatives feel prisons have become. Nor are they training grounds for the hardening of criminals, as some liberals contend.

5-5
THE URGENT NEED FOR COURT REFORM IN TEXAS
Truman Roberts

In 1876, which (as the older ones of us remember) was immediately after the War Between the States, we adopted our present Texas Constitution. We wrote this Constitution in 1875 after we had finally gotten rid of the carpetbaggers. We were distrustful of nearly all kinds of government. So we spelled out in the new Constitution specifically what should happen in regard to everything. In regard to the courts of this state, there has been no meaningful change made in that Constitution since 1891, when by an amendment we created the Court of Criminal Appeals. What was the population of Texas in 1891? A little over two million people. What is the population of Texas today? Over eleven million people. In 1891, the largest town in the State of Texas was the size of Temple, Texas, today. We had a rural society then. Today we have an urban society. Our present court system was designed for a rural society of two million people and not for an urban society of eleven million people.

I will warrant you that even the teachers of government in our high schools and in most of our universities can't tell you what the present court system's structure is in this state. And the average layman has no conception of what it is. We have our municipal courts; we have our j. p. courts; and we have our county courts. In many counties we have all kinds of county courts at law, including county courts at law for civil cases, county courts at law for criminal cases, county courts at law for criminal appeals, and county courts at law for traffic appeals. Also, we have district courts, 245 of them.* In addition to that, on the district level, we have courts of domestic relations, juvenile courts, family courts. You name them, we have them! Then we have fourteen courts of civil appeals, which are three-judge appellate courts; and we have the Court of Criminal Appeals, which is a five-judge court with two commissioners, the Supreme Court for criminal matters. Then we have the Supreme Court of Texas, which is the highest court for civil matters.

So, that is your court system. And if you draw a diagram of this court system, it's the worst messed-up thing that you have ever seen [see Figure 5-6]. The reason that it is messed up is because we do not have integration. We don't have

This is an edited version of a tape-recorded address given by Judge Truman Roberts, member of the Court of Criminal Appeals of Texas, on December 14, 1972, at the annual banquet of the Heart of Texas Council of Governments (HOTCOG). It is published with the permission of Judge Roberts. In his address the judge describes the proposed revision of Article V of the Texas constitution that was published in September, 1972, by the Chief Justice's Task Force for Court Improvement. On December 15 the Task Force met and adopted a final draft for submission to the 63rd Legislature. The co-authors of *Practicing Texas Politics* have supplied notes calling attention to significant changes that were incorporated into the final draft. For the text of this draft, see "Proposed Article V of the Texas Constitution: Draft of December 15, 1972," in the *Texas Bar Journal,* Vol. XXVI (January 22, 1973), pp. 25-26, 28, 44.

*In 1973 this number was increased to 258.

vertical integration; we don't have horizontal integration. If we have a domestic relations court and it's not busy, and our criminal courts are overrun with business, the domestic relations judge can't try criminal cases. If we have a county court that is overrun with cases and we don't have a county court at law, the district judges can't come down and sit on the county court. If the district court is busy and the county court at law is not busy, the county court at law judge can't go up and sit on that bench. We do not have the means by which we can make full use of our manpower.

Chief Justice Robert Calvert, recently retired as Chief Justice of the Supreme Court of Texas, has formed a task force. This task force has proposed a revision of Article V of the Constitution of the State of Texas [see Figure 5-7]. Of course the voters of the State of Texas at the last general election, quite wisely I thought, enabled the legislature to resolve itself into a constitutional convention in 1974 for the purpose of writing a new Constitution for this state. We need it. We've had to amend the present Constitution over 200 times. Over 200 amendments! And that is true because it is so specific in all of its detail. But I am here tonight to tell you that in truth and in fact we cannot wait 'til 1974 to do something about the court structure of this state.

In every state in these United States where there has been any meaningful restructuring and reform of the court system, it has come about after one thing has happened. And that one thing that has happened has been a scandal. In the state of Missouri, the Pendergast machine completely controlled the court system. But it was restructured and given back to the people. In the state of New Jersey, before court reform, the courts were corrupt and rotten. The people got tired and did something about it. In Illinois the same thing was true. And in Oklahoma, God bless their souls, two Supreme Court justices were caught taking bribes before the "Okies" were willing to do anything about their court structure. Colorado, the same; California, the same. I am not the least bit worried that we are going to have any Supreme Court justices in Texas taking bribes. I do not think that any political machine is going to gain control of the courts of this state. But I am here tonight to tell you that in this state we have a scandalous situation today.

The scandalous situation that we have is not in regard to civil cases, but it is in regard to criminal cases. During the calendar year 1972, the Court of Criminal Appeals, with five judges and the two commissioners that we got a year ago last September, handed down written opinions in 1,465 cases—which means about 200 opinions per judge per year. In addition to these, we decided 912 writs of habeas corpus. The average case load in the United States for appellate judges is approximately 30 cases per year. And I was out in California recently, at a judicial conference, and heard the cry of alarm because their appellate judges were having to write nearly 80 cases a year. My heart really bled for them. In addition to that, we have handled 880 writs of habeas corpus.

That would be fine if we were keeping current, but we're not. Each day that goes by, on the court which I am now privileged to serve, we fall further behind. From the day a case finally reaches our court from the trial court and is filed there, until the day that it is submitted to the court for its decision, nine months

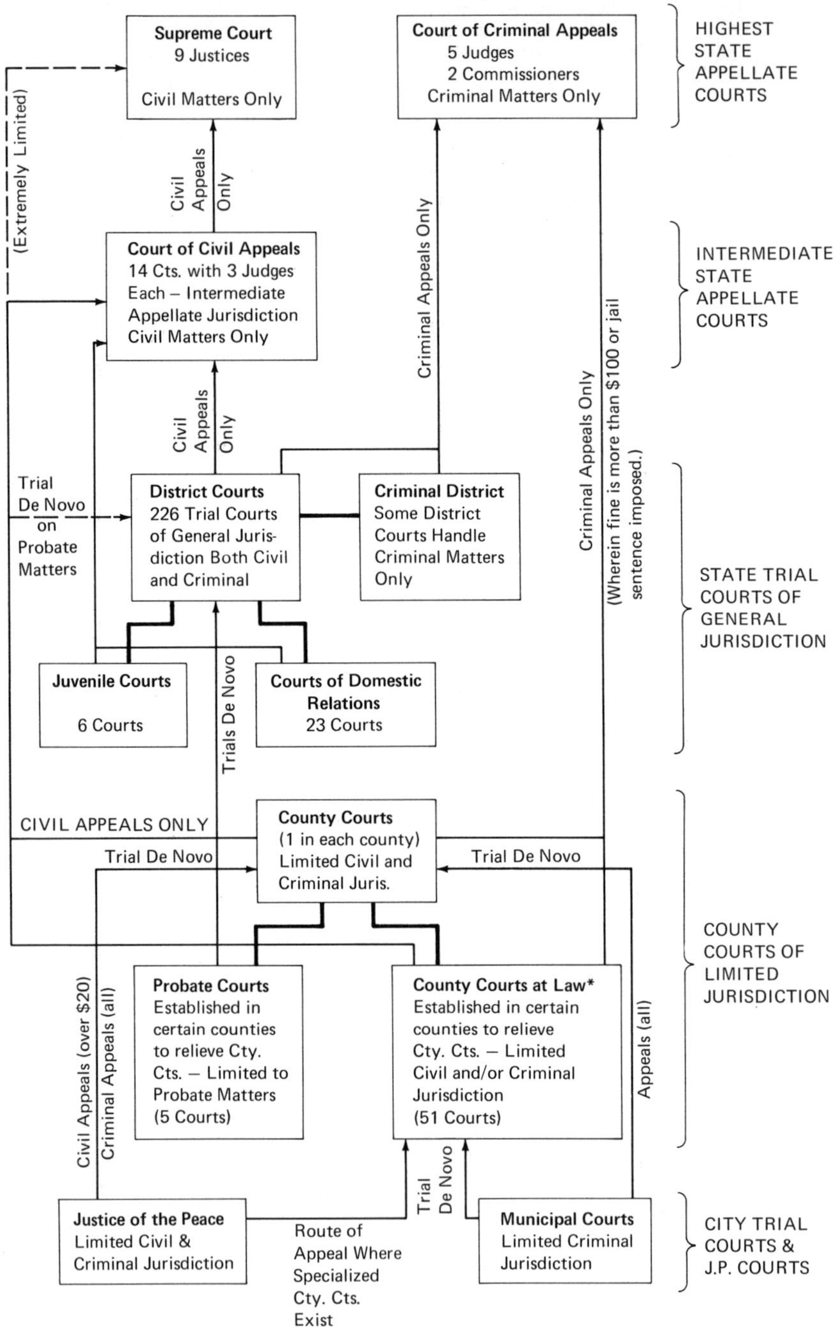

Figure 5-6
Present judicial system of Texas

Figure 5-6
Present judicial system of Texas.

Reproduced from the Chief Justice's Task Force for Court Improvement, Justice at the Crossroads: Court Improvement in Texas *(1972); compare with Figure 5-1. Note that thirteen additional district courts were created by the 63rd Legislature in 1973.*

**Some counties have separate civil and criminal county courts at law (34 county courts at law, 10 county criminal courts at law, 3 county civil courts at law, 1 county criminal court of appeal, 2 "county courts").*

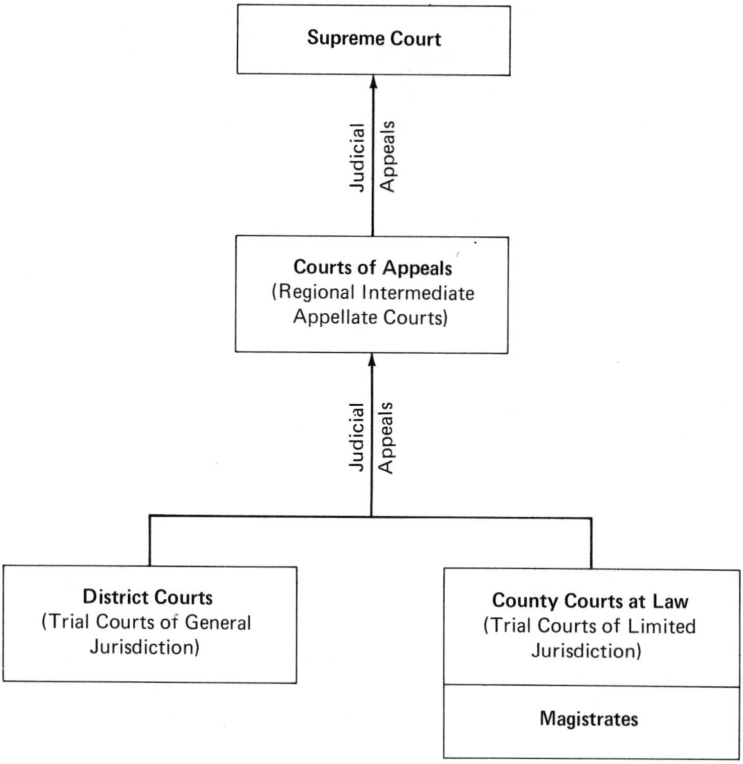

Figure 5-7
Proposed judicial system of Texas

Reproduced from the Chief Justice's Task Force for Court Improvement, Justice at the Crossroads: Court Improvement in Texas *(1972).*

elapse. That's not good. From the day that a case is tried in Dallas or Houston, 'til the day that it arrives in our court, approximately 19 months pass. Nineteen and nine, any way you cut it, is 28 months. And that is two years and four months. If a man is in the jailhouse and has been wrongfully convicted, two years and four months is too long to have to sit there. If a man is out on bond, and he had been rightfully convicted, two years and four months is too long for him to be walking the streets free to commit other burglaries, free to commit other armed robberies, free to do as he sees fit. And I have no figures on how long it is from the date of arrest for a crime 'til the date that the accused is finally tried. But I do know that in our larger metropolitan centers, in too many instances, people are in jail a year or two years, or in extreme cases (like when one got lost in Houston and they couldn't find him), four years before trial. Now if this is not a scandal, I don't know what it is!

This constitutional revision doesn't call for new judges. It calls for a two-level trial bench: district courts and county courts at law[1] on the trial level. It envisions taking the justices of the peace and the municipal court judges into the system. Those who are lawyers can try contested matters; those who are not lawyers cannot try contested matters. They will act as magistrates: setting bonds, holding preliminary hearings and that sort of thing. It envisions a two-level appellate situation. The fourteen courts of civil appeals, with their 42 judges, will become courts of intermediate appeal hearing both criminal and civil matters. So instead of a five-judge court (with two commissioners) hearing all the criminal appeals in the State of Texas, you will have 42 judges hearing the criminal appeals in the State of Texas. Then it envisions the Supreme Court and the Court of Criminal Appeals being merged into one Supreme Court of Texas, hearing both civil and criminal matters.

You may say, "Now wait just a minute, Judge. Are you going to take nine judges and have them hear what nine plus seven have been doing?" No. Because under this system the only way that you can get into the Supreme Court with a criminal case will be on a writ of certiorari. You can't go there as a matter of right. A court of appeals will be final except in those cases where there is a difference between two courts of appeals on a question of law or on some important constitutional matter.

The judiciary of the State of Texas (with 254 county judges, 57 judges of county courts at law, 245 district judges, over 800 justices of the peace, and I don't know how many municipal court judges) is without a head. There is no person, office or organization that is in charge of the judiciary of this state. I was a district judge for ten years; and, as a district judge, there was no one who had the authority to tell me, "Judge Roberts, you go down to Coryell County and clean up the docket there"; or "You go to Comanche County and clean it up there." A district judge in this state, well, he has his own little kingdom; and he runs it the way he wants to. If Truman Roberts was out there and didn't have enough work to do in the 52nd Judicial District, and Harris County was snowed under, nobody could tell me I had to go to Harris County. They could call me and ask me. If I wanted to go, I'd go; and if I didn't, I'd say "No, I'm not about to go." And some judges are afraid to go because they are afraid that their people will get mad at them and won't re-elect them.

So; this plan makes the Supreme Court's Chief Justice the head administrative officer of all the judiciary of the State of Texas, with authority to assign a judge and say, "Judge, they're snowed under in Harris County; they're snowed under in Dallas County; you go help. You go down there for two weeks." I know of no other organization this large without a head to it. We must have the ability to use our judicial manpower to its fullest extent wherever it's needed.

Now, concerning the methods of selection in this constitutional amendment, there are two of them. One, in the main amendment, calls for a non-partisan ballot to elect judges. That means that judges won't run as Democrats or run as Republicans. They will run on a judicial ballot to be voted on by the people of this state just exactly as they are now. There is an alternative method; and that is what is commonly known as the Missouri Plan, which many people dislike extremely. Under the Missouri Plan, there is a commission. When there's a vacancy, this commission recommends to the governor the names of three persons who they say are qualified; then the governor must appoint one of those three. Incidentally, the Missouri Plan only applies to appellate judges; it does not apply to district judges and the lower court judges. If this present proposed constitutional amendment is submitted to the people of Texas, they will have the opportunity to turn the whole kit and kaboodle down, keep it like it is now, or they will have the opportunity to adopt the amendment on non-partisan ballots, or, if they choose, they can also adopt one for the Missouri Plan. It's up to the people of Texas to do whatever they want.

Now this plan that Chief Justice Calvert has advocated has drawn a whole bunch of fire. There's not anybody much against it—except the sheriffs' association, the district and county attorneys' association, the county clerks' association, the district clerks' association, the j. p.'s and the constables. I don't know whether the county judges and commissioners have come out against it yet or not. Outside of that, there's nobody much against it! Of course, that's about the most powerful alignment that I can imagine. They are against it because they are all included in the present judicial order. And the Task Force Committee, in dealing with them, left it up to the good discretion of the legislature.

I was talking with Chief Justice Calvert the other day, and in this life in Texas you must face political realities. So, I think you are going to see a little bit of change. I think that when it finally gets down to the people in the legislature, we are going to find the j. p.'s are "grandfathered in." Those of you who don't know what "grandfathered in" means, ask some of your representatives and they'll tell you.[2] You are going to find possibly an amendment that deals more specifically with sheriffs, constables, district clerks, and county clerks.[3] That's a political reality. You see, the judiciary trusts the good judgment of these excellent legislators to do what is right; but evidently the j. p.'s and the sheriffs and the others don't have as much confidence in the legislators as we do. Now, I understand their concern; I really do. But there's one other matter: Many county authorities are afraid that all of the money that comes in from fines and forfeitures is going to be taken from the county and given to the state. That is not contemplated at all. Only such an amount as would be necessary to defray the expenses of the judiciary, which has been projected as about 75%, will go to the state. The remaining 25% will remain with the counties and the cities.[4]

I am sure that the 63rd Legislature of this state, having been elected as a reform legislature, will give to the people of Texas an opportunity to vote and to say what kind of a court system they want. In the words of Chief Justice Calvert, "They were willing to submit to the people of Texas on four occasions how much money the legislature should be paid, so they should at least let the people of Texas speak in regard to what kind of a court system they will have." That's all that anyone can ask—that the people be heard.

I submit to you that Texas does not need a scandal in the administration of criminal justice, and I further submit to you that a state as great as ours is deserving of the best judicial system that the mind of man can devise. These are your courts. The people who go to the legislature are your representatives and your senators. And I guarantee you one thing: you might not think so, but if you write them and tell them how you think, and what you feel (and if it's not a form letter that some organization sends out, but a personal letter written by you), if you think that they don't pay some attention to it, brother, you don't know! They read their mail from back home. They are there to represent you and what you want, and what you feel is needed for this state. I urge each of you to acquaint yourself as far as possible with what is needed in the area of court restructuring and court reform. Let your legislators know, so that the people of Texas can continue upward and onward with the finest judicial system in the nation.

NOTES

1. Section 4(b) of the final draft of December 15, 1972, uses the term "county court" rather than "county court at law."
2. Both justices of the peace and constables are "grandfathered in" under the terms of Section 10(f) of the final draft: "All offices of justice of the peace and constable shall continue temporarily in all respects as they exist at the time of adoption hereof; and each justice of the peace and constable in office at such time shall continue to occupy the office, performing such duties as provided by law, until his or her resignation, retirement, or death, at which time the particular office shall cease to exist. When an office of justice of the peace shall cease to exist, the duties of the office shall vest in the county court of the county in which the office was located. When an office of constable shall cease to exist, the duties of the office shall, unless otherwise provided by law, vest in the office of sheriff of the county in which the office was located."
3. Section 9(a) of the final draft states, "The Legislature shall provide for the election and duties of a district attorney and district clerks in each Judicial District, and for the election and duties of a sheriff and a county clerk in each county. The Legislature shall also provide for the election and duties of such county attorneys as it deems necessary."

4. A study by the Texas Research League shows that in 1972 the average Texas county received a little more than one dollar of court revenue for every two dollars spent to defray court costs; on the other hand, the average city government collected four times as much money in fines, forfeitures, and other revenues as it spent to maintain its judicial branch. Presently, state revenues from the court system are insignificant. See "Measuring Court Costs," *Texas in Action Report*, Vol. III (April 30, 1973), p. 2.

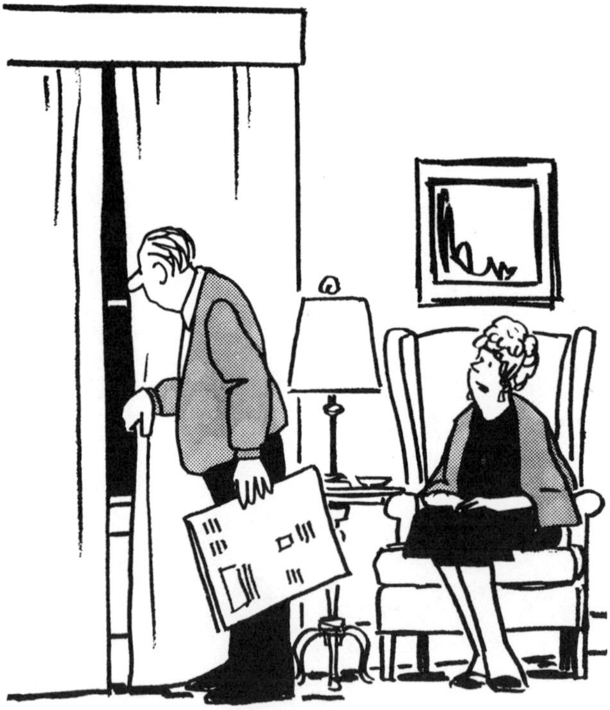

"O.K.! Crime is up in the suburbs. So what do we do now — move back to the city?"

6

Local Governments

There are two basic, related functions of government: (1) providing goods and services, and (2) resolving conflicts. These functions are most clearly seen at the grassroots level of American government, the cities and towns. As the United States has increasingly become an urban nation, public attention has concentrated on city government as the principal provider of goods and services and one of the many arbiters of conflict.

THE SOCIAL AND ECONOMIC CONTEXTS OF "GRASSROOTS" GOVERNMENT

In contrast to the traditionally rural domination of government at the state level, Texas has moved in step with the rest of the nation in becoming an urban state. According to the 1970 census, almost 83 per cent of the Texas population was living in cities of over 50,000. Houston and Dallas metropolitan areas boasted populations of 1,958,491 and 1,539,371, respectively. In the face of this increased urban growth, Texas cities have experienced the same dilemma that pervades all units of government on the national scene: demands for more and improved services paid for by increasingly limited revenue sources. Concomitant with their fiscal dilemma, cities face a human crisis expressed in both economic and sociological contexts. As New Orleans Mayor Landrieu indicates:

We must make it clear that two kinds of poverty exist in the cities: one is the poverty of the people who live in them. The other is the poverty of city governments themselves.[1]

RACIAL FACTORS

Increasingly Texas cities are being caught up in the national sociological problem of a racial conflict between the poor minorities of the inner city and the affluent whites of the suburbs. About one-third of Houston's and one-fourth of Dallas's population is black; over 50 per cent of San Antonio's is Mexican-American. The social and political unrest among these minority groups is compounded by the growing suburbs, which, because of their legal autonomy, are dominated by white citizens escaping the problems of the inner cities—e.g., massive, court-ordered school busing programs in Dallas, Corpus Christi, Austin, and Fort Worth; and the high incidence of major crimes (in 1972 Houston had 303 murders, Dallas 207). The "white flight" from city to suburb widens the political gulf between the races and compounds racial tension. The liberalism of the inner city versus the conservatism of the suburbs was clearly seen in the 1972 Democratic race for governor. In both the primary and run-off elections, liberal "Sissy" Farenthold carried Houston primarily because of its high concentration of blacks. On the other hand, her conservative opponent, Dolph Briscoe, carried such affluent suburbs and neighborhoods as Spring Branch (Harris County), Richardson (Dallas County), and Alamo Heights in San Antonio (Bexar County). Such a dichotomy in voting patterns, although easily explainable and inevitable, is counterproductive to bringing the entire metropolitan area together sociologically or politically. Robert Weaver, former Secretary of the Department of Housing and Urban Development, puts the matter in clear perspective:

Neither growth in the metropolitan fringes nor decay in the older areas of the central city can be conveniently sorted out and considered alone. The two components of the metropolitan complex are interdependent. . . .[2]

POVERTY

Underlying the sociological pattern of Texas cities, which sees an upward trend in the percentage of nonwhites in the central cities, is an economic poverty that accentuates the struggle between the "haves" and the "have-nots." Based on 1970 census figures, a recent United States Senate subcommittee report indicated that the percentage of the labor force in Texas cities earning less than $80 a week was as follows: San Antonio, 45.9 per cent; Fort Worth, 39.0 per cent; and Dallas, 37.3 per cent.[3] Furthermore, the economic disparity between the inner city and the suburb is reflected in housing patterns. As an example, the median value of a home in the Dallas suburb of Highland Park is $49,000, compared to $16,800 for a home in the central city.[4]

TRENDS

In summary, two significant population trends in Texas's metropolitan areas present a serious challenge to the future of their governments. First, the population cycle indicates a continuing rural-to-central city-to-suburb pattern. Recent supportive statistics of suburban growth are as follows:

Eight suburbs are now ranked among the state's 30 most populous cities. Led by Irving, 12th largest at 97,260; Arlington, 14th at 90,643; Pasadena, 16th at

89,277; and Garland, 17th at 81,437, the suburbs are making their presence felt as the most dynamic growth areas in the state.[5]

Second, even though the suburbs are increasing in population, the central cities also continue to grow, with the resulting problem of high-density population. For example, from 1960 to 1970 Austin realized the most rapid growth of Texas cities, with a 35 per cent increase. Many Texas *municipalities,* like their national counterparts, are thus forced to come to grips with the problem of growth and its many by-products. As Houston's Mayor Louie Welch has concluded:

> Our major problems are those of growth rather than stagnation. Air pollution, because of the rapid increase in the number of automobiles, is a major concern. The problem of growth is a challenge for us to keep up with basic city services such as fire and police protection, sewage treatment and streets.[6]

Legally, Texas cities are restricted by municipal charters, constitutional limitations, and state statutes. As a result of these restrictions, the problems of governing at the local level are compounded.

LEGAL STATUS OF MUNICIPALITIES

Historically Texas cities have been prisoners of the Texas constitution of 1876, which, in Article XI, gives municipal corporations their powers. A municipal corporation derives its powers from the state and is thus subject to both constitutional limitations and to statutory restrictions imposed by the state legislature. In 1912, however, a home-rule amendment allowed Texas cities with populations of 5,000 or above to determine their own form of government, pass ordinances, and establish local policies not inconsistent with the general laws of Texas and the state constitution. Thus, to all intents and purposes, there are two legal classifications of cities in Texas: *home-rule cities* and *general-law cities.* The former have greater flexibility in determining their structure and form of municipal government. A general-law city does not automatically become a home-rule city just because its population rises above 5,000; likewise, a home-rule city does not change just because its population drops below 5,000.

With the *Home-Rule Enabling Act of 1913,* home-rule cities can write their own charters, which are their legal bases in such areas as determining the procedure for passing city ordinances and for listing the powers, salaries, and terms of office for members of the city council. Also, the charter stipulates the powers, salary, qualifications, and methods of selection and removal of the mayor. Provisions for the city manager are included if the city has the council-manager form of municipal government. Amendments to the charter are submitted to the qualified voters of the city in either regular municipal elections or special elections called by the city council. A city may not adopt any charter provision which is inconsistent with the laws or constitution of Texas.

FORMS OF MUNICIPAL GOVERNMENT

Basically there are four principal forms of municipal government in operation in the United States, but the council-manager form prevails in most Texas cities. A brief comparison of the four structures gives one an insight into why most Texas cities have adopted the council-manager form.

STRONG MAYOR-COUNCIL

The *strong mayor-council form* has long been the dominant type of municipal government in the major cities of the United States. Of the ten largest cities in the country, only Los Angeles (weak mayor-council) and Dallas (council-manager) operate with structures other than the strong mayor-council. In New York, Chicago, Philadelphia, San Francisco, Detroit, Boston, and St. Louis, the mayor is the administrative as well as political head of the city. Nationally, many of these mayors wield tremendous political power, as exemplified in such personalities as New York City's John V. Lindsay and Chicago's Richard J. Daley.

In Texas, however, this form of government has not been adopted in the state's largest cities primarily because of the machine or ward-heeling kind of politics that has characterized northern cities. Even though the Boss Tweeds of New York City and Pendergasts of Kansas City have departed municipal politics, the memory of the graft and corruption that plagued those cities under a strong mayor-council government lingers among local practitioners in a majority of Texas's home-rule cities.

Instead of adopting this form, Texas's largest city, Houston, has implemented a variation known as the strong mayor-chief administrator-council form. Essentially, this type allows the mayor to delegate much of the city's administrative work to an assistant, whom he appoints and removes. The duties of this administrative assistant vary from city to city, but Houston's Mayor Louie Welch has placed the primary responsibility for budget coordination in the hands of his administrative assistant.

The forty home-rule cities in Texas that operate with the strong mayor-council form have the following characteristics:

1. A council elected either at large or by wards
2. An at-large elected mayor with power to appoint and remove department heads
3. Budgetary power given to the mayor, with council approval in most cities
4. Veto power over council actions given to the mayor

WEAK MAYOR-COUNCIL

As the term weak mayor-council implies, this model of local government places the mayor in a weak administrative position. Under this type, (1) the mayor is elected along with the city council, department heads, and other administrative bodies; and (2) the council has the power to override the mayor's veto. The mayor's position is weak because he has no control (appointment and removal power) over municipal government personnel. Instead of being chief executive, he is one of several elected officials who are responsible to the electorate. It is significant that none of the ten largest cities in Texas has adopted the *weak mayor-council structure.* Nationally, too, the trend is away from this form, which is characterized by the Jacksonian concept of popular election of a large number of local officials.

COMMISSION

In the wake of a 1900 tidal wave that all but destroyed Galveston, Texas, that city tried and later abandoned the commission type of government. Since the adoption of the home-rule amendment in 1912, none of Texas's larger cities has adopted the *commission structure.* Essentially, the commission system uses no executive but relies instead on a group of elected commissioners who, collectively, constitute a policy-making board and, separately, administer the various commissions or departments of public safety, finance, public works, welfare, legal, and other services. Most students of municipal government are critical of this type because of the lack of a chief executive and the unintegrated administrative structure. This structure has not been adopted on a widespread basis either nationally (only St. Paul, Minnesota, and Portland, Oregon, of the major cities) or in Texas (none of the major cities and only seven of the 195 home-rule cities).

COUNCIL-MANAGER

The most popular form of municipal government among Texas's 195 home-rule cities is the *council-manager plan,* which is characterized as follows:

1. A city council elected either at large or by district
2. A city manager appointed and removable by the city council
3. Department heads appointed and removable by the manager, who is responsible for budget coordination
4. An at-large elected mayor who is a member of the council

The principal advantage of this type is that it allows policies to be made by the city council after deliberation and debate on the issues that confront cities: taxation, police protection, zoning ordinances, and the like. Once the policy is made, the city manager and his staff administer its implementation.

As the policy-making arm of municipal government, the city council is a sounding board for many of the grievances and issues which arise in a city. Its meetings are open to the public on a weekly basis, though sometimes they are conducted in executive or closed sessions. Most city councils in Texas consist of five to nine members who are elected at large and who usually serve without pay or for a token remittance (Dallas pays its council members $50 a month).

When Amarillo and Terrell adopted the council-manager form in 1913, a new era began in Texas municipal administration with the appearance of the city manager. This position has become the key office in Texas's largest central cities and growing suburban communities; Houston is the only exception. Since the city manager is an appointed, professional administrator, the city council looks to him for general advice and recommendations and for the preparation of the annual budget.

The most delicate relationship under the council-manager form is that of manager-council rapport. The city manager on occasion finds himself in conflict with the council when he opposes a council policy and refuses to carry it out. This often results in a rapid turnover in city managers. It should be emphasized that with competitive salaries, larger staffs, the need for city planning, urban renewal, and the complex grant-in-aid programs from state and federal governments, the city manager's office has become the pivotal institution for effective city government under the council-manager form. City managers cannot divorce themselves completely from the politics of the community because their superiors are the elected council members, who represent different factions.

MUNICIPAL POLITICS

Under the leadership of chambers of commerce, civic clubs, service organizations, good-government leagues, and the League of Women Voters, municipal government in Texas has managed to improve since the adoption of home rule. Although not experiencing the heavy hand of the boss-controlled machine, local politics in Texas has been characterized by the inevitable conflict of personalities in municipal government and the awesome power of an oligarchy of business executives, popularly referred to as the "establishment" or "power structure." To be sure, every Texas city has its "power behind the throne," such as *Dallas's Citizens Council* (not to be confused with the city council). This voluntary and unofficial group of business leaders has great influence in the selection of city council members and mayors and in dealing with local issues. It has almost become axiomatic in Dallas politics that the presidents of the city's four largest banks (Republic National, First National, Mercantile National, and Texas Bank and Trust) wield as much power from their upper-echelon vantage point in the Citizens Council as any other four individuals in the city. A careful study of other Texas cities would probably reveal a similar type of oligarchy, which revolves around the individuals who control the purse strings of the city.

By state law municipal elections in Texas are non-partisan in nature. Most local elections find different political factions of a city organizing around racial, social, or economic interest-groups. As an example, the political arm of the Dallas business establishment is the Citizens Charter Association, which, since its founding forty years ago by the late R. L. Thornton, Sr., has dominated Dallas's municipal government (see Reading 6-1). The dominant position of big business in Dallas and other cities may decline in the future as minority groups, blue-collar workers, and middle-income groups become more active in local politics due to their increasing concern with such issues as housing, welfare, and lack of representation in city hall.

Perhaps the greatest barrier to an increase in minority-group representation on Texas's city councils is the fact that most of these deliberative bodies are elected on a citywide basis (see Reading 6-2). This prevents inhabitants of the racial ghetto from uniting behind candidates from their neighborhood districts. In view of this situation, which exists in many cities across the nation, a Dallas court case (*Lipscomb* v. *Wise*) is pending before a federal district court. Petitioners challenge the citywide or *at-large election* practice on the grounds of violation of the equal protection clause of the Fourteenth Amendment. A decision in favor of the Dallas plaintiffs could have a significant effect in changing the balance of power in Texas's cities.

FINANCING MUNICIPAL GOVERNMENT

Traditionally, American local governments have been strictly limited in raising and spending funds. Limitations are often embedded in long-outdated constitutional provisions that are difficult to change. Primarily for that reason, in response to strong public demands, local governmental services and activities have increased at a much more rapid rate than local revenues.

MUNICIPAL REVENUES

Texas local governments are constitutionally limited to raising funds from three tax sources: the general property tax, miscellaneous occupation taxes, and sales taxes. They may also acquire funds from such nontax sources as license fees, permits, fines, and penalties; the local share of state-collected taxes; and subsidies and other grants from federal and state governments. If these sources prove insufficient to meet current capital expenditures and operating expenses, local governments must resort to issuing bonds and other methods of borrowing.

Texas cities may charge a *franchise fee* based on the gross receipts of public utilities operating within their jurisdictions. The Texas courts have held that this is fundamentally a "street rental" or "alley rental" charge. The rates vary considerably, but most common is a 2 per cent levy on gross receipts for business conducted within the city.

In addition to those taxes, Texas municipalities are authorized to levy fees for a number of licenses and permits, the most important of which are beer and liquor licenses, and building and plumbing permits. Moreover, acting under their police power, cities are authorized to maintain police courts. The revenues from courts, in the form of court costs, fines, and forfeitures, are retained by the city. In the larger cities these revenues may be quite substantial, especially if the city conducts a vigorous program of enforcing traffic regulations. Fees derived from parking meters have been sustained by the courts, which designated them as police regulatory fees and not taxes; but under whatever guise, they have become a substantial source of revenue for many of the larger cities.

Texas municipalities have authority to own and operate water, electric, and gas utility systems. For such services some cities charge fees that are sufficiently large to permit their transfer from utility fees to general funds. Cities also levy charges against the patrons of other municipal enterprises. These include fees collected for such services as sewage disposal, garbage and trash collection, hospital services, and the use of municipal recreation facilities.

Taxes and fees normally produce enough revenue for Texas cities to meet their day-to-day operating expenses, but money for capital improvements to meet emergencies must often be obtained through the issuance and sale of municipal bonds. The state constitution provides that Texas municipalities may issue bonds in any amount provided such units of government assess and collect annually a sum sufficient to pay the interest and retire the principal without exceeding their legal tax limits. Cities are authorized to issue two types of bonds: general obligation and revenue. *General obligation bonds* are secured by the full faith and credit of the city and are redeemed out of its general revenue funds. *Revenue bonds* are backed by and redeemed out of the revenues of the property or activity financed by the sale of bonds. Money received from the sale of municipal bonds is used to finance such items as street improvements, storm sewers, water and sewer lines, airport expansion, municipal buildings, and recreation facilities.

Financial aid from state and federal governments is rapidly emerging as an important source of municipal revenue. According to the Texas Research League, federal aid increased more than 134 per cent from 1956-1957 to 1964-1965, while state aid rose over 90 per cent. Today Texas cities receive federal funds for hospital and airport construction, public works projects, urban development, and community action programs. They receive some state aid for employees' retirement programs and for the construction of expressways. State aid to municipalities is not yet a significant factor in their revenue schemes, as most of it goes to local school districts.

Even though the local-option city sales tax has provided some much-needed relief for Texas cities, the most important source of all municipal revenues continues to be the general property tax. The Texas Research League compared the revenues produced by sales and property taxes during the first year of sales taxation in the seven largest cities in the state. The conclusion was that although the sales tax produced \$65.4 million in those cities, the property tax aggregated \$202.7 million, or more than three times the sales tax revenue.

The state constitution authorizes smaller, general-law Texas cities to levy a maximum ad valorem property tax of \$1.50 on the \$100 valuation of all property in the city's limits, while allowing the larger, home-rule cities to increase that rate to a maximum of \$2.50 on the \$100 valuation. Like county governments, cities may tax any occupations already being taxed by the state government.

State statutes authorize municipal government to levy two additional taxes: sales and franchise. As of April, 1970, some 509 Texas cities had been granted the authority to levy a one-cent sales tax through a favorable vote of their citizens, despite the much-heralded belief that Texans are inherently opposed to higher taxes. The city sales tax continues to produce increasing revenues, and in 1970 Texas municipalities collected over \$199 million in sales taxes. Each quarter the total collected has increased because of a steady increase in the number of cities levying the tax and the inherent economic growth of this source of revenue.

MUNICIPAL EXPENDITURES

Many highly variable factors influence both the amounts spent by municipal governments and the items they select for expenditures. City administrations are motivated to spend by the demands of individuals and organized groups; by topographical features which affect, sometimes drastically, the costs of capital improvements or services; by competition between the city and other cities in close proximity to the same markets; by general wage and salary scales in the community; by the natural wealth of the city; and by changes in the nature and size of its population. The choice of what functions to support financially, and to what degree, is dependent upon the variables confronting the city's government.

A staff research report to the Legislative Council classifies Texas municipal expenditures according to function, as follows:

1. *General Administration:* expenses for the council, courts, manager (if any), legal department, planning, finance and personnel administration, conduct of elections, recording and reporting;
2. *Police:* expenses for the police department, custody of prisoners, and traffic control;
3. *Fire:* expenses for fire protection and prevention;
4. *Streets:* operation and maintenance costs of streets, alleys, sidewalks, curbs and gutters, and grade crossings;
5. *Sewer:* sewage-disposal plant expense and cost of maintenance and extension of sewer lines;
6. *Garbage:* expenses for equipment, operation and maintenance, and salaries for garbage-disposal workers;
7. *Welfare:* assistance to needy persons and expenses of institutions for the needy;
8. *Health:* expenses for the health department, clinics, food and sanitary inspections;
9. *Hospitals:* expenditures for city-owned hospitals, payments to other hospitals for municipal patients, and allocations to joint city-county hospitals;
10. *Libraries, Parks, and Recreation;*
11. *Contributions to Trust Funds:* retirement systems;
12. *Debt Service;*
13. *Utilities:* expenses of water, electric power, and natural gas distribution systems;
14. *Miscellaneous:* markets, warehouses, cemeteries, and airports.

Like their counterparts in other states, Texas cities are caught up in a vigorously rising spiral of expenditures as they must make greater outlays for capital investments but at a relatively static income level and as their residents demand more and better services. The recently authorized city sales tax has only partially resolved this dilemma.

When the city or county cannot provide a needed public service, special districts are often created. Their presence further strains the taxpayer, who must support the districts from his property tax or fees.

SPECIAL DISTRICTS

School districts and water districts, with their governing boards, constitute the majority of *special districts* in Texas. The justification for most of these districts is certainly valid in that they provide necessary services not offered by other units of government. But their proliferation has prompted the following conclusions from a report prepared for the Institute of Public Affairs at the University of Texas in Austin:

Special districts are major contributors "to the relatively low bond ratings accorded Texas cities."

Special districts tend to be inefficient and costly. They are used to evade legal tax and debt limits, and they are vehicles for speculating in land and municipal securities.

. . . their activities are obscured from the public eye by infrequent and little-publicized meetings, meager and misleading public reporting, disguised tax and service charges, the smallness of their operations, and the omnipresence of their numbers.[7]

A cogent example of the report's conclusions was recently revealed in the *Houston Post.* In 1971 there were twenty bond elections held in Harris County involving water and utility districts (water districts account for over 450 of Texas's 1,001 special districts, excluding school districts). Only six of the twenty bond proposals failed, which resulted in Harris County taxpayers' assuming a 60-million-dollar debt. Amazingly enough, only 585 persons participated in the twenty elections (see Reading 6-3).

HIDDEN GOVERNMENTS

Created to perform functions and services which the city or county are unwilling or unable to perform because of constitutional limitations, special districts have increased in number at an alarming rate. During the decade of 1960 to 1970, the number of special districts more than doubled.[8] Aside from their virtual anonymity vis-à-vis the general public, the principal indictment which can be laid at the feet of the special districts is that they are perhaps the most undemocratic level of government in existence. By passing a special law, the Legislature can create a special district without any notice to the voting taxpayers, although the voters must give their approval. This is one of the reasons why there is such a low voter turnout. Moreover, a city can extend services into an area where a proposed special district may have been voted down. A case in point was an attempt in 1968 to create Water Control and Improvement District 102 in the eastern part of Harris County. Voters in the area turned down the proposed district by a vote of 513-53. The city of Houston, however, working with influential private groups and Harris County legislators, devised a scheme whereby the city can authorize the installation of water and sewer lines in the area without voter approval either in the city or county. The city sold $5.2 million bonds for the construction of the lines. Eventually the bonds will become the obligation of the city. Then the city plans to annex the area. Such a scheme is being challenged in the state courts and is pending before the Texas Supreme Court. Many other examples of special-district abuse could be cited. For the reform of special districts the Texas Urban Development Commission has recommended that:

A constitutional procedure be established relieving the legislature from the responsibility for creating districts by special act.

Legislation be enacted consolidating existing statutes regarding special districts to carry out a particular governmental function.

Legislation be enacted requiring local review and approval of all proposals for the creation of special purpose governments.

Legislation be enacted designating the Texas Department of Community Affairs as the state agency responsible for establishing a continuing program of state-wide supervision over the activities of special districts.

Legislation be enacted conferring upon regional councils of governments authority over special districts.[9]

FINANCING GOVERNMENTS OF SPECIAL DISTRICTS

Most governments of special districts, of which there are several kinds in Texas, have the power to raise revenue through taxation. The most important exceptions are soil conservation districts, certain water districts, and public housing authorities. In almost every instance the power to tax is limited to an ad valorem tax on property. Some of the special districts—notably water-power control, levee improvement, and drainage districts—may levy an additional tax on the benefits derived from their operations. Special-district governments are usually required to secure advance approval from their electorates for property tax rates and are limited to maximum rates established by the law creating the district. Governments of these districts may issue either *general obligation* or *revenue bonds* (see Chapter 7 for definitions). Some may issue both; but their borrowing power usually requires special elections to approve all bonds issued, percentage limitations on the amount of bonds that may be outstanding at one time, or both.

Some special districts in Texas, for example, soil conservation districts and public housing authorities, depend heavily upon federal and state aid for their revenues. Soil conservation districts neither have taxing power nor are permitted to borrow, whereas public housing districts cannot tax and may issue only revenue bonds. Some districts obtain additional revenues from improvements and rentals of equipment or sale of services. Since most special districts are created to perform a single function, their expenditures are usually restricted to the direct cost of the service performed and the indirect costs incidental to performance.

Single-purpose designed as they are, special districts fail to come to grips with the problems of the total metropolitan milieu. Indeed they are counter-productive to serving the interdependent needs of the Texas urbanite.

THE PROBLEM OF METROPOLITAN AREAS

At the present time Texas has twenty-three standard metropolitan statistical areas (SMSAs), more than any other state in the United States. They are the focal point of attention in any discussion about the future of urban government in Texas. Occupying only 6.6 per cent of the land, almost 83 per cent of the state's 11 million population live in Texas's metropolitan areas. The late Marvin Hurley, former executive vice-president of the Houston Chamber of Commerce, gave a capsule description of the metropolitan situation when he said, "Whether we like the idea or not, the fact remains that about 90 per cent of our people are destined to live out their days not in some rural utopia but in a man-made environment of stores and office buildings and industries and freeways and parking lots."[10]

To be sure, the "metroplex" is a fact of life in Texas, and the overriding question of the future is how metropolitan areas are to be governed. In attempting to come to grips with this question, Texas encounters a problem which is common throughout the nation. That is the problem of a multiplicity of governments in a relatively small land-use area. In short, governments lie on top of governments in an overlapping manner that could produce an acute urban crisis for the state. Specifically, superimposed upon Texas's 254 counties are 977 municipalities, 1,177 school districts, and 1,681 special districts.

Crime, air-water pollution, housing, education, transportation, and land use are problems which are metropolitan in scope. Yet the fragmentation of local governmental units causes these issues to be dealt with in an uncoordinated manner. The only valid conclusion to the question of governing metropolitan areas is that there is no one answer. Existing approaches to the metropolitan problem, along with some future alternatives, need to be examined, however.

COUNCILS OF GOVERNMENTS

Currently the most successful approach to the metropolitan problem has been the creation of *Councils of Governments,* or COGs (see Reading 6-4). The COGs consist of representatives from the various local governmental units in the metropolitan areas. Membership in a COG is voluntary. Furthermore, the COGs do not attempt to usurp the legal autonomy of any governmental unit. According to Philip Barnes, the COGs have the following basic functions: "(1) to undertake regional planning activities and (2) to provide such other services as member governments may desire."[11] More than any other catalyst, stringent guidelines for federal grants to local governments have sparked the growth and utilization of the COGs. Through the "review and comment" procedure, local officials in cooperation with the COGs draft and implement state and federally funded programs. Some critics of the COGs argue that these regional forums are the first step toward *metro government,* such as is currently in use in Toronto, Canada, and Miami, Florida. Metro government results in "supergovernment," or the abolition of the current county, municipal, and special-district structure. Fears of such a development in Texas are largely unfounded because of the many political and attitudinal barriers against it. Apparent also is the fact that the COGs are not governments, in that they have no taxing or lawmaking authority. The COGs' most significant contribution has been to facilitate the total planning for a metropolitan area.

STOPGAP APPROACHES

Other approaches to the metropolitan problem include the consolidation of areawide functions under county government, increased annexation of unincorporated areas by existing cities to prevent further suburbanization, and expansion of interlocal contracts whereby local governments contract with each other for such services as water and police protection. Experience in the use of these programs doubtlessly will increase with time. None, however, provide a complete solution to the problem of governing metropolitan areas.

STATE-FEDERAL INVOLVEMENT

Both at the state and national levels there is a renewed emphasis on helping Texas cities to cope with the metropolitan problem. Significant examples are the creation of the Texas Department of Community Affairs by the Legislature in 1971 and the appointment of the Texas Urban Development Commission by Governor Preston Smith in 1970. At the federal level in 1972, Congress passed a five-year, $30-billion revenue-sharing bill. Texas's annual share of the bill is estimated at $244.5 million, with $40.9 million earmarked for the state government and the rest for cities and counties. Over the five-year period, Texas's largest cities would receive approximately the following amounts: Houston, $20.7 million; Dallas, $13.5 million; San Antonio, $12.8 million; Fort Worth, $8.2 million; and El Paso, $6.4 million. Local governments (city and county) must spend their allocations in the following areas, according to federal guidelines: police-fire protection, sewage disposal, pollution abatement, urban transit, and libraries.

Intergovernmental cooperation among all levels of government is perhaps the key to solving the metropolitan problem in Texas. Sparked by the expertise of COG staffs and revenue-sharing, Texas cities are certainly part of the new federalism, which sees the nation's urban centers being cajoled to solve their own problems with less dependence on Washington. Indeed the mayors of the United States are being challenged to promote "unity, cooperation, brotherhood, and sensitivity to the plight of others," as Indianapolis Mayor Richard Lugar pleaded in the opening address to the 49th annual convention of the National League of Cities.[12]

To be sure, in both governmental and human terms Texas cities stand at a crossroads. How they handle their common problems of land use, pollution, housing, mass transit, police protection, public health, and education will go a long way toward determining the quality of life for most Texans in the future. But the obstacles to metropolitan solutions for metropolitan problems are numerous, and not the least of them is county government in Texas.

THE COUNTY

For over fifty years textbook writers have referred to American county government as "The Dark Continent of American Politics." They have taken their cue from H. S. Gilbertson, who first used the term in 1917 in the title of his book, *The County, The Dark Continent of American Politics.*[13] Gilbertson's choice of title was no doubt justified by the reluctance of county government to modernize its operations to keep pace with changing demands. Three decades later the situation apparently had improved little. In 1952 Clyde F. Snider wrote that few basic structural and functional changes of note had occurred in county government in the United States during the first half of the twentieth century.[14] Another quarter-century later, in the mid-1970s, Gilbertson, if still around, would find little cause to alter his assessment of 1917. The aftermath of this failure of the American county to update its operations has left in the minds of many Americans a mental image of county government as consisting of "fat politicians sitting around a potbellied stove, spraying tobacco juice into a copper spittoon, and plotting how to grease the political machine."[15] Though the potbellied stove and copper spittoon are no longer visible at the county seat, how much greasing of the political machine still exists is open to question.

More recent spokesmen on the subject of county government have been less pessimistic about its value and role of service within the American system. James W. McGrew, writing for a publication of the Institute of Public Affairs of the University of Texas at Austin, believes that "the county is being seriously considered as the vehicle for handling urban problems of areawide concern."[16] The Texas Research League is of the opinion that where metropolitan areas stretch across most of a county, nothing can replace a general-purpose government like that of a county government to provide the public services to which its citizens are entitled.[17] In a speech before the 35th annual convention of the National Association of Counties in Atlanta in July, 1970, Laurence Roos, supervisor of St. Louis County, Missouri, boldly predicted that "what was once the dark continent of American politics will become, I believe, the salvation of our form of government." Minor B. Crager of the Institute of Public Affairs of the University of Texas at Austin believes that recent federal court decisions requiring equal apportionments of people in the county commissioner precincts will produce "a gradual modification of the image of county government: County government may no longer be regarded as basically rural government."[18] Such optimism could be interpreted as a hopeful sign that county government may come to be recognized as the governmental form best equipped to bring order out of the growing chaos in sprawling metropolitan areas, which are fragmented by multiple units of government whose trademark is duplication and overlapping of functions and services.

COUNTY-STATE RELATIONS

The county is an old institution of government, older than the United States. It was imported from England, where in Anglo-Saxon times it was known as the shire. Our county sheriff was once the "reeve," or chief officer, of the shire (hence "shire reeve," or "sheriff") in medieval England. English settlers brought county government to the New World, where they transplanted it in a variety of forms and functions, depending on where they settled. Those who came to the New England region preferred the smaller, more compact governmental form known there today as town government and characterized by the annual town meeting, where the citizens gather once or twice a year and directly conduct all their local governmental business. It follows, therefore, that the town in New England overshadows the county as a unit of local government; in fact, county government never was established in Rhode Island and was abolished in Connecticut in 1960. Farther south, English settlers arriving in New York and Pennsylvania looked with more favor on the county and hence gave it equal weight with the township in local governmental affairs. The township was a modification of the New England town and, like it, a geographical subdivision of the county. The county-township combination was carried westward across the Appalachians into the middle western states by pioneer migrants from New York and Pennsylvania.

In the South, where it never had to compete with the town or township, the county became the only local governmental form. As settlers from Virginia, Georgia, and the Carolinas moved westward, county government as they knew it went with them. Spreading ultimately across the Mississippi, it became the prevailing local governing unit, without competition from town or township, in all the trans-Mississippi states.

Today there are approximately 3,050 counties in the forty-eight states that now have county governments. Louisiana has the equivalent of the county in the parishes. These 3,050 counties vary in size and population. The largest in area is San Bernardino County, California, with 20,131 square miles. Arlington County, Virginia, in contrast, is 24 square miles in area. Texas counties vary almost as widely in area as those in the rest of the nation: Rockwall County is the smallest, with 147 square miles; and Brewster County the largest, with 6,208 square miles. Los Angeles County, California, is the most populous, with over 7 million people; while tiny *Loving County, Texas,* had only 226 residents in 1960 but was reduced to an embarrassing 164 by 1970. Texas, therefore, has the smallest county in the nation in population but the largest number of counties, 254; Delaware has the fewest, 3. Texas counties vary widely in population if we compare Loving County with Harris County, which has over 1 million people. See Table 6-1, which compares the least populous and most populous counties.

Unlike the American municipality, the *county* is essentially an administrative arm of the state, created by the state to serve its needs and purposes. Yet, paradoxically, the state exercises little administrative supervision over county government and provides few guidelines for its operation. The state assumes little or no obligation to see to it that its objectives are realized in the county. As an agent of the state, the county enforces the state's laws, conducts its elections, levies and collects its taxes, administers its justice, educates its citizens, and maintains its order. In the name of the state the county conducts programs of health and welfare (also in conjunction with the federal government), maintains

TABLE 6-1
Comparison of the smallest county in Texas (Loving) with the largest in Texas (Harris) and in the United States (Los Angeles)

Subject	Los Angeles County (California)	Harris County (Texas)	Loving County (Texas)
Population (1970)	7,032,075	1,722,533	164
Rank among 3,050 counties in U.S.	1	12	3,050
Area (sq.mi.)	4,069	1,723	648
Population per sq.mi.	1,728	1,011	.25

Source: U.S. Bureau of the Census, *1970 Census of Population: Number of Inhabitants Texas,* PC (1)-A45 Tex. (Washington, D.C.: U.S. Government Printing Office, August, 1971); U.S. Bureau of the Census, *1970 Census of Population: Number of Inhabitants California,* PC (1)-AG. Calif. (Washington, D.C.: U.S. Government Printing Office, September, 1971).

records of vital statistics, issues licenses, collects fees, and carries on a host of other services for the citizens of the state. Benefiting from these services, the residents tend to look upon the county governmental functions as being more local than state. At least it is difficult for them to distinguish between functions performed for the county residents and those performed for the state. For example, the county sheriff and county judge together administer and enforce state law, not county law. They are, therefore, state officers; yet they are elected by the voters of the county, who look upon them as county officers. As presently explained, some of the services and functions conducted by the county in Texas are mandatory under the state constitution or state statutes, and some are discretionary.

STRUCTURE AND OPERATION

In the forefront of county governmental machinery in the United States is a board most frequently referred to either as the county board of commissioners or county board of supervisors. From state to state it varies widely in size from a single member to over 250.

In all of Texas's 254 counties the governing body is composed of a board called the *commissioners court* (see Figure 6-1). The term "court" is a misnomer in that there are no judicial functions involved. The commissioners court is primarily an administrative body carrying out assigned duties for the state. It cannot pass ordinances, as a city council may. However, the county does exercise legislative functions, in a sense, when it decides whether or not to perform functions which are authorized but not required by the state. The commissioners courts in all 254 counties of Texas are identical in size and structure. Tiny rural Loving County, with its 164 residents, has essentially the same government as

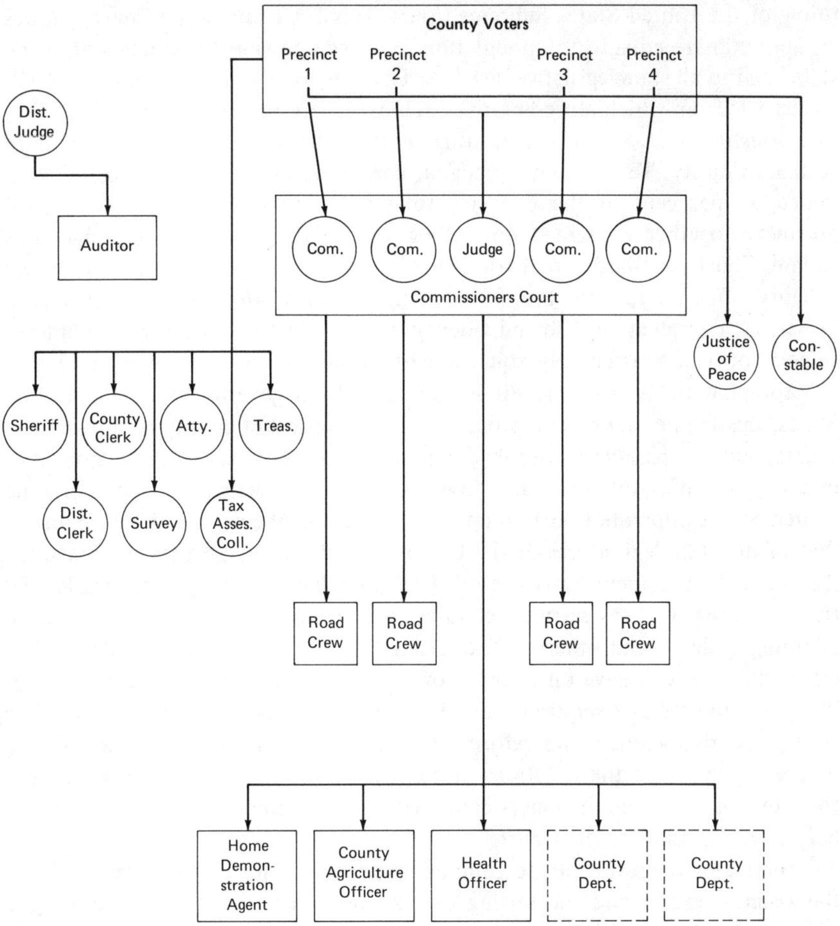

Figure 6-1
Organization of county government in Texas

Reproduced from George D. Braden, Citizens' Guide to the Texas Constitution, *prepared for the Texas Advisory Commission on Intergovernmental Relations by the Institute of Urban Studies, The University of Houston (Austin, Tex., 1972), p. 51.*

huge, urban Harris County with well over 1 million people. The commissioners court is composed of the county judge and four commissioners. Each commissioner is elected by the voters in one of four *commissioners precincts.* The *county judge* is elected at large and serves as chairman. All are elected for four-year terms; the terms of the commissioners are staggered so that two are elected every two years.

The boundary lines of the commissioners precincts are set by the commissioners court, but in so doing the court must observe the "*one man, one vote*" ruling of the United States Supreme Court. This 1964 rule of the Court requires an approximate equality of population in all congressional districts within the states and in all state legislative districts. The same rule was then applied in 1968 to districts from which representatives in local government are elected. The 1968 case sought to force the redistricting of the four commissioners precincts in Midland County, Texas.[19] One precinct, composed of the city of Midland, contained 97 per cent of the county's total population, while the other three precincts together contained only 3 per cent. Where population imbalances violate Court standards, redistricting will be necessary to achieve essential equality. "We hold," said the Court in the *Avery* v. *Midland* case, "that petitioner, as a resident of Midland County, has a right to a vote for the commissioners court of substantially equal weight to the vote of every other resident."

Applying to as many as 80,000 units of local government in the United States, this landmark decision promised to give control of county commissioners courts, and comparable bodies in other states, to the voters of the major cities in many counties in Texas and in the nation. In reaching this decision, the United States Supreme Court compared the work of the commissioners court to that of the state legislatures or the Congress of the United States. It concluded that the commissioners court is essentially a legislative body performing legislative functions, such as setting tax rates, equalizing assessments, issuing bonds, adopting budgets, and otherwise exercising "general governmental powers." The effect this case will have on county government in Texas is uncertain. It is not likely that the decision requiring equality of representation on the commissioners court will bring about major reform of county administration in the near future or the expansion of the functions of county government. Without state legislative approval the commissioners court will have no more authority than it had before the decision of the Court.

The major functions of the commissioners court include the preparation of the county budget and the setting of tax rates. In performing its duties, the court must observe the limitations prescribed by the state constitution on the taxes that may be collected by the county and what the maximum rates may be. However, this leaves a wide margin of discretion as to what taxes may be used for county revenue and how such revenue is to be expended. The commissioners court has considerable discretionary power in deciding how such tax revenue shall be used to finance functions prescribed by the state, such as building and maintaining county roads and bridges, operating a courthouse and a jail, and administering county health and welfare programs. Aside from mandatory functions imposed by the state, the county may use its discretion about entering other programs authorized but not required by the state. Within this latitude the commissioners court may establish county hospitals, libraries, parks, airports, museums, and other public facilities. Increasing public demands for services rendered by these agencies impose on the county an ever-expanding budgetary responsibility.

Another major function of the commissioners court is the conduct of elections. The state leaves the administration of virtually all elections—national, state, and local—to the county; the exceptions are those for municipal and special-district offices. The county must bear the cost of general and special elections, except those of municipal and school elections. The commissioners court divides the county into voting precincts based on equal population by law. It selects the polling places, election judges, and clerks. Finally, it canvasses the returns from the voting precincts. Other county officials are involved along with the commissioners court in the conduct of elections. The county clerk certifies the candidates for a place on the ballot and prepares the ballot, while the actual printing of ballots, securing of supplies, and other incidental duties are performed by the county election board, composed of the county judge, the county clerk, the sheriff, and the county chairmen of the major political parties.

Members of the commissioners court, in addition to their collective responsibilities as members of that body, have additional individual duties. Each serves as road and bridge administrator in his precinct. Frequently money allotted for roads and bridges in the county is divided among the four precincts regardless of need. Lack of coordination and faulty administration are the inevitable result. Since 1947, when the Legislature passed an optional county road law, voters in the county have been permitted to adopt the *county unit system,* which provides for a county-wide road system under the direction of a trained engineer. To date few counties (such as Dallas, Bexar, and Tarrant) have adopted the plan (see Reading 6-6).

The county judge presides over two courts, the commissioners court and the county court. He must, therefore, divide his time between judicial duties as county judge and administrative and legislative duties as presiding officer of the commissioners court. In his judicial capacity he presides over the county court, which has general jurisdiction in the probation of wills, appointment of guardians, and settlement of estates. In most counties the county judge hears other civil cases as well as misdemeanor criminal cases. As a member of the election board the county judge posts election notices, receives election returns from election judges in the precincts, presents these to the commissioners court for official canvassing, and then forwards the final results to the secretary of state. In counties with 225,000 population or less, he serves as county budget officer. He fills vacancies in the commissioners court, and in counties with less than 3,000 public school pupils he may serve as ex-officio school superintendent. Lastly, he is a notary public and is authorized to perform marriages.

Closely associated with the county judge in his judicial duties are the *county attorney* and the *county sheriff.* The former, elected for four years, serves as legal adviser to county and precinct officers; also, he represents the state in criminal cases and the county in civil cases. As chief law-enforcement officer, the sheriff is charged with keeping the peace of the county. In this capacity he appoints his own deputies and other staff aids and is in charge of the county jail and its prisoners.

Under the terms of the Texas constitution, each county is supposed to have at least four justices. Situated on the bottom rung of the state judicial ladder, the justice of the peace has jurisdiction only over minor civil and criminal suits. Because cases in his court are often decided in favor of the plaintiff, the term

"J.P." is frequently referred to in and out of Texas as "justice for the plaintiff." A *constable* is elected by the voters in each J.P. precinct to a four-year term to aid the justice of the peace by serving subpoenas, executing judgments, and otherwise performing the duties of a peace officer.

Each of the 254 counties elects a *county clerk* and a tax assessor-collector. The former is more than a court clerk. Elected for four years, he serves as clerk both of the county court and the commissioners court; and in counties of less than 8,000 population, he is also clerk of the district court when it is in session in that county. In addition, he is recorder of legal documents, such as deeds, mortgages, and contracts; and he is the keeper of vital statistics. Measured by the extent and variety of his duties, the county court clerk is one of the most important officers of the county. The *tax assessor-collector,* elected for four years in all counties of 10,000 or more population, is primarily occupied with the assessment and collection of the general property tax for both the county and the state. He issues certificates of title, collects fees for license plates for all motor vehicles, and administers voter registration. In counties of less than 10,000 population these duties are performed by the sheriff unless the voters approve of adding an assessor-collector of taxes.

The *county treasurer* receives and pays out all county funds according to the will of the commissioners court. Payments are made by warrants which are signed by the treasurer and drawn on the county treasury. Counties of 35,000 population or with tax valuations in excess of $15 million must have an *auditor* appointed by the district judge. The auditor is responsible for countersigning warrants issued by the county treasurer; and, in counties with more than 225,000 in population, he serves also as county budget officer. His auditing function involves checking account books and records of all county officials who handle county funds.

Some countywide elective offices in Texas have become, over the years, largely anachronistic. With nearly 100 per cent of the state's public school children attending schools in independent school districts, which have their own superintendents and trustees, there is little work to be done by county superintendents and trustees. Likewise, there is not enough public land left to warrant the employment of a full-time county surveyor. Election of a public weigher and an inspector of hides and animals is also provided for in the Texas constitution, but these county offices are usually vacant.

Several appointive officers are found in counties across the state, depending on the population of a county and the wishes of the voters and the commissioners court. Whenever a county engages in activities authorized but not required by the state constitution or statutes, the commissioners court must appoint an administrative head to oversee the program. Federal grants-in-aid also involve the counties in programs requiring an administrator. Health, welfare, home demonstration, and agricultural extension are examples. Each county commissioners court is required by the state constitution to appoint a health officer for a two-year term.

COUNTY REVENUES

The Texas constitution authorizes county governments to assess and collect taxes on property and occupations. Although counties may constitutionally tax all property, they are restricted to taxing only those occupations already taxed by the state. No other forms of tax revenue are available to these governments. As a consequence, more than 90 per cent of the *county's tax revenue* comes from the ad valorem tax on property within its jurisdiction.

All forms of property are subject to ad valorem taxation, whether they are being taxed by counties or other units of state and local government. Value for this purpose is defined as true and full value or fair market value in cost at private sale. The three broad categories of taxable property are *real property,* including land, building, structures, improvements, fixtures, and rights and privileges connected with the land, as well as mines, minerals, quarries, and fossils in and under the land; *tangible personal property,* including all goods, chattels, and effects owned by citizens of the state, ships, motor vehicles, airplanes, boats, and other vessels belonging to residents of the state and registered in Texas; and *intangible personal property,* including money in hand or on deposit in or out of the state, credits, bonds, securities, and shares. However, certain legal limitations restrict those definitions. They exempt government-owned property, holdings of certain designated private charitable, educational, and religious institutions, household furnishings up to a value of $250, homesteads up to a value of $3,000, farm products in the hands of the producer, and family supplies for farm and home use.

The commissioners court in each county must meet annually and determine the tax rate for that fiscal year. The base rate may not exceed 80 cents of the $100 valuation, or 0.8 per cent of the assessed value of the taxable property within the county. Revenue produced from that basic levy is distributed among the general revenue, permanent improvement, road and bridge, and jury funds in the county treasury. An additional levy of 15 cents for public roads in the county may be authorized by the Legislature and a majority of the qualified voters voting at a special countywide election. An additional 30 cents for farm-to-market roads and flood control may be authorized by the qualified voters in the county. The Legislature may allow the county to issue bonds and additional property taxes to pay for capital outlays, such as for a new county courthouse.

State statutes also permit the county to share in the revenue obtained from the state motor vehicle registration fee, the motor fuel tax, and the certificate-of-title fee for motor vehicles. The county receives some funds from what might be called subsidiary nontax revenues. Those revenues, rarely of great amount in the overall income picture of the typical Texas county, include: fees paid to county officers for their services in excess of the amounts allocated to those officers for their expenses; fines, fees, and forfeitures in justice of the peace, county, and district courts; and interest on county funds invested.

Federal grants-in-aid form the last important source of county revenues. Congress has usually made counties eligible to receive any and all aid extended to cities and towns. For example, such aid has been offered to counties by federal statutes for hospital construction, airport construction, and construction of public housing. Much of the extension and agricultural work of the federal government, aimed primarily at conservation and development of natural resources, is also channeled through the county governments.

Texas counties, like other units of local government, are caught in an ever-tightening revenue squeeze. Demands for county services, costs of goods and services, and population are increasing; but sources of tax revenue for counties have not been expanded significantly in many years, and other revenue sources have not bridged the widening gap.

COUNTY EXPENDITURES

Although highly ritualized by legal requirements and state administrative directives, the exact patterns of *county expenditures* vary considerably from county to county. Certain functional categories may be used, however, to indicate the general nature of county expenditures:

1. General administrative operations
   a. Administration of justice
   b. Administration of county finances
   c. Recording of public and private documents
   d. Holding state and local elections
   e. Collection of state and local taxes
2. Law-enforcement operations
3. Public welfare operations
4. Hospital and other public health operations
5. Soil conservation and other agricultural services
6. Construction and maintenance of roads and bridges
7. Payment of interest and principal on county debt

Since counties do not have complete control over their own expenditures, state statutes and administrative directives often require them to perform services or regulate activities. Thus they are required to raise funds and spend them for purposes and in amounts not fully understood by the taxpayer. (For the case history of the defeat of the Trinity River canalization project by aroused taxpayers and environmentalists, see Reading 6-5.)

PROPOSED REFORMS

What reforms are needed to change the face of county government in the United States in order to make it more efficient and accountable to the people in the performance of its duties? Even the superficial observer of the local government scene would be inclined to answer this question by naming several needed reforms, and probably the one most frequently mentioned would be that of providing for an executive head for county government. There is little doubt that among the several glaring deficiencies of county government, the need for some form of chief executive—county manager, supervisor, or president—should rank at the top of the list of proposed reforms. Today no county in Texas has a single administrative head who could direct responsible governing practices so sorely needed on the county level. Instead, each county officer, elected like most of his colleagues, largely goes his own way; he is responsible to no superior official, only to the voters. And rarely can voters hold any official responsible for his conduct in office except in glaring cases of malfeasance.

By a home-rule amendment to the state constitution, adopted in 1933, the state seemingly took a step forward to remedy this fault; but after thirty-six years passed without implementation of home rule in any county, this provision was removed from the Texas constitution by another amendment in 1969. Unless a new, progressive constitution is adopted, there appears to be no prospect of achieving significant and needed reforms in county government. Although many reforms might be suggested, there are at least four that appear obvious to most political scientists.

First of these is a single *chief executive* of the county, similar to that found in approximately 450 counties across the nation. Such an officer could be empowered to appoint most of the presently elected department heads. This badly needed reform would go far toward eliminating the "long ballot" and providing administrative responsibility centered in a single chief executive elected by the people of the county and responsible to them for the performance of his administration. This administrative practice now prevails in the offices of the President of the United States, most state governors, city managers, strong mayors, and a few county executive heads. With the adoption of a county executive in Texas, the present commissioners court could be retained as a legislative body similar to that of a city council.

A second sorely needed reform in Texas county government is the adoption of a *merit system* to replace the present "spoils" system. Apparently Texas's long outmoded constitution hampers the adoption of a merit system on the county level. The one attempt of a Texas county to adopt a merit system was ruled unconstitutional by the state Supreme Court. Although national, state, and municipal governments have long recognized the salutary effects of recruitment by means of competitive examination rather than by hiring "cronies" or using hiring as a reward for contributions toward the election of a public official, the lesson apparently cannot be applied to the Texas county. Until it can be applied, the more responsible and efficient personnel systems found in some state agencies and municipalities in Texas will be denied to the county, which will continue to operate on the basis of nineteenth-century Jacksonian methods of recruitment and management.

A third area of needed reform is that of the county road system, which in most counties is as inefficient and uncoordinated as personnel management. Where budget money for roads is divided four ways among precinct commissioners without regard for need, the end result must inevitably be inferior road services. If each commissioner is free to carry out his road and bridge program as he sees fit, there is no guarantee that plans and operations of the four commissioners will be coordinated and that funds will be spent in a businesslike fashion.

Passage of the Optional Road Law of 1947 allows the voters in a county to adopt a *county-unit plan* whereby a county road system can be operated under the direction of a county engineer appointed by the commissioners court. To date little headway has been made in county-unit road administration, since relatively few counties have adopted it (see Reading 6-6).

A fourth needed reform is reduction in the total number of counties. Of the 254 counties, according to the 1970 census, 106 are under 10,000 population, 59 are under 5,000, and 5 are under 1,000. Kenedy County has only 665 residents, while Loving County has a bare 164. With so few residents it is not possible to conduct any form of county government effectively.

Other needed reforms include decentralized purchasing practices and improvement in monetary and fiscal operations (including tax collection, property assessment, accounting and auditing practices, and bonded indebtedness). Reforms in these areas are discussed elsewhere in this book.

NOTES

1. Moon Landrieu, "The Real Crisis of the Cities," *U.S. News and World Report,* August 14, 1972, p. 58.
2. Robert C. Weaver, *Dilemmas of Urban America* (New York: Athenian Press, 1967), p. 8.
3. Texas Urban Development Commission, *Urban Texas: Policies for the Future* (Arlington, Tex.: Institute of Urban Studies, The University of Texas at Arlington, November, 1971), pp. 11-21.
4. *Ibid.,* p. 16.
5. *Ibid.,* p. 18.
6. "Big City Woes as the Mayors See Them," *U.S. News and World Report,* July 3, 1972, pp. 52-54.
7. Woodworth G. Thrombley, *Special Districts and Authorities in Texas* (Austin, Tex.: Institute of Public Affairs, The University of Texas, 1966). See also David W. Tees, *A Fresh Look at Special Districts in Texas,* a report prepared for the Texas Urban Development Commission (June, 1971).
8. Texas Urban Development Commission, *Urban Texas: Policies for the Future,* p. 26.
9. *Ibid.,* pp. 58-59.
10. *Dallas Morning News,* August 25, 1972.
11. Philip W. Barnes, *Councils of Governments in Texas: Changing Federal-Local Relations* (Austin, Tex.: Institute of Public Affairs, The University of Texas, 1968).
12. "The Changing Aspirations of Cities," *Wall Street Journal,* December 6, 1972.
13. Henry S. Gilbertson, *The County, The Dark Continent of American Politics* (New York: The National Short Ballot Association, 1917).
14. "American County Government: A Mid-Century Review," *American Political Science Review,* Vol. XLVI (March, 1952), pp. 66-80.

15. Bernard F. Hillenbrand, "County Government Is Reborn," *Public Administration Survey* (May, 1960), pp. 1-8, in Robert L. Morlan, *Capital, Courthouse and City Hall* (Boston: Houghton Mifflin, 1966), p. 216.
16. James W. McGrew, "The Texas Urban County in 1968: Problems and Issues," *Public Affairs Comment,* Vol. XIV (Austin, Tex.: Institute of Public Affairs, The University of Texas at Austin, March, 1968), pp. 1-4.
17. *Ibid.*
18. Minor B. Crager, "County Reapportionment in Texas," *Public Affairs Comment,* XVII (March 1972), 6.
19. *Avery* v. *Midland County, Texas, et al.*, 390 U.S. 474 (1968).

KEY TERMS AND CONCEPTS

municipality
home-rule cities
general-law cities
Home Rule Enabling Act of 1912
strong mayor-council form
weak mayor-council structure
commission structure
council-manager plan
Dallas Citizens Council
Lipscomb v. *Wise*
at-large election
franchise fee
special district
general obligation bonds
revenue bonds
Councils of Governments
metro government
The Dark Continent of American Politics
Loving County, Texas
county
commissioners court
commissioners precinct
county judge
"one man, one vote" rule
Avery v. *Midland County, Texas, et al.*
county attorney
county sheriff
constable
county clerk
county tax assessor-collector
county treasurer
county auditor
county's tax revenues
real property
tangible personal property
intangible personal property
county expenditures
county chief executive
merit system
county unit plan

REG HIDER

"How was the traffic?"

Selected Readings

6-1
INTERVIEW WITH WES WISE, MAYOR OF DALLAS

Robert S. Trotter, Jr. Would you briefly describe your official duties as Mayor of Dallas?

Wes Wise Well, in the council-manager form of government, the city council is the policy-making arm of the government. The city manager and the various departments under him are the functional branches of our city government. The

Interview conducted by Robert S. Trotter, Jr., City Hall, Dallas, Texas, August 25, 1972.

mayor in the city of Dallas has often been likened to the chairman of the board of a corporation, although I personally somewhat resent that description because I feel that in the modern times in which we live, people demand much more than a chairman of the board. They demand a citizen relations man, a person who has very close contact with the people from all walks, particularly in this era of protest from the young people, from blacks, from the underprivileged, etc. So, even though the original concept many years ago may have been that the mayor in the council-manager form of government would be a chairman of the board, it has now evolved and broadened into something much more than that. My Wednesday afternoon meetings, at which I open my office to any citizen who wishes to come to see me, are typical of that general change in the attitude and the function of the mayor of the city of Dallas.

Of course, I am the leader of the council, preside over the council, and do not have veto power. I have one vote, a single vote along with the rest of them; but I am expected to exert leadership in certain areas, such as the Open Housing Ordinance which Dallas passed rather strongly a few months ago.

Trotter Could you define specifically the role you do play on the Dallas city council and your relationship to the city manager and his staff?

Wise Well, with the city council, as I say, I am the leader of the council, and as far as the actual council meetings themselves are concerned, which are only the top of the iceberg, I am the man who wields the gavel, the man who directs the council proceedings. I think that where the real function of a mayor, in regards to the councilmen, is concerned, is on certain issues which may come up at any given time, to actually provide the leadership and guidance that he, the mayor, feels is necessary to achieve a goal. For example, the previous city council on which I served as a councilman was accused of vacillating somewhat in the building of our new city hall—the municipal administration building. When I came on as mayor, I charged the council with the responsibility of getting off dead center and told them that I felt it was our duty as the elected representatives of the city of Dallas, to move one way or the other—either give up the city hall or definitely commit ourselves to move forward on it, to open the bids; and if the bids did not come in within the specified amount that the people had already voted on, then to put whatever overrun was necessary in the then coming bond issue which is now passed. It did not become necessary to ask the public for any additional funds, since the advertised bids were under the amount which had already been voted by the public. But I think it was important for the mayor in this case to exert that leadership, and I did so. There are quite a few other examples. Again, the housing ordinance would be an example of that.

In relation to the city manager, we have a very close liaison. We converse daily as to the operational end of the city government, that is, his end, and the policy-making, leadership end of the city government, which is my end. We have a close coordination and a very excellent working relationship. Again, I'll try to give you an example to be specific on that, such as the case of the desegregation and/or busing issue, as you will, of some year ago. When it became something of a crisis, not just to Dallas, but in many different cities of the country, we met regularly, and he told me regularly what liaison or what the information he was getting from the school board (which is not under our city government), what information he was getting from the school administration, and what intelligence he was getting from the police department as to whether there was any racial strife or racial turmoil evolving. I, in turn, communicated to the city council this information, and our policy in regards to this whole thing was evolved; and we became an intervenor in the suit of the Dallas School Board with the Fifth Circuit Court of Appeals. So here again, there is a very close, and has to be a very close, liaison; but generally speaking, I consider the city manager the nuts-and-bolts operator of the city. The mayor is the leader of the policy-making body in our form of government.

Trotter Dallas is the only city of the ten largest cities in the United States to have a council-manager form of government. Do you feel this structure is adequate for Dallas now and in the future?

Wise I think there are going to have to be some rather dramatic adjustments to what we have known in the past. When the original council-manager form of government was instituted here some 35 to 40 years ago, the mayor was probably primarily a ribbon-cutter, speech-maker, and ceremonial figurehead. But this is no longer the case, nor could it be any longer the case. I think there is going to have to be a re-examination of both the pay structure and the matter of time consumed by a mayor in this type of government. We're in an era of younger mayors. Examples of this in addition to myself are Mayor Richard Lugar of Indianapolis, Mayor Moon Landrieu of New Orleans, Mayor Sam Massell of Atlanta—all of major, rising cities; Mayor Wilson in San Diego is probably an even better example. As we find ourselves in the middle of that era, younger people are not as likely to be independently wealthy as the mayors of other years in the history of Dallas have been—who could afford unlimited amounts of time from their personal affairs or personal business. In my case, for example, where I have my own public relations firm and export company, which are both starting companies, it is very difficult to carry on a business and continue serving as mayor of the city of Dallas on $50 a week or $50 a meeting. So there is going to have to be some adjustment there. What I've suggested is that after my term or terms of office are through, I would then like to sit down with the other former mayors living in the city of Dallas and try to come up with an answer to that situation, to something more reasonable.

Another problem here is that you run the risk of having certain accusations or conflicts of interest. Even though no conflicts may exist, you run the risk of having such conflicts or being accused of such conflicts; and this damages your image as the mayor of the community.

Another reason I think there is a trend toward younger mayors is, very frankly, because the strains of the office are such that it takes a younger, vigorous, more healthy person to withstand some of those rigors; and I think there are many older people who are not going to want to withstand those strains.

Trotter Your election as mayor represented a setback to the so-called "establishment" of Dallas. How do you explain your successful race for Mayor?

Wise Well, I don't think there is any question but what the fact that I had been in radio and television here for some number of years and had name identification to begin with was a definite plus-factor. However, it should be emphasized that many more people with television-radio backgrounds run for public office and lose than do run for public office and win. As a matter of fact, one of my opponents was a man who had been in television here much longer than I, and he came out, I believe, if I'm not mistaken, seventh in a nine-man field. So you still have to have plenty besides that name identification, and I did have what I consider to be a very strong record: first, when I ran for the city council; second, in civic affairs both preceding my city council term and including the city council term. And so when the accusation came up during the campaign, as it did, as I expected it to, that I was a TV talker, and my opponent said he was a doer, all I had to do was point to my record to prove that in addition to the television image, I also had a record to fall back on, and I think this was convincing. The people of Dallas, I believe, were somewhat disenchanted with the conception that a small handful of men controlled the fortunes of the city. I don't know whether this was true or not. All I know is it is not true now, and it has not been since I have been mayor.

I campaigned on the basis and I still feel this way—even more so perhaps—that it was important that an independent outside of the organization, i.e., the Citizens Charter Association, should be on every city council. And, indeed, in the runoff I pointed out that I was their last chance—the electorate's last chance—to provide an independent and that the office of mayor should not be a closed office for just a small group of wealthy businessmen. I pointed out that I was an average businessman, an average man, and could better relate to the silent majority—the blacks, the youth, and some of the dissident elements of our community. I feel that way even more strongly now.

So, I think I had some pluses going for me; and, of course, the minuses were the fact that I did not have the unlimited amounts of campaign funds that my opponents had.

Frankly, in the coming re-election, or the coming election for my re-election, if I decide to run, I don't think I will have as much opposition from the so-called "establishment" as might have been expected. It really doesn't matter to me one way or the other whether they run anybody against me, which it's rumored they don't intend to now. It really doesn't make any difference to me because my campaign would not be predicated upon opposition from a particular organization like that. I do think it has been very important for the "image" of the city of Dallas to have an average man in this office. I think it has helped to destroy, and indeed, I have tried aggressively to destroy, the image of this being a closely-held city. I know it is not because there is no man who can pick up the telephone and call me and tell me what decision to make, and the people of Dallas know that.

Trotter Could you relate briefly what your relationship is now to the CCA?

Wise It is healthy, but probably distant. I don't have any ambitions to run on the Citizens Charter Association ticket. I would accept their endorsement, even though I don't know whether it would be particularly beneficial to me; in fact, it might not be. But I have always maintained I would accept the endorsement of any legitimate organization, and that would have to include the CCA as well as the AFL-CIO, NAACP, etc. I needed everybody's help in passing this 172 million dollar bond issue. The fact that it passed overwhelmingly was due to both the so-called establishment and the silk stocking group support. I don't hesitate a second to pick up the telephone and call a member of the Citizens Charter Association or the Dallas Citizens Council or the "establishment" and ask for advice, and they respond very well indeed. Nor do I hesitate to do the same thing, though, and this is very important, with the people who support me and who voted for me. I feel like I am the mayor of all the people. I would say that the relationship could be summed up as cordial, but somewhat distant; but nevertheless, cooperative for what is good for the city of Dallas.

Trotter What are the major issues confronting Dallas today as you see them?

Wise: Probably still about the ones which I made the main issues during the campaign. Crime in the streets is certainly a main concern; and I'm very proud that Dallas was one of the eight cities selected for the LEAA High Impact crime grant of 20 million dollars over a three-year period, which is even a lot of money by Dallas standards.

Pollution continues to be a consideration; and I put recreation in with pollution because, for example, where water pollution of the Trinity is certainly a principal concern, an even greater concern to me is the navigation of the Trinity to provide water and recreation for people who couldn't afford it. Free recreation would be provided by the town lake, which would be largely dependent on the Trinity canal project and the town lake concept right outside of downtown Dallas, which would make Dallas an especially beautiful city—even more beautiful than it already is, in my opinion. Air pollution continues to be a concern, although Dallas is very fortunate in that respect. We have neither prevailing winds nor mountain ranges to hold in our air. We do have to look toward rapid transit though, both for that reason and for relief of downtown traffic glut.

Another issue is the polarization of young and old, of black and white, and Mexican-American segments of our community. I think it has improved greatly and I think that has occurred over the last year and four months of my administration. I feel that one of the reasons it is improved is that they genuinely feel I am accessible. They know I am available every Wednesday afternoon to anybody that walks in. I often go into the communities to take a look at the specific problems. So I think the polarization continues to be a problem, but I think we are working very well on it indeed.

And of course the economy and taxes are certainly a concern. I'm very proud of the city manager's work and the city council's determination to have no tax increase this year. I think it is remarkable that this city council provided the leadership to pass a 172-million-dollar bond issue and turned right around in a few days and came up with the biggest budget by far in the history of the city of Dallas—over 200 million dollars—that would not necessitate a tax increase. Now, of course, that bond issue is going to necessitate a slight tax increase three or four years from now. But I think it is remarkable that, at the same time we wanted to have progress, we also determined that we should watch the economy and keep the taxes down or hold the line on taxes. The person on a fixed income certainly has his back to the wall, and we have to seriously look at the whole property tax structure to be sure that this is really an equitable tax for all segments of the community. I doubt that it is, and to my way of thinking, there has to be a re-thinking of the total tax structure including the federal income tax, school taxes, and on down the line. The property tax may truly be an inequitable tax.

I was appointed to the Urban Financial Affairs Committee of the U.S. Conference of Mayors for my work and my determination in this area. I think it is a major committee assignment which I take very seriously because we've got to put our best brains forward to come up with a solution that will be fair, particularly to the underprivileged and give them the opportunity to pick themselves up by their bootstraps and get ahead. Also taxes have to be fairer to that tremendous swath of our community, the middle- or average-income man who really is probably getting the worst deal right now in taxation.

So, I would think revenue sharing would be a big help. Of course, I think that the city of Dallas has done a good job, but must continue to do a good job in really economizing on the city level.

6-2 ALTERNATIVE METHODS OF ELECTING CITY COUNCILS IN TEXAS HOME RULE CITIES

Philip W. Barnes

During every two-to-four-year period, voters in Texas' 185 home rule cities go to the polls and elect almost 1,000 city councilmen.[1] Collectively, these elected officials represent 7.5 million Texans, or about 70 per cent of the state's population. As councilmen, they are called upon to decide a myriad of questions. Texas city councils hire and fire city managers and other municipal officials, authorize contracts of various sorts, approve the granting of easements, extend city boundaries, set utility rates, and tax and spend according to their perceptions of the public interest. These public bodies are ultimately responsible for the management of our cities; so their decisions are important. Also important are the ways in which these public representatives are chosen for their jobs, for political institutions tend to shape the decisions city councils make. This article will describe

From *Public Affairs Comment*, Vol. XVI (Austin, Tex.: Institute of Public Affairs, The University of Texas at Austin, May, 1970), pp. 1-4. This is an abridged version. Reprinted by permission.

the alternative methods used to elect city councils in Texas home rule cities, review the arguments for and against the different electoral systems, and offer some suggestions for making existing electoral systems more representative.

THE REFORM MOVEMENT

All 185 home rule cities in Texas are reform cities, for all practical purposes. There are 176 council-manager cities; 148 are of the home rule type. Traditional partisan elections are almost unknown, and only four home rule cities operate under the ward system. Why is this so? One answer is suggested by the history of the growth of Texas' urban population. Unlike many states, Texas experienced early urbanization almost free of in-migration from other parts of the country. In their formative years, Texas cities were populated by immigrants from Texas farms and rural areas. Moreover, urbanization has occurred primarily between 1900 and 1960.[2] Two conclusions are suggested: first, most Texas cities were settled while and after the reform movement swept the country, with its emphasis on manager government, nonpartisan "politics," and at-large elections. Second, few of the people urbanizing the state brought with them established notions of how a city should be governed. Not surprisingly, then, the municipal reform movement found fertile soil in Texas. The pervasiveness of the reform movement is seen in the number of council-manager cities in Texas and in the number of Texas home rule cities that employ at-large electoral systems.

ALTERNATIVE ELECTORAL SYSTEMS

Historically, there are two basic systems of electing city councils: election by ward and election at-large. There are, however, several variations of each. Altogether there are six distinct electoral systems used in Texas home rule cities. The traditional ward system is patterned after the legislative model; each councilman is elected from a designated geographical area of the city by the qualified voters of the area or ward. The traditional at-large system, on the other hand, requires all members of the city council to be elected by the voters of the entire city. Thus, if there are five places on the council, the five candidates receiving the most votes are elected. Election by ward and at-large represent the two extremes among the systems discussed here. Table 1 is constructed to place each of the variations of these two basic systems on a scale, thus indicating their relative position to each of the others.

The most notable variation of the at-large system found in Texas cities is the place system. Among Texas cities of all sizes, the place system is the most widely used. It requires that each of the seats on the city council be assigned a number, such as a Place No. 1, No. 2, etc.; candidates are elected at-large for a particular place. The place system does have an impact on electoral politics, for it tends to pair candidates against each other. In many cases, elections for particular places are won uncontested, something that is impossible in simple at-large systems, assuming there are more candidates than seats on the council.[3]

TABLE 1
Basic electoral systems used in Texas home rule cities

At-Large Systems

Traditional At-Large System. All councilmen are elected at-large by the qualified voters of the entire city; the candidates receiving the most votes are elected, up to the number of seats to be filled.

Place System. All councilmen are elected at-large for specific places on the council.

Place System with Residency Requirements, Modified. All councilmen are elected at-large by the place system: candidates for some of the places must live in designated geographical areas of the city.

Place System with Residency Requirements. All councilmen are elected at-large by the place system: candidates for each place on the council must live in designated geographical areas of the city.

Ward Systems

Modified Ward System. Some councilmen are elected by wards, some are elected at-large by the place system.

Traditional Ward System. All councilmen are elected from designated geographical areas of the city.

Election at-large with a residency requirement is another variation. It is, in fact, a modification of the place system. Each candidate runs for a specific place on the council, but candidates must live in specified areas of the city. Even though all candidates are elected at-large, the residency requirement restricts candidates to given geographical areas. Therefore, they tend to reflect more accurately the social characteristics of those areas.

Table 2 displays the number of Texas cities, broken down by populations, using the various electoral systems. The preponderance of the at-large systems is clearly indicated. Among cities of 25,000 population or more, the place system is preferred to all others. As the table shows, the place system and the traditional at-large system dominate all cities in every population category. This is additional evidence of the pervasiveness of the reform movement in Texas. Because of the widespread use of at-large elections, it is necessary to examine some of the arguments favoring their use.

EVALUATING ELECTORAL SYSTEMS

The arguments for and against ward and at-large elections have appeared in the literature for many years.[4] Most people who favor ward elections are generally opposed to at-large systems and vice versa. Indeed, the arguments for and against various electoral systems are almost inextricably interwoven with arguments for

TABLE 2
Distribution of electoral systems used in Texas home rule cities: by population

Method of Election	Over 100,000	25,000-100,000	10,000-25,000	Under 10,000	Total
At-large system	2	10	28	27	67
Place system	7	16	29	25	77
Place system with residency requirements, modified	2	5	3	0	10
Place system with residency requirements	2	6	7	5	20
Modified ward system	0	0	1	1	2
Ward system	0	0	2	2	4
Totals	13	37	70	60	180[a]

Source: Institute of Public Affairs Questionnaire (1968) and home rule city charters.
[a]Information for five cities is unavailable.

and against various forms of municipal government, particularly the mayor-council and council-manager forms.

Since ward systems antedate at-large electoral systems, supporters of at-large elections begin by criticizing the use of wards. They argue that ward elections tend to accentuate social differences in the city and prevent the city council from developing a broad view of the city's interests. Ward elections, the critics continue, lead to log-rolling legislative tactics, large unwieldy councils, gerrymandering of election districts, and the election of "little men," i.e., those with narrow vision, incapable of seeing the city's interests as a whole. At-large elections, the proponents argue, have none of the limitations of the ward system; they tend to promote "better men" to office, those with "broad vision." Hence, parochialism is overcome and the interests of the city are protected. Moreover, at-large elections and small city councils are coordinate parts of the council-manager plan and are defended as essential to manager government.

As indicated, the critics of at-large elections are prone to favor the ward system. They point to the importance of providing an institutional forum for the expression of cultural, class, or ethnic differences in representative government. They contend that the reformers are impatient with the parochialism and perhaps also the "lack of polish and education" of many councilmen elected by the ward system. Those who favor ward elections maintain that this attitude—when coupled with at-large elections—sublimates basic community differences and virtually assures a one-sided control of government by a majority party or dominant group in the community. Because the electoral system is less representative of the genuine differences in the population, the city council is less responsive to community demands. Too, the "better man" argument has come under attack for its implicit class bias.[5]

What about the other electoral systems found in Texas? Since the place system does not reflect neighborhood diversities, it is the subject of criticisms similar to those directed at at-large elections.[6] However, the modified ward system and the two at-large systems that incorporate residency requirements are attempts at some compromise between the characteristics of ward and at-large election systems. Although all maintain some elements of at-large elections, each attempts to provide an institutional mechanism for reflecting community differences.

NOTES

1. The Texas Constitution, Art. 11, Sec. 5, provides for home rule cities. Any city of 5,000 or more population may adopt a city charter incorporating a government of its own design, so long as the charter is not inconsistent with any provisions of the Constitution or the General Laws of the State of Texas. All other towns and cities are governed under the General Laws.
2. Harley L. Browning, "Urban Population Trends and Changes," in *Proceedings of the Fifteenth Governmental Accounting and Finance Institute* (Austin, Tex.: Institute of Public Affairs, The University of Texas, 1969), pp. 20-27.
3. Roy E. Young, *The Place System in Texas Elections* (Austin, Tex.: Institute of Public Affairs, The University of Texas, 1965), p. 29.
4. Most of the textbooks in the field review the basic arguments for and against ward and at-large electoral systems. See, for example, Banfield and Wilson, *op. cit.*, pp. 87-100.
5. W. L. Miller, *The Fifteenth Ward and the Great Society* (Boston: Houghton Mifflin, 1966), pp. 39-40.
6. See Young, *op. cit.*, pp. 33-34, for a summary of the arguments for and against the place system.

6-3
THE WATER DISTRICT CONSPIRACIES
Harvey Katz

The water district conspiracy is an example of the high public cost paid for private gain. A water district in Texas is a quasi-public body created to finance and manage development of an area that lies outside a municipal jurisdiction.

Ordinarily, if residents of such an area wished to obtain municipal-type services, they would be required to hire a private contractor and pay him themselves. This, of course, would involve a substantial cash outlay for the residents. The water district offers a much more attractive alternative. Such a district has authority to issue public bonds. The revenue from the bond is used to develop the area and the bond debt is paid off gradually, in some cases over a period as long as thirty years. The district can tax the residents in the area in order to collect the funds with which to pay off the debt. And the district provides a central management for all municipal-type affairs that affect the district.

The original objective of the legislation creating this type of entity, passed early in the twentieth century, was to facilitate development of farm irrigation projects in rural areas. During the suburb boom following World War II, however, the water district concept was extended to include development of modern residential services such as sewers and water lines. Some water districts also provide firefighting and police protection services. Despite these modern touches, however, the theory behind these entities has supposedly remained unchanged through the century—that is, a cheap, convenient method for residents and landowners to provide themselves with services which their local government would supply if they had one. And the Texas statute books contain numerous provisions that are designed to implement the water district as an instrument by, of, and for residential landowners.

Under these statutes, a water district is created only after a petition from a majority of landowners is approved by a local court. The landowners must then hold an election for the district's board of directors. If public bonds are to be issued, this also must be submitted for approval of all landowners. Actions of the district must be recorded and filed with the court and the State Water Rights Commission. Scattered throughout these statutes are protective provisions requiring court hearings for various actions of the district, opportunities for appeals by unhappy residents, notices to all residents, audit reports to courts and state agencies, and so forth. If all those provisions were effective, they would be most worthwhile. But a water district is granted a great deal of authority, and it generally operates far from the public eye. Thus, there is a very real danger of that authority falling into the wrong hands or being directed toward the wrong objectives. The statute books seem to provide adequate protections against such threats. Unfortunately, those protections seldom extend beyond the paper on which they are written.

In 1969 close to one hundred water districts were created in the state of Texas without the benefit of landowner petitions, court supervision, or rights of appeal. The directors of these districts were selected without elections. In many other respects, such districts could completely ignore the statutory provisions that were enacted to protect the public from misuse of public power. In every case, this special status was obtained from the Texas legislature by means of a special bill that created the district and set forth a long list of exemptions from protective laws. Directors of the district were named in the bill, and they were given wide authority to use the district's public powers without approval of landowners and residents in the area. These creatures of the legislature are designated "municipal utility districts" in order to avoid confusing them with water districts subject to various statutory protections. The bills that create them originate in the House of Representatives and are sponsored by state representatives who are on very good terms with the House leadership. These bills are automatically assigned to the "consent calendar," which means that they ordinarily fly through the legislature without the benefit of committee hearing or record vote.

More than half of the utility districts created by the Texas legislature have been in areas surrounding the city of Houston (Harris County).

"It's no secret around here," a state representative told me, "if you're selected to sponsor one of those water bills, you get a fat campaign contribution for the next election. The most common figure is $750." According to a Houston contractor: "At one time, I was thinking of getting a utility district for an area. I went to a lawyer here—I can't tell you his name—and he told me right off that it would cost me two thousand bucks just to get the bill passed. Half for him and half for the representative who would sponsor the bill. And that didn't include other legal work he'd probably have to do." An employee of the State Water Rights Commission told me: "You hear it too much for it to be just a rumor. Two thousand dollars, split between the lawyer and the sponsor of the bill."

From these and similar statements, from court records and documents filed with state agencies, the pieces of a very ingenious scheme begin to emerge and fit together. It seems to work like this: A real estate developer who wants to finance residential construction by means of a utility district contacts a water district lawyer and plunks down his cash. The lawyer is compiling a list of districts he intends to create during the next legislative session. He selects a few candidates for the House and reaches an understanding with them regarding the passage of water district bills. Part of the deal is that, come what may, the legislator will remain on good terms with the House leadership throughout the session.

The bill that results from this private arrangement exempts the water district from most regulation and names the district's board of directors. Most often, this is a token list, devised to camouflage the real interests behind the district. The initial directors will usually step aside, after accepting a small payment for the use of their names. Many times, this payment is in the form of a piece of land within the district. On occasion, the initial list is really the permanent board of directors. In such cases, the real estate developer will have a representative on the board to protect his interests.

Many water districts that were annexed by Texas municipalities issued large amounts of public bonds just before annexation. Sometimes the bond revenue was used to complete construction that lagged until the district promoters were assured that the debt would be assumed by all taxpayers. One district annexed by Houston spent much of its initial bond revenue, designated for sewage construction, on some very questionable items, including a recreation hall, an office building, travel expenses for district board members, a fire station, and contributions to several local charities. Prospective home buyers saw a nice little community which, unbeknownst to them, had no sewer or water lines. Just before it was annexed, the district issued enough public bonds to provide funds for these essentials. The city of Houston took over the entire debt. There is, of course, no guarantee that the revenue from those last-minute bond issues will be pumped into the district's sewer system. As long as the developer is in control, he can direct the district directors to dispose of those funds in other ways—salaries, legal fees and a variety of conduits to the pockets of the developer and his friends. If such transactions do occur, they are buried beneath tons of figures inscribed in water district ledgers by employees of the real estate developer.

In 1950, a group of residents and real estate developers created Water Control and Improvement District No. 24 on the outskirts of Houston. Not much was done with the district until a man by the name of Frank Sharp bought out just about everyone else and set out to create Sharpstown. This was in 1954. Around the same time, the Houston City Council was considering a grand plan to annex large areas to the city. One of the council members was Louis Welch, who later became mayor. Welch and Sharp were good friends even then. In 1956, the council decided to annex Sharpstown along with several other water districts. A few months before the annexation, Sharp's district suddenly issued $7,300,000 in public bonds, raising the total bond debt to $11,000,000. All of this was assumed by the city. Houston officials are still sorting through the records. But it appears that very little of that bond revenue was left by the time annexation was effected. The last of it probably went on the day before annexation, when directors of the water district authorized $600,000 in expenditures, including a $50,000 legal fee to Cyril B. Smith.

The water district that later became Sharpstown was not created by the Texas legislature, but by petition and court approval. It is apparent, therefore, that full blame for the water district fiasco does not fall on the Austin Capitol. Real estate developers must obtain the cooperation of a number of people to make the scheme work, whether a particular water district is created by special legislation or court petition. In either case, mayors, city councilmen, contractors, lawyers, clerks, and many others must lend active support or perhaps just close their eyes to the obvious. During the late 1940s and early 1950s, Texas real estate developers established strong ties with the conservative Democrats and, since then, they have not hesitated to seek the help of their political friends. Even more important, the real estate people work together much more frequently than they do in competition with one another. They become partners in water districts, split up construction work, and aid each other when needed.

The water district conspirators have not been obtaining their legal advice from sleazy shysters, but from the cream of the Texas legal establishment. And the conspirators themselves are hardly disreputable types. If you add up all the land and banks and political friends of people like Frank Sharp and Walter Mischer, you have a pretty awesome social and political force. Since that force operates mostly in the shadows, it is very difficult for the average person to estimate accurately its scope and strength. But the water district conspiracy does provide a valuable clue. As evidenced by Frank Sharp's manipulation of the Sharpstown district, the land promoters could have operated successfully under existing statutes—finding the loopholes, skirting the protective provisions, and plucking favors from mayors and councilmen whenever necessary. But all this meant a lot of time and trouble. A broad governmental license from the legislature simply made things a lot easier.

Once men like Frank Sharp manage to cut themselves loose from the system and raise themselves above it, all the limits disappear. What use are protective laws when the perverters can obtain exemptions whenever they please? And how can we possibly know where the power of those people ends when there seems to be no institution that is too sacred to become their pawn? When the water district conspirators began to make their big move, they could reach above the laws and regulations that applied to everyone else, seize a chunk of the legislature's terrible power, and use it to accomplish their very private aims at public expense.

And they did.

6-4
TEXAS REGIONALISM–FUTURE PERSPECTIVES
John A. Gronouski

THE TEXAS EXPERIENCE

As early as 1965, the state government of Texas assumed a supportive posture toward COGs. Present state policy is aimed at strengthening local general-purpose government within the framework of a state-regional-local partnership. Councils of governments, rather than more traditional areawide agencies designed to serve narrow functional interests, are increasingly being called upon to carry out areawide health, transportation, criminal justice, and law-enforcement planning and development activities required or encouraged by the federal government. This vesting of responsibilities in councils of government has provided an institutional setting for local elected officials to negotiate with one another and with state and federal officials from a position of collective strength.

One measure of Texas' leadership is its technical assistance to COGs in the field of administrative management. In February, 1972, the Governor issued the first *Uniform Program Management and Accounting System Manual* for use by all Texas Regional councils.

The state's commitment is also reflected in the provision of $3.2 million of direct dollar support to councils of governments since 1965. This represented 14 per cent of their total resources during this period. The national average of direct state dollar support is only 5 per cent. For 1971, state funds allocated to Texas COGs totaled $612,751. Moreover, state departments and agencies with major functional responsibilities have often demonstrated a willingness to organize and deliver services on a regional basis. It is likely that councils will continue to

From *Public Affairs Comment,* Vol. XVIII (Austin, Tex.: Institute of Public Affairs, The University of Texas at Austin, February, 1972), pp. 1-5. This is an abridged version. Reprinted by permission.

be involved in the development of new or expanded service delivery systems.

It is also useful to note the extent to which local elected officials participate in COG governance. State officials consistently have stressed the importance of control by general-purpose local governments through their elected representatives. Approximately 84 per cent of the members of COG governing bodies are elected officials, and the vast majority of these are from city and county governments.

Through state leadership, particularly in the development phases, Texas COGs now include within their jurisdiction all of the state's 24 SMSAs and over 90 per cent of its eleven million people. The state's rural areas as well as its large urban complexes, such as the Dallas, Houston, and San Antonio areas, are now represented in regional forums. Fifteen of Texas' 24 COGs have service-area populations of less than 300,000, and some of these cover a geographical area equal to some states. Thus, a majority of Texas COGs reflect the rural heritage of the state; many of them deal primarily with problems of rural constituents. The fact that the regional council concept has considerable potential for coping with rural problems as well as those of metropolitan and urban areas is sometimes overlooked.

These positive signs should not suggest that Texas COGs are immune from problems similar to those facing regional councils elsewhere. There is evidence of dissatisfaction with COG performance on the part of member governments. There have been instances of financial support being withheld by local governments that are nominally COG members. Often simmering beneath the public consciousness in every major Texas city is racial discontent which could materially affect the character of Texas COGs, as it has affected regional councils elsewhere.

There are also questions of organization and authority that must be met and solved. While COGs are organizations of member governments, they must stand beside their member governments "as full partners in the processes of government." These questions of organizational structure and role identification become critical as COGs attempt to implement regional plans, establish an adequate local financial base, and provide for a governing body which is representative of their member governments and the people in the region whom they serve.

In response to these problems, the Sixty-second Texas Legislature, at the request of the Governor, increased the 1971-73 state appropriation for COGs, while altering the funding formula to reduce local matching requirement, and extended the scope of review and comment activities presently carried out in accordance with federal legislative and administration guidelines to include state-aided projects and programs of regional significance. Clearly, the evolving posture of state government—as well as that of the national government—will have an important influence on the development of COGs as effective instruments of regional governance.

CONCLUSIONS

Several years ago Norman Beckman referred to regional councils as "the silent revolution within intergovernmental relations."[1] The revolution is not so silent any longer and is being gradually carried out by federal, state, and local officials within existing political processes. The growth noted in regional organizations reflects the fact that citizens of Texas' larger metropolitan areas, as well as its rural areas, are increasingly a part of a definable areawide polity with shared interests. Local political boundaries begin to take on a new meaning as national and state programs dealing with education, land use, pollution control, environmental protection, transportation, welfare, law enforcement, and criminal justice systems take into account regional considerations. National and state finance, court decisions, program requirements and service delivery systems are likely to be thought of in areawide terms, rather than within existing political boundaries, as we attempt to resolve pressing urban problems.

The basic public policy shift that has occurred in Texas and in almost every other state underscores the fact that regionalism in some form is here to stay. This decade will see great strides and equally great failures until the regional revolution finds its place in inter-governmental history. One of the most significant questions to be answered is whether "grass roots democracy" can be retained and strengthened at the local government and neighborhood levels within a viable regional framework. Equally important, a regional approach to the solution of urban problems will gain greater acceptance if it can be demonstrated that development of successful regional delivery systems also will serve to improve the effectiveness of local government.

In the regional revolution, as in all other aspects of domestic public life, the genius of the American federal system lies in its ability to accommodate changes in public direction, the substance of public programs, and even governmental organization over time. Implementation of change tends to be uneven and sporadic in a pluralistic system, and the precise role and structural form of regional organization will continue to vary from state to state and region to region. This is the way it should and must be as elected representatives at every level struggle to comprehend fully and deal with the complex problems now on the national domestic agenda.

NOTE

1. Address by Norman Beckman before the National Conference of the American Society for Public Administration, Miami Beach, Florida, May 21, 1969.

6-5
THE UNHOLY TRINITY INCIDENT
Dave McNeely and Lyke Thompson

In 1965, with the help of then-President Lyndon B. Johnson, the Trinity River Project was authorized for construction. The project was to include the canal,

Dave McNeely and Lyke Thompson write for the *Dallas Morning News.* This is an abridged version of their article which was originally published in *Texas Monthly,* June, 1973, pp. 42-48. Reprinted by permission of *Texas Monthly.*

for what later was set as a cost of $1.1 billion. Other parts, totaling half a billion dollars, included stream channelization for four parts of the river, $135 million; a massive reservoir at Tennessee Colony midway down the river, $332 million; and a pipeline to carry water from Tennessee Colony back to Fort Worth for re-use, $109 million.

To transform the narrow, winding Trinity into a navigable river, the U.S. Army Corps of Engineers proposed 21 locks and three dams on the river to create a watery stairway of pools deep enough for barges with a nine-foot draft. It would have to be 200 feet wide so that barges going in opposite directions could pass each other. That meant at least doubling the width at its upper end, and straightening the bends so the barges (not the most maneuverable of vessels) would not have to twist and turn to follow the existing river. Bridges, of course, would have to be raised to allow room for barges to get under them. And so new bridges over the Trinity built since the late 1960's were built higher than they otherwise would have been; by early 1973, seven bridges had been constructed to accommodate the barge traffic expected to be moving under them by 1985.

The Corps said the canal would carry primarily sand and gravel, with iron, steel and grains making up most of the rest of the payloads. Sand and gravel are getting scarce in the Dallas-Fort Worth area, and it would be cheaper, the Corps said, to ship them by barge than by rail. Dallas doesn't have any heavy industry to speak of, so there would not have been much market for shipping out heavy finished goods.

The local sponsor for the federal project was the Trinity River Authority, a state agency whose directors are appointed by the governor of Texas. It has a somewhat interlocking relationship with the chamber-of-commerce style Trinity Improvement Association: Ben Carpenter and Amon Carter Jr. are on the boards of both groups; almost every director of the River Authority holds a similar position on the Improvement Association; and the River Authority's general manager, David Brune, is president of the Improvement Association. Among the canal's supporters were incumbent Dallas Congressmen Earle Cabell, a Democrat, and Jim Collins, a Republican; Fort Worth Congressman Jim Wright, a Democrat; newly elected Democratic Congressman Dale Milford of the new Mid-Cities Congressional District; Dallas Mayor Wes Wise; Fort Worth Mayor Sharkey Stovall; and virtually all of the Dallas downtown business establishment represented by the traditionally influential Citizens Charter Association. The pro-canal forces, listing virtually every traditional leader in Dallas among their supporters in large advertisements, were led by Tom Unis, a former Dallas City Councilman and former head of the powerful Citizens Charter Association.

During the late 1950's and on into the 1960's, a boy named Jim Bush was growing up in Kerens, Navarro County, a few miles from the Trinity. Bush hiked along the river, which cleansed itself to some extent of Dallas and Fort Worth pollution by the time it reached his home, 60 or 70 miles downriver. He and his friends fished in it, camped beside it, boated down it. They tramped through the forests that line its floodplains, trees left by farmers to keep their fields from washing away. Bush and his friends liked the river as it was.

In Dallas during those years, an owlish looking attorney, Ned Fritz, carried on a lonely battle trying to protect some of the natural areas in Dallas and the surrounding countryside from the ravages of development. When the Trinity project came up for congressional hearings in the mid-1960's, Fritz paid his way to Washington to testify against it. He talked of the beautiful spots downstream from Dallas, where hardwood forests left in the floodplains support plant communities and more wildlife than on upland areas. Below Lake Livingston, the once putrid water is almost clear as it courses between white sand banks and passes through portions of the Big Thicket. Fritz lost that battle, but he didn't give up the war.

By 1971, Jim Bush had gone on to Navarro County Junior College and began to think more and more about the proposed canal. He didn't like what he heard; he thought about the river he had enjoyed as a youngster, and what the proposed canal would do to it. He saw it as a great gouge through forests and farmlands, leaving much of the old river bed that he knew cut off from its sustaining flow. Bush decided that instead of dredging and straightening the river and scalping its forested banks to make a watery highway to Dallas for barge traffic, efforts should be directed at cleaning up the river and restoring it to a condition that other youngsters, years in the future, could enjoy as he had. Bush put together a group of students at the college to oppose the canal. They met that year with Mrs. Mary Wright, one of the leading Sierra Club members in Dallas. They shared their information about the river, and pondered the devastation to the ecology of the Trinity River that the canal would bring.

In the early spring of 1972, James F. White, a theology professor at SMU, hunched over his desk figuring up his income tax. He read the results of his unhappy computations, and figured he was working one day a week just to pay taxes. It is time, he decided, to cut down on all that pork-barrel boondoggling and wasteful federal spending that Richard Nixon talked about. White decided that he had one such boondoggle almost in his back yard: the proposed Trinity canal.

Don Smith, a young economics professor at SMU, puzzled over the cost accounting that had been applied to the Trinity project. Smith sports a mustache, owns a canoe, enjoys the outdoors, and wants to get his money's worth out of his tax dollars. He figured that the canal project would be economically profitable only if it were computed at the old rate of 3.5 per cent return on investments. If the Corps of Engineers calculated the benefits on the premise that the canal must return 10 per cent on its investment, as private industry computes its cost-benefit ratios, then the project would yield only 60 per cent of its original cost.

Henry Fulcher, a Dallas businessman and a Republican, thought government ought to be run on a basis that would provide the best possible return on government investment in public projects. He decided that the Trinity canal project was not wise economically.

On April 13, 1972, most of those people met at Don Smith's house, and formed an organization called Citizens Organization for a Sound Trinity (COST). They decided to do what they could to oppose canalization of the Trinity in Congress, where the project was coming up for funding consideration. In the spring of 1972, Mrs. Wright met a young man named Alan Steelman at a

Republican Women's Club gathering in Dallas. Steelman was seeking the Republican nomination in May to run against incumbent Congressman Earle Cabell in November. Mrs. Wright told Steelman about the Trinity River, and what it would do. Steelman listened—and nodded his head.

In 1964, Cabell had resigned as Dallas mayor to run a winning race for Congress, with one of his major pledges to bring the canal to Dallas. In 1972, he returned for his biennial endorsement by Dallas voters in his much-shrunken Northeast Dallas district. He was still, he said, 100 per cent for the canal.

Steelman had begun during the spring Republican primary to wonder aloud whether a bigger Dallas was necessarily a better one, and, after conversations with Mrs. Wright and others, whether Dallas needed barge transportation when the massive new regional airport between Dallas and Fort Worth was to begin operation in 1973. Heavy transportation is for heavy industry, Steelman said, which means pollution and crime. Steelman won the Republican nomination. Steelman dubbed the project a "billion-dollar ditch." Even with candidate Steelman on board, the opposition to the canal was still just a handful of relatively unknown people. Most Dallas residents didn't pay that much attention to it. The canal seemed one of those things that would probably be built, since everyone more or less assumed all along that it would. But in October, at a hearing of home owners fighting the Corps-planned channelization of Garland's Duck Creek, Trinity River Authority manager Brune let it slip that there would have to be a local bond issue to provide starter money for the canal.

The canal was now going to cost $1.6 billion. But to show their good faith and interest, as well as to account for their expected benefits, the 17 counties along the river were going to have to put up $150 million in seed money. Ten per cent down, and Uncle Sam would pick up the rest. But it was the first time that citizens in Dallas knew that the project was going to require some money from *their* pockets. All of a sudden it was a whole new ballgame. At a time when inflation had brought wage and price controls, when President Richard Nixon was calling for trimming wasteful federal spending, when Dallas' aerospace industry had fallen off with the cutback of the SuperSonic Transport, when belts were being tightened on many fronts, the canal seemed increasingly like largesse to many people—especially if they were going to have to dig into their own pockets to help pay for it. Then came Steelman's upset victory over Cabell with an unexpectedly high 56 per cent of the vote. Canal supporters read that weathervane with a definite feeling of queasiness. Could it be the canal might *not* happen? Not good, not good, the Dallas establishment could see. Better get to work and let the folks know how important this is to them, how important for *Dallas.* And so the big push started, and Unis was chosen to head it up.

The COST forces later applauded the choice of Unis for the lead role in selling the canal. He adopted the traditional Dallas "Big Daddy" downtown business leader approach: Don't ask questions; you don't need all that information to cast your vote. What's good for the downtown business folks is good for you. Always has been. Always will be. The COST forces later said that Unis' rasping criticism of canal opponents as "environmental extremists" won more active opponents to the canal project every time Unis uttered it. City councilmen in some of Dallas' suburbs said later they had been turned off on the canal by Unis' paternalistic attitude.

After it became obvious a local bond vote was necessary, and the Steelman victory had indicated at least a twinge of doubt about the canal project in voters' minds, COST shifted its focus from Washington to Dallas. Although the project had been tentatively authorized by Congress, before it could be built further study and appropriations hearings were necessary to clear the project for full construction allocations. Those hearings had been considered mere formalities. But the COST people made sure that it was made known that there were some people in the Trinity valley who weren't gung-ho for the canal.

Complaints that prophets of ecological doom like Fritz had made for years began to re-emerge. And lo and behold, even some semi-official sources of information began to bear him out. Environmental hearings on the project did not go smoothly. Environmentalists called the canal economically and environmentally unsound—"welfare for the rich." A representative of the Texas Parks and Wildlife Department said the project would cause "wholesale devastation" to the environment. (Two weeks before the canal bond vote, the parks department reversed its stand, apparently under the urging of Gov. Dolph Briscoe, who according to environmentalists brought pressure on the department at the behest of Ben Carpenter.)

Opponents of the canal argued that the Trinity canal idea was once necessary to help the heavy cotton market in Dallas avoid high railroad freight rates. But the shift to synthetic fibers, the interlacing of the Dallas area with interstate highways, and the growth of Dallas as the finance, banking and insurance capital of the Southwest, they said, made water transportation unnecessary. With those arguments in mind, the opponents asked *who* would benefit from the canal. It was learned that eight of the 24 River Authority directors had land holdings in the Trinity watershed. In addition, major utility companies represented on the board had holdings in the area.

By then the canal project backers were getting downright nervous. They decided to move as quickly as possible and set the bond vote before the canal opposition could develop additional strength. They set the vote on Tuesday, March 13—passing up an opportunity to hold it April 3 in conjunction with city council elections in Dallas and Fort Worth and several other cities, or on April 7, when the Dallas school board elections and several smaller city elections would be held. River Authority director Brune said the early date was necessary to demonstrate local funding support for the project before Congress went into appropriations hearings. He said the election was purposely held separately from any other elections because the Authority felt the people should not have the issue clouded with any other electoral matters.

The canal backers put together an advertising and promotion show reminiscent of bringing a new cigaret on the market. Brochures, billboards, testimonials from every Congressman in the area (except Steelman), a gala kickoff celebration with music and banners—the works. The estimated cost of the campaign was half a million dollars. COST went into action, too, although on a much smaller scale. The March 13 election date fell two weeks before an environmental impact study on the Trinity project was due to be released by the Corps of Engineers, and a few months before a revised Corps cost study was to be released. The COST troops insisted, with effectiveness, that voters were being asked by the business establishment to cast their votes blind—because they would never approve the project if they saw what it would cost and what it would do to the environment. A favorite COST slogan was "Your money, their canal."

In the midst of the campaign a federal court handed down a decision casting a large shadow over the entire Trinity project. Several groups—the Sierra Club, the Houston Sportsmen's Club, the Houston Audubon Society, the Texas Shrimp Association—and two fishermen had filed suit in September, 1971, in Houston challenging construction of the Wallisville reservoir project at the mouth of the Trinity. They charged that the Corps, by proceeding with plans for the Wallisville Dam (vital to the whole canal project), had failed to draw up an environmental impact statement, as the law required. Environmentalists said this project at the mouth of the Trinity would destroy the prime nursery grounds for shrimp, crabs and menhaden in one of the nation's most productive bays, resulting in an annual decline in fish catches of 7 million pounds. Although the Wallisville project had been funded separately from the rest of the Trinity project, they charged it was a vital link in the canal plans and therefore the ecological impact of the whole project should be judged before one of its parts was allowed to be built. Federal District Judge Carl O. Bue refused to stop the $24 million project at that time, but also refused to dismiss the suit.

On February 15, 1973, a cold Saturday morning, Steelman and Fritz and several other environmentally-minded folks huddled under a bridge on the Trinity River near Liberty. They had camped nearby the night before, and were preparing to take a canoe trip down the Trinity so Fritz could show Steelman how the proposed canal would devastate nature in the Big Thicket area. But Mother Nature herself had intervened with Fritz's plan. The temperature that morning was slightly below freezing, and flakes of snow wafted down from the leaden sky. An omen, perhaps? Mother Nature turning against those doing battle in her name?

A television crew that had come to film the departure brought a newspaper from Houston. The new arrivals asked if Fritz and Steelman had heard the news. What news? Steelman grabbed the paper, and read aloud to the shivering throng that Judge Bue on Friday had told the Corps it had not satisfied legal requirements for a comprehensive environmental impact statement on the Wallisville project. Although the dam was then 72 per cent complete, Bue said the Corps had to stop working on it until it considered the environmental impact of the whole project. And Bue scolded the Corps for "super-salesmanship" in promoting the project. The crowd cheered. Steelman told the television interviewers that this certainly emphasized what he and other canal opponents had been saying all along.

Dan Weiser, a liberal Democrat who makes a hobby of studying election returns, said that the canal opponents figured that if they could get 56 per cent in Dallas County, break even in Tarrant County (Fort Worth), then they could afford to lose 70-30 in the other 15 down-river counties that would vote on the project. A majority of all voters and a majority of the 17 counties had to approve the project for it to pass. But the truly massive pro-canal promotion began to worry the canal opponents, who until the last couple of weeks thought they had the election in the bag. We'll still win, they insisted. But as election day neared, their self-assurance sounded increasingly nervous. Could it be true? Could the Dallas establishment hype its way to victory again?

The vote turnout was overwhelming—almost twice as large in Dallas as three weeks later for the city council elections. And down the project went. Dallas voted 56 per cent against it; Tarrant County went 54 per cent against it; and opponents got 47 per cent of the vote in the other 15 counties, actually carrying seven of them. The show of economic power in promoting the project probably hurt pro-canal efforts, COST people said later. If *that* much money was being spent to push the project, voters may have wondered whether some folks were planning to get a rather hefty return on their investment.

The canal project was a sort of all-the-king's-horses-and-all-the-king's-men effort, but the barge channel turned out to be Humpty Dumpty. And there is no immediate likelihood that its backers will get it together again. Some canal proponents, including Senator John Tower, are nonetheless still talking about alternative means to finance the canal. They maintain that the voters rejected only the taxes required to pay for the canal, and not the canal itself. In some minds, the issue is apparently still not settled. The Corps of Engineers is still pursuing its cost studies and other research as if the canal were still on the drawing board, since they are under Congressional instructions to do so. New bridges that are built over the Trinity along the proposed canal route will still be required to allow clearance space for barges that may never go under them. And just as teenagers canoeing down the river a decade ago may have wondered what those concrete things that look like locks are, teenagers tracking their course a decade hence may wonder why the bridges are so damn high.

6-6
COUNTY ROADS . . . IS THE COST TOO HIGH?
Bill Modisett

Take one county roadman. Give him 15 miles of road to work and 3 pieces of machinery to keep that road in proper condition. Cost of maintaining those 15 miles of road per year—$2,745, according to figures in Tom Green County offices. In 1970, Tom Green County spent $183 for every mile of the estimated 550 miles of roads it maintained—a total expenditure of $100,617.80. But according to five other West Texas counties, that figure could be cut in half—even more than half. How? By implementation of the Optional County Road Law of 1947—the embattled county unit road system.

Tom Green County employs 33 men to maintain its roads and spends

From the *San Angelo Standard Times,* December 29, 1971. Reprinted by permission.

thousands more dollars giving them the equipment to work with, plus other equipment which apparently must stand idle. Namely, that equipment includes 28 pickups, 17 dump trucks, 14 road graders, 8 tractor-mowers, 7 water trucks, 4 power shovels, 4 grid rollers, 3 frontend loaders, 1 lawn mower, a plain truck, and one tractor. The growing list of equipment purchased here also includes a wide assortment of bulldozers, chain saws, power post-hole diggers, trailers, and shredders. In all, the number of pieces of heavy equipment alone totals more than 90–almost three pieces of machinery for every man.

At the beginning of 1971 Precincts 1 and 2, headed by commissioners Arley Guess and Ervin Young, Jr., respectively, entered into a joint roadwork operation. Precincts 3 and 4, under direction of Commissioners Harold Green and John Callison, remained single units. After one year the roadwork tab for the joint precincts was $206,059.15. The tab for Precinct 3, operating as a separate unit, was $98,085.74; and Precinct 4's bill amounted to $91,362.12. By their combined efforts Precincts 1 and 2 saved the county $40,000 by eliminating purchase of a power shovel for Guess' precinct. Both precincts used the power shovel already "owned" by Precinct 2. And Guess and Young agree service and efficiency have improved in both their precincts by implementation of the unit road system even on that small scale.

Howard, Sterling, Crane, Midland, and Crockett counties are using the unit road system. The system is apparently well received in those counties. In a recent poll, officials from those counties were asked their opinions on the unit road system. Here are their replies: Crane County Judge C. Bennett calls the system "the very best." That county uses less equipment and employees while getting "more and better use of the same and uniform roads." Sterling County officials replied, "Very satisfactory. If we were not on the system, it would cost 60 to 70 percent more to operate." Crockett Clerk Leta Powell noted the system "works real well for all concerned." Midland County Judge Barbara Culver says, "We all like it. We have had it so long comparative figures are unavailable." Howard County summed up its views on the system with one word–"good." An afternote on the Howard County reply indicated the unit system provides better utilization of men and equipment.

If these counties can make the unit system work with such impressive results, then why can't Tom Green County? Geographically the counties are all about the same. Nearly all six have one major metropolitan area surrounded by rural communities. The road networks are of basically the same makeup, and each county has approximately the same area: Howard, 912 square miles; Sterling, 914; Crane, 796; and Midland, 938. Tom Green County consists of 1,534 square miles, and Crockett County makes the unit system work effectively in its whopping 2,794 rocky, hilly square miles.

Voted in here, the unit system might provide the answer to a decrease in the number of road department personnel. Only one road foreman or road administrator would be needed. By pooling equipment and operating as a single unit, the four precincts feasibly could eliminate duplication of heavy equipment. Another advantage–delegating responsibility for maintenance of the roads to a qualified professional engineer could release commissioners for attention to their ever increasing loads of administrative duties.

The county unit road system—the Optional County Road Law of 1947—is nothing more than a team effort, a joint effort of four separate units to operate as a single unit. After taking a long hard look at the system of road maintenance in county government, the members of the 50th Legislature provided for the unit road system. Tom Green County has never used the unit road system. Precincts 1 and 2 in 1971 have operated as a single unit on a trial basis, and it has worked. Precincts 3 and 4 have never tried the joint roadwork effort.

What is the unit road system? Section 4, Article 6716-1 of *Vernon's Annotated Texas Statutes* describes it in this manner: "The construction and maintenance of county roads, the ownership and use of all county road department equipment, materials and supplies, and the administration of the county road department shall be on the basis of the county as a whole without regard to commissioners precincts." Under the unit system, the commissioners have no precinct boundaries, but remain the final word in all county road operations. The court becomes the "policy-determining body" only. The county road department, however, also includes a county road engineer, who is the chief executive officer; other administrative personnel; and road employees.

The unit road system takes at least a majority of the load of "politics," road responsibility, and necessary road education off the backs of commissioners and places it squarely on the back of a licensed professional engineer who is "experienced in road construction and maintenance" and who is required to meet the qualifications of engineers for the State Highway Department. Commissioners would appoint the engineer, who is responsible to the court for the efficient and economical construction and maintenance of county roads. Presently serving as county engineer for Tom Green County is Durham K. "Bull" Durham. Besides coordinating his services with those of commissioners and road foremen here, Durham also has responsibility for consultation with the remaining county operations—most departments. He does not serve in the capacity of a county engineer as specified by the statutes for the Optional County Road Law.

With implementation of the unit road system, a county can eliminate three of its precinct foremen, pool equipment, and work together as a single unit instead of four separate entities.

Expensive "Little Red Schoolhouse"

HERC FICKLEN FROM THE DALLAS NEWS

7

Financing the State's Governments

Caught in today's inflationary cycle and faced with sharply increased public demands for additional services, greater expenditures for many existing services, and increased activity in the regulation of individual and corporate conduct, Texas governments are particularly hard pressed. To meet these rising expectations, all units of Texas government will have to expand their operations, whether service or regulatory; but before any of them can do so to any degree, they will have to raise the necessary revenue.

SOME GROWING DEMANDS

Four major governmental functions—education, transportation, welfare, and health—will require more than 90 per cent of the state's revenues for the fiscal years of the early and mid-seventies. Each of them is an area of sharply increasing demands and rising expectations from large segments of the state's people.

STATE EXPENDITURES

Public education Expenditures for public education are currently increasing at a rate of more than $200 million in each fiscal year. Most of that increase is the result of improvements in the basic levels of support (e.g., teacher pay raises approved by the Legislature during the 1969 session, the creation of new institutions of higher education, greater emphasis on vocational-technical education) and a broader array of program offerings from kindergarten to graduate school. Should federal courts declare unconstitutional the present state-local financing scheme for public schools, a plan of full state support could cause the state's financial responsibility to increase markedly.

Public transportation Although declining as a percentage of total state expenditures, transportation demands, largely in the form of highway construction and maintenance, will necessitate spending more than $50 million each year in additional state funds.

Public welfare With the beginning of the Medical Assistance (Medicaid) Program in fiscal 1968, and increased costs of categorical assistance (e.g., old-age pensions and dependent children) and welfare administration, as well as increased support of other services such as vocational rehabilitation and aid to the blind, welfare expenditures have risen at the rate of over $100 million per fiscal year. The national government will take over many of these programs in 1974.

Public health As a percentage of the total state budget the public health area remains quite small; but ever-increasing demands from some influential sectors of the public are causing the state to respond by spending an additional $50 million each year.

LOCAL DEMANDS

Local governments will likewise face heavy demands for increased outlays of public money. The growing demand for "law and order" has occasioned greater budget demands for law enforcement at all levels, but notably in the county and city. Since federal courts have not required the state government to take over the full responsibility for financing public education, local school districts will be compelled to increase fiscal outlays during the next decade to meet higher standards established by the national government and increased expectations imposed by the Texas Education Agency and local school patrons.

Other problem areas will cause local governments to expand expenditures. Demand is increasing for expansion of water resources, in short supply because of uneven rainfall distribution and uneven underground water supplies; and solutions for environmental pollution of land, water, and air are being developed. Both of these areas will require vast sums of public money if they are to be handled effectively. Cities are congested; and new slums develop even as old ones are being torn down. In short, the needs of schools, colleges, technical-training facilities, and police and fire protection are threatening to outstrip the revenue sources now available.

THE FISCAL SYSTEM

To meet these increasing financial burdens, Texas governments are under the necessity of re-examining their fiscal systems and developing carefully planned fiscal programs along sound and politically attainable lines. The *fiscal system* of a state or local government consists of the means by which revenues are collected, expenditures are made, and the total financial policy is administered and controlled.

A *sound fiscal system* consists of sufficient revenue to carry out the functions undertaken by government while meeting the requirements that taxes be just and equitable. The system must, moreover, reduce to a minimum all of the problems involved in the custody and expenditure of state and local revenues. Finally, it must provide that revenues and expenditures be administered and controlled in a manner that gives the best services for the government. No matter how "sound" the system is, however, no matter how well it meets the criteria mentioned, no matter how fair and equitable it may in fact be, unless it is acceptable to the public in general it may not long be tolerated.

SOURCES OF STATE REVENUE

As a part of its present fiscal system the state of Texas seeks to obtain revenues from a wide variety of sources, which for convenience can be classified under two headings: *tax sources* and *nontax sources.* Chief among the tax sources are the sales taxes, the highway motor fuel tax, gross receipts and production taxes, the motor vehicle license fee, and the cigarette tax. Contrary to a widely held belief, the state obtains considerable amounts of revenue from sources other than taxation. Chief among these nontax sources are grants-in-aid obtained from the national government; but the state also receives revenue from public land sales, rentals, and royalties; ownership and operation of commercial enterprises; the sale of licenses and imposition of fees; and from such miscellaneous sources as special assessments, court fines, forfeitures and escheats, donations, pension assessments, highway privileges, rents on investment properties, interest, and the like. The state usually meets those fiscal obligations incurred but not covered by these several revenue sources by borrowing money. Borrowings by the state produce receipts in the state treasury which are subject to appropriation by the state legislature, but they also produce fixed charges from the future revenues of the state until the obligation has been paid. They often represent a present revenue but a future expenditure.

THE STATE TAX SYSTEM

Even though nontax sources have become increasingly important in recent years in Texas (see Figure 7-1), the bulk of its revenue, approximately 61.34 per cent in 1972 for state government, comes from tax sources. A *tax* is a compulsory contribution imposed by a public authority whose expenditure will be for the benefit of the public rather than individuals. The state of Texas imposes a variety of taxes, which taken together may be referred to as the *state tax system.* According to generally accepted standards of a sound fiscal system, each tax levied and the total tax structure should be just and equitable, but there are widely varying notions of what kinds of taxes and what sort of system can meet those standards.

BENEFITS RECEIVED PRINCIPLE

The crucial question is: What principles should guide the government in distributing the burden of its financial needs among its citizens? Many persons have

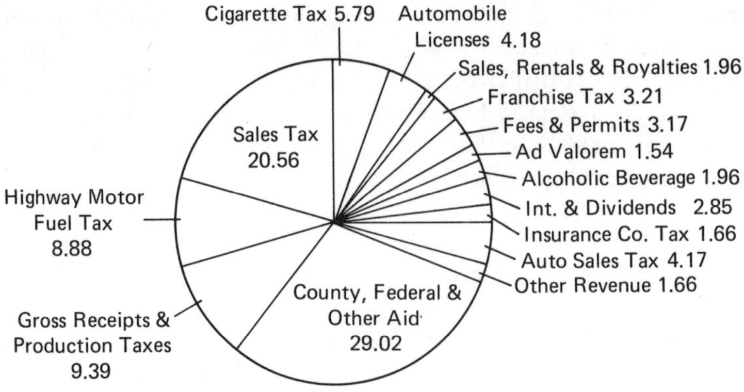

Figure 7-1
Sources of the Texas revenue dollar, fiscal year 1972. Source: Annual Report of the Comptroller of Public Accounts, State of Texas, *1972 Part IA. Note: the Texas fiscal year begins on September 1 and ends on the following August 31.*

advocated a principle drawn primarily from the business world and often referred to as the *benefits received principle:* that those who receive the benefits of the government's service or regulation should be required to pay for them. Three basic criticisms have usually been leveled at this principle. First, it is not possible to devise any definite, foolproof measurement of benefits received. Next, no one can determine adequately who receives the greatest benefit, directly or indirectly–the rich, the middle-income, or the poor classes of citizens. And finally, this principle is incompatible with wide consumption of government services, for the more one received, the more one would be called on to pay, and those who need the greatest shares of services are often the least prepared to support them.

ABILITY TO PAY PRINCIPLE

Probably the most fully accepted principle of taxation in twentieth-century America has been one drawn from social theory. This principle stresses the ability of each citizen-taxpayer to contribute and is usually referred to as the *ability to pay principle.* It is normally attacked on the grounds that it penalizes thrift, efficiency, and success, and that ability to pay is no easier to measure than benefits received. Its proponents usually advance the arguments that most, if not all, nonprofit organizations, such as churches, community chests, and the Red Cross, are financed on this basis and that the principle involves a minimum of sacrifice by the taxpayer.

SOCIAL EXPEDIENCY PRINCIPLE

A third principle advanced in recent years by those who take a pragmatic approach to social problems is the *social expediency principle.* In this view the best revenue sources and revenue system are those that work best, that come closest to accomplishing the ends or objectives of the society as a whole.

From the standpoint of the government a good tax is usually seen as one that produces sizable amounts of revenue, costs little to collect, and is paid without great resistance. A general sales tax seems to meet these criteria most effectively, and the ad valorem property tax least of all. But such a tax may not meet all the criteria necessary to make a tax just and equitable.

SOUND TAX SYSTEM

It is widely held among students of public finances as well as students of state government that a sound tax is one that produces a sufficient amount of revenue to meet the requirements of public expenditures—at least those portions not intended to be met by increased indebtedness. A sound tax is also characterized by a high degree of certainty; that is, it is generally simple and clear enough to enable the taxpayer to understand how much he must pay and on what basis his tax was computed. It should always be reasonably economical to collect.

In this view a *sound tax system* that is just and equitable should also be diverse enough to promote stability and adequacy of yield; it should be easy to adjust to either increased or decreased need for revenue. It must thus possess a degree of elasticity or flexibility. The burden of taxation, moreover, should fall equitably upon the various classes in the community; there should be some rough correlation between the burden of the tax and the ability of the taxpayer to meet it.

SALES TAXES

By far the most important single source of tax revenues in Texas is sales taxation (see Table 7-1). Altogether the state levies six or more different *sales taxes,* which account for more than two-thirds of its tax revenues.

Because Texas relies so heavily upon state sales taxes, the tax burden on individual taxpayers may vary greatly depending upon their pattern of consumption. Also, the effective rate of taxation declines as the income rate rises. Thus the Texas tax system tends to be sharply regressive, drawing a greater percentage from the income of individuals in lower income brackets than from those in higher income brackets and from businesses and corporations. (In Reading 7-1 a veteran Austin news analyst discusses the Texas tax effort, drawing on a recent national survey.) Whether or not such a *regressive tax system* is just and equitable depends upon the perspective from which it is viewed and upon the viewer's notions as to the purpose of taxation.

The limited sales, excise, and use tax, first imposed by the 57th Legislature in 1961, currently produces over 40 per cent of the state's tax revenue. Table

TABLE 7-1
Major Texas tax revenues, 1971-1972 fiscal year

Type of Tax	Per Cent of Total Revenue	Per Cent of Tax Revenue	Total Amount
Sales	41.58	67.78	$1,676,496,463
Limited Sales, Excise and Use			
Motor Fuels			
Cigarette and Tobacco			
Alcoholic Beverages			
Automobile Sales			
Hotel and Motel			
Business	14.50	22.01	585,316,894
Franchises			
Chain Store			
Insurance Companies			
Occupations			
Gross Receipts and Production			
Motor Vehicle Registration	4.18	6.81	167,551,484
Property	1.54	2.51	61,588,911
Totals	61.80	99.11	$2,490,953,753

Source: *Annual Report of the Comptroller of Public Accounts, State of Texas,* 1972, Part 1A. Totals in dollars have been rounded to the nearest dollar.

7-1a shows tax revenue estimates for the fiscal years 1973-75. Its base is the sale price of "all tangible personal property" and "the storage, use or other consumption of tangible personal property purchased, leased, or rented," but taxes on the sale of a number of items are exempted from payment. *General sales taxes* are currently exempted on receipts from water, telephone, and telegraph services; sales of goods otherwise taxed (e.g., cigarettes and motor fuels); food and food products (but not restaurant meals); medical supplies sold by prescription; and animals and supplies used in agricultural production. The current rate is 4 per cent, but local governments may by petition and election levy an additional 1 per cent. This tax is viewed by many state officials as a *selective sales tax* rather than a general sales tax because of the number and nature of its exemptions. The tax currently produces approximately one-fifth of the total revenues of the state.

Other items singled out for selective sales taxation include highway motor fuels, cigarettes, alcoholic beverages for consumption, and automobiles. The *motor fuel tax* alone brought in almost 12 per cent of the tax revenues in 1971-1972. The *alcoholic beverage tax*—that on beer was originally levied in 1933, that on distilled spirits and wines in 1935—can be counted on for some $70 to $80 million per year. In recent years the 4 per cent sales tax has also been imposed on the sale of alcoholic beverages to the consumer. The sale of both wines and ales is further subjected to the "limited" sales tax on purchases by

TABLE 7-1a
Estimated major tax revenues, 1973-1975 fiscal years

Type of Tax	Estimated Totals in Millions 1973	1974	1975
Sales			
Limited Sales, Excise, and Use	$925.2	$1,014.0	$1,110.5
Motor Fuels	371.9	396.4	422.6
Cigarette and Tobacco	213.1	215.0	217.3
Alcoholic Beverages	72.6	77.3	80.1
Automobile Sales	180.4	194.1	206.8
Hotel and Motel	9.1	9.7	10.4
Total Sales	1,772.5	1,906.5	1,967.7
Business			
Franchises	128.2	133.3	138.7
Chain Store	2.5	1.3	–0–
Insurance Companies	72.1	78.9	86.4
Occupations	87.1	88.1	89.2
Gross Receipts and Production	374.3	397.8	405.8
Total Business	664.2	703.4	720.1
Motor Vehicle Registration	175.3	186.2	197.9
Property	.025	.025	.025
Total	$2,612.0	$2,796.1	$2,885.7

Source: *Biennial Revenue Estimate, 1973-1975.*
Totals in dollars have been rounded to the nearest tenth of a million dollars.

consumers. The selected *tax on cigarette sales* was originally levied in 1931 as a depression emergency measure. Rates have been increased repeatedly, most recently in 1973. In 1959 the Legislature added a levy of 25 per cent on the wholesale price of all other tobacco products, except snuff. It was specifically excused on the ground that the tax would work a real hardship on those who could least afford to pay. A motor vehicle sales tax, first authorized in 1941, is now levied at the rate of 3 to 4 per cent on the retail sale price. An out-of-state vehicle applying for a certificate of title must pay a fee of $15.00 in place of the tax, while the fee on an even exchange of vehicles is $5.00 and that on a gift vehicle $10.00. A 3 per cent tax was imposed on hotel and motel room rentals in 1959. In the same year a retail sales tax of 1.5 per cent on boats and boat motors was imposed, to which the Legislature later added the "limited" sales tax.

BUSINESS TAXES

The second most productive group of taxes in terms of revenue produced for the state is the *severance or production tax* on crude oil, natural gas, sulphur, and cement, which is responsible for supplying another tenth of the state's total revenue. The crude oil tax alone currently brings in nearly 5 per cent. The crude oil production tax is assessed on gross production on the basis of market value. According to the Texas State Tax Study Commission the Texas crude oil tax, 4.6 per cent of the market value, is low compared with that of states that also impose the property tax. The natural gas production tax is assessed at the rate of 7.5 per cent of the value of gross production at the wellhead. This rate gives Texas the distinction of levying the highest permanent natural gas tax of any state in the Union. A severance tax on the mining of sulphur is also assessed at a rate of $1.03 per long ton (2,240 pounds) of gross production. Finally, the sale, use, and distribution of cement are subject to a tax of $0.0275 per hundredweight produced.

The third most productive group of taxes is that imposed on other business operations, including the organization of corporations and their privilege of doing business in the state; gross receipts of insurance companies, utilities, common carriers, and many other types of businesses; and, finally, chain stores. Such miscellaneous business taxes raise more than 6 per cent of the total revenue of the state.

Corporate franchise taxes, originally levied in 1907, constitute the nearest approximation to a statewide, or "general," business tax. They are assessed upon the invested capital, surplus, and long-term debt of each corporation to the extent that it does business in the state. The present rate of this tax is $3.00 per $1,000 of business transacted.

A special gross receipts tax on insurance company business is based on the premiums collected within the state. The rate varies between the smaller, Texas-based companies and the larger, out-of-state companies. Out-of-state companies may reduce their rates by investing a required portion of their assets in Texas securities. This tax on insurance premium receipts serves two distinct purposes: It provides needed revenue for the state treasury, and it encourages out-of-state companies to invest in Texas securities. This tax is levied on insurance companies in addition to any state and local ad valorem taxes they must pay on their real and personal property.

The state also taxes gross receipts on business transactions in Texas of telephone and telegraph companies, privately owned electric power and water companies, and transportation companies.

A tax on chain stores is apportioned according to the number of retail and wholesale outlets in the chain. Retailers and wholesalers are liable for payment at the rate of $5.00 annually for the first store up to a maximum of $826.00 for each store in excess of fifty. Exceptions are extended to some operations, principally to dairies and service stations. The operators of excepted businesses, however, must pay a fee of $5.00 for the first store and $10.00 for each additional store. The chain store tax is intended to discourage the operation of multi-unit businesses in the state and to provide incidental revenue for the treasury.

MOTOR VEHICLE REGISTRATION

The next most productive tax in terms of state revenue is that imposed on the registration of motor vehicles. It is chiefly a *highway use tax* and currently raises over 4 per cent of the state's total revenue. The first $50,000 collected from annual registration fees is retained by the county; the next $125,000 is divided equally between the county and the state; and all receipts over $175,000 go to the state for its use. Passenger cars account for more than three-fourths of total registration fees, though trucks and truck tractors, trailers, busses, and motorcycles and sidecars are also taxed. The rate is based on the weight of the vehicle, with no allowance for purchase price, depreciation, or use to which the vehicle is put. There would appear to be considerable room for inequity in this registration scheme.

STATE PROPERTY TAX

The state *property tax,* although steadily diminishing in importance, continues to produce some 2.5 per cent of the state's tax revenues. All forms of property—real and personal—are subject under the Texas constitution to taxation according to their market value. (Reading 7-2 analyzes the property tax as a source of revenue for state and local governments, emphasizing the need for reform.) A proposed constitutional amendment which failed to pass at the November, 1970, general election would have established a uniform method of assessing ranch, farm, and forest lands based on the amount of income they produced. The constitution of the state exempts certain types of property from this tax—$250 worth of household and kitchen furniture and $3,000 of the value of all homesteads. An amendment adopted at the 1972 general election permits local governments to extend the $3,000 homestead exemption to residence homesteads of all persons sixty-five years of age or older. Moreover, an amendment approved in 1966 stipulates that all land owned by natural persons which is designated and actually used for agricultural purposes may be assessed only as agricultural land regardless of its location or market value. (An evaluation of the general property tax is included in the discussion of local taxation in Chapter 6.)

MISCELLANEOUS TAXES

The most important among the miscellaneous tax sources is the fifty-year-old Texas *inheritance tax.* It is an ordinary inheritance tax levied on beneficiaries, graduated by the size of the inheritance and the degree of relationship between the beneficiary and the deceased. Husbands, wives, children, and other lineal descendants are allowed an exemption of $25,000; on the excess they are taxed on a sliding scale from 1 to 6 per cent. Brothers, sisters, or their descendants are allowed $10,000, and on all above that are taxed at a rate of 3 to 10 per cent. Uncles, aunts, or their descendants are allowed only $1,000 and are taxed at the rate of 4 to 15 per cent on the excess. All other heirs are allowed only $500 and are taxed 5 to 20 per cent on the remainder.

CONCLUSIONS ON TAX REVENUES

Two major conclusions emerge from this analysis of Texas tax revenues. Although the state levies a wide variety of types of taxes, it relies increasingly on sales taxation and miscellaneous business levies. These may very well have neared, if not reached, their practical limits–i.e., the limits established by adverse taxpayer reaction. Taxpayers may not be ready to accept additional burdens on these sources. Faced with ever-rising costs and the threat of diminishing returns from the above taxes, the state must continue its search for new tax sources and additional revenues. Some of the new taxes that the Legislature may turn to in the immediate future include a corporate income tax, a personal income tax, and additional taxes on natural resources. Some analysts have advanced the argument that a sound, properly balanced tax system in Texas can only be achieved when a greater proportion of the tax burden is derived from corporate and personal income taxes. However, a long-standing and deeply held animosity toward these tax sources among the Texas electorate has to be overcome before an income tax in any form would be accepted.

COLLECTION OF STATE TAXES

In spite of the fact that the state of Texas levies an almost bewildering array of taxes, it relies on three, or at most four, principal officers to assess and collect them. The only notable exception among major sources of tax revenues is the "limited sales, excise, and use tax," which is collected by the retailer making the sale and turned over to the state comptroller of public accounts, the state's chief tax collector. The table below indicates which of these state and local officers is charged with the responsibility of assessing and collecting the most important state taxes and fees.

State and Local Officers	Taxes Assessed and Collected
State Comptroller of Public Accounts	(1) Natural resources or severance taxes, (2) Motor fuels taxes, (3) Gross receipts taxes, (4) Public utilities taxes, (5) Franchise taxes, (6) Hotel and motel sales taxes, (7) Tobacco products sales taxes, (8) Chain store tax
State Treasurer	(1) Cigarette sales tax, (2) Alcoholic beverages sales taxes, except the beer tax, which is collected by the Alcoholic Beverage Commission
County Assessor and Collector of Taxes	(1) Ad valorem property tax, (2) Motor vehicle sales tax, (3) Motor vehicle registration fees
Board of Insurance Commissioners	(1) Gross receipts taxes on insurance companies

NONTAX REVENUES OF THE STATE

FEDERAL GRANTS

For two decades *federal grants-in-aid* have contributed more revenue to the state treasury than any single tax levied by the state. In the fiscal year 1971-1972 they produced almost as much as the two most productive taxes combined. They have regularly accounted for at least one-fourth of the state's total revenue (see Table 7-2). With the long-awaited advent of *revenue-sharing* in 1972, they will undoubtedly contribute an even greater percentage of the state's receipts. More than two-thirds of these federal funds were allocated to public welfare and highway programs. Other significant amounts went to public health, public education, and unemployment programs. In the fiscal year 1969-1970 Texas received the fourth largest total amount in federal grants (only California, New York, and Illinois received more).

TABLE 7-2
Federal grants to the state of Texas, 1971-1972 fiscal year

Object of Grant	Per Cent of State Revenue	Total Dollars
Highways	05.99	$240,262,282.00
Public Welfare	15.26	611,491,460.00
Public Education	04.76	190,765,415.00
Public Health	00.45	18,367,108.00
Others	02.24	90,238,484.00
Totals	29.02	$1,151,124,749.00

Source: *Annual Report of the Comptroller of Public Accounts, State of Texas, 1972,* Part 1A. Totals have been rounded to the nearest dollar.

Federal grants were originally offered to the states under two general conditions: that the federal money had to be matched dollar for dollar, and that the full amount had to be expended for the exact purpose specified in the federal legislation and in accordance with the stipulations prescribed by the national government. Today the first of those conditions has given way to the normal practice of allocating funds on the basis of a formula which uses such factors as lump sums, uniform sums, population, area, mileage, need and fiscal ability, cost of service, administrative discretion, and the special needs of the state. Under this arrangement the allocation can be as much as 90 per cent or more by the national government to 10 per cent or less by the state. Texans have traditionally been opposed to the principle of federal grants generally on the ground that they tend to drain away the rights and powers of the state. Nevertheless, the state has not been reluctant to take part in programs where it would receive large sums of money for projects that have the hearty approval of its people; for example, the highway construction and maintenance program. There does not appear to be any widespread disposition to refuse federal grants in these areas, even though many Texans oppose them in principle.

In late 1972 the national government added a new dimension to the federal grant picture by enacting the State and Local Government Fiscal Assistance Act, calling for $30.1 billion in revenue-sharing over the next five years. The 1972 allocation was $5.3 billion, of which Texas governments received $244.4 million, with $81.4 million going to the state government and $163.0 million to local governments. The 1973 allocation is $5.975 billion and the 1974 allocation $6.125 billion, of which Texas will receive about the same proportions as in 1972. The state comptroller estimates that federal grants will total $1,316,219,447 in fiscal 1974 and $1,575,685,612 in 1975. The Texas Research League, along with many other groups interested in Texas finance, originally considered revenue-sharing money as a windfall, as an extra bundle of funds to help ensure more expenditures without the necessity of increasing taxes during the 1973-1974 biennium. Soon after the amounts of Texas revenue-sharing funds were announced from Washington, however, President Nixon began withdrawing federal funds from a wide variety of programs financed at least in part by the federal government. The final result of this federal manipulation of funds very likely will be that Texas will emerge by 1975 with little more money, if any, to finance the state's operations.

Each allocation must be divided so that two-thirds of the funds are passed to local governments, with state governments retaining the other one-third. There are no strings attached to the expenditure of state shares, but local governments must spend their share within seven "high priority" categories: public safety, environmental protection, public transportation, health and recreation, social services, libraries, and cost of administration. The underlying principle behind this new revenue-sharing scheme, which had been strongly advocated by many for over a decade, is the belief that given sufficient resources, states and localities can be more responsive to the needs of the people and more responsible for identification of local priorities.

LAND REVENUES

The state also receives a substantial sum (almost 2 per cent of total revenue) from land sales, rentals, and royalties. Sales of land, sand, shell, and gravel; rentals on grazing lands, buildings and equipment; and prospecting permits account for nearly one-fourth of this revenue. The remaining three-fourths is received primarily from mineral leases and royalties.

MISCELLANEOUS SOURCES

Other important nontax sources are fees, permits, and investments. Major fee sources include motor vehicle inspection fees, college tuition fees, other student fees, patient fees at state hospitals, and certificate-of-title fees for motor vehicles.

The most significant sources of revenue based on permits are special truck and automobile permits; liquor, wine and beer permits; and cigarette tax permits. At any given moment, moreover, the state actually has on hand many millions of dollars that are invested in securities or interest-bearing bank accounts. The income from those investments produced over $100 million in 1972.

PUBLIC BORROWING

Since the state's revenues rarely exceed or even match its expenditures, an annual deficit is common in Texas. This is true despite a constitutional provision adopted in 1942 which seeks to prevent the Legislature from appropriating more money than the comptroller of public accounts certifies will be available in the treasury. Thus the people of Texas have tried through constitutional provisions to force the state to operate on the basis of a balanced budget, but their efforts have not always been successful.

An 1876 constitutional provision prevents the state from borrowing money "except to supply casual deficiencies of revenue, repel invasion, suppress insurrection, and defend the State in war." No limit was established for borrowing to repel invasion, suppress insurrection, or defend the state; but the "debt created to supply casual deficiencies in the revenue" can never exceed an accumulated total of $200,000. The 1942 provision sought to prevent deficiencies except in cases of emergency and imperative public necessity. The comptroller is required to submit to the Legislature in advance of each regular session a sworn statement of cash on hand and revenue anticipated for the coming biennium. The appropriations bills enacted at that regular session and any subsequent special sessions are limited to not more than the amount certified unless new revenue sources are provided.

Casual deficiencies in excess of $200,000, however, were incurred in the fiscal year 1959-1960. They occurred as the result of excessive estimates of anticipated revenue brought about by partial failure of many of the state's gross receipts and sales taxes to produce as expected. Deficits were common in the fifteen-year period from 1930-1944. Increased taxes and curtailed state expenditures during World War II produced a brief era of surpluses from 1945 through 1949. Each legislature that met from 1951 through 1958 in regular or special session had to increase taxes in an effort to avoid deficits. Despite their efforts and the enactment in 1959 of the largest tax bill in history up to that time, the state continued to fall deeper in debt. By 1961 the state was faced with a deficit of some $70 million, and its Legislature was forced to turn to a general sales tax to retire that indebtedness and finance current spending. Through increasing rates on existing taxes, casual deficiencies have been avoided throughout most of the 1960s. The pattern of biennial deficiencies could easily return in the 1970s as demands for increased spending grow in the state or massive resistance to more taxes appears.

Of the 445 funds that compose the state treasury, chronic deficits have occurred, for the most part, in only the *General Revenue Fund,* but it is the critical fund in that maze of accounts. Like a fever thermometer, it measures the state's fiscal health. If the fund shows a surplus, fiscal health is good; if a deficit, the state is fiscally ill. Although only some 20 per cent of the state's expenditures are paid from the General Revenue Fund, nearly all state spending affects it. For example, public school support is not paid for from the General Fund, but schools have a priority on revenues that would otherwise flow into that fund. If school support is increased, General Funds decrease. In a broad sense, most funds—other than those supported by specified taxes, such as the Highway Fund, which relies on gasoline taxes—keep solvent at the expense of the General Revenue Fund. On August 31, 1958, for example, the last day of that fiscal year, the State of Texas had on hand in its treasury some $1.3 million in other funds, but the General Fund was facing a sizable deficit.

Although the creation of bonded indebtedness appears to be precluded by stringent constitutional limitations, Texas had amassed a total authorized bonded indebtedness of $794.3 million on August 31, 1972. This paradoxical situation had been brought about by a series of amendments to the 1876 constitution authorizing the acquisition of bonded indebtedness. An amendment adopted in 1946 authorized the issue of $25 million in bonds backed by the credit of the state to finance the Veterans' Land Program. In 1951 a second amendment increased that amount by an additional $75 million, and it was increased to a total of $200 million in 1955, to $350 million in 1963, and to $400 million in 1967. Another amendment, adopted in 1947, authorized a bond issue of $15 million for buildings at the University of Texas at Austin and the Texas A & M University at College Station. The same amendment permitted other state colleges and universities to issue ten-year bonds for building purposes, backed by a five-cent state property tax. Other amendments in 1956 and 1965 expanded the scope of this program and extended it indefinitely. A 1965 amendment also authorized a maximum of $85 million to establish and fund a college student loan program. Still another amendment, adopted in 1957, called for the issue of $200 million (raised to $400 million in 1966) in bonds for water conservation projects. A bond issue of $75 million was approved in 1967 to finance state park development.

The exact amount of bonded debt owed by the state fluctuates from day to day as new bonds are issued and sold and old ones are redeemed and retired. Most of the outstanding bonded debt is in the form of *self-liquidating revenue bonds,* i.e., those guaranteed from income produced by the activity financed, such as Veterans' Land Bonds or College Student Loan Bonds, or *limited obligation bonds,* i.e., those guaranteed by income from specific taxes or assessments, such as College Building Bonds.

PLANNING AND SUPERVISING STATE EXPENDITURES

While it is important to be informed about how governments obtain money and the purposes for which they spend it, one must also be familiar with the techniques and procedures for handling public funds. Emphasis here will be placed on budgeting, accounting, purchasing, and auditing.

BUDGETING

A plan of financial operation is usually referred to as a *budget.* In modern state governments, budgets serve at least two distinct functions, each of which is important in its own right. The budget serves as a plan for spending. It also serves as a statement of the financial condition of the government at the end of the current fiscal year (the Texas fiscal year extends from September 1 to the following August 31), the anticipated condition at the close of the next fiscal year, and some recommendations for the coming fiscal year.

In 1949 the Texas Legislature created a Legislative Budget Board, whose director and staff prepare the biennial budget and help to prepare the general appropriations bills for introduction at each regular session of the Legislature (see Reading 7-7). Several attempts have been made in recent years to put the state appropriations on an annual basis, but each time constitutional amendments aimed at that objective have been submitted to the voters, they have been rejected. The reason most frequently given for rejection at the polls is that annual sessions of the Legislature will encourage more unnecessary and undesirable spending and bring about higher taxes, which are at least equally unnecessary and undesirable in the public view.

An Executive Budget Officer, under the direction and supervision of the governor, is also required by a 1951 statute to present a budget to the Legislature within five days after the opening of each regular session. The result of this dual arrangement is that two budgets, one legislative in origin and the other executive, are prepared each biennium—a fiscal oddity shared by no other state. The legislative budget normally contains more graphic presentations, more summary statements, and more detailed appendixes. The executive budget usually contains recommendations for greater amounts of expenditures and more new programs for spending.

Actual compilation of each biennial budget begins with the preparation of forms and instructions by the budget agencies. These forms are sent to each spending agency early in the even-numbered years. For five or six months thereafter, representatives of the budgeting agencies work closely with personnel in the operating agencies in the preparation of departmental requests. By early fall those departmental estimates are submitted to the two budget agencies. The budget agencies then carefully analyze all requests and hold hearings with representatives of the spending departments to clarify details and supply such additional information as may be needed. At the close of the hearings, normally in mid-December, the budget agencies compile their estimates of expenditures into their two separate proposed budgets.

At the beginning of each legislative session members of the Legislature are confronted with two sets of recommendations for all state expenditures for the coming biennium. Since the inception of the dual budget system, the Legislature has shown a steady inclination to prefer the recommendations of its own budget-making agents to those of the executive department.

Recently some important reforms have been made in the general budgeting process in Texas, making the budget in its final form more flexible and allowing for a greater degree of administrative discretion. A virtually complete picture of the state's spending and thus its revenue requirements is now obtained by including all expenditures and all receipts from whatever sources. Budgetary recommendations are now enacted in a single appropriations bill dealing with all items of expenditure. Line-item expenditures have been reduced sharply. Budgets today, moreover, include such information as program costs, character and object costs, work-load statistics, and other descriptive material not included a few years ago. These reforms have improved budgeting in Texas, but there is still a long way to go in the attempt to provide an efficient, modern budgetary process.

ACCOUNTING

The accounts of the state are under the supervision of the comptroller of public accounts. He is held responsible by statutory provisions for maintaining a double entry system of accounts with such ledgers and accounts as he believes necessary. The statutes, however, narrow his discretion by creating numerous *special funds* or accounts; but these are really nothing more than separate entries composed of designated revenues that must be used for financing specified activities of the state. They include constitutional trust funds, such as the Permanent School Fund and the Permanent University Fund; retirement and other trust funds, such as the Teachers' and State Employees' Retirement Funds; constitutionally dedicated funds, such as the State Highway and Available School Funds; and over two hundred more of these special funds. Into them pour millions of dollars annually, and from them 75 to 80 per cent of the state's expenditures are made. Since they are usually earmarked for special purposes, this means that they are not subject to appropriation by the Legislature on its own judgment.

Among the major accounting tasks of the Comptroller's Office are the preparation of warrants (i.e., checks) for the payment of state obligations, the acknowledgment of receipts from the various revenue sources of the state, and the recording of information concerning receipts and expenditures in the ledgers and other account books of the state. Contrary to the usual business practice, the accounts of the state are set up on a cash rather than an *accrual* basis. Expenditures are thus entered when the money is actually paid rather than when the obligation is incurred. *Cash accounting* permits the state to create obligations in one fiscal year and carry them over into the next before paying them; but it complicates the task of fiscal planning by failing to reflect a completely accurate picture of current finances at any given moment. The comptroller issues an annual report in three volumes in which he includes statements of operation for the various funds of the state treasury. The report does not constitute, however, a series of balance sheets but only a financial statement at the end of the fiscal year.

PURCHASING

Agencies of the state government must purchase through or under the supervision of the Board of Control, a three-member central body appointed by the governor with the advice and consent of the Senate. (The six-year terms of board members overlap.) All purchases fall into one of three classes—contract, open market (or local), and emergency (or spot)—and each is handled differently.

When contractors agree in advance to sell to the state at a stipulated price, this is known as *contract purchasing.* Contracts are usually entered into for the fiscal year. They are awarded on the basis of bids submitted to the Board of Control in conformity with board instructions. The board is normally obligated to accept the lowest bid meeting its specifications. It is physically impossible for the board to foresee all purchases needed by all agencies. The board is authorized by statute, therefore, to purchase in the *open market* where necessary. As in contract items, competitive bids are required and contracts awarded in each case.

Emergency purchases may be made, but they are discouraged and must be held to a minimum. Here again the normal forms must be completed and processed, even when purchases have been delivered. The lowest and best bid usually must be accepted, and under normal conditions the purchase is made from a closely located vendor. Spot purchases are those under $50 which may be made by each agency without prior board approval. *Local purchases* are those authorized by the board which involve perishable commodities.

AUDITING

Auditing in Texas is under the direct supervision of the state auditor, who is appointed to a two-year term by the Legislative Audit Committee with the approval of two-thirds of the Senate. The auditor may be removed by the committee at any time without the privilege of a hearing. His principal duty is that of checking all financial records and transactions after the transactions have been completed. He must, therefore, check all records and accounts of disbursing officers and those of the custodians of all state funds.

The purpose of this audit is a check by the legislative branch of the state government on the integrity and efficiency of the executive branch. The auditor has the authority to require changes in the accounting or record-keeping of any state agency in order to promote a more uniform system of accounts. He has access to all state records, books, accounts, and reports and may demand assistance from state officers and employees in the performance of his duty.

Another important duty of the auditor is to examine the activities of each state agency to determine the quality of its service and whether duplication of effort exists. Following each examination he makes a written report to the head of each state agency with recommendations for correction of deficiencies and suggestions for improvement. Copies of each report are sent to the speaker of the House of Representatives and to all members of the Legislature. The governor receives a summary report annually.

PURPOSES OF STATE EXPENDITURES

When the Texas constitution was adopted in 1876, the annual expenditure of the state government was only about $1 million; now it exceeds $4 billion. Some

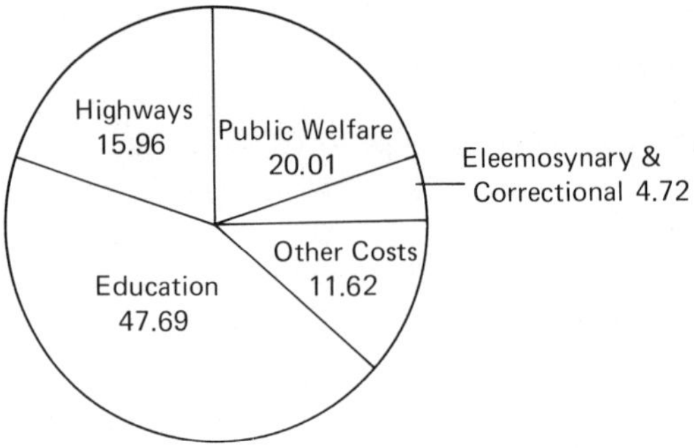

Figure 7-2
Objects of the Texas expenditure dollar, fiscal year 1972. Source: Annual Report of the Comptroller of Public Accounts, State of Texas, *1972, Part IA. All general expenditures made by the state government are included in these figures, whether from its own sources or from federal grants.*

of the items of expenditure in 1876 were payment of interest on bonded debt; erection and repairs of public buildings; support of public schools, colleges and universities; cost of assessing and collecting revenue; support of state eleemosynary institutions; enforcement of quarantine regulations along the coast; and protection of the frontier. Today more than 88 per cent of state expenditures are concentrated in only five areas—support of the public schools, construction and maintenance of highways, public welfare payments, support of higher education, and support of eleemosynary and correctional institutions (see Figure 7-2 and Table 7-2a).

TABLE 7-2a
Appropriations for major expenditure items, fiscal years 1974-1975

Item	1974	1975
Education	45.5%	47.0%
Public Welfare	21.9	20.9
Highways (Transportation)	15.6	15.5
Public Health	6.2	6.2
General Government	3.1	2.8
Natural Resources and Environmental Quality	2.7	2.7
Public Safety and Correctional	2.4	2.2
Miscellaneous	2.6	2.7
	100.0%	100.0%

Source: *General Appropriations Bill for 1974-1975 Fiscal Years,* House Bill 139, 63rd Legislature, Regular Session. One hundred per cent in 1974 equals $4,763,955,649 and in 1975 $4,940,567,353.

Table 7-3 shows another facet of the same situation, demonstrating expenditures by major function at regular intervals since 1950. It details the steady rise in state government costs for many years and the great increases since the end of World War II. Several factors have contributed to this condition, the most important being the expansion of social welfare functions into new areas, increased state subsidization of education, rising costs of highway construction and maintenance, police protection and other functions of government, and the decline in the purchasing power of the dollar. Much additional expenditure can also be attributed to man's search for security—economic and social as well as military.

EXPENDITURES FOR PUBLIC EDUCATION

For several decades the major item of expenditure for any state government has been support of its public school systems. Included in this item are subsidies for local public schools and the state's college and university systems. During the fiscal year ending August 31, 1972, over 47 cents of every dollar of state expenditure went to support public education—32.20 cents for local schools and 14.80 cents for institutions of higher education.

TABLE 7-3
Functional expenditures, state of Texas, selected fiscal years, 1950-1972

Function	1950	1955	1960	1965	1969	1972
Public Education	$211.8	$298.6	$426.3	$647.2	$1066.4	$1648.2
Highway Construction and Maintenance	123.5	190.6	386.7	436.4	557.0	605.2
Public Welfare	132.0	157.6	188.0	328.2	399.5	774.4
Charitable and Correctional	23.6	45.2	60.8	78.2	124.6	179.1
Protection of Persons and Property	6.1	9.1	14.3	15.4	35.8	45.0
Public Health and Sanitation	9.4	10.0	11.8	15.4	29.8	52.0

Source: *Annual Reports of the Comptroller of Public Accounts, State of Texas,* 1950-1972. Amounts have been rounded to the nearest tenth of a million dollars.

Recent court decisions in Texas and California threatened, however, to force drastic upward changes in state expenditures for public education. In 1971 the Supreme Court of California (in the case of *Serrano* v. *Priest*) ruled that a system of financing public schools that depended heavily upon local property taxes was in violation of the equal protection clause of the Fourteenth Amendment to the federal Constitution. The California court found that such a system made the quality of the child's education dependent upon the wealth of his parents and neighbors. As the decision was handed down on the West Coast, a taxpayers' suit was pending in San Antonio challenging a similar system in Texas.

In December, 1971, a three-member federal district court panel held unanimously in a case styled *Rodríguez* v. *San Antonio Independent School District* that the Texas system violated both the federal and state constitutions. Texas was given two years to adopt a financial scheme wherein variations in wealth among the state's school districts would not affect spending for the education of any child. Suit was filed by fifteen Mexican-American parents living in the Edgewood Independent School District in San Antonio. The state immediately announced an appeal to the Supreme Court of the United States.

Almost all of the money allocated for the support of state schools comes from three sources—general revenue funds, available school funds, and foundation school funds. Most of the funds directed to the Available School Fund come from portions of taxes on crude oil production, cigarettes, natural gas production, insurance gross premiums, motor vehicle sales, motor fuel sales, and property. Foundation School Fund money likewise comes almost entirely from the same sources, with the exception of taxes on motor fuel sales and general property (see Table 7-4).

Ultimately, on March 21, 1973, the nation's highest court overturned the decision in the *Rodríguez* case. By a 5-to-4 vote the Supreme Court ruled that the state could continue to finance its public schools, at least in part, through the use of local property taxes. Associate Justice Lewis F. Powell, Jr., for the majority, held that the present system of financing public education in Texas is concededly imperfect but that it bears a rational relationship to a legitimate state purpose. Justice Powell also held that the present Texas system assured basic education for every child in the state and that it also permitted and encouraged participation in and significant control of each district's school at the local level. (Reading 7-3 is a much condensed version of the Supreme Court's quite lengthy opinion.)

State officials appeared to recognize that the Supreme Court's decision was only a reprieve and not a mandate to ignore the manifold inequities that promoted the original San Antonio suit. During 1973 and 1974 at least seven different legislative and executive commissions, committees, and study groups were at work on the problem. (Readings 7-4 and 7-5 present a detailed analysis of the public school finance problem in Texas caused by growing costs and recent court decisions.) A 1972 plan offered by a Texas Education Agency study group (see Reading 7-6) went so far as to advocate that the state take over the financing of public schools without local taxation. Other alternatives will be given careful study over the next few years.

According to a survey conducted in 1969 by the Legislative Budget Office, the state of Texas has allocated a significantly larger proportion of expenditures for local public schools than the composite of all states. It continues, however, to lag behind seven other states in total outlay for such purposes, although only three states have a greater public school population.

The twenty-five state-supported institutions of higher education require an annual expenditure of well over $300 million, and their costs are increasing

TABLE 7-4
Major state funds

Inputs	Outputs
General Revenue Fund	
State Property Tax Inheritance Tax Sales and Use Taxes License Fees Transfers from Omnibus Tax Clearance Fund	Aid to Public Schools Public Welfare Programs Public Health Programs Public Safety Programs Cost of Legislative, Executive and Judicial Departments
Omnibus Tax Clearance Fund	
Severance Taxes Occupation Taxes Selective Sales Taxes Franchise Taxes	Farm- and Ranch-to-Market Roads Public Welfare Programs Teacher Retirement Payments Foundation School Program
Available School Fund	
Severance Taxes Selective Sales Taxes Insurance Gross Receipts Tax Motor Vehicle Sales Tax	Aid to Public Schools
Foundation School Fund	
Severance Taxes Selective Sales Taxes Insurance Gross Receipts Tax Motor Vehicle Sales Tax	Aid to Public Schools
Highway Trust Fund	
Motor Fuels Tax Motor Vehicle Registration Fees	Interstate Highways U.S. and State Highways Farm- and Ranch-to-Market Roads
College Building Fund	
State Property Tax	College Buildings
Permanent University Fund	
Land Sales, Rentals, and Royalties	University Buildings

rapidly as enrollments grow, new senior colleges are authorized, and inflation adds to fixed expenditures. State colleges and universities are supported by appropriations from the General Revenue Fund and from tuition and other fees collected by the local institutions from their students. Some college buildings are financed from the College Building Fund and the Permanent University Fund.

State aid to public junior colleges exceeded $47 million in the 1972 fiscal year. These institutions are funded from four major sources—state aid, local taxes, student fees, and federal and private grants. Had the *Rodríguez* decision referred to above been upheld in the United States Supreme Court, it is quite likely that the local tax funding portion of junior college financing would have been challenged in the federal courts on the same grounds.

COSTS OF HIGHWAY CONSTRUCTION AND MAINTENANCE

The cost of building and maintaining an adequate system of highways for so vast an area as Texas is sizable and has increased materially in recent years. The state's highway system comprises over 70,000 miles, covering three types of roads: interstate highways, United States and state-numbered highways, and farm- and ranch-to-market roads.

Texas highways are constructed and maintained on a "pay-as-you-ride" basis. For the most part they are thus paid for by highway users. Principal sources of the highway dollar are the motor fuel tax, motor vehicle registration fees, and the federal Highway Trust Fund, to which certain federal highway-user taxes are allocated. The Highway Trust Fund was created by Congress in 1956 to help finance the construction of a 41,000-mile federal highway system, the bulk of which is represented by the system of interstate highways currently being constructed. Taxes designated by Congress to be channeled into the fund were those on gasoline, diesel, and special motor fuels, on trucks and tires, on tread rubber, and on the use of heavy trucks and busses on the highways. Apportioning of this fund is made on the basis of a "needs" formula for interstate highways and an "area-population-mileage" formula for other types of federally subsidized highways. Nearly ninety cents of each highway dollar is spent on building and maintaining the roads, while the remainder is spent for equipment, support of the highway patrol, research, and administration. All federal aid is earmarked for construction (50 per cent on regular federal highways and 90 per cent on interstate highways), while maintenance and operating expenses on all highways are the state's responsibilities. For several years now Texas has received the lion's share of federal funds allocated for highway construction. Rural roads, except those designated as farm- or ranch-to-market roads, remain the fiscal responsibility of the county governments.

EXPENDITURES FOR PUBLIC WELFARE PROGRAMS

Funds for support of the various welfare programs of the Texas government amounted to approximately twenty-three cents of the expenditure dollar in the fiscal year 1972. Although welfare expenditures have increased steadily during the past three decades, they have failed by a wide margin to keep pace with increases in the cost of living. Major programs financed by the state include old age assistance, aid to the needy blind, aid to families with dependent children, aid to the permanently and totally disabled, and medical services to all recipients of public assistance. Welfare funds are primarily supplied by the federal government—almost 70 per cent in the fiscal year 1971-1972—in the form of grants-in-aid (see Table 7-5) and by allocations from oil production, natural gas production, cigarettes, insurance gross receipts, and motor vehicle sales taxes. In 1972 the Congress of the United States enacted the Supplemental Security Income Act, which will apparently abolish the existing state-administered welfare programs of old age assistance, aid to the needy blind, and aid to the disabled. Effective January 1, 1974, the statute provides for a $130-a-month minimum cash income for each single person eligible for old age assistance, and comparable incomes for persons in other categories.

Already consuming approximately one-fourth of the expenditure dollar, welfare payments and administration have been climbing at an exceedingly rapid rate in the 1970s. The national government will assume responsibility for the expenditures detailed in Table 7-5 in 1974.

TABLE 7-5
Public welfare payments, 1971-1972 fiscal year

Program	Average Number	Average Payment	State Funds	Federal Funds	Totals
Old Age Assistance	$232,166	$62.65	$45,555,563	$128,986,825	$174,542,388
Aid to Needy Blind	4,020	79.16	1,172,333	2,646,343	3,818,676
Aid to Permanently and Totally Disabled	23,871	66.43	5,404,236	13,624,764	19,029,000
Aid to Families with Dependent Children	85,369	118.15	29,290,752	91,745,412	121,036,164
Totals			$81,422,884	$237,003,344	$318,426,288

Source: Legislative Budget Office, *Fiscal Size-Up of Texas State Services, 1971-1972.*

EXPENDITURES FOR ELEEMOSYNARY AND CORRECTIONAL INSTITUTIONS

Almost five cents of every expenditure dollar in Texas goes to maintain the state's eleemosynary and correctional institutions. *Eleemosynary institutions* include schools for the mentally retarded; hospitals for the mentally ill; homes for senile patients; special educational institutions for the blind, the deaf, and the mute; homes for orphans; tuberculosis hospitals; and an institution for the cerebral-palsied. *Correctional institutions* include the state prison, prison farms, and juvenile correctional institutions. The addition of new and more modern units, as well as the improvement of existing ones in each of these areas, is a continuing project for the state and involves it in growing expenditures.

MISCELLANEOUS EXPENDITURES

Other significant expenditures include protection of persons and property, regulation of business and industry, conservation of health and sanitation, development and conservation of natural resources, and administrative costs of the legislative, executive, and judicial departments. None of them, however, involves the expenditure of as much as five cents of the expenditure dollar.

PROPOSED FISCAL REFORMS

As the costs of Texas governments increase steadily and as new sources of revenue become more difficult to discover, Texans will undoubtedly begin looking for ways to stretch their current tax dollars. Thus they may turn ultimately to fiscal reforms as one means of accomplishing their objective. Existing revenue sources, for example, might produce larger sums if they were not hamstrung by so many detailed and damaging constitutional and statutory restrictions, and were not subject to antiquated and crippling methods of tax assessment and collection. Existing accounting methods, moreover, fail to reflect up-to-the-minute conditions in Texas finances; and existing appropriations methods, also encumbered with constitutional restraints, fail to provide flexibility in the use of public funds. Texas taxpayers and their state and local representatives should therefore examine all facets of the state fiscal program with a view toward effecting savings and conservation of funds, proper administration of revenues and expenditures, and alternative sources of income.

TAX REFORMS

With over 250 funds earmarked for special purposes in the Texas treasury, the state legislature finds it exceedingly difficult to adapt a revenue program to changing needs. Many of these funds are established by the constitution and are supplied by revenue from a *dedicated tax.* Tax money thus pours into these funds in amounts beyond the control of the state's officers and can be spent only for the purpose for which it is assessed and collected. Surpluses often accumulate that cannot be immediately and easily used, especially in such funds as the Confederate Pension Fund. The number of these funds should be sharply reduced and their taxes repealed or the dedication removed so that the money can be channeled into the General Revenue Fund for use in meeting current needs.

Texas statutes and the constitution have imposed a substantial number of limitations on the taxing power of state and local governments. These limitations have, for example, conferred special privileges on persons engaged in agricultural pursuits. Other legal provisions limit tax rates, objects to be taxed, methods of taxation, and types of taxes. All these limitations should be examined carefully and their number reduced to a minimum. Privileged positions for individuals, corporations, occupational groups, or other categories of taxpayers should as a general rule be eliminated. Other source and rate limitations imposed by law should also be eliminated in order to allow each spending unit to impose taxes necessary to support its program. The only limits should be those imposed by citizen-taxpayers, to whom spending agents are legally and politically responsible. Spending agencies, moreover, should be subject again only to the citizens' permission.

Of all taxes imposed by state and local governments in Texas, the one most in need of reform is the *ad valorem tax* on property. In recent years an ever-increasing chorus has urged the state government to abandon the property tax, leaving it exclusively in the hands of local governments. Texas has already taken tentative steps in that direction by sharply limiting the rate that the state can charge for its treasury. Regardless of whether it is used by both levels of government or by only one of them, some fundamental changes in the ad valorem assessment and collection are necessary in order to make it both equitable and productive.

The first order of business should be the *equalization of assessments,* for the areas of injustice here are large. Taxing agencies must be given a free hand in improving the recruitment and training of personnel concerned with property tax assessments. The job of tax assessor-collector should be recognized as a professional, nonpartisan position to be filled by persons with professional training and experience. The post should be filled, therefore, by appointment, not election, as is that of the county tax assessor and collector, who levies the property tax for both the state and the county. Most other tax assessors—those for cities, schools, and other special districts—are already appointed. The assessor should be paid a salary that would attract professionally trained personnel, and he should be provided with a sufficient number of well-paid assistants and clerks to enable him to get the job done promptly and efficiently.

At this point a second suggestion seems in order: *consolidation of the number of tax offices.* In 1967 the Texas Committee on State and Local Tax Policy found at least 1,500 separate local tax offices in Texas. Twenty-four large urban counties had an average of 19 each, the other 230 counties an average of 5 or 6. These separate tax offices do not cooperate with each other. They do not share information concerning the location of taxable property, methods of assessment, or renditions of the same real or personal property. The committee therefore found that the vast majority of local property tax offices are too small to do a reasonable job of administering the tax in an equitable manner or to attract and pay qualified appraisers, and that they are financially unable to provide needed supporting personnel and equipment. The committee offered five alternatives to the present arrangement: (1) state administration of assessment and collection; (2) state assessment, with local levy and collection; (3) state assessment of railroads, utilities, minerals, and certain types of personal property, with local assessment of other kinds of property, and thus local levy and collection; (4) local assessment and collection, with state supervision of assessments;

or (5) areawide local assessment districts. The first and last courses would effect the greatest degree of consolidation. Probably the county would be the most practical unit for assessment and collection, with or without state supervision or assessment. Thus a single countywide property tax agency, headed by an appointed, well-paid assessor with the necessary staff and equipment, seems most desirable.

Consolidation of taxing units and employment of professional personnel should make it possible to equalize the burden on real and personal property. As things now stand, tax officers in different areas go through vastly different procedures to arrive at types of property to be assessed and valuations for tax purposes. In some areas only real property is taxed; in others real property and selected items of personal property—such as automobiles, furniture, and livestock; and in rare instances all real and personal property. Different tax offices employ different calculations to arrive at assessed value. The net effect is that different kinds of property are assessed at different fractions of full value by tax offices in the same geographical area. Texas, therefore, should develop procedures for assessing property taxes that can achieve uniform results.

Some dissatisfaction with the levy and collection of the general sales tax has been voiced since its adoption in 1961. From the beginning critics pointed out that sales of a large number of items were exempted from payment, and they demanded broadened coverage. Gradually some of the exempt items have been included, the latest of which were beer and liquor in 1969. Inclusion of other items could produce substantial sums of additional revenue. There is strong opposition, however, to the inclusion of subsistence items such as food because of the highly regressive nature of such levies.

Moreover, since state statutes require regular reports from businesses selling goods subject to the sales tax, and since the seller collects the tax, successful administration requires extensive auditing of at least the major sellers in order to make sure that all funds due the state are being collected and reported.

At present the state levies natural resource or severance taxes only on the production of a limited number of items—petroleum, natural gas, sulphur, and cement. Considerable additional revenue, as well as a more equitable distribution of the tax load, could be effected by expanding this type of levy to include such other minerals as stone, sand, gravel, salt, lime, clays, and gypsum. A "gas gathering" tax, assuming one could be designed that the courts would uphold, might also be added to present resource taxes. Such a tax would be imposed on the transportation of natural gas, after its severance, from the well to the first meter. It would require the users of the natural resource to help pay a direct amount for its depletion.

ALTERNATE SOURCES OF TAX REVENUE

In addition to tax reform, the state might continue its efforts to stretch its revenue dollars by considering some alternative sources of tax revenue. State and local income taxes and additional local sales taxes are the most promising options, for both will produce considerable sums of money and will cost comparatively little to administer.

If Texas chooses to follow the format employed by forty-six of the states, it will impose a *corporate income tax* in preference to a personal income tax. A state tax on corporate incomes would be levied on income attributable to business done in the state. It could be based on gross income, gross receipts, or net income; it would probably replace present gross receipts taxes; and it might well be accompanied by a companion tax to cover the income of unincorporated competing businesses.

Should the state choose instead, or in addition, to impose a *personal income tax,* the National Tax Association recommends that it be levied upon entire net incomes from all sources, that it be collected only from persons and at the places where they actually reside, that it allow deductions for operating expenses and interest on indebtedness, that it exempt all small incomes, and that the rate be uniform for all kinds of income. The association also suggests that rates be progressive, that administration be placed in the hands of a state tax officer, and that the tax be collected from the taxpayers on the basis of strictly enforced and controlled returns.

Local governments, often in dire need of more tax money, could be empowered to make use of a local income tax or even a local motor fuels tax in addition to the optional sales tax already authorized, or in place of that tax if they desired. If adopted, the local income tax should be limited to taxing what the local authority can reasonably administer; for example, gross wages of residents and net income of corporations and other businesses located in the taxing jurisdiction. The rate should probably be fixed at a small percentage, not over 2 per cent.

DEBT REFORMS

Nearly all Texas governments are limited in some way in their ability to acquire indebtedness. At a minimum, the ceiling on state indebtedness should be removed from the constitution and the decision as to the amount, if any, be left to the Legislature, which is responsible to the citizen-taxpayers who will be taxed to repay the debt. The state should be free to borrow when emergencies occur and to repay when conditions are more favorable. It is no longer necessary in this day to hamper a state government with debt restrictions designed to curb the irresponsible behavior of state officials in the past.

Local debt limitations should be modified to relate directly to the circumstances of time and place. Debt for capital improvements having a reasonable prospect for self-payment should not be limited arbitrarily but only by legitimate prospects for repayment. Other debt limits should be tied to average annual revenues, with periodic review by a state agency.

REFORM IN STATE AID TO LOCALITIES

The system of state grants to local governments has developed without much forethought in Texas. There is a growing need, therefore, for some effort to see the picture as a whole, to determine what portion of the state's total revenues can reasonably be allotted to local governments, and to decide how this sum should be apportioned among the purposes for which aid is granted. Under this recommendation the present Texas scheme of "per capita" grants in lump sums, such as those for public schools, and "shared taxes," such as the motor vehicle registration fee, would be replaced by "direct grants" to local units, with no strings attached. Thus responsibility for wise and proper use of the money would be placed where, in theory at least, it has always been—in the hands of local officials.

APPROPRIATIONS REFORMS

Students of public finance have long criticized the two customary methods state legislatures have used to appropriate money to state and local spending agencies. They have attacked *itemized appropriations* for not permitting administrators the discretion and flexibility of action thought to be essential to execute public policy with reasonable dispatch and efficiency. On the other hand, *lump sum appropriations* are extremely desirable in the hands of wise and experienced administrators but are subject to abuse in the hands of less dependable ones.

Although Texas appropriations statutes now carry fewer itemized grants than they did a decade ago, they still have to be characterized as semi-itemized at best. The state should consider adopting a third procedure, known as the *allotment plan,* which makes use of the lump sum kind of appropriation but combines it with quarterly or monthly allotments made only upon approval of an itemized quarterly or monthly work program. Such a scheme would emphasize financial planning and would place responsibility upon the chief executives of the state or local governments and their staffs for the supervision and reporting of expenditures in their areas. This procedure would force chief executives to see to it that their subordinates spent the money allotted to them wisely and in accordance with overall program needs.

REFORMS IN FISCAL ADMINISTRATION

Even if a state's revenue system is producing substantial sums adequate for the legitimate demands made upon it, the state may still face fiscal deficits, in part because of poor fiscal management. The cost of handling public funds cannot be avoided, but it must be reduced to a minimum. The relatively high cost of handling public funds in Texas should prompt the adoption of some or all of a group of administrative reforms.

Of primary importance is the collection of taxes and other fees. Today more than thirty state departments, boards, and commissions accept taxes, licenses, fees, and other miscellaneous revenues. The collection of the more important state revenues is divided among at least four of these agencies. In order to achieve better management of tax revenues, collection of taxes and other fees should be turned over to a single state department of revenue or to a state department of taxation and finance to which the duty would be assigned by law. In addition to collecting most, if not all, state taxes and fees, the department should assist and supervise local governments in the assessment and collection of local taxes; and it should conduct continuous research into methods and procedures that can facilitate the assessment and collection of taxes at the greatest return to the state and local governments.

Most authorities on state fiscal management recommend a consolidated state budget under executive supervision. Under the combined direction of an executive agency and a legislative agency, Texas has developed a comprehensive budget that takes cognizance of all income, expenditures, and financial requirements (see Reading 7-7). The activities of the present Executive Budget Office and the Legislative Budget Board should probably be combined in a single agency under executive supervision. If this cannot be achieved, then consideration should be given to consolidation under legislative direction. Moreover, some uniform plan for classifying items of expenditure, a uniform accounting system, and a means of preventing overspending, or spending so much in the early part of the fiscal year that not enough remains to maintain operations during the latter part, should be developed to aid in the overall budgeting process. The accrual system of accounting, consolidation of special funds, and the quarterly allotment system of fund distribution should help to meet these needs.

Although slight improvements have been made, more needs to be done in improving *financial reporting* in Texas. In the past those financial reports that were published were large and cumbersome, poorly bound, unattractive in appearance, and not widely distributed. Improved reports would be neat and attractive in appearance, interesting, and challenging in content. Reports should be readable and supplemented by charts, graphs, tables, and pictures whenever possible. The annual report of the Legislative Budget Board is an excellent example. A well-prepared, attractively printed report would not necessarily stretch tax dollars, but it would enable intelligent citizens to attain a clear understanding of major programs and policies, and how they are being implemented.

Finally, the state of Texas should establish some minimum standards of fiscal procedure and functional performance for local governments, but the local officials concerned should be given the opportunity and encouraged to exceed those standards. Those same local officials should be held responsible for results by the state. In keeping with this proposal, the state should lay down uniform budget procedures for localities and supervise the procedures through which they administer budgets. The state should also create and staff supervising agencies to interpret and enforce its legal requirements, and should assist local units in complying with them; ensure the enforcement of minimum budget and fiscal standards applicable to all local units; and promptly assume direct budgetary and fiscal control where local units break down. State supervision of local fiscal practices should also include a post-audit by state officers of all local accounts and uniform fiscal reports from all localities as a by-product of their uniform budgeting and accounting systems.

If Texas is to perpetuate its century-old principle of "pay-as-you-go" in fiscal affairs, it must solve a most perplexing problem—the critical need for significant, even massive, increases in revenue in a political atmosphere that has been traditionally hostile to tax increases and deficit financing. In the immediate future Texans must face their fiscal problems squarely. They may elect to adopt some, if not all, of the fiscal reforms suggested here; but even those heroic measures will not fully meet the demands for additional funds. It seems inescapable that they must accede to increases in present taxes, adoption of new taxes, or deficit financing. The other alternative—to sharply curtail expenditures—does not seem viable in the face of inflation and increasing public demands.

KEY TERMS AND CONCEPTS

fiscal system
sound fiscal system
tax sources of revenue
nontax sources of revenue
state tax system
benefits received principle
ability to pay principle
social expediency principle
sound tax system
sales tax
regressive tax system
general sales tax
selective sales tax
motor fuel tax
alcoholic beverage tax
tax on cigarette sales
severance or production tax
highway use tax
property tax
inheritance tax
federal grants-in-aid
revenue-sharing
General Revenue Fund
self-liquidating revenue bonds
limited obligation bonds
budget
special funds
accrual accounting
cash accounting
contract purchasing
open market purchasing
emergency purchasing
local purchasing
auditing
Rodríguez v. *San Antonio School District*
eleemosynary institutions
correctional institutions
dedicated tax
ad valorem tax
equalization of assessments
consolidated tax offices
corporate income tax
personal income tax
itemized appropriations
lump sum appropriations
allotment plan
financial reporting

BILL MC CLANAHAN FROM THE DALLAS NEWS

Selected Readings

7-1
TEXAS' TAX EFFORT SECOND LOWEST IN NATION
Stuart Long

Texas is No. 2 because it doesn't try harder than anybody except Nevada.

Avis says it tries harder because it is No. 2, but a new study made for a federal commission reveals that the Texas Legislature, the city councils, school boards and county commissioners courts in Texas try less hard than those in any other state except Nevada to extract taxes from the citizens. The study was made on "tax effort" by the Commission on Intergovernmental Relations as a part of the federal consideration of revenue-sharing and other ways of feeding federal tax dollars to the states and local governments. Statisticians naturally work a bit behind the times, so the figures do not take into account the general increases in taxes voted in 1969, 1970 and 1971. But, presumably, the legislatures and school boards of other states have been doing the same thing.

But what the report says, based on 1969-70 tax collections, is this:

From the *San Angelo Standard-Times,* October 10, 1971. Reprinted by permission.

Texans tax themselves only 72 per cent as high as all the U.S. citizens put together, when the taxes paid are related to the "ability to pay," the income of citizens. Only Nevada, at 71 per cent, taxes its citizens less. By contrast, New York "tried harder" and comes out at 139 per cent of the national average effort. New Mexico taxes at 91 per cent, Oklahoma at 74 per cent, Louisiana at 83 and Ohio at 82. California comes in second from the highest at 116 per cent of the average national effort. But perhaps more interesting to Texas taxpayers is the fact that Texas dropped 4 per cent in effort from 1966-1967 to 1968-1969, when Texas was taxing at 10 per cent less than its revenue capacity. . . .

The reported state-by-state comparisons reaffirm, in updated form and by reference to broader-based measures, some extremely significant findings of an earlier study: that the relative self-financing capacity of governments in various areas does not always correspond closely to the relative well-offness of people in such areas, as reflected by per capita income figures. The reason is, of course, that there is no measure of the relative needs of the various areas. A hard-pressed West Texas city, pipelining water 50 miles, will levy taxes or charges for that vital service far greater than cities blessed by ample, cheap and close-by water supplies like San Antonio. The variations are tremendous. Bexar County local government gets 14.7 per cent of its total revenues from utility profits, where Bell County gets only 5.9 per cent. Ector County gets 50 per cent of its revenue from property taxes on business property, where Denton County gets only 11 per cent, Gregg County 38 per cent and El Paso 27 per cent. Wichita County gets 2.2 per cent from farm property, while adjoining Archer County gets 24 per cent, Grayson gets 10 per cent and Taylor 1.8 per cent.

Residential property pays around a fourth of local revenue in most Texas areas, just about three-fourths of the portion paid by homeowners in the nation as a whole. But Texas cities and counties put on more "local and miscellaneous charges" than the nation on the average. But where they have industry tax, the homeowners get off lightly. Midland County's homeowners pay only 3.5 per cent of local taxes, while business pays 70.5 and the farmers and ranchers pay less than one per cent. Jones County farm property pays 34.9 per cent, while that in Taylor County pays only 18 per cent of local revenues.

What the whole thing shows is the tremendous variation of taxing patterns across Texas, which is really no news. Former Gov. John Connally's Committee on Public School Education reported that on school taxes, but Connally was not able to get the Legislature to change it. Now the Texas Association of School Boards wants the state government to pay all of local school costs, with local taxpayers paying none, as a means of equalizing the costs of public schools on a statewide basis.

7-2
PRESENT AND FUTURE SHOCK IN PROPERTY TAXATION
Mabel Walker

Repeated shock waves have been running through the property tax area, and both the most dramatic and the most numerous of these shocks have occurred within the past year. It is doubtful that any other major tax in this country has been subjected to so many onslaughts from so many different directions within a comparably short period. . . . The situation appears even more significant when we consider that the property tax is likely to have more direct economic and social effects upon the majority of the citizens than any other tax currently imposed.

Sales and income taxes have their undisputed effects upon consumption and investment, but probably cause relatively few persons to lose their homes, or to be unable to buy a home near their place of employment, or to suffer educational disadvantage. The property tax affects both owners and renters. It affects housing and industrial location, educational and recreational facilities, and the maintenance of ecological standards. Unlike other taxes, the burden that it imposes may become heavier, even though the taxpayer's income is shrinking or nonexistent and his standard of consumption declining.

Why have these long-standing effects suddenly become of paramount concern? There appear to be two predominant reasons. First, property tax pressures have been building up sharply during recent years, and the long-suffering taxpayers are becoming increasingly bitter. Second, this is an age of social activism, and many activists—particularly in the legal profession—are pointing up the adverse effects of the tax upon great numbers of citizens, whether or not they are property taxpayers. Legal actions are reaching the courts and resulting in momentous decisions. Complaints are reaching the ears of state governors and legislators . . . and are causing concern in those quarters. It seems reasonable to anticipate that future shock in this area will be even greater than the amount of present shock.

The most dramatic and immediately powerful shock force is represented by court decisions. . . . Current judicial decisions in the property tax area are like volcanic eruptions that will cause tremendous upheavals. The following categories are likely to have particular impact on property taxations: decisions demanding uniformity of assessments; decisions relating to equality of governmental services in different parts of a city; decisions relating to "exclusionary zoning," or as it is frequently dubbed, "snob zoning"; decisions bearing upon ecological considerations; decisions relating to educational and tax disparities resulting from local property tax financing of public schools. . . .

The property taxpayer is peculiarly vulnerable to taxation. Since World War II, property owners have been hit sharply both through increased assessments

From *Texas Town & City*, Vol. LIX (November, 1972), pp. 12-18. The author is Executive Director, Tax Institute of America. Reprinted by permission.

and by rising tax rates. Increased assessments are burdensome to owners who do not wish to sell their homes, particularly if their incomes have not increased proportionately, or if they have retired. In addition they suffer from rising tax rates, occasioned both by growth of services and by cost inflation. . . . Schools account for the major part of the property tax burden, and persons who can barely make ends meet bitterly resent rising salaries and fringe benefits for teachers, elaborate school buildings, and what they consider unnecessary frills in the educational process. Increasing taxpayers' resentment has made itself felt in the defeat of school budgets and of bond issues. In 1967 there were 23,390 school systems in the United States, and 21,782 were independent school districts having the power to levy property taxes. (Of these Texas had 1,308, or the fourth largest number among the American states.)

The more a state is subdivided into small units, the greater is the likelihood of marked fiscal disparities among these units. As education is the most costly local function, these disparities become particularly oppressive in the case of school districts. But the disparities are found not only in tax burdens, but also in the quality of governmental services. Disparities in educational services are particularly resented.

In the period of political activism the discrepancy among school districts, particularly in the states with a large number of such districts, proved an obvious target for social reformers. Most of the court actions relating to these disparities have resulted in verdicts on behalf of the plaintiffs. These decisions relating to educational disparities resulting from local financing of schools have aroused widespread interest. . . .

On December 23, 1971 [for example], a special panel of three federal judges declared the Texas public school financing system—based largely on the local property tax—unconstitutional because it makes educational expenditures a function of local wealth, and ordered the state legislature to devise a new one. (*Rodríguez* v. *San Antonio I.S.D.,* 334 F. Supp. 280.) The finding was essentially the same as one made last August by the California State Supreme Court, and last October by a United States District Court in Minnesota. But unlike either of these courts, the three-judge panel in Texas ordered the state to take remedial action. . . . The Texas State Board of Education voted unanimously on January 8, 1972, to appeal directly to the United States Supreme Court. Thirty states, plus a few local governments, have asked the Supreme Court to reverse the Texas ruling. The Supreme Court agreed on June 7, 1972, to review the ruling . . . in the term beginning in October. . . .

FUTURE OF PROPERTY TAX

Will the property tax disappear, as has been hinted by some journalists and advocated by some tax groups? Not a chance! It is doubtful that a single serious student of the property tax anticipates, or would advocate, such a development. Some of us who have been deeply concerned with the property tax for many years have been anticipating some radical developments, but the actual events have taken place faster and with greater impact than had been expected. Moreover, there have been concurrent and somewhat related developments that may not have been anticipated by anyone. . . .

The property tax has many faults. Administration is far from adequate. Too much property is exempt. Competition among local governmental units for tax-paying ratables results in bad land use planning as well as in great fiscal disparities—particularly with respect to education. Exclusionary zoning designed to keep out low-income groups unfairly restricts them in their search for housing. Vast fortunes are being made in land speculation. Finally, so much of the burden of supplying governmental services has been loaded upon the property tax that it is oppressive in many places and contributes to urban deterioration. But these disadvantages could be corrected, if there were a sufficient will to do so, and there seem no reasonable grounds whatever to downgrade the property tax, perhaps to the point of eventual extinction.

"What is a fair tax rate?" or "What should be the limit on property tax rates?" are questions that are often asked and seldom answered. Tax writers give little attention to such questions, although they are fundamental. The major evil of the property tax is the manipulation of the rate to meet burgeoning governmental needs. This is particularly unfair, as property ownership is, for most persons, a substantial long-term—perhaps lifetime—investment. They have checked on tax and mortgage rates and have tried to estimate whether they can assume the financial responsibilities involved in ownership of property. They know, of course, that if their property increases in value the *assessment* will be, or should be, increased. But a valid argument could be presented for maintaining a stable *rate.* A sharply increasing rate on their capital investment jeopardizes their solvency. It seems to this writer that juggling (can we use the term "juggling" for something that goes up but never down?) the property tax rate is far less defensible than changing the rate of income or sales taxes, since the former affects a long-term capital investment. It is this manipulation of the rate that makes the tax so onerous on the elderly, who thought that they had provided a home for their old age, only to find that they are being penalized beyond their most somber expectations.

If all property were always assessed accurately at full value and if the tax rate were kept constant, the homeowner would be relieved of a great load of anxiety. Some general recognition of the necessity for placing an ultimate limit on property tax rates would enable new owners to buy houses with more assurance that they could afford them and would tend to relieve the anxiety of the elderly homeowner. It would make individual financial planning more orderly. Either governmental authorities will exercise some restraint in loading ever-greater burdens on the property owner, or we shall witness a recurrence of the tax strikes and drastic tax limit legislation of the 1930's. . . .

In connection with some proposals for substantive changes, there has been much discussion as to whether the property tax is progressive or regressive. For the most part, such debating has been a largely meaningless exercise, affording pleasure to economists but actually serving as a red herring that diverts attention from more important aspects of the problem, because it is impossible to form any valid overall conclusion as to its regressivity as presently administered. How can we discuss progressivity or regressivity without considering assessment practices? If private homes are favored by many assessors over apartment houses and business and industrial properties—and there has been considerable evidence in this direction—the net effect of the tax may be progressive, except for apartments in low-income areas. If homes of modest value are assessed at a higher ratio than more expensive homes—and there has been considerable evidence to that effect—then the tax is regressive. But if assessments are highly erratic and houses of equal value are assessed at very different ratios of value—and they often are—then the incidence of the tax is erratic and it cannot be classified as progressive, regressive, or proportional. . . . A final decision on the progressivity or regressivity of this tax must wait upon the achievement of uniform and accurate assessing practices and the equalization of tax burdens among governmental units. . . .

SOME PREVALENT DOUBTS

Here and there commentators are raising the question as to whether huge additional funds are actually needed for education in view of the declining birth rate. The most conspicuously bright spot in this whole problem-studded situation is the falling birth rate, as poorer citizens are getting the opportunity to control the size of their families that the middle- and upper-income groups have long enjoyed. With most of our socio-economic difficulties, we are faced with a numbers game. The current financial resources, available know-how, and trained personnel resources may be adequate to assist and rehabilitate *x* millions of the disadvantaged (whether the disadvantaged arises through ignorance, poverty, or illness), but if these numbers become *x* times *x* millions, the entire social fabric is threatened with a breakdown.

A further question is being asked concerning the quality of the educational process and appropriate standards for evaluation. Educators traditionally equate educational quality with educational expenditure, but such a standard of evaluation ignores efficiency and innovation. Two teachers may have gone through the same educational treadmill for the same number of years and may be paid identical salaries and have comparable teaching tools, but one teacher may be getting far better results from pupils of the same natural abilities than the other. . . .

CONCLUSION

At some point in this accelerating tempo of demanding ever-greater expenditures and sweeping tax reductions, the American people will have to face their moment of truth. Where is the money coming from? Many states already have heavy sales and income taxes, and the federal government is being forced to reduce its present income tax. The property tax is a tough and dependable old workhorse. Although it needs a stiff currying, it is by no means ready for the slaughterhouse.

7-3
SAN ANTONIO INDEPENDENT SCHOOL DISTRICT ET AL. V. RODRIGUEZ ET AL., SUPREME COURT OF THE UNITED STATES (MARCH 21, 1973)

Mr. Justice [Lewis F.] Powell delivered the opinion of the Court.

This suit attacking the Texas system of financing public education was initiated by Mexican-American parents whose children attend the elementary and secondary schools in the Edgewood Independent School District, an urban school district in San Antonio, Texas. They brought a class action on behalf of school children throughout the State who are members of minority groups or who are poor and reside in school districts having a low property tax base. Named as defendants were the State Board of Education, the Commissioner of Education, the State Attorney General, and the Bexar County (San Antonio) Board of Trustees. The complaint was filed in the summer of 1968 and a three-judge court was impaneled in January 1969. In December 1971 the panel rendered its judgment in a *per curiam* opinion holding the Texas school finance system unconstitutional under the Equal Protection Clause of the Fourteenth Amendment. . . .

The first Texas Constitution, promulgated upon Texas' entry into the Union in 1845, provided for the establishment of a system of free schools. Early in its history, Texas adopted a dual approach to the financing of its schools, relying on mutual participation by the local school districts and the State. As early as 1883 the state constitution was amended to provide for the creation of local school districts empowered to levy *ad valorem* taxes with the consent of local taxpayers for the "erection of school buildings" and for the "further maintenance of public free schools." Such local funds as were raised were supplemented by funds distributed to each district from the State's Permanent and Available School Funds.

The Permanent School Fund, established in 1854, was endowed with millions of acres of public land set aside to assure a continued source of income for school support. The Available School Fund, which received income from the Permanent School Fund as well as from a state *ad valorem* property tax and other designated taxes, served as the disbursing arm for most state educational funds throughout the late 1800's and the first half of this century. Additionally, in 1918 an increase in state property taxes was used to finance a program providing free textbooks throughout the State.

Until recent times Texas was predominantly rural and its population and property wealth were spread relatively evenly across the State. Sizable differences in the value of assessable property between local school districts became increasingly evident as the State became more industrialized and as rural-to-urban population shifts became more pronounced. The location of commercial and industrial

Associate Justice Lewis F. Powell, Jr. delivered the opinion of the Court, in which Chief Justice Warren Burger, and Associate Justices Potter Stewart, Harry A. Blackmun, and William H. Rehnquist joined.

property began to play a significant role in determining the amount of tax resources available to each school district. These growing disparities in population and taxable property between districts were responsible in part for increasingly notable differences in levels of local expenditure for education. . . .

Recognizing the need for increased state funding to help offset disparities in local spending and to meet Texas' changing educational requirements, the state legislature in the late 1940's undertook a thorough evaluation of public education with an eye toward major reform. In 1947 . . . [the Texas Legislature created the Texas Minimum Foundation School Program].

The Program calls for state and local contributions to a fund ear-marked specifically for teacher salaries, operating expenses, and transportation costs. The State, supplying funds from its general revenues, finances approximately 80% of the Program, and the school districts are responsible—as a unit—for providing the remaining 20%. The district's share, known as the Local Fund Assignment, is apportioned among the school districts under a formula designed to reflect each district's relative taxpaying ability. . . .

The design of this complex system was twofold. First, it was an attempt to assure that the Foundation Program would have an equalizing influence on expenditure levels between school districts most capable of paying. Second, the Program's architects sought to establish a Local Fund Assignment that would force every school district to contribute to the education of its children but that would not by itself exhaust any district's resources. Today every school district does impose a property tax from which it derives locally expendable funds in excess of the amount necessary to satisfy its Local Fund Assignment under the Foundation Program. . . .

The school district in which appellees reside, the Edgewood Independent School District, has been compared throughout this litigation with the Alamo Heights Independent School District. This comparison between the least and the most affluent districts in the San Antonio area serves to illustrate the manner in which the dual system of finance operates and to indicate the extent to which substantial disparities exist despite the State's impressive progress in recent years. . . . And it was these disparities, largely attributable to differences in the amounts of money collected through local property taxation, that led the District Court to conclude that Texas' dual system of public school finance violated the Equal Protection Clause. The District Court held that the Texas system discriminates on the basis of wealth in the manner in which education is provided for its people. . . .

The State candidly admits that "[n]o one familiar with the Texas system would contend that it has yet achieved perfection." Apart from its concession that educational finance in Texas has "defects" and "imperfections," the State defends the system's rationality with vigor and disputes the District Court's finding that it lacks a "reasonable basis."

This, then, establishes the framework for our analysis. We must decide, first, whether the Texas system of financing public education operates to the disadvantage of some suspect class or impinges upon a fundamental right explicitly or implicitly protected by the Constitution. . . . If so, the judgment of the District

Court should be affirmed. If not, the Texas scheme must still be examined to determine whether it rationally furthers some legitimate, articulated state purpose and therefore does not constitute an invidious discrimination in violation of the Equal Protection Clause of the Fourteenth Amendment. . . .

Only appellees' first possible basis for describing the class disadvantaged by the Texas school finance system—discrimination against a class of definably "poor" persons—might arguably meet the criteria established in . . . prior cases. Even a cursory examination, however, demonstrates that neither of the two distinguishing characteristics of wealth classifications can be found here. First, in support of their charge that the system discriminates against the "poor" appellees have made no effort to demonstrate that it operates to the peculiar disadvantage of any class fairly definable as indigent, or as composed of persons whose incomes are beneath any designated poverty level. . . . Second, neither appellees nor the District Court addressed the fact that, unlike each of the foregoing cases, lack of personal resources has not occasioned an absolute deprivation of the desired benefit. . . .

For these two reasons—the absence of any evidence that the financing system discriminates against any definable category of "poor" people or that it results in the absolute deprivation of education—the disadvantaged class is not susceptible to identification in traditional terms. . . .

This brings us, then, to the third way in which the classification scheme might be defined—*district* wealth discrimination. Since the only correlation indicated by the evidence is between district property wealth and expenditures, it may be argued that discrimination might be found without regard to the individual income characteristics of district residents. . . . However described, it is clear that appellees' suit asks this Court to extend its most exacting scrutiny to review a system that allegedly discriminates against a large, diverse, and amorphous class, unified only by the common factor of residence in districts that happen to have less taxable wealth than other districts. The system of alleged discrimination and the class it defines have none of the traditional indicia of suspectness: the class is not saddled with such disabilities, or subjected to such a history of purposeful unequal treatment, or relegated to such a position of political powerlessness as to command extraordinary protection from the majoritarian political process.

We thus conclude that the Texas system does not operate to the peculiar disadvantage of any suspect class. But in recognition of the fact that this Court has never heretofore held that wealth discrimination alone provides an adequate basis for invoking strict scrutiny, appellees have not relied solely on this contention. They also assert that the State's system impermissibly interferes with the exercise of a "fundamental" right and that accordingly the prior decisions of this Court require the application of the strict standard of judicial review. It is this question—whether education is a fundamental right, in the sense that it is among the rights and liberties protected by the Constitution . . . to which the Court now turns.

Education, of course, is not among the rights afforded explicit protection under our Federal Constitution. Nor do we find any basis for saying it is implicitly so protected. . . . The Texas system . . . utilizes today–including the decisions permitting localities to tax and expend locally, and creating and continuously expanding state aid–every effort to *extend* public education and to improve its quality. Of course, every reform that benefits some more than others may be criticized for what it fails to accomplish. But we think it plain that, in substance, the thrust of the Texas system is affirmative and reformatory and, therefore, should be scrutinized under judicial principles sensitive to the nature of the State's efforts and to the rights reserved to the States under the Constitution. . . .

We need not rest our decision, however, solely on the inappropriateness of the strict scrutiny test. A century of Supreme Court adjudication under the Equal Protection Clause affirmatively supports the application of the traditional standard of review, which requires only that the State's system be shown to bear some rational relationship to legitimate state purposes. . . . We have here nothing less than a direct attack on the way in which Texas has chosen to raise and disburse state and local tax revenues. We are asked to condemn the State's judgment in conferring on political subdivisions the power to tax local property to supply revenues for local interests. . . . [W]e stand on familiar ground when we continue to acknowledge that the Justices of this Court lack both the expertise and the familiarity with local problems so necessary to the making of wise decisions with respect to the raising and disposition of public revenues. Yet we are urged to direct the State either to alter drastically the present system or throw out the property tax altogether in favor of some other form of taxation. No scheme of taxation, whether the tax is imposed on property, income, or purchase of goods and services, has yet been devised which is free of all discriminatory impact. . . . The foregoing considerations buttress our conclusion that Texas' system of public school finance is an inappropriate candidate for strict judicial scrutiny. . . .

[T]o the extent that the Texas system of school finance results in unequal expenditures between children who happen to reside in different districts, we cannot say that such disparities are the product of a system that is so irrational as to be invidiously discriminatory. Texas has acknowledged its shortcomings and has persistently endeavored–not without some success–to ameliorate the differences in levels of expenditures without sacrificing the benefits of local participation. . . . The constitutional standard under the Equal Protection Clause is whether the challenged state action rationally furthers a legitimate purpose or interest. . . . We hold that the Texas plan abundantly satisfies this standard. . . .

The need is apparent for reform in tax systems which may well have relied too long and too heavily on the local property tax. And certainly innovative new thinking as to public education, its methods and its funding, is necessary to assure both a higher level of quality and greater uniformity of opportunity. These matters merit the continued attention of the scholars who already have contributed much by their challenges. But the ultimate solutions must come from the lawmakers and from the democratic pressures of those who elect them.

Mr. Justice [Potter] Stewart, concurring.

The method of financing public schools in Texas, as in almost every other State, has resulted in a system of public education that can fairly be described as chaotic and unjust. It does not follow, however, and I cannot find, that this system violates the Constitution of the United States. I join the opinion and judgment of the court because I am convinced that any other course would mark an extraordinary departure from principled adjudication under the Equal Protection Clause of the Fourteenth Amendment. . . .

Mr. Justice [William J.] Brennan, dissenting.

Although I agree with my Brother White that the Texas statutory scheme is devoid of any rational basis, and for that reason is violative of the Equal Protection Clause, I also record my disagreement with the Court's rather distressing assertion that a right may be deemed "fundamental" for the purposes of equal protection analysis only if it is "explicitly or implicitly guaranteed by the Constitution."

Mr. Justice [Byron R.] White, with whom Mr. Justice [William O.] Douglas and Mr. Justice Brennan join, dissenting.

Perhaps the majority believes that the major disparity in revenues provided and permitted by the Texas system is inconsequential. I cannot agree, however, that the difference of the magnitude appearing in this case can sensibly be ignored, particularly since the State itself considers it so important to provide opportunities to exceed the minimum state educational expenditures.

There is no difficulty in identifying the class that is subject to the alleged discrimination and that is entitled to the benefits of the Equal Protection Clause. I need go no farther than the parents and children in the Edgewood district, who are plaintiffs here and who assert that they are entitled to the same choice as Alamo Heights to augment local expenditures for schools but are denied that choice by state law. This group constitutes a class sufficiently definite to invoke the protection of the Equal Protection Clause as were the voters in allegedly unrepresented counties in reapportionment cases. . . . Similarly, in the present case we would blink reality to ignore the fact that school districts, and students in the end, are differentially affected by the Texas financing scheme with respect to their capacity to supplement the Minimum Foundation School Program. At the very least, the law discriminates against those children and their parents who live in districts where the per-pupil tax base is sufficiently low to make impossible the provision of comparable school revenues by resort to the real property tax which is the only device the State extends for this purpose.

Mr. Justice [Thurgood] Marshall, with whom Mr. Justice Douglas concurs, dissenting.

The Court today decides, in effect, that a State may constitutionally vary the quality of education which it offers its children in accordance with the amount of taxable wealth located in the school districts within which they reside. The majority's decision represents an abrupt departure from the mainstream of recent state and federal court decisions concerning the unconstitutionality of state educational financing schemes dependent upon taxable local wealth. More unfortunately, though, the majority's holding can only be seen as a retreat from our historic commitment to equality of educational opportunity and as unsupportable acquiescence in a system which deprives children in their earliest years of the chance to reach their full potential as citizens. The Court does this despite the absence of any substantial justification for a scheme which arbitrarily channels educational resources in accordance with the fortuity of the amount of taxable wealth within each district.

In my judgment, the right of every American to an equal start in life, so far as the provision of a state service as important as education is concerned, is far too vital to permit state discrimination on grounds as tenuous as those presented by this record. Nor can I accept the notion that it is sufficient to remit these appellees to the vagaries of the political process which, contrary to majority's suggestion, has proven singularly unsuited to the task of providing a remedy for this discrimination. I, for one, am unsatisfied with the hope of an ultimate "political" solution sometime in the indefinite future while, in the meantime, countless children unjustifiably receive inferior educations that "may affect their hearts and minds in a way unlikely ever to be undone." *Brown* v. *Board of Education,* 347 U.S. 483, 494 (1954). I must therefore respectfully dissent. . . .

[I]t is essential to recognize that an end to the wide variations in taxable district property wealth inherent in the Texas financing scheme would entail none of the untoward consequences suggested by the Court . . . [or by the State of Texas].

First, affirmance of the District Court's decision would hardly sound the death knell for local control of education. It would mean neither centralized decisionmaking or federal court intervention in the operation of public schools. Clearly, this suit has nothing to do with local educational spending. It involves only a narrow aspect of local control—namely, local control over the raising of educational funds. In fact, in striking down interdistrict disparities in taxable local wealth, the District Court took the course which is most likely to make true local control over educational decisionmaking a reality for *all* Texas school districts.

Nor does the District Court's decision even necessarily eliminate local control of educational funding. The District Court struck down nothing more than the continued interdistrict wealth discrimination inherent in the present property tax. Both centralized and decentralized plans for educational funding not involving such interdistrict discrimination have been put forward. The choice among these or other alternatives remains with the State, not with the federal courts. In this regard, it should be evident that the degree of federal intervention in matters of local concern would be substantially less in this context than in previous decisions in which we have been asked effectively to impose a particular scheme upon the States under the guise of the Equal Protection Clause. . . .

The Court seeks solace for its action today in the possibility of legislative reform. The Court's suggestions of legislative redress and experimentation will doubtless be a great comfort to the school children of Texas' disadvantaged districts, but considering the vested interests of wealthy school districts in the preservation of the status quo, they are worth little more. The possibility of legislative action is, in all events, no answer to this Court's duty under the Constitution to eliminate unjustified state discrimination. In this case we have been presented with an instance of such discrimination, in a particularly invidious form, against an individual interest of large constitutional and practical importance. To support the demonstrated discrimination in the provision of educational opportunity the State has offered a justification which, on analysis, takes on at best an ephemeral character. Thus, I believe that the wide disparities in taxable district property wealth inherent in the local property tax element of the Texas financing scheme render that scheme violative of the Equal Protection Clause.

7-4
PUBLIC SCHOOL FINANCE PROBLEMS IN TEXAS
Texas Research League

TRENDS IN THE PAST DECADE

Expenditures for public school education in Texas totaled $2.1 billion in 1970-71—almost three times the $750 million spent in 1960. Although the number of students enrolled increased by 37 per cent during this period, expenditures per student more than doubled. The average salary for professional personnel increased 81 per cent, while the pupil-teacher ratio dropped. An additional 51,600 professional persons were employed to handle the enrollment increases and to lower staffing ratios. Payroll expenditures for nonprofessional school employees grew from $61.7 million to more than $221 million.

The cost of the Foundation School Program (paid 80 per cent by the State) increased from $379 million in 1960-61 to nearly $1.1 billion in 1970-71. While state aid was increasing, local school taxes (which support 20 per cent of the Foundation Program, finance all capital outlay and provide "enrichment" beyond the Foundation Program) also increased, from $340 million to $817 million. During the decade, federal aid jumped from about $38 million to $230 million.

A LOOK AT THE FUTURE

Because of the lower birth rates, the total enrollment in public schools is expected to decrease during the next five years, even though more than 100,000 additional children will be attending public kindergartens during that period. Nonetheless,

From *TRL Analyzes Developments in Texas State and Local Government,* Texas Research League Bulletin, June, 1972.

projections by the Texas Education Agency indicate that the number of professionals employed by the public schools will increase by more than 10,000 between now and 1977. While the number of regular elementary and secondary school teachers will decline, this will be more than offset by substantial increases in kindergarten, special education and vocational education teachers. All told, the projected personnel increases are expected to drop the pupil-professional ratio by about eight per cent in the next five years.

The cost of the Foundation School Program is projected to rise substantially because of (1) the additional teachers to be employed, and (2) higher salaries produced by mandated increments for experience and across-the-board salary increases of $600 in 1974-75 and $660 in 1978-79 guaranteed in legislation enacted in 1969.

THE RODRÍGUEZ DECISION

The mounting cost of the Foundation Program has been a matter of concern to state officials. . . . These concerns, however, were pushed into the background in December, 1971 when a three-judge federal panel sitting in San Antonio ruled that ". . . the current system of financing public education in Texas discriminates on the basis of wealth by permitting citizens of affluent districts to provide a higher quality of education for their children, while paying lower taxes. . . ." The Court held that such a system violates the equal protection clause of the Fourteenth Amendment to the United States Constitution and thus the public school finance system of Texas is invalid.

In essence, the San Antonio District Court declared that the resources available for educating each child in Texas' public schools must be equal. The Court did not say that spending on each child must be equal or that local property taxes must be abolished as a source of school support. The decision indicated that a wide variety of financing plans would be acceptable, including systems which incorporate local property taxes, "so long as the variations in wealth among the governmentally chosen units do not affect spending for the education of any child."

A two-year delay was granted by the Court to "afford the defendants and the Legislature an opportunity to take all steps reasonably feasible to make the school system comply with the applicable laws. . . ."

THE PROBLEM OF EQUALIZATION

Standing alone, the Foundation Program presumably meets the Court's standard of an educational system that is not a function of wealth other than the wealth of the State as a whole. Despite some imperfections, the Program does attempt to equalize resources up to the guaranteed Foundation level. However, the Foundation Program is only a part of a total system declared unconstitutional by the

Court, and it was never meant to restrict or balance local enrichment—primarily for extra personnel and higher salaries.

A WIDENING GAP

During the late 1950's and early 1960's, when the Nation was trying to educate students produced by the post-World War II "baby boom" with a teacher force recruited from the children born in the lean Depression years of the 1930's, all states suffered from a chronic shortage of well-qualified teachers. In the competition for new teachers, the standard of effort in Texas became the comparison with a calculated national average teacher salary.

To produce an average state salary in Texas which compared favorably with the national average, it was necessary to combine the minimum salaries guaranteed in all districts under the Foundation Program with the supplements paid in districts which "enriched" their salary schedules to attract better teachers. Whenever the Legislature increased the state minimum schedule, state officials encouraged local districts already paying above the minimum to "pass on" the increase—thereby maintaining the differential between rich and poor districts....

RESOURCE EQUALIZATION: THE TOUGH CHOICE

If the *Rodríguez* decision is upheld, and if it means that equal state-local resources must be provided behind each child in Texas, then equalizing resources among Texas' 1,149 operating districts would require a difficult choice between (1) reducing funds for some districts to raise the resource level for others, or (2) providing substantially increased funds to raise the poorer districts' resources up to the level enjoyed in the more affluent systems. . . .

THE COST OF "LEVELING UP"

Equalization at any level above the average would require a substantially greater net outlay of public funds. For example, if the equalization point were set at $100 above the state average (i.e., $804), the net additional cost to the taxpayers would be nearly $248 million per year. This would provide equalized resources behind 86 per cent of all Texas public school children, but still would entail revenue losses aggregating $59 million by 401 districts enrolling 14 per cent of all students.

The net cost grows very rapidly as the level of equalization is increased:

To equalize resources for 90 per cent of the children would cost $388 million, yet 324 districts would suffer revenue losses.

To equalize resources for 95 per cent of the children would cost $630 million, despite the fact that 233 districts would have less revenue per child.

To equalize resources for 99 per cent of the children would cost $1.4 billion in additional annual taxes, and still there would be 102 school districts with decreased revenues.

To provide equalized resources for 99.9 per cent of the children would increase annual costs by nearly $2.5 billion. Even so, 36 districts would lose revenue....

FULL STATE FINANCING OR A STATE-LOCAL PARTNERSHIP?

FULL STATE FINANCING

State assumption of full responsibility would require a vast amount of additional revenue from some source. For example, the *increased* state cost by 1973-74 under this approach might total nearly $1.5 billion—taking into account present state commitments and replacement of $1 billion in local school taxes and assuming that the equalization level were set only $100 per pupil above the 1970-71 average.

Compared to the 1970-71 state investment of one billion dollars in public education, the cost estimate above would represent a 150 per cent increase, and it is quite possible that full state assumption might be much more costly, depending on the equalization level required.

The magnitude of the cost of full state funding suggests careful consideration of a continued joint state-local financing plan. In addition, an impressive list of educational organizations and public officials have gone on record in favor of maintaining local property taxes for school support as a bulwark of local control in public education.

EQUALIZATION PROBLEMS IN A JOINT STATE-LOCAL SCHOOL FINANCE SYSTEM

Before Texas can comply with the *Rodríguez* resource-equalization requirement (if it is upheld) through a joint state-local finance system, three steps must be taken:

1. A reliable system must be established for estimating taxable values per pupil in each district on a comparable basis;
2. An enforceable definition of taxable property must be adopted and uniformly applied; and
3. The wide variations in per-student taxable resources among the districts must be substantially reduced.

At present, local district tax-paying ability is indirectly measured by the Texas Education Agency through a complex set of formulas based primarily on a county-by-county comparison of economic activity factors.

Within each county, the relative ability of each district is determined by computing its percentage of the total property values on the county tax roll. This system has, at best, only a remote correlation with a district's tax-paying capacity, and it will not yield the kind of full data per student on which the Court relied in the *Rodríguez* case. In addition, the present Economic Index-County Tax Roll system is under a separate attack in the federal courts in a case filed jointly by the Fort Worth, Dallas and Houston school districts. . . .

The problem of a uniform definition of taxable property . . . may involve the submission of one or more constitutional amendments. . . . Briefly, the problem is that school districts do not (and probably cannot) follow the constitutional and statutory provisions which require that *all* property be uniformly assessed and taxed. The solution might take either of two forms: (1) the property tax law might be amended to bring it into conformity with actual practice, or (2) steps might be taken to bring the administration of the property tax into conformity with the law.

The reduction of resource variations among the school districts is another complex problem.

If *Rodríguez* is upheld, the Court might accept as a "reasonably feasible" plan some state-local finance formula which would equalize resources for all but a small percentage of the students in the State—particularly if those students were in districts where high costs were unavoidable. However, it would be almost impossible for the State to match the continuing *potential* infusion of local funds unless that potential is limited in the more affluent districts. For example, even though it is already a high-cost district, affluent Deer Park could have doubled its revenue per pupil in 1972 had it elected to assess property at the constitutional standard of full market value.

There are four possible approaches to reduction of the wide variations in local resources potentials:

1. legal limits on spending or taxing tied to the state-guaranteed program level;
2. realignment of taxing jurisdiction to equalize per-student wealth;
3. a requirement that more affluent districts return some portion of their local tax collections to the State for reapportionment; or
4. modification of the local tax base to eliminate those classes of property which produce the greatest disparities in wealth per pupil.

These various options and their prospective impact on individual districts will . . . [need to be explored by public officials and private groups alike in the next few months].

7-5
TEXAS PUBLIC SCHOOL FINANCE: A MAJORITY OF EXCEPTIONS
Texas Research League

The U.S. Supreme Court on October 12, 1972, heard oral arguments on the State's appeal from the decision of the Federal District Court in the case of *Rodríguez* vs. *San Antonio, et al.* The outcome of that appeal is very much in doubt, but a number of education groups are preparing proposals aimed at solving what the Legislature in 1969 described as the "serious problem which exists in the financing of the Minimum Foundation Program and . . . [the] apparent inequities in the allocation of funds to be provided by local districts. . . ." These proposals will be urged for legislative action in 1973, regardless of the outcome in the *Rodríguez* case.

The court suit in *Rodríguez* attacks the product of the total school finance system in Texas (excluding Federal aid), measured in terms of fiscal resources per student among the districts. Plaintiffs concede that State aid to local districts has a "mildly equalizing effect," but they contend that wide variations in local property taxpaying capacity produce unreasonable disparities in combined State-local funds among districts.

REVIVING A 1957 LEAGUE PROPOSAL

Among the prospective solutions to the resource equalization problem, a proposal advanced by the Texas Research League in 1957 has drawn considerable attention by the various study groups. The League, reporting on a study requested by the State Board of Education in 1953, noted that ". . . many school districts are spending local tax money outside the minimum program for services and supplies which are, in reality, part of their basic minimum needs." To remedy that situation, the League report suggested that ". . . *parallel upward adjustments in both the minimum program and in local required tax shares toward that program may be desirable so as to strengthen the educational program in poorer school districts of the State.* By expanding the program coverage to include most local "enrichment" expenditures, while at the same time requiring the more affluent districts to pay a larger share of the cost of their own programs, this approach would substantially narrow the resource gap between rich and poor systems.

From *TRL Analyzes Developments in Texas State and Local Government,* Texas Research League Bulletin, November, 1972.

FOUNDATION PROGRAM VARIATIONS

Unfortunately, tinkering with the Foundation Program over the years has so eroded the basic formulas devised by the Gilmer-Aiken Committee in 1948 that the State school aid system no longer functions effectively as a rational plan for guaranteeing equal minimum educational opportunities among the districts. If the Foundation Program has a "mildly equalizing effect," it also produces some peculiar variations in fiscal resources for which there are no simple explanations.

In 1970-71, the Foundation Program cost per student averaged $427, but it exceeded $1,500 in one district with 38 pupils at one extreme, and dropped below $300 in another district with 51 pupils. Although 84 per cent of the districts containing 99 per cent of the students fell within a $300-600 per pupil cost range, that still left a 100 per cent gap from top to bottom.

Part of the variation in Foundation Program cost per pupil among districts may be explained by the formula favoritism built into the program for small districts, particularly for transportation and vocational education. . . . Higher costs for salary and operations, transportation and vocational education all contribute to the directly higher proportional costs per student of the Foundation Program in smaller districts. Special education costs do not correlate with district size. Some discrimination by district size might be permitted under a court-ordered resource equalization plan, but there are substantial differences in Foundation Program cost among districts of roughly comparable size. . . .

Houston's Foundation Program cost per student was $24 higher than Dallas' cost. That $24 multiplied by more than 200,000 students was worth nearly $4.9 million to Houston. Conversely, Dallas lost about $3.5 million compared to the funds it would have received at the Houston level. Austin, Waco and Alamo Heights enjoyed comparable advantages over Corpus Christi, Laredo and Mission, respectively. . . .

A MAJORITY OF EXCEPTIONS

Because Foundation Program costs are calculated separately from local contributions to the Program, increases in costs are reflected in higher State aid. Districts also may increase their State aid entitlement by taking advantage of various statutory "credits" designed to reduce the local share of the program responsibility in favored classes of districts. After examining the background and application of these "credit" provisions in some detail, the League . . . concludes that they have no demonstrable relationship to educational need or taxpaying ability.

When all of the special benefits, exceptions and adjustments are taken into account, the State-supported school finance system in Texas almost produces individually prescribed allocation formulas for the 1,149 taxpaying districts. In 1970-71:

433 districts were allotted 1,161 extra teachers, plus other personnel and operating funds worth $7.7 million beyond their current Foundation Program computed needs because these districts declined in attendance from 1969-70.

520 districts received $65 million for Special Education programs approved by the Texas Education Agency.

933 districts were given $54.5 million for Vocational programs, mostly on the basis of administrative formulas established by the Texas Education Agency.

94 districts had adjustments approved by the Texas Education Agency totalling $1.3 million in additional State aid because they were too small to operate with a regular formula allotment.

776 districts received about $4.6 million in supplemental State aid for variable salary plans above the minimum schedule.

85 districts received $1.9 million in State aid bonuses because some other district or districts had consolidated with them.

270 districts (with some overlap) received $5.9 million more in State aid because they received "credits" for government land (of certain special classes) in their district.

177 districts qualified for $15 million more in State aid because their calculated "legal" tax rates multiplied times county-assessed property values would not produce their assigned local shares of the Foundation Program cost. One hundred sixty-four of these were independent districts with their own tax rolls, and the "maximum tax rate credit" was only a legal fiction which has not been tested in the courts or ruled upon by the Attorney General.

There were at least seven other kinds of special program allotments or adjustments worth about $10 million to selected recipient districts.

THE RODRÍGUEZ TARGET: LOCAL TAX VARIATIONS

Despite the many fiscal idiosyncrasies of the Texas Foundation School program, its unequal impact was not the target of the *Rodríguez* case. The suit was aimed at eliminating the broad disparities in local property tax resources which combine with the Foundation Program to produce a total system characterized by substantially unequal funds available to local districts of similar size.

Plaintiffs in the *Rodríguez* suit did not ask, and the District Court order does not require, equality of treatment for taxpayers among local districts. However, taxpayer equity clearly is implied in the mandate that educational opportunity shall not be a function of wealth other than the wealth of the State as a whole. Under the Texas Constitution, all tangible and intangible property is taxable at its actual market value, but no school district tax assessor follows that standard. Treatment of tangible personal property such as automobiles, household furniture, farm machinery, boats and an endless variety of other items is very irregular. Intangible property such as stocks, bonds and bank deposits is almost never taxed, although some estimates suggest that such intangibles constitute more than half of the actual property wealth. Under such conditions, the property tax has become virtually a local option tax under which school district officials are free to decide what shall be included on the tax roll and at what percentage of true value.

If the Supreme Court upholds the *Rodríguez* decision, it seems unlikely that any new plan would be approved under which local taxpaying capacity was subject to manipulation at local option. Not only would the State be required to measure the local tax base actually in use, but it might also be necessary to insure that all school districts use a uniform tax base.

Data on the actual taxpaying ability of the school districts in Texas is limited, and its validity is subject to question. The substitute measures of economic activity used in the present system to measure taxpaying capacity have no demonstrated relation to the actual property tax base on which districts must rely for local funds.

7-6
PANEL ASKS TOTAL REVISION OF TEXAS' SCHOOL FINANCE SYSTEM

A State Board of Education Committee recommended Saturday a total revision of Texas' public school finance system, with the state picking up all basic educational costs. "Upon full implementation of this program, local districts would be able to reduce local property taxes for the support of educational programs," the committee report said. . . . In addition to shifting all of the burden of basic public school costs to state tax sources by the 1978-1979 school year, the proposal also would boost yearly expenditures by $400 million by increasing amounts spent on the "educationally disadvantaged," general operating expenses, buses and school staffs. Board approval would not put the proposal into effect but would merely send the recommendations on to the legislature with its blessing. The legislature convenes in a 140-day regular session January 9. A three-judge court in San Antonio ruled Dec. 23, 1971 that Texas' current system of public school finance—based on local property taxes—was unconstitutional because it gave children in

From the *San Antonio Light*, November 12, 1972.

wealthy districts educational advantages over those who live in poor districts. The court's decision is now on appeal to the U.S. Supreme Court, where the state's lawyers presented arguments Oct. 12.

TO REPLACE PROGRAM

Members of the board committee made clear, however, that they believe their recommendations should be adopted by the legislature regardless of how the Supreme Court rules. If adopted, the proposal would replace the Minimum Foundation School Program, adopted in 1949, under which the state pays an average of 80 per cent of certain basic costs, including minimum teacher salaries. Local districts now pay an average of 20 per cent of what the state determines to be basic costs. They also are free to exceed minimum standards, and a number of districts pay higher than the basic salary scale and provide certain "enrichment" programs. "Much of what is classified as 'enrichment' has, in reality, been necessary local expenditures to make up for the deficiencies in the present foundation school program," the committee said. "Expansion of the salary schedule, combined with the use of all of the authorized pay grades, may reduce the need for local salary supplements above the minimum schedule. Improved allotments for operating costs will offset most of the primary cause of local 'enrichment.'"

LOCAL TAXES

There still would be some need for local school taxes if the committee proposals were passed into law. "Local taxes would be levied only for those programs which the local community desires to expand beyond the level provided by the state, and for equipping and building school facilities," the report said. Counting recommended improvements and the state takeover of all basic expenses, the committee estimated that the impact of the foundation school program on state tax sources would rise from $1.13 billion in the coming school year to $2.075 billion in 1978-1979. This includes a $464 million increase already built into the program. Local taxpayers' share of the basic program would drop gradually from an estimated $282 million in the 1973-1974 school year to $183 million in 1976-1977 and then to zero in 1978-1979.

STATE'S JOB

"The provision of an adequate education is a state responsibility. . . . For too long there has been a distinction between 'state' taxpayers and 'local' taxpayers. Actually, all taxpayers share in the responsibility to provide funds for the support of education. The best way to guarantee fair and equitable treatment for all of the educational taxpayers of the state is to fund the entire cost of the educational program from state revenues," the committee said. The committee, headed by board chairman Ben Howell of El Paso, said that under its proposal the state would be in a position to guarantee that each district would receive the funds needed "for an adequate educational program." "Districts currently have the option of not raising their assigned share of the foundation school program and thus penalizing the children of the district," the report said. In addition to full state financing of basic school costs, the committee made five other recommendations: (1) Continue presently authorized increases in public school expenditures according to schedule, including teacher pay raises and the phasing in of state-supported kindergarten, both approved by the 1969 Legislature. (2) Provide more counselors, teacher aides, non-teaching personnel and special duty teachers, such as student activity sponsors, coaches and team teaching leaders. This recommendation would take effect next September, at a cost of $69.4 million the first year. (3) Spend more state funds starting next Sept. 1 for operating costs, such as library books, utilities, insurance, building upkeep, supplies and salaries of non-professional employees. The formula would be increased gradually from $50 per pupil in average daily attendance in 1973-1974 to $139 in 1978-1979, counting a 3 per cent inflation factor. The increased cost in 1973-1974 would be $45.7 million. The committee said the foundation program allotted only $72 million to these expenses in 1970-1971, while they actually cost an estimated $314 million. (4) Increase funds for school bus operation by about $800 per bus route, or $6.8 million in the coming school year. (5) Supplement federal funds for "compensatory education" for disadvantaged children in areas with high concentrations of poor families by $100 per pupil, starting in 1974-1975 with an expenditure of $44.4 million in additional funds.

ACHIEVEMENT LEVEL

"Several recent studies have indicated that at approximately $300 per child above the regular cost of education, compensatory programs have an impact upon the educational achievement level of the child. Less than this amount often produces no lasting effect, while funds above this level may be in excess of the amount needed to achieve the desired results. To achieve this level of total support, an additional $100 per . . . pupil would be required," the report said. Legislative committees also are studying the school finance problem. Barring a U.S. Supreme Court decision that Texas' school financing system is unconstitutional, the legislature has hoped to get through its 1973 session with a minimal tax bill, or even none at all. The committee's recommended new expenditures—not counting the added cost of phasing in a system of nearly total state support for public schools—would cost $176.7 million in the two fiscal years for which the 1973 Legislature must appropriate funds.

7-7
BETTER BUDGETING AND MONEY MANAGEMENT FOR TEXAS
Texas Research League

THE MONEY-MANAGEMENT CYCLE IN STATE GOVERNMENT

"Budget Execution" is the process by which a central authority in government supervises the implementation of a spending plan approved by the legislative branch. In state government, budget execution usually is vested in the Governor's Office or in a Department of Administration headed by the Governor's appointee. However, in some states, budget execution is entrusted to a staff responsible to a joint commission composed of the Governor (or his representative) and legislative leaders. *In all of the 33 states which practice some form of budget execution, the process is an integral part of a comprehensive money-management cycle,* including (1) budget preparation, (2) appropriation of funds, (3) expenditure approval (budget execution), and (4) post-audit of expenditures. In a few states, an additional phase of "fiscal review" to determine program effectiveness has been initiated.

Texas is the only major state which has not incorporated budget execution into its money-management cycle. It is the only state which divides budget-preparation responsibility between the Governor and a legislative board, acting separately and independently.

DEVELOPMENT OF THE TEXAS BUDGET SYSTEM

Before 1949, Texas had no budget "system." State agency spending proposals were compiled by the State Board of Control and forwarded to the Governor and the Legislature with no effort to develop a rational state spending plan. The Legislative Budget Board was established in 1949, composed of the Lt. Governor, the Speaker of the House of Representatives, the chairmen of the tax and appropriation committees in each House, and two additional Legislators from each House, appointed by the Lt. Governor and Speaker, respectively.

In 1951, the Legislature passed a bill designating the Governor as the "Chief Budget Officer" of the State and giving him a staff. Since that time, both the Governor and the Legislative Budget Board have submitted separate budget proposals for legislative consideration. *No other significant changes have been made in two decades while the total state budget has spiraled from approximately $500 million a year to around $4 billion a year. . . .*

From a report to Governor Preston Smith and the Texas Legislature on *Better Budgeting and Money Management for Texas,* Texas Research League Bulletin, February, 1971.

THE TEXAS BUDGET SYSTEM AND ITS PROBLEMS

Texas has made considerable progress in fiscal management during the past two decades, and the State continues to enjoy the most economical government among the major states. The dual budget-making system permits participation by both the Governor and the legislative leadership in the examination of state services and programs and the planning of expenditures.

But the dual budget-making process also produces two separate expenditure plans. [See accompanying diagram.] Most of the time in the past 20 years, the Governor's plan has been largely ignored in the legislative appropriation process except on a few specific issues where the Governor has taken a strong personal stand. The only general appropriations bill introduced is the one drafted by the Legislative Budget Board staff. It tracks the LBB budget proposals and usually provides only a minimum projection of existing programs and services. It invites every state agency, every organized interest group and every individual member of the Legislature to compete for expanded spending authority in their own areas of concern. The final appropriations bill is almost always completed in a "free conference" committee near the end of a legislative session. During most sessions in the past two decades, a tax bill had to be completed in a few hectic days *after the final outlines of the spending program had been determined.*

The present Texas system almost guarantees: (1) that the spending package will be built in more or less unrelated increments without the guidance of a rational plan of priorities; and (2) that the supporting tax bill will be hastily drawn without full consideration of its long-range effect on the economy of the State or its long-term ability to support state services. These conditions contribute to Texas' recurrent biennial fiscal crises. In addition, the absence of central supervision over expenditures by independent agencies and institutions prevents the implementation of operating economies to help meet these crises. Without budget-execution authority, it is virtually impossible for the Governor or the Legislature to know whether or not appropriated funds are expended for approved program objectives—or whether those objectives are attained. Yet it is virtually certain that the agencies and institutions will expend the appropriated funds rather than permit them to lapse at the end of the fiscal period.

OBSTACLES TO BUDGET EXECUTION IN TEXAS

Despite the obvious need for budget-execution authority in Texas government, grafting such authority onto the present dual budget-making system might cause as many problems as it could cure. In every state that employs budget execution, the responsibility is vested in the same professional staff that prepares the single budget proposal presented to the Legislature. In other words, this staff helps to implement a budget which it helped draft in the first place. The states that operate under a joint executive-legislative budget commission have a further

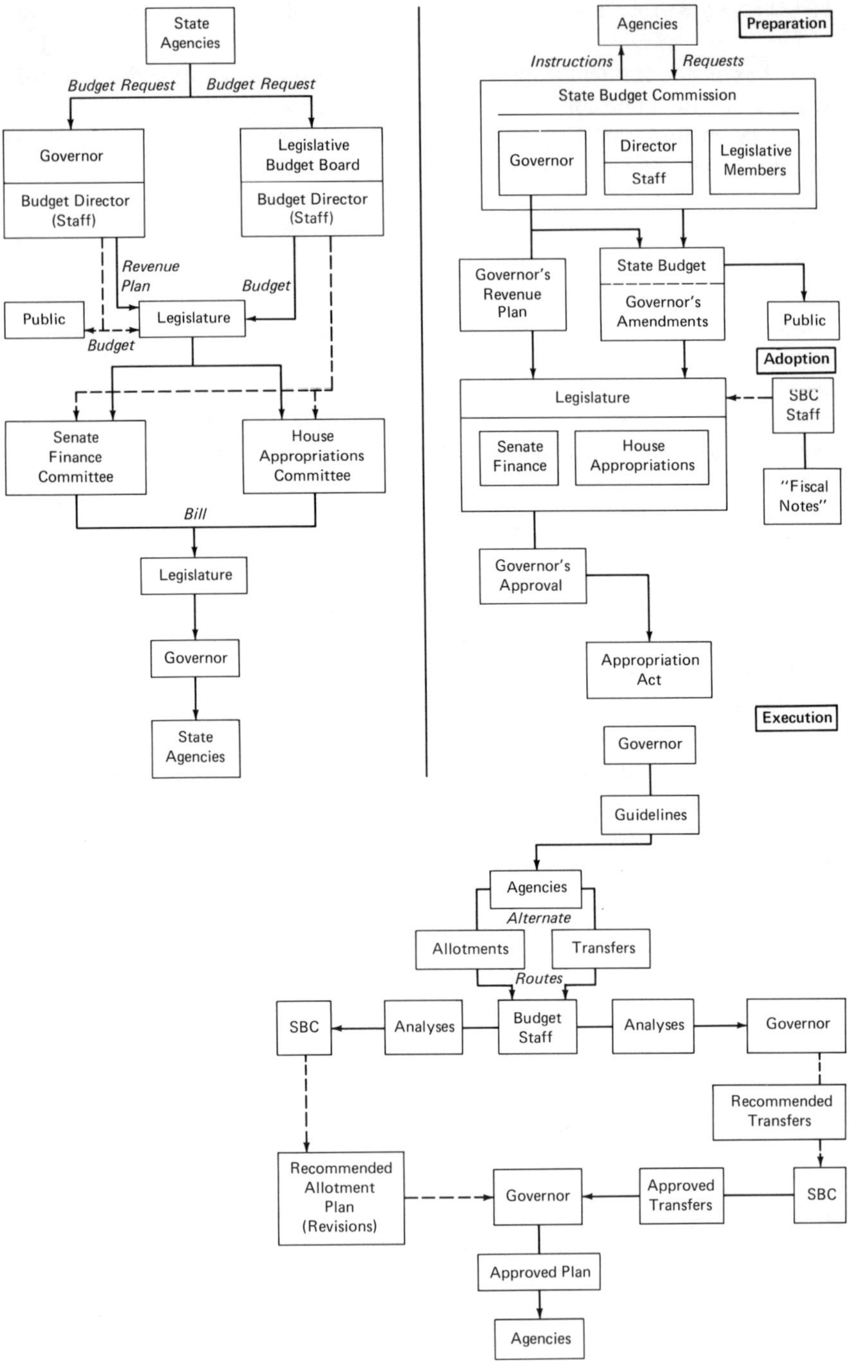

Figure 7-3
The present Texas budget system and a proposed budget system

advantage in budget execution. The staff which prepares the budget also serves the legislative appropriations committees during the hearing process. With this background, the staff may be expected to fulfill budget-execution responsibilities with reasonable confidence. . . .

If the Governor of Texas alone were charged with budget-execution responsibilities, his staff would enjoy none of these advantages. . . .

COSTLY STAFF DUPLICATION

By duplicating the budget-preparation process, the present Texas system effectively wastes perhaps a quarter of a million dollars a year. Yet, neither the Governor's staff nor the Legislative Budget Board staff, alone, is large enough to do a comprehensive job of budget request analysis. The Governor's staff would not be large enough to handle adequately the budget-execution function—even on a selective basis—while maintaining its responsibility for preparing the budget proposals for the following fiscal period. In combination, the Legislative and Executive Budget staff could do a much more effective job of budget request analysis and still undertake budget-execution responsibilities. . . .

A PROPOSED BUDGET SYSTEM FOR TEXAS

STRUCTURE

A State Budget Commission should be established including the members of the present Legislative Budget Board, with the Governor as Chairman. The present executive and legislative budget staffs should be combined under a Director appointed by the Governor for a two-year term with consent of the other members of the State Budget Commission.

BUDGET PREPARATION

A single proposed state budget should be prepared by the State Budget Commission staff following procedures and policies prescribed by the Commission. [See accompanying diagram.] The staff would issue instructions to state agencies and institutions for making budget requests and would hold hearings on those requests. Commission members might participate in the hearings, at least on a selective basis.

The Governor should be authorized to propose amendments to the Commission-approved budget recommendations, and these proposals should be included in the Commission's budget document. The Commission staff would prepare an appropriation bill to be submitted to the Legislature based on the Commission budget, with alternative attachments designed to implement the Governor's amendments. The Governor would continue to exercise his responsibility for recommending any revenue measures which might be required.

BUDGET ADOPTION

The State Budget Commission staff should serve the Appropriations Committees of the two Houses of the Legislature during the session. They would perform the functions now handled by the Legislative Budget Board staff members. In addition, the State Budget Commission staff should prepare "fiscal notes" on proposals for changes in the recommended appropriations and on major spending bills not included in the General Appropriations Bill. The "price tagging" service should provide a more realistic appraisal of the cost of prospective program changes under consideration. In addition to the services of the State Budget Commission staff, a "fiscal assistant" might be assigned to the Lt. Governor and Speaker, respectively, to schedule hearings, to keep records of Committee actions and to perform such special functions as might be delegated to them by the Committee Chairmen.

BUDGET EXECUTION

After adoption of the Appropriations Bill, the State Budget Commission staff would issue instructions to state agencies and institutions for submission of operating budgets to be approved by the Governor with advice of the Commission. Approval might be on an annual, a semiannual or a quarterly basis and should be used on a selective basis to ensure achievement of major program objectives as efficiently and economically as possible. Where economies can be effected, the Governor should have authority to reduce the proposed operating budget, with advice of the other members of the State Budget Commission—particularly on a large reduction. Where funds saved by economies in one program are needed for another purpose other than that approved in the Appropriations Bill, transfers should be proposed by the Governor, but should be made only with the approval of the State Budget Commission as a whole. . . .

State agencies and institutions should be required to report their expenditures to the State Budget Commission and to establish accounting procedures required by the budget-execution process.

BENEFITS OF A BALANCED SYSTEM

Legislative policy deliberations would begin with a single comprehensive spending plan with logical priorities and supporting revenue proposals (when needed).

Waste of funds on duplication of staff work would be avoided. After participating in budget preparation and adoption, the staff would be well equipped to carry out policy decisions in budget execution.

"Price tagging" major spending proposals would provide an accurate estimate of state commitments and revenue needs.

Significant economies could be achieved without sacrificing programs or services. . . .

A balanced coordinated money-management system with a rational plan of spending priorities coupled with efficient budget execution, can give better state services at lower cost and help avoid future fiscal crises.

'There's Work To Be Done!'

HERC FICKLEN FROM THE DALLAS NEWS

Epilogue

Participating in Texas Politics

This concluding portion of the text is directed to people, young and old, who would like to know how to become more involved in the politics of their state and of their local communities. In spite of the disappointingly low turnout of voters in the 1972 elections, many young people are anxious to participate actively in the political process but do not know where or how to begin. It is hoped that this epilogue will point the way for those citizens who wish to take a larger part in the political process than just casting a vote on election day. For, as the caption to a political cartoon appearing in a Dallas newspaper just before the 1972 general election proclaimed, "There's Work to Be Done."

FORMS OF PARTICIPATION

At the outset the interested citizen must realize that participation in today's politics may take many *forms.* For example, he may participate in the formal electoral processes through such activities as running for elective office; seeking nomination to an appointive office; taking part in a political campaign through contributions of time, energy, and money; or circulating a petition calling for a referendum on some current issue.*

On the other hand, the citizen may choose to participate in a multitude of less formal activities, many of which have as great or greater impact on the political process; e.g., contributing time or money to organizations that support or oppose candidates or take stands on public issues, influencing others by discussing candidates and issues, or wearing political buttons or placing bumper

*This epilogue will not attempt to provide detailed analyses of these and other political processes. Chapter 2 provides those interested with detailed descriptions, analyses, and historical backgrounds. Presented here, hopefully, is a foundation for meaningful participation.

stickers on cars. Finally, his participation may take the form of protest marches, "sit-ins," or other forms of direct action.

Even during a period of peak participation, i.e., the weeks immediately preceding an election, many people become only marginally involved, while most remain completely uninvolved. The degree and intensity of disinterest and non-involvement fluctuate with elections, issues, and geographical areas. (In Reading E-2 two distinguished political scientists analyze apathy in American politics and question the merits of "participatory democracy.")

SOME WAYS OF PARTICIPATING

In the event that an interested citizen decides to become a participant, his first step probably should be to take an inventory of himself. How much time and effort is he willing to commit to this undertaking? What skills does he have to offer? Is he willing to subordinate himself in a team effort? His answers to these and related questions will help to determine where, when, and to what extent he will participate. He should be realistic with himself and others who may come to count upon him, so that he does not promise too quickly and easily more than he is actually prepared to give.

BECOMING A VOTER

To participate most effectively in politics, one must become a *registered voter.* Of course there are ways of participating other than registering and voting. But registering to vote assures a citizen that he will have an opportunity to help select those persons into whose hands the power of his government is going to be placed for a given period of time.

Registering to vote involves some crucial questions: Who can register? Where does one register? How? When? How often?

All citizens of the United States who have reached their eighteenth birthday and who have resided in the state of Texas and in a voting precinct (district) for at least thirty days are now eligible to register to vote.

Potential voters may apply in person or by mail to the *registrar of voters* (county tax assessor and collector) in the county of their residence. Each applicant or his agent must fill out and submit to the registrar or his authorized deputy an application showing name, sex, age, address (post office address if a rural resident, street address if an urban resident), and citizenship. The applicant may submit his completed application in person or by mail to the registrar or his deputy. Husbands, wives, fathers, mothers, sons, or daughters of persons eligible to register may act as agents for the purpose of registration if they are also qualified voters in the same county. Upon receipt of a properly executed application, the registrar makes out a *registration certificate* and delivers it to the voter or to his agent in person or by mail. If the registrar refuses to issue a valid certificate following application, a prospective voter may appeal to the state district court having jurisdiction over the area.

Even though a potential voter is registered, the presiding judge, an election clerk, a poll watcher, or any other person may challenge the right of a voter to participate in any election. If challenged, the voter may be required by the presiding judge to swear under oath to the facts which are necessary to meet the objection, or he may be certified as eligible by the sworn oath of at least one well-known resident of the voting precinct.

A registered voter who changes his residence within the same election precinct should notify the registrar of the change and present his registration certificate for correction. One who moves to another precinct in the same county should present his certificate to the registrar together with a written, signed request for a transfer. After moving into another county, a voter must register again in the new county, and the new registrar should notify the former registrar and request a cancellation of the prior certificate.

Whenever a qualified voter votes in any party primary or in the November general election, his registration is automatically extended for a period of three voting years. If, however, he fails to vote in such an election for three consecutive years, his registration will be canceled, and he will need to re-register to become eligible again to participate in Texas elections.

VOTING

The process of voting also raises some crucial questions for the participant: When will I have an opportunity to vote? Where must I cast my ballot? How should I conduct myself at the polling place?

Thirty-one days after becoming a registered voter, one may cast a ballot in any election—national, state, or local—where the polls are open in his voting precinct. (Reading E-1 presents in tabular form the dates and other pertinent information concerning the voter's opportunities to participate in Texas elections.)

Texas election laws specify, without exception, that each voter must cast his ballot in the *voting precinct* of his legal residence. His registration certificate bears the number of the precinct, and public announcements indicate the place.

On election day, polls are open at 7:00 A.M. in the larger cities or at 8:00 A.M. in the smaller cities and rural areas; they remain open until 7:00 P.M. the same day. All voters remaining in line to vote when a polling place is declared closed must be given an opportunity to cast their ballots.

Where paper ballots are in use, the prospective voter should present his registration certificate to the election judge or his deputy, sign the *register of voters,* select a ballot and proceed to a vacant voting booth, mark his ballot by checking the party-column square to vote a straight ticket or by checking squares for individual candidates, detach the stub, place the ballot in the box provided and the stub in the small stub-box also provided, and leave the polls as quietly and as quickly as possible. In party primaries he must also sign an oath or affidavit (sometimes called the *loyalty oath*) stating that he is a member of the party holding the primary and that he has not participated in the primary of any other party that day. Those signing this pledge and voting in the first primary of one party may not legally participate in the second primary of any other party.

Where voting machines are being used, instead of selecting a ballot the voter enters a curtained booth surrounding the machine, pulls the levers corresponding to his choices, and then leaves the booth, thereby recording his vote on the automatic tally built into the machine. Otherwise his behavior should be very nearly the same as when using a paper ballot.

In marking his ballot, the voter should be particularly careful to read and observe all directions appearing on it and should not fail to question election officials when he does not understand what he is required to do.

RUNNING FOR OFFICE

Although a person may be elected to office in Texas without first being formally nominated, nomination by primary, convention, or petition is a practical requirement. If nomination is a virtual prerequisite to election, then how does an aspiring candidate get nominated? What method or methods of nomination afford him a chance of securing election?

Prior to 1974 the Texas Election Code required that all political parties whose candidates for the office of governor have received at least 200,000 votes in the most recent general election must hold *party primaries* to nominate all candidates for statewide, legislative district, judicial district, county, and precinct offices. Since only Democratic and Republican party candidates for governor now regularly poll more than the 200,000-vote minimum, nomination in one of those party primaries (especially the Democratic Party primary) is a practical necessity for election. (Reading E-1 supplies all relevant dates and deadlines for these primaries.) Effective in 1974 legislation enacted by the 63rd Legislature (1973) changed this primary election rule, requiring primaries only for those parties whose candidates for governor received at least twenty per cent of the votes cast for that office in the preceding general election.

The same statute reinstituted the filing fee system for party primaries. This new legislation stipulates that every candidate for public office must accompany his application for a place on the primary election ballot by a filing fee as indicated in the table below. In place of paying a filing fee, a candidate may file a nominating petition signed by qualified voters eligible to vote for the office he is seeking. Petitions for statewide office require 5,000 signatures; district, county, precinct, or other political subdivision officers need only 2 per cent of the vote cast for the party's candidate for governor in the preceding general election in the area. Minimum number of signatures required here is twenty-five; the maximum is five hundred.

Parties whose candidates for governor do not poll 200,000 votes at the same November general election may choose to nominate candidates for the next general election by *party conventions.* (Reading E-1 indicates the dates for such conventions.) Inasmuch as no major party uses this method of nomination in Texas, it affords little chance for election to office.

Candidates who are not nominated by political parties and who are styled

TABLE E-1
Primary filing fees

Offices	Filing Fees
All statewide offices	$1,000
United States Representative	500
State senator	400
State representative	200
State Board of Education	50
Justice, Court of Civil Appeals	400
District judge or other judge having the status of a district judge	400
District attorney or criminal district attorney	400
County offices, except county surveyor or inspector of hides and animals	150
County surveyor or inspector of hides and animals	50
County commissioner	100
Justice of the peace or constable	
counties over 200,000 population	100
counties under 200,000 population	50
Public weigher	50

nonpartisan or independent candidates in election statutes may be nominated as a result of submitting a written application, popularly known as a *petition,* which is delivered to the proper officer within thirty days after the second primary election day (see Reading E-1 for these dates). No candidate so nominated has been successful in many years.

A person wishing to run for a municipal or city office, such as mayor or councilman, may file a sworn statement declaring his candidacy at city hall at least thirty days before the election. This method might be designated by the term *self-announcement,* and it is by far the most frequently used method. Candidates may also be nominated by petition signed by qualified voters equaling 5 per cent of the entire vote cast for mayor in the last municipal election or twenty-five voters, whichever is the lesser number. Any political party may nominate candidates by primary or by convention, but these methods are rarely employed in Texas city politics.

Candidates for the office of trustee of an independent school district must apply for a place on the ballot with the county judge in districts with less than 150 scholastics (i.e., children of school age) or with the secretary of the school board in larger districts. Applications must be filed at least thirty days before the election. Candidates for the office of trustee for a common school district or a rural high school district must file with the county judge within the thirty-day limit. State statutes also provide that candidates for boards of trustees of junior (community) college districts must in general be nominated and elected according to the same rules governing the boards of independent school districts.

Securing a nomination is only part-way down the road to obtaining an elective public office. Those nominated must be elected. *General elections* are held regularly in November of even-numbered years for statewide, district, county, and precinct offices, and in April for municipal and school district offices. They may also be held at other times throughout the year as statutes or charters prescribe, especially in the case of school district offices. *Special elections* may be held at virtually any time on call by the state Legislature, county commissioners court, city council, or school board. At either type of election, voters may be called upon to vote for either candidates or issues, such as constitutional amendments, bond issues, or property tax increases.

CAMPAIGNING FOR ELECTION

One fundamental fact must be held uppermost in any analysis of political campaigning, namely, that the purpose of the campaign is to win an election. (Reading E-3 illustrates how a successful campaign was launched and managed in Houston in 1972.) Its purpose is not, therefore, to demonstrate intellectual brilliance or moral superiority. It must not be thought of as a debate between champions. Many, perhaps most, voters do not weigh alternatives or thoroughly inform themselves of all the facts. They are simply not issue-oriented; instead, they tend to be party-oriented or candidate-oriented.

Campaigns, no matter how well organized or energetic, are not likely to alter very many of the basic beliefs or attitudes of individual voters; nor are they likely to galvanize into action persons who have little or no interest in public matters. What campaigns can do is to reinforce effectively the convictions of the faithful and get them out to vote. Campaigns that accomplish those objectives to a significant degree are usually *successful campaigns.*

With these limits clearly in mind, then, what can one do to participate effectively in a political campaign? What practical steps can he take to help ensure victory for his candidate, party, or cause?

One of the first things that he might do is to contact the local party chairman, campaign manager, or candidate of his choice and volunteer his service. Chances are very good that his offer will be warmly received and that he will quickly be put to work. Persons with few skills and limited experience can be valuable workers in such areas as checking voting lists, stamping letters, distributing cards and leaflets, arranging meetings, getting out publicity releases, and putting up posters and other signs. Those with skills and experience can be utilized in developing newspaper and television advertising and campaign speeches, painting signs, raising funds, typing, organizing and directing door-to-door campaigns, transporting voters to the polls, and running errands of an almost endless variety.

Another important way that he may contribute to the success of his party, candidate, or cause is to organize, direct, or participate actively in a *drive to register voters*—especially those voters who are likely to support the party, candidate, or cause. In order to do so, he should first secure a copy of the current registration list from the registrar of voters, check it to determine who is registered, and then begin to compile a list of those persons he wants to approach or those areas of the county or city where he must concentrate his efforts. Registration lists may be compared with current telephone listings or membership rolls of organizations—e.g., the American Legion, A.F.L.-C.I.O. locals, or the Chamber of Commerce—for names of persons not registered. The astute campaigner will attempt to determine subtly how the unregistered citizen feels about his party, candidate, or cause before urging him to register. It certainly would not be politic to arouse and register too many who will find their way into the camp of the opposition.

An even more important contribution to one's campaign involves the conduct of a successful *voting drive.* A great deal of time, money, and effort can be expended in registering voters with few, if any, tangible results unless the registration drive is followed up by an equally determined drive to get voters committed to your persuasion to the polls on election day. In addition to providing transportation, this effort will involve telephone canvassing and checking at the polls to determine which and how many of the faithful are turning out.

Experience indicates that registration and voting drives should be directed at individual voters, that they be approached personally, and that the greatest degree of success is usually attained when the approach is part of a community-wide program. This is especially true, it would seem, of registration drives.

For the individual interested in active participation in campaigns and elections, the list[1] below provides some hints that should prove useful for the beginner and a good review for the more experienced.

1. Be a joiner, i.e., affiliate with a great variety of organizations and become active in their programs, for in this way you will make your name familiar, win friends, and learn the skills of the political arena.
2. Be "one of the boys."
3. Learn to remember names and faces.
4. Ignore unfriendly attacks.
5. Know your facts.
6. Never overestimate how much the people know or underestimate their intelligence.
7. Remember that a good personality and mastery of the "tricks of the trade" are no substitute for intelligence, integrity, and conviction.

Finally, those involved in Texas campaigns should bear in mind that each candidate must keep an accurate record of all gifts or loans of money or other valuable things received by him, his campaign manager, or assistant campaign managers; and of all gifts, loans and payments made, and of all debts incurred in connection with his candidacy. These records must include the names and addresses of all persons from whom money or anything of value has been received or borrowed. Contributions by banks and other business corporations are specially restricted. Candidates for county, precinct, or district office where the district does not contain more than one county must file their *financial reports* with the county clerk of the county; candidates for district office where the district contains more than one county, or for state office, file with the secretary of state; candidates for municipal office file with the city secretary; and candidates for a special district office—such as school trustee—file with the secretary of the governing board. These financial statements are public records and must be kept open for public inspection for at least two years.

WORKING ON ELECTION DAY

Assuming that on election day the volunteer groups that have agreed to work for candidates, parties, or causes have their drivers and their cars ready to roll, their telephone canvassers ready to follow up on reluctant voters, their headquarters manned, and their baby-sitters ready to do their jobs, are there other important tasks that can be performed on election day?

If one chooses to continue to work as a partisan on that day, there is at least one other job he may be asked to assume on behalf of his cause, i.e., serving as a *poll watcher.* Watchers may be appointed by political parties, by candidates, or by voters—fifty qualified voters or 5 per cent of the qualified voters in any election precinct, whichever number is smaller. Watchers must be present at the polls when they are opened and remain there until the polls are closed, except for meals and for periods of time permitted by the election judge. Acting under oath, the watcher is obligated to mention and to note any errors he may see in qualifying the voters, counting the votes or making out the returns of the election. He is required to report in writing all violations of the law and uncorrected irregularities that he may observe to the county executive committee in primary elections, to the county commissioners court in general elections, and to the body charged with the duty of canvassing the votes in other types of elections. He may also report in writing to the next session of the grand jury. Watchers must be qualified voters residing in the election precinct where the election is being held, and they must not be employees or employers of the election judge or any clerk of the election or too closely related to any officer of the election.

GETTING A PROPOSITION BEFORE THE PUBLIC

Aside from supporting a candidate or party committed to a proposition or issue, voters can take other kinds of actions designed to get their propositions before the public. Perhaps the most significant of these are preparing and circulating petitions, organizing and participating in campaigns to secure constitutional or charter revisions or amendments, and organizing and participating in peaceful demonstrations.

Through the use of petitions, interested citizens can often bring about a *public referendum* (vote) on some issue of concern. This petition-election process may be used to create new units of local government (e.g., cities, school districts, and hospital districts) or to abolish existing units; to approve or amend a city charter; to authorize or prohibit the sale of alcoholic beverages; to authorize the levy, or alter the rate of, some specific tax (e.g., city sales taxes or school district property tax); or to authorize the issue and sale of bonds by units of local government.

Referenda may also be included on primary election ballots by action of the party's state executive committee or by petition of 5 per cent of the voters of the party, as shown by the total number of votes cast for the office of governor in the last primary. Recent examples of this type of "straw vote" include the issues of liquor by the drink and school bussing. Results of these referenda are not binding but stand as expressions of popular sentiment.

INFLUENCING PARTY ACTIVITIES

Aside from voting in a party primary and thereby helping a party nominate many of its candidates for public and party offices, interested citizens may influence the activities of the party of their choice by taking an active part in its caucuses and conventions. There they will have an opportunity to help determine party policy, select some party officers, and nominate at least some party candidates. For the interested citizen the most critical of the party's meetings is the *primary caucus,* in Texas statutes referred to as the *precinct convention.* (Reading E-1 provides dates for all important party meetings.)

Primary caucuses are called in even-numbered years on the day of the first primary. (Chapter 2 describes in detail all Texas party meetings.) At this meeting party members are given opportunities to offer resolutions concerning party policy, to nominate and elect officers to govern the caucus, and to nominate and select delegates to represent them at other party meetings.

In states, such as Texas, that do not have any sort of presidential preference primary, the primary caucus also affords the most significant opportunity to express a preference for, and to influence the choice of, the party's candidates for President and Vice-President of the United States. Delegates committed to support certain candidates are selected at this meeting to attend the county convention; there delegates are chosen to attend the state convention; and finally, at the state convention delegates are chosen to attend the national convention, where the choice is made.

A voter who does not take part in a party primary and primary caucus has materially reduced his influence on his state's government and politics. He has, in large measure, tacitly agreed to leave some important facets of his state and national governments in the hands of those who do participate in party affairs.

SHOULD I PARTICIPATE?

The preceding discussion of participation has emphasized the mechanics of taking part in the political process in Texas. Its concluding statement concerning the impact of participation on government, however, suggests two important aspects of the subject that have been analyzed only incidentally, i.e., the advisability of participation and the consequences of nonparticipation.

Aside from the familiar arguments for participation based on Jeffersonian principles of democracy, there are other reasons for choosing to take an active part in Texas politics. For some the compelling motivations for political activity are self-interest; civic duty; loyalty to friends, neighbors, or family; social pressure; and commitment to an issue or principle. For others, however, another, more practical factor is the compelling one, namely, that if they fail to participate, then those taking active part will help to make decisions affecting all persons in the state. If they do participate, they may not be decisive in getting what they want out of government; but if they do not participate, they almost certainly will not have much material influence. The most obvious consequence of their nonparticipation, then, is the virtual loss of an opportunity to have some significant share in determining many of the rules and regulations by which their lives are governed. Those who do participate will be elected to public office and party positions, will be appointed to public boards, commissions and committees, and will help to choose those who are elected and appointed.

NOTE

1. James MacGregor Burns and Jack Walter Peltason, *Government by the People*, 7th ed. (Englewood Cliffs, N.J.: Prentice-Hall, 1969), p. 770.

KEY TERMS AND CONCEPTS

forms of participation
registered voter
registrar of voters
registration certificate
voting precinct
register of voters
loyalty oath
party primaries
party conventions
nonpartisan or independent candidates
petition
self-announcement
general elections
special elections
successful campaigns
voter registration drive
voting drive
campaign financial reports
poll watcher
public referendum
primary caucus
precinct convention

HERC FICKLEN FROM THE DALLAS NEWS

"It's an automatic handshaker for pooped politicians."

Selected Readings

E-1
CALENDAR OF OPPORTUNITIES FOR POLITICAL PARTICIPATION IN TEXAS
J. E. Ericson

In increasing numbers concerned citizens—especially student-voters—are inquiring concerning opportunities for participation in the Texas political process. Questions often voiced include: When is the last day to register? When does absentee voting begin? When does it end? The calendar that follows is intended to furnish answers to these and other similar questions. The information it contains is adapted from the *Texas Election Laws, 1972-1973,* published by Steck-Warlick Co. of Austin, and the *Texas Political Calendar, 1972,* published and distributed by the State Democratic Executive Committee of Texas. The compiler has also drawn heavily upon his many years as an election judge, precinct committeeman, and county chairman for clues as to what information would be most valuable to the concerned citizen.

TEXAS POLITICAL CALENDAR FOR POLITICAL PARTICIPATION

FEBRUARY	
First Monday	Last day to *file* for inclusion on the Primary Election ballot–even-numbered years.
MARCH	
First Week	Sixty days before the First Primary, period for absentee voting by mail begins–even-numbered years. Thirty days before Municipal and School Trustee elections; last day *to register* to vote in those elections.
APRIL	
First Week	Sixty days before the Second Primary, period for absentee voting by mail begins–even-numbered years.
First Tuesday*	*Municipal Elections* for general law and some home rule cities–annually. Thirty days before the First Primary, last day *to register* to vote in that primary.
First Saturday*	*School District Trustee Elections* for most County School Boards. Common School Boards, Boards of Independent School Districts, Rural High School Boards, and Boards of Junior Colleges Districts–annually.
Second or third week	Twenty days before the First Primary, period for *absentee voting* by personal appearance begins–even-numbered years.
MAY	
First Week	Three days before the First Primary, period for *absentee voting* by mail and personal appearance ends–even-numbered years. Thirty days before Second Primary; last day *to register* to vote in that primary.
First Saturday	*First Primary Election*–even-numbered years. *Precinct Conventions*–even-numbered years. Thirty days before Second Primary, period for last day *to register* to vote in that primary.

Third or fourth week	Ten days before the Second Primary, period for *absentee voting* by personal appearance begins—even-numbered years.
Last week	Four days before the Second Primary, period for *absentee voting* by mail and personal appearance ends—even-numbered years.
JUNE	
First Saturday	*Second Primary Election*—even-numbered years.
Second Saturday	*County Conventions*—even-numbered years.
Second Tuesday after first Saturday	*State Conventions* to select delegates to national presidential nominating conventions—quadrennially in even-numbered years.
SEPTEMBER	
Third Tuesday	*State Conventions*—regular party conventions—even-numbered years.
First week	Sixty days before the General Election, period for *absentee voting* by mail begins—even-numbered years.
OCTOBER	
First Week	Thirty days before General Election; last day *to register* to vote in that election.
Third week	Twenty days before the General Election, period for *absentee voting* by personal appearance begins—even-numbered years.
NOVEMBER	
First Week	Three days before the General Election, period for *absentee voting* by mail and personal appearance ends—even-numbered years.
First Tuesday after first Monday*	*General Election* for national, state, district, county, and precinct officers.

*Special elections may be called at other times by state, county, city, or special district governments. Moreover, special and local laws make exceptions as to the time and frequency of local elections. Those exceptions are too numerous to include here.

E-2
TOWARD PARTICIPATORY DEMOCRACY?
Nelson W. Polsby and Aaron Wildavsky

Whenever a democratic system falters or even seems to, somebody prescribes more democracy. These days, not any old kind of democracy will do; "participatory" democracy is the miracle drug that idealists like. . . .

Political resources and the men who possess them are important . . . because campaigns are important. And campaigns are important because . . . numerical majorities must be mobilized in a large, complex, and not terribly attentive society.

American politics responds to non-democratic resources because many, if not most, citizens are politically apathetic. If nearly everyone participated, no other resources would be necessary. Why is political apathy widespread? There are several alternative explanations. Perhaps it is because the system presents the citizenry with no real alternatives. . . .

Perhaps it is because the public has been imbued with a "false-consciousness" that blinds it to its "real" desires and interests. This is an explanation traditionally seized upon by the enlightened few to deny value to the preferences of the ignorant many. The people, we are told, are easily fooled; this testifies to their credulity; they do not know what is good for them; this makes them child-like; but when the people cannot trust their own feelings, when their desires are alleged to be unworthy, when their policy preferences should be ignored because they are not "genuine" or "authentic," they are being deprived as well of their humanity.

What is left for the people if they are deprived of judgment, wisdom, feeling, desire and preference? Such a premise would offer little hope for democracy of any sort. . . .

A more hopeful . . . explanation of political apathy might note that throughout American history a substantial number of American citizens have not wished to concern themselves continually with the problems and actions of government. Many citizens prefer to participate on their own terms, involving themselves with a particular issue-area or a specific problem. The participation of these citizens is necessarily sporadic and more narrow than that of the rare person interested in all public problems and actively involved in general political life.

Many other citizens (surely a majority) are more interested in the problems of their own personal lives than they are in any issue of public policy . . . [these] citizens who meet their public obligations by going to the polls at fairly regular intervals, making their selections on the basis of their own criteria, and then supporting the actions and policies of the winners—whether their first choice or not. In the intervals, unless they themselves are personally affected by some policy

From the *Wall Street Journal,* August 3, 1972. Polsby is Professor of Political Science and Wildavsky is Dean, Graduate School of Public Policy, at the University of California, Berkeley. Reprinted by permission.

proposal, most of these citizens simply wish to be left alone. Most citizens, in short, do not participate because they are concerned with other things important to them, like earning a living or painting a picture or cultivating a garden, not because they feel it is so difficult to influence outcomes. . . .

Imagine for a moment a situation where these conditions did not hold. Consider a society where all citizens are concerned about public matters as the most active of American party volunteers. Such a society would not require mobilization; all who were able would vote. The hoopla and gimcrackery associated with our political campaigns would have little effect; this citizenry would know the record of the party and the candidate and, presumably, would make their reasoned choice on this basis. Should such an active society be the goal . . . ?

This question should not and cannot be answered without first addressing the problem of how such a society could be achieved and what this achievement would require. Without attempting to be comprehensive, a few difficulties do merit some specific comment.

First and foremost, political participation . . . takes a great deal of time. . . . Most citizens lack the time, even if they had the temperament and training to continually engage in politics.

To the degree that mass representative institutions—political parties, legislatures, elected executives—are denigrated in favor of more direct modes of activity, to that degree the majority of the people will be without the means of participation through which they can most effectively make their will felt. In short, to impose requirements of direct participation on those desiring a voice in decisions would be to insure that the incessant few rather than the sporadic many would rule; thus the slogan "power to the people" really proposes to replace a representative few, who are elected, with an unrepresentative few, who are self-appointed.

We raise this issue not because we are opposed in principle to the idea of an active, participatory democratic society. By persuasion and political education the majority of our citizens might indeed be convinced that the quality of our shared existence could and should be improved through more continuous devotion to public activity. But to argue this is quite a different matter than to argue that the rules of the game should be changed so as to disenfranchise those who presently lack the opportunity or desire to be active in this sense. We do not favor efforts to implement ideal goals when the preconditions and the means of achieving these goals do not exist.

More importantly, we do not favor actions which in the name of democracy (or under any other disguise) restrict the ability of most of the people to have their political say.

E-3
GETTING ELECTED (HOUSTON, TEXAS: STATE REPRESENTATIVE RON WATERS)
Chester G. Atkins, Barry Hock, and Bob Martin

Being at the right place at the right time is the quickest way to prominence in any career, and nowhere is that more true than in politics. An appealing and competent candidate with a good organization has a fair chance of winning an election, but there are few politicians who attain office without a share of luck. In many cases, luck means the difference between having a chance to run and win and never having a decent chance at all.

In the case of Ron Waters, luck took the form of a state Supreme Court decision which put an end to the use of large, multi-member legislative districts. These districts had made the legislature a bastion of entrenched party polls having the wealth and power necessary to wage expensive campaigns over wide geographic areas.

In the fall of 1971, prior to the court decision, Waters was a twenty-two-year-old University of Houston senior with several years of political experience to his credit but with little chance of reaching office in the near future.

"I've wanted to run for some kind of office since I was eighteen. I was doing all of the things that you were supposed to do to work yourself up the ladder as a candidate," Waters states.

Indeed he was. He was president of the Young Democrats at the University, a member of the executive committee of the county Democratic Party, a veteran of campaigns for Ralph Yarborough and other liberals, and regional coordinator of Countdown '72, a nationwide youth registration effort. In addition, he was active in several community and statewide organizations.

In spite of these credentials, Waters had neither the money nor the recognition necessary to mount a campaign for municipal office in a city the size of Houston or for a legislative seat in a multi-member district.

"Under the old multi-member districts it would have taken me two to eight years to work my way into the position I'm in now where it is financially feasible for me to run a campaign," Waters stated during his campaign.

In October, 1971, however, a court ruling resulted in the creation of single-member legislative districts, and Waters immediately saw the significance of the ruling. The smaller districts suddenly made it possible for a candidate such as he to win without spending exorbitant amounts of money.

When the boundary lines of the new districts were announced, prospective candidates were thrown into a frenzy of speculation over their chances of winning in various districts. A two or three week game of political hopscotch ensued. Waters was living in what turned out to be a conservative district and was looking around for one where his prospects would be brighter. "At one point I had two or three apartments," he said of his search for a political base.

Casting his eyes across the district boundary into the nearby 79th district, Waters spotted his opportunity: "I couldn't believe they had put all those liberal Montrose precincts together. My first impression was 'Hell, a radical's going to get elected there.'" (Montrose is Houston's version of Greenwich Village.)

Asking around to find out who else might be running in the district, Waters learned of five or six prospective candidates. One of these was thirty-four-year-old Ann Lower, a writer and local party activist who would later become Waters' campaign manager. Ms. Lower urged Waters to run, saying she would bow out if he moved into the district.

Continuing his survey, Waters contacted the Democratic precinct judges (precinct leaders) in all twenty-one precincts of the district. "Out of twenty-one precinct judges, there were eleven who were liberal, and I got commitments from nine of them," Waters recalls. With that much support, he found an apartment in the district and went to work.

"I didn't know how I was going to raise the money," he said of his decision to run, but he did know that if he waited two more years it was likely that someone else would gain a grip on the district and Waters would be shut out.

The 79th legislative district, in which Waters and five other Democrats were to vie for their party's nomination in May, is roughly ten miles long and two miles wide, embracing a 70,000 person segment of Houston's population of 1.2 million. While it does contain the several liberal Montrose precincts that attracted Waters to it (including large contingents of freaks and homosexuals), the remainder of the district is a mixed bag. Of the twenty-one precincts, four are solidly black, one is Chicano, two consist of wealthy, conservative whites, and seven or eight more of older low-income Wallacite whites. "The majority of the district is poor, overwhelmingly poor," says Waters.

As he soon realized, various factions in the district were bitterly hostile to one another: the whites hated the blacks, the blacks hated the Chicanos, and the freaks just wanted to be left alone. Solidly Democratic (with only 2000 Republicans among 26,000 registered voters), the district was still not likely to go to a liberal without a fight. A conservative Democrat who played his cards right could easily send the liberal camp into confusion by playing off one out-group against another.

That, apparently, was just what Waters' chief opponent had in mind. He was a former state representative who, after being defeated in 1970, had gone to work as an aide to two other legislators. He had helped draw the boundary lines for the new district, and had earmarked it for himself.

The remarkable aspect of Waters' victory is how wide a spectrum of support he was able to bring together in this diverse district, and how he did so while adhering to what must have been one of the most liberal platforms in the state of Texas. While taking outspoken stands in favor of gay liberation and the legalization of abortion and marijuana, Waters was also able to attract the support of the Houston firefighters' and teachers' unions and the local chapter of the Steelworkers of America.

Very early in the campaign Waters realized that the only way to win was to find the common denominator of the several mutually alienated groups in the district. "The only thing the people in this district had in common was economics," he found.

Accordingly, Waters' speeches, his campaign literature, and the activity of his canvassers all focused on a series of economic issues bound to strike a chord in any voter's mind:

1. Waters favored the use of a corporate income tax to replace the state sales tax. The only other candidate who made any real headway had supported the sales tax during his previous time in the legislature.
2. With property taxes a thorn in every voter's side, Waters advocated equalization of the tax rates for residential and commercial property. He also proposed tax rebates for elderly homeowners, a measure the former legislator had voted against.
3. Long before his campaign, Waters had organized a Nader-style group to work for reform of the state's auto insurance rate-setting system. Carrying the issue into the campaign, he found that even the most conservative elements in the district were willing to ignore his youth and relative radicalism when he began talking about insurance. "Per person, per house," he discovered, "they picked that as the most important issue."
4. Waters also aroused community interest, especially among blacks, in his proposals for state action in the construction of low-cost housing, medical facilities, and recreation areas.

With his economic issues and with frequent emphasis on the need to reform the corruption-ridden Texas legislature of which his leading opponent had been part, Waters found a wide base that was relatively unworried by his stands on marijuana, abortion, gay liberation, women's rights, and police brutality. He won the support of unions with a strong pro-labor stance and the endorsement of the Houston teachers' union with his views on education. He forged a coalition out of as unlikely an assembly of backers as could be found in American politics.

The campaign was stretched out over a long period. Waters decided to run in November 1971, and the final election was not until November 1972. The primary was held in May, however, and in such a solidly Democratic district it was the primary that would determine the election. (The final election, in which Waters defeated his Republican opponent with 61 per cent of the vote, took place in November 1972. This discussion concerns only the primary and runoff races.)

The real kickoff for the campaign was a February meeting between the candidate, his campaign manager, and local party workers, party leaders from seven precincts, and candidates for leadership posts in five others, together with a state senate candidate whose campaign would be linked with Waters'. The outcome of that meeting was a series of decisions on campaign strategy, including plans for a precinct organization of the district.

The key decision made at that meeting—to have campaign workers contact every registered voter in the district before the primary—was to determine the nature of the campaign.

"Ann was convinced that block-walking was the only way to win," Waters states, and her view prevailed. With the exception of three conservative precincts which were written off, virtually every voter was reached by campaign volunteers. (There were 26,000 voters in the district.)

"We stressed that we wanted in-depth discussion with the people. We did not want people to just drop a leaflet," Ms. Lower said in discussing the campaign. "Our block-walkers were enthused. It's what kept the campaign going."

While Waters had originally pledged to walk every street of the district himself, he gave up on that idea after covering about 5 per cent of the district. Finding that his progress was too slow, and believing himself to be ineffective on a one to one basis, Waters decided that the best forum for him was a large group or rally. (He had been a champion debater.)

Having realized that the four black precincts would be crucial in determining the outcome of the primary, he did stick with the door to door tour in those areas.

Turning to what seemed his forte, Waters appeared before a series of large gatherings ranging in attendance from 150 to 2000. One of these was a rock concert at which he spoke alongside gubernatorial candidate Sissy Farenthold, whose candidacy rocked the Texas political establishment to its foundations.

For all the effort put into the Waters' campaign, there were numerous potential campaign tools it ignored. No headcount of Waters' supporters was attempted, nor did the campaign conduct a major effort to bring out the vote on election day. There was no effort to poll public opinion about the campaign.

In retrospect, Waters said he believed that a poll or a headcount would have been of great value. Having overestimated the response he was to get in the primary, he said he was shocked to be outpolled by the former legislator. The latter received 3518 to Waters' 3120, while the other four candidates received a combined total of 1600 votes. Fortunately for Waters, the crowded primary field meant that there would be a runoff in which he would have a second shot.

One aspect of the primary results that Waters might have discovered in advance was the fact that in the most liberal of the district's twenty-one precincts he received 300 fewer votes than Farenthold. The reason, he would learn, was that it was not generally realized there that he was more liberal than Farenthold. Similarly, Waters had been beaten in four precincts he thought were solidly for him and which he had taken for granted. While this failing was remedied before the runoff, it could have been avoided entirely by more careful study of voter attitudes. After his rude awakening in the primary, Waters ended up winning in the runoff with a vote of 5824 to 5030.

The significant point about Waters' campaign is that on a budget of $5000 he was able to run a six-month primary campaign that mobilized a broad coalition around a relatively radical platform, and that he won against an opponent estimated to have a budget of more than $20,000 at his disposal.

Equally important, that Waters' victory was not the fruit of a campaign put together at the spur of the moment: he had put enough time into earlier political activities so that he was familiar with his district and the issues affecting it. He also knew enough to seek the backing of other local leaders. While it was a matter of luck that he had the opportunity to run when he did, Waters had gone to great lengths to be ready for such an opportunity when it came.

Selected Bibliography

REFERENCES

Bibliography on Texas Government. Austin: Institute of Public Affairs, University of Texas, 1964.

Black's Law Dictionary. 4th ed. St. Paul, Minn.: West Publishing Co., 1951.

Book of the States. Lexington, Ky.: Council of State Governments, annual.

Guide to Texas State Agencies. 4th ed. Austin: Bureau of Government Research, Lyndon B. Johnson School of Public Affairs, University of Texas, 1972.

The Handbook of Texas. Edited by Walter Prescott Webb and H. Bailey Carroll. 2 vols. Austin: Texas State Historical Association, 1952.

Municipal Yearbook. Washington, D.C.: International City Managers Association, annual.

Texas Almanac and State Industrial Guide. Dallas: A. H. Belo Corp., biannual.

Texas State Directory. Austin: Texas State Directory, Inc., biannual.

PERIODICALS

Austin Report. Edited by Stuart Long, weekly newsletter. Address: P.O. Box 12368, Capitol Station, Austin.

Municipal Matrix. Edited by Charldean Newell. Published quarterly by the University Center for Community Services. Address: 1510 Maple Street, Denton.

Public Affairs Comment. Edited by Lynn F. Anderson, quarterly. Lyndon B. Johnson School of Public Affairs, University of Texas at Austin.

Texas Government Newsletter. Edited by Charles Deaton. Published weekly by the editor since January, 1973, this two-page newsletter is designed especially for classroom use; each issue includes a summary of current developments and in-depth treatment of a selected topic. Address: P.O. Box 12814, Capitol Station, Austin.

The Texas in Action Report. Published weekly by Executive Services, Inc. Address: Suite 207, Westgate Bldg., 1122 Colorado, Austin.

Texas Monthly. Edited by William Broyles. Published monthly beginning in 1973. Address: P.O. Box 13366, Austin.

Texas Observer. Edited by Kaye Northcott, biweekly. Address: 600 West 7th Street, Austin.

GENERAL

Anderson, James E.; Murray, Richard W.; and Farley, Edward L. *Texas Politics: An Introduction.* 2nd ed. New York: Harper & Row, 1974.

Benton, Wilbourn E. *Texas: Its Government and Politics.* 3rd ed. Englewood Cliffs, N.J.: Prentice-Hall, 1972.

Box, Jim. *Your Texas Government in Pictures.* 2d ed. Austin: Graphic Ideas, 1971.

Conner, Seymour V. *Texas: A History.* New York: Thomas Y. Crowell, 1971.

Gantt, Fred, Jr.; Dawson, Irving O.; and Hagard, Luther G., Jr., eds. *Governing Texas: Documents and Readings.* 3rd ed. New York: Thomas Y. Crowell, 1974.

Kraemer, Richard H., and Barnes, Philip W., eds. *Texas: Readings in Politics, Government, and Public Policy.* San Francisco: Chandler Publishing Co., 1971.

MacCorkle, Stuart A., and Smith, Dick. *Texas Government.* 6th ed. New York: McGraw-Hill, 1968.

McCleskey, Clifton. *The Government and Politics of Texas.* 4th ed. Boston: Little, Brown, 1972.

Nimmo, Dan, and Oden, William E. *The Texas Political System.* Englewood Cliffs, N.J.: Prentice-Hall, 1971.

Richardson, Rupert Norval; Wallace, Ernest; and Anderson, Adrian N. *Texas: The Lone Star State.* 3rd ed. Englewood Cliffs, N.J.: Prentice-Hall, 1970.

THE CONTEXT OF TEXAS POLITICS: Environment

Acuna, Rodolfo. *Occupied America: The Chicano's Struggle Toward Liberation.* San Francisco: Canfield Press, 1972.

Arbingast, Stanley. "Texas Industry, 1973." *Texas Business Review,* vol. XLVII (February, 1973), pp. 33-38.

Big Town, Big Money: The Business of Houston. Houston, Cordovan Press, 1973.

Briggs, Vernon M., Jr. *Chicanos and Rural Poverty.* Baltimore: Johns Hopkins University Press, 1973.

"The Chicano Experience in the United States." *Social Science Quarterly,* vol. LIII (March, 1973), pp. 652-942 (a special topical issue with twenty-two articles and research notes).

De Are, Deana, and Poston, Dudley L., Jr. "Texas Population in 1970: 5. Trends and Variations in the Populations of Nonmetropolitan Towns, 1950-1970," *Texas Business Review,* vol. XLVII (January, 1973), pp. 11-16.

Goodman, Mary Ellen, et al. *The Mexican American Population of Houston.* Rice University Studies No. 57. Houston: Rice University, 1971.

Grebler, Leo; Moore, Joan W.; and Guzman, Ralph G. *The Mexican-American People: The Nation's Second Largest Minority.* New York: The Free Press, 1970.

Haddox, John. *Los Chicanos: An Awakening People.* Southwestern Studies No. 28. El Paso: University of Texas at El Paso, 1970.

McCleskey, Clifton. "Texas." *Encyclopedia Americana.* International ed. Vol. XXVI (1971), pp. 541-560.

Nevin, David. *The Texans: What They Are—and Why.* New York: William Morrow, 1968.

Peirce, Neal R. *The Megastates of America: People, Places and Power in the Ten Great States.* New York: W. W. Norton, 1972.

Rangel, Jorge C., and Alcala, Carlos M. "Project Report: De Jure Segregation of Chicanos in Texas Schools." *Harvard Civil Rights-Civil Liberties Law Review,* vol. VII (March, 1972), pp. 307-391.

Ryan, Robert H., et al. *Texas 90: An Economic Profile of Texas to 1990.* Austin: Bureau of Business Research, University of Texas at Austin, 1969.

Schmidt, Fred H. *Spanish Surnamed American Employment in the Southwest.* Washington, D.C.: U.S. Government Printing Office, 1970.

THE CONTEXT OF TEXAS POLITICS: Federalism and the Texas Constitution

Bebout, John E. "The Problem of the Texas Constitution" in *The Texas Constitution: Problems and Prospects for Revision.* A report prepared for the Texas Urban Development Commission, Institute of Urban Studies, University of Texas at Arlington, 1971.

Braden, George D. *Citizen's Guide to the Texas Constitution.* Prepared for the Texas Advisory Commission on Intergovernmental Relations by the Institute for Urban Studies, University of Houston, 1972.

Marburger, Harold J. *Amendments to the Texas Constitution of 1876.* Austin: Legislative Reference Division, Texas State Library, 1956.

May, Janice C. *Amending the Texas Constitution.* Austin: Texas Advisory Commission on Intergovernmental Relations, 1972.

McKay, Seth S. *Debates in the Texas Constitutional Convention of 1875.* Austin: University of Texas Press, 1930.

——. *Making the Texas Constitution of 1876.* Philadelphia: University of Pennsylvania Press, 1924.

——. *Seven Decades of the Texas Constitution of 1876.* Lubbock: n.p., 1942.

Smith, Dick. "Constitutional Revision in Texas, 1876-1961." *Public Affairs Comment,* vol. VII (September, 1961), pp. 1-4.

——. "Constitutional Revision: Attempts to Unshackle Texas." *Public Affairs Comment,* vol. XV (November, 1969), pp. 1-6.

Storey, Robert G. "Does Texas Need a New Constitution?" *Texas Bar Journal,* vol. XXXI (22 May 1968), pp. 363-364, 399-406.

Texas Advisory Commission on Intergovernmental Relations. *The Texas Constitutional Revision Commission of 1973: A Report and Proposal.* Austin: 1972.

——. *Amending the Texas Constitution, 1951-1972.* Austin, February, 1973.

THE POLITICS OF PARTIES AND ELECTIONS

Castro, Tony. "Viva, Ramsey Muniz!" *Saturday Review: The Arts,* November, 1972, pp. 16, 18, 21.

Cuellar, Alfredo. "Perspective on Politics" in Joan Moore, *Mexican Americans.* Englewood Cliffs, N.J.: Prentice-Hall, 1970.

Deaton, Charles. *The Year They Threw the Rascals Out.* Austin: Shoal Creek Publishers, 1973.

Espinosa, John L. "Raza Unida Conference: Unidos Ganaremos." *La Luz,* November, 1972, pp. 10-12.

Green, George Norris. "Some Aspects of the Far Right Wing in Texas Politics" in *Essays on Recent Southern Politics* edited by Harold M. Hollingsworth. Austin and London: University of Texas Press, 1970.

Holloway, Harry. *The Politics of the Southern Negro from Exclusion to Big City Organization.* New York: Random House, 1969.

Ivins, Molly. "How Much Financial Disclosure Does a Financial Disclosure Disclose?" *Texas Observer,* May 12, 1972, pp. 1, 3.

May, Janice C. "The Texas Voter Registration System." *Public Affairs Comment,* vol. XVII (July, 1970), pp. 1-5.

Mohn, N. Carroll. "Potential Voting Population in Texas: The Young and the Old of It." *Texas Business Review,* vol. XLVI (September, 1972), pp. 189-195.

Nicolaides, Philip. "Texas Can Do It–but Didn't" [postmortem on Grover's gubernatorial campaign]. *National Review,* February 2, 1973, p. 150.

La Raza Unida Party in Texas. Speeches by Mario Compean and José Angel Gutiérrez, with an introduction by Antonio Camejo. New York: Pathfinder Press, 1970.

Rivera, George, Jr. "Social Change in the Barrio: The Chicano Movement in South Texas." *Aztlan,* vol. III (Fall, 1973), pp. 205-214.

Shinn, Allen M., Jr. "Note on Voter Registration and Turnout in Texas, 1960-1970." *Journal of Politics,* vol. XXXIII (November, 1971), pp. 1120-1129.

Shockley, John. "Los Cinco Mexicanos" and "Crystal City: La Raza Unida and the Second Revolt." In *Chicano: The Evolution of a People,* edited by Renato Rosaldo, Robert Calvert, and Gustav L. Seligmann. Minneapolis, Minn.: Winston Press, 1973.

——. *Chicano Revolt in a Texas Town.* Notre Dame, Ind.: University of Notre Dame Press, 1973.

Soukup, James R.; McCleskey, Clifton; and Holloway, Harry. *Party and Factional Division in Texas.* Austin: University of Texas Press, 1964.

Tarrance, V. Lance, comp. and ed. *Texas Precinct Votes '70: 1970 General Election Returns, Analysis, and Maps.* Arnold Foundation for the Study of Democratic Process. Austin and London: University of Texas Press, 1972.

Vidal, Mirta. *Chicano Liberation and Revolutionary Youth.* New York: Pathfinder Press, 1971.

Waldron, Ann, and Sherrill, Robert. "Sissy Farenthold of Texas: She Just Might Be Governor." *Nation,* April 24, 1972, pp. 528-531.

Weeks, O. Douglas. "Texas." In *The Changing Politics of the South,* edited by William C. Havard. Baton Rouge: Louisiana State University Press, 1972.

Wrinkle, Robert D., and Elliott, Charles. "Wallace Party Activists in Texas." *Social Science Quarterly,* vol. LII (June, 1971), pp. 197-203.

THE LEGISLATURE

Banks, Jimmy. *Money, Marbles and Chalk: The Wondrous World of Texas Politics.* Austin: Texas Publishing Co., 1971.

Burns, John. *The Sometimes Governments: A Critical Study of the 50 American Legislatures.* Citizens Conference on State Legislatures. New York: Bantam Books, 1971.

Cobb, Edwin L. "Representative Theory and the Flotorial District: The Case of Texas." *Western Political Quarterly,* vol. XXII (December, 1969), pp. 790-805.

Dugger, Ronnie. "Money and Ben Barnes." *Texas Observer,* March 3, 1972, pp. 14-16.

Ferguson, John. "Half-loaves from the House." *Texas Observer,* February 16, 1973, pp. 12-13.

Green, Wayne E., and Shaffer, Richard A. "Anatomy of a Scandal: Collapse of Texas Financial Empire." *Wall Street Journal,* September 28, 1971, p. 38.

Ivins, Molly. "Mr. Speaker Daniel." *Texas Observer,* February 2, 1973, pp. 3-7.

Jamison, Alonzo W. "The Education of a Legislator." *Southwestern Journal of Social Education,* vol. I (Fall, 1970), pp. 41-47.

Katz, Harvey. "How the Dirty Thirty Cleaned Up Texas." *Washington Monthly,* July, 1972, pp. 37-48, 50-52.

——. *Shadow on the Alamo: New Heroes Fight Old Corruption in Texas Politics.* Garden City, N.Y.: Doubleday, 1972.

Kinch, Sam, Jr., and Proctor, Ben. *Texas Under a Cloud: Story of the Texas Stock Fraud Scandal.* Austin and New York: Jenkins Publishing Co., 1972.

Oden, William E. "Some Characteristics of Recent Texas Legislators." *Rocky Mountain Social Science Journal,* vol. IV (October, 1967), pp. 110-119.

Reichly, A. James. "The Texas Banker Who Bought Politicians." *Fortune,* December, 1971, pp. 37-48, 50-52.

Taebel, Delbert A. "Administering the Legislative Interim Committee: A Case Study." *Public Affairs Comment,* vol. XVII (January, 1971), pp. 1-4.

Texas Legislative Council. *Texas Legislative Manual* (loose-leaf). Austin, 1971.

The . . . Texas Legislature: A Review of Its Work. Austin: Institute of Public Affairs, University of Texas, 1953- ("Public Affairs Series" studies of each Texas Legislature beginning with the 53rd).

Texas Monthly Staff. "The Ten Best (and, Sigh, the Ten Worst) Legislators." *Texas Monthly,* July, 1973, pp. 42-50.

West, Richard. "Inside the Lobby." *Texas Monthly,* July, 1973, pp. 50-59.

Young, Stanley K. *Texas Legislative Handbook.* Austin: Texas Legislative Council, 1973.

THE EXECUTIVE

Boyle, Robert H.; Graves, John; and Walkins, T. H. *The Water Hustlers.* San Francisco: Sierra Club, 1971.

Dickson, James Galen, Jr. "Decision-Making in a Restrictive Constitutional Environment: Impact on the Texas Governor of High Court Decisions and Attorney General Opinions." *Rocky Mountain Social Science Journal,* vol. X (January, 1973), pp. 51-60.

——. "The Office of the Attorney General in Texas." *Public Affairs Comment,* vol. XVII (May, 1971), pp. 1-5.

Flawn, Peter T. "The Environmental Problem, Government Agencies, and Public Policy." *Public Affairs Comment,* vol. XVIII (May, 1972), pp. 1-4.

Gantt, Fred, Jr. "Special Legislative Sessions in Texas: The Governor's Bane or Blessing." *Public Affairs Comment,* vol. XVI (November, 1970), pp. 1-6.

League of Women Voters of Texas. *The Texas Executive Department.* Houston, 1967.

McKay, Seth Shepard. *W. Lee O'Daniel and Texas Politics, 1938-1942.* Lubbock: Texas Technological College Press, 1944.

Miller, Thomas Lloyd. *The Public Lands of Texas, 1519-1970.* Norman: University of Oklahoma Press, 1972.
Mills, Warner E., Jr. *Martial Law in East Texas.* University, Ala.: University of Alabama Press, 1960.
Northcott, Kaye. "Briscoe's First Hurrah." *Texas Observer,* January 19, 1973, pp. 6-7.
Stewart, Frank M. "Impeachment in Texas." *American Political Science Review,* vol. XXIV (August, 1930), pp. 652-658.

THE JUDICIARY

Arnold, J. D. "The Dallas Jail." *Texas Observer,* July 7, 1972, pp. 6-10.
Baker, Dick. "The Texas Indigent–Is the Time Ripe for a Public Defender System?" *Baylor Law Review,* vol. XXV (Winter, 1973), pp. 55-70.
Brown, Clinton Giddings. *You May Take the Witness.* Austin: University of Texas Press, 1955.
Calvert, Robert W. "Summary of Major Changes Proposed by Chief Justice's Task Force for Court Improvement." *Texas Bar Journal,* vol. XXXVI (January 22, 1973), pp. 24-25.
Greenhill, Joe R., and Odom, John W., Jr. "Judicial Reform of Our Texas Courts: A Re-examination of Three Important Aspects." *Baylor Law Review,* vol. XXIII (Spring, 1971), pp. 204-226.
Henderson, Bancroft C., and Sinclair, T. C. *The Selection of Judges in Texas: An Exploratory Study.* Houston: Public Affairs Research Center, University of Houston, 1965.
Ivins, Molly. "The Trial of the Abilene Three." *Texas Observer,* March 31, 1972, pp. 1, 3-4.
Jackson, Bruce. *In the Life.* New York: Holt, Rinehart and Winston, 1972.
Mabry, James E. "The Texas Department of Corrections–Two Decades of Progress. *State Government,* vol. XLVI (Spring, 1971), pp. 77-81.
MacCorkle, Stuart A. *The Texas Grand Jury.* Austin: Institute of Public Affairs, University of Texas, 1964.
"Proposed Revision [of] Article V, Texas Constitution [a symposium of articles defending and attacking the proposed reform of the state judicial system]." *Texas Bar Journal,* vol. XXXV (November 22, 1972), pp. 1001-1018.
Reid, Don. *Eyewitness.* Houston: Cordovan Press, 1973.
Smith, Griffin, Jr. "Empires of Paper." *Texas Monthly,* November, 1973, pp. 53-60, 62-63, 98-100, 102-103, 105-109.
Stracinsky, Gary C., et al. *Texas Jails: Problems and Reformation.* Huntsville: Institute of Contemporary Corrections and the Behavioral Sciences, Sam Houston State University, 1971.
Texas Commission on Law Enforcement Procedure of 60th Legislature. *Handbook for Texas Law Enforcement Officers.* Rev. ed. Austin, 1972.
Texas Criminal Justice Council, Office of the Governor. *1973 Criminal Justice Plan for Texas.* Austin, 1973.
Texas Research League. *Measuring Court Performance: A Report on the Data Collection Process of the Texas Civil Judicial Council.* Austin, 1972.
United States Commission on Civil Rights. *Mexican Americans and the Administration of Justice in the Southwest.* Washington, D.C.: U.S. Government Printing Office, 1970.

LOCAL GOVERNMENTS

Anderson, Lynn F. "Texas Local Government: The Numbers Game." *Public Affairs Comment*, vol. XV (January, 1969), pp. 1-6.

Bryant, Mavis. "The Emerging Councils of Government." *Dallas*, July, 1972, pp. 25-27.

Crane, Bill. "San Antonio: Pluralistic City and Monolithic Government" in *Urban Politics in the Southwest* edited by Leonard E. Goodall. Tempe: Institute of Public Administration, Arizona State University, 1967.

Durham, John. "Marvin Zindler, Consumer Lawman." *Texas Monthly*, February, 1973, pp. 52-57.

Montgomery, Dave. "Air-born New Texas Metropolis" [Impact of the Dallas-Fort Worth Airport]. *City*, Fall, 1972, pp. 27-31.

Newell, Charldean. *County Representation and Legislative Apportionment*. Austin: Institute of Public Affairs, University of Texas, 1965.

Spain, August O. "Fort Worth: Great Expectations–Cowtown Hares and Tortoises" in *Urban Politics in the Southwest* edited by Leonard E. Goodall. Tempe: Institute of Public Administration, Arizona State University, 1967.

Tees, David, and Stanford, Jay G. *Handbook for Interlocal Contracting in Texas*. Arlington: Institute of Urban Studies, University of Texas at Arlington, with cooperation of the Texas Municipal League, 1972.

Texas Advisory Commission on Intergovernmental Relations. *Land Use Standards in Unincorporated Areas: Proposed State Legislation for Local Governments*. Austin: Institute of Urban Studies, University of Texas at Arlington, 1972.

Texas Rural Development Commission. *Rural Texas at the Crossroads*. Austin, January, 1973.

Texas Urban Development Commission. *Urban Texas: Policies for the Future*. Arlington: Institute of Urban Studies, University of Texas at Arlington, November, 1971.

Wall, Mary Kate. *Texas Municipal Election Law*. Rev. ed. Denton: University Center for Community Services, North Texas State University, 1972.

Wrinkle, Robert D. *Politics in the Urban Southwest*. Albuquerque: Division of Government Research, University of New Mexico, 1971.

FINANCING THE STATE'S GOVERNMENTS

Allen, William. "The Case of Demetrio Rodríguez." *Saturday Review: The Society*, September 9, 1972, pp. 6-8, 13-14.

Back, Kenneth. "The Property Tax Under Fire: Views on Strengths, Weaknesses, and Future Role." *Public Affairs Comment*, vol. XIX (February, 1973), pp. 1-4.

Ivins, Molly. "School Financing Is *Good* for You." *Texas Observer*, December 15, 1972, pp. 1, 3-6.

——. "Through the Appropriations Maze with Neil Caldwell." *Texas Observer*, March 16, 1973, pp. 1, 3-6.

League of Women Voters of Texas. *Texas School Finance*. Dickinson, Tex., September, 1972.

Maxwell, James A. *Financing State and Local Governments*. Rev. ed. Washington, D.C.: The Brookings Institution, 1969.

Oates, Wallace E. *Fiscal Federalism.* New York: Harcourt Brace Jovanovich, 1972.
"Revenue Sharing Provides $30.1 Billion to State, Localities Over the Next 5 Years." *State Government News,* October, 1972, pp. 2-5.
Solomon, Burt. "Revolution in School Financing." *Texas Observer,* March 31, 1972, pp. 7-9.
Texas Research League. "Property Tax Reform: Where It Must Begin." *TRL Analyzes Developments in Texas State and Local Government,* December, 1972.
——. *Public School Finance Problems in Texas.* An Interim Report to the Texas Legislature. June, 1972.
Wright, Neil S. "Federal Revenue Sharing: Problems and Prospects." *Public Affairs Comment,* vol. XVII (July, 1971), pp. 1-6.

EPILOGUE

Blevins, Leon W. *A Topical Dictionary of American Government and Politics: The Young Voter's Manual.* Totowa, N.J.: Littlefield, Adams, 1973.
Burkhart, James; Eisenstein, James; Fleming, Theodore; and Kendrick, Frank. *Strategies for Political Participation.* Cambridge, Mass.: Winthrop, 1972.
Claunch, R. G.; Dickson, J. G.; and Cox, J. D. "Opportunity and Motivation: Why Students Register to Vote in Their University Community." *The Municipal Matrix,* October, 1972, pp. 1-4.
Cook, Terrence E., and Morgan, Patrick M. *Participatory Democracy.* New York: Canfield Press, 1971.
Herzberg, Donald G., and Peltason, J. W. *A Student Guide to Campaign Politics.* New York: McGraw-Hill, 1970.
Manatos, Andrew E. "What Do You Get When You Get-Out-the-Vote?" *Politeía,* vol. I (Summer, 1972), pp. 41-42.
Mitchell, W. C. *Why Vote?* Chicago: Markham Publishing Co., 1972.
Shadegg, Stephen C. *How to Win an Election: The Art of Political Victory.* New York: Taplinger, 1964.
Texas Secretary of State. *Handbook for Election Judges and Clerks for Use in Primary and General Elections for State and County Officers in Precincts Using Paper Ballots.* April, 1972.
Van Riper, Paul. *Handbook of Practical Politics.* 3rd ed. New York: Harper and Row, 1967.

Index